DIRECTORY

OF

VENTURE CAPITAL

SECOND EDITION

DIRECTORY

OF

VENTURE CAPITAL

SECOND EDITION

KATE LISTER
TOM HARNISH

JOHN WILEY & SONS, INC.
New York • Chichester • Weinheim • Brisbane • Singapore • Toronto

Copyright © 2000 by Kate Lister and Tom Harnish. All rights reserved.

Published by John Wiley & Sons, Inc.

Published simultaneously in Canada.

This publication is designed to provide accurate and authoritative information in regard to the subject matter covered. It is sold with the understanding that the publisher is not engaged in rendering professional services. If professional advice or other expert assistance is required, the services of a competent professional person should be sought.

Library of Congress Cataloging-in-Publication Data:

Lister, Kate, 1959-

Directory of venture capital / Catherine E. Lister and Thomas D. Harnish.-- 2nd ed.
    p. cm.
    Includes index.
    ISBN 0-471-36104-6 (paper : alk. paper).
    1. Venture capital--United States--Directories. 2. Small business investment companies--United States--Directories. I. Harnish, Tom, 1945- II. Title.

HG4963.L57 2000
332.66--dc21   99-057988

Printed in the United States of America.

10 9 8 7 6 5 4 3 2 1

ABOUT THE AUTHORS

Catherine E. Lister (Kate) is an authority on small-business finance. An experienced banker, business owner, private investor, and venture capitalist, she has advised fast-growing companies on management and finance strategies since 1986, and has helped find millions of dollars for her clients. A popular speaker on financing, financial management, and business planning, Kate has conducted hundreds of workshops and seminars including programs for numerous associations, banks, the Wharton School, Eastman Kodak, many others.

During her 15-year career, Kate has served as an advisor and board member for entrepreneurial groups and organizations, including the Wharton Small Business Development Center, the Temple University Entrepreneurial Institute, and the Philadelphia Chamber of Commerce Small Business Council, where she received the Business Advocate of the Year Award. She also received the SBA's Business Advocate Award, and was a finalist in the prestigious *Inc.* magazine/Arthur Young Entrepreneur of the Year Award program.

Kate graduated from the Philadelphia College of Textiles and Science in 1980 with a Bachelor of Science Degree in business management and a minor in computer science.

Thomas D. Harnish (Tom) has a 20-year history of leading technology development. An experienced entrepreneur and executive, he started his first business, a computer service bureau, while still in college. As scientist and consultant for companies including Booz, Allen & Hamilton, Reynolds & Reynolds, and OCLC, he conceived and directed the development of home information services, interactive cable television, electronic automotive parts catalogs, and multimedia systems. Over the years he has started, managed, and funded a variety of businesses, including a home healthcare company, a medical imaging company, and an aviation CD-ROM publishing company funded by private investors.

A frequent speaker at national and international conferences on information technology and new business development, Tom was host of "Future File," a weekly program about emerging technology broadcast on public radio. A member of the National Advisory Board on the Use of Computers in Education and as Senior Scientist for the Online Computer Library Center (OCLC); he has testified on emerging technology before Congress and at the White House.

Tom graduated from the University of New Mexico in 1969 with a Bachelor of Science Degree in aerospace psychology and with minors in chemistry, math, and physics. In 1988 he established an aviation world speed record.

TABLE OF CONTENTS

ACKNOWLEDGMENTS

Paul E. Kreutz, Partner
Gray Cary Ware & Freidenrich
4365 Executive Drive, Suite 1600
San Diego CA 92121-2189
619-677-1400

Gray Cary Ware & Freidenrich is one of California's largest law firms with principal offices in Silicon Valley and San Diego County. The firm focuses on emerging companies and providing litigation, business, corporate, finance, real estate, employment, tax, trust and estate planning, and patent law services.

Matt Quilter, Partner
Heller, Ehrman, White, & McAuliffe
525 University Avenue, Suite 1100
Palo Alto CA 94301-1900
650-324-7000

Heller, Ehrman, White, & McAuliffe is one of the nation's largest law firms. The firm serves an international clientele ranging in size from individual entrepreneurs to publicly held multinational corporations. The firm assists high-technology clients in public and private financings, strategic alliances, technology licensing, intellectual property protection and general business matters.

James D. Atwell, Managing Partner
PricewaterhouseCoopers, Venture Capital Practice,
Global Technology Industry Group
10 Almaden Boulevard, Suite 1600
San Jose CA 95113
408-534-2316

PricewaterhouseCoopers is the world's leading professional services organization. The Global Technology Industry Group delivers a broad spectrum of services in Computers & Peripherals, Internet, Life Sciences, Networking & Communications, Semiconductors, Software, and Venture Capital. PricewaterhouseCoopers is a recognized leader in each industry segment with services for technology clients in all stages of growth.

David Gleba, President
Jean Yakemchuk, VP of Research & Technology
VentureOne
345 Spear Street, East Tower, Suite 520
San Francisco CA 94105-1657
650-357-2100

VentureOne is the leading investment research firm providing the venture capital industry with immediate access to information on thousands of venture capital–backed companies. This information is used to review entrepreneurial companies for potential investment. Access to VentureOne's services is restricted to their clients, who rank among the nation's leading venture capital and professional services firms.

ABOUT THIS DIRECTORY

This directory is designed to help business owners, advisors, and others determine if they, or their clients, are candidates for professional venture capital and, if so, which venture firms to approach.

Over 600 offices for the nation's most active venture capital firms are included in this directory. Unlike other databases and directories that may include more firms and offices, this one focuses only on active investors. We intentionally omit service firms such as investment bankers, consultants, and finders unless they also make direct investments. This directory also omits funds that are fully invested, that are inactive, or that invest primarily in foreign countries.

For more help in understanding venture capital investors, what they want, how they evaluate proposals, deal pricing and structure, contract negotiation, and other issues, pick up a copy of *Finding Money—The Small Business Guide to Financing* also published by John Wiley & Sons.

This directory is a resource for planning an organized, targeted search for capital. We recommend that you not use it to mass mail copies of your business plan or financing proposal. Venture capitalists are busy people. They don't have the time to read every business plan they receive. What they will look at is a business plan that fits their investment criteria, industry and geographic preferences, and deal size requirements. Mail it to the wrong people and you'll look foolish, lazy, or unprepared . . . and the word will get around.

An electronic version of this directory is available. See page 379 if you would like to purchase the data in this directory in a form that is easily imported into a word processor, database, or spreadsheet computer program on any personal computer.

1

THE VENTURE CAPITAL INDUSTRY

During just the first half of 1999 venture firms invested $11.4 billion, an amount which exceeded 90 percent of 1998's record annual high and all venture investment in 1997. For the second quarter of 1999, the number of companies receiving funds increased 30 percent to 992 compared to 763 companies a year earlier. At the same time, average funding per company increased 57 percent to $7.4 million versus $4.9 million a year earlier. Phenomenal growth and the stock market success in the information and communications industries, especially the Internet, fueled this unparalleled volume.

In 1998 the venture capital industry raised over $14 billion for 2,853 deals, an average of nearly $5 million per deal, up slightly from an average deal size of about $4.7 million in 1997, according to the PricewaterhouseCoopers Money Tree™ Survey. Exhibit 1.1 shows that the majority of venture capital funding went to emerging technologies in communications and software & information.

Exhibit 1.1 1998 Venture Capital Investments

1998 Venture Capital Investments in Millions of Dollars

Industry	Number of Deals	Dollars Raised	Percent Total
Biotechnology	139	$635.0	4.5%
Business Services	137	$636.6	4.5%
Communications	583	$3,994.6	27.7%
Computers & Peripherals	86	$436.6	3.1%
Consumer	118	$580.1	4.1%
Distribution/Retailing	87	$383.8	2.7%
Electronics & Instrumentation	96	$306.2	2.1%
Environmental	14	$13.2	0.1%
Health Care	255	$1,099.2	7.7%
Industrial	118	$420.4	2.9%
Medical Instrumentation & Devices	173	$686.6	4.8%
Pharmaceuticals	51	$324.7	2.3%
Semiconductors/Equipment	40	$226.9	1.6%
Software & Information	952	$4,548.8	31.9%
Other	4	$9.4	0.1%
Total	**2853**	**$14,252.1**	**100.0%**

Source: PricewaterhouseCoopers Money Tree ™ Survey, PricewaterhouseCoopers, Global Technology Industry Group, Austin TX. Used with permission.

The venture capital community is composed of about 1,000 firms whose goal is to invest in companies that will produce extraordinary returns on their investment. Venture firms include public and private venture capital partnerships, Small Business Investment Companies (SBICs), Special Small Business Investment Companies (SSBICs), and venture leasing companies. This directory includes approximately 600 actively investing venture firm offices.

Due to the dynamic nature of venture capital, the industry's investment mix changes substantially from year to year. In 1992, for example, more venture capital went to biotech deals than to any other category, but by 1994 biotechnology was only third in both dollars raised and number of deals, and just 4.5 percent of the deals in the first half of 1999. Retail and consumer investments, while still far from the top of the list, more than doubled from 1992 to 1994, but still only represented 6.8 percent of total funding in 1998. In 1999 technology-based companies were setting records and accounted for 90 percent of all investments in the second quarter. Investment in Internet-related companies had grown to over half of all deals and 56 percent of the amount raised, according to VentureOne, the leading investment research firm serving the venture capital community.

While Later Stage companies still receive the bulk of venture funding, almost 60 percent in 1998, the competition for Early Stage dollars is heating up. According to David Gleba, president of VentureOne, "The investment focus of the venture capital industry is being driven by the pressures associated with managing ever larger funds in an increasingly competitive environment." During the first half of 1999 almost 10 percent of the funding went to Seed and Start-up companies, and another 30 percent went to Early Stage companies.

While some venture firms seek majority interests in the firms they finance, most take a minority position. And the longer you can hold on, the less you'll give up. A VentureOne report on all companies in their database five years ago indicated that Start-up Phase companies gave up an average of 50 percent ownership, while profitable companies gave up an average of only 16 percent. Exhibit 1.2 shows that more experienced companies landing VC funding in 1998 still gave up less ownership and control than Early Stage ventures, but the difference has narrowed.

Exhibit 1.2 Investment as a Percent of Company Valuation

**First Round Investment
as a Percentage of Company Valuation**

Start-up	45.45%
Development	44.44%
Beta testing	44.76%
Clinical trials	42.75%
Shipping	31.18%
Profitable	31.45%

Source: VentureOne. Cohort of companies entering the VC space in 1998.
VentureOne, San Francisco, CA 1999. Used with permission.

VENTURE CAPITAL FIRMS

Private and public partnerships represent the bulk of the venture capital community. The partners and principals in these funds act as investment managers for money they've raised from pension funds, corporations, foreign investors, insurance companies, trust funds, foundations, and wealthy individuals or families. Typically, a handful of partners manage between several million and several hundred million dollars of invested funds.

The success of a venture capital partnership depends on the success of the companies in which it invests. Unless some of the companies in a fund's portfolio reach the point of a successful public offering or other lucrative exit, the fund will not be able to generate the kind of returns it promises its investors.

The kinds of deals a particular fund will consider will be determined by a combination of the:
- Nature of the investors
- Technological and societal trends
- Recent stock market successes or failures
- Fund's own successes and failures
- Backgrounds of the firm's decision makers
- Activities of other venture firms
- Mix of current portfolio companies (industry, location, stage of business)
- Size of the fund
- Fund's own life-cycle stage

SMALL BUSINESS INVESTMENT COMPANIES (SBICs)

Small Business Investment Companies (SBICs) leverage private money with federal dollars to establish venture funds. Special Small Business Investment Companies (SSBICs) fund businesses owned and operated by socially or economically disadvantaged people. SBICs and SSBICs are privately owned and operated, but are licensed, regulated, and partially funded by the Small Business Administration.

Banks invested in nearly 20 percent of SBIC financings in 1998, representing 65 percent of the investment dollars. Financial companies, including established venture capital firms, individuals, and other organizations, manage the balance of SBIC funds. SBIC and SSBIC funds tend to be smaller than the average venture capital fund—almost half with less than $25 million under management.

The official goal of the SBIC/SSBIC program is to stimulate the flow of equity capital and long-term debt funding (five– to 20–year terms) for small-business growth and development. At one time, the structure of the SBIC program encouraged mostly debt-based investment for expansion, management buyouts, or strategic acquisitions. The program has been restructured to encourage SBICs to make equity-based investments in companies in all growth stages, but most still favor Later Stage deals. They generally look for a 20 to 30 percent return on their investment, slightly lower than the expectation of traditional venture capitalists.

SBICs collectively invested over $2 billion in FY1998. The average investment was just under $1 million. As of January 1999, the SBA reported 196 SBICs were managing approximately $6.7 billion in investment funds, and 66 SSBICs managed another $329 million.

In the directory portion of this book, there is an SBIC/SSBIC indicator. Only those that make equity or convertible debt investments have been included. Because some firms operate multiple funds, the SBIC/SSBIC indicator does not necessarily mean that the firm makes only SBIC investments.

VENTURE LEASING FIRMS

This nontraditional form of leasing allows venture-backed companies to qualify for leases that would otherwise be impossible. Venture leasing companies work closely with a venture firm to structure a lease that works for both the lessor and the lessee. Typically, the lessor eases its standard underwriting criteria in exchange for an equity position or rights to a future equity position in the lessee's company.

2

THE BUSINESS OF VENTURE CAPITAL

Venture capital firms, in general, invest in businesses with products or services that utilize, are based on, or serve emerging technologies and trends. They are primarily interested in proprietary products or services, proven management teams, huge market potential, and companies with the ability to produce extraordinary returns. In addition, individual venture firms, and even individual partners within firms, develop strong preferences for particular types of deals.

PROPRIETARY PRODUCTS OR SERVICES

A venture capital candidate must have some significant advantage over existing or potential competitors so it can achieve and maintain a dominant position in its industry. Companies with proprietary products or services often enjoy a desirable "unfair" competitive advantage by virtue of the exclusivity. Patents, trademarks, copyrights, exclusive distributorships, or other special rights protect a company's unique position in the market. Sometimes, an unprotected product or service with an exceptional head start on potential competition can fit this criterion as well.

HUGE MARKET POTENTIAL

Venture-funded companies are expected to be able to grow from nothing to $30 million, $50 million, or even $100 million in three to seven years. Therefore, the size of the potential market has to be big enough to support such growth. Many venture proposals fail to adequately convince investors of the market potential while others naively project that they'll capture 10, 20, or even 50 percent market share in a very short period. Even the iMac, which dominated sales for months after its release in August 1998, still only achieved 5.6 percent market share of new personal computer sales for the period by year's end.

PROVEN MANAGEMENT TALENT

Management may be the most important element in a venture capitalist's decision to invest in a company. Are the people running the company capable of building a $50 million business? Has the team managed similar growth in the past? Does the staff include, or is the company able to hire, top people in the field? Real depth in the company's principals and advisors is a prerequisite for venture financing.

EXTRAORDINARY RETURNS

Financial return requirements vary from firm to firm and deal to deal, but venture capitalists generally look for average returns at exit of 20 to 50 percent per year. As Exhibit 2.1 shows, in order to produce a 50 percent annual return on a $1 million investment, that investment must grow to $5 million in four years. Most businesses, even highfliers, won't achieve that kind of return through profits. In fact, most will lose money in the early years. Therefore, a venture prospect will have to be willing and able to sell the company or complete a successful public offering in three to seven years.

Exhibit 2.1 Return on Investment Multiples

Return on Investment Multiples				
A) If your investors want a return of	20%	30%	40%	50%
B) And they want to cash out in year:	C) They'll need their original investment to grow by the following multiple by the end of the period			
3	1.7	2.2	2.7	3.4
4	2.1	2.9	3.8	5.1
5	2.5	3.7	5.4	7.6
6	3.0	4.8	7.5	11.4
7	3.6	6.3	10.5	17.1

To earn a 50% return on investment, and cash out in four years, investors' money will have to grow by 5.1 times during the period

VENTURE FIRM PREFERENCES

Venture funds differ in their interests, likes, dislikes, wants, and needs. Most develop strong preferences for certain industries, technologies, locations, life stages of the companies in which they invest, and size of investment. While firms are often willing to stretch their criteria, it's best to find a match with the stated interests of the investors. Thanks to the Internet, a great deal of information is available on the background of the principals who decide which proposal is funded and which one is not. The electronic version of this directory (see page 385) contains URLs for those firms with Web sites.

INDUSTRY PREFERENCES

The investment interests of the venture community change with the times. In the 1980s and even the early 1990s, most venture firms turned their noses up at entertainment deals, but by the mid-1990s CD-ROM, multimedia entertainment, interactive television, and the Internet had become the talk of the industry.

Still, venture firms tend to focus on certain types of deals, such as computer hardware, software, telecommunications, biotechnology, health care, pharmaceuticals, electronics, environmental products and services, retailing, consumer products and services, media, and even environmentally and socially responsible projects. While few firms specialize in just one type of investing, specialty funds are particularly prevalent in health care, biotechnology, consumer products, and retailing.

This directory uses the following primary and subcategory industry preferences:

Information Industry
      Communications
      Computer Equipment
      Computer Services
      Computer Components
      Computer Entertainment
      Computer Education
      Information Technologies
      Computer Media

Software
Internet

Medical/Health Care
Biotechnology
Health Care Services
Life Sciences
Medical Products

Industrial
Advanced Materials
Chemicals
Instruments/Controls

Basic Industries
Consumer
Distribution
Manufacturing
Retail
Service
Wholesale

Specific Industries
Energy
Environmental
Financial
Real Estate
Transportation
Publishing
Food
Franchises

Diversified

Miscellaneous

In the directory section of this book, if a venture firm indicates an interest in any of the subcategories (e.g., communications, computer hardware, software, and so forth) the primary category (e.g., Information Industry) will also indicate an interest.

If a firm indicates an interest in more than one primary category (e.g., Industrial Products and Medical/Health Care), the firm will also be labeled "Diversified." A diversified fund does not necessarily have an interest in all areas.

LIFE STAGE PREFERENCES

Venture firms tend to invest in *rounds* of financing that match the company's growth needs. Sometimes early investors may commit to multiple rounds when, and if, certain benchmarks are met. Funds are generally added at the following stages of a company's life:

Early Stage

Seed Stage—Earliest and riskiest stage of funding. At this stage, the business may not even have been established. Funds are often needed for feasibility analysis, market testing, early product development, and business formation.

Start-up Stage—Funds are typically needed to build an organization and continue product development.

First Stage—Organization is in place. Funds are needed for manufacturing and marketing.

Later Stage

Second Stage—Company is fully operational. Products are being shipped, but funds are needed to expand into high-growth mode. The company may or may not have made a profit at this stage.

Mature Stage—Funds are needed to support major expansion of manufacturing and marketing, or for new product development. The company is making a profit at this stage.

Mezzanine—Bridges the gap between senior bank financing and equity capital for established Later Stage companies. Typically structured as debt with options for equity.

LBO/MBO—Funding for leveraged or management buyouts.

Turnaround—Funding for troubled businesses with new management and direction.

International Expansion—Funding for expansion into foreign markets or offshore manufacturing.

Venture Leasing

Be aware there are no universally agreed upon definitions of the various stages. One firm's definition of a start-up may include Seed Stage companies while another's may not. Therefore, it's best to clarify the interests of firms before pursuing them.

In the directory portion of this book, if a firm indicates it is willing to do Seed Stage, Start-up, or First Stage deals, the Early Stage category will also be indicated. Likewise, if a firm indicates an interest in Second Stage or Mature Stage, LBO/MBO, Mezzanine, Turnaround, or International Expansion, the Later Stage category will be indicated. Venture Leasing is indicated as a category by itself.

GEOGRAPHIC PREFERENCES

Practically speaking, it's easier for venture capitalists to evaluate and invest in deals that are within a couple of hours of one of their offices. This is particularly true for Seed Stage deals where a venture firm is more likely to take a more active role in the company's development. Nevertheless, many larger venture capital firms, and some smaller ones, are willing to consider investments throughout the United States and even internationally.

SIZE PREFERENCES

Because it takes just as much due diligence and paperwork to invest $100,000 as it does $1 million, most firms prefer larger deals. However, some firms, particularly those that invest in Early Stage deals, are willing to invest smaller sums (a few will even consider investments of less than $100,000) with the intent of investing additional sums as the company's progress warrants.

In the directory portion of this book, minimum investment is listed. Before approaching a venture firm, be sure your financing requirements fit the firm's specified criteria.

PERSONAL PREFERENCES

In addition to a firm's industry focus, the partners also tend to specialize in, or at least favor, certain types of deals. Before sending a business plan to a venture firm be sure to research its specific interests, and especially try to determine which partner(s) reviews which kind of deals. One partner might be rich in health care industry experience, while another might specialize in software. If the health care specialist receives your software deal, it might be passed along to the right partner, but then again it might not. The same goes for the personal interests of the partners.

PORTFOLIO PREFERENCES

The backgrounds and interests of a venture firm's investors may also influence its choice of investments. For example, The Yankee Group, a prominent computer and telecommunications consulting firm, operates Battery Ventures. TTC Ventures is a subsidiary of The Thompson Corporation, one of the largest information publishers in the world. Not surprisingly, these venture firms favor information technology deals and offer a wealth of resources to their portfolio companies.

The technologies, distribution channels, or industries in which any venture firm has already invested will bias future investments. On one hand, familiarity may pave the way for complementary investments. On the other hand, similarities can backfire if the venture firm's management feels another deal in the same industry would create too much concentration or if their investments in that industry aren't doing well.

Finally, the venture firm's own life-cycle stage may bias investment interests. If a fund is almost fully invested, fund managers may be more cautious or picky about their last few investments. In fact, most fund managers will hold back a portion of their uninvested funds so they don't miss out on later rounds of financing needed by their own portfolio companies. Newer funds, in contrast, may be more eager and aggressive.

3

THE DEAL

When negotiating with venture firms, entrepreneurs often mistakenly focus solely on retaining majority ownership. However, even without majority ownership, a venture firm can effectively control and obtain a greater than pro rata share of the financial returns in a company through provisions in the fine print of the closing documents.

Since few business owners have experience negotiating with a venture capitalist, most are unprepared for the experience. Thus, we offer one important piece of advice—hire competent professionals. Specifically, hire an attorney and accountant who have extensive experience with the venture capital industry. Inexperienced advisors will not only cost you money, they could cost you the deal. Additional information about the professionals that we used in the preparation of this book is included in the Acknowledgments on page ix.

SAMPLE TERM SHEET

Once a venture firm has decided to invest in a company, it will issue a Term Sheet to summarize the proposed deal structure. Keep in mind that deal structure varies substantially from one financing to the next and among different venture firms. Our sample represents a typical first-round financing.

The following sample Term Sheet was prepared by Matt Quilter, a partner with Heller Ehrman White & McAuliffe based in Palo Alto, California. Explanations of the key issues are provided in italics following each major section.

Keep in mind that a Term Sheet represents only a summary of the proposed terms that, once negotiated, will be covered in much greater detail in the closing documents. Samples of some of these documents including the Stock Purchase Agreement, Shareholders Agreement, and amended and restated Articles of Incorporation follow the Term Sheet.

Hi Tech Widget, Inc. is a fictitious company. The company is closing on an investment of $2.5 million, representing 2 million shares of a new Series A Preferred Stock to be issued in favor of a venture firm investor. Post-financing, the venture firm will own one-third of the company.

Summary of Terms
This Memorandum summarizes the principal terms of venture capital financing for Hi Tech Widget, Inc. (the "Company").

Description of Financing

Amount		$2,500,000
Type Security	Series A Preferred Stock	
# Shares		2,000,000
Price Per Share		$1.25
Closing		December 31, 1995

Post-Financing Capitalization

	# of Shares	Percent
Shares of Common held by Founders	3,200,000	53.34%
Shares Reserved for Future Employees	800,000	13.33%
Series A Preferred Stock	2,000,000	33.33%
Total	6,000,000	100.00%

This Description of Financing section spells out the amount to be invested, the structure of the investment, the number of shares of stock to be purchased, the price per share, the closing date, and ownership of the company post-investment. The capitalization table identifies the "pre-money" and "post-money" valuation of Hi Tech Widget, Inc.

Pre-money valuation refers to the value of the company prior to an investment. This value is a major point of negotiation in venture capital financings. Pre-money valuation is calculated by multiplying the price per share to be paid by the investors, by the number of shares outstanding prior to the financing (calculated on a fully diluted basis so as to include the employee reserve pool). In this example, the pre-money valuation of the company was $5 million ($1.25 per share times 4 million shares). "Post-money" valuation refers to the value of the company immediately after the financing and is calculated by adding the amount of the new investment to the pre-money valuation. The $2.5 million financing of Hi Tech Widget, Inc. yields a post-money valuation of $7.5 million.

Series A Preferred Stock is simply the name given to stock sold in this particular transaction, under these particular terms. Investors generally insist on issuance of preferred stock because of the accompanying preferred rights to dividends and preferential treatment upon liquidation or sale of the business. The next investment round will usually include different terms and conditions, and is likely to be called Series B Preferred Stock.

A reserve for future employee stock grants is typical in these deals. Ten to 15 percent of the shares are usually reserved at this stage.

Dividend Preference: Prior to any payment of dividends on the Common Stock, dividends will be paid to the holders of Series A Preferred at the rate of 7 percent per annum from funds legally available. No dividend shall be paid on the Common at a rate greater than the rate at which dividends are paid on Series A

Preferred (based on the number of shares of Common into which the Series A Preferred is convertible on the date the dividend is declared). Dividends on the Series A Preferred will be noncumulative.

The dividend preference section has two purposes: 1) it spells out details about dividends that will be paid or accrued on the Series A preferred shares, typically dividends are noncumulative; 2) it establishes that the investors have a priority over holders of common stock for the payment of dividends. When investors convert their preferred stock into common stock (typically at the time of an initial public offering [IPO] or upon acquisition of the venture-backed company), some agreements allow them to collect unpaid dividends in the form of additional shares of common stock. These provisions effectively enable investors to increase their percentage ownership in the company.

Liquidation Preference: In the event of any liquidation or winding up of the Company, the holders of Series A Preferred will be entitled to receive in preference to holders of Common an amount equal to the purchase price of the Series A Preferred per share plus declared but unpaid dividends. All remaining proceeds shall be shared pro rata by all the holders of Common and Series A Preferred until the holders of Series A Preferred have received $3.75 per share. Thereafter, the remaining proceeds shall be shared pro rata by all holders of Common. A consolidation or merger of the Company or sale of substantially all of its assets shall be deemed to be a liquidation or winding up for the purposes of the liquidation preference.

The liquidation preference section gives investors the right to recoup their investment if the company ceases operation, is liquidated, or sold. For example, if the company is liquidated for $3 million, investors would receive the first $2.5 million of proceeds to repay their investment (plus more if they've accrued the right to additional common shares through the dividend provisions), plus 33.3 percent (their percentage ownership) of the remaining $500,000.

The structure of the liquidation preference determines the allocation of the proceeds between you and your investors when your company is sold. That is, investors may have the opportunity to participate in the amount of proceeds in excess of their investment on a pro rata basis, a pro rata basis up to some predefined cap (here the cap is three times the initial investment), or not at all. If there is no right of participation in proceeds in excess of the amount invested, and if the per share return to all shareholders exceeds the $1.25 per share investment by the Series A preferred shareholders, they will convert their shares of Series A preferred stock into common stock, and receive a pro rata distribution. Because so many more venture-backed companies achieve liquidity through acquisition rather than initial public offering [IPO], the scope of the liquidation preference is a critical term to be negotiated.

Conversion Rights: (1) Series A Preferred may be converted into Common Stock at any time at the option of the holders and will automatically convert to Common in the event of an underwritten public offering of the Company's Common Stock in excess of

$7,500,000 and at a public offering price of at least $6 per share. (2) The conversion price of the Preferred Stock will be subject to proportional adjustment for stock splits, reverse stock splits, and the like, and will be subject to adjustment on a weighted average formula basis upon future issuances of shares at a price less than the then current Series A conversion price.

The investors may convert to common stock at any time, but must convert if a public offering will bring them their required return. In this case, a $6 per share price would yield a 4.7 times return on their investment ($6 ÷ $1.25 per share purchase price). This feature is included because public offerings are rarely successful if preferred stockholders do not convert their holdings to common stock before the public offering is completed, and instead retain the special voting rights and other preferences of the preferred stock.

If future financings occur at a price lower than that paid by earlier investors, the early investors' shares will be devalued and thus their ownership will be diluted. Therefore, investors will almost always require some form of dilution protection as a condition to investing in a company. A wide variety of dilution protection mechanisms are used by investors, so be sure you understand the math and consequences to the founders' ownership position should a downfinancing (one that's priced lower than the per share price paid by earlier investors) occur. Poorly structured or overly aggressive anti-dilution provisions can reduce founders' equity incentives and complicate future financings.

Sometimes investors will rely on the protection afforded by their right of participation in future financings (see Right of Participation). More often, however, investors will seek "ratchet" or "weighted-average" formula dilution protection.

Absent agreement to the contrary, dilution benefits apply equally to all Series A investors, whether or not they continue to support the company by participating in a downfinancing. As a result, investors often require co-investors to participate in future financings in order to receive the dilution protection. This requirement is referred to as "pay to play."

The most common form of dilution protection is "weighted-average" formula protection. A formula is used to determine the dilutive effect of a downfinancing by calculating how many more shares are issued in the new financing than would have been issued had the new investors bought at the same price as the Series A investors.

A less common form of dilution protection is known as "ratchet" protection. It gives the investor the benefit of any lower-priced issuances during the term of the ratchet. For example, if a Series B financing of the company occurred at $.75 per share, the Series A investors would be able to convert their preferred stock into common stock as if they had purchased it at $.75 per share rather than $1.25 per share. Thus, instead of owning 2,000,000 shares, they would own 3,333,333 shares.

With ratchet protection, the size of the downfinancing generally does not affect the size of the adjustment. The benefit conferred on all earlier investors will be the same. By contrast, with weighted-average formula dilution, the magnitude of the benefit to investors, and accompanying dilution to founders, is based on the size of the dilutive financing and on whether the formula is broad-based, medium-based, or narrow-based as described below.

The following examples demonstrate weighted-average formula dilution protection. Using the terms of the Series A financing (described in the Summary of Terms section), assume a Series B financing of $7.5 million at $.75 per share (versus the Series A price of $1.25 per share).

Basic Formula: NCP = CCP X ((CSO + DS) ÷ (CSO + NS))

NCP	=	*New conversion price (to be determined by the formula)*
CCP	=	*Current conversion p rice ($1.25 per share)*
CSO	=	*Number of shares of common stock considered to be outstanding prior to the dilutive financing (under a broad-based formula, this includes all Series A preferred shares, all common shares, and all employee reserve shares, or 6 million shares; under a medium-based formula, employee reserve shares are excluded for a total of 5.2 million shares; and under a narrow-based formula, only Series A preferred shares purchased with the dilution protection are included, totaling 2 million shares in this example). As more series of preferred stock are issued, the variety of formulas increases as well.*
DS	=	*Number of shares of "deemed" to be issued in the dilutive financing—that is, the number of shares that would have been issued had the new financing been done at a price per share paid in the earlier financing (7,500,000 ÷ $1.25 = 6,000,000)*
NS	=	*Number of new shares actually issued in the dilutive financing ($7,500,000 ÷ $.75 = 10,000,000)*

Example (1) Broad-based weighted-average dilution formula

NCP	=	1.25 X ((6,000,000 + 6,000,000) ÷ (6,000,000 + 10,000,000))
NCP	=	1.25 X .75
NCP	=	.94

Thus each share of Series A Preferred will convert to 1.25 ÷ .94 or 1.3298 shares of Common; a total of 2,659,574 shares.

Example (2) Medium-based weighted-average dilution formula

NCP	=	1.25 X ((5,200,000 + 6,000,000) ÷ (5,200,000 + 10,000,000))
NCP	=	1.25 X .7368
NCP	=	.92

Thus each share of Series A Preferred will convert to 1.25 ÷ .92 or 1.3587 shares of Common; a total of 2,717,391 shares.

Example (3) Narrow-based weighted-average dilution formula

NCP	=	1.25 X ((2,000,000 + 6,000,000) ÷ (2,000,000 + 10,000,000))
NCP	=	1.25 X .6667
NCP	=	.83

Thus each share of Series A Preferred will convert to 1.25 ÷ .83 or 1.506 shares of Common; a total of 3,012,084 shares.

If ratchet protection were in effect, each share of Series A Preferred would convert to 1.6667 shares of Common, a total of 3,333,333 shares. The examples illustrate the great difference in the effect on the founders' equity of the application of different dilution formulas. The narrower the base of shares against which the dilutive issuance is applied, the greater the adjustment given to the Series A investors. The larger the size of the Series B financing, the greater the adjustment given to the Series A investor; a Series B financing of, say, $4 million would result in a smaller adjustment.

Because a new investor's pre-money valuation is independent of the effects of any dilution protection (e.g., "We will invest $5 million in your company for 25 percent of its fully diluted post-financing equity), dilution adjustments become a transfer of equity from common shareholders and others who invested before *the dilution protection was granted. The following demonstrates the extent of ownership loss suffered by the founders, assuming a narrow-based, weighted-average, anti-dilution formula:*

 # Shares Ownership Percent

Ownership before Anti-dilution Adjustment and before Series B Financing

	# Shares	Ownership Percent
Founders	3,200,000	53.34%
Future Employee Reserve	800,000	13.33%
Series A Preferred	2,000,000	33.33%
Total	6,000,000	100.00%

Ownership giving effect to Anti-dilution Adjustment immediately before Series B Financing

	# Shares	Ownership Percent
Founders	3,200,000	45.64%
Future Employee Reserve	800,000	11.41%
Series A Preferred	3,012,084	42.95%
Total	7,012,084	100.00%

Ownership after Anti-dilution Adjustment and after Series B Financing

	# Shares	Ownership Percent
Founders	3,200,000	18.81%
Future Employee Reserve	800,000	4.70%
Series A Preferred	3,012,084	17.71%
Series B Preferred	10,000,000	58.78%
Total	17,012,084	100.00%

> Voting Rights: A holder of Series A Preferred will have the right to that number of votes equal to the number of shares of Common issuable upon conversion of the Series A Preferred. Holders of Series A Preferred shall have the right to elect one director, the holders of Common shall have the right to elect one director, and one shall be chosen at the mutual consent of both. On all other matters, the Preferred and the Common shall vote together, except as provided by law.

The voting rights section gives the investors voting rights as though they owned an equivalent number of common shares. But, by getting to choose one board member, and influencing the choice of another, they can effectively exert much more control over the company. Since the board legally oversees the management of the business, controlling a majority of the board enables your investors to control the company. At the extreme, this means they can replace the founders if things aren't going well. Some investment agreements will include a provision to "flip" control if certain benchmarks aren't met; others will include a voting agreement where founders and investors agree to vote their shares to elect certain persons or designees to the board, notwithstanding their relative shareholdings. As a company matures, management and investors often seek to add outside board members, people with relevant industry or other experience and stature who can assist the company in anticipating and meeting the challenges of growth.

> Protective Covenants: Consent of the holders of a majority of Preferred Stock will be required for: (i) creation of any new class or series of shares having preference over or being on parity with the Series A Preferred, (ii) any increase in the authorized number of shares of Preferred Stock, (iii) any amendment to the Articles of Incorporation, (iv) any change in the authorized number of directors, or (v) any transaction in which control of the Company is transferred or the Company is acquired.

Protective covenants set forth certain events that will require consent of the investors. In addition to those previously cited, investors' consent might also be required for financing, pledging of assets, any material change in the company's business, transactions with related parties, payment of dividends, employee compensation, and the signing of certain contracts. This is more often the case with strategic or corporate investors than with venture capital investors. Again, these rights allow investors to exert more control than their ownership percentage implies.

Financial Information: The Company will deliver annual and monthly financial statements and annual budgets to each holder of Series A Preferred. These obligations will terminate upon a public offering of Common Stock.

The financial information section stipulates financial information to be provided to investors. This information is not required to be delivered to shareholders as a matter of law, and thus investors seek to acquire these rights as a matter of contract. Founders should be sure that they can produce and distribute the required reports.

Registration Rights:

(1) Beginning at the earlier of September 30, 2000, or six months after the Company's initial public offering, persons holding at least 40 percent of the Series A Preferred may request that the Company file a Registration Statement for at least 33 1/3 percent of the Preferred (or any lesser percentage if the anticipated aggregate offering price, net of underwriting discounts and commissions, would exceed $7,500,000), and the Company will use its best efforts to cause such shares to be registered. The Company will not be obligated to effect more than two demand registrations (other than on Form S-3).

(2) Holders of at least 25 percent of the Series A Preferred will have the right to require the Company to file Form S-3 registrations provided that (i) the Company is able to utilize such form, (ii) the aggregate proposed public offering price is in excess of $1 million dollars ($1,000,000), and (iii) the Company shall not be required to effect more than one such registration within any six-month period.

(3) Holders of Series A Preferred will be entitled to piggyback registration rights on Company Registrations, subject to the right of Company and its underwriters to reduce the number of such shares proposed to be registered, but not below 25 percent of the total number of shares to be offered in any offering subsequent to the company's initial registered public offering. There will be a 180-day lockup agreement with respect to the Company's first two public offerings provided that similar agreements are in effect with each of the Company's directors, officers, and holders of one percent or more of its shares.

To many investors, registration rights and the subsequent public offering are one of the most important issues in a financing. If the investor holds a minority position in a nonpublic company, the exit possibilities depend on the decisions made by others. If the founder is happy for the business to remain a private company, as long as additional funds aren't needed, the investor cannot force a public offering except by exercising a contractual registration right.

Investors typically look for two kinds of rights: demand registration rights, which are described in paragraphs (1) and (2) in the preceding box, and piggyback rights, which are described in paragraph (3). Demand rights, as the name implies, allow investors to require that the company file a public offering; usually a demand registration right is structured so that it cannot be exercised until a sufficient amount of time has elapsed for the company to mature and become an attractive candidate for a public financing. Piggyback rights allow investors to tag their shares onto other shares (usually being sold by the company itself) offered in a public offering. Investors will also want your company to pay expenses of a public offering.

> Reserved Employee Shares: The Company has reserved 1,000,000 shares of Common for issuance to Employees (the "Reserved Employee Shares"). The Reserved Employee Shares will be issued from time to time under such arrangements, contracts, or plans as are recommended by management and approved by the Board. All such shares will be issued subject to vesting restrictions.

This section creates a pool of shares to be used as employment incentives at a later date. It's a good idea to provide for these shares now so that you won't have to negotiate with investors when you want to grant shares to employees at a later time. Employee shares up to the agreed amount for the pool will not be subject to ant-dilution protection. Employee shares will be subject to vesting or repurchase right in favor of the company. Typically vesting occurs over four years, with the first 25 percent of the shares vesting at the end of one year of employment ("cliff" vesting), and the remaining vesting in equal monthly increments over the next three years.

> Right of Participation: Investors shall have a pro rata right (based on their percentage equity ownership of the company calculated on a fully diluted basis), to participate in future equity financings of the Company (subject to the employee reserve pool and customary exclusions).

Frequently, first-round investors will secure dilution protection via a right to participate in future financing rounds at a level sufficient to maintain their share ownership level. The right of participation provides the same economic benefit to those investors who continue to support the company by participating in a downfinancing as does, say, weighted-average formula dilution protection. Early-round investors often prefer the right of participation over ratchet or weighted-average formula protection because it protects only those investors who continue to support the company by participating in a downfinancing and because the principal beneficiaries of the other forms of dilution protection are usually the later investors.

Often the price paid in a downfinancing is low enough to trigger ratchet or formula dilution protection for later investors who bought at a higher price, but it still exceeds the price paid by the early investors. Accordingly, the early investors are entitled to no adjustment. Even when a downfinancing is at a price less than that paid by early investors, later investors will be the principal beneficiaries of ratchet and formula dilution protection if they bought at a higher price than earlier investors, as is usually the case. In such a scenario, later investors will receive a greater equity adjustment than early-round investors. Thus the stake of the founders and early investors will be reduced.

> Right of Co-Sale: Investors shall have the right to participate in transfers of stock for value by the Founders.

Investors may require certain rights in the event that the founders cash in some of their shares prior to an IPO or to acquisition of the company. For example, if the founder wants to sell 100 shares of stock to a new investor, current investors might require the right to sell a pro rata portion of the shares to be sold to that new investor. If investors exercise their right of co-sale, the founder will be able to sell fewer of your shares.

> Confidential Information and Inventions Agreement: Each officer, director, and key employee of the Company has entered, and each person serving in any such capacity in the future will enter, into the Company's standard Employee Confidential Information and Inventions Agreement.

Investors want to know that all owners and employees will keep company information confidential. Moreover, they want to know that the company will own all intellectual property rights in the technology developed by its employees and contractors.

> The Purchase Agreement: The purchase of the Series A Preferred will be made pursuant to a Stock Purchase Agreement and Shareholders Agreement drafted by counsel to the Company and reasonably acceptable to the investors. The Purchase Agreement will contain, among other things, appropriate representations and warranties of the Company, and covenants of the Company reflecting the provisions set forth herein. An opinion of counsel to the Company as to the validity of the shares being issued and other customary matters will also be delivered at the closing.

The key here is to recognize that the Term Sheet is only a summary of a whole lot of details that will be memorialized in later documents, principally the Stock Purchase Agreement, Shareholders Agreement (sometimes referred to as the Information and Registration Rights Agreement), and Articles of Incorporation.

Rather than waiting until the eleventh hour for those documents, be sure that all of the principal terms and understandings with the investors are captured in the Term Sheet. Because of the dynamics of negotiations, "surprises" at the time of signing may put the founder in the position of agreeing to be bound by unfavorable terms that would have been rejected had they been raised in the Term Sheet.

> Expenses: The Company will pay at Closing reasonable legal fees and expenses, in an amount not to exceed $10,000 incurred by a single counsel to all investors.

The company, not the investors, pays closing fees. Typically, the lead investor selects counsel for the investors and is responsible for negotiating the principal terms of the financing.

> Counsel to the Company:
> Matthew P. Quilter
> Heller Ehrman White & McAuliffe
> 525 University Avenue, Suite 1100
> Palo Alto, California 94301
> 650-324-7029

Counsel to be used on behalf of the company is named here. Sometimes founders will secure separate counsel to represent their interests, but this is not common in a venture financing.

SAMPLE STOCK PURCHASE AGREEMENT

The Stock Purchase Agreement sets forth the basic terms of the financing transaction and identifies the parties to the financing, the terms of the financing, the conditions of the closing of the financing, and the time and place of the closing. Most importantly, this agreement includes the representations and warranties of the issuer upon which the investors will rely in making their investment. The agreement typically also includes representations and warranties from the investors (helpful in establishing an exemption from federal and state securities laws), covenants by the issuer concerning the provision of financial information after the closing, and the terms upon which the issuer will agree to register the securities for future public resale by the investors.

Paul E. Kreutz, a partner in the Silicon Valley law firm of Gray Cary Ware & Freidenrich, prepared the following documents.

HI TECH WIDGET, INC.

SERIES A PREFERRED STOCK PURCHASE AGREEMENT

THIS AGREEMENT is made as of _____ , 20 __ , by and among HI TECH WIDGET, INC., a _____ corporation (the "Company"), and the persons and entities listed on the Schedule of Purchasers attached hereto as Exhibit A (the "Purchasers"). The parties hereby agree as follows:

1.   Authorization and Sale of Preferred Shares.

1.1   Authorization; Amended and Restated Articles [Certificate] of Incorporation. The Company has authorized the issuance and sale to the Purchasers, pursuant to the terms and conditions hereof, of up to 2,000,000 shares of its Series A Preferred Stock (the "Preferred Shares") at a purchase price of $1.25 per share. The Preferred Shares have the rights, preferences, and provisions as set forth in the Company's Amended and Restated Articles [Certificate] of Incorporation (the "Articles") attached hereto as Exhibit B.

1.2   Sale and Issuance of the Preferred Shares. Subject to the terms and conditions hereof, the Company will issue and sell to each Purchaser and each Purchaser will purchase the number of Preferred Shares set forth opposite the name of each Purchaser on Exhibit A at the purchase price per Preferred Share as indicated in Section 1.1.

2.   Closing Date; Delivery.

2.1   Closing Date.

(a)   Purchase and Sale. The closing of the purchase and sale of the Preferred Shares shall be held at the offices of _____ at _____ m. on _____ , 20__ , or at such other time and place as the Company and the Purchasers may agree in writing.

(b)   Closing. The closing referred to in subsection (a) above is hereinafter referred to as the "Closing" and the date of the Closing is hereinafter referred to as the "Closing Date."

2.2   Delivery. Subject to the terms of this Agreement, at the Closing the Company will deliver to each Purchaser the certificates representing the Preferred Shares to be purchased by the Purchasers from the Company, against payment of the purchase price therefor by a check or checks payable to the order of the Company or by wire transfer.

3.   Representations and Warranties of the Company. The Company hereby represents and warrants to the Purchasers that except as set forth on a Schedule of Exceptions attached hereto as Exhibit C, which exceptions shall be deemed to be representations and warranties as if made hereunder:

3.1   Organization and Standing; Articles [Certificate] and Bylaws. The Company is a corporation duly organized, validly existing, and in good standing under the laws of the State of _____ and has all requisite corporate power and authority to carry on its businesses as now conducted and as proposed to be conducted. The Company is qualified or licensed to do business as a foreign corporation in all jurisdictions where such qualification or licensing is required, except where the failure to so qualify would not have a material adverse effect upon the Company. Copies of the Company's Articles [Certificate] of Incorporation, Bylaws, minutes, and consents of shareholders and of the Board of Directors are available for inspection at the Company's offices and have been previously provided to special counsel for the Purchasers.

3.2   Corporate Power. The Company has now, or will have at the Closing Date, all requisite corporate power to enter into this Agreement and the Shareholders Agreement (the "Shareholders Agreement") in the form attached hereto as Exhibit D and to sell and issue the Preferred Shares and to issue the Common Stock upon conversion of the Preferred Shares. This Agreement and the Shareholders Agreement are valid and binding obligations of the Company enforceable in accordance with their respective terms, except as the same may be limited by bankruptcy, insolvency, moratorium, and other laws of general application affecting the enforcement of creditors' rights.

3.3   Subsidiaries. The Company does not control, directly or indirectly, any other corporation, association, or business entity.

3.4   Capitalization. The authorized capital stock of the Company is _____ shares of Common Stock, par value $_____ per share, of which _____ shares are outstanding and _____ shares of Preferred Stock, par value $_____ per share, of which _____ shares are designated Series A Preferred Stock, none of which are issued and outstanding. The holders of record of the presently issued and outstanding Common Stock immediately prior to the Closing are as set forth on Exhibit E. All such issued and outstanding shares have been duly authorized and validly issued, are fully paid and nonassessable, and were issued in compliance with all applicable state and federal laws concerning the issuance of securities. The Company has reserved _____ shares of Common Stock for issuance to employees, directors, and consultants pursuant to a stock option plan providing for vesting over a _____ month period of which _____ are outstanding. The holders of any and all rights, warrants, or conversion rights to purchase or acquire from the Company any of its capital stock, along with the number of shares of capital stock issuable upon exercise of such rights, are set forth on Exhibit F hereto. Except for such rights, there are no outstanding rights, warrants, conversion rights, or agreements for the purchase or acquisition from the Company of any shares of its capital stock.

3.5   Authorization.

(a)   Corporate Action. All corporate action on the part of the Company, its officers, directors, and shareholders necessary for the sale and issuance of the Preferred Shares and the issuance of the Common Stock issuable upon conversion of the Preferred Shares and the performance of the Company's obligations hereunder and under the Shareholders Agreement has been taken or will be taken prior to the Closing. The Company has duly reserved an aggregate of _____ shares of Common Stock for issuance upon conversion of the Preferred Shares.

(b)   Valid Issuance. The Preferred Shares, when issued in compliance with the provisions of this Agreement and the shares of Common Stock issuable upon conversion of the Preferred Shares when issued in accordance with the provisions of the Articles, will be duly authorized, validly issued, fully paid and nonassessable, and will be free of any liens or encumbrances caused or created by the Company; provided, however, that all such shares may be subject to restrictions on transfer under state and/or federal securities laws as set forth herein, and as may be required by future changes in such laws. The rights, preferences, privileges, and restrictions of the Preferred Shares are as set forth in the Articles.

(c)   No Preemptive Rights. No person has any right of first refusal or any preemptive rights in connection with the issuance of the Preferred Shares, the issuance of the Common Stock upon conversion of the Preferred Shares, or any future issuances of securities by the Company.

3.6   Patents, Trademarks, etc. The Company owns and possesses or is licensed (or is able to obtain adequate licenses, rights, or purchase options on terms that will not materially and adversely affect its business) under all patents, patent applications, licenses, trademarks, trade names, brand names, inventions, and copyrights reasonably necessary for the operation of its business as now conducted and as proposed to be conducted, with no infringement of or conflict with the rights of others respecting any of the same. The operation of the Company's business as now conducted or as proposed to be conducted does not and will not infringe any patent or other proprietary rights of others respecting any of the same. The Company is not obligated to make any payments by way of royalties, fees, or otherwise to any owner, licensor of, or other claimant to any patent, trademark, trade name, copyright, or other intangible asset, with respect to the use thereof or in connection with the conduct of its business, or otherwise. The Company has not received any communications alleging that it has violated or, by conducting its business as proposed, would violate any of the patents, trademarks, service marks, trade names, copyrights, trade secrets, or other proprietary rights of any other person or entity, nor is the Company aware of any basis for the foregoing.

3.7   Compliance with Other Instruments, None Burdensome, etc. The Company is not in violation of any term of the Articles [Certificate] or Bylaws, nor is the Company in violation of or in default in any material respect under the terms of any mortgage, indenture, contract, agreement, instrument, judgment, or decree, the violation of which would have a material adverse effect on the Company as a whole, and to the knowledge of the Company, is not in violation of any order, statute, rule, or regulation applicable to the Company, the violation of which would have a material adverse effect on the Company. The execution, delivery and performance of and compliance with this Agreement or the Shareholders Agreement, and the issuance and sale of the Preferred Shares will not (a) result in any such violation, or (b) be in conflict with or constitute a default under any such term, or (c) result in the creation of any mortgage, pledge, lien, encumbrance, or charge upon any of the properties or assets of the Company pursuant to any such term. To the knowledge of the Company, there is no such term which materially adversely affects, or, so far as the Company may now foresee, in the future may materially adversely affect, the business, condition, affairs, or operations of the Company or any of its properties or assets.

3.8   Proprietary Agreements; Employees. All technical and management personnel presently employed by the Company have executed an agreement regarding confidentiality and proprietary information, the form of which has been provided to the Purchasers. The Company is not aware that any of its employees is in violation thereof and will use reasonable efforts to prevent any such violation. The Company is not aware that any of its employees is obligated under any contract (including licenses, covenants, or commitments of any nature) or other agreement, or subject to any judgment, decree, or order of any court or administrative agency, that would interfere with the use of his or her best efforts to promote the interests of the Company or that would conflict with the Company's business as conducted or as proposed to be conducted or that would prevent any such employee from assigning inventions to the Company. The Company does not believe that it is or will be necessary for the Company to utilize any inventions of any of its employees (or people it currently intends to hire) made prior to their employment by the Company.

3.9   Litigation, etc. There is no action, proceeding, or investigation pending against the Company or, to the Company's knowledge, its officers, directors, or shareholders, or to the Company's knowledge, against employees or consultants of the Company (or, to the Company's knowledge, any basis therefor or threat thereof): (1) which might result, either individually or in the aggregate, in (a) any material adverse change in the business, conditions, affairs, or operations of the Company or in any of its properties or assets, or (b) any material adverse impairment of the right or ability of the Company to carry on its business as now conducted or as proposed to be conducted, or (c) any material liability on the part of the Company; or (2) which questions the validity of this Agreement, the Shareholders Agreement or any action taken or to be taken in connection herewith, including in each case, without limitation, actions pending or threatened involving the prior employment of any of the Company's employees, the use in connection with the Company's business of any information or techniques allegedly proprietary to any of its former employees, or their obligations under any agreements with prior employers. The Company is not a party to or subject to the provisions of any order, writ, injunction, judgment, or decree of any court or government agency or instrumentality. There is no action, suit, proceeding, or investigation by the Company currently pending or which the Company currently intends to initiate.

3.10   Governmental Consent, etc. Based in part upon the representations and warranties of the Purchasers in Section 4 hereof, no consent, approval or authorization of or designation, declaration, or filing with any governmental authority on the part of the Company is required in connection with: (a) the valid execution and delivery of this Agreement or the Shareholders Agreement; or (b) the offer, sale, or issuance of the Preferred Shares or the issuance of the shares of Common Stock issuable upon conversion of the Preferred Shares, or (c) the obtaining of the consents, permits, and waivers specified in subsection 5.1(b) hereof, except the filing of the Articles [Certificate] and, if required, filings or qualifications under applicable blue sky laws, which filings or qualifications, if required, will have been timely filed or obtained after the sale of the Preferred Shares.

3.11   Offering. In reliance on the representations and warranties of the Purchasers in Section 4 hereof, the offer, sale, and issuance of the Preferred Shares in conformity with the terms of this Agreement will not result in a violation of the requirements of Section 5 of the Securities Act of 1933, as amended (the "Securities Act") or the qualification or registration requirements of the Law or other applicable blue sky laws.

3.12   Taxes. The Company has filed all tax returns that are required to have been filed with appropriate federal, state, county, and local governmental agencies or instrumentalities, except where the failure to do so would not have a material adverse effect upon the Company, taken as a whole. The Company has paid or established reserves for all material income, franchise, and other taxes, assessments, governmental charges, penalties, interest, and fines due and payable by them on or before the Closing. There is no pending dispute with any taxing authority relating to any of such returns and the Company has no knowledge of any proposed liability for any tax to be imposed upon the properties or assets of the Company for which there is not an adequate reserve reflected in the Financial Statements (as defined below) or, if adversely determined against the Company, would have a material adverse effect.

3.13   Title. The Company owns its properties and assets, including the properties and assets reflected in the Financial Statements, free and clear of all liens, mortgages, loans, or encumbrances except liens for current taxes, and such encumbrances and liens which arise in the ordinary course of business and do not materially impair the Company's ownership or use of such property or assets. With respect to the property and assets leased by the Company, the Company is in compliance with such leases and holds valid leasehold interests free and clear of any liens, claims, or encumbrances.

3.14   Material Contracts and Commitments. All of the contracts, mortgages, indentures, agreements, instruments, and transactions to which the Company is a party or by which it is bound (including purchase orders to the Company or placed by the Company) which involve obligations of, or payments to, the Company in excess of Ten Thousand Dollars ($10,000) and all agreements between the Company and its officers, directors, consultants, and employees are either (i) attached as exhibits to this Agreement, or (ii) set forth on the list attached hereto as Exhibit G (the "Contracts"), copies of which have been made available to special counsel to the Purchasers. All of the Contracts are valid, binding, and in full force and effect in all material respects and enforceable by the Company in accordance with their respective terms in all material respects, subject to the effect of applicable bankruptcy, insolvency, reorganization, moratorium, or other laws of general application relating to or affecting enforcement of creditors' rights and rules or laws concerning equitable remedies. The Company is not in material default under any of such Contracts. To the Company's knowledge, no other party to any of the Contracts is in material default thereunder.

3.15   Financial Statements. The Company has delivered to the Purchasers (i) its audited financial statements for the fiscal year ended _____, 20 ____ , and (ii) its unaudited financial statements for the _____ months ended _____ , 20 ___ (the "Balance Sheet Date") (hereinafter collectively referred to as the "Financial Statements"). The Financial Statements are complete and correct in all material respects and have been prepared on a consistent basis throughout the relevant periods. The Financial Statements accurately set out and describe the financial condition and operating results of the Company as of the dates, and during the periods, indicated therein. Except as set forth in the Financial Statements, as of the Closing Date the Company has no material liabilities of any nature (matured or unmatured, fixed or contingent). The Company maintains and will continue to maintain a standard system of accounting established and administered in accordance with generally accepted accounting principles.

3.16   Absence of Changes. Except as contemplated by this Agreement since the Balance Sheet Date: (a) the Company has not entered into any transaction which was not in the ordinary course of business, (b) there has been no material adverse change in the condition (financial or otherwise) of the business, property, assets, or liabilities of the Company other than changes in the ordinary course of business, none of which, individually or in the aggregate, has been materially adverse, (c) there has been no damage to, destruction of, or loss of physical property (whether or not covered by insurance) materially adversely affecting the assets, financial condition, operating results, business, or operations of the Company, (d) the Company has not declared or paid any dividend or made any distribution on its stock, or redeemed, purchased, or otherwise acquired any of its stock, (e) the Company has not materially changed any compensation arrangement or agreement with any of its key employees or executive officers, or materially changed the rate of pay of its employees as a group, (f) the Company has not received notice that there has been a cancellation of an order for the Company's products or a loss of a customer of the Company, the cancellation or loss of which would materially adversely affect the business of the Company, (g) the Company has not changed or amended any material contract by which the Company or any of its assets are bound or subject, (h) there has been no resignation or termination of employment of any key officer or employee of the Company and the Company does not know of any impending resignation or termination of employment of any such officer or employee that if consummated would have a material adverse effect on the business of the Company, (i) there has been no labor dispute involving the Company or its employees and none is pending or, to the best of the Company's knowledge, threatened, (j) there has been no change, except in the ordinary course of business, in the material contingent obligations of the Company (nor in any contingent obligation of the Company regarding any director, shareholder, key employee, or officer of the Company) by way of guaranty, endorsement, indemnity, warranty, or otherwise, (k) there have been no loans made by the Company to any of its employees, officers, or directors other than travel advances and other advances made in the ordinary course of business, (l) there has been no waiver by the Company of a valuable right or of a material debt owing to it, (m) there has not been any satisfaction or discharge of any lien, claims, encumbrance, or any payment of any obligation by the Company, except in the ordinary course of business and which is not material to the assets, properties, financial condition, operating results, or business of the Company, and (n) to the best of the knowledge of the Company, there has been no other event or condition of any character pertaining to and materially adversely affecting the assets or business of the Company.

3.17   Outstanding Indebtedness. Except as disclosed in the Financial Statements, the Company has no indebtedness for borrowed money which it has directly or indirectly created, incurred, assumed, or guaranteed, or with respect to which it has otherwise become liable, directly or indirectly. The Company has no material liability or obligation in excess of $10,000, absolute or contingent, which is not shown or provided for in the latest Financial Statements, except obligations under purchase orders, sales contracts, real property leases, equipment leases, or similar obligations incurred in the ordinary course of business.

3.18   Registration Rights. Other than as granted pursuant to Section 7 hereof, the Company has not granted or agreed to grant any rights to register as that term is defined in Section 7, including piggyback registration rights, to any person or entity.

3.19   Certain Transactions. The Company is not indebted, directly or indirectly, to any of its officers, directors, or shareholders or to their spouses or children, in any amount whatsoever; and none of said officers, directors, or, to the best of the Company's knowledge, shareholders, or any member of their immediate families, are indebted to the Company or have any direct or indirect ownership interest in any firm or corporation with which the Company is affiliated or with which the Company has a business relationship (except as a holder of securities of a corporation whose securities are publicly traded and which is subject to the reporting requirements of the Securities Exchange Act of 1934, to the extent of owning not more than two percent (2%) of the issued and outstanding securities of such corporation). No such officer, director, or shareholder, or any member of their immediate families, is, directly or indirectly, interested in any material contract with the Company. The Company is not guarantor or indemnitor of any indebtedness of any other person, firm, or corporation.

3.20   Corporate Documents; Minute Books. Except for amendments necessary to satisfy representations and warranties or conditions contained herein (the form of which amendments has been approved by the Purchasers), the Articles [Certificate] and Bylaws of the Company are in the form previously provided to the Purchasers. The minute books of the

Company previously made available to the Purchasers contain a complete summary of all meetings of directors and shareholders since the time of incorporation of the Company.

3.21   Employee Benefit Plans. The Company does not have any "employee benefit plan" as defined in the Employee Retirement Income Security Act of 1974, as amended.

3.22   Real Property Holding Corporation. The Company is not a "real property holding corporation" within the meaning of Section 897(c)(2) of the United States Internal Revenue Code of 1986, as amended.

3.23   Disclosure. No representation or warranty by the Company in this Agreement, or in any document or certificate furnished or to be furnished to the Purchasers pursuant hereto or in connection with the transactions contemplated hereby, when taken together, contains or will contain any untrue statement of a material fact or omits or will omit to state a material fact necessary to make the statements made herein and therein, in the light of the circumstances under which they were made, not misleading.

3.24   Insurance. The Company maintains insurance covering property damage and liability reasonably prudent under commercially reasonable practices.

3.25   Shareholder Agreements. Except as otherwise contemplated by this Agreement, (a) there are no agreements or arrangements between the Company and any of the Company's shareholders or to the Company's knowledge, between any of the Company's shareholders which materially and adversely affect any shareholder's ability or right freely to alienate or vote such shares, and (b) to the Company's knowledge, none of the Company's shareholders is affiliated with or has any agreements or arrangements with any customer of, or supplier to, the Company.

4.   Representations and Warranties of Purchasers and Restrictions on Transfer Imposed by the Securities Act.

4.1   Representations and Warranties by the Purchasers. Each of the Purchasers represents and warrants to the Company as of the date hereof and as of the Closing Date as follows:

(a)   Investment Intent. This Agreement is made with the Purchasers in reliance upon such Purchasers' representations to the Company, evidenced by the Purchasers' execution of this Agreement, that Purchasers are acquiring the Preferred Shares and the Common Stock issuable upon conversion of the Preferred Shares (collectively the "Securities") for investment for each Purchaser's own account, not as nominee or agent, and not with a view to, or for resale in connection with, any distribution or public offering thereof within the meaning of the Securities Act and the Law. Purchasers have the full right, power, and authority to enter into and perform this Agreement and the Shareholders Agreement, and this Agreement and the Shareholders Agreement constitute valid and binding obligations upon it.

(b)   Preferred Shares Not Registered. Purchasers understand and acknowledge that the offering of the Preferred Shares pursuant to this Agreement will not be registered under the Securities Act or qualified under the Law on the grounds that the offering and sale of securities contemplated by this Agreement are exempt from registration under the Securities Act pursuant to Section 4(2) thereof and exempt from registration pursuant to Section 25102(f) of the Law, and other applicable state securities or blue sky laws, and that the Company's reliance upon such exemptions is predicated upon such Purchasers' representations set forth in this Agreement. The Purchasers acknowledge and understand that the Securities must be held indefinitely unless the Securities are subsequently registered under the Securities Act and qualified under the Law or an exemption from such registration and such qualification is available.

(c)   No Transfer. Purchasers covenant that in no event will they dispose of any of the Securities (other than in conjunction with an effective registration statement for the Securities under the Securities Act or in compliance with Rule 144 promulgated under the Securities Act) unless and until (i) the Purchasers shall have notified the Company of the proposed disposition and shall have furnished the Company with a statement of the circumstances surrounding the proposed disposition, and (ii) if reasonably requested by the Company, the Purchasers shall have furnished the Company with an opinion of counsel satisfactory in form and substance to the Company to the effect that (x) such disposition will not require registration under the Securities Act, and (y) appropriate action necessary for compliance with the Securities Act, the Law, and any other applicable state, local, or foreign law has been taken. It is agreed that the Company will not require opinions of counsel for transactions made pursuant to Rule 144.

(d)   Knowledge and Experience. Purchasers (i) have such knowledge and experience in financial and business matters as to be capable of evaluating the merits and risks of the Purchasers' prospective investment in the Securities; (ii) have the ability to bear the economic risks of the Purchasers' prospective investment; (iii) have been furnished with and have had access to such information as the Purchasers have considered necessary to make a determination as to the purchase of the Securities together with such additional information as is necessary to verify the accuracy of the information supplied; (iv) have had all questions which have been asked by the Purchasers satisfactorily answered by the Company; and (v) have not been offered the Securities by any form of advertisement, article, notice, or other communication published in any newspaper, magazine, or similar medium; or broadcast over television or radio; or any seminar or meeting whose attendees have been invited by any such medium.

(e)   Not Organized to Purchase. Purchasers have not been organized for the purpose of purchasing the Securities.

(f)   Holding Requirements. Purchasers understand that if the Company does not (i) register its Common Stock with the Securities and Exchange Commission ("SEC") pursuant to Section 12 of the Securities Exchange Act of 1934, as amended (the "Exchange Act"), (ii) become subject to Section 15(d) of the Exchange Act, (iii) supply information pursuant to Rule 15c2-11 thereunder, or (iv) have a registration statement covering the Securities (or a filing pursuant to the exemption from registration under Regulation A of the Securities Act covering the Securities) under the Securities Act in effect when it desires to sell the Securities, the Purchasers may be required to hold the Securities for an indeterminate period.

4.2   Legends. Each certificate representing the Securities may be endorsed with the following legends:

(a)   Federal Legend. THE SECURITIES REPRESENTED BY THESE ARTICLES HAVE NOT BEEN REGISTERED UNDER THE SECURITIES ACT OF 1933, AS AMENDED (THE "ACT") AND ARE "RESTRICTED SECURITIES" AS DEFINED IN RULE 144 PROMULGATED UNDER THE ACT. THE SECURITIES MAY NOT BE SOLD OR OFFERED FOR SALE OR OTHERWISE DISTRIBUTED EXCEPT (i) IN CONJUNCTION WITH AN EFFECTIVE REGISTRATION STATEMENT FOR THE SHARES UNDER THE ACT, OR (ii) IN COMPLIANCE WITH RULE 144, OR (iii) PURSUANT TO AN OPINION OF COUNSEL, SATISFACTORY TO THE COMPANY, THAT SUCH REGISTRATION OR COMPLIANCE IS NOT REQUIRED AS TO SAID SALE, OFFER, OR DISTRIBUTION.

(b)   Other Legends. Any other legends required by the Law or other applicable state blue sky laws. The Company need not register a transfer of legended Securities, and may also instruct its transfer agent not to register the transfer of the Securities, unless the conditions specified in each of the foregoing legends are satisfied.

4.3   Removal of Legend and Transfer Restrictions. Any legend endorsed on a certificate pursuant to subsection 4.2(a) and the stop transfer instructions with respect to such legended Securities shall be removed, and the Company shall issue a certificate without such legend to the holder of such Securities if such Securities are registered and sold under the Securities Act and a prospectus meeting the requirements of Section 10 of the Securities Act is available or if such holder satisfies the requirements of Rule 144(k) and, where reasonably deemed necessary by the Company, provides the Company with an opinion of counsel for such holder of the Securities, reasonably satisfactory to the Company, to the effect that (i) such holder meets the requirements of Rule 144(k), or (ii) a public sale, transfer, or assignment of such Securities may be made without registration.

4.4   Rule 144. Purchasers are aware of the adoption of Rule 144 by the SEC promulgated under the Securities Act, which permits limited public resales of securities acquired in a nonpublic offering, subject to the satisfaction of certain conditions. Purchasers understand that under Rule 144, the conditions include, among other things: the availability of certain current public information about the issuer and the resale occurring not less than two years after the party has purchased and paid for the securities to be sold.

5.   Conditions to Closing.

5.1   Conditions to Purchasers' Obligations. The obligations of the Purchasers to purchase the Preferred Shares at the Closing are subject to the fulfillment to its satisfaction, on or prior to the Closing Date, of the following conditions, any of which may be waived in accordance with the provisions of subsection 8.1 hereof:

(a)   Representations and Warranties Correct; Performance of Obligations. The representations and warranties made by the Company in Section 3 hereof shall be true and correct when made, and shall be true and correct in all material respects on the Closing Date with the same force and effect as if they had been made on and as of said date. The Company's business and assets shall not have been adversely affected in any material way prior to the Closing Date. The Company shall have performed in all material respects all obligations and conditions herein required to be performed or observed by it on or prior to the Closing Date.

(b)   Consents and Waivers. The Company shall have obtained in a timely fashion any and all consents, permits, and waivers necessary or appropriate for consummation of the transactions contemplated by this Agreement.

(c)   Election of Director. Effective upon the Closing, _____ shall have been appointed to the Company's Board of Directors.

(d)   Filing of the Articles. The Articles [Certificate] shall have been filed with the Secretary of State of _____.

(e)   Shareholders Agreement. The Company, the Employee Holders (as defined), and the Purchasers shall have executed and delivered the Shareholders Agreement in the form attached as Exhibit D hereto.

(f)   Stock Purchase Agreements. The employees of the Company who are parties to the Shareholders Agreement, and all other employees of the Company who are shareholders shall have entered into Stock Purchase Agreements with the Company which shall have vesting and other terms acceptable to the Purchasers.

       (g)   <u>Compliance Certificate</u>. The Company shall have delivered a Certificate, executed by the President of the Company, dated the Closing Date, certifying to the fulfillment of the conditions specified in subsections (a), (b), (c), and (d) of this Section 5.1.

       (h)   <u>Opinion of Counsel</u>. The Purchasers shall have received an opinion from the Company's counsel, in substantially the form attached hereto as <u>Exhibit H</u>.

       (i)   <u>Reservation of Common Stock</u>. The shares of Common Stock issuable upon conversion of the Preferred Shares shall have been duly authorized and reserved for issuance upon such conversion.

       5.2   <u>Conditions to Obligations of the Company</u>. The Company's obligation to sell and issue the Preferred Shares at the Closing is subject to the condition that the representations and warranties made by the Purchasers in Section 4 hereof shall be true and correct when made, and shall be true and correct on the Closing Date with the same force and effect as if they had been made on and as of said date.

       6.   <u>Affirmative Covenants of the Company</u>. The Company hereby covenants and agrees as follows:

       6.1   <u>Financial Information</u>. Until the first to occur of (a) the date on which the Company is required to file a report with the SEC pursuant to Section 13(a) of the Exchange Act, by reason of the Company having registered any of its securities pursuant to Section 12(g) of the Exchange Act, or (b) quotations for the Common Stock of the Company are reported by the automated quotations system operated by the National Association of Securities Dealers, Inc. or by an equivalent quotations system, or (c) shares of the Common Stock of the Company are listed on a national securities exchange registered under Section 6 of the Exchange Act, the Company will furnish to each Purchaser:

       (a)   as soon as practicable after the end of each fiscal year, and in any event within 120 days thereafter, consolidated balance sheets of the Company and its subsidiaries, if any, as at the end of such fiscal year, and consolidated statements of operations and consolidated statements of changes in financial position (or equivalent cash flow statements if required by the Financial Accounting Standards Board) of the Company and its subsidiaries, if any, for such year, prepared in accordance with generally accepted accounting principles, all in reasonable detail and certified by independent public accountants of recognized national standing selected by the Company, and

       (b)   so long as each Purchaser owns an aggregate of at least ten percent (10%) of the Preferred Shares acquired at the Closing (including any Common Stock issued upon conversion of any Preferred Shares) as soon as practicable after the end of each month and each quarter (except the last month and last quarter of the fiscal year), and in any event within 30 and 45 days, respectively, thereafter, consolidated balance sheets of the Company and its subsidiaries, if any, as of the end of such month or quarter; and consolidated statements of income (or equivalent cash flow statements if required by the Financial Accounting Standards Board), for such month or quarter and for the current fiscal year to date, prepared in accordance with generally accepted accounting principles (except for required footnotes), all in reasonable detail and signed, subject to changes resulting from year-end audit adjustments, by the principal financial officer or chief executive officer of the Company, and

(c)   so long as each Purchaser owns an aggregate of at least ten percent (10%) of the Preferred Shares acquired at the Closing (including any Common Stock issued upon conversion of any Preferred Shares) as soon as practicable after its adoption or approval by the Company's Board of Directors, but not later than the commencement of such fiscal year, an annual plan for each fiscal year which shall include monthly capital and operating expense budgets, cash flow statements, projected balance sheets, and profit and loss projections for each such month and for the end of the year, itemized in such detail as the Board of Directors may reasonably determine.

6.2   Conflicts of Interests. The Company shall use its best efforts to ensure that the Company's employees, during the term of their employment with the Company, do not engage in activities which would result in a conflict of interest with the Company. The Company's obligations hereunder include, but are not limited to, requiring that the Company's employees devote their primary productive time, ability, and attention to the business of the Company (provided, however, the Company's employees may engage in other business activity if such activity does not materially interfere with their obligations to the Company), requiring that the Company's employees enter into agreements regarding proprietary information and confidentiality and preventing the Company's employees from engaging or participating in any business that is in competition with the business of the Company.

6.3   Key-Man Insurance. The Company shall use reasonable efforts to obtain at commercially reasonable rates within thirty (30) days of the Closing and maintain in force, until canceled or modified with the written consent of Purchasers holding fifty-one percent (51%) of the Preferred Shares issued at the Closing, an insurance policy on the lives of _____ and _____ , in the amounts of $_____ and $_____ , respectively, naming the Company as holder and beneficiary. The Company shall use similar efforts to obtain an insurance policy on similar terms and conditions and in the same amount on the life of any person who shall serve as the chief executive officer or chief operating officer of the Company or in a comparable management position, within thirty (30) days of the commencement of such person's employment with the Company.

6.4   Proprietary Agreements. The Company will use reasonable efforts to prevent any employee from violating the confidentiality and proprietary information agreement entered into between the Company and each of its employees.

6.5   Future Stock Issuances. The Company agrees that after the Closing it will not issue any shares of Common Stock (or grant any options, warrants, or other rights to purchase the same) to any employee, officer, or director except pursuant to written agreements which provide for vesting over a period of at least forty-eight (48) months with the initial vesting date to occur at least after twelve (12) months and a right of first refusal in favor of the Company in the event of any proposed transfer unless such issuance or grant is approved by the director elected by the holders of the Preferred Shares and provided that no such agreement will require the Company to repurchase or redeem any of such shares. This Section 6.5 will terminate upon the termination of Section 6.1.

6.6   Rule 144. The Company covenants that (i) at all times after the Company first becomes subject to the reporting requirements of Section 13 or 15(d) of the Securities Exchange Act of 1934, the Company will use its best efforts to comply with the current public information requirements of Rule 144(c)(1) under the Securities Act; and (ii) at all such times as Rule 144 is available for use by the Purchasers, the Company will furnish the Purchasers upon request with all information within the possession of the Company required for the preparation and filing of Form 144.

7.   Registration.

   7.1   Definitions. As used in this Section 7:

      (a) The terms "register," "registered," and "registration" refer to a registration effected by preparing and filing a registration statement in compliance with the Securities Act and the declaration or ordering of the effectiveness of such registration statement;

      (b) The term "Registrable Securities" means: (i) any Common Stock issued or to be issued pursuant to conversion of the Preferred Shares issued hereunder, and (ii) any other Common Stock issued as a dividend or other distribution with respect to, or in exchange for or in replacement of, the Preferred Shares or the shares of Common Stock issued pursuant to conversion of the Preferred Shares;

      (c) The term "Holder" means any holder of outstanding Registrable Securities who acquired such Registrable Securities in a transaction or series of transactions not involving any registered public offering;

      (d) The term "Initiating Holders" means any Holder or Holders making a request for registration pursuant to the provisions of Section 7.2;

      (e) The term "Substantial Amount of Registrable Securities" means at least forty percent (40%) of the Registrable Securities which have not been resold to the public in a registered public offering.

   7.2   Requested Registration.

      (a) Request for Registration. If at any time after the date that is the earlier of _____ years after the Closing Date or three months after the first registration effected by the Company of any of its securities the Company shall receive from the Holders of a Substantial Amount of Registrable Securities a written request that the Company effect any registration, qualification, or compliance with respect to all or a part of the Registrable Securities, the Company will:

         (i) promptly give written notice of the proposed registration, qualification or compliance to all other Holders; and

         (ii) as soon as practicable, use its diligent best efforts to effect all such registrations, qualifications, and compliances (including, without limitation, the execution of an undertaking to file post-effective amendments, appropriate qualification under the applicable state securities laws, and appropriate compliance with exemptive regulations issued under the Securities Act and any other governmental requirements or regulations) as may be so requested and as would permit the sale and distribution of such portion of such Holders' Registrable Securities as are specified in such request, together with such portion of the Registrable Securities of any other Holder or Holders joining in such request as are specified in a written notice given within thirty (30) days after receipt of written notice from the Company; provided that the Company shall not be obligated to take any action to effect any such registration, qualification, or compliance pursuant to this Section 7.2 (1) after the Company has effected two registrations under this Section 7.2, or (2) within three months after the filing date of any other registration filed under the Securities Act (other than registration statements relating to employee stock or stock purchase plans or relating solely to Rule 145 transactions or to debt securities).

      (b) Underwriting. If the Initiating Holders intend to distribute the Registrable Securities covered by their request by means of an underwriting, they shall so advise the Company as a part of their request made pursuant to Section 7.2(a) and the Company shall include such information in the written notice referred to in Section 7.2(a)(i). The Company may require that any registration of shares constituting more than one percent (1%) of the total number of shares then outstanding be firmly underwritten. The right of any Holder to registration pursuant to Section 7.2 shall be conditioned upon the inclusion of such Holder's Registrable Securities in the underwriting. The Company shall (together with all Holders proposing to distribute their securities) enter into an underwriting agreement in customary form with the underwriter or underwriters selected for such underwriting by the Company. Notwithstanding any other provision of this Section 7.2, if the underwriter advises the Initiating Holders in writing that marketing factors require a limitation of the number of shares to be underwritten, then the Initiating Holders shall so advise all Holders of Registrable Securities which would otherwise be registered and underwritten pursuant hereto, and the number of shares included in the registration and underwriting shall be allocated among the Holders of Registrable Securities requesting registration in proportion, as nearly as practicable, to the total number of Registrable Securities held by such Holders at the time of filing of the registration statement. In no event, however, shall any Registrable Shares be eliminated from the registration until any and all shares being sold for the account of the Company and for the account of shareholders who are not Holders are first eliminated. If any Holder disapproves of the terms of the underwriting, he or she may elect to withdraw therefrom by written notice to the Company, the underwriter, and the Initiating Holders. The Registrable Securities so withdrawn shall also be withdrawn from registration.

(c)   Delay of Registration. The Company shall not be required to effect a registration pursuant to this Section 7.2 if the Company shall furnish to the Holders a certificate signed by the President of the Company stating that in the good faith judgment of the Board of Directors of the Company, it would be seriously detrimental to the Company and its shareholders for such registration to be effected at such time, in which event the Company shall have the right to defer the filing of the registration statement for a period of not more than 90 days after the receipt of the request of the Holder or Holders under this Section 7.2; provided, however, that the Company shall not utilize this right more than once in any 12-month period.

7.3   Company Registration.

(a) Notice of Registration. If at any time or from time to time, the Company shall determine to register any of its securities, either for its own account or the account of a security Holder or Holders (other than a registration relating solely to employee stock option or purchase plans or relating solely to an SEC Rule 145 transaction or to debt securities), the Company will:

(i) promptly give to each Holder written notice thereof; and

(ii) include in such registration (and any related qualification under state securities laws or other compliance), and in any underwriting involved therein, all the Registrable Securities specified in a written request or requests, received within twenty (20) days after such written notice from the Company, by any Holder or Holders, except as set forth in Section 7.3(b) below.

(b) Underwriting. If the registration of which the Company gives notice is for a registered public offering involving an underwriting, the Company shall so advise the Holders as a part of the written notice given pursuant to Section 7.3(a)(i). In such event the right of any Holder to registration pursuant to Section 7.3 shall be conditioned upon the inclusion of such Holder's Registrable Securities in the underwriting. All Holders proposing to distribute their securities shall (together with the Company and other Holders distributing their securities through such underwriting) enter into an underwriting agreement in customary form with the underwriter or underwriters selected for such underwriting by the Company. Notwithstanding any other provision of this Section 7.3, if the underwriter determines that marketing factors require a limitation of the number of Registrable Securities to be included in the registration on a pro rata basis based on the total number of the Registrable Securities held by the Holders and based on the total number of securities (other than Registrable Securities) entitled to registration held by other persons or organizations selling securities pursuant to registration rights granted them by the Company, provided that no such reduction shall be made with respect to securities being offered by Holders of securities who have requested the Company to register such securities pursuant to a mandatory registration obligation of the Company similar to the one contained in Section 7.2 hereof ("Other Shareholder Demand Offering"), and provided further that if such offering is other than the first registered offering of the Company's securities to the public or is not an Other Shareholder Demand Offering, the underwriter may not limit the Registrable Securities to be included in such offering to less than thirty percent (30%) of the securities included therein (based on aggregate market values.) The Company shall advise all Holders of Registrable Securities which would otherwise be registered and underwritten pursuant hereto of any such limitations, and the number of shares of Registrable Securities that may be included in the registration. If any Holder disapproves of the terms of any such underwriting, he or she may elect to withdraw therefrom by written notice to the Company and the underwriter. Any securities excluded or withdrawn from such underwriting shall not be transferred prior to 90 days after the effective date of the registration statement for such underwriting, or such shorter period as the underwriter may require.

7.4 Form S-3. The Company shall use its best efforts to qualify for registration on Form S-3 or its successor form. After the Company has qualified for the use of Form S-3, Holders of not less than twenty percent (20%) of the aggregate number of Registrable Securities then outstanding shall have the right to request registrations on Form S-3 (which request shall be in writing and shall state the number of shares of Registrable Securities to be disposed of and the intended method of disposition of Shares by such Holders), subject only to the following:

(a) The Company shall not be required to effect a registration pursuant to this subsection 7.4 within 90 days of the effective date of any registration referred to in subsections 7.2 and 7.3 above.

(b) The Company shall not be required to effect a registration pursuant to this subsection 7.4 if it has, within the 12-month period preceding the date of any request under this subsection 7.4, already effected two registrations pursuant to this subsection 7.4.

(c) The Company shall not be required to effect a registration pursuant to this Section 7.4 unless the Holder or Holders requesting registration propose to dispose of shares of Registrable Securities having an aggregate price to the public (before deduction of underwriting discounts and expenses of sale) of at least $750,000.

(d) The Company shall not be required to effect a registration pursuant to this Section 7.4 if the Company shall furnish to the Holders a certificate signed by the President of the Company stating that in the good faith judgment of the Board of Directors of the Company, it would be seriously detrimental to the Company and its shareholders for such Form S-3 registration to be effected at such time, in which event the Company shall have the right to defer the filing of the Form S-3 registration statement for a period of not more than 90 days after receipt of the request of the Holder or Holders under this Section 7.4; provided, however, that the Company shall not utilize this right more than once in any 12-month period.

The Company shall give written notice to all Holders of Registrable Securities of the receipt of a request for registration pursuant to this Section 7.4 and shall provide a reasonable opportunity for other Holders to participate in the registration, provided that if the registration is for an underwritten offering, the terms of subsection 7.2(b) shall apply to all participants in such offering. Subject to the foregoing, the Company will use its best efforts to effect promptly the registration of all shares of Registrable Securities on Form S-3 to the extent requested by the Holder or Holders thereof for purposes of disposition.

7.5   Expenses of Registration. All expenses incurred in connection with any registration, qualification, or compliance pursuant to this Section 7, including all registration, filing and qualification fees, printing expenses, fees and disbursements of counsel for the Company, and expenses of any special audits incidental to such registration, shall be borne by the Company; provided, however:

(a) The Company shall not be required to pay for expenses of any registration proceeding begun pursuant to Section 7.2 or 7.4, the request of which has been subsequently withdrawn by the Initiating Holders, in which case, such expenses shall be borne by the Holders of securities (including Registrable Securities) requesting or causing such withdrawal;

(b) The Company shall not be required to pay underwriters' discounts, commissions, or stock transfer taxes relating to Registrable Securities or the fees of any counsel retained by the Holders.

7.6   Registration Procedures. In the case of each registration, qualification or compliance effected by the Company pursuant to Section 7, the Company will keep each Holder participating therein advised in writing as to the initiation of each registration, qualification, and compliance and as to the completion thereof. At its expense the Company will:

(a) keep such registration, qualification, or compliance pursuant to Section 7.2, 7.3, or 7.4 effective for a period of three months or until the Holder or Holders have completed the distribution described in the registration statement relating thereto, whichever first occurs; and

(b) furnish such number of prospectuses and other documents incident thereto as a Holder from time to time may reasonably request.

7.7   Indemnification.

(a) The Company will indemnify each Holder of Registrable Securities, each of its officers, directors, and partners, and each person controlling such Holder, with respect to which registration, qualification, or compliance has been effected pursuant to this Section 7 and each underwriter, if any, and each person who controls any underwriter of the Registrable Securities held by or issuable to such Holder, against all claims, losses, damages, costs, expenses, and liabilities whatsoever (or actions in respect thereof) arising out of or based on any untrue statement (or alleged untrue statement) of a material fact contained in any registration statement, prospectus, offering circular, or other documents (including any related registration, statement, notification, or the like) incident to any such registration, qualification, or compliance, or based on any omission (or alleged omission) to state therein a material fact required to be stated therein or necessary to make the statements therein not misleading, or any violation by the Company of the Securities Act or any state securities law or of any rule or regulation promulgated under the Securities Act or any state securities law applicable to the Company and relating to action or inaction required of the Company in connection with any such registration, qualification, or compliance, and will reimburse each such Holder, each of its officers and directors, and each person controlling such Holder, each such underwriter, and each person who controls any such underwriter, for any legal and any other expenses reasonably incurred in connection with investigating or defending any such claim, loss, damage, cost, expense, liability, or action, provided that the Company will not be liable in any such case to the extent that any such claim, loss, damage, cost, expense, or liability arises out of or is based on any untrue statement or omission based upon written information furnished to the Company by an instrument duly executed by any Holder or underwriter and stated to be specifically for use therein.

(b) Each Holder will, if Registrable Securities held by or issuable to such Holder are included in the securities as to which such registration, qualification, or compliance is being effected, indemnify the Company, each of its directors and officers who sign such registration statement, each underwriter, if any, of the Company's securities covered by such a registration statement, each person who controls the Company within the meaning of the Securities Act, and each other Holder, each of such other Holder's officers and directors, and each person controlling such other Holder, against all claims, losses, damages, costs, expenses, and liabilities whatsoever (or actions in respect thereof) arising out of or based on any untrue statement (or alleged untrue statement) of a material fact contained in any such registration statement, prospectus, offering circular, or other documents (including any related registration statement, notification, or the like) incident to any such registration, qualification or compliance, or based on any omission (or alleged omission) to state therein a material fact required to be stated therein or necessary to make the statements therein not misleading, and will reimburse the Company, such other Holders, such directors, officers, persons, or underwriters for any legal or any other expenses reasonably incurred in connection with investigating or defending any such claim, loss, damage, cost, expense, liability, or action, in each case to the extent, but only to the extent, that such untrue statement (or alleged untrue statement) or omission (or alleged omission) is made in such registration statement, prospectus, offering circular or other document in reliance upon and in conformity with written information furnished to the Company by an instrument duly executed by such Holder and stated to be specifically for use therein; provided, however, that the foregoing indemnity agreement is subject to the condition that, insofar as it relates to any such untrue statement (or alleged untrue statement) or omission (or alleged omission) made in the preliminary prospectus but eliminated or remedied in the amended prospectus on file with the SEC at the time the registration statement becomes effective or the amended prospectus filed with the SEC pursuant to Rule 424(b) (the "Final Prospectus"), such indemnity agreement shall not inure to the benefit of any underwriter or any Holder, if there is no underwriter, if a copy of the Final Prospectus was furnished to the person or entity asserting the loss, liability, claim, or damage at or prior to the time such action is required by the Securities Act; and provided further, the total amount for which any Holder shall be liable under this Section 7.7 shall not in any event exceed the aggregate proceeds received by such Holder from the sale of Registrable Securities held by such Holder in such registration.

(c) Each party entitled to indemnification under this Section 7.7 (the "Indemnified Party") shall give notice to the party required to provide indemnification (the "Indemnifying Party") promptly after such Indemnified Party has actual knowledge of any claim as to which indemnity may be sought, and shall permit the Indemnifying Party to assume the defense of any such claim or any litigation resulting therefrom, provided that counsel for the Indemnifying Party, who shall conduct the defense of such claim or litigation, shall be approved by the Indemnified Party (whose approval shall not unreasonably be withheld), and the Indemnified Party may participate in such defense at such party's expense, and provided further that the failure of any Indemnified Party to give notice as provided herein shall not relieve the Indemnifying Party of its obligations under this Section 7. No Indemnifying Party, in the defense of any such claim or litigation, shall, except with the consent of each Indemnified Party, consent to entry of any judgment or enter into any settlement which does not include as an unconditional term thereof the giving by the claimant or plaintiff to such Indemnified Party of a release from all liability in respect to such claim or litigation. If any such Indemnified Party shall have been advised by counsel chosen by it that there may be one or more legal defenses available to such Indemnified Party which are different from or additional to those available to the Indemnifying Party, the Indemnifying Party shall not have the right to assume the defense of such action on behalf of such Indemnified Party and will reimburse such Indemnified Party and any person controlling such Indemnified Party for the reasonable fees and expenses of any counsel retained by the Indemnified Party, it being understood that the Indemnifying Party shall not, in connection with any one action or separate but similar or related actions in the same jurisdiction arising out of the same general allegations or circumstances, be liable for the reasonable fees and expenses of more than one separate firm of attorneys for such Indemnified Party or controlling person, which firm shall be designated in writing by the Indemnified Party to the Indemnifying Party.

7.8   Information by Holder. The Holder or Holders of Registrable Securities included in any registration shall furnish to the Company such information regarding such Holder or Holders and the distribution proposed by such Holder or Holders as the Company may request in writing and as shall be required in connection with any registration, qualification or compliance referred to in this Section 7.

7.9   Sale without Registration. If at the time of any transfer (other than a transfer not involving a change in beneficial ownership) of any Shares or Registrable Securities, such Shares or Registrable Securities shall not be registered under the Securities Act, the Company may require, as a condition of allowing such transfer, that the Holder or transferee furnish to the Company (a) such information as is necessary in order to establish that such transfer may be made without registration under the Securities Act; and (b) at the expense of the Holder or transferee, an opinion by legal counsel designated by such Holder or transferee and satisfactory to the Company, satisfactory in form and substance to the Company, to the effect that such transfer may be made without registration under such Act; provided that nothing contained in this Section 7.9 shall relieve the Company from complying with any request for registration, qualification, or compliance made pursuant to the other provisions of this Section 7.

7.10   Rule 144 Reporting. With a view to making available to the Purchasers the benefits of certain rules and regulations of the U.S. Securities and Exchange Commission ("SEC") which may permit the sale of the Shares or Registrable Securities to the public without registration, the Company agrees to:

(a) make and keep public information available, as those terms are understood and defined in SEC Rule 144, at all times after 90 days after the effective date of the first registration filed by the Company which involves a sale of securities of the Company to the general public;

(b) file with the SEC in a timely manner all reports and other documents required of the Company under the Securities Act and the Securities Exchange Act of 1934, as amended (the "Securities Exchange Act");

(c) furnish to Purchasers so long as Purchasers own any Preferred Shares or Registrable Securities forthwith upon request a written statement by the Company that it has complied with the reporting requirements of said Rule 144 (at any time after 90 days after the effective date of said first registration statement filed by the Company) and of the Securities Act and the Securities Exchange Act (at any time after it has become subject to such reporting requirements), a copy of the most recent annual or quarterly report of the Company, and such other reports and documents so filed by the Company as may be reasonably requested in availing Purchasers of any rule or regulation of the SEC permitting the selling of any such securities without registration.

7.11   Transfer of Registration Rights. The rights to cause the Company to register securities granted by the Company under Sections 7.2, 7.3, and 7.4 may be assigned by any Purchaser to a transferee or assignee who acquires at least _____ of the Preferred Shares or an equivalent amount of Registrable Securities issued upon conversion thereof (adjusted for any dividends, subdivisions, combinations, or reclassifications with respect to such shares), provided that such transfer may otherwise be effected in accordance with applicable securities laws and provided further that the Company is given written notice by such Purchaser at the time of or within a reasonable time after said transfer, stating the name and address of said transferee or assignee and identifying the securities with respect to which such registration rights are being assigned.

7.12   Limitations on Subsequent Registration Rights. From and after the date hereof, the Company shall not, without the prior written consent of the Holders (which consent will not be unreasonably withheld) of not less than a majority of the Registrable Securities then held by Holders, enter into any agreement with any holder or prospective holder of any securities of the Company which would allow such holder or prospective holder (a) to include such securities in any registration filed under Sections 7.2, 7.3 or 7.4 hereof, unless under the terms of such agreement, such holder or prospective holder may include such securities in any such registration only to the extent that the inclusion of his securities will not reduce the amount of the Registrable Securities of the Holders which is included or (b) to make a demand registration which could result in such registration statement being declared effective prior to the earlier of either of the dates set forth in Section 7.2 or within 120 days of the effective date of any registration effected pursuant to Sections 7.3 or 7.4.

7.13   "Market Stand-Off" Agreement. Each Holder hereby agrees that, during the period of duration specified by the Company and an underwriter of Common Stock or other securities of the Company (such period shall not exceed 180 days), following the effective date of a registration statement of the Company filed under the Securities Act, it shall not, to the extent requested by the Company and such underwriter, directly or indirectly sell, offer to sell, contract to sell (including, without limitation, any short sale), grant any option to purchase, or otherwise transfer or dispose of (other than to donees who agree to be similarly bound) any securities of the Company held by it at any time during such period except Common Stock included in such registration; provided, however, that:

(a)   such agreement shall be applicable only to the first such registration statement of the Company which covers Common Stock (or other securities) to be sold on its behalf to the public in an underwritten offering; and

(b)   such agreement shall not be required unless all officers and directors of the Company and all other persons with registration rights (whether or not pursuant to this Agreement) or purchasing Common Stock of the Company enter into similar agreements.

In order to enforce the foregoing covenant, the Company may impose stop-transfer instructions with respect to the Registrable Securities of each Holder (and the shares of securities of every other person subject to the foregoing restriction) until the end of such period.

7.14   Expiration of Rights. All registration rights shall expire and not apply to any Holder upon the earlier of the date seven years from the Closing Date or the date such Holder is eligible to sell in a three-month period pursuant to SEC Rule 144 all Registrable Securities held by such Holder.

8.   Miscellaneous.

8.1   Waivers and Amendments. With the written consent of the record Holders of at least a majority of the Preferred Shares, the obligations of the Company and the rights of the Holders of the Preferred Shares under this Agreement may be waived or amended (either generally or in a particular instance); provided, however, that no such waiver or amendment shall reduce the aforesaid proportion of Preferred Shares, the Holders of which are required to consent to any waiver or supplemental agreement, without the consent of the record Holders of all of the Preferred Shares. Upon the effectuation of each such waiver or amendment, the Company shall promptly give written notice thereof to the record Holders of the Preferred Shares who have not previously consented thereto in writing. Except to the extent provided in this subsection 8.1, this Agreement or any provision hereof may be amended, waived, discharged, or terminated only by a statement in writing signed by the party against which enforcement of the amendment, waiver, discharge, or termination is sought.

8.2   Governing Law. This Agreement shall be governed in all respects by the laws of the State of _____ as such laws are applied to agreements between _____ _____ residents entered into and to be performed entirely within _____.

8.3   Survival. The representations, warranties, covenants and agreements made herein shall survive the Closing of the transactions contemplated hereby, notwithstanding any investigation made by the Purchasers. All statements as to factual matters contained in any certificate or other instrument delivered by or on behalf of the Company pursuant hereto or in connection with the transactions contemplated hereby shall be deemed to be representations and warranties by the Company hereunder as of the date of such certificate or instrument.

8.4   Successors and Assigns. Except as otherwise expressly provided herein, the provisions hereof shall inure to the benefit of, and be binding upon, the successors, assigns, heirs, executors, and administrators of the parties hereto.

8.5   Entire Agreement. This Agreement and the other documents delivered pursuant hereto constitute the full and entire understanding and agreement between the parties with regard to the subjects hereof and thereof and they supersede, merge, and render void every other prior written and/or oral understanding or agreement among or between the parties hereto.

8.6   Notices, etc. All notices and other communications required or permitted hereunder shall be in writing and shall be delivered personally, mailed by first class mail, postage prepaid, or delivered by courier or overnight delivery, addressed (a) if to a Purchaser, at such Purchaser's address set forth on the Schedule of Purchasers, or at such other address as such Purchaser shall have furnished to the Company in writing, or (b) if to the Company, at its address set forth at the beginning of this Agreement, or at such other address as the Company shall have furnished to the Purchasers in writing. Notices that are mailed shall be deemed received five (5) days after deposit in the United States mail. Notices sent by courier or overnight delivery shall be deemed received two (2) days after they have been so sent.

8.7   Severability. In case any provision of this Agreement shall be found by a court of law to be invalid, illegal, or unenforceable, the validity, legality, and enforceability of the remaining provisions of this Agreement shall not in any way be affected or impaired thereby.

8.8   Finder's Fees and Other Fees.

(a)   The Company (i) represents and warrants that it has retained no finder or broker in connection with the transactions contemplated by this Agreement, and

(ii) hereby agrees to indemnify and to hold Purchasers harmless from and against any liability for commission or compensation in the nature of a finder's fee to any broker or other person or firm (and the costs and expenses of defending against such liability or asserted liability) for which the Company, or any of its employees or representatives, is responsible.

(b)   Each Purchaser (i) represents and warrants that the Purchaser has retained no finder or broker in connection with the transactions contemplated by this Agreement, and (ii) hereby agrees to indemnify and to hold the Company harmless from and against any liability for any commission or compensation in the nature of a finder's fee to any broker or other person or firm (and the costs and expenses of defending against such liability or asserted liability) for which such Purchaser is responsible.

8.9   Expenses. The Company and the Purchasers shall each bear their own expenses and legal fees in connection with the consummation of this transaction; provided, however, that the Company will pay the reasonable fees of special counsel for the Purchasers in an amount not to exceed $_____ , together with disbursements and expenses incurred by special counsel in connection with all transactions leading up to and including the Closing.

8.10   Titles and Subtitles. The titles of the sections and subsections of this Agreement are for convenience of reference only and are not to be considered in construing this Agreement.

8.11   Counterparts. This Agreement may be executed in any number of counterparts, each of which shall be an original, but all of which together shall constitute one instrument.

8.12   Delays or Omissions. No delay or omission to exercise any right, power, or remedy accruing to the Company or to any Holder of any securities issued or to be issued hereunder shall impair any such right, power, or remedy of the Company or such Holder, nor shall it be construed to be a waiver of any breach or default under this Agreement, or an acquiescence therein, or of or in any similar breach or default thereafter occurring; nor shall any delay or omission to exercise any right, power, or remedy or any waiver of any single breach or default be deemed a waiver of any other right, power, or remedy or breach or default theretofore or thereafter occurring. All remedies, either under this Agreement, or by law otherwise afforded to the Company or any Holder, shall be cumulative and not alternative.

IN WITNESS WHEREOF, the parties hereto have executed this Agreement as of the date first written above.

HI TECH WIDGET, INC.

By:_____

_____ , President

PURCHASERS:

_____

_____

_____

SAMPLE SHAREHOLDERS AGREEMENT

This agreement sets forth the rights of the investors to participate in future private equity offerings of the issuer. This agreement also fixes the rights of investors (a) to purchase shares held by key employees in the event of a proposed future transfer or, in the alternative, b) to participate, pro rata, with employees in the proposed sale. Whether or not these provisions are included in a separate agreement (as proposed in the following) or in the basic stock purchase agreement is primarily a "form over substance" decision.

HI TECH WIDGET, INC.
SHAREHOLDERS AGREEMENT

SHAREHOLDERS AGREEMENT dated effective as of the _____ day of _____, 20___, by and among HI TECH WIDGET, INC., a _____ corporation (the "Company"), the undersigned holders of the Company's Common Stock (the "Employee Holders"), and the undersigned holders (the "Purchasers") of Preferred Stock of the Company (the "Preferred Shares").

WITNESSETH:

WHEREAS, the parties desire to set forth certain rights and restrictions related to the ownership and disposition of their respective shares of stock in the Company (referred to from time to time as "shares");

NOW, THEREFORE, in consideration of the premises and the mutual promises set forth in this Agreement,

THE PARTIES AGREE AS FOLLOWS:

1.   Restrictions on Transfer of Shares by Employee Holder. Except as otherwise provided in this Agreement, the Employee Holders will not sell, assign, transfer, pledge, hypothecate, or otherwise encumber or dispose of in any way, all or any part of or interest in the shares now or hereafter owned or held by them. Any sale, assignment, transfer, pledge, hypothecation, or other encumbrance or disposition of shares not made in conformance with this Agreement shall be null and void, shall not be recorded on the books of the Company, and shall not be recognized by the Company.

2.   Pre-emptive Right.

2.1   Definitions.

(a)   Equity Securities. The term "Equity Securities" shall mean any securities having voting rights in the election of the Board of Directors not contingent upon default, or any securities evidencing an ownership interest in the Company, or any securities convertible into or exercisable for any shares of the foregoing, or any agreement or commitment to issue any of the foregoing.

        (b)   Holders. For purposes of this Section 2 the term "Holders" shall mean the Purchasers or persons who have acquired shares from any of the Purchasers or their transferees in a transaction not involving a public offering and in compliance with this Section 2.

        2.2   The Right. If at any time prior to termination of this Agreement the Company shall issue any Equity Securities, it shall offer to sell to each Holder a Ratable Portion of such Equity Securities on the same terms and conditions and at the lowest price as such Equity Securities are issued to any person. "Ratable Portion" shall mean that portion of such Equity Securities that bears the same ratio to all such Equity Securities (including for this purpose all Equity Securities which may be purchased by all Holders pursuant to this Section 2) as the number of shares of Common Stock held by the Holder from conversion of Preferred Shares and the number of shares of Common Stock into which the Preferred Shares held by the Holder are then convertible bears to the Outstanding Common Shares. "Outstanding Common Shares" means all shares of Common Stock then outstanding and all shares of Common Stock issuable upon conversion of all convertible securities then outstanding or issuable upon exercise of warrants then outstanding (except the Equity Securities so issued).

        2.3   Notice. The Company shall give notice of the issuance of Equity Securities to each Holder not later than ten (10) days after the issuance. Such notice shall contain all material terms and conditions of the issuance and of the Equity Securities. Each Holder may elect to exercise all or any portion of its rights under this Section 2 by giving written notice to the Company within twenty (20) days of the Company's notice. If the consideration paid by others for the Equity Securities is not cash, the value of the consideration shall be determined in good faith by the Company's Board of Directors, and any electing Holder which cannot for any reason pay for the Equity Securities in the form of noncash consideration may pay the cash equivalent thereof, as determined by the Board of Directors. All payments shall be delivered by electing Holders to the Company not later than the date specified by the Company in its notice, but in no event earlier than 30 days after the Company's notice.

        2.4   Limitation. The provisions of this Section 2 shall not apply to (i) issuances after the date of this Agreement of up to _____ shares of Common Stock (and options to purchase such Common Stock) to employees, officers, directors, or consultants (adjusted for any stock splits, stock dividends, recapitalizations, and the like after the date hereof); (ii) issuances pursuant to a bona fide firmly underwritten public offering registered under the Securities Act of 1933, as amended; (iii) issuances of Equity Securities in connection with the acquisition or merger of another business entity or majority ownership thereof provided that no director and no relative or Affiliate (as defined below) of a director of the Company has a material interest in such other business entity; (iv) issuances of Common Stock upon conversion of the Preferred Shares; and (v) the issuances of warrants to purchase Common Stock (and shares of Common Stock upon exercise thereof) to commercial lending institutions and equipment lessors.

        2.5   Termination. The rights of Holders under this Section 2 shall terminate (i) as to any Holder which has sold or otherwise disposed of (except to an Affiliate and except by conversion into Common Stock) more than forty percent (40%) of the highest number of shares of Preferred Shares (and/or Common Stock issuable upon conversion of Preferred Shares) owned by such Holder, and (ii) as to all Holders immediately prior to the closing of a firmly underwritten public offering of securities by the Company under the Securities Act.

        2.6   Assignment. Holder's rights under this Section 2 shall be assignable only to an assignee who following such assignment holds at least ____ Preferred Shares (or ___ shares of Common Stock issued upon conversion of Preferred Shares, or any combination thereof), adjusted for any stock splits, stock dividends, recapitalizations, and the like after the date hereof.

2.7   Affiliate. For purposes of this Section 2, the term "Affiliate" means any person or entity controlling, controlled by, or under common control with such Purchaser.

3.   Agreements among the Company, the Purchasers, and the Employee Holders.

3.1   Right of Last Refusal.

(a)   The Right. If at any time any of the Employee Holders proposes to sell Equity Securities (as defined in Section 2) to one or more third parties pursuant to an understanding with such third parties in a transaction not registered under the Securities Act in reliance upon a claimed exemption thereunder (the "Transfer"), then the Employee Holder shall give the Company and each Investor (as defined below) written notice of his or her intention (the "Transfer Notice"), describing the offered shares ("Offered Shares"), the identity of the prospective transferee, and the consideration and the material terms and conditions upon which the proposed Transfer is to be made. The Transfer Notice shall certify that the Employee Holder has received a firm offer from the prospective transferee and in good faith believes a binding agreement for Transfer is obtainable on the terms set forth, and shall also include a copy of any written proposal or letter of intent or other agreement relating to the proposed Transfer. The Company, upon request of the Employee Holder, will provide a list of the addresses of the Investors.

(b)   Investors. For purposes of this Section 3, the term "Investors" shall mean the Purchasers or persons who have acquired shares from any of the Purchasers or their transferees in a transaction not involving a public offering and in compliance with Section 3.4 below.

(c)   Investor Option. The Investors shall have an option for a period of thirty (30) days from receipt of the Transfer Notice to purchase their respective pro rata shares of the Offered Shares at the same price and subject to the same material terms and conditions as described in the Transfer Notice. Each of such persons may only exercise such purchase option and, thereby, purchase all or any portion of his, her, or its pro rata shares (with any reallotments as provided below) of the Offered Shares, by notifying the Employee Holder and the Company in writing, before expiration of the initial thirty (30) day period as to the number of such shares which he, she, or it wishes to purchase. Each Investor's pro rata share of the Offered Shares shall be a fraction of the Offered Shares, of which the number of shares of Common Stock held and issued to such Investor or issuable upon conversion of the Preferred Shares held by such Investor on the date of the Transfer Notice (the "Notice Date") shall be the numerator and the total number of shares of Common Stock issued or issuable upon conversion and/or exercise of all outstanding Equity Securities held by all on the Notice Date shall be the denominator. Each Investor shall have a right of overallotment such that, if any other Investor fails to exercise the right to purchase his, her, or its full pro rata share of the Offered Shares, the other participating Investors may, before the date ten (10) days following the expiration of the initial thirty (30) day period, exercise an additional right to purchase, on a pro rata basis, the Offered Shares not previously purchased by so notifying the Employee Holder and the Company, in writing, within such ten (10) day period. Each Investor shall be entitled to apportion Offered Shares to be purchased among its partners and affiliates, provided that such Investor notifies the Employee Holder of such allocation, and provided that such allocation does not threaten the Company's ability to rely upon an exemption from the Securities Act or the qualification provisions of applicable state securities laws. If an Investor gives the Employee Holder notice that it desires to purchase its share and, as the case may be, its overallotment, then payment for the Offered Shares shall be by check, or wire transfer, against delivery of the Offered Shares to be purchased at a place agreed upon between the parties and at the time of the scheduled closing therefor.

(d)   <u>Failure to Notify</u>. If the Investors fail to purchase all of the Offered Shares by exercising the options granted in this Section 3.1 within the periods provided, the Employee Holder shall be entitled for a period of ninety (90) days thereafter to complete the proposed Transfer of the balance of such shares not purchased by the Investors upon the terms and conditions specified in the Transfer Notice. If the Employee Holder has not so transferred the Offered Shares during such period, the Employee Holder shall not thereafter make a Transfer of shares without again first offering such shares to the other parties in the manner provided in this Section 3.1.

3.2   <u>Right of Co-Sale</u>.

(a)   <u>The Right</u>. If at any time any of the Employee Holders proposes to sell shares of Equity Securities to parties other than the Investors in a transaction (the "Transaction") not registered under the Securities Act in reliance upon a claimed exemption thereunder, and the Investors as a group do not exercise their right of last refusal as to the Offered Shares pursuant to Section 3.1, then any Investor (a "Selling Investor" for purposes of this subsection 3.2) which notifies the Employee Holder in writing within thirty (30) days after receipt of the Transfer Notice referred to in Section 3.1(a), shall have the opportunity to sell a pro rata portion of Equity Securities which the Employee Holder proposes to sell to such third party in the Transaction. In such instance, the Employee Holder shall assign so much of his or her interest in the proposed agreement of sale as the Selling Investor shall be entitled to and shall request hereunder, and the Selling Investor shall assume such part of the obligations of the Employee Holder under such agreement as shall relate to the sale of the securities by the Selling Investor. For the purposes of this Section 3.2, the "pro rata portion" which the Selling Investor shall be entitled to sell shall be an amount of Equity Securities (assuming the exercise and conversion of all such securities to Common Stock) equal to a fraction of the total amount of Equity Securities (assuming the exercise and conversion of all such securities to Common Stock) proposed to be sold. The numerator of such fraction shall be the number of Equity Securities (assuming the exercise and conversion of all such securities to Common Stock) owned by a Selling Investor and the denominator shall be the total number of Equity Securities (assuming the exercise and conversion of all such securities to Common Stock) owned by all participating Selling Investors and the Employee Holder. Each Selling Investor shall notify the Employee Holder whether it elects to sell an amount equal to, more than, or less than its pro rata share of the Equity Securities so offered. Each Selling Investor shall be entitled to apportion Equity Securities to be sold among its partners and affiliates, provided that such Selling Investor notifies the Employee Holder of such allocation, and provided that such allocation does not threaten the Company's reliance on any exemption from the registration provisions of the Securities Act or the qualification provisions of applicable state securities laws.

(b)   <u>Failure to Notify</u>. If within thirty (30) days after the Employee Holder gives the aforesaid notice to the Investors, the Investors do not notify the Employee Holder that they desire to sell all of their pro rata portions of the Equity Securities described in such notice for the price and on the terms and conditions set forth therein, then the Employee Holder may, subject to Section 3.1 hereof, sell during the period set forth in Section 3.1(d) such Equity Securities as to which the Investors do not elect to sell. Any such sale shall be made only to persons identified in the Employee Holder's notice and at the same price and upon the same terms and conditions as those set forth in the notice. In the event the Employee Holder has not sold the Equity Securities or entered into an agreement to sell the Equity Securities within the period set forth in Section 3.1(d), the Employee Holder shall not thereafter sell any Equity Securities without first notifying the Investors in the manner provided above.

3.3   <u>Limitations to Rights of Last Refusal and Co-Sale</u>. Without regard and not subject to the provisions of Sections 3.1 and 3.2;

(a)   Each Employee Holder may sell or otherwise assign, with or without consideration, Equity Securities to any or all of his or her ancestors, descendants, spouse, or members of his or her immediate family, or to a custodian, trustee (including a trustee of a voting trust), executor, or other fiduciary for the account of his or her ancestors, descendants, spouse, or members of his or her immediate family, provided that each such transferee or assignee, prior to the completion of the sale, transfer, or assignment, shall have executed documents assuming the obligations of the Employee Holder under this Agreement with respect to the transferred securities;

(b)   In addition to any transfers pursuant to subsections 3.3(a) and 3.3(c), each Employee Holder may sell, assign, or otherwise transfer, with or without consideration, in any twelve (12) month period after the date of this Agreement up to five percent (5%) of the Equity Securities owned by the Employee Holder as of such date and such transferred securities shall be free of the provisions of this Agreement; provided, however, the Employee Holder may not transfer Equity Securities pursuant to this subsection 3.3(b) aggregating more than ten percent (10%) of the Equity Securities owned as of the date of this Agreement; and

(c)   Each Employee Holder may sell Equity Securities to the Company upon exercise by the Company of its rights to repurchase Common Stock issued pursuant to stock purchase or option agreements entered into between the Company and the Employee Holder.

3.4   Assignment. Upon written notice to the Employee Holders, the rights granted pursuant to this Section 3 may be assigned by an Investor or its transferees upon a sale or transfer (other than a sale thereof to the public) of at least ten thousand (10,000) shares of the Preferred Stock and/or shares of Common Stock issuable upon conversion thereof (adjusted for stock splits, stock dividends, reorganizations, and the like after the date hereof) held by such Investor or transferee; provided that any transferee of an Investor shall agree to become subject to the obligations of the Investors hereunder.

4.   Legend. Each existing or replacement certificate for shares now owned by an Employee Holder shall bear the following legend upon its face:

"The ownership, transfer, encumbrance, pledge, assignment, or other disposition of this certificate and the share of stock represented thereby, are subject to the restrictions contained in a Shareholders Agreement dated _____ , 20____ , a copy of which is on file at the office of the Company."

5.   Effect of Change in Company's Capital Structure. Appropriate adjustments shall be made in the number, exercise price, and class of shares in the event of a stock dividend, stock split, reverse stock split, combination, reclassification, or like change in the capital structure of the Company. If, from time to time, there is any stock dividend, stock split, or other change in the character or amount of any of the outstanding stock of the Company, then in such event any and all new, substituted, or additional securities to which the Employee Holders are entitled by reason of the Employee Holders' ownership of the stock shall be immediately subject to the rights set forth in Sections 2 and 3 with the same force and effect as the stock subject to such rights immediately before such event.

6.   Notices. Any notice required or permitted by any provision of this Agreement shall be given in writing, and shall be delivered either personally or by registered or certified mail, postage prepaid, addressed (i) in the case of the Employee Holders and the Purchasers to their addresses as set forth on the stock records of the Company or such other addresses as are designated in writing from time to time by any such party, (ii) in the case of the Company, to its principal office, and (iii) in the case of any permitted transferee of a party to this Agreement or its

transferee, to such transferee at its address as designated in writing by such transferee to the Company from time to time.

7.   <u>Binding Effect</u>. This Agreement and each and every term, covenant, and condition thereof, including all restrictions herein contained upon the sale, transfer, assignment, or other disposition or encumbrance of stock, shall be binding upon and inure to the benefit of the transferees, legatees, donees, heirs, executors, administrators, personal representatives, successors, and assigns of each of the parties.

8.   <u>Term</u>. The term of this Agreement shall expire (i) immediately prior to the closing of the Company's first firmly underwritten public offering registered under the Securities Act from which the Company receives net proceeds of not less than $_____ at a purchase price of not less than $_____ per share (as adjusted for stock dividends, stock splits, recapitalizations, and the like after the date hereof), or (ii) upon shareholder approval of any merger or consolidation of the Company with any other corporation in which more than fifty percent (50%) of the voting control of the Company is transferred to a third party.

9.   <u>Entire Agreement, etc</u>. This instrument contains the entire understanding of the parties with respect to the subject matter thereof, supersedes all other agreements between any of the parties with respect to the subject matter hereof, and cannot be altered or otherwise amended except pursuant to an instrument in writing signed by each of the parties. This Agreement shall be interpreted under the laws of the State of _____ , without reference to its principles of conflicts of law.

10.   <u>Severability</u>. The invalidity or unenforceability of any provision hereof shall not in any way affect the validity or enforceability of any other provision.

IN WITNESS WHEREOF, this Agreement has been duly executed effective as of the date and year first above written.

HI TECH WIDGET, INC.

By: _____

_____ , President

PURCHASERS:

_____

_____

EMPLOYEE HOLDERS:

_____

_____

_____

_____

SAMPLE AMENDED AND RESTATED ARTICLES OF INCORPORATION

This document, when filed with the appropriate state agency (typically the secretary of state), fixes the rights and preferences of the preferred stock being issued to the investors. This document must conform to the laws of the state in which it is filed and becomes a matter of public record thereafter. Generally, approval of both the board of directors and shareholders of the issuer are required before this filing can be made. Key provisions included in this document include the rights of the holders of preferred stock to receive dividends, receive distributions in the event of the sale or liquidation of the issuer, convert into common stock, vote at shareholders meetings, and approve future corporate transactions such as the sale or merger of the issuer.

AMENDED AND RESTATED

ARTICLES **[CERTIFICATE]** OF INCORPORATION OF

HI TECH WIDGET, INC.

A _____ Corporation

The undersigned, _____ and _____ , hereby certify that:

1. They are the President and Secretary, respectively, of Hi Tech Widget, Inc., a

_____ corporation.

2. The Articles **[Certificate]** of Incorporation of said corporation are amended and

restated to read as follows:

ARTICLE I

The name of this corporation is Hi Tech Widget, Inc. (the "Corporation").

ARTICLE II

The purpose of the Corporation is to engage in any lawful act or activity for which a corporation may be organized under the General Corporation Law of _____ other than the banking business, the trust company business, or the practice of a profession permitted to be incorporated by the _____ Corporations Code.

ARTICLE III

The name and address in the State of _____ of the Corporation's initial agent for service of process are:

_____

_____

_____

ARTICLE IV

The Corporation is authorized to issue two classes of shares to be designated respectively "Preferred" and "Common." The total number of Preferred shares authorized is 10,000,000, and the total number of Common shares authorized is 20,000,000.

The Preferred shares authorized by these Articles **[Certificate]** of Incorporation may be issued from time to time in one or more series. The Board of Directors is authorized to determine or alter any or all of the rights, preferences, privileges, and restrictions granted to or imposed upon any wholly unissued series of Preferred shares, and to fix or alter the number of shares comprising any such series and the designation thereof, or any of them, and to provide for rights and terms of redemption or conversion of the shares of any such series.

The first such series of Preferred shares shall be designated "Series A Preferred Stock," and shall consist of 2,000,000 shares. The rights, preferences, privileges, restrictions, and other matters relating to the Series A Preferred Stock are as follows:

Section 1. Dividends Rights of Series A Preferred. The holders of the Series A Preferred shall be entitled, *pari passu*, to receive, out of any funds legally available therefor, dividends at the rate of $0.0875 per share of Series A Preferred, per annum, and no more, on each outstanding share of Series A Preferred, payable in preference and priority to any payment of any dividend on Common, when, as, and if declared by the Board of Directors. The right to such dividends on the Series A Preferred shall not be cumulative, and no right shall accrue to holders of Series A Preferred by reason of the fact that dividends on such shares are not declared or paid in any prior year. In the event that the Board of Directors shall have declared and paid or set apart dividends on the Series A Preferred at the rate specified in this section in any one fiscal year and shall elect to declare additional dividends in that fiscal year out of funds legally available therefor, such additional dividends shall be declared on the Common.

Section 2. Liquidation Preference.

(a)   (i)   In the event of any liquidation, dissolution, or winding up of the Corporation, either voluntary or involuntary, the holders of the Series A Preferred shall be entitled to receive, prior and in preference to any distribution of any of the assets or surplus funds of the Corporation to the holders of Common by reason of their ownership thereof, the amount of $1.25 per share of Series A Preferred (as such amount shall be adjusted to reflect subdivisions and combinations of shares and stock dividends) for each share of Series A Preferred then held by them, plus an amount equal to all declared but unpaid dividends on the Series A Preferred. If upon any such liquidation, dissolution, or winding up of the Corporation, the assets and funds available for distribution among the holders of the Series A Preferred shall be insufficient to permit the payment to such holders of the full preferential amount, then such assets and funds of the Corporation legally available for distribution shall be distributed ratably among the holders of the Series A Preferred in proportion to the preferential amount each such holder is entitled to receive.

(ii) After payment has been made to the holders of the Series A Preferred of the full amounts to which they shall be entitled as aforesaid, the assets of the Corporation available for distribution to shareholders, if any, shall be distributed ratably among the holders of Common and Series A Preferred (on an as converted basis) until the holders of Series A Preferred have received (pursuant to Sections, 2[a][i] and [ii]) the aggregate amount of $3.75 for each share of Series A Preferred. Thereafter, all remaining assets of the Corporation available for distribution to the shareholders, if any, shall be distributed ratably among the holders of Common.

(b) (i) For purposes of this Section 2, a liquidation shall be deemed to be occasioned by, or to include, the Corporation's sale of all or substantially all of its assets or the acquisition of the Corporation by another entity by means of merger or consolidation (other than a consolidation or merger in which the holders of voting securities of the Corporation immediately prior to the consolidation or merger own [immediately after the consolidation or merger] voting securities of the surviving or acquiring entity, or of a parent of such entity, representing more than fifty percent (50%) of the voting power of the surviving or acquiring entity or such parent) resulting in the exchange of the outstanding shares of the Corporation for securities or consideration issued, or caused to be issued, by the acquiring entity.

(ii) In any of such events, if the consideration received by the Corporation is other than cash or indebtedness, its value will be deemed to be its fair market value. In the case of publicly traded securities, fair market value shall mean the closing market price for such securities on the date such consolidation, merger, or sale is consummated. If the consideration is in a form other than publicly traded securities, its value will be determined in good faith by agreement between the Board of Directors of the Corporation and the holders of a majority of the outstanding shares of Series A Preferred.

Section 3. Conversion. The holders of the Series A Preferred shall have conversion rights as follows (the "Conversion Rights"):

(a) Right to Convert.

(i) Optional Conversion. Each share of Series A Preferred shall be convertible, at the option of the holder thereof, at any time after the date of issuance of such share, at the office of the Corporation or any transfer agent for the Series A Preferred, into such number of fully paid and nonassessable shares of Common, as is determined by dividing $1.25 by the Series A Conversion Price in effect at the time of conversion. The Series A Conversion Price shall initially be $1.25, and shall be subject to adjustment as hereinafter provided.

(ii) Automatic Conversion. Each share of Series A Preferred shall automatically be converted into shares of Common, at the then effective Series A Conversion Price, upon the earlier of (i) the date specified by vote or written consent of the holders of not less than seventy-five percent (75%) of the then outstanding shares of Series A Preferred, or (ii) the closing of a firm commitment underwritten public offering pursuant to an effective registration statement on Form S-1 (or a successor form) under the Securities Act of 1933, as amended, covering the offer and sale of Common for the account of the Corporation to the public at an aggregate offering price of not less than $7,500,000. In the event of such a public offering, the person(s) entitled to receive the Common issuable upon such conversion of Series A Preferred shall not be deemed to have converted such Series A Preferred until immediately prior to the closing of such sale of Common, at which time the Series A Preferred shall be converted automatically without any further action by the holders of such shares and whether or not the certificates representing such shares are surrendered to the Corporation or its transfer agent; provided, however, that the Corporation shall not be obligated to issue certificates evidencing the shares of Common issuable upon such conversion unless certificates evidencing such shares of Series A Preferred being converted are either delivered to the Corporation or its transfer agent, as hereinafter provided, or the holder notifies the Corporation or any transfer agent, as hereinafter provided, that such certificates have been lost, stolen, or destroyed and executes an agreement satisfactory to the Corporation to indemnify the Corporation from any loss incurred by it in connection therewith. Upon the occurrence of such automatic conversion of Series A Preferred, the holders of the Series A Preferred shall surrender the certificates representing such shares at the office of the Corporation or of any transfer agent for the Series A Preferred. Thereupon, there shall be issued and delivered to such holder, promptly at such office and in the name as shown on such surrendered certificate or certificates, a certificate or certificates for the number of shares of Common into which the shares of Series A Preferred surrendered are convertible on the date on which said automatic conversion occurred.

(b) <u>Mechanics of Conversion</u>. No fractional shares of Common shall be issued upon conversion of Series A Preferred. In lieu of any fractional shares to which the holder would otherwise be entitled, the Corporation shall pay cash equal to such fraction multiplied by the then effective Conversion Price. Except as provided in Section 3(a)(ii), before any holder of Series A Preferred shall be entitled to convert the same into full shares of Common, he or she shall surrender the certificate or certificates therefor, duly endorsed, at the office of the Corporation or of any transfer agent for the Series A Preferred, and shall give written notice to the Corporation at such office that he or she elects to convert the same. The Corporation shall, as soon as practicable thereafter, issue and deliver at such office to such holder of Series A Preferred, a certificate or certificates for the number of shares of Common to which he or she shall be entitled as aforesaid and a check payable to the holder in the amount of any cash payable in lieu of fractional shares of Common (after aggregating all shares of Common issuable to such holder of Series A Preferred upon conversion of the number of shares of Series A Preferred at the time being converted). In addition, if less than all of the shares represented by such certificates are surrendered for conversion pursuant to Section 3(a)(i), the Corporation shall issue and deliver to such holder a new certificate for the balance of the shares of Series A Preferred not so converted. Except as provided in Section 3(a)(ii), such conversion shall be deemed to have been made immediately prior to the close of business on the date of the surrender of the certificate for the shares of Series A Preferred to be converted, and the person or persons entitled to receive the shares of Common issuable upon such conversion shall be treated for all purposes as the record holder or holders of such shares of Common on such date.

(c) <u>Adjustment to Conversion Price for Diluting Issues</u>.

(i) <u>Special Definitions</u>. For purposes of this Section 3(c), the following definitions shall apply:

(1) "<u>Options</u>" shall mean rights, options, or warrants to subscribe for, purchase, or otherwise acquire either Common or Convertible Securities.

(2) "<u>Original Issue Date</u>" shall mean the date on which the first share of Series A Preferred is issued.

(3) "<u>Convertible Securities</u>" shall mean any evidences of indebtedness, shares, or other securities directly or indirectly convertible into or exchangeable for Common.

(4) "<u>Additional Shares of Common</u>" shall mean all shares of Common issued (or, pursuant to Section 3[c][iii], deemed to be issued) by the Corporation after the Original Issue Date, other than shares of Common issued or issuable:

(A)   upon conversion of shares of Series A Preferred;

(B)   to officers or employees of, or consultants to, the Corporation pursuant to a stock grant, stock option plan, stock purchase plan, or other stock incentive agreement (collectively, the "Plans") approved by the Board of Directors;

(C)   as a dividend or distribution on Series A Preferred; and

(D)   by way of dividend or other distribution on shares of Common excluded from the definition of Additional Shares of Common by the foregoing clauses (A), (B), and (C) or this clause (D) or on shares of Common so excluded.

(ii)   <u>No Adjustment of Conversion Price</u>. No adjustment in the Series A Conversion Price shall be made in respect of the issuance of Additional Shares of Common unless the consideration per share for an Additional Share of Common issued or deemed to be issued by the Corporation is less than the Series A Conversion Price in effect on the date of, and immediately prior to, the issuance of such Additional Shares of Common.

(iii)   <u>Deemed Issue of Additional Shares of Common</u>.

(1)   <u>Options and Convertible Securities</u>. In the event the Corporation at any time or from time to time after the Original Issue Date shall issue any Options or Convertible Securities or shall fix a record date for the determination of holders of any class of securities entitled to receive any such Options or Convertible Securities, then the maximum number of shares (as set forth in the instrument relating thereto without regard to any provisions contained therein for a subsequent adjustment of such number) of Common issuable upon the exercise of such Options or, in the case of Convertible Securities and Options therefor, the conversion or exchange of such Convertible Securities, shall be deemed to be Additional Shares of Common issued as of the time of such issue or, in case such a record date shall have been fixed, as of the close of business on such record date, provided that Additional Shares of Common shall not be deemed to have been issued unless the consideration per share (determined pursuant to Section 4[c][v] hereof) of such Additional Shares of Common would be less than the Series A Conversion Price in effect on the date of and immediately prior to such issue, or such record date, as the case may be, and provided further that in any such case in which Additional Shares of Common are deemed to be issued:

(A)   no further adjustment in the Series A Conversion Price shall be made upon the subsequent issue of Convertible Securities or shares of Common upon the exercise of such Options or conversion or exchange of such Convertible Securities;

(B)   if such Options or Convertible Securities by their terms provide, with the passage of time or otherwise, for any increase or decrease in the consideration payable to the Corporation, or increase or decrease in the number of shares of Common issuable, upon the exercise, conversion, or exchange thereof, the Series A Conversion Price computed upon the original issue thereof (or upon the occurrence of a record date with respect thereto), and any subsequent adjustments based thereon, shall, upon any such increase or decrease becoming effective, be recomputed to reflect such increase or decrease insofar as it affects such Series A Conversion Price, but no further change in the Series A Conversion Price shall be made upon the exercise, conversion, or exchange of such Options or Convertible Securities;

(C)   if any such Options or Convertible Securities shall expire without having been exercised or converted, the Series A Conversion Price as adjusted upon the issuance of such Options or Convertible Securities shall be readjusted to the Series A Conversion Price which would have been in effect had an adjustment been made on the basis that the only Additional Shares of Common so issued were the Additional Shares of Common, if any, actually issued or sold on the exercise of such Options or the conversion of such Convertible Securities, and such Additional Shares of Common, if any, were issued or sold for the consideration actually received by the Corporation upon such exercise, plus the consideration, if any, actually received by the Corporation for the granting of all such Options, whether or not exercised, plus the consideration received for issuing or selling the Convertible Securities actually converted plus the consideration, if any, actually received by the Corporation (other than by cancellation of liabilities or obligations evidenced by such Convertible Securities) on the conversion of such Convertible Securities; and

(D)   no readjustment pursuant to clauses (B) or (C) above shall have the effect of increasing the Series A Conversion Price to an amount which exceeds the lower of (i) the Series A Conversion Price on the original adjustment date (immediately prior to the adjustment), or (ii) the Series A Conversion Price that would have resulted from any actual issuance of Additional Shares of Common between the original adjustment date and such readjustment date.

(2)   Stock Dividends and Subdivisions. In the event the Corporation at any time or from time to time after the Original Issue Date shall declare or pay any dividend on the Common payable in Common, or effect a subdivision of the outstanding shares of Common into a greater number of shares of Common (by reclassification or otherwise than by payment of a dividend in Common), then and in any such event, Additional Shares of Common shall be deemed to have been issued:

(A)   in the case of any such dividend, immediately after the close of business on the record date for the determination of holders of any class of securities entitled to receive such dividend; or

(B)   in the case of any such subdivision, at the close of business on the date immediately prior to the date upon which such corporate action becomes effective.

(iv)   Adjustment of Conversion Price upon Issuance of Additional Shares of Common. In the event that the Corporation shall, at any time after the Original Issue Date, issue Additional Shares of Common (including Additional Shares of Common deemed to be issued pursuant to Section 3[c][iii]), without consideration or for a consideration per share less than the Series A Conversion Price in effect on the date of and immediately prior to such issue, then and in such event, such Series A Conversion Price shall be reduced, concurrently with such issue, to a price (calculated to the nearest cent) determined by multiplying such Series A Conversion Price by a fraction (A) the numerator of which shall be the number of shares of Common outstanding immediately prior to such issue plus the number of shares of Common which the aggregate consideration received by the Corporation for the total number of Additional Shares of Common so issued would purchase at such Series A Conversion Price; and (B) the denominator of which shall be the number of shares of Common outstanding immediately prior to such issue plus the number of such Additional Shares of Common so issued. For purposes of this Section 3(c)(iv), all shares of Common issuable upon conversion of outstanding shares of Series A Preferred and shares of Common issuable upon conversion of outstanding Convertible Securities shall be deemed to be outstanding, and provided further that immediately after any Additional Shares of Common are deemed issued pursuant to Section 3(c)(iii), such Additional Shares of Common shall be deemed to be outstanding.

(v)   <u>Determination of Consideration</u>. For purposes of this Section 3(c), the consideration received by the Corporation for the issue of any Additional Shares of Common shall be computed as follows:

(1)   <u>Cash and Property</u>. Such consideration shall:

(A)   insofar as it consists of cash, be computed at the aggregate amount of cash received by the Corporation excluding amounts paid or payable for accrued interest or accrued dividends;

(B)   insofar as it consists of property other than cash, be computed at the fair value thereof at the time of such issue, as determined in good faith by the Board of Directors; and

(C)   in the event Additional Shares of Common are issued together with other shares or securities or other assets of the Corporation for consideration which covers both, by the proportion of such consideration so received, computed as provided in clauses (A) and (B) above, as determined in good faith by the Board of Directors.

(2)   <u>Options and Convertible Securities</u>. The consideration per share received by the Corporation for Additional Shares of Common deemed to have been issued pursuant to Section 3(c)(iii)(1), relating to Options and Convertible Securities, shall be determined by dividing:

(A)   the total amount, if any, received or receivable by the Corporation as consideration for the issue of such Options or Convertible Securities, plus the minimum aggregate amount of additional consideration (as set forth in the instruments relating thereto, without regard to any provisions contained therein for a subsequent adjustment of such consideration) payable to the Corporation upon the exercise of such Options or the conversion or exchange of such Convertible Securities, or in the case of Options for Convertible Securities, the exercise of such Options for Convertible Securities and the conversion or exchange of such Convertible Securities, by

(B)   the maximum number of shares of Common (as set forth in the instruments relating thereto, without regard to any provisions contained therein for a subsequent adjustment of such number) issuable upon the exercise of such Options or the conversion or exchange of such Convertible Securities.

(3)   <u>Stock Dividends and Stock Subdivisions</u>. Any Additional Shares of Common deemed to have been issued, relating to stock dividends and stock subdivisions, shall be deemed to have been issued for no consideration.

(vi)   <u>Adjustments for Combinations or Consolidation of Common</u>. In the event the outstanding shares of Common shall be combined or consolidated, by reclassification or otherwise, into a lesser number of shares of Common, the Series A Conversion Price in effect immediately prior to such combination or consolidation shall, concurrently with the effectiveness of such combination or consolidation, be proportionately increased.

(d)   <u>No Impairment</u>. The Corporation will not, by amendment of its Articles **[Certificate]** of Incorporation or through any reorganization, transfer of assets, consolidation, merger, dissolution, issue, or sale of securities or any other voluntary action, avoid or seek to avoid the observance or performance of any of the terms to be observed or performed hereunder by the Corporation but will at all times in good faith assist in the carrying out of all the provisions of this Section 3 and in the taking of all such action as may be necessary or appropriate in order to protect the Conversion Rights of the holders of the Series A Preferred against impairment.

(e)   Certificate as to Adjustments. Upon the occurrence of each adjustment or readjustment of the Series A Conversion Price pursuant to this Section 3, the Corporation at its expense shall promptly compute such adjustment or readjustment in accordance with the terms hereof and furnish to each holder of Series A Preferred a certificate setting forth such adjustment or readjustment and showing in detail the facts upon which such adjustment or readjustment is based. The Corporation shall, upon the written request at any time of any holder of Series A Preferred, furnish or cause to be furnished to such holder a like certificate setting forth (i) all such adjustments and readjustments, (ii) the Series A Conversion Price at the time in effect, and (iii) the number of shares of Common and the amount, if any, of other property which at the time would be received upon the conversion of such holder's Series A Preferred.

(f)   Notices of Record Date. In the event that the Corporation shall propose at any time:

(i)   to declare any dividend or distribution upon the Common, whether in cash, property, stock, or other securities, whether or not a regular cash dividend and whether or not out of earnings or earned surplus, other than distributions to shareholders in connection with the repurchase of shares of former employees or consultants, to which the holders of Series A Preferred have consented in Section 5 hereof; or

(ii)   to offer for subscription to the holders of any class or series of its capital stock any additional shares of stock of any class or series or any other rights; or

(iii)   to effect any reclassification or recapitalization; or

(iv)   to merge or consolidate with or into any other corporation, or sell, lease, or convey all or substantially all its property or business, or to liquidate, dissolve or wind up;

then, in connection with each such event, the Corporation shall send to the holders of the Series A Preferred:

(1)   written notice at least 20 days prior to the date on which a record shall be taken for such dividend, distribution, or subscription rights (and specifying the date on which the holders of Common shall be entitled thereto) or for determining rights to vote in respect of the matters referred to in clauses (iii) and (iv) above; and

(2)   in the case of the matters referred to in clauses (iii) and (iv) above, written notice at least 20 days prior to the date when the same shall take place (and specifying the date on which the holders of Common shall be entitled to exchange their Common for securities or other property deliverable upon the occurrence of such event).

Each such written notice shall be given by first class mail, postage prepaid, addressed to the holders of Series A Preferred at the address for each such holder as shown on the books of the Corporation.

Section 4. Voting Rights. Except as otherwise provided herein or required by law, each share of Common issued and outstanding shall have one vote and each share of Series A Preferred issued and outstanding shall have the number of votes equal to the number of Common shares into which the Series A Preferred is convertible, as adjusted from time to time pursuant to Section 3 hereof. Holders of Series A Preferred shall be entitled to vote on all matters as to which holders of Common shall be entitled to vote, in the same manner and with the same effect as the holders of Common, voting together with the holders of Common as one class. The foregoing notwithstanding, holders of Series A Preferred shall have the right, voting as a separate class, to elect one member to the Board of Directors of the Corporation.

Section 5. No Reissuance of Series A Preferred. No share or shares of Series A Preferred acquired by the Corporation by reason of redemption, purchase, conversion or otherwise shall be reissued, and all such shares shall be cancelled, retired, and eliminated from the shares which the Corporation shall be authorized to issue.

Section 6. Residual Rights. All rights accruing to the outstanding shares of this Corporation not expressly provided for to the contrary herein shall be vested in the Common.

Section 7. Covenants. Except as otherwise required by law or these Articles **[Certificate]** of Incorporation, so long as any shares of Series A Preferred shall be outstanding, the Corporation shall not, without first obtaining the affirmative vote or written consent of the holders of not less than a majority of such outstanding shares of Series A Preferred voting as a single class:

(a)   Authorize or issue shares of any class or series of stock having any rights, preferences, or privileges superior to or on a parity with the Series A Preferred;

(b)   Repurchase, redeem, acquire, or retire any shares of Common, except from employees, directors, or consultants of this Corporation upon termination upon terms approved by the Board of Directors of the Corporation;

(c)   Undertake or effect any consolidation or merger of this Corporation with or into another entity or any conveyance of all or substantially all of the assets of the Corporation to another person or persons in any transaction or series of transactions if, as a result of any consolidation, merger, or conveyance, the shareholders of this Corporation shall own less than a majority of the voting securities or power of the surviving entity or person; or

(d)   Amend or repeal any provision of, or add any provision to, the Corporation's Articles **[Certificate]** of Incorporation or Bylaws.

ARTICLE V

The liability of the directors of the Corporation for monetary damages shall be eliminated to the fullest extent permissible under _____ law. Any repeal or modification of this Article V, or the adoption of any provision of the Articles **[Certificate]** of Incorporation inconsistent with this Article V, shall only be prospective and shall not adversely affect the rights under this Article V in effect at the time of the alleged occurrence of any act or omission to act giving rise to liability.

ARTICLE VI

The Corporation is authorized to provide indemnification of agents (as defined in Section _____ of the _____ Corporations Code) through bylaw provisions, agreements with agents, vote of shareholders or disinterested directors, or otherwise, in excess of the indemnification otherwise permitted by Section _____ of the _____ Corporations Code, subject only to the applicable limits on indemnification set forth in Section ___ of the _____ Corporations Code with respect to actions for breach of duty to the Corporation or its shareholders. Any repeal or modification of this Article VI, or the adoption of any provision of the Articles **[Certificate]** of Incorporation inconsistent with this Article VI, shall only be prospective and shall not adversely affect the rights under this Article VI in effect at the time of the alleged occurrence of any action or omission to act giving rise to indemnification.

1.   The foregoing amendment and restatement of the Articles **[Certificate]** of Incorporation has been duly approved by the Board of Directors of said Corporation.

2.   The foregoing amendment and restatement of the Articles **[Certificate]** of Incorporation has been duly approved by the required vote of the shareholders of said Corporation in accordance with Section _____ of the _____ Corporations Code. The total number of outstanding shares of said Corporation entitled to vote with respect to the foregoing amendment was _____ shares of Common. The number of shares voting in favor of the amendment equaled or exceeded the vote required, such required vote being more than a majority of the outstanding shares of Common.

4 USING THIS DIRECTORY

In this Directory venture firms are organized by state and listed within each state alphabetically by firm name.

CONTENTS

Venture firm listings include the following information (if disclosed):

- Firm name
- Address
- Telephone number
- Fax number
- Affiliation with other companies
- Cross-reference to other firm locations
- Capital under management range
- Minimum investment range
- Names of key professionals and their titles
- Industry preference
- Life stage preference
- Geographic preference
- An SBIC or SSBIC indicator

To find firms that are likely to favor your particular investment opportunity, start with the geographic listing and look for venture funds with offices not more than a few hours away. Then fine-tune your list by looking for those that indicate an interest in the industry, stage of business, and minimum investment criteria that matches your company's needs. If the industry, stage, or deal size almost fits, keep those companies on the list for further clarification and a second-tier effort.

Once you have a target list, rather than sending business plans out blindly, call each of the firms for a copy of its brochure (or obtain a cyber-brochure on the Internet or other online services). If it has one, the brochure will include valuable information about what companies it has invested in, the background and experience of the partners, the fund's investors, and additional details about its strategies and interests. Based on that information, target your efforts toward not just the right firms, but toward the right principals at the right firm . . . the one who is most likely to understand and appreciate your business and your deal.

USING A COMPUTER TO SPEED YOUR SEARCH

An electronic version of the directory portion of this book, including the names and interests of the more than 600 venture firms' offices included in this directory, is available for purchase at http://www.findingmoney.com/order1 or may be ordered via mail or fax. See page 385.

Used properly the electronic version of this directory will help you quickly narrow your search for the perfect venture capital match. Used improperly the electronic version of this directory will help you quickly convince hundreds of venture capitalists that you are incompetent or lazy. Don't use the electronic version to create a mail-merge list of firms and then send every one a copy of your plan or resumé.

Venture capitalists operate in a very small community. Different funds often have the same investors, partners, directors, and offices. Just a few buildings on Sand Hill Road in Menlo Park, for example, are home to over 60 venture capital firms. When the same office receives several copies of your plan or resume it makes you look, at best, naive or, worse, incompetent. You'll save yourself embarrassment, money, paper, and the unnecessary exposure of confidential concepts by conducting a thoughtful, informed, and organized search. The advertising adage that it takes seven exposures to get someone's attention does not work with VCs.

VENTURE FIRMS
LISTED BY STATE

FJC GROWTH CAPITAL CORP.

200 Westside Square
Suite 340
Huntsville AL 35801

Phone (256) 922-2918   Fax (256) 922-2909

PROFESSIONALS	TITLE
William B. Noojin	Vice President

INDUSTRY PREFERENCE

☐ INFORMATION INDUSTRY	☒ BASIC INDUSTRIES
☐ Communications	☒ Consumer
☐ Computer Equipment	☒ Distribution
☐ Computer Services	☒ Manufacturing
☐ Computer Components	☒ Retail
☐ Computer Entertainment	☐ Service
☐ Computer Education	☒ Wholesale
☐ Information Technologies	☒ SPECIFIC INDUSTRIES
☐ Computer Media	☐ Energy
☐ Software	☐ Environmental
☐ Internet	☐ Financial
☐ MEDICAL/HEALTHCARE	☒ Real Estate
☐ Biotechnology	☐ Transportation
☐ Healthcare Services	☐ Publishing
☐ Life Sciences	☐ Food
☐ Medical Products	☐ Franchises
☐ INDUSTRIAL	☒ DIVERSIFIED
☐ Advanced Materials	☐ MISCELLANEOUS
☐ Chemicals	
☐ Instruments & Controls	

STAGE PREFERENCE

☐ EARLY STAGE
☐ Seed
☐ Start-up
☐ 1st Stage
☒ LATER STAGE
☒ 2nd Stage
☒ Mature
☐ Mezzanine
☐ LBO/MBO
☐ Turnaround
☐ INT'L EXPANSION
☐ WILL CONSIDER ALL
☐ VENTURE LEASING

SSBIC
Other Locations:

Affiliation:
Minimum Investment: $1 Million or more
Capital Under Management: Less than $100 Million

GEOGRAPHIC PREF

☐ East Coast
☐ West Coast
☐ Northeast
☐ Mid Atlantic
☐ Gulf States
☐ Northwest
☒ Southeast
☐ Southwest
☐ Midwest
☐ Central
☐ Local to Office
☐ Other Geo Pref

HICKORY VENTURE GROUP

301 Washington Street NW
Suite 100
Huntsville AL 35801-4816

Phone (256) 539-1931   Fax (256) 539-5130

PROFESSIONALS	TITLE
J. Thomas Noojin	President
Monro B. Lanier	Vice President
John R. Bise	Vice President

INDUSTRY PREFERENCE

☒ INFORMATION INDUSTRY	☒ BASIC INDUSTRIES
☒ Communications	☐ Consumer
☐ Computer Equipment	☒ Distribution
☒ Computer Services	☐ Manufacturing
☐ Computer Components	☐ Retail
☐ Computer Entertainment	☐ Service
☐ Computer Education	☐ Wholesale
☒ Information Technologies	☒ SPECIFIC INDUSTRIES
☐ Computer Media	☐ Energy
☒ Software	☐ Environmental
☒ Internet	☐ Financial
☒ MEDICAL/HEALTHCARE	☐ Real Estate
☐ Biotechnology	☐ Transportation
☒ Healthcare Services	☐ Publishing
☐ Life Sciences	☐ Food
☒ Medical Products	☐ Franchises
☒ INDUSTRIAL	☒ DIVERSIFIED
☐ Advanced Materials	☒ MISCELLANEOUS
☐ Chemicals	Security
☒ Instruments & Controls	

STAGE PREFERENCE

☒ EARLY STAGE
☐ Seed
☐ Start-up
☒ 1st Stage
☒ LATER STAGE
☒ 2nd Stage
☒ Mature
☒ Mezzanine
☐ LBO/MBO
☐ Turnaround
☐ INT'L EXPANSION
☐ WILL CONSIDER ALL
☐ VENTURE LEASING

SBIC
Other Locations:

Affiliation:
Minimum Investment: $1 Million or more
Capital Under Management: Less than $100 Million

GEOGRAPHIC PREF

☐ East Coast
☐ West Coast
☐ Northeast
☐ Mid Atlantic
☐ Gulf States
☐ Northwest
☒ Southeast
☐ Southwest
☐ Midwest
☐ Central
☐ Local to Office
☐ Other Geo Pref

TD JAVELIN CAPITAL FUND LP

2850 Cahaba Road
Suite 240
Birmingham AL 35223

Phone (205) 870-4811   Fax (205) 870-4822

PROFESSIONALS	TITLE
Lyle Hohnke	Partner
Joan Neuscheler	Partner

INDUSTRY PREFERENCE

☒ INFORMATION INDUSTRY	☐ BASIC INDUSTRIES
☐ Communications	☐ Consumer
☐ Computer Equipment	☐ Distribution
☐ Computer Services	☐ Manufacturing
☐ Computer Components	☐ Retail
☐ Computer Entertainment	☐ Service
☐ Computer Education	☐ Wholesale
☒ Information Technologies	☒ SPECIFIC INDUSTRIES
☐ Computer Media	☐ Energy
☐ Software	☐ Environmental
☒ Internet	☐ Financial
☒ MEDICAL/HEALTHCARE	☐ Real Estate
☒ Biotechnology	☐ Transportation
☒ Healthcare Services	☐ Publishing
☒ Life Sciences	☐ Food
☒ Medical Products	☐ Franchises
☐ INDUSTRIAL	☒ DIVERSIFIED
☐ Advanced Materials	☐ MISCELLANEOUS
☐ Chemicals	Animal Healthcare,
☐ Instruments & Controls	Agricultural Research

STAGE PREFERENCE

☒ EARLY STAGE
☒ Seed
☒ Start-up
☒ 1st Stage
☐ LATER STAGE
☐ 2nd Stage
☐ Mature
☐ Mezzanine
☐ LBO/MBO
☐ Turnaround
☐ INT'L EXPANSION
☐ WILL CONSIDER ALL
☐ VENTURE LEASING
SBIC
Other Locations:

Affiliation:
Minimum Investment: Less than $1 Million
Capital Under Management: Less than $100 Million

GEOGRAPHIC PREF

☐ East Coast
☐ West Coast
☐ Northeast
☐ Mid Atlantic
☐ Gulf States
☐ Northwest
☒ Southeast
☐ Southwest
☐ Midwest
☐ Central
☐ Local to Office
☐ Other Geo Pref

BIO-VENTURES WEST

101 North Wilmott
Suite 600
Tucson AZ 85711

Phone (520) 748-4400

PROFESSIONALS	TITLE
John Perchorowicz	Partner

INDUSTRY PREFERENCE

☐ INFORMATION INDUSTRY	☐ BASIC INDUSTRIES
☐ Communications	☐ Consumer
☐ Computer Equipment	☐ Distribution
☐ Computer Services	☐ Manufacturing
☐ Computer Components	☐ Retail
☐ Computer Entertainment	☐ Service
☐ Computer Education	☐ Wholesale
☐ Information Technologies	☐ SPECIFIC INDUSTRIES
☐ Computer Media	☐ Energy
☐ Software	☐ Environmental
☐ Internet	☐ Financial
☒ MEDICAL/HEALTHCARE	☐ Real Estate
☒ Biotechnology	☐ Transportation
☒ Healthcare Services	☐ Publishing
☒ Life Sciences	☐ Food
☒ Medical Products	☐ Franchises
☐ INDUSTRIAL	☐ DIVERSIFIED
☐ Advanced Materials	☒ MISCELLANEOUS
☐ Chemicals	
☐ Instruments & Controls	

STAGE PREFERENCE

☐ EARLY STAGE
☐ Seed
☐ Start-up
☐ 1st Stage
☐ LATER STAGE
☐ 2nd Stage
☐ Mature
☐ Mezzanine
☐ LBO/MBO
☐ Turnaround
☐ INT'L EXPANSION
☐ WILL CONSIDER ALL
☐ VENTURE LEASING

Other Locations: Carlsbad CA

Affiliation:
Minimum Investment: Less than $1 Million
Capital Under Management: Less than $100 Million

GEOGRAPHIC PREF

☐ East Coast
☒ West Coast
☐ Northeast
☐ Mid Atlantic
☐ Gulf States
☐ Northwest
☐ Southeast
☐ Southwest
☐ Midwest
☐ Central
☐ Local to Office
☐ Other Geo Pref

21ST CENTURY INTERNET VENTURE PARTNERS

Two South Park
Second Floor
San Francisco CA 94107

Phone (415) 512-1221   Fax (415) 512-2650

PROFESSIONALS	TITLE
J. Neil Weintraut	Partner
Peter Ziebelman	Partner

INDUSTRY PREFERENCE

☒ INFORMATION INDUSTRY	☐ BASIC INDUSTRIES
☐ Communications	☐ Consumer
☐ Computer Equipment	☐ Distribution
☐ Computer Services	☐ Manufacturing
☐ Computer Components	☐ Retail
☐ Computer Entertainment	☐ Service
☐ Computer Education	☐ Wholesale
☐ Information Technologies	☒ SPECIFIC INDUSTRIES
☐ Computer Media	☐ Energy
☐ Software	☐ Environmental
☐ Internet	☐ Financial
☐ MEDICAL/HEALTHCARE	☐ Real Estate
☐ Biotechnology	☐ Transportation
☐ Healthcare Services	☐ Publishing
☐ Life Sciences	☐ Food
☐ Medical Products	☐ Franchises
☐ INDUSTRIAL	☐ DIVERSIFIED
☐ Advanced Materials	☒ MISCELLANEOUS
☐ Chemicals	
☐ Instruments & Controls	

STAGE PREFERENCE

☒ EARLY STAGE
☒ Seed
☒ Start-up
☒ 1st Stage
☒ LATER STAGE
☒ 2nd Stage
☐ Mature
☒ Mezzanine
☐ LBO/MBO
☐ Turnaround
☐ INT'L EXPANSION
☐ WILL CONSIDER ALL
☐ VENTURE LEASING

Other Locations:

Affiliation:
Minimum Investment: $1 Million or more
Capital Under Management: Less than $100 Million

GEOGRAPHIC PREF

☐ East Coast
☐ West Coast
☐ Northeast
☐ Mid Atlantic
☐ Gulf States
☐ Northwest
☐ Southeast
☐ Southwest
☐ Midwest
☐ Central
☐ Local to Office
☐ Other Geo Pref

2M INVEST, INC.

1875 S. Grant Street
Suite 750
San Mateo CA 94402

Phone (650) 655-3765   Fax (650) 372-9107

PROFESSIONALS	TITLE
Michael Mathiesen	President
Henrick Albertsen	Investment Manager
Soren J. Bruun	Managing Director
William R. Hipp	Managing Director
Robert C. Hsieh	Managing Director

INDUSTRY PREFERENCE

☒ INFORMATION INDUSTRY	☐ BASIC INDUSTRIES
☒ Communications	☐ Consumer
☐ Computer Equipment	☐ Distribution
☒ Computer Services	☐ Manufacturing
☐ Computer Components	☐ Retail
☐ Computer Entertainment	☐ Service
☐ Computer Education	☐ Wholesale
☒ Information Technologies	☒ SPECIFIC INDUSTRIES
☒ Computer Media	☐ Energy
☒ Software	☐ Environmental
☒ Internet	☐ Financial
☐ MEDICAL/HEALTHCARE	☐ Real Estate
☐ Biotechnology	☐ Transportation
☐ Healthcare Services	☐ Publishing
☐ Life Sciences	☐ Food
☐ Medical Products	☐ Franchises
☐ INDUSTRIAL	☐ DIVERSIFIED
☐ Advanced Materials	☒ MISCELLANEOUS
☐ Chemicals	
☐ Instruments & Controls	

STAGE PREFERENCE

☒ EARLY STAGE
☐ Seed
☒ Start-up
☒ 1st Stage
☒ LATER STAGE
☒ 2nd Stage
☒ Mature
☒ Mezzanine
☒ LBO/MBO
☒ Turnaround
☐ INT'L EXPANSION
☐ WILL CONSIDER ALL
☒ VENTURE LEASING

Other Locations:

Affiliation:
Minimum Investment: $1 Million or more
Capital Under Management: Less than $100 Million

GEOGRAPHIC PREF

☐ East Coast
☐ West Coast
☐ Northeast
☐ Mid Atlantic
☐ Gulf States
☐ Northwest
☐ Southeast
☐ Southwest
☐ Midwest
☐ Central
☐ Local to Office
☐ Other Geo Pref

ABS CAPITAL PARTNERS

101 California Street
San Francisco CA 94111

Phone (415) 477-4249   Fax (415) 477-3229

PROFESSIONALS	TITLE
John Stobo	General Partner

INDUSTRY PREFERENCE

- ☒ INFORMATION INDUSTRY
- ☒ Communications
- ☒ Computer Equipment
- ☒ Computer Services
- ☐ Computer Components
- ☐ Computer Entertainment
- ☒ Computer Education
- ☒ Information Technologies
- ☒ Computer Media
- ☒ Software
- ☒ Internet
- ☒ MEDICAL/HEALTHCARE
- ☒ Biotechnology
- ☒ Healthcare Services
- ☒ Life Sciences
- ☒ Medical Products
- ☒ INDUSTRIAL
- ☒ Advanced Materials
- ☒ Chemicals
- ☒ Instruments & Controls

- ☒ BASIC INDUSTRIES
- ☐ Consumer
- ☐ Distribution
- ☐ Manufacturing
- ☐ Retail
- ☒ Service
- ☐ Wholesale
- ☒ SPECIFIC INDUSTRIES
- ☒ Energy
- ☐ Environmental
- ☐ Financial
- ☐ Real Estate
- ☐ Transportation
- ☒ Publishing
- ☐ Food
- ☐ Franchises
- ☒ DIVERSIFIED
- ☒ MISCELLANEOUS

STAGE PREFERENCE

- ☐ EARLY STAGE
- ☐ Seed
- ☐ Start-up
- ☐ 1st Stage
- ☒ LATER STAGE
- ☒ 2nd Stage
- ☐ Mature
- ☒ Mezzanine
- ☒ LBO/MBO
- ☐ Turnaround
- ☐ INT'L EXPANSION
- ☐ WILL CONSIDER ALL
- ☐ VENTURE LEASING

Other Locations: Baltimore MD

Affiliation:
Minimum Investment: $1 Million or more
Capital Under Management: Over $500 Million

GEOGRAPHIC PREF

- ☐ East Coast
- ☐ West Coast
- ☐ Northeast
- ☐ Mid Atlantic
- ☐ Gulf States
- ☐ Northwest
- ☐ Southeast
- ☐ Southwest
- ☐ Midwest
- ☐ Central
- ☐ Local to Office
- ☐ Other Geo Pref

ACACIA VENTURE PARTNERS

101 California Street
Suite 3160
San Francisco CA 94111

Phone (415) 433-4200   Fax (415) 433-4250

PROFESSIONALS	TITLE
C. Sage Givens	General Partner
David S. Heer	General Partner
C. Ted Paff	General Partner

INDUSTRY PREFERENCE

- ☒ INFORMATION INDUSTRY
- ☐ Communications
- ☐ Computer Equipment
- ☐ Computer Services
- ☐ Computer Components
- ☐ Computer Entertainment
- ☐ Computer Education
- ☐ Information Technologies
- ☐ Computer Media
- ☐ Software
- ☒ Internet
- ☒ MEDICAL/HEALTHCARE
- ☐ Biotechnology
- ☒ Healthcare Services
- ☐ Life Sciences
- ☐ Medical Products
- ☐ INDUSTRIAL
- ☐ Advanced Materials
- ☐ Chemicals
- ☐ Instruments & Controls

- ☐ BASIC INDUSTRIES
- ☐ Consumer
- ☐ Distribution
- ☐ Manufacturing
- ☐ Retail
- ☐ Service
- ☐ Wholesale
- ☒ SPECIFIC INDUSTRIES
- ☐ Energy
- ☐ Environmental
- ☐ Financial
- ☐ Real Estate
- ☐ Transportation
- ☐ Publishing
- ☐ Food
- ☐ Franchises
- ☒ DIVERSIFIED
- ☐ MISCELLANEOUS
  - e-Health

STAGE PREFERENCE

- ☒ EARLY STAGE
- ☒ Seed
- ☒ Start-up
- ☒ 1st Stage
- ☒ LATER STAGE
- ☒ 2nd Stage
- ☒ Mature
- ☒ Mezzanine
- ☒ LBO/MBO
- ☐ Turnaround
- ☐ INT'L EXPANSION
- ☐ WILL CONSIDER ALL
- ☐ VENTURE LEASING

Other Locations:

Affiliation:
Minimum Investment: $1 Million or more
Capital Under Management: $100 to $500 Million

GEOGRAPHIC PREF

- ☐ East Coast
- ☐ West Coast
- ☐ Northeast
- ☐ Mid Atlantic
- ☐ Gulf States
- ☐ Northwest
- ☐ Southeast
- ☐ Southwest
- ☐ Midwest
- ☐ Central
- ☐ Local to Office
- ☐ Other Geo Pref

ACCEL PARTNERS

428 University Avenue
Palo Alto CA 94301

Phone (650) 614-4800   Fax (650) 614-4880

PROFESSIONALS	TITLE
Bud Colligan	Partner
Luke Evnin	General Partner
Arthur C. Patterson	General Partner
James W. Breyer	Managing General Partner
James Schwartz	Managing General Partner
Jim Flach	Partner
Bruce Golden	Partner
Mitch Capor	Partner

INDUSTRY PREFERENCE

- ☒ INFORMATION INDUSTRY
- ☒ Communications
- ☒ Computer Equipment
- ☒ Computer Services
- ☒ Computer Components
- ☐ Computer Entertainment
- ☒ Computer Education
- ☒ Information Technologies
- ☒ Computer Media
- ☒ Software
- ☒ Internet
- ☐ MEDICAL/HEALTHCARE
- ☐ Biotechnology
- ☐ Healthcare Services
- ☐ Life Sciences
- ☐ Medical Products
- ☐ INDUSTRIAL
- ☐ Advanced Materials
- ☐ Chemicals
- ☐ Instruments & Controls

- ☒ BASIC INDUSTRIES
- ☐ Consumer
- ☐ Distribution
- ☐ Manufacturing
- ☐ Retail
- ☒ Service
- ☐ Wholesale
- ☐ SPECIFIC INDUSTRIES
- ☐ Energy
- ☐ Environmental
- ☐ Financial
- ☐ Real Estate
- ☐ Transportation
- ☐ Publishing
- ☐ Food
- ☐ Franchises
- ☒ DIVERSIFIED
- ☐ MISCELLANEOUS

STAGE PREFERENCE

- ☒ EARLY STAGE
- ☒ Seed
- ☒ Start-up
- ☒ 1st Stage
- ☒ LATER STAGE
- ☒ 2nd Stage
- ☒ Mature
- ☒ Mezzanine
- ☒ LBO/MBO
- ☐ Turnaround
- ☐ INT'L EXPANSION
- ☐ WILL CONSIDER ALL
- ☐ VENTURE LEASING

Other Locations: Princeton NJ

Affiliation:
Minimum Investment: Less than $1 Million
Capital Under Management: $100 to $500 Million

GEOGRAPHIC PREF

- ☐ East Coast
- ☐ West Coast
- ☐ Northeast
- ☐ Mid Atlantic
- ☐ Gulf States
- ☐ Northwest
- ☐ Southeast
- ☐ Southwest
- ☐ Midwest
- ☐ Central
- ☐ Local to Office
- ☐ Other Geo Pref

ADVANCED TECHNOLOGY VENTURES

485 Ramona Street
Suite 200
Palo Alto CA 94301

Phone (650) 321-8601   Fax (650) 321-0934

PROFESSIONALS	TITLE
Jos C. Henkens	General Partner
Steven Baloff	General Partner
Peter Schiller	General Partner
Michael Carusi	Principal
Michael Frank	General Partner

INDUSTRY PREFERENCE

- ☒ INFORMATION INDUSTRY
- ☒ Communications
- ☒ Computer Equipment
- ☒ Computer Services
- ☒ Computer Components
- ☐ Computer Entertainment
- ☒ Computer Education
- ☒ Information Technologies
- ☒ Computer Media
- ☒ Software
- ☒ Internet
- ☒ MEDICAL/HEALTHCARE
- ☒ Biotechnology
- ☒ Healthcare Services
- ☒ Life Sciences
- ☒ Medical Products
- ☒ INDUSTRIAL
- ☒ Advanced Materials
- ☒ Chemicals
- ☒ Instruments & Controls

- ☒ BASIC INDUSTRIES
- ☐ Consumer
- ☐ Distribution
- ☐ Manufacturing
- ☐ Retail
- ☒ Service
- ☐ Wholesale
- ☒ SPECIFIC INDUSTRIES
- ☒ Energy
- ☐ Environmental
- ☐ Financial
- ☐ Real Estate
- ☐ Transportation
- ☐ Publishing
- ☐ Food
- ☐ Franchises
- ☒ DIVERSIFIED
- ☐ MISCELLANEOUS

STAGE PREFERENCE

- ☒ EARLY STAGE
- ☒ Seed
- ☒ Start-up
- ☒ 1st Stage
- ☒ LATER STAGE
- ☒ 2nd Stage
- ☐ Mature
- ☒ Mezzanine
- ☐ LBO/MBO
- ☐ Turnaround
- ☐ INT'L EXPANSION
- ☐ WILL CONSIDER ALL
- ☐ VENTURE LEASING

Other Locations: Waltham MA

Affiliation:
Minimum Investment: Less than $1 Million
Capital Under Management: Less than $100 Million

GEOGRAPHIC PREF

- ☐ East Coast
- ☒ West Coast
- ☐ Northeast
- ☐ Mid Atlantic
- ☐ Gulf States
- ☐ Northwest
- ☐ Southeast
- ☐ Southwest
- ☐ Midwest
- ☐ Central
- ☐ Local to Office
- ☐ Other Geo Pref

ADVENT INTERNATIONAL CORP.

2180 Sand Hill Road
Suite 420
Menlo Park CA 94025

Phone (650) 233-7500   Fax (650) 233-7515

PROFESSIONALS	TITLE
John Rockwell	Partner

INDUSTRY PREFERENCE

☒ INFORMATION INDUSTRY	☒ BASIC INDUSTRIES
☒ Communications	☒ Consumer
☒ Computer Equipment	☐ Distribution
☒ Computer Services	☐ Manufacturing
☐ Computer Components	☒ Retail
☒ Computer Entertainment	☒ Service
☒ Computer Education	☐ Wholesale
☒ Information Technologies	☐ SPECIFIC INDUSTRIES
☐ Computer Media	☐ Energy
☒ Software	☐ Environmental
☒ Internet	☐ Financial
☒ MEDICAL/HEALTHCARE	☐ Real Estate
☒ Biotechnology	☐ Transportation
☒ Healthcare Services	☐ Publishing
☒ Life Sciences	☐ Food
☒ Medical Products	☐ Franchises
☒ INDUSTRIAL	☒ DIVERSIFIED
☒ Advanced Materials	☐ MISCELLANEOUS
☒ Chemicals	
☒ Instruments & Controls	

STAGE PREFERENCE

☒ EARLY STAGE
☒ Seed
☒ Start-up
☒ 1st Stage
☒ LATER STAGE
☒ 2nd Stage
☒ Mature
☒ Mezzanine
☒ LBO/MBO
☒ Turnaround
☒ INT'L EXPANSION
☐ WILL CONSIDER ALL
☒ VENTURE LEASING

Other Locations: Boston MA

Affiliation:
Minimum Investment: Less than $1 Million
Capital Under Management: Over $500 Million

GEOGRAPHIC PREF

☐ East Coast
☐ West Coast
☐ Northeast
☐ Mid Atlantic
☐ Gulf States
☐ Northwest
☐ Southeast
☐ Southwest
☐ Midwest
☐ Central
☐ Local to Office
☐ Other Geo Pref

ALPINE TECHNOLOGY VENTURES

20300 Steven Creek Boulevard
Suite 495
Cupertino CA 95014

Phone (408) 725-1810   Fax (408) 725-1207

PROFESSIONALS	TITLE
Chuck K . Chan	General Partner
David A. Lane	General Partner

INDUSTRY PREFERENCE

☒ INFORMATION INDUSTRY	☒ BASIC INDUSTRIES
☒ Communications	☒ Consumer
☒ Computer Equipment	☒ Distribution
☒ Computer Services	☐ Manufacturing
☒ Computer Components	☐ Retail
☐ Computer Entertainment	☐ Service
☐ Computer Education	☐ Wholesale
☐ Information Technologies	☐ SPECIFIC INDUSTRIES
☐ Computer Media	☐ Energy
☒ Software	☐ Environmental
☒ Internet	☐ Financial
☐ MEDICAL/HEALTHCARE	☐ Real Estate
☐ Biotechnology	☐ Transportation
☐ Healthcare Services	☐ Publishing
☐ Life Sciences	☐ Food
☐ Medical Products	☐ Franchises
☒ INDUSTRIAL	☒ DIVERSIFIED
☐ Advanced Materials	☒ MISCELLANEOUS
☐ Chemicals	
☒ Instruments & Controls	

STAGE PREFERENCE

☐ EARLY STAGE
☐ Seed
☐ Start-up
☐ 1st Stage
☐ LATER STAGE
☐ 2nd Stage
☐ Mature
☐ Mezzanine
☐ LBO/MBO
☐ Turnaround
☐ INT'L EXPANSION
☐ WILL CONSIDER ALL
☐ VENTURE LEASING

Other Locations:

Affiliation:
Minimum Investment: $1 Million or more
Capital Under Management: Less than $100 Million

GEOGRAPHIC PREF

☐ East Coast
☐ West Coast
☐ Northeast
☐ Mid Atlantic
☐ Gulf States
☐ Northwest
☐ Southeast
☒ Southwest
☐ Midwest
☐ Central
☐ Local to Office
☐ Other Geo Pref

ALTA PARTNERS MANAGEMENT

One Embarcadero Center
Suite 4050
San Francisco CA 94111

Phone (415) 362-4022   Fax (415) 362-6178

PROFESSIONALS	TITLE
Jean Deleage	Partner
Marino Polestra	Partner
Garrett Gruener	General Partner
Guy Paul Nohra	Partner

INDUSTRY PREFERENCE

☒ INFORMATION INDUSTRY
☒ Communications
☒ Computer Equipment
☒ Computer Services
☒ Computer Components
☐ Computer Entertainment
☐ Computer Education
☒ Information Technologies
☒ Computer Media
☒ Software
☒ Internet
☒ MEDICAL/HEALTHCARE
☒ Biotechnology
☒ Healthcare Services
☒ Life Sciences
☒ Medical Products
☒ INDUSTRIAL
☐ Advanced Materials
☒ Chemicals
☐ Instruments & Controls

☐ BASIC INDUSTRIES
☐ Consumer
☐ Distribution
☐ Manufacturing
☐ Retail
☐ Service
☐ Wholesale
☐ SPECIFIC INDUSTRIES
☐ Energy
☐ Environmental
☐ Financial
☐ Real Estate
☐ Transportation
☐ Publishing
☐ Food
☐ Franchises
☒ DIVERSIFIED
☒ MISCELLANEOUS

STAGE PREFERENCE

☒ EARLY STAGE
☒ Seed
☒ Start-up
☒ 1st Stage
☒ LATER STAGE
☒ 2nd Stage
☐ Mature
☒ Mezzanine
☐ LBO/MBO
☐ Turnaround
☐ INT'L EXPANSION
☐ WILL CONSIDER ALL
☐ VENTURE LEASING

Other Locations:

Affiliation:
Minimum Investment: $1 Million or more
Capital Under Management: $100 to $500 Million

GEOGRAPHIC PREF

☐ East Coast
☒ West Coast
☐ Northeast
☐ Mid Atlantic
☐ Gulf States
☐ Northwest
☐ Southeast
☐ Southwest
☐ Midwest
☐ Central
☐ Local to Office
☐ Other Geo Pref

APV TECHNOLOGY PARTNERS

535 Middlefield Road
Suite 150
Menlo Park CA 94025

Phone (650) 327-7871   Fax (650) 327-7631

PROFESSIONALS	TITLE
Will Stewart	Managing Member
Spencer Tall	Managing Member
Pete Bodine	Managing Member
Helen Ingerson	Managing Member

INDUSTRY PREFERENCE

☒ INFORMATION INDUSTRY
☒ Communications
☐ Computer Equipment
☐ Computer Services
☒ Computer Components
☐ Computer Entertainment
☐ Computer Education
☒ Information Technologies
☐ Computer Media
☒ Software
☒ Internet
☐ MEDICAL/HEALTHCARE
☐ Biotechnology
☐ Healthcare Services
☐ Life Sciences
☐ Medical Products
☐ INDUSTRIAL
☐ Advanced Materials
☐ Chemicals
☐ Instruments & Controls

☐ BASIC INDUSTRIES
☐ Consumer
☐ Distribution
☐ Manufacturing
☐ Retail
☐ Service
☐ Wholesale
☐ SPECIFIC INDUSTRIES
☐ Energy
☐ Environmental
☐ Financial
☐ Real Estate
☐ Transportation
☐ Publishing
☐ Food
☐ Franchises
☐ DIVERSIFIED
☒ MISCELLANEOUS

STAGE PREFERENCE

☒ EARLY STAGE
☒ Seed
☒ Start-up
☒ 1st Stage
☐ LATER STAGE
☐ 2nd Stage
☐ Mature
☐ Mezzanine
☐ LBO/MBO
☐ Turnaround
☐ INT'L EXPANSION
☐ WILL CONSIDER ALL
☐ VENTURE LEASING

Other Locations:

Affiliation:
Minimum Investment: Less than $1 Million
Capital Under Management: Less than $100 Million

GEOGRAPHIC PREF

☐ East Coast
☐ West Coast
☐ Northeast
☐ Mid Atlantic
☐ Gulf States
☐ Northwest
☐ Southeast
☐ Southwest
☐ Midwest
☐ Central
☐ Local to Office
☐ Other Geo Pref

ASPEN VENTURES

1000 Fremont Street
Suite 200
Menlo Park CA 94025-7116

Phone (650) 917-5670   Fax (650) 917-5677

PROFESSIONALS	TITLE
Alexander P. Cilento	General Partner
David Crockett	General Partner
Thaddeus J. Whalen	Partner

INDUSTRY PREFERENCE

- ☒ INFORMATION INDUSTRY
- ☒ Communications
- ☒ Computer Equipment
- ☒ Computer Services
- ☒ Computer Components
- ☒ Computer Entertainment
- ☒ Computer Education
- ☒ Information Technologies
- ☒ Computer Media
- ☒ Software
- ☒ Internet
- ☐ MEDICAL/HEALTHCARE
- ☐ Biotechnology
- ☐ Healthcare Services
- ☐ Life Sciences
- ☐ Medical Products
- ☐ INDUSTRIAL
- ☐ Advanced Materials
- ☐ Chemicals
- ☐ Instruments & Controls

- ☐ BASIC INDUSTRIES
- ☐ Consumer
- ☐ Distribution
- ☐ Manufacturing
- ☐ Retail
- ☐ Service
- ☐ Wholesale
- ☐ SPECIFIC INDUSTRIES
- ☐ Energy
- ☐ Environmental
- ☐ Financial
- ☐ Real Estate
- ☐ Transportation
- ☐ Publishing
- ☐ Food
- ☐ Franchises
- ☐ DIVERSIFIED
- ☐ MISCELLANEOUS

STAGE PREFERENCE

- ☒ EARLY STAGE
- ☒ Seed
- ☒ Start-up
- ☒ 1st Stage
- ☐ LATER STAGE
- ☐ 2nd Stage
- ☐ Mature
- ☐ Mezzanine
- ☐ LBO/MBO
- ☐ Turnaround
- ☐ INT'L EXPANSION
- ☐ WILL CONSIDER ALL
- ☐ VENTURE LEASING

Other Locations:

Affiliation:
Minimum Investment: Less than $1 Million
Capital Under Management: Less than $100 Million

GEOGRAPHIC PREF

- ☐ East Coast
- ☒ West Coast
- ☐ Northeast
- ☐ Mid Atlantic
- ☐ Gulf States
- ☐ Northwest
- ☐ Southeast
- ☐ Southwest
- ☐ Midwest
- ☐ Central
- ☐ Local to Office
- ☐ Other Geo Pref

ASSET MANAGEMENT COMPANY VENTURE CAPITAL

2275 East Bayshore Road
Suite 150
Palo Alto CA 94303

Phone (650) 494-7400   Fax (650) 856-1826

PROFESSIONALS	TITLE
Franklin P. Johnson, Jr.	General Partner
Bennett S. Dubin	General Partner
Dr. David M. Mauney, MD	General Partner

INDUSTRY PREFERENCE

- ☒ INFORMATION INDUSTRY
- ☒ Communications
- ☒ Computer Equipment
- ☒ Computer Services
- ☒ Computer Components
- ☒ Computer Entertainment
- ☒ Computer Education
- ☒ Information Technologies
- ☐ Computer Media
- ☒ Software
- ☒ Internet
- ☒ MEDICAL/HEALTHCARE
- ☐ Biotechnology
- ☒ Healthcare Services
- ☐ Life Sciences
- ☒ Medical Products
- ☒ INDUSTRIAL
- ☒ Advanced Materials
- ☐ Chemicals
- ☐ Instruments & Controls

- ☒ BASIC INDUSTRIES
- ☐ Consumer
- ☒ Distribution
- ☐ Manufacturing
- ☐ Retail
- ☒ Service
- ☐ Wholesale
- ☒ SPECIFIC INDUSTRIES
- ☒ Energy
- ☒ Environmental
- ☒ Financial
- ☐ Real Estate
- ☐ Transportation
- ☐ Publishing
- ☐ Food
- ☐ Franchises
- ☒ DIVERSIFIED
- ☐ MISCELLANEOUS

STAGE PREFERENCE

- ☒ EARLY STAGE
- ☒ Seed
- ☒ Start-up
- ☒ 1st Stage
- ☐ LATER STAGE
- ☒ 2nd Stage
- ☐ Mature
- ☐ Mezzanine
- ☐ LBO/MBO
- ☐ Turnaround
- ☐ INT'L EXPANSION
- ☐ WILL CONSIDER ALL
- ☐ VENTURE LEASING

Other Locations:

Affiliation:
Minimum Investment: Less than $1 Million
Capital Under Management: $100 to $500 Million

GEOGRAPHIC PREF

- ☒ East Coast
- ☒ West Coast
- ☒ Northeast
- ☐ Mid Atlantic
- ☐ Gulf States
- ☒ Northwest
- ☐ Southeast
- ☐ Southwest
- ☐ Midwest
- ☐ Central
- ☐ Local to Office
- ☐ Other Geo Pref

AT&T VENTURES

3000 Sand Hill Road
Building One - Suite 285
Menlo Park CA 94025

Phone (650) 233-0617   Fax (650) 854-4923

PROFESSIONALS	TITLE
Neal Douglas	General Partner
Tom Rosch	Partner

INDUSTRY PREFERENCE

☒ INFORMATION INDUSTRY	☐ BASIC INDUSTRIES
☒ Communications	☐ Consumer
☐ Computer Equipment	☐ Distribution
☐ Computer Services	☐ Manufacturing
☒ Computer Components	☐ Retail
☐ Computer Entertainment	☐ Service
☐ Computer Education	☐ Wholesale
☒ Information Technologies	☐ SPECIFIC INDUSTRIES
☐ Computer Media	☐ Energy
☒ Software	☐ Environmental
☒ Internet	☐ Financial
☐ MEDICAL/HEALTHCARE	☐ Real Estate
☐ Biotechnology	☐ Transportation
☐ Healthcare Services	☐ Publishing
☐ Life Sciences	☐ Food
☐ Medical Products	☐ Franchises
☐ INDUSTRIAL	☐ DIVERSIFIED
☐ Advanced Materials	☒ MISCELLANEOUS
☐ Chemicals	
☐ Instruments & Controls	

STAGE PREFERENCE

☒ EARLY STAGE	
☒ Seed	
☒ Start-up	
☒ 1st Stage	
☒ LATER STAGE	
☒ 2nd Stage	
☐ Mature	
☐ Mezzanine	
☐ LBO/MBO	
☐ Turnaround	
☐ INT'L EXPANSION	
☐ WILL CONSIDER ALL	
☐ VENTURE LEASING	

Other Locations: Basking Ridge NJ, Chevy Chase MD

Affiliation: AT&T
Minimum Investment: Less than $1 Million
Capital Under Management: $100 to $500 Million

GEOGRAPHIC PREF

☐ East Coast	
☐ West Coast	
☐ Northeast	
☐ Mid Atlantic	
☐ Gulf States	
☐ Northwest	
☐ Southeast	
☐ Southwest	
☐ Midwest	
☐ Central	
☐ Local to Office	
☐ Other Geo Pref	

AUGUST CAPITAL MANAGEMENT

2480 Sand Hill Road
Suite 101
Menlo Park CA 94025-6940

Phone (650) 234-9900   Fax (650) 234-9910

PROFESSIONALS	TITLE
John R. Johnson	Co-Founder
David F. Marquardt	Co-Founder
Mark G. Wilson	Chief Financial Officer
Won H. Chung	Research Partner
Andrew Rappaport	Partner
Andrew Anker	Partner

INDUSTRY PREFERENCE

☒ INFORMATION INDUSTRY	☐ BASIC INDUSTRIES
☒ Communications	☐ Consumer
☒ Computer Equipment	☐ Distribution
☒ Computer Services	☐ Manufacturing
☒ Computer Components	☐ Retail
☐ Computer Entertainment	☐ Service
☐ Computer Education	☐ Wholesale
☐ Information Technologies	☐ SPECIFIC INDUSTRIES
☐ Computer Media	☐ Energy
☒ Software	☐ Environmental
☒ Internet	☐ Financial
☐ MEDICAL/HEALTHCARE	☐ Real Estate
☐ Biotechnology	☐ Transportation
☐ Healthcare Services	☐ Publishing
☐ Life Sciences	☐ Food
☐ Medical Products	☐ Franchises
☐ INDUSTRIAL	☒ DIVERSIFIED
☐ Advanced Materials	☒ MISCELLANEOUS
☐ Chemicals	
☐ Instruments & Controls	

STAGE PREFERENCE

☒ EARLY STAGE	
☐ Seed	
☒ Start-up	
☒ 1st Stage	
☐ LATER STAGE	
☐ 2nd Stage	
☐ Mature	
☐ Mezzanine	
☐ LBO/MBO	
☐ Turnaround	
☐ INT'L EXPANSION	
☐ WILL CONSIDER ALL	
☐ VENTURE LEASING	

Other Locations:

Affiliation:
Minimum Investment: $1 Million or more
Capital Under Management: $100 to $500 Million

GEOGRAPHIC PREF

☐ East Coast	
☒ West Coast	
☐ Northeast	
☐ Mid Atlantic	
☐ Gulf States	
☒ Northwest	
☐ Southeast	
☒ Southwest	
☐ Midwest	
☐ Central	
☐ Local to Office	
☐ Other Geo Pref	

AVI MANAGEMENT PARTNERS

One First Street
Suite 2
Los Altos CA 94022

Phone (650) 949-9862   Fax (650) 949-8510

PROFESSIONALS	TITLE
Peter Wolken	General Partner
Barry Weinman	General Partner
Brian Grossi	General Partner

INDUSTRY PREFERENCE

- ☒ INFORMATION INDUSTRY
- ☒ Communications
- ☒ Computer Equipment
- ☒ Computer Services
- ☒ Computer Components
- ☐ Computer Entertainment
- ☒ Computer Education
- ☒ Information Technologies
- ☒ Computer Media
- ☒ Software
- ☒ Internet
- ☐ MEDICAL/HEALTHCARE
- ☐ Biotechnology
- ☐ Healthcare Services
- ☐ Life Sciences
- ☐ Medical Products
- ☐ INDUSTRIAL
- ☐ Advanced Materials
- ☐ Chemicals
- ☐ Instruments & Controls

- ☐ BASIC INDUSTRIES
- ☐ Consumer
- ☐ Distribution
- ☐ Manufacturing
- ☐ Retail
- ☐ Service
- ☐ Wholesale
- ☐ SPECIFIC INDUSTRIES
- ☐ Energy
- ☐ Environmental
- ☐ Financial
- ☐ Real Estate
- ☐ Transportation
- ☐ Publishing
- ☐ Food
- ☐ Franchises
- ☐ DIVERSIFIED
- ☐ MISCELLANEOUS

STAGE PREFERENCE

- ☒ EARLY STAGE
- ☒ Seed
- ☒ Start-up
- ☒ 1st Stage
- ☒ LATER STAGE
- ☒ 2nd Stage
- ☐ Mature
- ☐ Mezzanine
- ☐ LBO/MBO
- ☐ Turnaround
- ☐ INT'L EXPANSION
- ☐ WILL CONSIDER ALL
- ☐ VENTURE LEASING

SBIC
Other Locations:

Affiliation:
Minimum Investment: $1 Million or more
Capital Under Management: $100 to $500 Million

GEOGRAPHIC PREF

- ☐ East Coast
- ☒ West Coast
- ☐ Northeast
- ☐ Mid Atlantic
- ☐ Gulf States
- ☐ Northwest
- ☐ Southeast
- ☐ Southwest
- ☐ Midwest
- ☐ Central
- ☐ Local to Office
- ☐ Other Geo Pref

BACCHARIS CAPITAL, INC.

2420 Sand Hill Road
Suite 100
Menlo Park CA 94025

Phone (650) 324-6844   Fax (650) 854-3025

PROFESSIONALS	TITLE
Mary Bechmann	Managing Director
F. Noel Perry	

INDUSTRY PREFERENCE

- ☒ INFORMATION INDUSTRY
- ☒ Communications
- ☐ Computer Equipment
- ☐ Computer Services
- ☐ Computer Components
- ☐ Computer Entertainment
- ☐ Computer Education
- ☒ Information Technologies
- ☐ Computer Media
- ☒ Software
- ☐ Internet
- ☐ MEDICAL/HEALTHCARE
- ☐ Biotechnology
- ☐ Healthcare Services
- ☐ Life Sciences
- ☐ Medical Products
- ☐ INDUSTRIAL
- ☐ Advanced Materials
- ☐ Chemicals
- ☐ Instruments & Controls

- ☒ BASIC INDUSTRIES
- ☒ Consumer
- ☐ Distribution
- ☐ Manufacturing
- ☐ Retail
- ☐ Service
- ☐ Wholesale
- ☒ SPECIFIC INDUSTRIES
- ☒ Energy
- ☒ Environmental
- ☐ Financial
- ☐ Real Estate
- ☐ Transportation
- ☐ Publishing
- ☐ Food
- ☐ Franchises
- ☒ DIVERSIFIED
- ☐ MISCELLANEOUS

STAGE PREFERENCE

- ☒ EARLY STAGE
- ☐ Seed
- ☒ Start-up
- ☒ 1st Stage
- ☒ LATER STAGE
- ☒ 2nd Stage
- ☒ Mature
- ☒ Mezzanine
- ☒ LBO/MBO
- ☒ Turnaround
- ☐ INT'L EXPANSION
- ☐ WILL CONSIDER ALL
- ☒ VENTURE LEASING

Other Locations:

Affiliation:
Minimum Investment: $1 Million or more
Capital Under Management: Less than $100 Million

GEOGRAPHIC PREF

- ☐ East Coast
- ☒ West Coast
- ☐ Northeast
- ☐ Mid Atlantic
- ☐ Gulf States
- ☐ Northwest
- ☐ Southeast
- ☐ Southwest
- ☐ Midwest
- ☐ Central
- ☐ Local to Office
- ☐ Other Geo Pref

BANCBOSTON VENTURES, INC

**435 Tasso Street
Palo Alto CA 94301**

Phone (650) 470-4140   Fax (650) 853-1425

PROFESSIONALS	TITLE
Maia Heymann	
Julian Alesander	
A. J. Shanley	

INDUSTRY PREFERENCE

☒	INFORMATION INDUSTRY	☐	BASIC INDUSTRIES
☒	Communications	☐	Consumer
☒	Computer Equipment	☐	Distribution
☒	Computer Services	☐	Manufacturing
☒	Computer Components	☐	Retail
☐	Computer Entertainment	☐	Service
☒	Computer Education	☐	Wholesale
☒	Information Technologies	☐	SPECIFIC INDUSTRIES
☒	Computer Media	☐	Energy
☒	Software	☐	Environmental
☒	Internet	☐	Financial
☒	MEDICAL/HEALTHCARE	☐	Real Estate
☐	Biotechnology	☐	Transportation
☒	Healthcare Services	☐	Publishing
☐	Life Sciences	☐	Food
☐	Medical Products	☐	Franchises
☐	INDUSTRIAL	☒	DIVERSIFIED
☐	Advanced Materials	☒	MISCELLANEOUS
☐	Chemicals		
☐	Instruments & Controls		

STAGE PREFERENCE

☒	EARLY STAGE
☒	Seed
☒	Start-up
☒	1st Stage
☒	LATER STAGE
☒	2nd Stage
☒	Mature
☒	Mezzanine
☒	LBO/MBO
☐	Turnaround
☐	INT'L EXPANSION
☐	WILL CONSIDER ALL
☐	VENTURE LEASING

SBIC
Other Locations: Boston MA

Affiliation: Bank of Boston
Minimum Investment: Less than $1 Million
Capital Under Management: Over $500 Million

GEOGRAPHIC PREF

☐	East Coast
☐	West Coast
☐	Northeast
☐	Mid Atlantic
☐	Gulf States
☐	Northwest
☐	Southeast
☐	Southwest
☐	Midwest
☐	Central
☐	Local to Office
☐	Other Geo Pref

BANKAMERICA VENTURES

**950 Tower Lane
Suite 700
Foster City CA 94404**

Phone (650) 378-6000   Fax (650) 378-6040

PROFESSIONALS	TITLE
James D. Murphy	Managing Director
Anchie Y. Kuo	Managing Director
Kate D. Mitchell	Managing Director
Robert M. Obuch	Principal
Rory O'Driscoll	Principal
Carla Perumean	Contact Person

INDUSTRY PREFERENCE

☒	INFORMATION INDUSTRY	☐	BASIC INDUSTRIES
☒	Communications	☐	Consumer
☐	Computer Equipment	☐	Distribution
☐	Computer Services	☐	Manufacturing
☐	Computer Components	☐	Retail
☐	Computer Entertainment	☐	Service
☐	Computer Education	☐	Wholesale
☐	Information Technologies	☐	SPECIFIC INDUSTRIES
☐	Computer Media	☐	Energy
☒	Software	☐	Environmental
☒	Internet	☐	Financial
☒	MEDICAL/HEALTHCARE	☐	Real Estate
☒	Biotechnology	☐	Transportation
☐	Healthcare Services	☐	Publishing
☐	Life Sciences	☐	Food
☒	Medical Products	☐	Franchises
☐	INDUSTRIAL	☒	DIVERSIFIED
☐	Advanced Materials	☒	MISCELLANEOUS
☐	Chemicals		
☐	Instruments & Controls		

STAGE PREFERENCE

☒	EARLY STAGE
☐	Seed
☒	Start-up
☒	1st Stage
☒	LATER STAGE
☒	2nd Stage
☐	Mature
☒	Mezzanine
☐	LBO/MBO
☐	Turnaround
☐	INT'L EXPANSION
☐	WILL CONSIDER ALL
☐	VENTURE LEASING

SBIC
Other Locations:

Affiliation:
Minimum Investment: $1 Million or more
Capital Under Management: $100 to $500 Million

GEOGRAPHIC PREF

☐	East Coast
☐	West Coast
☐	Northeast
☐	Mid Atlantic
☐	Gulf States
☐	Northwest
☐	Southeast
☐	Southwest
☐	Midwest
☐	Central
☐	Local to Office
☐	Other Geo Pref

BASTION CAPITAL CORP.

1999 Avenue of the Stars
Suite 2960
Los Angeles CA 90067

Phone (310) 788-5700   Fax (310) 277-7582

PROFESSIONALS	TITLE
Guillermo Bron	Partner
Daniel Villanueva	Partner

INDUSTRY PREFERENCE

☒ INFORMATION INDUSTRY	☒ BASIC INDUSTRIES	
☒ Communications	☒ Consumer	
☐ Computer Equipment	☒ Distribution	
☐ Computer Services	☒ Manufacturing	
☒ Computer Components	☐ Retail	
☐ Computer Entertainment	☐ Service	
☐ Computer Education	☐ Wholesale	
☐ Information Technologies	☒ SPECIFIC INDUSTRIES	
☐ Computer Media	☒ Energy	
☐ Software	☐ Environmental	
☐ Internet	☒ Financial	
☒ MEDICAL/HEALTHCARE	☐ Real Estate	
☐ Biotechnology	☒ Transportation	
☐ Healthcare Services	☐ Publishing	
☐ Life Sciences	☐ Food	
☒ Medical Products	☐ Franchises	
☐ INDUSTRIAL	☒ DIVERSIFIED	
☐ Advanced Materials	☒ MISCELLANEOUS	
☐ Chemicals		
☐ Instruments & Controls		

STAGE PREFERENCE

☐ EARLY STAGE
☐ Seed
☐ Start-up
☐ 1st Stage
☒ LATER STAGE
☐ 2nd Stage
☐ Mature
☐ Mezzanine
☒ LBO/MBO
☒ Turnaround
☐ INT'L EXPANSION
☐ WILL CONSIDER ALL
☒ VENTURE LEASING

Other Locations:

Affiliation:
Minimum Investment: $1 Million or more
Capital Under Management: $100 to $500 Million

GEOGRAPHIC PREF

☐ East Coast
☐ West Coast
☐ Northeast
☐ Mid Atlantic
☐ Gulf States
☐ Northwest
☐ Southeast
☐ Southwest
☐ Midwest
☐ Central
☐ Local to Office
☐ Other Geo Pref

BATTERY VENTURES

901 Mariner's Island Boulevard
Suite 475
San Mateo CA 94404

Phone (650) 372-3939   Fax (650) 372-3930

PROFESSIONALS	TITLE
David Hartwig	
Dennis Phelps	
Marc Woodward	

INDUSTRY PREFERENCE

☒ INFORMATION INDUSTRY	☐ BASIC INDUSTRIES	
☒ Communications	☐ Consumer	
☒ Computer Equipment	☐ Distribution	
☒ Computer Services	☐ Manufacturing	
☒ Computer Components	☐ Retail	
☐ Computer Entertainment	☐ Service	
☒ Computer Education	☐ Wholesale	
☒ Information Technologies	☐ SPECIFIC INDUSTRIES	
☒ Computer Media	☐ Energy	
☒ Software	☐ Environmental	
☒ Internet	☐ Financial	
☐ MEDICAL/HEALTHCARE	☐ Real Estate	
☐ Biotechnology	☐ Transportation	
☐ Healthcare Services	☐ Publishing	
☐ Life Sciences	☐ Food	
☐ Medical Products	☐ Franchises	
☐ INDUSTRIAL	☐ DIVERSIFIED	
☐ Advanced Materials	☒ MISCELLANEOUS	
☐ Chemicals		
☐ Instruments & Controls		

STAGE PREFERENCE

☒ EARLY STAGE
☒ Seed
☒ Start-up
☒ 1st Stage
☒ LATER STAGE
☒ 2nd Stage
☒ Mature
☐ Mezzanine
☒ LBO/MBO
☐ Turnaround
☐ INT'L EXPANSION
☐ WILL CONSIDER ALL
☐ VENTURE LEASING

Other Locations: Boston MA

Affiliation:
Minimum Investment: Less than $1 Million
Capital Under Management: Over $500 Million

GEOGRAPHIC PREF

☐ East Coast
☐ West Coast
☐ Northeast
☐ Mid Atlantic
☐ Gulf States
☐ Northwest
☐ Southeast
☐ Southwest
☐ Midwest
☐ Central
☐ Local to Office
☐ Other Geo Pref

BAY PARTNERS SBIC, LP

10600 North De Anza Boulevard
Suite 100
Cupertino CA 95014-2031

Phone (408) 725-2444   Fax (408) 446-4502

PROFESSIONALS	TITLE
John Freidenrich	General Partner
Neal Dempsey	General Partner

INDUSTRY PREFERENCE

☒ INFORMATION INDUSTRY	☒ BASIC INDUSTRIES
☒ Communications	☐ Consumer
☒ Computer Equipment	☐ Distribution
☒ Computer Services	☐ Manufacturing
☐ Computer Components	☐ Retail
☐ Computer Entertainment	☒ Service
☐ Computer Education	☐ Wholesale
☒ Information Technologies	☐ SPECIFIC INDUSTRIES
☐ Computer Media	☐ Energy
☒ Software	☐ Environmental
☒ Internet	☐ Financial
☐ MEDICAL/HEALTHCARE	☐ Real Estate
☐ Biotechnology	☐ Transportation
☐ Healthcare Services	☐ Publishing
☐ Life Sciences	☐ Food
☐ Medical Products	☐ Franchises
☐ INDUSTRIAL	☒ DIVERSIFIED
☐ Advanced Materials	☐ MISCELLANEOUS
☐ Chemicals	
☐ Instruments & Controls	

STAGE PREFERENCE

☒ EARLY STAGE
☐ Seed
☒ Start-up
☒ 1st Stage
☒ LATER STAGE
☒ 2nd Stage
☐ Mature
☐ Mezzanine
☐ LBO/MBO
☐ Turnaround
☐ INT'L EXPANSION
☐ WILL CONSIDER ALL
☐ VENTURE LEASING

SBIC
Other Locations:

Affiliation:
Minimum Investment: $1 Million or more
Capital Under Management: $100 to $500 Million

GEOGRAPHIC PREF

☐ East Coast
☒ West Coast
☒ Northeast
☐ Mid Atlantic
☐ Gulf States
☐ Northwest
☐ Southeast
☐ Southwest
☐ Midwest
☐ Central
☐ Local to Office
☐ Other Geo Pref

BENTLEY CAPITAL

592 Vallejo Street
Suite #2
San Francisco CA 94133

Phone (415) 362-2868   Fax (415) 398-8209

PROFESSIONALS	TITLE
John Hung	President

INDUSTRY PREFERENCE

☐ INFORMATION INDUSTRY	☐ BASIC INDUSTRIES
☐ Communications	☐ Consumer
☐ Computer Equipment	☐ Distribution
☐ Computer Services	☐ Manufacturing
☐ Computer Components	☐ Retail
☐ Computer Entertainment	☐ Service
☐ Computer Education	☐ Wholesale
☐ Information Technologies	☒ SPECIFIC INDUSTRIES
☐ Computer Media	☐ Energy
☐ Software	☐ Environmental
☐ Internet	☐ Financial
☐ MEDICAL/HEALTHCARE	☐ Real Estate
☐ Biotechnology	☐ Transportation
☐ Healthcare Services	☐ Publishing
☐ Life Sciences	☐ Food
☐ Medical Products	☐ Franchises
☐ INDUSTRIAL	☒ DIVERSIFIED
☐ Advanced Materials	☒ MISCELLANEOUS
☐ Chemicals	Import/Export
☐ Instruments & Controls	

STAGE PREFERENCE

☒ EARLY STAGE
☒ Seed
☒ Start-up
☒ 1st Stage
☐ LATER STAGE
☐ 2nd Stage
☐ Mature
☐ Mezzanine
☐ LBO/MBO
☐ Turnaround
☐ INT'L EXPANSION
☐ WILL CONSIDER ALL
☐ VENTURE LEASING

SSBIC
Other Locations:

Affiliation:
Minimum Investment: $1 Million or more
Capital Under Management: Less than $100 Million

GEOGRAPHIC PREF

☐ East Coast
☒ West Coast
☐ Northeast
☐ Mid Atlantic
☐ Gulf States
☐ Northwest
☐ Southeast
☐ Southwest
☐ Midwest
☐ Central
☐ Local to Office
☐ Other Geo Pref

BERKELEY INTERNATIONAL CAPITAL CORPORATION

650 California Street
Suite 2800
San Francisco CA 94108-2609

Phone (415) 249-0450   Fax (415) 392-3929

PROFESSIONALS	TITLE
Arthur Trueger	Chairman / Founder
Michael Mayer	President

INDUSTRY PREFERENCE

☒ INFORMATION INDUSTRY	☒ BASIC INDUSTRIES
☒ Communications	☐ Consumer
☒ Computer Equipment	☒ Distribution
☒ Computer Services	☒ Manufacturing
☒ Computer Components	☐ Retail
☐ Computer Entertainment	☐ Service
☒ Computer Education	☐ Wholesale
☐ Information Technologies	☒ SPECIFIC INDUSTRIES
☐ Computer Media	☐ Energy
☒ Software	☐ Environmental
☐ Internet	☐ Financial
☒ MEDICAL/HEALTHCARE	☐ Real Estate
☐ Biotechnology	☐ Transportation
☒ Healthcare Services	☐ Publishing
☐ Life Sciences	☐ Food
☒ Medical Products	☐ Franchises
☐ INDUSTRIAL	☒ DIVERSIFIED
☐ Advanced Materials	☒ MISCELLANEOUS
☐ Chemicals	
☐ Instruments & Controls	

STAGE PREFERENCE

☐ EARLY STAGE
☐ Seed
☐ Start-up
☐ 1st Stage
☒ LATER STAGE
☒ 2nd Stage
☐ Mature
☒ Mezzanine
☒ LBO/MBO
☐ Turnaround
☐ INT'L EXPANSION
☐ WILL CONSIDER ALL
☐ VENTURE LEASING

Other Locations:

Affiliation:
Minimum Investment: $1 Million or more
Capital Under Management: $100 to $500 Million

GEOGRAPHIC PREF

☐ East Coast
☐ West Coast
☐ Northeast
☐ Mid Atlantic
☐ Gulf States
☐ Northwest
☐ Southeast
☐ Southwest
☐ Midwest
☐ Central
☐ Local to Office
☐ Other Geo Pref

BESSEMER VENTURE PARTNERS

535 Middlefield Road
Menlo Park CA 94025

Phone (650) 853-7000   Fax (650) 853-7001

PROFESSIONALS	TITLE
David Cowan	Partner

INDUSTRY PREFERENCE

☒ INFORMATION INDUSTRY	☒ BASIC INDUSTRIES
☒ Communications	☒ Consumer
☒ Computer Equipment	☐ Distribution
☒ Computer Services	☐ Manufacturing
☒ Computer Components	☒ Retail
☐ Computer Entertainment	☒ Service
☒ Computer Education	☒ Wholesale
☒ Information Technologies	☒ SPECIFIC INDUSTRIES
☒ Computer Media	☒ Energy
☒ Software	☒ Environmental
☒ Internet	☐ Financial
☒ MEDICAL/HEALTHCARE	☐ Real Estate
☒ Biotechnology	☐ Transportation
☒ Healthcare Services	☐ Publishing
☒ Life Sciences	☐ Food
☒ Medical Products	☐ Franchises
☒ INDUSTRIAL	☒ DIVERSIFIED
☒ Advanced Materials	☐ MISCELLANEOUS
☒ Chemicals	
☒ Instruments & Controls	

STAGE PREFERENCE

☒ EARLY STAGE
☒ Seed
☒ Start-up
☒ 1st Stage
☒ LATER STAGE
☒ 2nd Stage
☒ Mature
☒ Mezzanine
☒ LBO/MBO
☐ Turnaround
☐ INT'L EXPANSION
☐ WILL CONSIDER ALL
☐ VENTURE LEASING

Other Locations: Wellesley Hills MA, Westbury NY

Affiliation: Bessemer Securities Corp.
Minimum Investment: Less than $1 Million
Capital Under Management: $100 to $500 Million

GEOGRAPHIC PREF

☐ East Coast
☐ West Coast
☐ Northeast
☐ Mid Atlantic
☐ Gulf States
☐ Northwest
☐ Southeast
☐ Southwest
☐ Midwest
☐ Central
☐ Local to Office
☐ Other Geo Pref

BEST FINANCE CORPORATION

3540 Wilshire Boulevard
Suite 804
Los Angeles CA 90010

Phone (213) 385-7030   Fax (213) 385-7130

PROFESSIONALS	TITLE
James Hong	General Manager

INDUSTRY PREFERENCE

☐ INFORMATION INDUSTRY	☐ BASIC INDUSTRIES
☐ Communications	☐ Consumer
☐ Computer Equipment	☐ Distribution
☐ Computer Services	☐ Manufacturing
☐ Computer Components	☐ Retail
☐ Computer Entertainment	☐ Service
☐ Computer Education	☐ Wholesale
☐ Information Technologies	☐ SPECIFIC INDUSTRIES
☐ Computer Media	☐ Energy
☐ Software	☐ Environmental
☐ Internet	☐ Financial
☐ MEDICAL/HEALTHCARE	☐ Real Estate
☐ Biotechnology	☐ Transportation
☐ Healthcare Services	☐ Publishing
☐ Life Sciences	☐ Food
☐ Medical Products	☐ Franchises
☐ INDUSTRIAL	☒ DIVERSIFIED
☐ Advanced Materials	☐ MISCELLANEOUS
☐ Chemicals	
☐ Instruments & Controls	

STAGE PREFERENCE

☒ EARLY STAGE
☒   Seed
☒   Start-up
☒   1st Stage
☒ LATER STAGE
☒   2nd Stage
☐   Mature
☐   Mezzanine
☐   LBO/MBO
☐   Turnaround
☐ INT'L EXPANSION
☐ WILL CONSIDER ALL
☐ VENTURE LEASING
SSBIC
Other Locations:

Affiliation:
Minimum Investment: $1 Million or more
Capital Under Management: Less than $100 Million

GEOGRAPHIC PREF

☐ East Coast
☒ West Coast
☐ Northeast
☐ Mid Atlantic
☐ Gulf States
☐ Northwest
☐ Southeast
☐ Southwest
☐ Midwest
☐ Central
☐ Local to Office
☐ Other Geo Pref

BIO-VENTURES WEST

2131 Palomar Airport Road
Carlsbad CA 92009

Phone (760) 431-5104   Fax (760) 431-5105

PROFESSIONALS	TITLE
Robert Robb	President

INDUSTRY PREFERENCE

☐ INFORMATION INDUSTRY	☐ BASIC INDUSTRIES
☐ Communications	☐ Consumer
☐ Computer Equipment	☐ Distribution
☐ Computer Services	☐ Manufacturing
☐ Computer Components	☐ Retail
☐ Computer Entertainment	☐ Service
☐ Computer Education	☐ Wholesale
☐ Information Technologies	☐ SPECIFIC INDUSTRIES
☐ Computer Media	☐ Energy
☐ Software	☐ Environmental
☐ Internet	☐ Financial
☒ MEDICAL/HEALTHCARE	☐ Real Estate
☒ Biotechnology	☐ Transportation
☒ Healthcare Services	☐ Publishing
☒ Life Sciences	☐ Food
☒ Medical Products	☐ Franchises
☐ INDUSTRIAL	☐ DIVERSIFIED
☐ Advanced Materials	☒ MISCELLANEOUS
☐ Chemicals	
☐ Instruments & Controls	

STAGE PREFERENCE

☐ EARLY STAGE
☐   Seed
☐   Start-up
☐   1st Stage
☐ LATER STAGE
☐   2nd Stage
☐   Mature
☐   Mezzanine
☐   LBO/MBO
☐   Turnaround
☐ INT'L EXPANSION
☐ WILL CONSIDER ALL
☐ VENTURE LEASING

Other Locations: Tucson AZ

Affiliation:
Minimum Investment: Less than $1 Million
Capital Under Management: Less than $100 Million

GEOGRAPHIC PREF

☐ East Coast
☒ West Coast
☐ Northeast
☐ Mid Atlantic
☐ Gulf States
☐ Northwest
☐ Southeast
☐ Southwest
☐ Midwest
☐ Central
☐ Local to Office
☐ Other Geo Pref

BRENTWOOD ASSOCIATES

1920 Main Street
Suite 820
Irvine CA 92614

Phone (949) 251-1010   Fax (949) 251-1011

PROFESSIONALS	TITLE
Bill Link	General Partner
G. Bradford Jones	General Partner
John Walecka	General Partner
Ross Jaffe	General Partner
Jeffrey Brody	General Partner
Brian Atwood	General Partner

INDUSTRY PREFERENCE

- ☒ INFORMATION INDUSTRY
- ☒ Communications
- ☒ Computer Equipment
- ☒ Computer Services
- ☒ Computer Components
- ☐ Computer Entertainment
- ☒ Computer Education
- ☒ Information Technologies
- ☐ Computer Media
- ☒ Software
- ☒ Internet
- ☒ MEDICAL/HEALTHCARE
- ☒ Biotechnology
- ☒ Healthcare Services
- ☒ Life Sciences
- ☒ Medical Products
- ☐ INDUSTRIAL
- ☐ Advanced Materials
- ☐ Chemicals
- ☐ Instruments & Controls

- ☒ BASIC INDUSTRIES
- ☐ Consumer
- ☐ Distribution
- ☐ Manufacturing
- ☐ Retail
- ☒ Service
- ☐ Wholesale
- ☐ SPECIFIC INDUSTRIES
- ☐ Energy
- ☐ Environmental
- ☐ Financial
- ☐ Real Estate
- ☐ Transportation
- ☐ Publishing
- ☐ Food
- ☐ Franchises
- ☒ DIVERSIFIED
- ☐ MISCELLANEOUS

STAGE PREFERENCE

- ☒ EARLY STAGE
- ☒ Seed
- ☒ Start-up
- ☒ 1st Stage
- ☒ LATER STAGE
- ☒ 2nd Stage
- ☐ Mature
- ☐ Mezzanine
- ☐ LBO/MBO
- ☐ Turnaround
- ☐ INT'L EXPANSION
- ☐ WILL CONSIDER ALL
- ☐ VENTURE LEASING

Other Locations: Menlo Park CA, Los Angeles CA

Affiliation:
Minimum Investment: Less than $1 Million
Capital Under Management: $100 to $500 Million

GEOGRAPHIC PREF

- ☐ East Coast
- ☒ West Coast
- ☐ Northeast
- ☐ Mid Atlantic
- ☐ Gulf States
- ☐ Northwest
- ☐ Southeast
- ☐ Southwest
- ☐ Midwest
- ☐ Central
- ☐ Local to Office
- ☐ Other Geo Pref

BRENTWOOD ASSOCIATES

11150 Santa Monica Boulevard
Suite 1200
Los Angeles CA 90025-3380

Phone (310) 477-7678   Fax (310) 312-1868

PROFESSIONALS	TITLE
G. Bradford Jones	Venture Partner
B. Kipling Hagopian	Venture Partner
Dave Chonette	Special Limited Partner

INDUSTRY PREFERENCE

- ☒ INFORMATION INDUSTRY
- ☒ Communications
- ☒ Computer Equipment
- ☒ Computer Services
- ☒ Computer Components
- ☐ Computer Entertainment
- ☒ Computer Education
- ☒ Information Technologies
- ☐ Computer Media
- ☒ Software
- ☒ Internet
- ☒ MEDICAL/HEALTHCARE
- ☒ Biotechnology
- ☒ Healthcare Services
- ☒ Life Sciences
- ☒ Medical Products
- ☐ INDUSTRIAL
- ☐ Advanced Materials
- ☐ Chemicals
- ☐ Instruments & Controls

- ☒ BASIC INDUSTRIES
- ☐ Consumer
- ☐ Distribution
- ☐ Manufacturing
- ☐ Retail
- ☒ Service
- ☐ Wholesale
- ☐ SPECIFIC INDUSTRIES
- ☐ Energy
- ☐ Environmental
- ☐ Financial
- ☐ Real Estate
- ☐ Transportation
- ☐ Publishing
- ☐ Food
- ☐ Franchises
- ☒ DIVERSIFIED
- ☐ MISCELLANEOUS

STAGE PREFERENCE

- ☒ EARLY STAGE
- ☒ Seed
- ☒ Start-up
- ☒ 1st Stage
- ☒ LATER STAGE
- ☒ 2nd Stage
- ☐ Mature
- ☐ Mezzanine
- ☐ LBO/MBO
- ☐ Turnaround
- ☐ INT'L EXPANSION
- ☐ WILL CONSIDER ALL
- ☐ VENTURE LEASING

Other Locations: Menlo Park CA, Irvine CA

Affiliation:
Minimum Investment: Less than $1 Million
Capital Under Management: $100 to $500 Million

GEOGRAPHIC PREF

- ☐ East Coast
- ☒ West Coast
- ☐ Northeast
- ☐ Mid Atlantic
- ☐ Gulf States
- ☐ Northwest
- ☐ Southeast
- ☐ Southwest
- ☐ Midwest
- ☐ Central
- ☐ Local to Office
- ☐ Other Geo Pref

BRENTWOOD ASSOCIATES

3000 Sand Hill Road
Building One, Suite 260
Menlo Park CA 94025-7020

Phone (650) 854-7691   Fax (650) 854-9513

PROFESSIONALS	TITLE
Dr. Ross A. Jaffe	General Partner
John L. Walecka	General Partner
Jeff Brody	General Partner
Brian Atwood	General Partner
Stewart Schuster	Venture Partner

INDUSTRY PREFERENCE

☒ INFORMATION INDUSTRY	☒ BASIC INDUSTRIES
☒ Communications	☐ Consumer
☒ Computer Equipment	☐ Distribution
☒ Computer Services	☐ Manufacturing
☒ Computer Components	☐ Retail
☐ Computer Entertainment	☒ Service
☒ Computer Education	☐ Wholesale
☒ Information Technologies	☐ SPECIFIC INDUSTRIES
☐ Computer Media	☐ Energy
☒ Software	☐ Environmental
☒ Internet	☐ Financial
☒ MEDICAL/HEALTHCARE	☐ Real Estate
☒ Biotechnology	☐ Transportation
☒ Healthcare Services	☐ Publishing
☒ Life Sciences	☐ Food
☒ Medical Products	☐ Franchises
☐ INDUSTRIAL	☒ DIVERSIFIED
☐ Advanced Materials	☐ MISCELLANEOUS
☐ Chemicals	
☐ Instruments & Controls	

STAGE PREFERENCE

☒ EARLY STAGE	
☒ Seed	
☒ Start-up	
☒ 1st Stage	
☒ LATER STAGE	
☒ 2nd Stage	
☐ Mature	
☐ Mezzanine	
☐ LBO/MBO	
☐ Turnaround	
☐ INT'L EXPANSION	
☐ WILL CONSIDER ALL	
☐ VENTURE LEASING	

Other Locations: Los Angeles CA, Irvine CA

Affiliation:
Minimum Investment: Less than $1 Million
Capital Under Management: $100 to $500 Million

GEOGRAPHIC PREF

☐ East Coast	
☒ West Coast	
☐ Northeast	
☐ Mid Atlantic	
☐ Gulf States	
☐ Northwest	
☐ Southeast	
☐ Southwest	
☐ Midwest	
☐ Central	
☐ Local to Office	
☐ Other Geo Pref	

BURR, EGAN, DELEAGE & CO.

One Embarcadero Center
Suite 4050
San Francisco CA 94111-3729

Phone (415) 362-4022   Fax (415) 362-6178

PROFESSIONALS	TITLE
Garrett Gruener	Partner
Jean Deleage	Partner
Guy Paul Nohra	Partner

INDUSTRY PREFERENCE

☒ INFORMATION INDUSTRY	☒ BASIC INDUSTRIES
☒ Communications	☐ Consumer
☒ Computer Equipment	☐ Distribution
☒ Computer Services	☐ Manufacturing
☒ Computer Components	☐ Retail
☒ Computer Entertainment	☒ Service
☒ Computer Education	☐ Wholesale
☒ Information Technologies	☐ SPECIFIC INDUSTRIES
☒ Computer Media	☐ Energy
☐ Software	☐ Environmental
☒ Internet	☐ Financial
☒ MEDICAL/HEALTHCARE	☐ Real Estate
☒ Biotechnology	☐ Transportation
☒ Healthcare Services	☐ Publishing
☐ Life Sciences	☐ Food
☐ Medical Products	☐ Franchises
☒ INDUSTRIAL	☒ DIVERSIFIED
☒ Advanced Materials	☐ MISCELLANEOUS
☒ Chemicals	
☒ Instruments & Controls	

STAGE PREFERENCE

☒ EARLY STAGE	
☒ Seed	
☒ Start-up	
☒ 1st Stage	
☒ LATER STAGE	
☒ 2nd Stage	
☒ Mature	
☐ Mezzanine	
☒ LBO/MBO	
☒ Turnaround	
☐ INT'L EXPANSION	
☐ WILL CONSIDER ALL	
☒ VENTURE LEASING	

Other Locations: Boston MA

Affiliation:
Minimum Investment: Less than $1 Million
Capital Under Management: Over $500 Million

GEOGRAPHIC PREF

☐ East Coast	
☒ West Coast	
☒ Northeast	
☐ Mid Atlantic	
☐ Gulf States	
☐ Northwest	
☐ Southeast	
☐ Southwest	
☐ Midwest	
☐ Central	
☐ Local to Office	
☐ Other Geo Pref	

CALSAFE CAPITAL CORP.

245 East Main Street
Suite 107
Alhambra CA 91801

Phone (626) 289-3400   Fax (626) 300-8025

PROFESSIONALS	TITLE
Ming-Min Su	President

INDUSTRY PREFERENCE

- ☐ INFORMATION INDUSTRY
- ☐ Communications
- ☐ Computer Equipment
- ☐ Computer Services
- ☐ Computer Components
- ☐ Computer Entertainment
- ☐ Computer Education
- ☐ Information Technologies
- ☐ Computer Media
- ☐ Software
- ☐ Internet
- ☐ MEDICAL/HEALTHCARE
- ☐ Biotechnology
- ☐ Healthcare Services
- ☐ Life Sciences
- ☐ Medical Products
- ☐ INDUSTRIAL
- ☐ Advanced Materials
- ☐ Chemicals
- ☐ Instruments & Controls

- ☐ BASIC INDUSTRIES
- ☐ Consumer
- ☐ Distribution
- ☐ Manufacturing
- ☐ Retail
- ☐ Service
- ☐ Wholesale
- ☐ SPECIFIC INDUSTRIES
- ☐ Energy
- ☐ Environmental
- ☐ Financial
- ☐ Real Estate
- ☐ Transportation
- ☐ Publishing
- ☐ Food
- ☐ Franchises
- ☒ DIVERSIFIED
- ☐ MISCELLANEOUS

STAGE PREFERENCE

- ☐ EARLY STAGE
- ☐ Seed
- ☐ Start-up
- ☐ 1st Stage
- ☒ LATER STAGE
- ☒ 2nd Stage
- ☒ Mature
- ☐ Mezzanine
- ☐ LBO/MBO
- ☐ Turnaround
- ☐ INT'L EXPANSION
- ☐ WILL CONSIDER ALL
- ☐ VENTURE LEASING

SSBIC
Other Locations:

Affiliation:
Minimum Investment: $1 Million or more
Capital Under Management: Less than $100 Million

GEOGRAPHIC PREF

- ☐ East Coast
- ☐ West Coast
- ☐ Northeast
- ☐ Mid Atlantic
- ☐ Gulf States
- ☐ Northwest
- ☐ Southeast
- ☐ Southwest
- ☐ Midwest
- ☐ Central
- ☐ Local to Office
- ☐ Other Geo Pref

CANAAN PARTNERS

2884 Sand Hill Road
Suite 115
Menlo Park CA 94025

Phone (650) 854-8092   Fax (650) 854-8127

PROFESSIONALS	TITLE
Eric Young	General Partner
Deepak Kamra	General Partner
John Balen	Principal

INDUSTRY PREFERENCE

- ☒ INFORMATION INDUSTRY
- ☒ Communications
- ☒ Computer Equipment
- ☒ Computer Services
- ☒ Computer Components
- ☐ Computer Entertainment
- ☒ Computer Education
- ☒ Information Technologies
- ☒ Computer Media
- ☒ Software
- ☒ Internet
- ☒ MEDICAL/HEALTHCARE
- ☒ Biotechnology
- ☒ Healthcare Services
- ☒ Life Sciences
- ☒ Medical Products
- ☒ INDUSTRIAL
- ☒ Advanced Materials
- ☒ Chemicals
- ☒ Instruments & Controls

- ☒ BASIC INDUSTRIES
- ☒ Consumer
- ☐ Distribution
- ☐ Manufacturing
- ☒ Retail
- ☒ Service
- ☐ Wholesale
- ☒ SPECIFIC INDUSTRIES
- ☐ Energy
- ☒ Environmental
- ☒ Financial
- ☐ Real Estate
- ☐ Transportation
- ☐ Publishing
- ☐ Food
- ☐ Franchises
- ☒ DIVERSIFIED
- ☐ MISCELLANEOUS

STAGE PREFERENCE

- ☒ EARLY STAGE
- ☐ Seed
- ☐ Start-up
- ☒ 1st Stage
- ☒ LATER STAGE
- ☒ 2nd Stage
- ☒ Mature
- ☒ Mezzanine
- ☒ LBO/MBO
- ☒ Turnaround
- ☐ INT'L EXPANSION
- ☐ WILL CONSIDER ALL
- ☒ VENTURE LEASING

SBIC
Other Locations: Rowayton CT

Affiliation:
Minimum Investment: Less than $1 Million
Capital Under Management: Over $500 Million

GEOGRAPHIC PREF

- ☐ East Coast
- ☐ West Coast
- ☐ Northeast
- ☐ Mid Atlantic
- ☐ Gulf States
- ☐ Northwest
- ☐ Southeast
- ☐ Southwest
- ☐ Midwest
- ☐ Central
- ☐ Local to Office
- ☐ Other Geo Pref

CAPSTONE VENTURES

3000 Sand Hill Road
Building One, Suite 290
Menlo Park CA 94025

Phone (650) 854-2523   Fax (650) 854-9010

PROFESSIONALS	TITLE
Eugene Fisher	Managing Member
Barbara Santry	Managing Member
Richard Capen	Venture Manager

INDUSTRY PREFERENCE

- ☒ INFORMATION INDUSTRY
- ☒ Communications
- ☒ Computer Equipment
- ☒ Computer Services
- ☐ Computer Components
- ☐ Computer Entertainment
- ☐ Computer Education
- ☐ Information Technologies
- ☐ Computer Media
- ☒ Software
- ☒ Internet
- ☒ MEDICAL/HEALTHCARE
- ☐ Biotechnology
- ☒ Healthcare Services
- ☐ Life Sciences
- ☒ Medical Products
- ☐ INDUSTRIAL
- ☐ Advanced Materials
- ☐ Chemicals
- ☐ Instruments & Controls

- ☐ BASIC INDUSTRIES
- ☐ Consumer
- ☐ Distribution
- ☐ Manufacturing
- ☐ Retail
- ☐ Service
- ☐ Wholesale
- ☒ SPECIFIC INDUSTRIES
- ☐ Energy
- ☐ Environmental
- ☐ Financial
- ☐ Real Estate
- ☐ Transportation
- ☐ Publishing
- ☐ Food
- ☐ Franchises
- ☒ DIVERSIFIED
- ☒ MISCELLANEOUS
- Outsourcing

STAGE PREFERENCE

- ☒ EARLY STAGE
- ☒ Seed
- ☒ Start-up
- ☒ 1st Stage
- ☐ LATER STAGE
- ☐ 2nd Stage
- ☐ Mature
- ☐ Mezzanine
- ☐ LBO/MBO
- ☐ Turnaround
- ☐ INT'L EXPANSION
- ☐ WILL CONSIDER ALL
- ☐ VENTURE LEASING

SBIC
Other Locations: Minneapolis MN

Affiliation:
Minimum Investment: Less than $1 Million
Capital Under Management: Less than $100 Million

GEOGRAPHIC PREF

- ☐ East Coast
- ☒ West Coast
- ☐ Northeast
- ☐ Mid Atlantic
- ☐ Gulf States
- ☐ Northwest
- ☐ Southeast
- ☒ Southwest
- ☐ Midwest
- ☐ Central
- ☐ Local to Office
- ☐ Other Geo Pref

CATTERTON-SIMON PARTNERS LP

10990 Wilshire Boulevard
Suite 500
Los Angeles CA 90024

Phone (310) 996-8780   Fax (310) 575-3174

PROFESSIONALS	TITLE
Wiliam Simon	General Partner

INDUSTRY PREFERENCE

- ☒ INFORMATION INDUSTRY
- ☐ Communications
- ☐ Computer Equipment
- ☐ Computer Services
- ☐ Computer Components
- ☐ Computer Entertainment
- ☒ Computer Education
- ☐ Information Technologies
- ☐ Computer Media
- ☐ Software
- ☒ Internet
- ☐ MEDICAL/HEALTHCARE
- ☐ Biotechnology
- ☐ Healthcare Services
- ☐ Life Sciences
- ☐ Medical Products
- ☐ INDUSTRIAL
- ☐ Advanced Materials
- ☐ Chemicals
- ☐ Instruments & Controls

- ☒ BASIC INDUSTRIES
- ☒ Consumer
- ☐ Distribution
- ☐ Manufacturing
- ☐ Retail
- ☐ Service
- ☐ Wholesale
- ☐ SPECIFIC INDUSTRIES
- ☐ Energy
- ☐ Environmental
- ☐ Financial
- ☐ Real Estate
- ☐ Transportation
- ☐ Publishing
- ☐ Food
- ☐ Franchises
- ☒ DIVERSIFIED
- ☒ MISCELLANEOUS

STAGE PREFERENCE

- ☐ EARLY STAGE
- ☐ Seed
- ☐ Start-up
- ☐ 1st Stage
- ☒ LATER STAGE
- ☒ 2nd Stage
- ☐ Mature
- ☐ Mezzanine
- ☒ LBO/MBO
- ☐ Turnaround
- ☐ INT'L EXPANSION
- ☐ WILL CONSIDER ALL
- ☐ VENTURE LEASING

Other Locations: Greenwich CT, Charleston WV

Affiliation:
Minimum Investment: $1 Million or more
Capital Under Management: $100 to $500 Million

GEOGRAPHIC PREF

- ☐ East Coast
- ☐ West Coast
- ☐ Northeast
- ☐ Mid Atlantic
- ☐ Gulf States
- ☐ Northwest
- ☐ Southeast
- ☐ Southwest
- ☐ Midwest
- ☐ Central
- ☐ Local to Office
- ☐ Other Geo Pref

CHARTER VENTURE CAPITAL

525 University Avenue
Suite 1400
Palo Alto CA 94301

Phone (650) 325-6953   Fax (650) 325-4762

PROFESSIONALS	TITLE
A. Barr Dolan	Partner
Johnson Cha	Partner
Steven Bird	Parnter
James Boettcher	Partner
Eric Lassila	Partner

INDUSTRY PREFERENCE

☒ INFORMATION INDUSTRY
☒ Communications
☒ Computer Equipment
☒ Computer Services
☒ Computer Components
☐ Computer Entertainment
☒ Computer Education
☒ Information Technologies
☒ Computer Media
☒ Software
☒ Internet
☒ MEDICAL/HEALTHCARE
☒ Biotechnology
☒ Healthcare Services
☒ Life Sciences
☒ Medical Products
☒ INDUSTRIAL
☒ Advanced Materials
☒ Chemicals
☒ Instruments & Controls

☒ BASIC INDUSTRIES
☐ Consumer
☐ Distribution
☐ Manufacturing
☐ Retail
☒ Service
☐ Wholesale
☒ SPECIFIC INDUSTRIES
☒ Energy
☐ Environmental
☐ Financial
☐ Real Estate
☐ Transportation
☐ Publishing
☐ Food
☐ Franchises
☒ DIVERSIFIED
☐ MISCELLANEOUS

STAGE PREFERENCE

☒ EARLY STAGE
☒ Seed
☒ Start-up
☒ 1st Stage
☒ LATER STAGE
☒ 2nd Stage
☒ Mature
☒ Mezzanine
☒ LBO/MBO
☐ Turnaround
☐ INT'L EXPANSION
☐ WILL CONSIDER ALL
☐ VENTURE LEASING

Other Locations:

Affiliation:
Minimum Investment: Less than $1 Million
Capital Under Management: $100 to $500 Million

GEOGRAPHIC PREF

☐ East Coast
☐ West Coast
☐ Northeast
☐ Mid Atlantic
☐ Gulf States
☐ Northwest
☐ Southeast
☐ Southwest
☐ Midwest
☐ Central
☐ Local to Office
☐ Other Geo Pref

CHASE CAPITAL PARTNERS

50 California Street
Suite 2940
San Francisco CA 94111

Phone (415) 591-1200   Fax (415) 591-1205

PROFESSIONALS	TITLE
Shahan D. Soghikian	General Partner

INDUSTRY PREFERENCE

☒ INFORMATION INDUSTRY
☒ Communications
☒ Computer Equipment
☒ Computer Services
☒ Computer Components
☐ Computer Entertainment
☒ Computer Education
☒ Information Technologies
☒ Computer Media
☒ Software
☒ Internet
☒ MEDICAL/HEALTHCARE
☒ Biotechnology
☒ Healthcare Services
☒ Life Sciences
☒ Medical Products
☒ INDUSTRIAL
☐ Advanced Materials
☒ Chemicals
☐ Instruments & Controls

☒ BASIC INDUSTRIES
☐ Consumer
☐ Distribution
☐ Manufacturing
☒ Retail
☐ Service
☐ Wholesale
☒ SPECIFIC INDUSTRIES
☒ Energy
☐ Environmental
☐ Financial
☒ Real Estate
☐ Transportation
☐ Publishing
☐ Food
☐ Franchises
☒ DIVERSIFIED
☒ MISCELLANEOUS

STAGE PREFERENCE

☒ EARLY STAGE
☐ Seed
☒ Start-up
☒ 1st Stage
☒ LATER STAGE
☒ 2nd Stage
☒ Mature
☒ Mezzanine
☒ LBO/MBO
☒ Turnaround
☒ INT'L EXPANSION
☐ WILL CONSIDER ALL
☒ VENTURE LEASING

SBIC
Other Locations: New York NY, Vail CO

Affiliation:
Minimum Investment: $1 Million or more
Capital Under Management: Over $500 Million

GEOGRAPHIC PREF

☐ East Coast
☐ West Coast
☐ Northeast
☐ Mid Atlantic
☐ Gulf States
☐ Northwest
☐ Southeast
☐ Southwest
☐ Midwest
☐ Central
☐ Local to Office
☐ Other Geo Pref

CMEA VENTURES

235 Montgomery Street
Suite 920
San Francisco CA 94104

Phone (415) 352-1520   Fax (415) 352-1524

PROFESSIONALS	TITLE
Tom Baruch	General Partner
Gordon Hull	General Partner

INDUSTRY PREFERENCE

☒ INFORMATION INDUSTRY	☐ BASIC INDUSTRIES
☒ Communications	☐ Consumer
☐ Computer Equipment	☐ Distribution
☐ Computer Services	☐ Manufacturing
☒ Computer Components	☐ Retail
☐ Computer Entertainment	☐ Service
☐ Computer Education	☐ Wholesale
☒ Information Technologies	☐ SPECIFIC INDUSTRIES
☐ Computer Media	☐ Energy
☒ Software	☐ Environmental
☒ Internet	☐ Financial
☒ MEDICAL/HEALTHCARE	☐ Real Estate
☒ Biotechnology	☐ Transportation
☒ Healthcare Services	☐ Publishing
☒ Life Sciences	☐ Food
☒ Medical Products	☐ Franchises
☒ INDUSTRIAL	☒ DIVERSIFIED
☒ Advanced Materials	☒ MISCELLANEOUS
☒ Chemicals	
☐ Instruments & Controls	

STAGE PREFERENCE

☒ EARLY STAGE
☒ Seed
☒ Start-up
☒ 1st Stage
☒ LATER STAGE
☒ 2nd Stage
☐ Mature
☐ Mezzanine
☐ LBO/MBO
☐ Turnaround
☐ INT'L EXPANSION
☐ WILL CONSIDER ALL
☐ VENTURE LEASING

Other Locations:

Affiliation:
Minimum Investment: Less than $1 Million
Capital Under Management: $100 to $500 Million

GEOGRAPHIC PREF

☐ East Coast
☐ West Coast
☐ Northeast
☐ Mid Atlantic
☐ Gulf States
☐ Northwest
☐ Southeast
☐ Southwest
☐ Midwest
☐ Central
☐ Local to Office
☐ Other Geo Pref

COMDISCO VENTURES

3000 Sand Hill Road
Building One, Suite 155
Menlo Park CA 94025

Phone (650) 854-9484   Fax (650) 854-4026

PROFESSIONALS	TITLE
Manuel Heariguez	Managing Director

INDUSTRY PREFERENCE

☒ INFORMATION INDUSTRY	☒ BASIC INDUSTRIES
☒ Communications	☒ Consumer
☒ Computer Equipment	☐ Distribution
☒ Computer Services	☐ Manufacturing
☒ Computer Components	☐ Retail
☐ Computer Entertainment	☒ Service
☒ Computer Education	☐ Wholesale
☒ Information Technologies	☐ SPECIFIC INDUSTRIES
☒ Computer Media	☐ Energy
☒ Software	☐ Environmental
☒ Internet	☐ Financial
☒ MEDICAL/HEALTHCARE	☐ Real Estate
☒ Biotechnology	☐ Transportation
☒ Healthcare Services	☐ Publishing
☒ Life Sciences	☐ Food
☒ Medical Products	☐ Franchises
☒ INDUSTRIAL	☒ DIVERSIFIED
☒ Advanced Materials	☐ MISCELLANEOUS
☒ Chemicals	
☒ Instruments & Controls	

STAGE PREFERENCE

☒ EARLY STAGE
☒ Seed
☒ Start-up
☒ 1st Stage
☒ LATER STAGE
☒ 2nd Stage
☒ Mature
☒ Mezzanine
☐ LBO/MBO
☐ Turnaround
☐ INT'L EXPANSION
☐ WILL CONSIDER ALL
☐ VENTURE LEASING

Other Locations: Rosemont IL, Waltham MA

Affiliation:
Minimum Investment: Less than $1 Million
Capital Under Management: Over $500 Million

GEOGRAPHIC PREF

☐ East Coast
☐ West Coast
☐ Northeast
☐ Mid Atlantic
☐ Gulf States
☐ Northwest
☐ Southeast
☐ Southwest
☐ Midwest
☐ Central
☐ Local to Office
☐ Other Geo Pref

COMPASS TECHNOLOGY GROUP, INC.

1550 El Camino Real
Suite 275
Menlo Park CA 94025-4111

Phone (650) 322-7595   Fax (650) 322-0588

PROFESSIONALS	TITLE
David G. Arscott	General Partner
Alain S. Harrus	General Partner
Martha P. E. Arscott	General Partner

INDUSTRY PREFERENCE

☒ INFORMATION INDUSTRY	☒ BASIC INDUSTRIES
☒ Communications	☐ Consumer
☒ Computer Equipment	☒ Distribution
☒ Computer Services	☒ Manufacturing
☒ Computer Components	☐ Retail
☐ Computer Entertainment	☐ Service
☐ Computer Education	☐ Wholesale
☒ Information Technologies	☐ SPECIFIC INDUSTRIES
☐ Computer Media	☐ Energy
☐ Software	☐ Environmental
☒ Internet	☐ Financial
☒ MEDICAL/HEALTHCARE	☐ Real Estate
☒ Biotechnology	☐ Transportation
☐ Healthcare Services	☐ Publishing
☐ Life Sciences	☐ Food
☒ Medical Products	☐ Franchises
☒ INDUSTRIAL	☒ DIVERSIFIED
☐ Advanced Materials	☒ MISCELLANEOUS
☐ Chemicals	
☒ Instruments & Controls	

STAGE PREFERENCE

- ☒ EARLY STAGE
- ☐ Seed
- ☒ Start-up
- ☒ 1st Stage
- ☒ LATER STAGE
- ☒ 2nd Stage
- ☐ Mature
- ☒ Mezzanine
- ☒ LBO/MBO
- ☐ Turnaround
- ☐ INT'L EXPANSION
- ☐ WILL CONSIDER ALL
- ☐ VENTURE LEASING

Other Locations:

Affiliation:
Minimum Investment: Less than $1 Million
Capital Under Management: Less than $100 Million

GEOGRAPHIC PREF

- ☐ East Coast
- ☒ West Coast
- ☐ Northeast
- ☐ Mid Atlantic
- ☐ Gulf States
- ☐ Northwest
- ☐ Southeast
- ☐ Southwest
- ☐ Midwest
- ☐ Central
- ☐ Local to Office
- ☐ Other Geo Pref

COMVENTURES

505 Hamilton
Suite 305
Palo Alto CA 94301

Phone (650) 325-9600   Fax (650) 325-9608

PROFESSIONALS	TITLE
Roland A. Van der Meer	Partner
Clifford Higgerson	Partner
David Helfrich	Partner

INDUSTRY PREFERENCE

☒ INFORMATION INDUSTRY	☐ BASIC INDUSTRIES
☒ Communications	☐ Consumer
☒ Computer Equipment	☐ Distribution
☒ Computer Services	☐ Manufacturing
☐ Computer Components	☐ Retail
☐ Computer Entertainment	☐ Service
☐ Computer Education	☐ Wholesale
☒ Information Technologies	☐ SPECIFIC INDUSTRIES
☐ Computer Media	☐ Energy
☐ Software	☐ Environmental
☒ Internet	☐ Financial
☐ MEDICAL/HEALTHCARE	☐ Real Estate
☐ Biotechnology	☐ Transportation
☐ Healthcare Services	☐ Publishing
☐ Life Sciences	☐ Food
☐ Medical Products	☐ Franchises
☐ INDUSTRIAL	☐ DIVERSIFIED
☐ Advanced Materials	☐ MISCELLANEOUS
☐ Chemicals	
☐ Instruments & Controls	

STAGE PREFERENCE

- ☒ EARLY STAGE
- ☒ Seed
- ☒ Start-up
- ☒ 1st Stage
- ☐ LATER STAGE
- ☐ 2nd Stage
- ☐ Mature
- ☐ Mezzanine
- ☐ LBO/MBO
- ☐ Turnaround
- ☐ INT'L EXPANSION
- ☐ WILL CONSIDER ALL
- ☐ VENTURE LEASING

Other Locations:

Affiliation:
Minimum Investment: Less than $1 Million
Capital Under Management: $100 to $500 Million

GEOGRAPHIC PREF

- ☐ East Coast
- ☐ West Coast
- ☐ Northeast
- ☐ Mid Atlantic
- ☐ Gulf States
- ☐ Northwest
- ☐ Southeast
- ☐ Southwest
- ☐ Midwest
- ☐ Central
- ☐ Local to Office
- ☐ Other Geo Pref

CORAL VENTURES

**3000 Sand Hill Road
Building 3, Suite 220
Menlo Park CA 94025**

Phone (650) 854-5227   Fax (650) 854-4625

PROFESSIONALS	TITLE
Karen Boezi	Venture Partner
Yuval Alomg	Managing Partner

INDUSTRY PREFERENCE

☒ INFORMATION INDUSTRY	☒ BASIC INDUSTRIES
☒ Communications	☐ Consumer
☒ Computer Equipment	☐ Distribution
☒ Computer Services	☐ Manufacturing
☒ Computer Components	☐ Retail
☐ Computer Entertainment	☒ Service
☒ Computer Education	☐ Wholesale
☒ Information Technologies	☒ SPECIFIC INDUSTRIES
☒ Computer Media	☐ Energy
☒ Software	☐ Environmental
☒ Internet	☐ Financial
☒ MEDICAL/HEALTHCARE	☐ Real Estate
☒ Biotechnology	☐ Transportation
☒ Healthcare Services	☐ Publishing
☒ Life Sciences	☐ Food
☒ Medical Products	☐ Franchises
☐ INDUSTRIAL	☒ DIVERSIFIED
☐ Advanced Materials	☐ MISCELLANEOUS
☐ Chemicals	
☐ Instruments & Controls	

STAGE PREFERENCE

☒ EARLY STAGE
☒ Seed
☒ Start-up
☒ 1st Stage
☒ LATER STAGE
☒ 2nd Stage
☒ Mature
☒ Mezzanine
☒ LBO/MBO
☐ Turnaround
☐ INT'L EXPANSION
☐ WILL CONSIDER ALL
☐ VENTURE LEASING

Other Locations:

Affiliation:
Minimum Investment: Less than $1 Million
Capital Under Management: $100 to $500 Million

GEOGRAPHIC PREF

☐ East Coast
☐ West Coast
☐ Northeast
☐ Mid Atlantic
☐ Gulf States
☐ Northwest
☐ Southeast
☐ Southwest
☐ Midwest
☐ Central
☐ Local to Office
☐ Other Geo Pref

CRESCENDO VENTURES

**480 Cowper Street
Suite 300
Palo Alto CA 94301**

Phone (650) 470-1200   Fax (650) 470-1201

PROFESSIONALS	TITLE
R. David Spreng	Managing General Partner
Jeffrey R. Tollefson	General Partner
Anthony S. Daffer	General Partner
Lorraine Fox	General Partner
Roeland E. Boonstoppel	General Partner

INDUSTRY PREFERENCE

☒ INFORMATION INDUSTRY	☐ BASIC INDUSTRIES
☒ Communications	☐ Consumer
☒ Computer Equipment	☐ Distribution
☒ Computer Services	☐ Manufacturing
☒ Computer Components	☐ Retail
☐ Computer Entertainment	☐ Service
☒ Computer Education	☐ Wholesale
☒ Information Technologies	☐ SPECIFIC INDUSTRIES
☒ Computer Media	☐ Energy
☒ Software	☐ Environmental
☒ Internet	☐ Financial
☒ MEDICAL/HEALTHCARE	☐ Real Estate
☒ Biotechnology	☐ Transportation
☒ Healthcare Services	☐ Publishing
☒ Life Sciences	☐ Food
☒ Medical Products	☐ Franchises
☐ INDUSTRIAL	☒ DIVERSIFIED
☐ Advanced Materials	☒ MISCELLANEOUS
☐ Chemicals	
☐ Instruments & Controls	

STAGE PREFERENCE

☒ EARLY STAGE
☒ Seed
☒ Start-up
☒ 1st Stage
☒ LATER STAGE
☒ 2nd Stage
☐ Mature
☐ Mezzanine
☒ LBO/MBO
☐ Turnaround
☐ INT'L EXPANSION
☐ WILL CONSIDER ALL
☐ VENTURE LEASING

Other Locations:

Affiliation:
Minimum Investment: Less than $1 Million
Capital Under Management: $100 to $500 Million

GEOGRAPHIC PREF

☐ East Coast
☐ West Coast
☐ Northeast
☐ Mid Atlantic
☐ Gulf States
☐ Northwest
☐ Southeast
☐ Southwest
☐ Midwest
☐ Central
☐ Local to Office
☐ Other Geo Pref

CROCKER CAPITAL

1 Post Street
Room 2500
San Francisco CA 94104

Phone (415) 956-5250   Fax (415) 956-5710

PROFESSIONALS	TITLE
Charles Crocker	General Partner
William R. Dawson	Partner

INDUSTRY PREFERENCE

☒ INFORMATION INDUSTRY	☒ BASIC INDUSTRIES
☒ Communications	☒ Consumer
☒ Computer Equipment	☒ Distribution
☒ Computer Services	☐ Manufacturing
☒ Computer Components	☐ Retail
☐ Computer Entertainment	☐ Service
☒ Computer Education	☐ Wholesale
☒ Information Technologies	☒ SPECIFIC INDUSTRIES
☐ Computer Media	☐ Energy
☒ Software	☐ Environmental
☒ Internet	☐ Financial
☒ MEDICAL/HEALTHCARE	☐ Real Estate
☒ Biotechnology	☐ Transportation
☒ Healthcare Services	☐ Publishing
☒ Life Sciences	☐ Food
☒ Medical Products	☐ Franchises
☐ INDUSTRIAL	☒ DIVERSIFIED
☐ Advanced Materials	☐ MISCELLANEOUS
☐ Chemicals	
☐ Instruments & Controls	

STAGE PREFERENCE

☒ EARLY STAGE
☒ Seed
☒ Start-up
☒ 1st Stage
☒ LATER STAGE
☒ 2nd Stage
☒ Mature
☒ Mezzanine
☒ LBO/MBO
☐ Turnaround
☐ INT'L EXPANSION
☐ WILL CONSIDER ALL
☐ VENTURE LEASING

Other Locations:

Affiliation:
Minimum Investment: Less than $1 Million
Capital Under Management: Less than $100 Million

GEOGRAPHIC PREF

☐ East Coast
☒ West Coast
☐ Northeast
☐ Mid Atlantic
☐ Gulf States
☐ Northwest
☐ Southeast
☐ Southwest
☐ Midwest
☐ Central
☐ Local to Office
☐ Other Geo Pref

CROSSPOINT VENTURE PARTNERS

18552 MacArthur Boulevard
Suite 400
Irvine CA 92612

Phone (949) 852-1611   Fax (949) 852-9804

PROFESSIONALS	TITLE
Jim Dorrian	General Partner
Bob Lisbonne	General Partner
Donald B. Milder	General Partner Emeritus
Robert A. Hoff	General Partner
Barbara Lubash	Venture Partner

INDUSTRY PREFERENCE

☒ INFORMATION INDUSTRY	☒ BASIC INDUSTRIES
☒ Communications	☐ Consumer
☐ Computer Equipment	☒ Distribution
☐ Computer Services	☐ Manufacturing
☒ Computer Components	☐ Retail
☐ Computer Entertainment	☒ Service
☒ Computer Education	☐ Wholesale
☒ Information Technologies	☒ SPECIFIC INDUSTRIES
☒ Computer Media	☐ Energy
☒ Software	☐ Environmental
☒ Internet	☒ Financial
☒ MEDICAL/HEALTHCARE	☐ Real Estate
☒ Biotechnology	☐ Transportation
☒ Healthcare Services	☐ Publishing
☒ Life Sciences	☐ Food
☒ Medical Products	☐ Franchises
☒ INDUSTRIAL	☒ DIVERSIFIED
☐ Advanced Materials	☐ MISCELLANEOUS
☐ Chemicals	
☒ Instruments & Controls	

STAGE PREFERENCE

☒ EARLY STAGE
☒ Seed
☒ Start-up
☐ 1st Stage
☐ LATER STAGE
☐ 2nd Stage
☐ Mature
☐ Mezzanine
☐ LBO/MBO
☐ Turnaround
☐ INT'L EXPANSION
☐ WILL CONSIDER ALL
☐ VENTURE LEASING

Other Locations: Woodside CA

Affiliation: Crosspoint Corp.
Minimum Investment: Less than $1 Million
Capital Under Management: $100 to $500 Million

GEOGRAPHIC PREF

☐ East Coast
☒ West Coast
☐ Northeast
☐ Mid Atlantic
☐ Gulf States
☐ Northwest
☐ Southeast
☐ Southwest
☐ Midwest
☐ Central
☐ Local to Office
☐ Other Geo Pref

CROSSPOINT VENTURE PARTNERS

**The Pioneer Buliding
2925 Woodside Road
Woodside CA 94062**

Phone (650) 851-7600   Fax (650) 851-7661

PROFESSIONALS	TITLE
Rich Shapero	General Partner
John B. Mumford	General Partner
Seth Nieman	General Partner

INDUSTRY PREFERENCE

- ☒ INFORMATION INDUSTRY
- ☒ Communications
- ☒ Computer Equipment
- ☒ Computer Services
- ☒ Computer Components
- ☐ Computer Entertainment
- ☒ Computer Education
- ☒ Information Technologies
- ☒ Computer Media
- ☒ Software
- ☒ Internet
- ☒ MEDICAL/HEALTHCARE
- ☒ Biotechnology
- ☒ Healthcare Services
- ☒ Life Sciences
- ☒ Medical Products
- ☒ INDUSTRIAL
- ☐ Advanced Materials
- ☐ Chemicals
- ☒ Instruments & Controls

- ☒ BASIC INDUSTRIES
- ☐ Consumer
- ☒ Distribution
- ☐ Manufacturing
- ☐ Retail
- ☒ Service
- ☐ Wholesale
- ☒ SPECIFIC INDUSTRIES
- ☒ Energy
- ☒ Environmental
- ☒ Financial
- ☐ Real Estate
- ☐ Transportation
- ☐ Publishing
- ☐ Food
- ☐ Franchises
- ☒ DIVERSIFIED
- ☐ MISCELLANEOUS

STAGE PREFERENCE

- ☒ EARLY STAGE
- ☒ Seed
- ☒ Start-up
- ☐ 1st Stage
- ☐ LATER STAGE
- ☐ 2nd Stage
- ☐ Mature
- ☐ Mezzanine
- ☐ LBO/MBO
- ☐ Turnaround
- ☐ INT'L EXPANSION
- ☐ WILL CONSIDER ALL
- ☐ VENTURE LEASING

Other Locations: Irvine CA

Affiliation: Crosspoint Corp.
Minimum Investment: Less than $1 Million
Capital Under Management: $100 to $500 Million

GEOGRAPHIC PREF

- ☐ East Coast
- ☒ West Coast
- ☐ Northeast
- ☐ Mid Atlantic
- ☐ Gulf States
- ☐ Northwest
- ☐ Southeast
- ☐ Southwest
- ☐ Midwest
- ☐ Central
- ☐ Local to Office
- ☐ Other Geo Pref

CW GROUP, INC.

**2187 Newcastle Avenue
Suite 101
San Diego CA 92007**

Phone (760) 942-4535   Fax (760) 942-4530

PROFESSIONALS	TITLE
Lawrence A. Bock	General Partner

INDUSTRY PREFERENCE

- ☐ INFORMATION INDUSTRY
- ☐ Communications
- ☐ Computer Equipment
- ☐ Computer Services
- ☐ Computer Components
- ☐ Computer Entertainment
- ☐ Computer Education
- ☐ Information Technologies
- ☐ Computer Media
- ☐ Software
- ☐ Internet
- ☒ MEDICAL/HEALTHCARE
- ☒ Biotechnology
- ☒ Healthcare Services
- ☒ Life Sciences
- ☒ Medical Products
- ☐ INDUSTRIAL
- ☐ Advanced Materials
- ☐ Chemicals
- ☐ Instruments & Controls

- ☐ BASIC INDUSTRIES
- ☐ Consumer
- ☐ Distribution
- ☐ Manufacturing
- ☐ Retail
- ☐ Service
- ☐ Wholesale
- ☐ SPECIFIC INDUSTRIES
- ☐ Energy
- ☐ Environmental
- ☐ Financial
- ☐ Real Estate
- ☐ Transportation
- ☐ Publishing
- ☐ Food
- ☐ Franchises
- ☐ DIVERSIFIED
- ☒ MISCELLANEOUS

STAGE PREFERENCE

- ☒ EARLY STAGE
- ☒ Seed
- ☒ Start-up
- ☒ 1st Stage
- ☒ LATER STAGE
- ☒ 2nd Stage
- ☐ Mature
- ☐ Mezzanine
- ☐ LBO/MBO
- ☐ Turnaround
- ☐ INT'L EXPANSION
- ☐ WILL CONSIDER ALL
- ☐ VENTURE LEASING

Other Locations: New York NY

Affiliation:
Minimum Investment: Less than $1 Million
Capital Under Management: $100 to $500 Million

GEOGRAPHIC PREF

- ☐ East Coast
- ☐ West Coast
- ☐ Northeast
- ☐ Mid Atlantic
- ☐ Gulf States
- ☐ Northwest
- ☐ Southeast
- ☐ Southwest
- ☐ Midwest
- ☐ Central
- ☐ Local to Office
- ☐ Other Geo Pref

DELPHI VENTURES

**3000 Sand Hill Road
Building One, Suite 135
Menlo Park CA 94025**

Phone (650) 854-9650   Fax (650) 854-2961

PROFESSIONALS	TITLE
James J. Bochnowski	General Partner
David L. Douglass	General Partner
Donald J. Lothrop	General Partner

INDUSTRY PREFERENCE

☒ INFORMATION INDUSTRY	☒ BASIC INDUSTRIES
☐ Communications	☐ Consumer
☐ Computer Equipment	☐ Distribution
☐ Computer Services	☐ Manufacturing
☐ Computer Components	☐ Retail
☐ Computer Entertainment	☒ Service
☐ Computer Education	☐ Wholesale
☐ Information Technologies	☒ SPECIFIC INDUSTRIES
☐ Computer Media	☐ Energy
☒ Software	☐ Environmental
☒ Internet	☐ Financial
☒ MEDICAL/HEALTHCARE	☐ Real Estate
☒ Biotechnology	☐ Transportation
☒ Healthcare Services	☐ Publishing
☒ Life Sciences	☐ Food
☒ Medical Products	☐ Franchises
☐ INDUSTRIAL	☒ DIVERSIFIED
☐ Advanced Materials	☐ MISCELLANEOUS
☐ Chemicals	All Medical Related
☐ Instruments & Controls	

STAGE PREFERENCE

☒ EARLY STAGE
☒ Seed
☒ Start-up
☒ 1st Stage
☒ LATER STAGE
☒ 2nd Stage
☒ Mature
☒ Mezzanine
☒ LBO/MBO
☐ Turnaround
☐ INT'L EXPANSION
☐ WILL CONSIDER ALL
☐ VENTURE LEASING

Other Locations:

Affiliation:
Minimum Investment: Less than $1 Million
Capital Under Management: $100 to $500 Million

GEOGRAPHIC PREF

☐ East Coast
☒ West Coast
☐ Northeast
☐ Mid Atlantic
☐ Gulf States
☐ Northwest
☐ Southeast
☐ Southwest
☐ Midwest
☐ Central
☐ Local to Office
☐ Other Geo Pref

DOMAIN ASSOCIATES

**28202 Cabot Road
Suite 200
Laguna Niguel CA 92677**

Phone (949) 347-2446   Fax (949) 347-9720

PROFESSIONALS	TITLE
Richard S. Schneider	General Partner
Arthur Klausner	General Partner

INDUSTRY PREFERENCE

☐ INFORMATION INDUSTRY	☒ BASIC INDUSTRIES
☐ Communications	☐ Consumer
☐ Computer Equipment	☐ Distribution
☐ Computer Services	☐ Manufacturing
☐ Computer Components	☐ Retail
☐ Computer Entertainment	☒ Service
☐ Computer Education	☐ Wholesale
☐ Information Technologies	☐ SPECIFIC INDUSTRIES
☐ Computer Media	☐ Energy
☐ Software	☐ Environmental
☐ Internet	☐ Financial
☒ MEDICAL/HEALTHCARE	☐ Real Estate
☒ Biotechnology	☐ Transportation
☒ Healthcare Services	☐ Publishing
☒ Life Sciences	☐ Food
☒ Medical Products	☐ Franchises
☒ INDUSTRIAL	☒ DIVERSIFIED
☒ Advanced Materials	☐ MISCELLANEOUS
☐ Chemicals	
☒ Instruments & Controls	

STAGE PREFERENCE

☒ EARLY STAGE
☒ Seed
☒ Start-up
☒ 1st Stage
☒ LATER STAGE
☒ 2nd Stage
☐ Mature
☐ Mezzanine
☐ LBO/MBO
☐ Turnaround
☐ INT'L EXPANSION
☐ WILL CONSIDER ALL
☐ VENTURE LEASING

Other Locations: Princeton NJ

Affiliation:
Minimum Investment: Less than $1 Million
Capital Under Management: $100 to $500 Million

GEOGRAPHIC PREF

☐ East Coast
☐ West Coast
☐ Northeast
☐ Mid Atlantic
☐ Gulf States
☐ Northwest
☐ Southeast
☐ Southwest
☐ Midwest
☐ Central
☐ Local to Office
☐ Other Geo Pref

DOMINION VENTURES, INC.

44 Montgomery Street
Suite 4200
San Francisco CA 94104-4602

Phone (415) 362-4890   Fax (415) 394-9245

PROFESSIONALS	TITLE
Geoffrey Woolley	Managing General Partner

INDUSTRY PREFERENCE

☒ INFORMATION INDUSTRY	☐ BASIC INDUSTRIES		
☒ Communications	☐ Consumer		
☒ Computer Equipment	☐ Distribution		
☒ Computer Services	☐ Manufacturing		
☒ Computer Components	☐ Retail		
☐ Computer Entertainment	☐ Service		
☒ Computer Education	☐ Wholesale		
☒ Information Technologies	☐ SPECIFIC INDUSTRIES		
☒ Computer Media	☐ Energy		
☒ Software	☐ Environmental		
☒ Internet	☐ Financial		
☐ MEDICAL/HEALTHCARE	☐ Real Estate		
☐ Biotechnology	☐ Transportation		
☐ Healthcare Services	☐ Publishing		
☐ Life Sciences	☐ Food		
☐ Medical Products	☐ Franchises		
☒ INDUSTRIAL	☒ DIVERSIFIED		
☒ Advanced Materials	☐ MISCELLANEOUS		
☒ Chemicals			
☒ Instruments & Controls			

STAGE PREFERENCE

☒ EARLY STAGE
☐ Seed
☐ Start-up
☒ 1st Stage
☒ LATER STAGE
☒ 2nd Stage
☒ Mature
☒ Mezzanine
☒ LBO/MBO
☐ Turnaround
☐ INT'L EXPANSION
☐ WILL CONSIDER ALL
☐ VENTURE LEASING

Other Locations: Boston MA, Menlo Park CA

Affiliation:
Minimum Investment: $1 Million or more
Capital Under Management: $100 to $500 Million

GEOGRAPHIC PREF

☐ East Coast
☐ West Coast
☐ Northeast
☐ Mid Atlantic
☐ Gulf States
☐ Northwest
☐ Southeast
☐ Southwest
☐ Midwest
☐ Central
☐ Local to Office
☐ Other Geo Pref

DOMINION VENTURES, INC.

3000 Sand Hill Road
Building 2, Suite 235
Menlo Park CA 94025

Phone (650) 854-5932   Fax (650) 854-1957

PROFESSIONALS	TITLE
Renee Baker	Managing Director
Brian Smith	General Partner

INDUSTRY PREFERENCE

☒ INFORMATION INDUSTRY	☒ BASIC INDUSTRIES		
☒ Communications	☒ Consumer		
☒ Computer Equipment	☐ Distribution		
☒ Computer Services	☒ Manufacturing		
☒ Computer Components	☒ Retail		
☐ Computer Entertainment	☐ Service		
☒ Computer Education	☐ Wholesale		
☒ Information Technologies	☒ SPECIFIC INDUSTRIES		
☒ Computer Media	☐ Energy		
☒ Software	☐ Environmental		
☒ Internet	☒ Financial		
☐ MEDICAL/HEALTHCARE	☐ Real Estate		
☐ Biotechnology	☐ Transportation		
☐ Healthcare Services	☐ Publishing		
☐ Life Sciences	☐ Food		
☐ Medical Products	☐ Franchises		
☒ INDUSTRIAL	☒ DIVERSIFIED		
☒ Advanced Materials	☒ MISCELLANEOUS		
☒ Chemicals			
☒ Instruments & Controls			

STAGE PREFERENCE

☒ EARLY STAGE
☐ Seed
☐ Start-up
☒ 1st Stage
☒ LATER STAGE
☒ 2nd Stage
☒ Mature
☒ Mezzanine
☒ LBO/MBO
☐ Turnaround
☐ INT'L EXPANSION
☐ WILL CONSIDER ALL
☐ VENTURE LEASING

Other Locations: San Francisco CA , Boston MA

Affiliation:
Minimum Investment: $1 Million or more
Capital Under Management: $100 to $500 Million

GEOGRAPHIC PREF

☐ East Coast
☐ West Coast
☐ Northeast
☐ Mid Atlantic
☐ Gulf States
☐ Northwest
☐ Southeast
☐ Southwest
☐ Midwest
☐ Central
☐ Local to Office
☐ Other Geo Pref

DRAPER, FISHER, JURVETSON

400 Seaport Court
Suite 250
Redwood City CA 94063

Phone (650) 599-9000   Fax (650) 599-9726

PROFESSIONALS

Timothy Draper
John Fisher
Steven Jurvetson

TITLE

Managing Director
Managing Director
Managing Director

INDUSTRY PREFERENCE

☒ INFORMATION INDUSTRY	☒ BASIC INDUSTRIES
☒ Communications	☐ Consumer
☒ Computer Equipment	☐ Distribution
☒ Computer Services	☐ Manufacturing
☒ Computer Components	☐ Retail
☐ Computer Entertainment	☒ Service
☒ Computer Education	☐ Wholesale
☒ Information Technologies	☐ SPECIFIC INDUSTRIES
☒ Computer Media	☐ Energy
☒ Software	☐ Environmental
☒ Internet	☐ Financial
☐ MEDICAL/HEALTHCARE	☐ Real Estate
☐ Biotechnology	☐ Transportation
☐ Healthcare Services	☐ Publishing
☐ Life Sciences	☐ Food
☐ Medical Products	☐ Franchises
☐ INDUSTRIAL	☒ DIVERSIFIED
☐ Advanced Materials	☐ MISCELLANEOUS
☐ Chemicals	
☐ Instruments & Controls	

STAGE PREFERENCE

☒ EARLY STAGE
☒ Seed
☒ Start-up
☒ 1st Stage
☐ LATER STAGE
☐ 2nd Stage
☐ Mature
☐ Mezzanine
☐ LBO/MBO
☐ Turnaround
☐ INT'L EXPANSION
☐ WILL CONSIDER ALL
☐ VENTURE LEASING
SBIC
Other Locations:

Affiliation:
Minimum Investment: Less than $1 Million
Capital Under Management: $100 to $500 Million

GEOGRAPHIC PREF

☐ East Coast
☐ West Coast
☐ Northeast
☐ Mid Atlantic
☐ Gulf States
☐ Northwest
☐ Southeast
☐ Southwest
☐ Midwest
☐ Central
☐ Local to Office
☐ Other Geo Pref

DSV PARTNERS

1920 Main Street
Suite 820
Irvine CA 92614

Phone (949) 475-4242   Fax (949) 475-1950

PROFESSIONALS

James Bergman

TITLE

Partner

INDUSTRY PREFERENCE

☒ INFORMATION INDUSTRY	☒ BASIC INDUSTRIES
☒ Communications	☐ Consumer
☒ Computer Equipment	☐ Distribution
☒ Computer Services	☐ Manufacturing
☒ Computer Components	☐ Retail
☐ Computer Entertainment	☒ Service
☒ Computer Education	☐ Wholesale
☒ Information Technologies	☒ SPECIFIC INDUSTRIES
☒ Computer Media	☒ Energy
☒ Software	☐ Environmental
☒ Internet	☐ Financial
☒ MEDICAL/HEALTHCARE	☐ Real Estate
☒ Biotechnology	☐ Transportation
☒ Healthcare Services	☐ Publishing
☒ Life Sciences	☐ Food
☒ Medical Products	☐ Franchises
☒ INDUSTRIAL	☒ DIVERSIFIED
☒ Advanced Materials	☐ MISCELLANEOUS
☒ Chemicals	
☒ Instruments & Controls	

STAGE PREFERENCE

☒ EARLY STAGE
☒ Seed
☒ Start-up
☒ 1st Stage
☐ LATER STAGE
☐ 2nd Stage
☐ Mature
☐ Mezzanine
☐ LBO/MBO
☐ Turnaround
☐ INT'L EXPANSION
☐ WILL CONSIDER ALL
☐ VENTURE LEASING

Other Locations: Princeton NJ

Affiliation:
Minimum Investment: Less than $1 Million
Capital Under Management: $100 to $500 Million

GEOGRAPHIC PREF

☐ East Coast
☒ West Coast
☐ Northeast
☐ Mid Atlantic
☐ Gulf States
☐ Northwest
☐ Southeast
☐ Southwest
☐ Midwest
☐ Central
☐ Local to Office
☐ Other Geo Pref

EL DORADO VENTURES

2400 Sand Hill Road
Suite 100
Menlo Park CA 94025

Phone (650) 854-1200   Fax (650) 854-1202

PROFESSIONALS	TITLE
Ms. Shanda Bahles	General Partner
Gary W. Kalbach	General Partner
Tom Peterson	General Partner

INDUSTRY PREFERENCE

☒	INFORMATION INDUSTRY	☐	BASIC INDUSTRIES
☒	Communications	☐	Consumer
☒	Computer Equipment	☐	Distribution
☒	Computer Services	☐	Manufacturing
☐	Computer Components	☐	Retail
☐	Computer Entertainment	☐	Service
☐	Computer Education	☐	Wholesale
☒	Information Technologies	☐	SPECIFIC INDUSTRIES
☒	Computer Media	☐	Energy
☒	Software	☐	Environmental
☒	Internet	☐	Financial
☐	MEDICAL/HEALTHCARE	☐	Real Estate
☐	Biotechnology	☐	Transportation
☐	Healthcare Services	☐	Publishing
☐	Life Sciences	☐	Food
☐	Medical Products	☐	Franchises
☐	INDUSTRIAL	☒	DIVERSIFIED
☐	Advanced Materials	☐	MISCELLANEOUS
☐	Chemicals		
☐	Instruments & Controls		

STAGE PREFERENCE

☒	EARLY STAGE
☒	Seed
☒	Start-up
☐	1st Stage
☐	LATER STAGE
☐	2nd Stage
☐	Mature
☐	Mezzanine
☐	LBO/MBO
☐	Turnaround
☐	INT'L EXPANSION
☐	WILL CONSIDER ALL
☐	VENTURE LEASING

Other Locations:

Affiliation:
Minimum Investment: $1 Million or more
Capital Under Management: $100 to $500 Million

GEOGRAPHIC PREF

☐	East Coast
☒	West Coast
☐	Northeast
☐	Mid Atlantic
☐	Gulf States
☐	Northwest
☐	Southeast
☐	Southwest
☐	Midwest
☐	Central
☐	Local to Office
☐	Other Geo Pref

ENTERPRISE PARTNERS

7979 Ivanhoe Avenue
Suite 550
La Jolla CA 92037

Phone (858) 454-8833   Fax (858) 454-2489

PROFESSIONALS	TITLE
James H. Berglund	General Partner
Drew Senyei	General Partner
Ron Taylor	General Partner
Bill Stensrud	General Partner

INDUSTRY PREFERENCE

☒	INFORMATION INDUSTRY	☒	BASIC INDUSTRIES
☒	Communications	☒	Consumer
☒	Computer Equipment	☐	Distribution
☒	Computer Services	☐	Manufacturing
☒	Computer Components	☐	Retail
☒	Computer Entertainment	☒	Service
☐	Computer Education	☐	Wholesale
☒	Information Technologies	☒	SPECIFIC INDUSTRIES
☒	Computer Media	☐	Energy
☒	Software	☐	Environmental
☒	Internet	☐	Financial
☒	MEDICAL/HEALTHCARE	☐	Real Estate
☒	Biotechnology	☐	Transportation
☒	Healthcare Services	☐	Publishing
☒	Life Sciences	☐	Food
☒	Medical Products	☐	Franchises
☒	INDUSTRIAL	☒	DIVERSIFIED
☒	Advanced Materials	☐	MISCELLANEOUS
☒	Chemicals		
☒	Instruments & Controls		

STAGE PREFERENCE

☐	EARLY STAGE
☐	Seed
☐	Start-up
☐	1st Stage
☒	LATER STAGE
☐	2nd Stage
☐	Mature
☐	Mezzanine
☒	LBO/MBO
☐	Turnaround
☐	INT'L EXPANSION
☐	WILL CONSIDER ALL
☐	VENTURE LEASING

Other Locations: Newport Beach CA

Affiliation:
Minimum Investment: $1 Million or more
Capital Under Management: Less than $100 Million

GEOGRAPHIC PREF

☐	East Coast
☒	West Coast
☐	Northeast
☐	Mid Atlantic
☐	Gulf States
☐	Northwest
☐	Southeast
☐	Southwest
☐	Midwest
☐	Central
☐	Local to Office
☐	Other Geo Pref

ENTERPRISE PARTNERS

5000 Birch Street
Suite 6200
Newport Beach CA 92660

Phone (949) 833-3650   Fax (949) 833-3652

PROFESSIONALS	TITLE
Tom Clancy	Venture Partner

INDUSTRY PREFERENCE

- ☒ INFORMATION INDUSTRY
- ☒ Communications
- ☒ Computer Equipment
- ☒ Computer Services
- ☒ Computer Components
- ☐ Computer Entertainment
- ☒ Computer Education
- ☒ Information Technologies
- ☒ Computer Media
- ☒ Software
- ☒ Internet
- ☒ MEDICAL/HEALTHCARE
- ☒ Biotechnology
- ☒ Healthcare Services
- ☒ Life Sciences
- ☒ Medical Products
- ☒ INDUSTRIAL
- ☒ Advanced Materials
- ☒ Chemicals
- ☒ Instruments & Controls

- ☒ BASIC INDUSTRIES
- ☐ Consumer
- ☐ Distribution
- ☐ Manufacturing
- ☐ Retail
- ☒ Service
- ☐ Wholesale
- ☒ SPECIFIC INDUSTRIES
- ☐ Energy
- ☐ Environmental
- ☐ Financial
- ☐ Real Estate
- ☐ Transportation
- ☐ Publishing
- ☐ Food
- ☐ Franchises
- ☒ DIVERSIFIED
- ☐ MISCELLANEOUS

STAGE PREFERENCE

- ☐ EARLY STAGE
- ☐ Seed
- ☐ Start-up
- ☐ 1st Stage
- ☒ LATER STAGE
- ☐ 2nd Stage
- ☐ Mature
- ☐ Mezzanine
- ☒ LBO/MBO
- ☐ Turnaround
- ☐ INT'L EXPANSION
- ☐ WILL CONSIDER ALL
- ☐ VENTURE LEASING

Other Locations: La Jolla CA

Affiliation:
Minimum Investment: $1 Million or more
Capital Under Management: $100 to $500 Million

GEOGRAPHIC PREF

- ☐ East Coast
- ☒ West Coast
- ☐ Northeast
- ☐ Mid Atlantic
- ☐ Gulf States
- ☐ Northwest
- ☐ Southeast
- ☐ Southwest
- ☐ Midwest
- ☐ Central
- ☐ Local to Office
- ☐ Other Geo Pref

FAR EAST CAPITAL CORP.

2001 Gateway Plaza
Suite 101E
San Jose CA 95110

Phone (408) 487-0321   Fax (408) 487-0333

PROFESSIONALS	TITLE
Daniel Mitchner	Manager

INDUSTRY PREFERENCE

- ☐ INFORMATION INDUSTRY
- ☐ Communications
- ☐ Computer Equipment
- ☐ Computer Services
- ☐ Computer Components
- ☐ Computer Entertainment
- ☐ Computer Education
- ☐ Information Technologies
- ☐ Computer Media
- ☐ Software
- ☐ Internet
- ☐ MEDICAL/HEALTHCARE
- ☐ Biotechnology
- ☐ Healthcare Services
- ☐ Life Sciences
- ☐ Medical Products
- ☐ INDUSTRIAL
- ☐ Advanced Materials
- ☐ Chemicals
- ☐ Instruments & Controls

- ☐ BASIC INDUSTRIES
- ☐ Consumer
- ☐ Distribution
- ☐ Manufacturing
- ☐ Retail
- ☐ Service
- ☐ Wholesale
- ☐ SPECIFIC INDUSTRIES
- ☐ Energy
- ☐ Environmental
- ☐ Financial
- ☐ Real Estate
- ☐ Transportation
- ☐ Publishing
- ☐ Food
- ☐ Franchises
- ☒ DIVERSIFIED
- ☐ MISCELLANEOUS

STAGE PREFERENCE

- ☐ EARLY STAGE
- ☐ Seed
- ☐ Start-up
- ☐ 1st Stage
- ☒ LATER STAGE
- ☒ 2nd Stage
- ☒ Mature
- ☒ Mezzanine
- ☒ LBO/MBO
- ☐ Turnaround
- ☒ INT'L EXPANSION
- ☐ WILL CONSIDER ALL
- ☐ VENTURE LEASING

SSBIC
Other Locations:

Affiliation:
Minimum Investment: $1 Million or more
Capital Under Management: Less than $100 Million

GEOGRAPHIC PREF

- ☐ East Coast
- ☒ West Coast
- ☐ Northeast
- ☐ Mid Atlantic
- ☐ Gulf States
- ☐ Northwest
- ☐ Southeast
- ☐ Southwest
- ☐ Midwest
- ☐ Central
- ☐ Local to Office
- ☐ Other Geo Pref

FORREST, BINKLEY & BROWN

840 Newport Center Drive
Suite 480
Newport Beach CA 92660

Phone (949) 729-3222   Fax (949) 729-3226

PROFESSIONALS	TITLE
Greg Forrest	Partner
Jeff Brown	Partner

INDUSTRY PREFERENCE

☒ INFORMATION INDUSTRY	☒ BASIC INDUSTRIES
☒ Communications	☒ Consumer
☐ Computer Equipment	☒ Distribution
☐ Computer Services	☐ Manufacturing
☒ Computer Components	☐ Retail
☐ Computer Entertainment	☐ Service
☐ Computer Education	☐ Wholesale
☐ Information Technologies	☐ SPECIFIC INDUSTRIES
☐ Computer Media	☐ Energy
☒ Software	☐ Environmental
☒ Internet	☐ Financial
☒ MEDICAL/HEALTHCARE	☐ Real Estate
☒ Biotechnology	☐ Transportation
☒ Healthcare Services	☐ Publishing
☐ Life Sciences	☐ Food
☐ Medical Products	☐ Franchises
☒ INDUSTRIAL	☒ DIVERSIFIED
☐ Advanced Materials	☒ MISCELLANEOUS
☒ Chemicals	
☒ Instruments & Controls	

STAGE PREFERENCE

☐ EARLY STAGE	
☐ Seed	
☐ Start-up	
☐ 1st Stage	
☒ LATER STAGE	
☒ 2nd Stage	
☐ Mature	
☒ Mezzanine	
☒ LBO/MBO	
☐ Turnaround	
☐ INT'L EXPANSION	
☐ WILL CONSIDER ALL	
☐ VENTURE LEASING	

Other Locations: Solano Beach CA

Affiliation:
Minimum Investment: $1 Million or more
Capital Under Management: $100 to $500 Million

GEOGRAPHIC PREF

☐ East Coast	
☐ West Coast	
☐ Northeast	
☐ Mid Atlantic	
☐ Gulf States	
☐ Northwest	
☐ Southeast	
☐ Southwest	
☐ Midwest	
☐ Central	
☐ Local to Office	
☐ Other Geo Pref	

FORREST, BINKLEY & BROWN

265 Saint Helena
Suite 110
Solano Beach CA 92075

Phone (858) 259-4105   Fax (858) 259-4108

PROFESSIONALS	TITLE
Nick Binkley	Partner

INDUSTRY PREFERENCE

☒ INFORMATION INDUSTRY	☒ BASIC INDUSTRIES
☒ Communications	☒ Consumer
☐ Computer Equipment	☒ Distribution
☐ Computer Services	☐ Manufacturing
☒ Computer Components	☐ Retail
☐ Computer Entertainment	☐ Service
☐ Computer Education	☐ Wholesale
☐ Information Technologies	☐ SPECIFIC INDUSTRIES
☐ Computer Media	☐ Energy
☒ Software	☐ Environmental
☒ Internet	☐ Financial
☒ MEDICAL/HEALTHCARE	☐ Real Estate
☒ Biotechnology	☐ Transportation
☒ Healthcare Services	☐ Publishing
☐ Life Sciences	☐ Food
☐ Medical Products	☐ Franchises
☒ INDUSTRIAL	☒ DIVERSIFIED
☐ Advanced Materials	☒ MISCELLANEOUS
☒ Chemicals	
☒ Instruments & Controls	

STAGE PREFERENCE

☐ EARLY STAGE	
☐ Seed	
☐ Start-up	
☐ 1st Stage	
☒ LATER STAGE	
☒ 2nd Stage	
☐ Mature	
☒ Mezzanine	
☒ LBO/MBO	
☐ Turnaround	
☐ INT'L EXPANSION	
☐ WILL CONSIDER ALL	
☐ VENTURE LEASING	

Other Locations: Newport Beach CA

Affiliation:
Minimum Investment: $1 Million or more
Capital Under Management: $100 to $500 Million

GEOGRAPHIC PREF

☐ East Coast	
☐ West Coast	
☐ Northeast	
☐ Mid Atlantic	
☐ Gulf States	
☐ Northwest	
☐ Southeast	
☐ Southwest	
☐ Midwest	
☐ Central	
☐ Local to Office	
☐ Other Geo Pref	

FORWARD VENTURES

9255 Towne Center Drive
Suite 300
San Diego CA 92121

Phone (858) 677-6077   Fax (858) 452-8799

PROFESSIONALS	TITLE
Standish Fleming	Partner
Ivor Royston	Partner

INDUSTRY PREFERENCE

☐ INFORMATION INDUSTRY
☐ Communications
☐ Computer Equipment
☐ Computer Services
☐ Computer Components
☐ Computer Entertainment
☐ Computer Education
☐ Information Technologies
☐ Computer Media
☐ Software
☐ Internet
☒ MEDICAL/HEALTHCARE
☒ Biotechnology
☒ Healthcare Services
☐ Life Sciences
☒ Medical Products
☐ INDUSTRIAL
☐ Advanced Materials
☐ Chemicals
☐ Instruments & Controls

☐ BASIC INDUSTRIES
☐ Consumer
☐ Distribution
☐ Manufacturing
☐ Retail
☐ Service
☐ Wholesale
☐ SPECIFIC INDUSTRIES
☐ Energy
☐ Environmental
☐ Financial
☐ Real Estate
☐ Transportation
☐ Publishing
☐ Food
☐ Franchises
☐ DIVERSIFIED
☐ MISCELLANEOUS

STAGE PREFERENCE

☒ EARLY STAGE
☒ Seed
☒ Start-up
☒ 1st Stage
☐ LATER STAGE
☐ 2nd Stage
☐ Mature
☐ Mezzanine
☐ LBO/MBO
☐ Turnaround
☐ INT'L EXPANSION
☐ WILL CONSIDER ALL
☐ VENTURE LEASING

Other Locations:

Affiliation:
Minimum Investment: Less than $1 Million
Capital Under Management: Less than $100 Million

GEOGRAPHIC PREF

☐ East Coast
☒ West Coast
☐ Northeast
☐ Mid Atlantic
☐ Gulf States
☐ Northwest
☐ Southeast
☐ Southwest
☐ Midwest
☐ Central
☐ Local to Office
☐ Other Geo Pref

FOUNDATION CAPITAL

70 Willow Road
Suite 200
Menlo Park CA 94025

Phone (650) 614-0500   Fax (650) 614-0505

PROFESSIONALS	TITLE
Jim Anderson	General Partner
Bill Elmore	General Partner
Kathryn Gould	General Partner
Paul Koontz	General Partner
Mike Schuh	General Partner

INDUSTRY PREFERENCE

☒ INFORMATION INDUSTRY
☒ Communications
☒ Computer Equipment
☒ Computer Services
☒ Computer Components
☐ Computer Entertainment
☐ Computer Education
☐ Information Technologies
☐ Computer Media
☒ Software
☒ Internet
☐ MEDICAL/HEALTHCARE
☐ Biotechnology
☐ Healthcare Services
☐ Life Sciences
☐ Medical Products
☐ INDUSTRIAL
☐ Advanced Materials
☐ Chemicals
☐ Instruments & Controls

☐ BASIC INDUSTRIES
☐ Consumer
☐ Distribution
☐ Manufacturing
☐ Retail
☐ Service
☐ Wholesale
☐ SPECIFIC INDUSTRIES
☐ Energy
☐ Environmental
☐ Financial
☐ Real Estate
☐ Transportation
☐ Publishing
☐ Food
☐ Franchises
☐ DIVERSIFIED
☒ MISCELLANEOUS

STAGE PREFERENCE

☒ EARLY STAGE
☒ Seed
☒ Start-up
☒ 1st Stage
☒ LATER STAGE
☒ 2nd Stage
☐ Mature
☐ Mezzanine
☐ LBO/MBO
☐ Turnaround
☐ INT'L EXPANSION
☐ WILL CONSIDER ALL
☐ VENTURE LEASING

Other Locations:

Affiliation:
Minimum Investment: $1 Million or more
Capital Under Management: $100 to $500 Million

GEOGRAPHIC PREF

☐ East Coast
☐ West Coast
☐ Northeast
☐ Mid Atlantic
☐ Gulf States
☐ Northwest
☐ Southeast
☐ Southwest
☐ Midwest
☐ Central
☐ Local to Office
☐ Other Geo Pref

FREMONT GROUP

50 Fremont Street
Suite 3700
San Francisco CA 94105

Phone (415) 284-8500   Fax (415) 284-8191

PROFESSIONALS	TITLE
Robert Jaunich II	Managing Director

INDUSTRY PREFERENCE

☒ INFORMATION INDUSTRY	☒ BASIC INDUSTRIES
☒ Communications	☒ Consumer
☐ Computer Equipment	☒ Distribution
☒ Computer Services	☐ Manufacturing
☐ Computer Components	☐ Retail
☐ Computer Entertainment	☒ Service
☐ Computer Education	☐ Wholesale
☒ Information Technologies	☒ SPECIFIC INDUSTRIES
☐ Computer Media	☒ Energy
☐ Software	☒ Environmental
☐ Internet	☐ Financial
☒ MEDICAL/HEALTHCARE	☐ Real Estate
☐ Biotechnology	☒ Transportation
☐ Healthcare Services	☐ Publishing
☒ Life Sciences	☐ Food
☒ Medical Products	☐ Franchises
☒ INDUSTRIAL	☒ DIVERSIFIED
☒ Advanced Materials	☐ MISCELLANEOUS
☒ Chemicals	
☐ Instruments & Controls	

STAGE PREFERENCE

☐ EARLY STAGE
☐ Seed
☐ Start-up
☐ 1st Stage
☒ LATER STAGE
☐ 2nd Stage
☐ Mature
☒ Mezzanine
☒ LBO/MBO
☒ Turnaround
☒ INT'L EXPANSION
☐ WILL CONSIDER ALL
☒ VENTURE LEASING

Other Locations:

Affiliation: Direct Investments, Trinity Ventures
Minimum Investment: $1 Million or more
Capital Under Management: Over $500 Million

GEOGRAPHIC PREF

☐ East Coast
☐ West Coast
☐ Northeast
☐ Mid Atlantic
☐ Gulf States
☐ Northwest
☐ Southeast
☐ Southwest
☐ Midwest
☐ Central
☐ Local to Office
☐ Other Geo Pref

FULCRUM VENTURE CAPITAL CORPORATION

300 Corporate Pointe
Suite 380
Culver City CA 90230

Phone (310) 645-1271   Fax (310) 645-1272

PROFESSIONALS	TITLE
Brian Argrett	President
Cedric Penix	Advisor

INDUSTRY PREFERENCE

☒ INFORMATION INDUSTRY	☒ BASIC INDUSTRIES
☒ Communications	☐ Consumer
☐ Computer Equipment	☒ Distribution
☐ Computer Services	☒ Manufacturing
☐ Computer Components	☐ Retail
☐ Computer Entertainment	☒ Service
☐ Computer Education	☐ Wholesale
☐ Information Technologies	☒ SPECIFIC INDUSTRIES
☐ Computer Media	☐ Energy
☐ Software	☐ Environmental
☐ Internet	☐ Financial
☐ MEDICAL/HEALTHCARE	☐ Real Estate
☐ Biotechnology	☒ Transportation
☐ Healthcare Services	☐ Publishing
☐ Life Sciences	☐ Food
☐ Medical Products	☐ Franchises
☐ INDUSTRIAL	☒ DIVERSIFIED
☐ Advanced Materials	☐ MISCELLANEOUS
☐ Chemicals	
☐ Instruments & Controls	

STAGE PREFERENCE

☐ EARLY STAGE
☐ Seed
☐ Start-up
☐ 1st Stage
☒ LATER STAGE
☒ 2nd Stage
☒ Mature
☒ Mezzanine
☒ LBO/MBO
☐ Turnaround
☐ INT'L EXPANSION
☐ WILL CONSIDER ALL
☐ VENTURE LEASING

SSBIC
Other Locations:

Affiliation:
Minimum Investment: Less than $1 Million
Capital Under Management: Less than $100 Million

GEOGRAPHIC PREF

☐ East Coast
☒ West Coast
☐ Northeast
☐ Mid Atlantic
☐ Gulf States
☐ Northwest
☐ Southeast
☐ Southwest
☐ Midwest
☐ Central
☐ Local to Office
☐ Other Geo Pref

GLYNN CAPITAL MANAGEMENT

3000 Sand Hill Road
Suite 235, Building 4
Menlo Park CA 94025

Phone (650) 854-2215   Fax (650) 854-8083

PROFESSIONALS	TITLE
John Glynn, Jr.	General Partner

INDUSTRY PREFERENCE

☒ INFORMATION INDUSTRY	☒ BASIC INDUSTRIES
☒ Communications	☒ Consumer
☒ Computer Equipment	☐ Distribution
☒ Computer Services	☒ Manufacturing
☒ Computer Components	☐ Retail
☐ Computer Entertainment	☒ Service
☒ Computer Education	☐ Wholesale
☒ Information Technologies	☒ SPECIFIC INDUSTRIES
☐ Computer Media	☐ Energy
☒ Software	☒ Environmental
☒ Internet	☐ Financial
☒ MEDICAL/HEALTHCARE	☐ Real Estate
☒ Biotechnology	☐ Transportation
☒ Healthcare Services	☐ Publishing
☒ Life Sciences	☐ Food
☒ Medical Products	☐ Franchises
☒ INDUSTRIAL	☒ DIVERSIFIED
☐ Advanced Materials	☐ MISCELLANEOUS
☐ Chemicals	
☒ Instruments & Controls	

STAGE PREFERENCE

☒ EARLY STAGE
☐ Seed
☒ Start-up
☒ 1st Stage
☒ LATER STAGE
☒ 2nd Stage
☒ Mature
☒ Mezzanine
☒ LBO/MBO
☐ Turnaround
☐ INT'L EXPANSION
☐ WILL CONSIDER ALL
☐ VENTURE LEASING

Other Locations:

Affiliation: Glynn Capital Management
Minimum Investment: Less than $1 Million
Capital Under Management: Less than $100 Million

GEOGRAPHIC PREF

☐ East Coast
☐ West Coast
☐ Northeast
☐ Mid Atlantic
☐ Gulf States
☐ Northwest
☐ Southeast
☐ Southwest
☐ Midwest
☐ Central
☐ Local to Office
☐ Other Geo Pref

GREYLOCK MANAGEMENT

755 Page Mill Road
Suite A100
Palo Alto CA 94304

Phone (650) 423-5525   Fax (650) 493-5575

PROFESSIONALS	TITLE
Roger Evans	General Partner
Dave Strohm	General Partner
Chris Surowiec	General Partner
Aneel Bhusri	General Partner

INDUSTRY PREFERENCE

☒ INFORMATION INDUSTRY	☒ BASIC INDUSTRIES
☒ Communications	☒ Consumer
☐ Computer Equipment	☐ Distribution
☐ Computer Services	☐ Manufacturing
☐ Computer Components	☒ Retail
☐ Computer Entertainment	☒ Service
☐ Computer Education	☐ Wholesale
☐ Information Technologies	☒ SPECIFIC INDUSTRIES
☐ Computer Media	☐ Energy
☒ Software	☐ Environmental
☐ Internet	☒ Financial
☒ MEDICAL/HEALTHCARE	☐ Real Estate
☐ Biotechnology	☐ Transportation
☒ Healthcare Services	☐ Publishing
☐ Life Sciences	☐ Food
☒ Medical Products	☐ Franchises
☒ INDUSTRIAL	☒ DIVERSIFIED
☐ Advanced Materials	☒ MISCELLANEOUS
☐ Chemicals	
☒ Instruments & Controls	

STAGE PREFERENCE

☒ EARLY STAGE
☒ Seed
☒ Start-up
☒ 1st Stage
☒ LATER STAGE
☒ 2nd Stage
☒ Mature
☒ Mezzanine
☒ LBO/MBO
☐ Turnaround
☐ INT'L EXPANSION
☐ WILL CONSIDER ALL
☐ VENTURE LEASING

Other Locations: Boston MA

Affiliation:
Minimum Investment: Less than $1 Million
Capital Under Management: Over $500 Million

GEOGRAPHIC PREF

☐ East Coast
☐ West Coast
☐ Northeast
☐ Mid Atlantic
☐ Gulf States
☐ Northwest
☐ Southeast
☐ Southwest
☐ Midwest
☐ Central
☐ Local to Office
☐ Other Geo Pref

H&Q VENTURE ASSOCIATES

One Bush Street
San Francisco CA 94104

Phone (415) 439-3000   Fax (415) 439-3621

PROFESSIONALS	TITLE
Standish O'Grady	Managing Director

INDUSTRY PREFERENCE

- ☒ INFORMATION INDUSTRY
- ☒ Communications
- ☒ Computer Equipment
- ☒ Computer Services
- ☒ Computer Components
- ☒ Computer Entertainment
- ☐ Computer Education
- ☒ Information Technologies
- ☐ Computer Media
- ☒ Software
- ☒ Internet
- ☒ MEDICAL/HEALTHCARE
- ☒ Biotechnology
- ☒ Healthcare Services
- ☒ Life Sciences
- ☒ Medical Products
- ☒ INDUSTRIAL
- ☐ Advanced Materials
- ☐ Chemicals
- ☒ Instruments & Controls

- ☒ BASIC INDUSTRIES
- ☒ Consumer
- ☐ Distribution
- ☐ Manufacturing
- ☐ Retail
- ☒ Service
- ☐ Wholesale
- ☐ SPECIFIC INDUSTRIES
- ☐ Energy
- ☐ Environmental
- ☐ Financial
- ☐ Real Estate
- ☐ Transportation
- ☐ Publishing
- ☐ Food
- ☐ Franchises
- ☒ DIVERSIFIED
- ☒ MISCELLANEOUS

STAGE PREFERENCE

- ☒ EARLY STAGE
- ☒ Seed
- ☒ Start-up
- ☒ 1st Stage
- ☒ LATER STAGE
- ☒ 2nd Stage
- ☒ Mature
- ☒ Mezzanine
- ☒ LBO/MBO
- ☒ Turnaround
- ☒ INT'L EXPANSION
- ☐ WILL CONSIDER ALL
- ☒ VENTURE LEASING

Other Locations:

Affiliation:
Minimum Investment: Less than $1 Million
Capital Under Management: $100 to $500 Million

GEOGRAPHIC PREF

- ☐ East Coast
- ☐ West Coast
- ☐ Northeast
- ☐ Mid Atlantic
- ☐ Gulf States
- ☐ Northwest
- ☐ Southeast
- ☐ Southwest
- ☐ Midwest
- ☐ Central
- ☐ Local to Office
- ☐ Other Geo Pref

HALLADOR VENTURE PARTNERS

740 University Avenue
Suite 110
Sacramento CA 92825

Phone (916) 920-0191   Fax (916) 920-5188

PROFESSIONALS	TITLE
David Hardie	Managing Director
Chris L. Branscum	Managing Director

INDUSTRY PREFERENCE

- ☒ INFORMATION INDUSTRY
- ☒ Communications
- ☐ Computer Equipment
- ☐ Computer Services
- ☐ Computer Components
- ☐ Computer Entertainment
- ☐ Computer Education
- ☒ Information Technologies
- ☐ Computer Media
- ☐ Software
- ☒ Internet
- ☐ MEDICAL/HEALTHCARE
- ☐ Biotechnology
- ☐ Healthcare Services
- ☐ Life Sciences
- ☐ Medical Products
- ☐ INDUSTRIAL
- ☐ Advanced Materials
- ☐ Chemicals
- ☐ Instruments & Controls

- ☐ BASIC INDUSTRIES
- ☐ Consumer
- ☐ Distribution
- ☐ Manufacturing
- ☐ Retail
- ☐ Service
- ☐ Wholesale
- ☐ SPECIFIC INDUSTRIES
- ☐ Energy
- ☐ Environmental
- ☐ Financial
- ☐ Real Estate
- ☐ Transportation
- ☐ Publishing
- ☐ Food
- ☐ Franchises
- ☐ DIVERSIFIED
- ☐ MISCELLANEOUS

STAGE PREFERENCE

- ☒ EARLY STAGE
- ☒ Seed
- ☐ Start-up
- ☐ 1st Stage
- ☐ LATER STAGE
- ☐ 2nd Stage
- ☐ Mature
- ☐ Mezzanine
- ☐ LBO/MBO
- ☐ Turnaround
- ☐ INT'L EXPANSION
- ☐ WILL CONSIDER ALL
- ☐ VENTURE LEASING

Other Locations:

Affiliation:
Minimum Investment: Less than $1 Million
Capital Under Management: Less than $100 Million

GEOGRAPHIC PREF

- ☐ East Coast
- ☒ West Coast
- ☐ Northeast
- ☐ Mid Atlantic
- ☐ Gulf States
- ☐ Northwest
- ☐ Southeast
- ☐ Southwest
- ☐ Midwest
- ☐ Central
- ☐ Local to Office
- ☐ Other Geo Pref

HAMBRECHT & QUIST

One Bush Street
San Francisco CA 94104

Phone (415) 439-3000   Fax (415) 439-3621

PROFESSIONALS	TITLE
Charles Walker	

INDUSTRY PREFERENCE

☒ INFORMATION INDUSTRY	☒ BASIC INDUSTRIES
☒ Communications	☒ Consumer
☒ Computer Equipment	☐ Distribution
☒ Computer Services	☐ Manufacturing
☒ Computer Components	☐ Retail
☒ Computer Entertainment	☒ Service
☐ Computer Education	☐ Wholesale
☒ Information Technologies	☒ SPECIFIC INDUSTRIES
☐ Computer Media	☐ Energy
☒ Software	☐ Environmental
☒ Internet	☐ Financial
☒ MEDICAL/HEALTHCARE	☐ Real Estate
☒ Biotechnology	☐ Transportation
☒ Healthcare Services	☐ Publishing
☒ Life Sciences	☐ Food
☒ Medical Products	☐ Franchises
☒ INDUSTRIAL	☒ DIVERSIFIED
☐ Advanced Materials	☐ MISCELLANEOUS
☐ Chemicals	
☒ Instruments & Controls	

STAGE PREFERENCE

- ☒ EARLY STAGE
- ☒ Seed
- ☒ Start-up
- ☒ 1st Stage
- ☒ LATER STAGE
- ☒ 2nd Stage
- ☒ Mature
- ☒ Mezzanine
- ☒ LBO/MBO
- ☒ Turnaround
- ☒ INT'L EXPANSION
- ☐ WILL CONSIDER ALL
- ☒ VENTURE LEASING

Other Locations:

Affiliation:
Minimum Investment: Less than $1 Million
Capital Under Management: $100 to $500 Million

GEOGRAPHIC PREF

- ☐ East Coast
- ☐ West Coast
- ☐ Northeast
- ☐ Mid Atlantic
- ☐ Gulf States
- ☐ Northwest
- ☐ Southeast
- ☐ Southwest
- ☐ Midwest
- ☐ Central
- ☐ Local to Office
- ☐ Other Geo Pref

HUMMER WINBLAD VENTURE PARTNERS

Two South Park
Second Floor
San Francisco CA 94107

Phone (415) 979-9600   Fax (415) 979-9601

PROFESSIONALS	TITLE
John Hummer	Partner
Ann Winblad	Partner
Mark Gorenberg	Partner

INDUSTRY PREFERENCE

☒ INFORMATION INDUSTRY	☐ BASIC INDUSTRIES
☐ Communications	☐ Consumer
☐ Computer Equipment	☐ Distribution
☐ Computer Services	☐ Manufacturing
☐ Computer Components	☐ Retail
☐ Computer Entertainment	☐ Service
☐ Computer Education	☐ Wholesale
☒ Information Technologies	☐ SPECIFIC INDUSTRIES
☐ Computer Media	☐ Energy
☒ Software	☐ Environmental
☐ Internet	☐ Financial
☐ MEDICAL/HEALTHCARE	☐ Real Estate
☐ Biotechnology	☐ Transportation
☐ Healthcare Services	☐ Publishing
☐ Life Sciences	☐ Food
☐ Medical Products	☐ Franchises
☐ INDUSTRIAL	☐ DIVERSIFIED
☐ Advanced Materials	☐ MISCELLANEOUS
☐ Chemicals	
☐ Instruments & Controls	

STAGE PREFERENCE

- ☒ EARLY STAGE
- ☒ Seed
- ☒ Start-up
- ☒ 1st Stage
- ☒ LATER STAGE
- ☒ 2nd Stage
- ☒ Mature
- ☐ Mezzanine
- ☐ LBO/MBO
- ☐ Turnaround
- ☐ INT'L EXPANSION
- ☐ WILL CONSIDER ALL
- ☐ VENTURE LEASING

Other Locations:

Affiliation:
Minimum Investment: Less than $1 Million
Capital Under Management: $100 to $500 Million

GEOGRAPHIC PREF

- ☐ East Coast
- ☒ West Coast
- ☐ Northeast
- ☐ Mid Atlantic
- ☐ Gulf States
- ☐ Northwest
- ☐ Southeast
- ☐ Southwest
- ☐ Midwest
- ☐ Central
- ☐ Local to Office
- ☐ Other Geo Pref

IDANTA PARTNERS LTD.

4660 La Jolla Village Drive
Suite 850
San Diego CA 92122

Phone (858) 452-9690   Fax (858) 452-2013

PROFESSIONALS

David J. Dunn
Johnathon S. Huberman

TITLE

Managing Partner
General Partner

INDUSTRY PREFERENCE

- ☒ INFORMATION INDUSTRY
- ☒ Communications
- ☒ Computer Equipment
- ☒ Computer Services
- ☐ Computer Components
- ☐ Computer Entertainment
- ☐ Computer Education
- ☐ Information Technologies
- ☐ Computer Media
- ☒ Software
- ☒ Internet
- ☒ MEDICAL/HEALTHCARE
- ☐ Biotechnology
- ☒ Healthcare Services
- ☒ Life Sciences
- ☒ Medical Products
- ☐ INDUSTRIAL
- ☐ Advanced Materials
- ☐ Chemicals
- ☐ Instruments & Controls

- ☒ BASIC INDUSTRIES
- ☒ Consumer
- ☐ Distribution
- ☒ Manufacturing
- ☐ Retail
- ☒ Service
- ☐ Wholesale
- ☒ SPECIFIC INDUSTRIES
- ☐ Energy
- ☐ Environmental
- ☒ Financial
- ☐ Real Estate
- ☐ Transportation
- ☐ Publishing
- ☐ Food
- ☐ Franchises
- ☒ DIVERSIFIED
- ☐ MISCELLANEOUS

STAGE PREFERENCE

- ☒ EARLY STAGE
- ☐ Seed
- ☒ Start-up
- ☒ 1st Stage
- ☒ LATER STAGE
- ☒ 2nd Stage
- ☐ Mature
- ☐ Mezzanine
- ☒ LBO/MBO
- ☐ Turnaround
- ☐ INT'L EXPANSION
- ☐ WILL CONSIDER ALL
- ☐ VENTURE LEASING

Other Locations:

Affiliation:
Minimum Investment: Less than $1 Million
Capital Under Management: $100 to $500 Million

GEOGRAPHIC PREF

- ☐ East Coast
- ☐ West Coast
- ☐ Northeast
- ☐ Mid Atlantic
- ☐ Gulf States
- ☐ Northwest
- ☐ Southeast
- ☐ Southwest
- ☐ Midwest
- ☐ Central
- ☐ Local to Office
- ☐ Other Geo Pref

IDEALAB CAPITAL PARTNERS (ICP)

130 West Union Street
Pasadena CA 91103

Phone (626) 535-2880   Fax (626) 535-2881

PROFESSIONALS

Bill Elkus
Bill Gross
Jim Armstrong
William Quigley

TITLE

Managing Director
Managing Director
Principal
Principal

INDUSTRY PREFERENCE

- ☒ INFORMATION INDUSTRY
- ☒ Communications
- ☐ Computer Equipment
- ☐ Computer Services
- ☐ Computer Components
- ☐ Computer Entertainment
- ☐ Computer Education
- ☐ Information Technologies
- ☐ Computer Media
- ☐ Software
- ☒ Internet
- ☐ MEDICAL/HEALTHCARE
- ☐ Biotechnology
- ☐ Healthcare Services
- ☐ Life Sciences
- ☐ Medical Products
- ☐ INDUSTRIAL
- ☐ Advanced Materials
- ☐ Chemicals
- ☐ Instruments & Controls

- ☐ BASIC INDUSTRIES
- ☐ Consumer
- ☐ Distribution
- ☐ Manufacturing
- ☐ Retail
- ☐ Service
- ☐ Wholesale
- ☐ SPECIFIC INDUSTRIES
- ☐ Energy
- ☐ Environmental
- ☐ Financial
- ☐ Real Estate
- ☐ Transportation
- ☐ Publishing
- ☐ Food
- ☐ Franchises
- ☐ DIVERSIFIED
- ☒ MISCELLANEOUS

STAGE PREFERENCE

- ☒ EARLY STAGE
- ☒ Seed
- ☒ Start-up
- ☒ 1st Stage
- ☒ LATER STAGE
- ☒ 2nd Stage
- ☒ Mature
- ☒ Mezzanine
- ☐ LBO/MBO
- ☐ Turnaround
- ☐ INT'L EXPANSION
- ☐ WILL CONSIDER ALL
- ☐ VENTURE LEASING

Other Locations:

Affiliation:
Minimum Investment: Less than $1 Million
Capital Under Management: Less than $100 Million

GEOGRAPHIC PREF

- ☐ East Coast
- ☐ West Coast
- ☐ Northeast
- ☐ Mid Atlantic
- ☐ Gulf States
- ☐ Northwest
- ☐ Southeast
- ☐ Southwest
- ☐ Midwest
- ☐ Central
- ☐ Local to Office
- ☐ Other Geo Pref

IMPERIAL VENTURE CAPITAL

9920 South La Cienega Boulevard
14th Floor
Los Angeles CA 90009-2991

Phone (408) 451-8555   Fax (408) 451-8586

PROFESSIONALS	TITLE
Jim Retter	Senior Vice President

INDUSTRY PREFERENCE

- ☒ INFORMATION INDUSTRY
- ☐ Communications
- ☐ Computer Equipment
- ☐ Computer Services
- ☐ Computer Components
- ☐ Computer Entertainment
- ☐ Computer Education
- ☒ Information Technologies
- ☐ Computer Media
- ☐ Software
- ☐ Internet
- ☒ MEDICAL/HEALTHCARE
- ☐ Biotechnology
- ☒ Healthcare Services
- ☐ Life Sciences
- ☒ Medical Products
- ☐ INDUSTRIAL
- ☐ Advanced Materials
- ☐ Chemicals
- ☐ Instruments & Controls

- ☐ BASIC INDUSTRIES
- ☐ Consumer
- ☐ Distribution
- ☐ Manufacturing
- ☐ Retail
- ☐ Service
- ☐ Wholesale
- ☒ SPECIFIC INDUSTRIES
- ☐ Energy
- ☐ Environmental
- ☒ Financial
- ☐ Real Estate
- ☐ Transportation
- ☐ Publishing
- ☐ Food
- ☐ Franchises
- ☒ DIVERSIFIED
- ☐ MISCELLANEOUS

STAGE PREFERENCE

- ☐ EARLY STAGE
- ☐ Seed
- ☐ Start-up
- ☐ 1st Stage
- ☒ LATER STAGE
- ☒ 2nd Stage
- ☒ Mature
- ☒ Mezzanine
- ☒ LBO/MBO
- ☐ Turnaround
- ☐ INT'L EXPANSION
- ☐ WILL CONSIDER ALL
- ☐ VENTURE LEASING

SBIC
Other Locations:

Affiliation:
Minimum Investment: Less than $1 Million
Capital Under Management: Less than $100 Million

GEOGRAPHIC PREF

- ☐ East Coast
- ☒ West Coast
- ☐ Northeast
- ☐ Mid Atlantic
- ☐ Gulf States
- ☐ Northwest
- ☐ Southeast
- ☐ Southwest
- ☐ Midwest
- ☐ Central
- ☐ Local to Office
- ☐ Other Geo Pref

INDOSUEZ VENTURES

2180 Sand Hill Road
Suite 450
Menlo Park CA 94025

Phone (650) 854-0587   Fax (650) 323-5561

PROFESSIONALS	TITLE
David E. Gold	General Partner
Guy H. Conger	General Partner
Nancy D. Burrus	General Partner

INDUSTRY PREFERENCE

- ☒ INFORMATION INDUSTRY
- ☒ Communications
- ☒ Computer Equipment
- ☒ Computer Services
- ☒ Computer Components
- ☐ Computer Entertainment
- ☐ Computer Education
- ☒ Information Technologies
- ☒ Computer Media
- ☒ Software
- ☒ Internet
- ☒ MEDICAL/HEALTHCARE
- ☐ Biotechnology
- ☒ Healthcare Services
- ☒ Life Sciences
- ☒ Medical Products
- ☐ INDUSTRIAL
- ☐ Advanced Materials
- ☐ Chemicals
- ☐ Instruments & Controls

- ☒ BASIC INDUSTRIES
- ☐ Consumer
- ☒ Distribution
- ☐ Manufacturing
- ☐ Retail
- ☒ Service
- ☐ Wholesale
- ☒ SPECIFIC INDUSTRIES
- ☐ Energy
- ☐ Environmental
- ☐ Financial
- ☐ Real Estate
- ☐ Transportation
- ☐ Publishing
- ☐ Food
- ☐ Franchises
- ☒ DIVERSIFIED
- ☐ MISCELLANEOUS

STAGE PREFERENCE

- ☒ EARLY STAGE
- ☐ Seed
- ☒ Start-up
- ☒ 1st Stage
- ☒ LATER STAGE
- ☒ 2nd Stage
- ☒ Mature
- ☒ Mezzanine
- ☐ LBO/MBO
- ☐ Turnaround
- ☐ INT'L EXPANSION
- ☐ WILL CONSIDER ALL
- ☐ VENTURE LEASING

Other Locations:

Affiliation: Banque INDOSUEZ, Paris
Minimum Investment: Less than $1 Million
Capital Under Management: $100 to $500 Million

GEOGRAPHIC PREF

- ☐ East Coast
- ☒ West Coast
- ☐ Northeast
- ☐ Mid Atlantic
- ☐ Gulf States
- ☐ Northwest
- ☐ Southeast
- ☐ Southwest
- ☐ Midwest
- ☐ Central
- ☐ Local to Office
- ☐ Other Geo Pref

INFORMATION TECHNOLOGY VENTURES, LP

3000 Sand Hill Road
Building One Suite 280
Menlo Park CA 94025

Phone (650) 854-5500   Fax (650) 234-0130

PROFESSIONALS	TITLE
Mark Dubovoy	General Partner
Sam Lee	General Partner
Virginia Turezyn	General Partner

INDUSTRY PREFERENCE

☒ INFORMATION INDUSTRY
☒ Communications
☒ Computer Equipment
☒ Computer Services
☒ Computer Components
☐ Computer Entertainment
☐ Computer Education
☒ Information Technologies
☐ Computer Media
☒ Software
☒ Internet
☐ MEDICAL/HEALTHCARE
☐ Biotechnology
☐ Healthcare Services
☐ Life Sciences
☐ Medical Products
☐ INDUSTRIAL
☐ Advanced Materials
☐ Chemicals
☐ Instruments & Controls

☐ BASIC INDUSTRIES
☐ Consumer
☐ Distribution
☐ Manufacturing
☐ Retail
☐ Service
☐ Wholesale
☐ SPECIFIC INDUSTRIES
☐ Energy
☐ Environmental
☐ Financial
☐ Real Estate
☐ Transportation
☐ Publishing
☐ Food
☐ Franchises
☐ DIVERSIFIED
☒ MISCELLANEOUS

STAGE PREFERENCE

☒ EARLY STAGE
☒ Seed
☒ Start-up
☒ 1st Stage
☒ LATER STAGE
☒ 2nd Stage
☐ Mature
☒ Mezzanine
☐ LBO/MBO
☐ Turnaround
☐ INT'L EXPANSION
☐ WILL CONSIDER ALL
☐ VENTURE LEASING

Other Locations:

Affiliation:
Minimum Investment: Less than $1 Million
Capital Under Management: Less than $100 Million

GEOGRAPHIC PREF

☐ East Coast
☐ West Coast
☐ Northeast
☐ Mid Atlantic
☐ Gulf States
☐ Northwest
☐ Southeast
☐ Southwest
☐ Midwest
☐ Central
☐ Local to Office
☐ Other Geo Pref

INNOCAL ASSOCIATES

600 Anton Boulevard
Suite 1270, Plaza Tower
Costa Mesa CA 92626

Phone (714) 850-6784   Fax (714) 850-6798

PROFESSIONALS	TITLE
Jay Houlihan	General Partner
Russell Robelen	General Partner
Harry D. Lambert	General Partner

INDUSTRY PREFERENCE

☒ INFORMATION INDUSTRY
☒ Communications
☒ Computer Equipment
☒ Computer Services
☒ Computer Components
☐ Computer Entertainment
☒ Computer Education
☒ Information Technologies
☒ Computer Media
☒ Software
☒ Internet
☒ MEDICAL/HEALTHCARE
☒ Biotechnology
☒ Healthcare Services
☒ Life Sciences
☒ Medical Products
☐ INDUSTRIAL
☐ Advanced Materials
☐ Chemicals
☐ Instruments & Controls

☒ BASIC INDUSTRIES
☒ Consumer
☐ Distribution
☐ Manufacturing
☒ Retail
☒ Service
☐ Wholesale
☒ SPECIFIC INDUSTRIES
☒ Energy
☒ Environmental
☒ Financial
☐ Real Estate
☐ Transportation
☐ Publishing
☐ Food
☐ Franchises
☒ DIVERSIFIED
☐ MISCELLANEOUS

STAGE PREFERENCE

☒ EARLY STAGE
☒ Seed
☒ Start-up
☒ 1st Stage
☒ LATER STAGE
☒ 2nd Stage
☒ Mature
☒ Mezzanine
☒ LBO/MBO
☐ Turnaround
☐ INT'L EXPANSION
☐ WILL CONSIDER ALL
☐ VENTURE LEASING

Other Locations:

Affiliation:
Minimum Investment: Less than $1 Million
Capital Under Management: Less than $100 Million

GEOGRAPHIC PREF

☐ East Coast
☐ West Coast
☐ Northeast
☐ Mid Atlantic
☐ Gulf States
☐ Northwest
☐ Southeast
☐ Southwest
☐ Midwest
☐ Central
☐ Local to Office
☐ Other Geo Pref

INSTITUTIONAL VENTURE PARTNERS

3000 Sand Hill Road
Building Two, Suite 290
Menlo Park CA 94025

Phone (650) 854-0132   Fax (650) 854-5762

PROFESSIONALS	TITLE
Mary Jane Elmore	General Partner
Peter Gotcher	General Partner
W. Allen Beasley	General Partner
Ruthann Quindlen	General Partner
Rebecca B. Robertson	General Partner
T. Peter Thomas	General Partner
Norman A. Fogelsong	General Partner
Reid W. Dennis	General Partner
Samuel D. Colella	General Partner

INDUSTRY PREFERENCE

☒ INFORMATION INDUSTRY
☒ Communications
☒ Computer Equipment
☒ Computer Services
☒ Computer Components
☐ Computer Entertainment
☒ Computer Education
☒ Information Technologies
☒ Computer Media
☒ Software
☒ Internet
☒ MEDICAL/HEALTHCARE
☒ Biotechnology
☐ Healthcare Services
☒ Life Sciences
☒ Medical Products
☐ INDUSTRIAL
☐ Advanced Materials
☐ Chemicals
☐ Instruments & Controls

☒ BASIC INDUSTRIES
☐ Consumer
☐ Distribution
☐ Manufacturing
☒ Retail
☐ Service
☐ Wholesale
☐ SPECIFIC INDUSTRIES
☐ Energy
☐ Environmental
☐ Financial
☐ Real Estate
☐ Transportation
☐ Publishing
☐ Food
☐ Franchises
☒ DIVERSIFIED
☐ MISCELLANEOUS

STAGE PREFERENCE

☒ EARLY STAGE
☒ Seed
☒ Start-up
☒ 1st Stage
☒ LATER STAGE
☒ 2nd Stage
☒ Mature
☒ Mezzanine
☒ LBO/MBO
☒ Turnaround
☒ INT'L EXPANSION
☐ WILL CONSIDER ALL
☒ VENTURE LEASING

Other Locations:

Affiliation:
Minimum Investment: Less than $1 Million
Capital Under Management: Over $500 Million

GEOGRAPHIC PREF

☐ East Coast
☐ West Coast
☐ Northeast
☐ Mid Atlantic
☐ Gulf States
☐ Northwest
☐ Southeast
☐ Southwest
☐ Midwest
☐ Central
☐ Local to Office
☐ Other Geo Pref

INTERNET CAPITAL GROUP

44 Montgomery Street
Floor 37, Suite 3700
San Francisco CA 94104

Phone (415) 358-3200   Fax (415) 358-3240

PROFESSIONALS	TITLE
Kenneth A. Fox	Managing Director

INDUSTRY PREFERENCE

☒ INFORMATION INDUSTRY
☐ Communications
☐ Computer Equipment
☐ Computer Services
☐ Computer Components
☐ Computer Entertainment
☐ Computer Education
☒ Information Technologies
☐ Computer Media
☐ Software
☒ Internet
☐ MEDICAL/HEALTHCARE
☐ Biotechnology
☐ Healthcare Services
☐ Life Sciences
☐ Medical Products
☐ INDUSTRIAL
☐ Advanced Materials
☐ Chemicals
☐ Instruments & Controls

☐ BASIC INDUSTRIES
☐ Consumer
☐ Distribution
☐ Manufacturing
☐ Retail
☐ Service
☐ Wholesale
☐ SPECIFIC INDUSTRIES
☐ Energy
☐ Environmental
☐ Financial
☐ Real Estate
☐ Transportation
☐ Publishing
☐ Food
☐ Franchises
☐ DIVERSIFIED
☒ MISCELLANEOUS

STAGE PREFERENCE

☒ EARLY STAGE
☐ Seed
☐ Start-up
☒ 1st Stage
☒ LATER STAGE
☒ 2nd Stage
☐ Mature
☐ Mezzanine
☐ LBO/MBO
☐ Turnaround
☐ INT'L EXPANSION
☐ WILL CONSIDER ALL
☐ VENTURE LEASING

Other Locations: Boston MA, Wayne PA

Affiliation:
Minimum Investment: Less than $1 Million
Capital Under Management: $100 to $500 Million

GEOGRAPHIC PREF

☐ East Coast
☐ West Coast
☐ Northeast
☐ Mid Atlantic
☐ Gulf States
☐ Northwest
☐ Southeast
☐ Southwest
☐ Midwest
☐ Central
☐ Local to Office
☐ Other Geo Pref

INTERWEST PARTNERS

3000 Sand Hill Road
Building Three, Suite 255
Menlo Park CA 94025-7116

Phone (650) 854-8585   Fax (650) 854-4706

PROFESSIONALS	TITLE
W. Scott Hedrick	General Partner
Gilbert H. Kliman	General Partner
Robert R. Momsen	General Partner
H. Berry Cash	General Partner
Arnold Oronsky	General Partner
Alan W. Crites	General Partner
Philip T. Gianos	General Partner
Stephen Bowsher	Venture Partner
Rodney Ferguson	Venture Partner

INDUSTRY PREFERENCE

☒	INFORMATION INDUSTRY	☒	BASIC INDUSTRIES
☒	Communications	☒	Consumer
☒	Computer Equipment	☐	Distribution
☒	Computer Services	☐	Manufacturing
☒	Computer Components	☒	Retail
☐	Computer Entertainment	☒	Service
☒	Computer Education	☒	Wholesale
☒	Information Technologies	☐	SPECIFIC INDUSTRIES
☒	Computer Media	☐	Energy
☒	Software	☐	Environmental
☒	Internet	☐	Financial
☒	MEDICAL/HEALTHCARE	☐	Real Estate
☒	Biotechnology	☐	Transportation
☒	Healthcare Services	☐	Publishing
☒	Life Sciences	☐	Food
☒	Medical Products	☐	Franchises
☐	INDUSTRIAL	☒	DIVERSIFIED
☐	Advanced Materials	☐	MISCELLANEOUS
☐	Chemicals		
☐	Instruments & Controls		

STAGE PREFERENCE

☒	EARLY STAGE
☒	Seed
☒	Start-up
☒	1st Stage
☒	LATER STAGE
☒	2nd Stage
☒	Mature
☒	Mezzanine
☐	LBO/MBO
☐	Turnaround
☐	INT'L EXPANSION
☐	WILL CONSIDER ALL
☐	VENTURE LEASING

Other Locations: Dallas TX

Affiliation: Berry Cash Southwest Partnership
Minimum Investment: $1 Million or more
Capital Under Management: Over $500 Million

GEOGRAPHIC PREF

☐	East Coast
☐	West Coast
☐	Northeast
☐	Mid Atlantic
☐	Gulf States
☐	Northwest
☐	Southeast
☐	Southwest
☐	Midwest
☐	Central
☐	Local to Office
☐	Other Geo Pref

INVESTECH

6743 Montia Court
Suite One
Carlsbad CA 92009

Phone (760) 438-8304   Fax (760) 931-2664

PROFESSIONALS	TITLE
K. E. Lister	CEO
T. Dale Harnish	President

INDUSTRY PREFERENCE

☒	INFORMATION INDUSTRY	☒	BASIC INDUSTRIES
☒	Communications	☒	Consumer
☒	Computer Equipment	☒	Distribution
☒	Computer Services	☒	Manufacturing
☒	Computer Components	☒	Retail
☒	Computer Entertainment	☒	Service
☒	Computer Education	☒	Wholesale
☒	Information Technologies	☒	SPECIFIC INDUSTRIES
☒	Computer Media	☒	Energy
☒	Software	☒	Environmental
☒	Internet	☒	Financial
☒	MEDICAL/HEALTHCARE	☒	Real Estate
☒	Biotechnology	☒	Transportation
☒	Healthcare Services	☒	Publishing
☒	Life Sciences	☐	Food
☒	Medical Products	☐	Franchises
☒	INDUSTRIAL	☒	DIVERSIFIED
☒	Advanced Materials	☐	MISCELLANEOUS
☒	Chemicals		
☒	Instruments & Controls		

STAGE PREFERENCE

☒	EARLY STAGE
☒	Seed
☒	Start-up
☒	1st Stage
☒	LATER STAGE
☒	2nd Stage
☒	Mature
☒	Mezzanine
☒	LBO/MBO
☒	Turnaround
☒	INT'L EXPANSION
☐	WILL CONSIDER ALL
☒	VENTURE LEASING

Other Locations:

Affiliation:
Minimum Investment: Less than $1 Million
Capital Under Management: Less than $100 Million

GEOGRAPHIC PREF

☒	East Coast
☒	West Coast
☒	Northeast
☐	Mid Atlantic
☐	Gulf States
☒	Northwest
☒	Southeast
☒	Southwest
☐	Midwest
☐	Central
☐	Local to Office
☐	Other Geo Pref

JAFCO AMERICA VENTURES

505 Hamilton Avenue
Suite 310
Palo Alto CA 94301

Phone (650) 463-8800   Fax (650) 463-8801

PROFESSIONALS	TITLE
Hitoshi Imuta	Managing Director
Barry Schiffman	President, Chief Investment
Stephen Hill	Managing Principal
Andy Goldfarb	Managing Principal

INDUSTRY PREFERENCE

☒ INFORMATION INDUSTRY
☒ Communications
☒ Computer Equipment
☒ Computer Services
☒ Computer Components
☐ Computer Entertainment
☒ Computer Education
☒ Information Technologies
☒ Computer Media
☒ Software
☒ Internet
☒ MEDICAL/HEALTHCARE
☒ Biotechnology
☒ Healthcare Services
☒ Life Sciences
☒ Medical Products
☒ INDUSTRIAL
☒ Advanced Materials
☐ Chemicals
☒ Instruments & Controls

☒ BASIC INDUSTRIES
☐ Consumer
☐ Distribution
☐ Manufacturing
☐ Retail
☒ Service
☐ Wholesale
☒ SPECIFIC INDUSTRIES
☐ Energy
☐ Environmental
☐ Financial
☐ Real Estate
☐ Transportation
☐ Publishing
☐ Food
☐ Franchises
☒ DIVERSIFIED
☐ MISCELLANEOUS

STAGE PREFERENCE

☒ EARLY STAGE
☐ Seed
☐ Start-up
☒ 1st Stage
☒ LATER STAGE
☒ 2nd Stage
☒ Mature
☒ Mezzanine
☐ LBO/MBO
☒ Turnaround
☒ INT'L EXPANSION
☐ WILL CONSIDER ALL
☒ VENTURE LEASING

Other Locations:

Affiliation: Japan Associated Finance Co., Ltd.
Minimum Investment: Less than $1 Million
Capital Under Management: $100 to $500 Million

GEOGRAPHIC PREF

☐ East Coast
☐ West Coast
☐ Northeast
☐ Mid Atlantic
☐ Gulf States
☐ Northwest
☐ Southeast
☐ Southwest
☐ Midwest
☐ Central
☐ Local to Office
☐ Other Geo Pref

KLEINER PERKINS CAUFIELD AND BYERS

2750 Sand Hill Road
Menlo Park CA 94025

Phone (650) 233-2750   Fax (650) 233-0300

PROFESSIONALS	TITLE
Brook H. Byers	Partner
Joseph S. Lacob	Partner
Kevin R. Compton	Partner
E. Floyd Kvamme	Partner
Dr. L. John Doerr	Partner
Bernard J. Lacroute	Partner
James P. Lally	Partner

INDUSTRY PREFERENCE

☒ INFORMATION INDUSTRY
☒ Communications
☒ Computer Equipment
☒ Computer Services
☒ Computer Components
☐ Computer Entertainment
☒ Computer Education
☒ Information Technologies
☒ Computer Media
☒ Software
☒ Internet
☒ MEDICAL/HEALTHCARE
☒ Biotechnology
☒ Healthcare Services
☒ Life Sciences
☒ Medical Products
☐ INDUSTRIAL
☐ Advanced Materials
☐ Chemicals
☐ Instruments & Controls

☒ BASIC INDUSTRIES
☐ Consumer
☐ Distribution
☐ Manufacturing
☐ Retail
☒ Service
☐ Wholesale
☐ SPECIFIC INDUSTRIES
☐ Energy
☐ Environmental
☐ Financial
☐ Real Estate
☐ Transportation
☐ Publishing
☐ Food
☐ Franchises
☒ DIVERSIFIED
☐ MISCELLANEOUS

STAGE PREFERENCE

☒ EARLY STAGE
☒ Seed
☒ Start-up
☒ 1st Stage
☒ LATER STAGE
☒ 2nd Stage
☐ Mature
☐ Mezzanine
☐ LBO/MBO
☐ Turnaround
☐ INT'L EXPANSION
☐ WILL CONSIDER ALL
☐ VENTURE LEASING

Other Locations: San Francisco CA

Affiliation:
Minimum Investment: Less than $1 Million
Capital Under Management: $100 to $500 Million

GEOGRAPHIC PREF

☐ East Coast
☒ West Coast
☐ Northeast
☐ Mid Atlantic
☐ Gulf States
☐ Northwest
☐ Southeast
☐ Southwest
☐ Midwest
☐ Central
☐ Local to Office
☐ Other Geo Pref

KLEINER PERKINS CAUFIELD AND BYERS

Four Embarcadero Center
Suite 1880
San Francisco CA 94111-4106

Phone (415) 421-3110   Fax (415) 421-3128

PROFESSIONALS	TITLE
Frank J. Caufield	Partner
Thomas J. Perkins	Partner

INDUSTRY PREFERENCE

☒ INFORMATION INDUSTRY	☒ BASIC INDUSTRIES	
☒ Communications	☐ Consumer	
☒ Computer Equipment	☐ Distribution	
☒ Computer Services	☐ Manufacturing	
☒ Computer Components	☐ Retail	
☐ Computer Entertainment	☒ Service	
☒ Computer Education	☐ Wholesale	
☒ Information Technologies	☐ SPECIFIC INDUSTRIES	
☒ Computer Media	☐ Energy	
☒ Software	☐ Environmental	
☒ Internet	☐ Financial	
☒ MEDICAL/HEALTHCARE	☐ Real Estate	
☒ Biotechnology	☐ Transportation	
☒ Healthcare Services	☐ Publishing	
☒ Life Sciences	☐ Food	
☒ Medical Products	☐ Franchises	
☐ INDUSTRIAL	☒ DIVERSIFIED	
☐ Advanced Materials	☐ MISCELLANEOUS	
☐ Chemicals		
☐ Instruments & Controls		

STAGE PREFERENCE

☒ EARLY STAGE
☒ Seed
☒ Start-up
☒ 1st Stage
☒ LATER STAGE
☒ 2nd Stage
☐ Mature
☐ Mezzanine
☐ LBO/MBO
☐ Turnaround
☐ INT'L EXPANSION
☐ WILL CONSIDER ALL
☐ VENTURE LEASING

Other Locations: Menlo Park CA

Affiliation:
Minimum Investment: Less than $1 Million
Capital Under Management: $100 to $500 Million

GEOGRAPHIC PREF

☐ East Coast
☒ West Coast
☐ Northeast
☐ Mid Atlantic
☐ Gulf States
☐ Northwest
☐ Southeast
☐ Southwest
☐ Midwest
☐ Central
☐ Local to Office
☐ Other Geo Pref

KLINE HAWKES CALIFORNIA SBIC, LP

11726 San Vicente Boulevard
Suite 300
Los Angeles CA 90049

Phone (310) 442-4700   Fax (310) 442-4707

PROFESSIONALS	TITLE
Frank R. Kline	Managing Partner
Jay Ferguson	Partner

INDUSTRY PREFERENCE

☒ INFORMATION INDUSTRY	☐ BASIC INDUSTRIES	
☒ Communications	☐ Consumer	
☒ Computer Equipment	☐ Distribution	
☒ Computer Services	☐ Manufacturing	
☒ Computer Components	☐ Retail	
☐ Computer Entertainment	☐ Service	
☒ Computer Education	☐ Wholesale	
☒ Information Technologies	☐ SPECIFIC INDUSTRIES	
☒ Computer Media	☐ Energy	
☒ Software	☐ Environmental	
☒ Internet	☐ Financial	
☒ MEDICAL/HEALTHCARE	☐ Real Estate	
☒ Biotechnology	☐ Transportation	
☒ Healthcare Services	☐ Publishing	
☒ Life Sciences	☐ Food	
☒ Medical Products	☐ Franchises	
☐ INDUSTRIAL	☒ DIVERSIFIED	
☐ Advanced Materials	☐ MISCELLANEOUS	
☐ Chemicals		
☐ Instruments & Controls		

STAGE PREFERENCE

☐ EARLY STAGE
☐ Seed
☐ Start-up
☐ 1st Stage
☒ LATER STAGE
☐ 2nd Stage
☐ Mature
☒ Mezzanine
☒ LBO/MBO
☒ Turnaround
☐ INT'L EXPANSION
☐ WILL CONSIDER ALL
☒ VENTURE LEASING

SBIC
Other Locations:

Affiliation:
Minimum Investment: $1 Million or more
Capital Under Management: $100 to $500 Million

GEOGRAPHIC PREF

☐ East Coast
☒ West Coast
☐ Northeast
☐ Mid Atlantic
☐ Gulf States
☐ Northwest
☐ Southeast
☐ Southwest
☐ Midwest
☐ Central
☐ Local to Office
☐ Other Geo Pref

LEVINE LEICHTMAN CAPITAL PARTNERS

335 N. Maple Drive
Suite 240
Beverly Hills CA 90210

Phone (310) 275-5335   Fax (310) 275-1441

PROFESSIONALS	TITLE
Arthur Levine	President
Lauren Leichtman	CEO
Stephen Hogan	
Mark Mickelson	
Robert Foletti	
Steven Hartman	
Mark Sampson	
Anna Halloran	
Lewis Schoenwetter	

INDUSTRY PREFERENCE

- ☐ INFORMATION INDUSTRY
- ☐ Communications
- ☐ Computer Equipment
- ☐ Computer Services
- ☐ Computer Components
- ☐ Computer Entertainment
- ☐ Computer Education
- ☐ Information Technologies
- ☐ Computer Media
- ☐ Software
- ☐ Internet
- ☐ MEDICAL/HEALTHCARE
- ☐ Biotechnology
- ☐ Healthcare Services
- ☐ Life Sciences
- ☐ Medical Products
- ☐ INDUSTRIAL
- ☐ Advanced Materials
- ☐ Chemicals
- ☐ Instruments & Controls

- ☐ BASIC INDUSTRIES
- ☐ Consumer
- ☐ Distribution
- ☐ Manufacturing
- ☐ Retail
- ☐ Service
- ☐ Wholesale
- ☐ SPECIFIC INDUSTRIES
- ☐ Energy
- ☐ Environmental
- ☐ Financial
- ☐ Real Estate
- ☐ Transportation
- ☐ Publishing
- ☐ Food
- ☐ Franchises
- ☒ DIVERSIFIED
- ☒ MISCELLANEOUS

STAGE PREFERENCE

- ☐ EARLY STAGE
- ☐ Seed
- ☐ Start-up
- ☐ 1st Stage
- ☒ LATER STAGE
- ☒ 2nd Stage
- ☒ Mature
- ☒ Mezzanine
- ☒ LBO/MBO
- ☐ Turnaround
- ☐ INT'L EXPANSION
- ☐ WILL CONSIDER ALL
- ☐ VENTURE LEASING

Other Locations:

Affiliation:
Minimum Investment: $1 Million or more
Capital Under Management: $100 to $500 Million

GEOGRAPHIC PREF

- ☐ East Coast
- ☒ West Coast
- ☐ Northeast
- ☐ Mid Atlantic
- ☐ Gulf States
- ☐ Northwest
- ☐ Southeast
- ☐ Southwest
- ☐ Midwest
- ☐ Central
- ☐ Local to Office
- ☐ Other Geo Pref

LF VENTURE CAPITAL

360 Post Street
Suite 705
San Francisco CA 94108

Phone (415) 399-0110   Fax (415) 399-9222

PROFESSIONALS	TITLE
Michael Hsieh	President
Harrison Chang	Vice President

INDUSTRY PREFERENCE

- ☐ INFORMATION INDUSTRY
- ☐ Communications
- ☐ Computer Equipment
- ☐ Computer Services
- ☐ Computer Components
- ☐ Computer Entertainment
- ☐ Computer Education
- ☐ Information Technologies
- ☐ Computer Media
- ☐ Software
- ☐ Internet
- ☐ MEDICAL/HEALTHCARE
- ☐ Biotechnology
- ☐ Healthcare Services
- ☐ Life Sciences
- ☐ Medical Products
- ☐ INDUSTRIAL
- ☐ Advanced Materials
- ☐ Chemicals
- ☐ Instruments & Controls

- ☒ BASIC INDUSTRIES
- ☒ Consumer
- ☐ Distribution
- ☐ Manufacturing
- ☐ Retail
- ☐ Service
- ☐ Wholesale
- ☐ SPECIFIC INDUSTRIES
- ☐ Energy
- ☐ Environmental
- ☐ Financial
- ☐ Real Estate
- ☐ Transportation
- ☐ Publishing
- ☐ Food
- ☐ Franchises
- ☐ DIVERSIFIED
- ☒ MISCELLANEOUS

STAGE PREFERENCE

- ☐ EARLY STAGE
- ☐ Seed
- ☐ Start-up
- ☐ 1st Stage
- ☒ LATER STAGE
- ☐ 2nd Stage
- ☐ Mature
- ☒ Mezzanine
- ☒ LBO/MBO
- ☒ Turnaround
- ☒ INT'L EXPANSION
- ☐ WILL CONSIDER ALL
- ☒ VENTURE LEASING

Other Locations:

Affiliation:
Minimum Investment: $1 Million or more
Capital Under Management: Less than $100 Million

GEOGRAPHIC PREF

- ☐ East Coast
- ☐ West Coast
- ☐ Northeast
- ☐ Mid Atlantic
- ☐ Gulf States
- ☐ Northwest
- ☐ Southeast
- ☐ Southwest
- ☐ Midwest
- ☐ Central
- ☐ Local to Office
- ☐ Other Geo Pref

MARWIT CAPITAL, LLC

180 Newport Center Drive
Suite 200
Newport Beach CA 92660

Phone (949) 640-6234   Fax (949) 720-8077

PROFESSIONALS	TITLE
Matthew L. Witte	Principal
Chris L. Britt	Principal
Tom Windser	Principal

INDUSTRY PREFERENCE

☒ INFORMATION INDUSTRY	☒ BASIC INDUSTRIES
☒ Communications	☐ Consumer
☐ Computer Equipment	☒ Distribution
☐ Computer Services	☒ Manufacturing
☐ Computer Components	☐ Retail
☐ Computer Entertainment	☐ Service
☐ Computer Education	☒ Wholesale
☐ Information Technologies	☐ SPECIFIC INDUSTRIES
☐ Computer Media	☐ Energy
☒ Software	☐ Environmental
☒ Internet	☐ Financial
☐ MEDICAL/HEALTHCARE	☐ Real Estate
☐ Biotechnology	☐ Transportation
☐ Healthcare Services	☐ Publishing
☐ Life Sciences	☐ Food
☐ Medical Products	☐ Franchises
☐ INDUSTRIAL	☒ DIVERSIFIED
☐ Advanced Materials	☐ MISCELLANEOUS
☐ Chemicals	
☐ Instruments & Controls	

STAGE PREFERENCE

☐ EARLY STAGE
☐ Seed
☐ Start-up
☐ 1st Stage
☒ LATER STAGE
☒ 2nd Stage
☒ Mature
☒ Mezzanine
☒ LBO/MBO
☐ Turnaround
☐ INT'L EXPANSION
☐ WILL CONSIDER ALL
☐ VENTURE LEASING

SBIC
Other Locations:

Affiliation:
Minimum Investment: Less than $1 Million
Capital Under Management: Less than $100 Million

GEOGRAPHIC PREF

☐ East Coast
☐ West Coast
☐ Northeast
☐ Mid Atlantic
☐ Gulf States
☐ Northwest
☐ Southeast
☐ Southwest
☐ Midwest
☐ Central
☐ Local to Office
☐ Other Geo Pref

MATRIX PARTNERS

2500 Sand Hill Road
Suite 113
Menlo Park CA 94025

Phone (650) 854-3131   Fax (650) 854-3296

PROFESSIONALS	TITLE
Andrew Verhalen	General Partner
Mark Vershal	General Partner

INDUSTRY PREFERENCE

☒ INFORMATION INDUSTRY	☐ BASIC INDUSTRIES
☒ Communications	☐ Consumer
☒ Computer Equipment	☐ Distribution
☒ Computer Services	☐ Manufacturing
☒ Computer Components	☐ Retail
☐ Computer Entertainment	☐ Service
☒ Computer Education	☐ Wholesale
☒ Information Technologies	☐ SPECIFIC INDUSTRIES
☐ Computer Media	☐ Energy
☒ Software	☐ Environmental
☒ Internet	☐ Financial
☐ MEDICAL/HEALTHCARE	☐ Real Estate
☐ Biotechnology	☐ Transportation
☐ Healthcare Services	☐ Publishing
☐ Life Sciences	☐ Food
☐ Medical Products	☐ Franchises
☐ INDUSTRIAL	☐ DIVERSIFIED
☐ Advanced Materials	☒ MISCELLANEOUS
☐ Chemicals	
☐ Instruments & Controls	

STAGE PREFERENCE

☒ EARLY STAGE
☒ Seed
☒ Start-up
☒ 1st Stage
☒ LATER STAGE
☒ 2nd Stage
☒ Mature
☒ Mezzanine
☒ LBO/MBO
☐ Turnaround
☐ INT'L EXPANSION
☐ WILL CONSIDER ALL
☐ VENTURE LEASING

Other Locations: Waltham MA

Affiliation:
Minimum Investment: Less than $1 Million
Capital Under Management: $100 to $500 Million

GEOGRAPHIC PREF

☐ East Coast
☐ West Coast
☐ Northeast
☐ Mid Atlantic
☐ Gulf States
☐ Northwest
☐ Southeast
☐ Southwest
☐ Midwest
☐ Central
☐ Local to Office
☐ Other Geo Pref

MAYFIELD FUND

**2800 Sand Hill Road
Suite 250
Menlo Park CA 94025**

Phone (650) 854-5560   Fax (650) 854-5712

PROFESSIONALS	TITLE
Yogen Dalal	General Partner
Kevin Fong	General Partner
A. Grant Hedrich III	General Partner
Michael Levinthal	General Partner
F. Gibson Myers, Jr.	General Partner
William Unger	General Partner
Wendell Van Auken	General Partner
Wende Hutton	General Partner
Russell C. Hirsch	General Partner

INDUSTRY PREFERENCE

- ☒ INFORMATION INDUSTRY
- ☒ Communications
- ☒ Computer Equipment
- ☒ Computer Services
- ☒ Computer Components
- ☐ Computer Entertainment
- ☒ Computer Education
- ☒ Information Technologies
- ☒ Computer Media
- ☒ Software
- ☒ Internet
- ☒ MEDICAL/HEALTHCARE
- ☒ Biotechnology
- ☒ Healthcare Services
- ☒ Life Sciences
- ☒ Medical Products
- ☐ INDUSTRIAL
- ☐ Advanced Materials
- ☐ Chemicals
- ☐ Instruments & Controls

- ☒ BASIC INDUSTRIES
- ☒ Consumer
- ☐ Distribution
- ☐ Manufacturing
- ☐ Retail
- ☒ Service
- ☐ Wholesale
- ☐ SPECIFIC INDUSTRIES
- ☐ Energy
- ☐ Environmental
- ☐ Financial
- ☐ Real Estate
- ☐ Transportation
- ☐ Publishing
- ☐ Food
- ☐ Franchises
- ☒ DIVERSIFIED
- ☐ MISCELLANEOUS

STAGE PREFERENCE

- ☒ EARLY STAGE
- ☒ Seed
- ☒ Start-up
- ☒ 1st Stage
- ☐ LATER STAGE
- ☒ 2nd Stage
- ☐ Mature
- ☐ Mezzanine
- ☐ LBO/MBO
- ☐ Turnaround
- ☐ INT'L EXPANSION
- ☐ WILL CONSIDER ALL
- ☐ VENTURE LEASING

Other Locations:

Affiliation:
Minimum Investment: Less than $1 Million
Capital Under Management: Over $500 Million

GEOGRAPHIC PREF

- ☐ East Coast
- ☒ West Coast
- ☐ Northeast
- ☐ Mid Atlantic
- ☐ Gulf States
- ☐ Northwest
- ☐ Southeast
- ☐ Southwest
- ☐ Midwest
- ☐ Central
- ☐ Local to Office
- ☐ Other Geo Pref

MCCOWN DE LEEUW AND COMPANY

**3000 Sand Hill Road
Building Three, Suite 290
Menlo Park CA 94025**

Phone (650) 854-6000   Fax (650) 854-0853

PROFESSIONALS	TITLE
George E. McCown	Managing Director
Robert B. Hellman	Managing Director
Steven A. Zuckerman	Managing Director
Phil Collins	Managing Director

INDUSTRY PREFERENCE

- ☐ INFORMATION INDUSTRY
- ☐ Communications
- ☐ Computer Equipment
- ☐ Computer Services
- ☐ Computer Components
- ☐ Computer Entertainment
- ☐ Computer Education
- ☐ Information Technologies
- ☐ Computer Media
- ☐ Software
- ☐ Internet
- ☐ MEDICAL/HEALTHCARE
- ☐ Biotechnology
- ☐ Healthcare Services
- ☐ Life Sciences
- ☐ Medical Products
- ☐ INDUSTRIAL
- ☐ Advanced Materials
- ☐ Chemicals
- ☐ Instruments & Controls

- ☒ BASIC INDUSTRIES
- ☒ Consumer
- ☒ Distribution
- ☒ Manufacturing
- ☒ Retail
- ☒ Service
- ☐ Wholesale
- ☒ SPECIFIC INDUSTRIES
- ☐ Energy
- ☐ Environmental
- ☒ Financial
- ☐ Real Estate
- ☐ Transportation
- ☐ Publishing
- ☐ Food
- ☐ Franchises
- ☒ DIVERSIFIED
- ☐ MISCELLANEOUS

STAGE PREFERENCE

- ☐ EARLY STAGE
- ☐ Seed
- ☐ Start-up
- ☐ 1st Stage
- ☒ LATER STAGE
- ☒ 2nd Stage
- ☒ Mature
- ☐ Mezzanine
- ☒ LBO/MBO
- ☒ Turnaround
- ☐ INT'L EXPANSION
- ☐ WILL CONSIDER ALL
- ☒ VENTURE LEASING

Other Locations: New York NY

Affiliation:
Minimum Investment: $1 Million or more
Capital Under Management: Over $500 Million

GEOGRAPHIC PREF

- ☐ East Coast
- ☐ West Coast
- ☐ Northeast
- ☐ Mid Atlantic
- ☐ Gulf States
- ☐ Northwest
- ☐ Southeast
- ☐ Southwest
- ☐ Midwest
- ☐ Central
- ☐ Local to Office
- ☐ Other Geo Pref

MEDIA TECHNOLOGY VENTURES

One First Street
Suite Two
Los Altos CA 94022

Phone (650) 917-5900   Fax (650) 917-5901

PROFESSIONALS	TITLE
Barry Weinman	Managing Director

INDUSTRY PREFERENCE

☒ INFORMATION INDUSTRY	☐ BASIC INDUSTRIES
☒ Communications	☐ Consumer
☒ Computer Equipment	☐ Distribution
☒ Computer Services	☐ Manufacturing
☒ Computer Components	☐ Retail
☐ Computer Entertainment	☐ Service
☐ Computer Education	☐ Wholesale
☒ Information Technologies	☐ SPECIFIC INDUSTRIES
☐ Computer Media	☐ Energy
☒ Software	☐ Environmental
☒ Internet	☐ Financial
☒ MEDICAL/HEALTHCARE	☐ Real Estate
☒ Biotechnology	☐ Transportation
☒ Healthcare Services	☐ Publishing
☒ Life Sciences	☐ Food
☒ Medical Products	☐ Franchises
☒ INDUSTRIAL	☒ DIVERSIFIED
☐ Advanced Materials	☒ MISCELLANEOUS
☐ Chemicals	
☒ Instruments & Controls	

STAGE PREFERENCE

☐ EARLY STAGE
☒ Seed
☒ Start-up
☒ 1st Stage
☐ LATER STAGE
☐ 2nd Stage
☐ Mature
☐ Mezzanine
☐ LBO/MBO
☐ Turnaround
☐ INT'L EXPANSION
☐ WILL CONSIDER ALL
☐ VENTURE LEASING

Other Locations: Los Angeles CA, San Francisco CA

Affiliation:
Minimum Investment: $1 Million or more
Capital Under Management: $100 to $500 Million

GEOGRAPHIC PREF

☐ East Coast
☒ West Coast
☐ Northeast
☐ Mid Atlantic
☐ Gulf States
☐ Northwest
☐ Southeast
☐ Southwest
☐ Midwest
☐ Central
☐ Local to Office
☐ Other Geo Pref

MEDIA TECHNOLOGY VENTURES

746 W. Adams Boulevard
Los Angeles CA 90089

Phone (213) 743-2938   Fax (213) 745-7255

PROFESSIONALS	TITLE
Jonathan Funk	General Partner

INDUSTRY PREFERENCE

☒ INFORMATION INDUSTRY	☐ BASIC INDUSTRIES
☒ Communications	☐ Consumer
☒ Computer Equipment	☐ Distribution
☒ Computer Services	☐ Manufacturing
☒ Computer Components	☐ Retail
☐ Computer Entertainment	☐ Service
☐ Computer Education	☐ Wholesale
☒ Information Technologies	☐ SPECIFIC INDUSTRIES
☐ Computer Media	☐ Energy
☒ Software	☐ Environmental
☒ Internet	☐ Financial
☒ MEDICAL/HEALTHCARE	☐ Real Estate
☒ Biotechnology	☐ Transportation
☒ Healthcare Services	☐ Publishing
☒ Life Sciences	☐ Food
☒ Medical Products	☐ Franchises
☒ INDUSTRIAL	☒ DIVERSIFIED
☐ Advanced Materials	☒ MISCELLANEOUS
☐ Chemicals	
☒ Instruments & Controls	

STAGE PREFERENCE

☒ EARLY STAGE
☒ Seed
☒ Start-up
☒ 1st Stage
☐ LATER STAGE
☐ 2nd Stage
☐ Mature
☐ Mezzanine
☐ LBO/MBO
☐ Turnaround
☐ INT'L EXPANSION
☐ WILL CONSIDER ALL
☐ VENTURE LEASING

Other Locations: Los Altos CA, San Francisco CA

Affiliation:
Minimum Investment: $1 Million or more
Capital Under Management: $100 to $500 Million

GEOGRAPHIC PREF

☐ East Coast
☒ West Coast
☐ Northeast
☐ Mid Atlantic
☐ Gulf States
☐ Northwest
☐ Southeast
☐ Southwest
☐ Midwest
☐ Central
☐ Local to Office
☐ Other Geo Pref

MEDIA TECHNOLOGY VENTURES

185 Berry Street
Suite 3600
San Francisco CA 94107

Phone (415) 977-0500   Fax (415) 977-0502

PROFESSIONALS	TITLE
Robert Ackerman, Jr.	General Partner

INDUSTRY PREFERENCE

☒ INFORMATION INDUSTRY	☐ BASIC INDUSTRIES
☒ Communications	☐ Consumer
☒ Computer Equipment	☐ Distribution
☒ Computer Services	☐ Manufacturing
☒ Computer Components	☐ Retail
☐ Computer Entertainment	☐ Service
☐ Computer Education	☐ Wholesale
☒ Information Technologies	☒ SPECIFIC INDUSTRIES
☐ Computer Media	☐ Energy
☒ Software	☐ Environmental
☒ Internet	☐ Financial
☒ MEDICAL/HEALTHCARE	☐ Real Estate
☒ Biotechnology	☐ Transportation
☒ Healthcare Services	☐ Publishing
☒ Life Sciences	☐ Food
☒ Medical Products	☐ Franchises
☒ INDUSTRIAL	☒ DIVERSIFIED
☐ Advanced Materials	☒ MISCELLANEOUS
☐ Chemicals	
☒ Instruments & Controls	

STAGE PREFERENCE

☒ EARLY STAGE
☒ Seed
☒ Start-up
☒ 1st Stage
☐ LATER STAGE
☐ 2nd Stage
☐ Mature
☐ Mezzanine
☐ LBO/MBO
☐ Turnaround
☐ INT'L EXPANSION
☐ WILL CONSIDER ALL
☐ VENTURE LEASING

Other Locations: Los Angeles CA, Los Altos CA

Affiliation:
Minimum Investment: $1 Million or more
Capital Under Management: $100 to $500 Million

GEOGRAPHIC PREF

☐ East Coast
☒ West Coast
☐ Northeast
☐ Mid Atlantic
☐ Gulf States
☐ Northwest
☐ Southeast
☐ Southwest
☐ Midwest
☐ Central
☐ Local to Office
☐ Other Geo Pref

MEDICUS VENTURE PARTNERS

2882 Sand Hill Road
Suite 116
Menlo Park CA 94025

Phone (650) 854-7100   Fax (650) 854-5700

PROFESSIONALS	TITLE
John M. Reher	General Partner
Frederick J. Dotzler	General Partner

INDUSTRY PREFERENCE

☐ INFORMATION INDUSTRY	☒ BASIC INDUSTRIES
☐ Communications	☐ Consumer
☐ Computer Equipment	☐ Distribution
☐ Computer Services	☐ Manufacturing
☐ Computer Components	☐ Retail
☐ Computer Entertainment	☒ Service
☐ Computer Education	☐ Wholesale
☐ Information Technologies	☐ SPECIFIC INDUSTRIES
☐ Computer Media	☐ Energy
☐ Software	☐ Environmental
☐ Internet	☐ Financial
☒ MEDICAL/HEALTHCARE	☐ Real Estate
☒ Biotechnology	☐ Transportation
☒ Healthcare Services	☐ Publishing
☐ Life Sciences	☐ Food
☒ Medical Products	☐ Franchises
☐ INDUSTRIAL	☒ DIVERSIFIED
☐ Advanced Materials	☐ MISCELLANEOUS
☐ Chemicals	
☐ Instruments & Controls	

STAGE PREFERENCE

☒ EARLY STAGE
☒ Seed
☒ Start-up
☐ 1st Stage
☐ LATER STAGE
☐ 2nd Stage
☐ Mature
☐ Mezzanine
☐ LBO/MBO
☐ Turnaround
☐ INT'L EXPANSION
☐ WILL CONSIDER ALL
☐ VENTURE LEASING

Other Locations:

Affiliation: Hillman Partnership
Minimum Investment: Less than $1 Million
Capital Under Management: Less than $100 Million

GEOGRAPHIC PREF

☐ East Coast
☒ West Coast
☐ Northeast
☐ Mid Atlantic
☐ Gulf States
☐ Northwest
☐ Southeast
☐ Southwest
☐ Midwest
☐ Central
☐ Local to Office
☐ Other Geo Pref

MEDVENTURE ASSOCIATES

Four Orinda Way
Building D Suite 150
Orinda CA 94563

Phone (925) 253-0155   Fax (925) 253-0156

PROFESSIONALS	TITLE
Annette Campbell-White	Managing General Partner
George Choi	General Partner
Gary Stroy	Partner

INDUSTRY PREFERENCE

- ☐ INFORMATION INDUSTRY
- ☐ Communications
- ☐ Computer Equipment
- ☐ Computer Services
- ☐ Computer Components
- ☐ Computer Entertainment
- ☐ Computer Education
- ☐ Information Technologies
- ☐ Computer Media
- ☐ Software
- ☐ Internet
- ☒ MEDICAL/HEALTHCARE
- ☒ Biotechnology
- ☒ Healthcare Services
- ☒ Life Sciences
- ☒ Medical Products
- ☐ INDUSTRIAL
- ☐ Advanced Materials
- ☐ Chemicals
- ☐ Instruments & Controls

- ☐ BASIC INDUSTRIES
- ☐ Consumer
- ☐ Distribution
- ☐ Manufacturing
- ☐ Retail
- ☐ Service
- ☐ Wholesale
- ☐ SPECIFIC INDUSTRIES
- ☐ Energy
- ☐ Environmental
- ☐ Financial
- ☐ Real Estate
- ☐ Transportation
- ☐ Publishing
- ☐ Food
- ☐ Franchises
- ☐ DIVERSIFIED
- ☒ MISCELLANEOUS

STAGE PREFERENCE

- ☒ EARLY STAGE
- ☒ Seed
- ☒ Start-up
- ☒ 1st Stage
- ☒ LATER STAGE
- ☒ 2nd Stage
- ☒ Mature
- ☐ Mezzanine
- ☐ LBO/MBO
- ☐ Turnaround
- ☐ INT'L EXPANSION
- ☐ WILL CONSIDER ALL
- ☐ VENTURE LEASING

Other Locations:

Affiliation:
Minimum Investment: Less than $1 Million
Capital Under Management: $100 to $500 Million

GEOGRAPHIC PREF

- ☐ East Coast
- ☒ West Coast
- ☐ Northeast
- ☐ Mid Atlantic
- ☐ Gulf States
- ☒ Northwest
- ☐ Southeast
- ☒ Southwest
- ☐ Midwest
- ☐ Central
- ☐ Local to Office
- ☐ Other Geo Pref

MEIER MITCHELL & CO.

Four Orinda Way
Suite 200B
Orinda CA 94563

Phone (925) 254-9520   Fax (925) 254-9528

PROFESSIONALS	TITLE
Lee Meier	Managing Director
James Mitchell	Managing Director
Ms. Patricia Leicher	Managing Director

INDUSTRY PREFERENCE

- ☒ INFORMATION INDUSTRY
- ☒ Communications
- ☒ Computer Equipment
- ☒ Computer Services
- ☒ Computer Components
- ☒ Computer Entertainment
- ☒ Computer Education
- ☒ Information Technologies
- ☒ Computer Media
- ☒ Software
- ☒ Internet
- ☒ MEDICAL/HEALTHCARE
- ☒ Biotechnology
- ☒ Healthcare Services
- ☒ Life Sciences
- ☒ Medical Products
- ☒ INDUSTRIAL
- ☒ Advanced Materials
- ☒ Chemicals
- ☒ Instruments & Controls

- ☒ BASIC INDUSTRIES
- ☐ Consumer
- ☐ Distribution
- ☐ Manufacturing
- ☐ Retail
- ☒ Service
- ☐ Wholesale
- ☒ SPECIFIC INDUSTRIES
- ☒ Energy
- ☒ Environmental
- ☐ Financial
- ☐ Real Estate
- ☐ Transportation
- ☐ Publishing
- ☐ Food
- ☐ Franchises
- ☒ DIVERSIFIED
- ☐ MISCELLANEOUS

STAGE PREFERENCE

- ☒ EARLY STAGE
- ☒ Seed
- ☒ Start-up
- ☒ 1st Stage
- ☐ LATER STAGE
- ☐ 2nd Stage
- ☐ Mature
- ☐ Mezzanine
- ☐ LBO/MBO
- ☐ Turnaround
- ☐ INT'L EXPANSION
- ☐ WILL CONSIDER ALL
- ☐ VENTURE LEASING

Other Locations:

Affiliation:
Minimum Investment: Less than $1 Million
Capital Under Management: Less than $100 Million

GEOGRAPHIC PREF

- ☐ East Coast
- ☐ West Coast
- ☐ Northeast
- ☐ Mid Atlantic
- ☐ Gulf States
- ☐ Northwest
- ☐ Southeast
- ☐ Southwest
- ☐ Midwest
- ☐ Central
- ☐ Local to Office
- ☐ Other Geo Pref

MELLON VENTURES, INC.

Mellon Bank Center
400 Hope Street, 5th Floor
Los Angeles CA 90071-2806

Phone (213) 553-9685   Fax (213) 553-9690

PROFESSIONALS	TITLE
John Geer	Managing Director
Jeffery Anderson	Principal
Mark Patton	Associate

INDUSTRY PREFERENCE

- [x] INFORMATION INDUSTRY
- [x] Communications
- [x] Computer Equipment
- [x] Computer Services
- [x] Computer Components
- [x] Computer Entertainment
- [x] Computer Education
- [x] Information Technologies
- [x] Computer Media
- [x] Software
- [x] Internet
- [x] MEDICAL/HEALTHCARE
- [ ] Biotechnology
- [x] Healthcare Services
- [ ] Life Sciences
- [ ] Medical Products
- [x] INDUSTRIAL
- [x] Advanced Materials
- [x] Chemicals
- [x] Instruments & Controls

- [x] BASIC INDUSTRIES
- [x] Consumer
- [x] Distribution
- [x] Manufacturing
- [x] Retail
- [x] Service
- [x] Wholesale
- [x] SPECIFIC INDUSTRIES
- [ ] Energy
- [ ] Environmental
- [x] Financial
- [ ] Real Estate
- [x] Transportation
- [ ] Publishing
- [ ] Food
- [ ] Franchises
- [x] DIVERSIFIED
- [x] MISCELLANEOUS

STAGE PREFERENCE

- [ ] EARLY STAGE
- [ ] Seed
- [ ] Start-up
- [ ] 1st Stage
- [x] LATER STAGE
- [ ] 2nd Stage
- [ ] Mature
- [x] Mezzanine
- [x] LBO/MBO
- [x] Turnaround
- [ ] INT'L EXPANSION
- [ ] WILL CONSIDER ALL
- [x] VENTURE LEASING

SBIC

Other Locations: Atlanta GA, Pittsburgh PA, Radnor PA

Affiliation: Mellon Bank, NA
Minimum Investment: $1 Million or more
Capital Under Management: Less than $100 Million

GEOGRAPHIC PREF

- [ ] East Coast
- [ ] West Coast
- [ ] Northeast
- [ ] Mid Atlantic
- [ ] Gulf States
- [ ] Northwest
- [ ] Southeast
- [ ] Southwest
- [ ] Midwest
- [ ] Central
- [ ] Local to Office
- [ ] Other Geo Pref

MENLO VENTURES

3000 Sand Hill Road
Building Four, Suite 100
Menlo Park CA 94025

Phone (650) 854-8540   Fax (650) 854-7059

PROFESSIONALS	TITLE
Douglas C. Carlisle	General Partner
H. DuBose Montgomery	General Partner
Thomas H. Bredt	General Partner
Dr. Michael Laufer	General Partner
John W. Jarve	General Partner
Sonja L. Hoel	General Partner

INDUSTRY PREFERENCE

- [x] INFORMATION INDUSTRY
- [x] Communications
- [x] Computer Equipment
- [x] Computer Services
- [x] Computer Components
- [x] Computer Entertainment
- [ ] Computer Education
- [x] Information Technologies
- [x] Computer Media
- [x] Software
- [x] Internet
- [x] MEDICAL/HEALTHCARE
- [x] Biotechnology
- [x] Healthcare Services
- [x] Life Sciences
- [x] Medical Products
- [ ] INDUSTRIAL
- [ ] Advanced Materials
- [ ] Chemicals
- [ ] Instruments & Controls

- [x] BASIC INDUSTRIES
- [ ] Consumer
- [ ] Distribution
- [ ] Manufacturing
- [ ] Retail
- [x] Service
- [ ] Wholesale
- [ ] SPECIFIC INDUSTRIES
- [ ] Energy
- [ ] Environmental
- [ ] Financial
- [ ] Real Estate
- [ ] Transportation
- [ ] Publishing
- [ ] Food
- [ ] Franchises
- [x] DIVERSIFIED
- [ ] MISCELLANEOUS

STAGE PREFERENCE

- [x] EARLY STAGE
- [ ] Seed
- [x] Start-up
- [x] 1st Stage
- [x] LATER STAGE
- [x] 2nd Stage
- [x] Mature
- [x] Mezzanine
- [x] LBO/MBO
- [ ] Turnaround
- [ ] INT'L EXPANSION
- [ ] WILL CONSIDER ALL
- [ ] VENTURE LEASING

Other Locations:

Affiliation:
Minimum Investment: $1 Million or more
Capital Under Management: Over $500 Million

GEOGRAPHIC PREF

- [ ] East Coast
- [ ] West Coast
- [ ] Northeast
- [ ] Mid Atlantic
- [ ] Gulf States
- [ ] Northwest
- [ ] Southeast
- [ ] Southwest
- [ ] Midwest
- [ ] Central
- [ ] Local to Office
- [ ] Other Geo Pref

MISSION VENTURES

**11512 El Camino Real
Suite 215
San Diego CA 92130-2046**

Phone (858) 259-0100 Fax (858) 259-0112

PROFESSIONALS	TITLE
David Holder	Venture Partner
Robert Kibble	Managing Director
David Ryan	Managing Director
Jeff Starr	Entreprenuer in Residence

INDUSTRY PREFERENCE

☒ INFORMATION INDUSTRY	☒ BASIC INDUSTRIES
☒ Communications	☐ Consumer
☒ Computer Equipment	☒ Distribution
☒ Computer Services	☐ Manufacturing
☒ Computer Components	☐ Retail
☐ Computer Entertainment	☐ Service
☐ Computer Education	☐ Wholesale
☐ Information Technologies	☐ SPECIFIC INDUSTRIES
☒ Computer Media	☐ Energy
☒ Software	☐ Environmental
☒ Internet	☐ Financial
☐ MEDICAL/HEALTHCARE	☐ Real Estate
☐ Biotechnology	☐ Transportation
☐ Healthcare Services	☐ Publishing
☐ Life Sciences	☐ Food
☐ Medical Products	☐ Franchises
☐ INDUSTRIAL	☒ DIVERSIFIED
☐ Advanced Materials	☒ MISCELLANEOUS
☐ Chemicals	
☐ Instruments & Controls	

STAGE PREFERENCE

☒ EARLY STAGE
☒ Seed
☒ Start-up
☒ 1st Stage
☒ LATER STAGE
☒ 2nd Stage
☐ Mature
☐ Mezzanine
☐ LBO/MBO
☐ Turnaround
☐ INT'L EXPANSION
☐ WILL CONSIDER ALL
☐ VENTURE LEASING

Other Locations:

Affiliation:
Minimum Investment: Less than $1 Million
Capital Under Management: Less than $100 Million

GEOGRAPHIC PREF

☐ East Coast
☐ West Coast
☐ Northeast
☐ Mid Atlantic
☐ Gulf States
☐ Northwest
☐ Southeast
☐ Southwest
☐ Midwest
☐ Central
☐ Local to Office
☐ Other Geo Pref

MK GLOBAL VENTURES

**2471 East Bayshore
Suite 520
Palo Alto CA 94303**

Phone (650) 424-0151 Fax (650) 494-2753

PROFESSIONALS	TITLE
Michael Kaufman	Managing General Partner

INDUSTRY PREFERENCE

☒ INFORMATION INDUSTRY	☒ BASIC INDUSTRIES
☒ Communications	☐ Consumer
☒ Computer Equipment	☐ Distribution
☒ Computer Services	☐ Manufacturing
☒ Computer Components	☐ Retail
☐ Computer Entertainment	☒ Service
☒ Computer Education	☐ Wholesale
☒ Information Technologies	☐ SPECIFIC INDUSTRIES
☒ Computer Media	☐ Energy
☒ Software	☐ Environmental
☒ Internet	☐ Financial
☒ MEDICAL/HEALTHCARE	☐ Real Estate
☒ Biotechnology	☐ Transportation
☒ Healthcare Services	☐ Publishing
☒ Life Sciences	☐ Food
☒ Medical Products	☐ Franchises
☒ INDUSTRIAL	☒ DIVERSIFIED
☒ Advanced Materials	☐ MISCELLANEOUS
☒ Chemicals	
☒ Instruments & Controls	

STAGE PREFERENCE

☒ EARLY STAGE
☒ Seed
☒ Start-up
☒ 1st Stage
☒ LATER STAGE
☒ 2nd Stage
☒ Mature
☒ Mezzanine
☒ LBO/MBO
☐ Turnaround
☐ INT'L EXPANSION
☐ WILL CONSIDER ALL
☐ VENTURE LEASING

Other Locations:

Affiliation:
Minimum Investment: Less than $1 Million
Capital Under Management: Less than $100 Million

GEOGRAPHIC PREF

☐ East Coast
☒ West Coast
☐ Northeast
☐ Mid Atlantic
☐ Gulf States
☐ Northwest
☐ Southeast
☐ Southwest
☐ Midwest
☐ Central
☐ Local to Office
☐ Other Geo Pref

MOHR, DAVIDOW VENTURES

2775 Sand Hill Road
Suite 240
Menlo Park CA 94025

Phone (650) 854-7236   Fax (650) 854-7365

PROFESSIONALS	TITLE
William H. Davidow	Partner
George Zachary	Partner
Jonathan D. Feiber	Partner
Ms. Nancy Schoendorf	Partner

INDUSTRY PREFERENCE

☒ INFORMATION INDUSTRY
☒ Communications
☒ Computer Equipment
☒ Computer Services
☒ Computer Components
☐ Computer Entertainment
☒ Computer Education
☒ Information Technologies
☐ Computer Media
☒ Software
☒ Internet
☒ MEDICAL/HEALTHCARE
☐ Biotechnology
☒ Healthcare Services
☒ Life Sciences
☒ Medical Products
☒ INDUSTRIAL
☒ Advanced Materials
☒ Chemicals
☒ Instruments & Controls

☒ BASIC INDUSTRIES
☐ Consumer
☐ Distribution
☐ Manufacturing
☐ Retail
☒ Service
☐ Wholesale
☐ SPECIFIC INDUSTRIES
☐ Energy
☐ Environmental
☐ Financial
☐ Real Estate
☐ Transportation
☐ Publishing
☐ Food
☐ Franchises
☒ DIVERSIFIED
☐ MISCELLANEOUS

STAGE PREFERENCE

☒ EARLY STAGE
☒ Seed
☒ Start-up
☐ 1st Stage
☐ LATER STAGE
☐ 2nd Stage
☐ Mature
☐ Mezzanine
☐ LBO/MBO
☐ Turnaround
☐ INT'L EXPANSION
☐ WILL CONSIDER ALL
☐ VENTURE LEASING

Other Locations:

Affiliation:
Minimum Investment: Less than $1 Million
Capital Under Management: $100 to $500 Million

GEOGRAPHIC PREF

☐ East Coast
☒ West Coast
☐ Northeast
☐ Mid Atlantic
☐ Gulf States
☐ Northwest
☐ Southeast
☐ Southwest
☐ Midwest
☐ Central
☐ Local to Office
☐ Other Geo Pref

MORGAN STANLEY DEAN WITTER VENTURE PARTNERS

3000 Sand Hill Road
Building 4, Suite 250
Menlo Park CA 94025

Phone (650) 233-2600   Fax (650) 233-2626

PROFESSIONALS	TITLE
William J. Harding	General Partner
Robert J. Loarie	General Partner
Scott S. Halsted	General Partner

INDUSTRY PREFERENCE

☒ INFORMATION INDUSTRY
☒ Communications
☒ Computer Equipment
☒ Computer Services
☒ Computer Components
☐ Computer Entertainment
☒ Computer Education
☒ Information Technologies
☒ Computer Media
☒ Software
☒ Internet
☒ MEDICAL/HEALTHCARE
☒ Biotechnology
☒ Healthcare Services
☒ Life Sciences
☒ Medical Products
☒ INDUSTRIAL
☐ Advanced Materials
☐ Chemicals
☒ Instruments & Controls

☒ BASIC INDUSTRIES
☒ Consumer
☐ Distribution
☐ Manufacturing
☒ Retail
☒ Service
☐ Wholesale
☐ SPECIFIC INDUSTRIES
☐ Energy
☐ Environmental
☐ Financial
☐ Real Estate
☐ Transportation
☐ Publishing
☐ Food
☐ Franchises
☒ DIVERSIFIED
☐ MISCELLANEOUS

STAGE PREFERENCE

☐ EARLY STAGE
☐ Seed
☐ Start-up
☐ 1st Stage
☒ LATER STAGE
☒ 2nd Stage
☒ Mature
☒ Mezzanine
☒ LBO/MBO
☒ Turnaround
☐ INT'L EXPANSION
☐ WILL CONSIDER ALL
☒ VENTURE LEASING

Other Locations: New York NY

Affiliation: Morgan Stanley & Co.
Minimum Investment: $1 Million or more
Capital Under Management: $100 to $500 Million

GEOGRAPHIC PREF

☐ East Coast
☐ West Coast
☐ Northeast
☐ Mid Atlantic
☐ Gulf States
☐ Northwest
☐ Southeast
☐ Southwest
☐ Midwest
☐ Central
☐ Local to Office
☐ Other Geo Pref

MORGENTHALER VENTURES

2730 Sand Hill Road
Suite 280
Menlo Park CA 94025

Phone (650) 388-7600   Fax (650) 388-7606

PROFESSIONALS	TITLE
G. Gary Shaffer	General Partner
Robert Bellas, Jr.	General Partner

INDUSTRY PREFERENCE

☒ INFORMATION INDUSTRY	☒ BASIC INDUSTRIES		
☒ Communications	☐ Consumer		
☒ Computer Equipment	☐ Distribution		
☒ Computer Services	☒ Manufacturing		
☒ Computer Components	☐ Retail		
☐ Computer Entertainment	☒ Service		
☒ Computer Education	☐ Wholesale		
☒ Information Technologies	☒ SPECIFIC INDUSTRIES		
☐ Computer Media	☐ Energy		
☒ Software	☐ Environmental		
☒ Internet	☐ Financial		
☒ MEDICAL/HEALTHCARE	☐ Real Estate		
☒ Biotechnology	☐ Transportation		
☒ Healthcare Services	☐ Publishing		
☒ Life Sciences	☐ Food		
☒ Medical Products	☐ Franchises		
☒ INDUSTRIAL	☒ DIVERSIFIED		
☐ Advanced Materials	☐ MISCELLANEOUS		
☐ Chemicals			
☒ Instruments & Controls			

STAGE PREFERENCE

☒ EARLY STAGE
☒ Seed
☒ Start-up
☒ 1st Stage
☒ LATER STAGE
☒ 2nd Stage
☒ Mature
☒ Mezzanine
☒ LBO/MBO
☐ Turnaround
☐ INT'L EXPANSION
☐ WILL CONSIDER ALL
☐ VENTURE LEASING

Other Locations: Cleveland OH

Affiliation:
Minimum Investment: $1 Million or more
Capital Under Management: $100 to $500 Million

GEOGRAPHIC PREF

☐ East Coast
☐ West Coast
☐ Northeast
☐ Mid Atlantic
☐ Gulf States
☐ Northwest
☐ Southeast
☐ Southwest
☐ Midwest
☐ Central
☐ Local to Office
☐ Other Geo Pref

NATIONAL INVESTMENT MANAGEMENT INC

2601 Airport Drive
Suite 210
Torrance CA 90505

Phone (310) 784-7600   Fax (310) 784-7605

PROFESSIONALS	TITLE
Richard Robins	President

INDUSTRY PREFERENCE

☒ INFORMATION INDUSTRY	☒ BASIC INDUSTRIES
☐ Communications	☐ Consumer
☐ Computer Equipment	☒ Distribution
☐ Computer Services	☒ Manufacturing
☐ Computer Components	☐ Retail
☐ Computer Entertainment	☐ Service
☐ Computer Education	☒ Wholesale
☐ Information Technologies	☒ SPECIFIC INDUSTRIES
☒ Computer Media	☐ Energy
☐ Software	☐ Environmental
☐ Internet	☐ Financial
☐ MEDICAL/HEALTHCARE	☐ Real Estate
☐ Biotechnology	☐ Transportation
☐ Healthcare Services	☐ Publishing
☐ Life Sciences	☐ Food
☐ Medical Products	☐ Franchises
☒ INDUSTRIAL	☒ DIVERSIFIED
☐ Advanced Materials	☒ MISCELLANEOUS
☒ Chemicals	
☒ Instruments & Controls	

STAGE PREFERENCE

☐ EARLY STAGE
☐ Seed
☐ Start-up
☐ 1st Stage
☒ LATER STAGE
☐ 2nd Stage
☐ Mature
☐ Mezzanine
☒ LBO/MBO
☒ Turnaround
☐ INT'L EXPANSION
☐ WILL CONSIDER ALL
☒ VENTURE LEASING

Other Locations:

Affiliation:
Minimum Investment: $1 Million or more
Capital Under Management: Less than $100 Million

GEOGRAPHIC PREF

☐ East Coast
☐ West Coast
☐ Northeast
☐ Mid Atlantic
☐ Gulf States
☐ Northwest
☐ Southeast
☐ Southwest
☐ Midwest
☐ Central
☐ Local to Office
☐ Other Geo Pref

NEW ENTERPRISE ASSOCIATES

2490 Sand Hill Road
Menlo Park CA 94025

Phone (650) 854-9499   Fax (650) 854-9397

PROFESSIONALS	TITLE
Peter Morris	Partner

INDUSTRY PREFERENCE

- ☒ INFORMATION INDUSTRY
- ☒ Communications
- ☒ Computer Equipment
- ☒ Computer Services
- ☒ Computer Components
- ☒ Computer Entertainment
- ☒ Computer Education
- ☒ Information Technologies
- ☒ Computer Media
- ☒ Software
- ☒ Internet
- ☒ MEDICAL/HEALTHCARE
- ☒ Biotechnology
- ☒ Healthcare Services
- ☒ Life Sciences
- ☒ Medical Products
- ☒ INDUSTRIAL
- ☒ Advanced Materials
- ☒ Chemicals
- ☐ Instruments & Controls

- ☒ BASIC INDUSTRIES
- ☐ Consumer
- ☐ Distribution
- ☐ Manufacturing
- ☐ Retail
- ☒ Service
- ☐ Wholesale
- ☐ SPECIFIC INDUSTRIES
- ☐ Energy
- ☐ Environmental
- ☐ Financial
- ☐ Real Estate
- ☐ Transportation
- ☐ Publishing
- ☐ Food
- ☐ Franchises
- ☒ DIVERSIFIED
- ☐ MISCELLANEOUS

STAGE PREFERENCE

- ☒ EARLY STAGE
- ☒ Seed
- ☒ Start-up
- ☒ 1st Stage
- ☐ LATER STAGE
- ☐ 2nd Stage
- ☐ Mature
- ☐ Mezzanine
- ☐ LBO/MBO
- ☐ Turnaround
- ☐ INT'L EXPANSION
- ☐ WILL CONSIDER ALL
- ☐ VENTURE LEASING

Other Locations: Baltimore MD, Reston VA

Affiliation:
Minimum Investment: Less than $1 Million
Capital Under Management: Over $500 Million

GEOGRAPHIC PREF

- ☐ East Coast
- ☐ West Coast
- ☐ Northeast
- ☐ Mid Atlantic
- ☐ Gulf States
- ☐ Northwest
- ☐ Southeast
- ☐ Southwest
- ☐ Midwest
- ☐ Central
- ☐ Local to Office
- ☐ Other Geo Pref

NEWTEK VENTURES

500 Washington Street
Suite 720
San Francisco CA 94111

Phone (415) 986-5711   Fax (415) 986-4618

PROFESSIONALS	TITLE
John Hall	General Partner
Peter Wardle	General Partner

INDUSTRY PREFERENCE

- ☐ INFORMATION INDUSTRY
- ☐ Communications
- ☐ Computer Equipment
- ☐ Computer Services
- ☐ Computer Components
- ☐ Computer Entertainment
- ☐ Computer Education
- ☐ Information Technologies
- ☐ Computer Media
- ☐ Software
- ☐ Internet
- ☒ MEDICAL/HEALTHCARE
- ☐ Biotechnology
- ☒ Healthcare Services
- ☐ Life Sciences
- ☒ Medical Products
- ☒ INDUSTRIAL
- ☒ Advanced Materials
- ☐ Chemicals
- ☐ Instruments & Controls

- ☐ BASIC INDUSTRIES
- ☐ Consumer
- ☐ Distribution
- ☐ Manufacturing
- ☐ Retail
- ☐ Service
- ☐ Wholesale
- ☐ SPECIFIC INDUSTRIES
- ☐ Energy
- ☐ Environmental
- ☐ Financial
- ☐ Real Estate
- ☐ Transportation
- ☐ Publishing
- ☐ Food
- ☐ Franchises
- ☒ DIVERSIFIED
- ☐ MISCELLANEOUS

STAGE PREFERENCE

- ☒ EARLY STAGE
- ☒ Seed
- ☒ Start-up
- ☒ 1st Stage
- ☒ LATER STAGE
- ☐ 2nd Stage
- ☐ Mature
- ☐ Mezzanine
- ☒ LBO/MBO
- ☐ Turnaround
- ☐ INT'L EXPANSION
- ☐ WILL CONSIDER ALL
- ☐ VENTURE LEASING

Other Locations:

Affiliation:
Minimum Investment: Less than $1 Million
Capital Under Management: Less than $100 Million

GEOGRAPHIC PREF

- ☐ East Coast
- ☒ West Coast
- ☐ Northeast
- ☐ Mid Atlantic
- ☐ Gulf States
- ☐ Northwest
- ☐ Southeast
- ☐ Southwest
- ☐ Midwest
- ☐ Central
- ☐ Local to Office
- ☐ Other Geo Pref

NOKIA VENTURES

535 Middlefield Road
Suite 180
Menlo Park CA 94025

Phone (650) 462-7250   Fax (650) 462-7252

PROFESSIONALS	TITLE
John Malloy	Partner
W. Peter Buhl	Partner
John Gardner	Partner
Antti Kokkinen	Partner

INDUSTRY PREFERENCE

☒ INFORMATION INDUSTRY	☐ BASIC INDUSTRIES
☒ Communications	☐ Consumer
☒ Computer Equipment	☐ Distribution
☒ Computer Services	☐ Manufacturing
☒ Computer Components	☐ Retail
☒ Computer Entertainment	☐ Service
☒ Computer Education	☐ Wholesale
☒ Information Technologies	☐ SPECIFIC INDUSTRIES
☒ Computer Media	☐ Energy
☒ Software	☐ Environmental
☒ Internet	☐ Financial
☐ MEDICAL/HEALTHCARE	☐ Real Estate
☐ Biotechnology	☐ Transportation
☐ Healthcare Services	☐ Publishing
☐ Life Sciences	☐ Food
☐ Medical Products	☐ Franchises
☐ INDUSTRIAL	☐ DIVERSIFIED
☐ Advanced Materials	☒ MISCELLANEOUS
☐ Chemicals	
☐ Instruments & Controls	

STAGE PREFERENCE

☒ EARLY STAGE
☒ Seed
☒ Start-up
☒ 1st Stage
☒ LATER STAGE
☒ 2nd Stage
☐ Mature
☐ Mezzanine
☐ LBO/MBO
☐ Turnaround
☐ INT'L EXPANSION
☐ WILL CONSIDER ALL
☐ VENTURE LEASING

Other Locations:

Affiliation:
Minimum Investment: $1 Million or more
Capital Under Management: $100 to $500 Million

GEOGRAPHIC PREF

☐ East Coast
☐ West Coast
☐ Northeast
☐ Mid Atlantic
☐ Gulf States
☐ Northwest
☐ Southeast
☐ Southwest
☐ Midwest
☐ Central
☐ Local to Office
☐ Other Geo Pref

NORWEST VENTURE CAPITAL

245 Lytton Avenue
Suite 250
Palo Alto CA 94301

Phone (650) 321-8000   Fax (650) 321-8010

PROFESSIONALS	TITLE
George J. Still, Jr.	General Partner
Kevin G. Hall	General Partner
Promod Hague	
Robert Abbott	
Colin Savage	

INDUSTRY PREFERENCE

☒ INFORMATION INDUSTRY	☐ BASIC INDUSTRIES
☒ Communications	☐ Consumer
☒ Computer Equipment	☐ Distribution
☐ Computer Services	☐ Manufacturing
☐ Computer Components	☐ Retail
☐ Computer Entertainment	☐ Service
☐ Computer Education	☐ Wholesale
☒ Information Technologies	☐ SPECIFIC INDUSTRIES
☐ Computer Media	☐ Energy
☒ Software	☐ Environmental
☒ Internet	☐ Financial
☐ MEDICAL/HEALTHCARE	☐ Real Estate
☐ Biotechnology	☐ Transportation
☐ Healthcare Services	☐ Publishing
☐ Life Sciences	☐ Food
☐ Medical Products	☐ Franchises
☐ INDUSTRIAL	☐ DIVERSIFIED
☐ Advanced Materials	☐ MISCELLANEOUS
☐ Chemicals	
☐ Instruments & Controls	

STAGE PREFERENCE

☒ EARLY STAGE
☒ Seed
☒ Start-up
☒ 1st Stage
☒ LATER STAGE
☒ 2nd Stage
☒ Mature
☒ Mezzanine
☒ LBO/MBO
☒ Turnaround
☐ INT'L EXPANSION
☐ WILL CONSIDER ALL
☒ VENTURE LEASING
SBIC
Other Locations: Wellesley MA, Minneapolis MN

Affiliation: Norwest Corp.
Minimum Investment: Less than $1 Million
Capital Under Management: Over $500 Million

GEOGRAPHIC PREF

☐ East Coast
☐ West Coast
☐ Northeast
☐ Mid Atlantic
☐ Gulf States
☐ Northwest
☐ Southeast
☐ Southwest
☐ Midwest
☐ Central
☐ Local to Office
☐ Other Geo Pref

NOVUS VENTURES, LP

20111 Stevens Creek Boulevard
Suite 130
Cupertino CA 95014

Phone (408) 252-3900   Fax (408) 252-1713

PROFESSIONALS	TITLE
Daniel D. Tompkins	General Partner
Shirley Cerrudo	General Partner
Thomas van Overbeek	General Partner

INDUSTRY PREFERENCE

☒ INFORMATION INDUSTRY	☒ BASIC INDUSTRIES
☒ Communications	☐ Consumer
☒ Computer Equipment	☐ Distribution
☒ Computer Services	☐ Manufacturing
☒ Computer Components	☐ Retail
☐ Computer Entertainment	☒ Service
☒ Computer Education	☐ Wholesale
☒ Information Technologies	☐ SPECIFIC INDUSTRIES
☒ Computer Media	☐ Energy
☒ Software	☐ Environmental
☒ Internet	☐ Financial
☐ MEDICAL/HEALTHCARE	☐ Real Estate
☐ Biotechnology	☐ Transportation
☐ Healthcare Services	☐ Publishing
☐ Life Sciences	☐ Food
☐ Medical Products	☐ Franchises
☐ INDUSTRIAL	☒ DIVERSIFIED
☐ Advanced Materials	☐ MISCELLANEOUS
☐ Chemicals	
☐ Instruments & Controls	

STAGE PREFERENCE

☒ EARLY STAGE
☐ Seed
☐ Start-up
☒ 1st Stage
☒ LATER STAGE
☒ 2nd Stage
☒ Mature
☒ Mezzanine
☒ LBO/MBO
☒ Turnaround
☐ INT'L EXPANSION
☐ WILL CONSIDER ALL
☒ VENTURE LEASING
SBIC
Other Locations:

Affiliation:
Minimum Investment: Less than $1 Million
Capital Under Management: Less than $100 Million

GEOGRAPHIC PREF

☐ East Coast
☒ West Coast
☐ Northeast
☐ Mid Atlantic
☐ Gulf States
☐ Northwest
☐ Southeast
☐ Southwest
☐ Midwest
☐ Central
☐ Local to Office
☐ Other Geo Pref

OAK INVESTMENT PARTNERS

525 University Avenue
Suite 1300
Palo Alto CA 94301

Phone (650) 614-3700   Fax (650) 328-6345

PROFESSIONALS	TITLE
Fredric Harman	General Partner

INDUSTRY PREFERENCE

☒ INFORMATION INDUSTRY	☒ BASIC INDUSTRIES
☒ Communications	☐ Consumer
☒ Computer Equipment	☐ Distribution
☒ Computer Services	☐ Manufacturing
☒ Computer Components	☒ Retail
☐ Computer Entertainment	☒ Service
☒ Computer Education	☐ Wholesale
☒ Information Technologies	☐ SPECIFIC INDUSTRIES
☐ Computer Media	☐ Energy
☒ Software	☐ Environmental
☒ Internet	☐ Financial
☒ MEDICAL/HEALTHCARE	☐ Real Estate
☒ Biotechnology	☐ Transportation
☒ Healthcare Services	☐ Publishing
☒ Life Sciences	☐ Food
☒ Medical Products	☐ Franchises
☐ INDUSTRIAL	☒ DIVERSIFIED
☐ Advanced Materials	☐ MISCELLANEOUS
☐ Chemicals	
☐ Instruments & Controls	

STAGE PREFERENCE

☒ EARLY STAGE
☒ Seed
☒ Start-up
☒ 1st Stage
☒ LATER STAGE
☒ 2nd Stage
☒ Mature
☐ Mezzanine
☒ LBO/MBO
☐ Turnaround
☐ INT'L EXPANSION
☐ WILL CONSIDER ALL
☐ VENTURE LEASING

Other Locations: Minneapolis MN

Affiliation:
Minimum Investment: Less than $1 Million
Capital Under Management: Over $500 Million

GEOGRAPHIC PREF

☐ East Coast
☐ West Coast
☐ Northeast
☐ Mid Atlantic
☐ Gulf States
☐ Northwest
☐ Southeast
☐ Southwest
☐ Midwest
☐ Central
☐ Local to Office
☐ Other Geo Pref

ONSET VENTURES

2490 Sand Hill Road
Menlo Park CA 94025

Phone (650) 529-0700   Fax (650) 529-0777

PROFESSIONALS	TITLE
Robert Kuhling	General Partner
Darlene Mann	General Partner
Terry Opedendyk	General Partner
Susan Mason	Partner
Tom Winter	General Partner
Leslie Bottorff	Venture Investor

INDUSTRY PREFERENCE

☒ INFORMATION INDUSTRY	☐ BASIC INDUSTRIES	
☒ Communications	☐ Consumer	
☐ Computer Equipment	☐ Distribution	
☐ Computer Services	☐ Manufacturing	
☐ Computer Components	☐ Retail	
☐ Computer Entertainment	☐ Service	
☐ Computer Education	☐ Wholesale	
☒ Information Technologies	☐ SPECIFIC INDUSTRIES	
☐ Computer Media	☐ Energy	
☒ Software	☐ Environmental	
☒ Internet	☐ Financial	
☒ MEDICAL/HEALTHCARE	☐ Real Estate	
☐ Biotechnology	☐ Transportation	
☐ Healthcare Services	☐ Publishing	
☐ Life Sciences	☐ Food	
☒ Medical Products	☐ Franchises	
☐ INDUSTRIAL	☒ DIVERSIFIED	
☐ Advanced Materials	☒ MISCELLANEOUS	
☐ Chemicals		
☐ Instruments & Controls		

STAGE PREFERENCE

- ☒ EARLY STAGE
- ☒ Seed
- ☒ Start-up
- ☐ 1st Stage
- ☐ LATER STAGE
- ☐ 2nd Stage
- ☐ Mature
- ☐ Mezzanine
- ☐ LBO/MBO
- ☐ Turnaround
- ☐ INT'L EXPANSION
- ☐ WILL CONSIDER ALL
- ☐ VENTURE LEASING

Other Locations:

Affiliation:
Minimum Investment: Less than $1 Million
Capital Under Management: $100 to $500 Million

GEOGRAPHIC PREF

- ☐ East Coast
- ☐ West Coast
- ☐ Northeast
- ☐ Mid Atlantic
- ☐ Gulf States
- ☐ Northwest
- ☐ Southeast
- ☐ Southwest
- ☐ Midwest
- ☐ Central
- ☐ Local to Office
- ☐ Other Geo Pref

OPPORTUNITY CAPITAL CORPORATION

2201 Walnut Avenue
Suite 210
Fremont CA 94538

Phone (510) 795-7000   Fax (510) 494-5439

PROFESSIONALS	TITLE
J. Peter Thompson	President

INDUSTRY PREFERENCE

☒ INFORMATION INDUSTRY	☒ BASIC INDUSTRIES	
☒ Communications	☐ Consumer	
☐ Computer Equipment	☐ Distribution	
☐ Computer Services	☒ Manufacturing	
☐ Computer Components	☐ Retail	
☐ Computer Entertainment	☐ Service	
☐ Computer Education	☐ Wholesale	
☐ Information Technologies	☐ SPECIFIC INDUSTRIES	
☐ Computer Media	☐ Energy	
☐ Software	☐ Environmental	
☐ Internet	☐ Financial	
☒ MEDICAL/HEALTHCARE	☐ Real Estate	
☐ Biotechnology	☐ Transportation	
☒ Healthcare Services	☐ Publishing	
☐ Life Sciences	☐ Food	
☒ Medical Products	☐ Franchises	
☐ INDUSTRIAL	☒ DIVERSIFIED	
☐ Advanced Materials	☐ MISCELLANEOUS	
☐ Chemicals		
☐ Instruments & Controls		

STAGE PREFERENCE

- ☐ EARLY STAGE
- ☐ Seed
- ☐ Start-up
- ☐ 1st Stage
- ☒ LATER STAGE
- ☒ 2nd Stage
- ☒ Mature
- ☒ Mezzanine
- ☒ LBO/MBO
- ☐ Turnaround
- ☐ INT'L EXPANSION
- ☐ WILL CONSIDER ALL
- ☐ VENTURE LEASING

SSBIC
Other Locations:

Affiliation:
Minimum Investment: Less than $1 Million
Capital Under Management: Less than $100 Million

GEOGRAPHIC PREF

- ☐ East Coast
- ☒ West Coast
- ☐ Northeast
- ☐ Mid Atlantic
- ☐ Gulf States
- ☐ Northwest
- ☐ Southeast
- ☐ Southwest
- ☐ Midwest
- ☐ Central
- ☐ Local to Office
- ☐ Other Geo Pref

OXFORD BIOSCIENCE PARTNERS

650 Town Center Drive
Suite 810
Costa Mesa CA 92626

Phone (714) 754-5719   Fax (714) 754-6802

PROFESSIONALS	TITLE
Ned Olivier	
William Greenman	

INDUSTRY PREFERENCE

- ☐ INFORMATION INDUSTRY
- ☐ Communications
- ☐ Computer Equipment
- ☐ Computer Services
- ☐ Computer Components
- ☐ Computer Entertainment
- ☐ Computer Education
- ☐ Information Technologies
- ☐ Computer Media
- ☐ Software
- ☐ Internet
- ☒ MEDICAL/HEALTHCARE
- ☒ Biotechnology
- ☒ Healthcare Services
- ☒ Life Sciences
- ☒ Medical Products
- ☐ INDUSTRIAL
- ☐ Advanced Materials
- ☐ Chemicals
- ☐ Instruments & Controls

- ☐ BASIC INDUSTRIES
- ☐ Consumer
- ☐ Distribution
- ☐ Manufacturing
- ☐ Retail
- ☐ Service
- ☐ Wholesale
- ☐ SPECIFIC INDUSTRIES
- ☐ Energy
- ☐ Environmental
- ☐ Financial
- ☐ Real Estate
- ☐ Transportation
- ☐ Publishing
- ☐ Food
- ☐ Franchises
- ☐ DIVERSIFIED
- ☐ MISCELLANEOUS

STAGE PREFERENCE

- ☒ EARLY STAGE
- ☒ Seed
- ☒ Start-up
- ☒ 1st Stage
- ☒ LATER STAGE
- ☒ 2nd Stage
- ☐ Mature
- ☒ Mezzanine
- ☒ LBO/MBO
- ☐ Turnaround
- ☐ INT'L EXPANSION
- ☐ WILL CONSIDER ALL
- ☐ VENTURE LEASING

Other Locations: Westport CT

Affiliation:
Minimum Investment: Less than $1 Million
Capital Under Management: $100 to $500 Million

GEOGRAPHIC PREF

- ☒ East Coast
- ☒ West Coast
- ☐ Northeast
- ☐ Mid Atlantic
- ☐ Gulf States
- ☐ Northwest
- ☐ Southeast
- ☐ Southwest
- ☐ Midwest
- ☐ Central
- ☐ Local to Office
- ☐ Other Geo Pref

PACIFIC MEZZANINE FUND, LP

2200 Powell street
Suite 1250
Emeryville CA 94608

Phone (510) 595-9800   Fax (510) 595-9801

PROFESSIONALS	TITLE
Nathan Bell	General Partner

INDUSTRY PREFERENCE

- ☐ INFORMATION INDUSTRY
- ☐ Communications
- ☐ Computer Equipment
- ☐ Computer Services
- ☐ Computer Components
- ☐ Computer Entertainment
- ☐ Computer Education
- ☐ Information Technologies
- ☐ Computer Media
- ☐ Software
- ☐ Internet
- ☐ MEDICAL/HEALTHCARE
- ☐ Biotechnology
- ☐ Healthcare Services
- ☐ Life Sciences
- ☐ Medical Products
- ☐ INDUSTRIAL
- ☐ Advanced Materials
- ☐ Chemicals
- ☐ Instruments & Controls

- ☐ BASIC INDUSTRIES
- ☐ Consumer
- ☐ Distribution
- ☐ Manufacturing
- ☐ Retail
- ☐ Service
- ☐ Wholesale
- ☐ SPECIFIC INDUSTRIES
- ☐ Energy
- ☐ Environmental
- ☐ Financial
- ☐ Real Estate
- ☐ Transportation
- ☐ Publishing
- ☐ Food
- ☐ Franchises
- ☒ DIVERSIFIED
- ☐ MISCELLANEOUS

STAGE PREFERENCE

- ☐ EARLY STAGE
- ☐ Seed
- ☐ Start-up
- ☐ 1st Stage
- ☒ LATER STAGE
- ☒ 2nd Stage
- ☒ Mature
- ☒ Mezzanine
- ☒ LBO/MBO
- ☐ Turnaround
- ☐ INT'L EXPANSION
- ☐ WILL CONSIDER ALL
- ☐ VENTURE LEASING

SBIC
Other Locations:

Affiliation:
Minimum Investment: $1 Million or more
Capital Under Management: Less than $100 Million

GEOGRAPHIC PREF

- ☐ East Coast
- ☒ West Coast
- ☐ Northeast
- ☐ Mid Atlantic
- ☐ Gulf States
- ☐ Northwest
- ☐ Southeast
- ☐ Southwest
- ☐ Midwest
- ☐ Central
- ☐ Local to Office
- ☐ Other Geo Pref

PACIFIC VENTURE GROUP

**16830 Ventura Boulevard
Suite 244
Encino CA 91436**

Phone (818) 990-4141   Fax (818) 990-6556

PROFESSIONALS	TITLE
Layton Crouch	Managing Director
Eve Kurtin	Managing Director
William West	Finance Director

INDUSTRY PREFERENCE

- ☐ INFORMATION INDUSTRY
- ☐ Communications
- ☐ Computer Equipment
- ☐ Computer Services
- ☐ Computer Components
- ☐ Computer Entertainment
- ☐ Computer Education
- ☐ Information Technologies
- ☐ Computer Media
- ☐ Software
- ☐ Internet
- ☒ MEDICAL/HEALTHCARE
- ☒ Biotechnology
- ☒ Healthcare Services
- ☐ Life Sciences
- ☒ Medical Products
- ☐ INDUSTRIAL
- ☐ Advanced Materials
- ☐ Chemicals
- ☐ Instruments & Controls

- ☐ BASIC INDUSTRIES
- ☐ Consumer
- ☐ Distribution
- ☐ Manufacturing
- ☐ Retail
- ☐ Service
- ☐ Wholesale
- ☐ SPECIFIC INDUSTRIES
- ☐ Energy
- ☐ Environmental
- ☐ Financial
- ☐ Real Estate
- ☐ Transportation
- ☐ Publishing
- ☐ Food
- ☐ Franchises
- ☐ DIVERSIFIED
- ☒ MISCELLANEOUS

STAGE PREFERENCE

- ☒ EARLY STAGE
- ☒ Seed
- ☒ Start-up
- ☒ 1st Stage
- ☒ LATER STAGE
- ☒ 2nd Stage
- ☐ Mature
- ☒ Mezzanine
- ☒ LBO/MBO
- ☐ Turnaround
- ☐ INT'L EXPANSION
- ☐ WILL CONSIDER ALL
- ☐ VENTURE LEASING

Other Locations: Redwood Shores CA, Irvine CA

Affiliation:
Minimum Investment: $1 Million or more
Capital Under Management: $100 to $500 Million

GEOGRAPHIC PREF

- ☐ East Coast
- ☐ West Coast
- ☐ Northeast
- ☐ Mid Atlantic
- ☐ Gulf States
- ☐ Northwest
- ☐ Southeast
- ☐ Southwest
- ☐ Midwest
- ☐ Central
- ☐ Local to Office
- ☐ Other Geo Pref

PACIFIC VENTURE GROUP

**303 Twin Dolphin Drive
Suite 600
Redwood Shores CA 94065**

Phone (650) 632-4254   Fax (650) 632-4256

PROFESSIONALS	TITLE
Annette Bianchi	Managing Director

INDUSTRY PREFERENCE

- ☐ INFORMATION INDUSTRY
- ☐ Communications
- ☐ Computer Equipment
- ☐ Computer Services
- ☐ Computer Components
- ☐ Computer Entertainment
- ☐ Computer Education
- ☐ Information Technologies
- ☐ Computer Media
- ☐ Software
- ☐ Internet
- ☒ MEDICAL/HEALTHCARE
- ☒ Biotechnology
- ☒ Healthcare Services
- ☐ Life Sciences
- ☒ Medical Products
- ☐ INDUSTRIAL
- ☐ Advanced Materials
- ☐ Chemicals
- ☐ Instruments & Controls

- ☐ BASIC INDUSTRIES
- ☐ Consumer
- ☐ Distribution
- ☐ Manufacturing
- ☐ Retail
- ☐ Service
- ☐ Wholesale
- ☐ SPECIFIC INDUSTRIES
- ☐ Energy
- ☐ Environmental
- ☐ Financial
- ☐ Real Estate
- ☐ Transportation
- ☐ Publishing
- ☐ Food
- ☐ Franchises
- ☐ DIVERSIFIED
- ☒ MISCELLANEOUS

STAGE PREFERENCE

- ☒ EARLY STAGE
- ☒ Seed
- ☒ Start-up
- ☒ 1st Stage
- ☒ LATER STAGE
- ☒ 2nd Stage
- ☐ Mature
- ☒ Mezzanine
- ☒ LBO/MBO
- ☐ Turnaround
- ☐ INT'L EXPANSION
- ☐ WILL CONSIDER ALL
- ☐ VENTURE LEASING

Other Locations: Encino CA, Irvine CA

Affiliation:
Minimum Investment: $1 Million or more
Capital Under Management: $100 to $500 Million

GEOGRAPHIC PREF

- ☐ East Coast
- ☐ West Coast
- ☐ Northeast
- ☐ Mid Atlantic
- ☐ Gulf States
- ☐ Northwest
- ☐ Southeast
- ☐ Southwest
- ☐ Midwest
- ☐ Central
- ☐ Local to Office
- ☐ Other Geo Pref

PACIFIC VENTURE GROUP

15635 Alton Parkway
Suite 230
Irvine CA 92618

Phone (949) 753-0490   Fax (949) 753-8932

PROFESSIONALS	TITLE
Ralph Sabin	Managing Director

INDUSTRY PREFERENCE

☒ INFORMATION INDUSTRY	☐ BASIC INDUSTRIES
☐ Communications	☐ Consumer
☐ Computer Equipment	☐ Distribution
☐ Computer Services	☐ Manufacturing
☐ Computer Components	☐ Retail
☐ Computer Entertainment	☐ Service
☐ Computer Education	☐ Wholesale
☒ Information Technologies	☐ SPECIFIC INDUSTRIES
☐ Computer Media	☐ Energy
☐ Software	☐ Environmental
☒ Internet	☐ Financial
☒ MEDICAL/HEALTHCARE	☐ Real Estate
☒ Biotechnology	☐ Transportation
☒ Healthcare Services	☐ Publishing
☒ Life Sciences	☐ Food
☒ Medical Products	☐ Franchises
☐ INDUSTRIAL	☒ DIVERSIFIED
☐ Advanced Materials	☒ MISCELLANEOUS
☐ Chemicals	
☐ Instruments & Controls	

STAGE PREFERENCE

☒ EARLY STAGE
☒ Seed
☒ Start-up
☒ 1st Stage
☒ LATER STAGE
☒ 2nd Stage
☐ Mature
☒ Mezzanine
☒ LBO/MBO
☐ Turnaround
☐ INT'L EXPANSION
☐ WILL CONSIDER ALL
☐ VENTURE LEASING

Other Locations: Encino CA , Redwood Shores CA

Affiliation:
Minimum Investment: $1 Million or more
Capital Under Management: $100 to $500 Million

GEOGRAPHIC PREF

☐ East Coast
☒ West Coast
☐ Northeast
☐ Mid Atlantic
☐ Gulf States
☐ Northwest
☐ Southeast
☐ Southwest
☐ Midwest
☐ Central
☐ Local to Office
☐ Other Geo Pref

PARAGON VENTURE PARTNERS

3000 Sand Hill Road
Building One, Suite 275
Menlo Park CA 94025

Phone (650) 854-8000   Fax (650) 854-7260

PROFESSIONALS	TITLE
Robert Kibble	General Partner
John Lewis	General Partner

INDUSTRY PREFERENCE

☒ INFORMATION INDUSTRY	☒ BASIC INDUSTRIES
☒ Communications	☐ Consumer
☒ Computer Equipment	☐ Distribution
☒ Computer Services	☐ Manufacturing
☒ Computer Components	☐ Retail
☐ Computer Entertainment	☒ Service
☒ Computer Education	☐ Wholesale
☒ Information Technologies	☒ SPECIFIC INDUSTRIES
☒ Computer Media	☐ Energy
☒ Software	☐ Environmental
☒ Internet	☒ Financial
☒ MEDICAL/HEALTHCARE	☐ Real Estate
☒ Biotechnology	☐ Transportation
☒ Healthcare Services	☐ Publishing
☒ Life Sciences	☐ Food
☒ Medical Products	☐ Franchises
☒ INDUSTRIAL	☒ DIVERSIFIED
☒ Advanced Materials	☐ MISCELLANEOUS
☒ Chemicals	
☒ Instruments & Controls	

STAGE PREFERENCE

☒ EARLY STAGE
☒ Seed
☒ Start-up
☒ 1st Stage
☒ LATER STAGE
☒ 2nd Stage
☒ Mature
☒ Mezzanine
☒ LBO/MBO
☐ Turnaround
☐ INT'L EXPANSION
☐ WILL CONSIDER ALL
☐ VENTURE LEASING

Other Locations:

Affiliation:
Minimum Investment: Less than $1 Million
Capital Under Management: Less than $100 Million

GEOGRAPHIC PREF

☐ East Coast
☒ West Coast
☐ Northeast
☐ Mid Atlantic
☐ Gulf States
☐ Northwest
☐ Southeast
☐ Southwest
☐ Midwest
☐ Central
☐ Local to Office
☐ Other Geo Pref

PARTECH INTERNATIONAL

50 California Street
Suite 3200
San Francisco CA 94111-5802

Phone (415) 788-2929   Fax (415) 788-6763

PROFESSIONALS	TITLE
Philippe Cases	Partner
Vincent Worms	Partner
Thomas G. McKinley	Partner
Glenn Solomon	Partner
Nicolas El Baze	Partner

INDUSTRY PREFERENCE

- ☒ INFORMATION INDUSTRY
- ☒ Communications
- ☒ Computer Equipment
- ☒ Computer Services
- ☒ Computer Components
- ☐ Computer Entertainment
- ☐ Computer Education
- ☒ Information Technologies
- ☐ Computer Media
- ☒ Software
- ☒ Internet
- ☒ MEDICAL/HEALTHCARE
- ☒ Biotechnology
- ☒ Healthcare Services
- ☒ Life Sciences
- ☒ Medical Products
- ☒ INDUSTRIAL
- ☐ Advanced Materials
- ☐ Chemicals
- ☒ Instruments & Controls

- ☐ BASIC INDUSTRIES
- ☐ Consumer
- ☐ Distribution
- ☐ Manufacturing
- ☐ Retail
- ☐ Service
- ☐ Wholesale
- ☐ SPECIFIC INDUSTRIES
- ☐ Energy
- ☐ Environmental
- ☐ Financial
- ☐ Real Estate
- ☐ Transportation
- ☐ Publishing
- ☐ Food
- ☐ Franchises
- ☒ DIVERSIFIED
- ☐ MISCELLANEOUS

STAGE PREFERENCE

- ☒ EARLY STAGE
- ☒ Seed
- ☒ Start-up
- ☒ 1st Stage
- ☒ LATER STAGE
- ☒ 2nd Stage
- ☒ Mature
- ☒ Mezzanine
- ☒ LBO/MBO
- ☐ Turnaround
- ☒ INT'L EXPANSION
- ☐ WILL CONSIDER ALL
- ☐ VENTURE LEASING

Other Locations:

Affiliation: Banque Paribas, France
Minimum Investment: Less than $1 Million
Capital Under Management: $100 to $500 Million

GEOGRAPHIC PREF

- ☐ East Coast
- ☐ West Coast
- ☐ Northeast
- ☐ Mid Atlantic
- ☐ Gulf States
- ☐ Northwest
- ☐ Southeast
- ☐ Southwest
- ☐ Midwest
- ☐ Central
- ☐ Local to Office
- ☐ Other Geo Pref

PATRICOF AND COMPANY

2100 Geng Road
Suite 150
Palo Alto CA 94303

Phone (650) 494-9944   Fax (650) 494-6751

PROFESSIONALS	TITLE
Janet G. Effland	Managing Director

INDUSTRY PREFERENCE

- ☒ INFORMATION INDUSTRY
- ☒ Communications
- ☒ Computer Equipment
- ☒ Computer Services
- ☒ Computer Components
- ☐ Computer Entertainment
- ☒ Computer Education
- ☒ Information Technologies
- ☒ Computer Media
- ☒ Software
- ☒ Internet
- ☒ MEDICAL/HEALTHCARE
- ☒ Biotechnology
- ☒ Healthcare Services
- ☒ Life Sciences
- ☒ Medical Products
- ☒ INDUSTRIAL
- ☒ Advanced Materials
- ☒ Chemicals
- ☒ Instruments & Controls

- ☒ BASIC INDUSTRIES
- ☒ Consumer
- ☐ Distribution
- ☒ Manufacturing
- ☒ Retail
- ☒ Service
- ☒ Wholesale
- ☒ SPECIFIC INDUSTRIES
- ☒ Energy
- ☒ Environmental
- ☒ Financial
- ☐ Real Estate
- ☐ Transportation
- ☐ Publishing
- ☐ Food
- ☐ Franchises
- ☒ DIVERSIFIED
- ☐ MISCELLANEOUS

STAGE PREFERENCE

- ☒ EARLY STAGE
- ☒ Seed
- ☒ Start-up
- ☒ 1st Stage
- ☒ LATER STAGE
- ☒ 2nd Stage
- ☒ Mature
- ☒ Mezzanine
- ☒ LBO/MBO
- ☒ Turnaround
- ☐ INT'L EXPANSION
- ☐ WILL CONSIDER ALL
- ☒ VENTURE LEASING

Other Locations: New York NY, Radnor PA

Affiliation: MMG Patricof & Co., Inc.
Minimum Investment: Less than $1 Million
Capital Under Management: Over $500 Million

GEOGRAPHIC PREF

- ☐ East Coast
- ☐ West Coast
- ☐ Northeast
- ☐ Mid Atlantic
- ☐ Gulf States
- ☐ Northwest
- ☐ Southeast
- ☐ Southwest
- ☐ Midwest
- ☐ Central
- ☐ Local to Office
- ☐ Other Geo Pref

PAUL CAPITAL PARTNERS

**50 California Street
Suite 3000
San Francisco CA 94111**

Phone (415) 283-4300   Fax (415) 283-4301

PROFESSIONALS	TITLE
Philip Paul	Chairman
David Park	Partner
David DeWeese	Chief Financial Officer
Byron Sheets	Partner

INDUSTRY PREFERENCE

- ☐ INFORMATION INDUSTRY
- ☐ Communications
- ☐ Computer Equipment
- ☐ Computer Services
- ☐ Computer Components
- ☐ Computer Entertainment
- ☐ Computer Education
- ☐ Information Technologies
- ☐ Computer Media
- ☐ Software
- ☐ Internet
- ☐ MEDICAL/HEALTHCARE
- ☐ Biotechnology
- ☐ Healthcare Services
- ☐ Life Sciences
- ☐ Medical Products
- ☐ INDUSTRIAL
- ☐ Advanced Materials
- ☐ Chemicals
- ☐ Instruments & Controls

- ☐ BASIC INDUSTRIES
- ☐ Consumer
- ☐ Distribution
- ☐ Manufacturing
- ☐ Retail
- ☐ Service
- ☐ Wholesale
- ☐ SPECIFIC INDUSTRIES
- ☐ Energy
- ☐ Environmental
- ☐ Financial
- ☐ Real Estate
- ☐ Transportation
- ☐ Publishing
- ☐ Food
- ☐ Franchises
- ☒ DIVERSIFIED
- ☒ MISCELLANEOUS

STAGE PREFERENCE

- ☐ EARLY STAGE
- ☐ Seed
- ☐ Start-up
- ☐ 1st Stage
- ☒ LATER STAGE
- ☐ 2nd Stage
- ☐ Mature
- ☐ Mezzanine
- ☒ LBO/MBO
- ☐ Turnaround
- ☐ INT'L EXPANSION
- ☐ WILL CONSIDER ALL
- ☐ VENTURE LEASING

Other Locations:

Affiliation:
Minimum Investment: Less than $1 Million
Capital Under Management: $100 to $500 Million

GEOGRAPHIC PREF

- ☐ East Coast
- ☐ West Coast
- ☐ Northeast
- ☐ Mid Atlantic
- ☐ Gulf States
- ☐ Northwest
- ☐ Southeast
- ☐ Southwest
- ☐ Midwest
- ☐ Central
- ☐ Local to Office
- ☐ Other Geo Pref

PHOENIX GROWTH CAPITAL CORP.

**2401 Kerner Boulevard
San Rafael CA 94901**

Phone (415) 485-4569   Fax (415) 485-4663

PROFESSIONALS	TITLE
Norm Nelson	Manager

INDUSTRY PREFERENCE

- ☒ INFORMATION INDUSTRY
- ☒ Communications
- ☒ Computer Equipment
- ☒ Computer Services
- ☒ Computer Components
- ☐ Computer Entertainment
- ☒ Computer Education
- ☒ Information Technologies
- ☐ Computer Media
- ☒ Software
- ☒ Internet
- ☒ MEDICAL/HEALTHCARE
- ☒ Biotechnology
- ☒ Healthcare Services
- ☒ Life Sciences
- ☒ Medical Products
- ☒ INDUSTRIAL
- ☐ Advanced Materials
- ☐ Chemicals
- ☒ Instruments & Controls

- ☒ BASIC INDUSTRIES
- ☐ Consumer
- ☐ Distribution
- ☐ Manufacturing
- ☐ Retail
- ☒ Service
- ☐ Wholesale
- ☒ SPECIFIC INDUSTRIES
- ☒ Energy
- ☒ Environmental
- ☐ Financial
- ☐ Real Estate
- ☐ Transportation
- ☐ Publishing
- ☐ Food
- ☐ Franchises
- ☒ DIVERSIFIED
- ☐ MISCELLANEOUS

STAGE PREFERENCE

- ☒ EARLY STAGE
- ☐ Seed
- ☐ Start-up
- ☒ 1st Stage
- ☒ LATER STAGE
- ☒ 2nd Stage
- ☒ Mature
- ☒ Mezzanine
- ☒ LBO/MBO
- ☐ Turnaround
- ☐ INT'L EXPANSION
- ☐ WILL CONSIDER ALL
- ☐ VENTURE LEASING

Other Locations:

Affiliation:
Minimum Investment: $1 Million or more
Capital Under Management: Less than $100 Million

GEOGRAPHIC PREF

- ☐ East Coast
- ☐ West Coast
- ☐ Northeast
- ☐ Mid Atlantic
- ☐ Gulf States
- ☐ Northwest
- ☐ Southeast
- ☐ Southwest
- ☐ Midwest
- ☐ Central
- ☐ Local to Office
- ☐ Other Geo Pref

PINECREEK CAPITAL PARTNERS LP

24 Corporate Plaza
Suite 160
Newport Beach CA 92660

Phone (949) 720-4620   Fax (949) 720-4629

PROFESSIONALS	TITLE
Randall Zurbach	President

INDUSTRY PREFERENCE

☐ INFORMATION INDUSTRY
☐ Communications
☐ Computer Equipment
☐ Computer Services
☐ Computer Components
☐ Computer Entertainment
☐ Computer Education
☐ Information Technologies
☐ Computer Media
☐ Software
☐ Internet
☐ MEDICAL/HEALTHCARE
☐ Biotechnology
☐ Healthcare Services
☐ Life Sciences
☐ Medical Products
☐ INDUSTRIAL
☐ Advanced Materials
☐ Chemicals
☐ Instruments & Controls

☐ BASIC INDUSTRIES
☐ Consumer
☐ Distribution
☐ Manufacturing
☐ Retail
☐ Service
☐ Wholesale
☐ SPECIFIC INDUSTRIES
☐ Energy
☐ Environmental
☐ Financial
☐ Real Estate
☐ Transportation
☐ Publishing
☐ Food
☐ Franchises
☒ DIVERSIFIED
☐ MISCELLANEOUS

STAGE PREFERENCE

☐ EARLY STAGE
☐ Seed
☐ Start-up
☐ 1st Stage
☒ LATER STAGE
☐ 2nd Stage
☒ Mature
☒ Mezzanine
☒ LBO/MBO
☐ Turnaround
☐ INT'L EXPANSION
☐ WILL CONSIDER ALL
☐ VENTURE LEASING

SBIC
Other Locations:

Affiliation:
Minimum Investment: Less than $1 Million
Capital Under Management: Less than $100 Million

GEOGRAPHIC PREF

☐ East Coast
☒ West Coast
☐ Northeast
☐ Mid Atlantic
☐ Gulf States
☐ Northwest
☐ Southeast
☐ Southwest
☐ Midwest
☐ Central
☐ Local to Office
☐ Other Geo Pref

POSITIVE ENTERPRISES, INC.

1489 Webster Street
Suite 228
San Francisco CA 94115

Phone (415) 885-6600   Fax (415) 928-6363

PROFESSIONALS	TITLE
Kwok Szeto	President

INDUSTRY PREFERENCE

☐ INFORMATION INDUSTRY
☐ Communications
☐ Computer Equipment
☐ Computer Services
☐ Computer Components
☐ Computer Entertainment
☐ Computer Education
☐ Information Technologies
☐ Computer Media
☐ Software
☐ Internet
☐ MEDICAL/HEALTHCARE
☐ Biotechnology
☐ Healthcare Services
☐ Life Sciences
☐ Medical Products
☐ INDUSTRIAL
☐ Advanced Materials
☐ Chemicals
☐ Instruments & Controls

☒ BASIC INDUSTRIES
☐ Consumer
☐ Distribution
☒ Manufacturing
☐ Retail
☐ Service
☐ Wholesale
☐ SPECIFIC INDUSTRIES
☐ Energy
☐ Environmental
☐ Financial
☐ Real Estate
☐ Transportation
☐ Publishing
☐ Food
☐ Franchises
☒ DIVERSIFIED
☒ MISCELLANEOUS
Senior Home Care, Rest Home

STAGE PREFERENCE

☒ EARLY STAGE
☐ Seed
☐ Start-up
☒ 1st Stage
☒ LATER STAGE
☒ 2nd Stage
☒ Mature
☐ Mezzanine
☐ LBO/MBO
☐ Turnaround
☐ INT'L EXPANSION
☐ WILL CONSIDER ALL
☐ VENTURE LEASING

SSBIC
Other Locations:

Affiliation:
Minimum Investment: Less than $1 Million
Capital Under Management: Less than $100 Million

GEOGRAPHIC PREF

☐ East Coast
☐ West Coast
☐ Northeast
☐ Mid Atlantic
☐ Gulf States
☒ Northwest
☐ Southeast
☐ Southwest
☐ Midwest
☐ Central
☐ Local to Office
☐ Other Geo Pref

PREMIER MEDICAL PARTNER FUND

12225 El Camino Real
San Diego CA 92130

Phone (858) 509-6550   Fax (858) 481-8919

PROFESSIONALS	TITLE
Richard Kuntz	Sr. Managing Director
Palmer Ford	Managing Director
Douglas Lee	Managing Director

INDUSTRY PREFERENCE

☐ INFORMATION INDUSTRY
☐ Communications
☐ Computer Equipment
☐ Computer Services
☐ Computer Components
☐ Computer Entertainment
☐ Computer Education
☐ Information Technologies
☐ Computer Media
☐ Software
☐ Internet
☒ MEDICAL/HEALTHCARE
☒ Biotechnology
☒ Healthcare Services
☒ Life Sciences
☒ Medical Products
☐ INDUSTRIAL
☐ Advanced Materials
☐ Chemicals
☐ Instruments & Controls

☐ BASIC INDUSTRIES
☐ Consumer
☐ Distribution
☐ Manufacturing
☐ Retail
☐ Service
☐ Wholesale
☒ SPECIFIC INDUSTRIES
☐ Energy
☐ Environmental
☐ Financial
☐ Real Estate
☐ Transportation
☐ Publishing
☐ Food
☐ Franchises
☐ DIVERSIFIED
☒ MISCELLANEOUS

STAGE PREFERENCE

☒ EARLY STAGE
☐ Seed
☐ Start-up
☒ 1st Stage
☒ LATER STAGE
☒ 2nd Stage
☒ Mature
☒ Mezzanine
☐ LBO/MBO
☐ Turnaround
☐ INT'L EXPANSION
☐ WILL CONSIDER ALL
☐ VENTURE LEASING

Other Locations:

Affiliation:
Minimum Investment: $1 Million or more
Capital Under Management: Less than $100 Million

GEOGRAPHIC PREF

☐ East Coast
☐ West Coast
☐ Northeast
☐ Mid Atlantic
☐ Gulf States
☐ Northwest
☐ Southeast
☐ Southwest
☐ Midwest
☐ Central
☐ Local to Office
☐ Other Geo Pref

QUEST VENTURES

333 Bush Street
Suite 1750
San Francisco CA 94104

Phone (415) 782-1414   Fax (415) 782-1415

PROFESSIONALS	TITLE
William A. Boeger III	General Partner
Lucien Ruby	General Partner

INDUSTRY PREFERENCE

☒ INFORMATION INDUSTRY
☒ Communications
☒ Computer Equipment
☒ Computer Services
☒ Computer Components
☐ Computer Entertainment
☒ Computer Education
☒ Information Technologies
☒ Computer Media
☒ Software
☒ Internet
☒ MEDICAL/HEALTHCARE
☒ Biotechnology
☒ Healthcare Services
☒ Life Sciences
☒ Medical Products
☒ INDUSTRIAL
☒ Advanced Materials
☒ Chemicals
☒ Instruments & Controls

☒ BASIC INDUSTRIES
☒ Consumer
☒ Distribution
☒ Manufacturing
☒ Retail
☒ Service
☒ Wholesale
☒ SPECIFIC INDUSTRIES
☒ Energy
☐ Environmental
☒ Financial
☐ Real Estate
☒ Transportation
☐ Publishing
☐ Food
☐ Franchises
☒ DIVERSIFIED
☐ MISCELLANEOUS

STAGE PREFERENCE

☒ EARLY STAGE
☒ Seed
☒ Start-up
☒ 1st Stage
☒ LATER STAGE
☒ 2nd Stage
☒ Mature
☒ Mezzanine
☒ LBO/MBO
☒ Turnaround
☐ INT'L EXPANSION
☐ WILL CONSIDER ALL
☒ VENTURE LEASING

Other Locations:

Affiliation:
Minimum Investment: Less than $1 Million
Capital Under Management: Less than $100 Million

GEOGRAPHIC PREF

☐ East Coast
☐ West Coast
☐ Northeast
☐ Mid Atlantic
☐ Gulf States
☐ Northwest
☐ Southeast
☐ Southwest
☐ Midwest
☐ Central
☐ Local to Office
☐ Other Geo Pref

RECOVERY EQUITY INVESTORS, LP

901 Mariners Island Boulevard
Suite 465
San Mateo CA 94404

Phone (650) 578-9752   Fax (650) 578-9842

PROFESSIONALS	TITLE
Jeffrey A. Lipkin	General Partner
Joseph J. Finn-Egan	General Partner

INDUSTRY PREFERENCE

☒ INFORMATION INDUSTRY	☒ BASIC INDUSTRIES
☒ Communications	☐ Consumer
☒ Computer Equipment	☐ Distribution
☒ Computer Services	☐ Manufacturing
☐ Computer Components	☐ Retail
☐ Computer Entertainment	☒ Service
☒ Computer Education	☐ Wholesale
☒ Information Technologies	☒ SPECIFIC INDUSTRIES
☒ Computer Media	☒ Energy
☒ Software	☐ Environmental
☒ Internet	☐ Financial
☒ MEDICAL/HEALTHCARE	☐ Real Estate
☒ Biotechnology	☐ Transportation
☒ Healthcare Services	☐ Publishing
☒ Life Sciences	☐ Food
☒ Medical Products	☐ Franchises
☒ INDUSTRIAL	☒ DIVERSIFIED
☒ Advanced Materials	☐ MISCELLANEOUS
☒ Chemicals	
☒ Instruments & Controls	

STAGE PREFERENCE

☐ EARLY STAGE
☐ Seed
☐ Start-up
☐ 1st Stage
☒ LATER STAGE
☐ 2nd Stage
☐ Mature
☐ Mezzanine
☒ LBO/MBO
☒ Turnaround
☐ INT'L EXPANSION
☐ WILL CONSIDER ALL
☒ VENTURE LEASING

Other Locations:

Affiliation:
Minimum Investment: $1 Million or more
Capital Under Management: $100 to $500 Million

GEOGRAPHIC PREF

☐ East Coast
☐ West Coast
☐ Northeast
☐ Mid Atlantic
☐ Gulf States
☐ Northwest
☐ Southeast
☐ Southwest
☐ Midwest
☐ Central
☐ Local to Office
☐ Other Geo Pref

ROSEWOOD CAPITAL

1 Maritime Plaza
Suite 1330
San Francisco CA 94111

Phone (415) 362-5526   Fax (415) 362-1192

PROFESSIONALS	TITLE
Chip Adams	Principal
Kyle Anderson	Principal

INDUSTRY PREFERENCE

☒ INFORMATION INDUSTRY	☒ BASIC INDUSTRIES
☐ Communications	☒ Consumer
☐ Computer Equipment	☒ Distribution
☐ Computer Services	☐ Manufacturing
☐ Computer Components	☒ Retail
☐ Computer Entertainment	☒ Service
☐ Computer Education	☐ Wholesale
☐ Information Technologies	☐ SPECIFIC INDUSTRIES
☐ Computer Media	☐ Energy
☐ Software	☐ Environmental
☒ Internet	☐ Financial
☐ MEDICAL/HEALTHCARE	☐ Real Estate
☐ Biotechnology	☐ Transportation
☐ Healthcare Services	☐ Publishing
☐ Life Sciences	☐ Food
☐ Medical Products	☐ Franchises
☐ INDUSTRIAL	☒ DIVERSIFIED
☐ Advanced Materials	☐ MISCELLANEOUS
☐ Chemicals	
☐ Instruments & Controls	

STAGE PREFERENCE

☐ EARLY STAGE
☐ Seed
☐ Start-up
☐ 1st Stage
☒ LATER STAGE
☒ 2nd Stage
☒ Mature
☐ Mezzanine
☒ LBO/MBO
☐ Turnaround
☐ INT'L EXPANSION
☐ WILL CONSIDER ALL
☐ VENTURE LEASING

Other Locations:

Affiliation:
Minimum Investment: $1 Million or more
Capital Under Management: $100 to $500 Million

GEOGRAPHIC PREF

☐ East Coast
☒ West Coast
☐ Northeast
☐ Mid Atlantic
☐ Gulf States
☐ Northwest
☐ Southeast
☐ Southwest
☐ Midwest
☐ Central
☐ Local to Office
☐ Other Geo Pref

ROSSEIN VENTURES

268 Bush Street
Suite 4300
San Francisco CA 94101

Phone (415) 292-9920   Fax (415) 292-9920

PROFESSIONALS	TITLE

INDUSTRY PREFERENCE

☒ INFORMATION INDUSTRY	☐ BASIC INDUSTRIES	
☒ Communications	☐ Consumer	
☒ Computer Equipment	☐ Distribution	
☒ Computer Services	☐ Manufacturing	
☒ Computer Components	☐ Retail	
☐ Computer Entertainment	☐ Service	
☐ Computer Education	☐ Wholesale	
☒ Information Technologies	☒ SPECIFIC INDUSTRIES	
☒ Computer Media	☐ Energy	
☒ Software	☐ Environmental	
☒ Internet	☒ Financial	
☒ MEDICAL/HEALTHCARE	☐ Real Estate	
☒ Biotechnology	☐ Transportation	
☒ Healthcare Services	☐ Publishing	
☒ Life Sciences	☐ Food	
☒ Medical Products	☐ Franchises	
☒ INDUSTRIAL	☒ DIVERSIFIED	
☐ Advanced Materials	☒ MISCELLANEOUS	
☐ Chemicals		
☒ Instruments & Controls		

STAGE PREFERENCE

☒ EARLY STAGE
☒ Seed
☒ Start-up
☒ 1st Stage
☒ LATER STAGE
☒ 2nd Stage
☐ Mature
☐ Mezzanine
☐ LBO/MBO
☐ Turnaround
☐ INT'L EXPANSION
☐ WILL CONSIDER ALL
☐ VENTURE LEASING

Other Locations:

Affiliation:
Minimum Investment: Less than $1 Million
Capital Under Management: Less than $100 Million

GEOGRAPHIC PREF

☐ East Coast
☐ West Coast
☐ Northeast
☐ Mid Atlantic
☐ Gulf States
☐ Northwest
☐ Southeast
☐ Southwest
☐ Midwest
☐ Central
☐ Local to Office
☐ Other Geo Pref

SANDERLING VENTURES

2730 Sand Hill Road
Suite 200
Menlo Park CA 94025-7067

Phone (650) 854-9855   Fax (650) 854-3648

PROFESSIONALS	TITLE
Dr. Robert G. McNeil, PhD	General Partner
Fred A. Middleton	General Partner
Dr. James Healy, MD, PhD	Partner
Dr. Timothy Mills, PhD	Partner

INDUSTRY PREFERENCE

☐ INFORMATION INDUSTRY	☐ BASIC INDUSTRIES	
☐ Communications	☐ Consumer	
☐ Computer Equipment	☐ Distribution	
☐ Computer Services	☐ Manufacturing	
☐ Computer Components	☐ Retail	
☐ Computer Entertainment	☐ Service	
☐ Computer Education	☐ Wholesale	
☐ Information Technologies	☐ SPECIFIC INDUSTRIES	
☐ Computer Media	☐ Energy	
☐ Software	☐ Environmental	
☐ Internet	☐ Financial	
☒ MEDICAL/HEALTHCARE	☐ Real Estate	
☒ Biotechnology	☐ Transportation	
☒ Healthcare Services	☐ Publishing	
☒ Life Sciences	☐ Food	
☒ Medical Products	☐ Franchises	
☐ INDUSTRIAL	☐ DIVERSIFIED	
☐ Advanced Materials	☐ MISCELLANEOUS	
☐ Chemicals		
☐ Instruments & Controls		

STAGE PREFERENCE

☒ EARLY STAGE
☒ Seed
☒ Start-up
☒ 1st Stage
☐ LATER STAGE
☐ 2nd Stage
☐ Mature
☐ Mezzanine
☐ LBO/MBO
☐ Turnaround
☐ INT'L EXPANSION
☐ WILL CONSIDER ALL
☐ VENTURE LEASING

Other Locations:

Affiliation:
Minimum Investment: Less than $1 Million
Capital Under Management: Less than $100 Million

GEOGRAPHIC PREF

☐ East Coast
☒ West Coast
☐ Northeast
☐ Mid Atlantic
☐ Gulf States
☐ Northwest
☐ Southeast
☐ Southwest
☐ Midwest
☐ Central
☐ Local to Office
☐ Other Geo Pref

SEACOAST CAPITAL PARTNERS, LP

One Sansome Street
Suite 2100
San Francisco CA 94104

Phone (415) 956-1400   Fax (415) 956-1459

PROFESSIONALS	TITLE
Jeffrey J. Holland	Managing Director

INDUSTRY PREFERENCE

☐ INFORMATION INDUSTRY	☐ BASIC INDUSTRIES
☐ Communications	☐ Consumer
☐ Computer Equipment	☐ Distribution
☐ Computer Services	☐ Manufacturing
☐ Computer Components	☐ Retail
☐ Computer Entertainment	☐ Service
☐ Computer Education	☐ Wholesale
☐ Information Technologies	☐ SPECIFIC INDUSTRIES
☐ Computer Media	☐ Energy
☐ Software	☐ Environmental
☐ Internet	☐ Financial
☐ MEDICAL/HEALTHCARE	☐ Real Estate
☐ Biotechnology	☐ Transportation
☐ Healthcare Services	☐ Publishing
☐ Life Sciences	☐ Food
☐ Medical Products	☐ Franchises
☐ INDUSTRIAL	☒ DIVERSIFIED
☐ Advanced Materials	☒ MISCELLANEOUS
☐ Chemicals	
☐ Instruments & Controls	

STAGE PREFERENCE

☐ EARLY STAGE
☐ Seed
☐ Start-up
☐ 1st Stage
☒ LATER STAGE
☒ 2nd Stage
☒ Mature
☒ Mezzanine
☒ LBO/MBO
☐ Turnaround
☐ INT'L EXPANSION
☐ WILL CONSIDER ALL
☐ VENTURE LEASING

SBIC
Other Locations: Danvers MA

Affiliation:
Minimum Investment: $1 Million or more
Capital Under Management: $100 to $500 Million

GEOGRAPHIC PREF

☐ East Coast
☐ West Coast
☐ Northeast
☐ Mid Atlantic
☐ Gulf States
☐ Northwest
☐ Southeast
☐ Southwest
☐ Midwest
☐ Central
☐ Local to Office
☐ Other Geo Pref

SEQUOIA CAPITAL

3000 Sand Hill Road
Building Four, Suite 280
Menlo Park CA 94025

Phone (650) 854-3927   Fax (650) 854-2977

PROFESSIONALS	TITLE
Donald T. Valentine	Partner
Thomas F. Stephenson	Partner
Timothy Connors	Partner
Mark Stevens	Partner
Micheal Goguen	Partner
Douglas Leone	Partner
Michael Moritz	Partner
Gordon Russell	Partner
Pierre R. Lamond	Partner

INDUSTRY PREFERENCE

☒ INFORMATION INDUSTRY	☒ BASIC INDUSTRIES
☒ Communications	☐ Consumer
☒ Computer Equipment	☐ Distribution
☒ Computer Services	☐ Manufacturing
☒ Computer Components	☐ Retail
☐ Computer Entertainment	☒ Service
☒ Computer Education	☐ Wholesale
☒ Information Technologies	☒ SPECIFIC INDUSTRIES
☒ Computer Media	☐ Energy
☒ Software	☒ Environmental
☒ Internet	☐ Financial
☒ MEDICAL/HEALTHCARE	☐ Real Estate
☒ Biotechnology	☐ Transportation
☒ Healthcare Services	☐ Publishing
☒ Life Sciences	☐ Food
☒ Medical Products	☐ Franchises
☒ INDUSTRIAL	☒ DIVERSIFIED
☒ Advanced Materials	☐ MISCELLANEOUS
☒ Chemicals	
☒ Instruments & Controls	

STAGE PREFERENCE

☒ EARLY STAGE
☒ Seed
☒ Start-up
☒ 1st Stage
☒ LATER STAGE
☒ 2nd Stage
☒ Mature
☒ Mezzanine
☒ LBO/MBO
☒ Turnaround
☐ INT'L EXPANSION
☐ WILL CONSIDER ALL
☒ VENTURE LEASING

Other Locations:

Affiliation:
Minimum Investment: Less than $1 Million
Capital Under Management: Over $500 Million

GEOGRAPHIC PREF

☐ East Coast
☒ West Coast
☐ Northeast
☐ Mid Atlantic
☐ Gulf States
☐ Northwest
☐ Southeast
☐ Southwest
☐ Midwest
☐ Central
☐ Local to Office
☐ Other Geo Pref

SEVIN ROSEN MANAGEMENT CO.

169 University Avenue
Palo Alto CA 94301

Phone (650) 326-0550   Fax (650) 326-0707

PROFESSIONALS	TITLE
Stephen Dow	Partner
Steve Domenik	Partner
Jennifer Gill Roberts	Partner

INDUSTRY PREFERENCE

☒ INFORMATION INDUSTRY	☒ BASIC INDUSTRIES
☒ Communications	☐ Consumer
☒ Computer Equipment	☐ Distribution
☒ Computer Services	☐ Manufacturing
☒ Computer Components	☐ Retail
☐ Computer Entertainment	☒ Service
☒ Computer Education	☐ Wholesale
☒ Information Technologies	☐ SPECIFIC INDUSTRIES
☐ Computer Media	☐ Energy
☒ Software	☐ Environmental
☒ Internet	☐ Financial
☒ MEDICAL/HEALTHCARE	☐ Real Estate
☒ Biotechnology	☐ Transportation
☒ Healthcare Services	☐ Publishing
☒ Life Sciences	☐ Food
☒ Medical Products	☐ Franchises
☒ INDUSTRIAL	☒ DIVERSIFIED
☐ Advanced Materials	☐ MISCELLANEOUS
☒ Chemicals	
☐ Instruments & Controls	

STAGE PREFERENCE

☒ EARLY STAGE
☒ Seed
☒ Start-up
☒ 1st Stage
☐ LATER STAGE
☐ 2nd Stage
☐ Mature
☐ Mezzanine
☐ LBO/MBO
☐ Turnaround
☐ INT'L EXPANSION
☐ WILL CONSIDER ALL
☐ VENTURE LEASING

Other Locations: Dallas TX

Affiliation: Sevin Rosen Funds
Minimum Investment: Less than $1 Million
Capital Under Management: $100 to $500 Million

GEOGRAPHIC PREF

☐ East Coast
☐ West Coast
☐ Northeast
☐ Mid Atlantic
☐ Gulf States
☐ Northwest
☐ Southeast
☐ Southwest
☐ Midwest
☐ Central
☐ Local to Office
☐ Other Geo Pref

SIENNA HOLDINGS

2330 Marinship Way
Suite 220
Sausalito CA 94965

Phone (415) 339-2800   Fax (415) 339-2805

PROFESSIONALS	TITLE
Daniel Skaff	Chairman and CEO
Nancy Roset	Principal

INDUSTRY PREFERENCE

☒ INFORMATION INDUSTRY	☐ BASIC INDUSTRIES
☒ Communications	☐ Consumer
☒ Computer Equipment	☐ Distribution
☒ Computer Services	☐ Manufacturing
☐ Computer Components	☐ Retail
☐ Computer Entertainment	☐ Service
☐ Computer Education	☐ Wholesale
☒ Information Technologies	☐ SPECIFIC INDUSTRIES
☐ Computer Media	☐ Energy
☒ Software	☐ Environmental
☒ Internet	☐ Financial
☐ MEDICAL/HEALTHCARE	☐ Real Estate
☐ Biotechnology	☐ Transportation
☐ Healthcare Services	☐ Publishing
☐ Life Sciences	☐ Food
☐ Medical Products	☐ Franchises
☐ INDUSTRIAL	☐ DIVERSIFIED
☐ Advanced Materials	☒ MISCELLANEOUS
☐ Chemicals	
☐ Instruments & Controls	

STAGE PREFERENCE

☒ EARLY STAGE
☐ Seed
☒ Start-up
☒ 1st Stage
☒ LATER STAGE
☒ 2nd Stage
☒ Mature
☐ Mezzanine
☐ LBO/MBO
☐ Turnaround
☐ INT'L EXPANSION
☐ WILL CONSIDER ALL
☐ VENTURE LEASING

Other Locations:

Affiliation:
Minimum Investment: $1 Million or more
Capital Under Management: $100 to $500 Million

GEOGRAPHIC PREF

☐ East Coast
☐ West Coast
☐ Northeast
☐ Mid Atlantic
☐ Gulf States
☐ Northwest
☐ Southeast
☐ Southwest
☐ Midwest
☐ Central
☐ Local to Office
☐ Other Geo Pref

SIERRA VENTURES

3000 Sand Hill Road
Building Four, Suite 210
Menlo Park CA 94025

Phone (650) 854-1000   Fax (650) 854-5593

PROFESSIONALS	TITLE
Jeffrey M. Drazan	General Partner
Peter C. Wendell	General Partner
Petri Vainio	General Partner
David Schwab	General Partner

INDUSTRY PREFERENCE

☒ INFORMATION INDUSTRY	☒ BASIC INDUSTRIES
☒ Communications	☐ Consumer
☒ Computer Equipment	☐ Distribution
☒ Computer Services	☐ Manufacturing
☒ Computer Components	☐ Retail
☐ Computer Entertainment	☒ Service
☒ Computer Education	☐ Wholesale
☒ Information Technologies	☒ SPECIFIC INDUSTRIES
☒ Computer Media	☐ Energy
☒ Software	☐ Environmental
☒ Internet	☒ Financial
☒ MEDICAL/HEALTHCARE	☐ Real Estate
☒ Biotechnology	☐ Transportation
☒ Healthcare Services	☐ Publishing
☒ Life Sciences	☐ Food
☒ Medical Products	☐ Franchises
☐ INDUSTRIAL	☒ DIVERSIFIED
☐ Advanced Materials	☐ MISCELLANEOUS
☐ Chemicals	
☐ Instruments & Controls	

STAGE PREFERENCE

☒ EARLY STAGE
☒ Seed
☒ Start-up
☒ 1st Stage
☐ LATER STAGE
☐ 2nd Stage
☐ Mature
☐ Mezzanine
☐ LBO/MBO
☐ Turnaround
☐ INT'L EXPANSION
☐ WILL CONSIDER ALL
☐ VENTURE LEASING

Other Locations:

Affiliation: The Prospect Group
Minimum Investment: Less than $1 Million
Capital Under Management: $100 to $500 Million

GEOGRAPHIC PREF

☐ East Coast
☐ West Coast
☐ Northeast
☐ Mid Atlantic
☐ Gulf States
☐ Northwest
☐ Southeast
☐ Southwest
☐ Midwest
☐ Central
☐ Local to Office
☐ Other Geo Pref

SIGMA PARTNERS

2884 Sand Hill Road
Suite 121
Menlo Park CA 94025

Phone (650) 854-1300   Fax (650) 854-1323

PROFESSIONALS	TITLE
C. Bradford Jeffries	General Partner
J. Burgess Jamieson	General Partner
Lawrence G. Finch	General Partner
Wade Woodson	General Partner
Clifford L. Haas	General Partner

INDUSTRY PREFERENCE

☒ INFORMATION INDUSTRY	☒ BASIC INDUSTRIES
☒ Communications	☐ Consumer
☒ Computer Equipment	☐ Distribution
☒ Computer Services	☐ Manufacturing
☒ Computer Components	☒ Retail
☐ Computer Entertainment	☒ Service
☒ Computer Education	☐ Wholesale
☒ Information Technologies	☐ SPECIFIC INDUSTRIES
☒ Computer Media	☐ Energy
☒ Software	☐ Environmental
☒ Internet	☐ Financial
☒ MEDICAL/HEALTHCARE	☐ Real Estate
☐ Biotechnology	☐ Transportation
☒ Healthcare Services	☐ Publishing
☐ Life Sciences	☐ Food
☒ Medical Products	☐ Franchises
☐ INDUSTRIAL	☒ DIVERSIFIED
☐ Advanced Materials	☐ MISCELLANEOUS
☐ Chemicals	
☐ Instruments & Controls	

STAGE PREFERENCE

☒ EARLY STAGE
☒ Seed
☒ Start-up
☒ 1st Stage
☒ LATER STAGE
☒ 2nd Stage
☒ Mature
☐ Mezzanine
☒ LBO/MBO
☐ Turnaround
☐ INT'L EXPANSION
☐ WILL CONSIDER ALL
☐ VENTURE LEASING

Other Locations: Boston MA

Affiliation:
Minimum Investment: Less than $1 Million
Capital Under Management: $100 to $500 Million

GEOGRAPHIC PREF

☐ East Coast
☐ West Coast
☐ Northeast
☐ Mid Atlantic
☐ Gulf States
☐ Northwest
☐ Southeast
☐ Southwest
☐ Midwest
☐ Central
☐ Local to Office
☐ Other Geo Pref

SOFINNOVA, INC.

140 Geary Street
10th Floor
San Francisco CA 94108

Phone (415) 228-3380   Fax (415) 228-3390

PROFESSIONALS	TITLE
Alain Azan	President
Robert Carr	Information Technology
Dr. Michael Powell	Life Sciences

INDUSTRY PREFERENCE

☒ INFORMATION INDUSTRY	☐ BASIC INDUSTRIES
☒ Communications	☐ Consumer
☒ Computer Equipment	☐ Distribution
☒ Computer Services	☐ Manufacturing
☒ Computer Components	☐ Retail
☐ Computer Entertainment	☐ Service
☐ Computer Education	☐ Wholesale
☒ Information Technologies	☐ SPECIFIC INDUSTRIES
☐ Computer Media	☐ Energy
☒ Software	☐ Environmental
☒ Internet	☐ Financial
☒ MEDICAL/HEALTHCARE	☐ Real Estate
☒ Biotechnology	☐ Transportation
☐ Healthcare Services	☐ Publishing
☒ Life Sciences	☐ Food
☒ Medical Products	☐ Franchises
☐ INDUSTRIAL	☒ DIVERSIFIED
☐ Advanced Materials	☒ MISCELLANEOUS
☐ Chemicals	
☐ Instruments & Controls	

STAGE PREFERENCE

☒ EARLY STAGE
☒ Seed
☒ Start-up
☒ 1st Stage
☒ LATER STAGE
☒ 2nd Stage
☐ Mature
☒ Mezzanine
☐ LBO/MBO
☐ Turnaround
☐ INT'L EXPANSION
☐ WILL CONSIDER ALL
☐ VENTURE LEASING

Other Locations:

Affiliation:
Minimum Investment: Less than $1 Million
Capital Under Management: Less than $100 Million

GEOGRAPHIC PREF

☐ East Coast
☒ West Coast
☐ Northeast
☐ Mid Atlantic
☐ Gulf States
☐ Northwest
☐ Southeast
☐ Southwest
☐ Midwest
☐ Central
☐ Local to Office
☐ Other Geo Pref

SOFTBANK TECHNOLOGY VENTURES

333 W. San Carlos
Suite 1225
San Jose CA 95110

Phone (408) 271-2265   Fax (408) 271-2270

PROFESSIONALS	TITLE
Gary Rieschel	Managing Director
Scott Russell	Managing Director

INDUSTRY PREFERENCE

☒ INFORMATION INDUSTRY	☒ BASIC INDUSTRIES
☒ Communications	☐ Consumer
☒ Computer Equipment	☐ Distribution
☐ Computer Services	☐ Manufacturing
☒ Computer Components	☐ Retail
☐ Computer Entertainment	☒ Service
☐ Computer Education	☐ Wholesale
☒ Information Technologies	☒ SPECIFIC INDUSTRIES
☒ Computer Media	☐ Energy
☒ Software	☐ Environmental
☒ Internet	☐ Financial
☐ MEDICAL/HEALTHCARE	☐ Real Estate
☐ Biotechnology	☐ Transportation
☐ Healthcare Services	☐ Publishing
☐ Life Sciences	☐ Food
☐ Medical Products	☐ Franchises
☐ INDUSTRIAL	☒ DIVERSIFIED
☐ Advanced Materials	☒ MISCELLANEOUS
☐ Chemicals	
☐ Instruments & Controls	

STAGE PREFERENCE

☒ EARLY STAGE
☒ Seed
☒ Start-up
☒ 1st Stage
☒ LATER STAGE
☒ 2nd Stage
☒ Mature
☒ Mezzanine
☒ LBO/MBO
☐ Turnaround
☐ INT'L EXPANSION
☐ WILL CONSIDER ALL
☐ VENTURE LEASING

Other Locations: Newton Center MA, Eldorado Springs CO

Affiliation:
Minimum Investment: $1 Million or more
Capital Under Management: Over $500 Million

GEOGRAPHIC PREF

☐ East Coast
☐ West Coast
☐ Northeast
☐ Mid Atlantic
☐ Gulf States
☐ Northwest
☐ Southeast
☐ Southwest
☐ Midwest
☐ Central
☐ Local to Office
☐ Other Geo Pref

SORRENTO ASSOCIATES

4370 La Jolla Village Drive
Suite 1040
San Diego CA 92122-1253

Phone (858) 452-3100   Fax (858) 452-7607

PROFESSIONALS	TITLE
Robert M. Jaffe	President & CEO
Vincent Burgess	Vice President

INDUSTRY PREFERENCE

- ☒ INFORMATION INDUSTRY
- ☒ Communications
- ☒ Computer Equipment
- ☐ Computer Services
- ☒ Computer Components
- ☐ Computer Entertainment
- ☐ Computer Education
- ☐ Information Technologies
- ☐ Computer Media
- ☐ Software
- ☒ Internet
- ☒ MEDICAL/HEALTHCARE
- ☒ Biotechnology
- ☒ Healthcare Services
- ☒ Life Sciences
- ☒ Medical Products
- ☐ INDUSTRIAL
- ☐ Advanced Materials
- ☐ Chemicals
- ☐ Instruments & Controls

- ☒ BASIC INDUSTRIES
- ☒ Consumer
- ☒ Distribution
- ☐ Manufacturing
- ☒ Retail
- ☐ Service
- ☐ Wholesale
- ☐ SPECIFIC INDUSTRIES
- ☐ Energy
- ☐ Environmental
- ☐ Financial
- ☐ Real Estate
- ☐ Transportation
- ☐ Publishing
- ☐ Food
- ☐ Franchises
- ☒ DIVERSIFIED
- ☐ MISCELLANEOUS

STAGE PREFERENCE

- ☐ EARLY STAGE
- ☐ Seed
- ☐ Start-up
- ☐ 1st Stage
- ☒ LATER STAGE
- ☒ 2nd Stage
- ☒ Mature
- ☐ Mezzanine
- ☒ LBO/MBO
- ☐ Turnaround
- ☐ INT'L EXPANSION
- ☐ WILL CONSIDER ALL
- ☐ VENTURE LEASING

SBIC
Other Locations:

Affiliation:
Minimum Investment: Less than $1 Million
Capital Under Management: $100 to $500 Million

GEOGRAPHIC PREF

- ☐ East Coast
- ☒ West Coast
- ☐ Northeast
- ☐ Mid Atlantic
- ☐ Gulf States
- ☐ Northwest
- ☐ Southeast
- ☐ Southwest
- ☐ Midwest
- ☐ Central
- ☐ Local to Office
- ☐ Other Geo Pref

SPECTRUM EQUITY INVESTORS

245 Lytton Avenue
Suite 175
Palo Alto CA 94301

Phone (415) 464-4600   Fax (415) 464-4601

PROFESSIONALS	TITLE
Brion Applegate	Managing General Partner
Randy Henderson	General Partner
Matthew Mochary	Partner
Vic Parker	Vice President

INDUSTRY PREFERENCE

- ☒ INFORMATION INDUSTRY
- ☒ Communications
- ☒ Computer Equipment
- ☒ Computer Services
- ☒ Computer Components
- ☐ Computer Entertainment
- ☐ Computer Education
- ☒ Information Technologies
- ☒ Computer Media
- ☒ Software
- ☒ Internet
- ☐ MEDICAL/HEALTHCARE
- ☐ Biotechnology
- ☐ Healthcare Services
- ☐ Life Sciences
- ☐ Medical Products
- ☐ INDUSTRIAL
- ☐ Advanced Materials
- ☐ Chemicals
- ☐ Instruments & Controls

- ☐ BASIC INDUSTRIES
- ☐ Consumer
- ☐ Distribution
- ☐ Manufacturing
- ☐ Retail
- ☐ Service
- ☐ Wholesale
- ☐ SPECIFIC INDUSTRIES
- ☐ Energy
- ☐ Environmental
- ☐ Financial
- ☐ Real Estate
- ☐ Transportation
- ☐ Publishing
- ☐ Food
- ☐ Franchises
- ☒ DIVERSIFIED
- ☒ MISCELLANEOUS

STAGE PREFERENCE

- ☒ EARLY STAGE
- ☒ Seed
- ☒ Start-up
- ☒ 1st Stage
- ☒ LATER STAGE
- ☒ 2nd Stage
- ☒ Mature
- ☒ Mezzanine
- ☒ LBO/MBO
- ☐ Turnaround
- ☐ INT'L EXPANSION
- ☐ WILL CONSIDER ALL
- ☐ VENTURE LEASING

Other Locations: Boston MA

Affiliation:
Minimum Investment: $1 Million or more
Capital Under Management: $100 to $500 Million

GEOGRAPHIC PREF

- ☐ East Coast
- ☐ West Coast
- ☐ Northeast
- ☐ Mid Atlantic
- ☐ Gulf States
- ☐ Northwest
- ☐ Southeast
- ☐ Southwest
- ☐ Midwest
- ☐ Central
- ☐ Local to Office
- ☐ Other Geo Pref

SPROUT GROUP

3000 Sand Hill Road
Building Three, Suite 170
Menlo Park CA 94025-7116

Phone (650) 234-2700   Fax (650) 234-2779

PROFESSIONALS	TITLE
Kathleen LaPorte	General Partner
Keith B. Geeslin	General Partner
Robert Finzi	General Partner
Robert E. Curry	General Partner
Philippe O. Chambon	General Partner
Stephen M. Diamond	General Partner
Alexander Rosen	General Partner
Farrokh Billimoria	General Partner

INDUSTRY PREFERENCE

- ☒ INFORMATION INDUSTRY
- ☒ Communications
- ☒ Computer Equipment
- ☒ Computer Services
- ☒ Computer Components
- ☐ Computer Entertainment
- ☒ Computer Education
- ☒ Information Technologies
- ☐ Computer Media
- ☒ Software
- ☒ Internet
- ☒ MEDICAL/HEALTHCARE
- ☒ Biotechnology
- ☒ Healthcare Services
- ☐ Life Sciences
- ☒ Medical Products
- ☒ INDUSTRIAL
- ☐ Advanced Materials
- ☒ Chemicals
- ☐ Instruments & Controls

- ☒ BASIC INDUSTRIES
- ☒ Consumer
- ☒ Distribution
- ☐ Manufacturing
- ☐ Retail
- ☒ Service
- ☐ Wholesale
- ☒ SPECIFIC INDUSTRIES
- ☐ Energy
- ☐ Environmental
- ☒ Financial
- ☐ Real Estate
- ☐ Transportation
- ☐ Publishing
- ☐ Food
- ☐ Franchises
- ☒ DIVERSIFIED
- ☐ MISCELLANEOUS

STAGE PREFERENCE

- ☒ EARLY STAGE
- ☒ Seed
- ☒ Start-up
- ☒ 1st Stage
- ☒ LATER STAGE
- ☒ 2nd Stage
- ☒ Mature
- ☒ Mezzanine
- ☒ LBO/MBO
- ☐ Turnaround
- ☐ INT'L EXPANSION
- ☐ WILL CONSIDER ALL
- ☐ VENTURE LEASING

Other Locations: New York NY

Affiliation: Donaldson, Lufkin & Jenrette, Inc.
Minimum Investment: $1 Million or more
Capital Under Management: Over $500 Million

GEOGRAPHIC PREF

- ☐ East Coast
- ☐ West Coast
- ☐ Northeast
- ☐ Mid Atlantic
- ☐ Gulf States
- ☐ Northwest
- ☐ Southeast
- ☐ Southwest
- ☐ Midwest
- ☐ Central
- ☐ Local to Office
- ☐ Other Geo Pref

ST. PAUL VENTURE CAPITAL, INC.

Three Lagoon Drive
Suite 130
Redwood City CA 94065

Phone (650) 596-5630   Fax (650) 596-5711

PROFESSIONALS	TITLE
Nancy Olsen	General Partner

INDUSTRY PREFERENCE

- ☒ INFORMATION INDUSTRY
- ☒ Communications
- ☒ Computer Equipment
- ☒ Computer Services
- ☒ Computer Components
- ☐ Computer Entertainment
- ☒ Computer Education
- ☒ Information Technologies
- ☐ Computer Media
- ☒ Software
- ☒ Internet
- ☒ MEDICAL/HEALTHCARE
- ☒ Biotechnology
- ☒ Healthcare Services
- ☒ Life Sciences
- ☒ Medical Products
- ☒ INDUSTRIAL
- ☐ Advanced Materials
- ☐ Chemicals
- ☒ Instruments & Controls

- ☒ BASIC INDUSTRIES
- ☒ Consumer
- ☐ Distribution
- ☐ Manufacturing
- ☐ Retail
- ☐ Service
- ☐ Wholesale
- ☐ SPECIFIC INDUSTRIES
- ☐ Energy
- ☐ Environmental
- ☐ Financial
- ☐ Real Estate
- ☐ Transportation
- ☐ Publishing
- ☐ Food
- ☐ Franchises
- ☒ DIVERSIFIED
- ☒ MISCELLANEOUS

STAGE PREFERENCE

- ☒ EARLY STAGE
- ☒ Seed
- ☒ Start-up
- ☒ 1st Stage
- ☒ LATER STAGE
- ☒ 2nd Stage
- ☒ Mature
- ☒ Mezzanine
- ☒ LBO/MBO
- ☐ Turnaround
- ☐ INT'L EXPANSION
- ☐ WILL CONSIDER ALL
- ☐ VENTURE LEASING

Other Locations: Eden Prairie MN, Andover MA

Affiliation:
Minimum Investment: $1 Million or more
Capital Under Management: Over $500 Million

GEOGRAPHIC PREF

- ☐ East Coast
- ☐ West Coast
- ☐ Northeast
- ☐ Mid Atlantic
- ☐ Gulf States
- ☐ Northwest
- ☐ Southeast
- ☐ Southwest
- ☐ Midwest
- ☐ Central
- ☐ Local to Office
- ☐ Other Geo Pref

SUMMIT PARTNERS

499 Hamilton Avenue
Suite 200
Palo Alto CA 94301

Phone (650) 321-1166 Fax (650) 321-1188

PROFESSIONALS	TITLE
Walter Kortschak	Managing Partner
Gregory M. Avis	Managing Partner
Peter Y. Chung	General Partner

INDUSTRY PREFERENCE

☒ INFORMATION INDUSTRY	☒ BASIC INDUSTRIES
☒ Communications	☐ Consumer
☒ Computer Equipment	☐ Distribution
☒ Computer Services	☐ Manufacturing
☒ Computer Components	☐ Retail
☐ Computer Entertainment	☒ Service
☒ Computer Education	☐ Wholesale
☒ Information Technologies	☐ SPECIFIC INDUSTRIES
☒ Computer Media	☐ Energy
☒ Software	☐ Environmental
☒ Internet	☐ Financial
☒ MEDICAL/HEALTHCARE	☐ Real Estate
☒ Biotechnology	☐ Transportation
☒ Healthcare Services	☐ Publishing
☒ Life Sciences	☐ Food
☒ Medical Products	☐ Franchises
☐ INDUSTRIAL	☒ DIVERSIFIED
☐ Advanced Materials	☐ MISCELLANEOUS
☐ Chemicals	
☐ Instruments & Controls	

STAGE PREFERENCE

☒ EARLY STAGE	
☐ Seed	
☐ Start-up	
☒ 1st Stage	
☒ LATER STAGE	
☒ 2nd Stage	
☒ Mature	
☒ Mezzanine	
☐ LBO/MBO	
☐ Turnaround	
☐ INT'L EXPANSION	
☐ WILL CONSIDER ALL	
☐ VENTURE LEASING	

Other Locations: Boston MA

Affiliation:
Minimum Investment: Less than $1 Million
Capital Under Management: Over $500 Million

GEOGRAPHIC PREF

☐ East Coast	
☐ West Coast	
☐ Northeast	
☐ Mid Atlantic	
☐ Gulf States	
☐ Northwest	
☐ Southeast	
☐ Southwest	
☐ Midwest	
☐ Central	
☐ Local to Office	
☐ Other Geo Pref	

SUTTER HILL VENTURES

755 Page Mill Road
Suite A-200
Palo Alto CA 94304-1005

Phone (650) 493-5600 Fax (650) 858-1854

PROFESSIONALS	TITLE
G. Leonard Baker, Jr.	Managing Director
Tench Coxe	Managing Director
William H. Younger, Jr.	Managing Director
David L. Anderson	Managing Director
Gregory P. Sands	Managing Director

INDUSTRY PREFERENCE

☒ INFORMATION INDUSTRY	☒ BASIC INDUSTRIES
☒ Communications	☐ Consumer
☒ Computer Equipment	☒ Distribution
☒ Computer Services	☒ Manufacturing
☒ Computer Components	☒ Retail
☐ Computer Entertainment	☒ Service
☒ Computer Education	☐ Wholesale
☒ Information Technologies	☒ SPECIFIC INDUSTRIES
☐ Computer Media	☐ Energy
☒ Software	☐ Environmental
☒ Internet	☒ Financial
☒ MEDICAL/HEALTHCARE	☐ Real Estate
☒ Biotechnology	☐ Transportation
☒ Healthcare Services	☐ Publishing
☒ Life Sciences	☐ Food
☒ Medical Products	☐ Franchises
☒ INDUSTRIAL	☒ DIVERSIFIED
☒ Advanced Materials	☐ MISCELLANEOUS
☒ Chemicals	
☒ Instruments & Controls	

STAGE PREFERENCE

☒ EARLY STAGE	
☐ Seed	
☐ Start-up	
☒ 1st Stage	
☒ LATER STAGE	
☒ 2nd Stage	
☒ Mature	
☐ Mezzanine	
☒ LBO/MBO	
☐ Turnaround	
☐ INT'L EXPANSION	
☐ WILL CONSIDER ALL	
☐ VENTURE LEASING	

Other Locations:

Affiliation:
Minimum Investment: Less than $1 Million
Capital Under Management: $100 to $500 Million

GEOGRAPHIC PREF

☐ East Coast	
☐ West Coast	
☐ Northeast	
☐ Mid Atlantic	
☐ Gulf States	
☐ Northwest	
☐ Southeast	
☐ Southwest	
☐ Midwest	
☐ Central	
☐ Local to Office	
☐ Other Geo Pref	

TA ASSOCIATES, INC.

70 Willow Road
Suite 100
Palo Alto CA 94025

Phone (650) 328-1210   Fax (650) 326-4933

PROFESSIONALS	TITLE
Michael C. Child	Managing Director
Jeffrey T. Chambers	Managing Director

INDUSTRY PREFERENCE

☒ INFORMATION INDUSTRY
☒ Communications
☒ Computer Equipment
☒ Computer Services
☒ Computer Components
☐ Computer Entertainment
☒ Computer Education
☒ Information Technologies
☒ Computer Media
☒ Software
☒ Internet
☒ MEDICAL/HEALTHCARE
☒ Biotechnology
☒ Healthcare Services
☒ Life Sciences
☒ Medical Products
☒ INDUSTRIAL
☐ Advanced Materials
☐ Chemicals
☒ Instruments & Controls

☒ BASIC INDUSTRIES
☒ Consumer
☒ Distribution
☐ Manufacturing
☒ Retail
☒ Service
☐ Wholesale
☒ SPECIFIC INDUSTRIES
☒ Energy
☒ Environmental
☒ Financial
☐ Real Estate
☐ Transportation
☐ Publishing
☐ Food
☐ Franchises
☒ DIVERSIFIED
☐ MISCELLANEOUS

STAGE PREFERENCE

☐ EARLY STAGE
☐ Seed
☐ Start-up
☐ 1st Stage
☒ LATER STAGE
☒ 2nd Stage
☒ Mature
☒ Mezzanine
☒ LBO/MBO
☐ Turnaround
☐ INT'L EXPANSION
☐ WILL CONSIDER ALL
☐ VENTURE LEASING

Other Locations: Boston MA, Pittsburgh PA

Affiliation:
Minimum Investment: $1 Million or more
Capital Under Management: Over $500 Million

GEOGRAPHIC PREF

☐ East Coast
☐ West Coast
☐ Northeast
☐ Mid Atlantic
☐ Gulf States
☐ Northwest
☐ Southeast
☐ Southwest
☐ Midwest
☐ Central
☐ Local to Office
☐ Other Geo Pref

TECHNOLOGY CROSSOVER VENTURES (TCV)

575 High Street
Suite 400
Palo Alto CA 94301

Phone (650) 614-8200   Fax (650) 614-8222

PROFESSIONALS	TITLE
Jay Hoag	General Partner
Richard Kimball	General Partner
Tom Newby	General Partner
Michael Linnert	General Partner
Jake Reynolds	General Partner

INDUSTRY PREFERENCE

☒ INFORMATION INDUSTRY
☒ Communications
☒ Computer Equipment
☒ Computer Services
☒ Computer Components
☐ Computer Entertainment
☐ Computer Education
☒ Information Technologies
☐ Computer Media
☒ Software
☒ Internet
☐ MEDICAL/HEALTHCARE
☐ Biotechnology
☐ Healthcare Services
☐ Life Sciences
☐ Medical Products
☐ INDUSTRIAL
☐ Advanced Materials
☐ Chemicals
☐ Instruments & Controls

☐ BASIC INDUSTRIES
☐ Consumer
☐ Distribution
☐ Manufacturing
☐ Retail
☐ Service
☐ Wholesale
☐ SPECIFIC INDUSTRIES
☐ Energy
☐ Environmental
☐ Financial
☐ Real Estate
☐ Transportation
☐ Publishing
☐ Food
☐ Franchises
☐ DIVERSIFIED
☒ MISCELLANEOUS

STAGE PREFERENCE

☐ EARLY STAGE
☐ Seed
☐ Start-up
☐ 1st Stage
☒ LATER STAGE
☐ 2nd Stage
☐ Mature
☒ Mezzanine
☒ LBO/MBO
☐ Turnaround
☐ INT'L EXPANSION
☐ WILL CONSIDER ALL
☐ VENTURE LEASING

Other Locations:

Affiliation:
Minimum Investment: $1 Million or more
Capital Under Management: Over $500 Million

GEOGRAPHIC PREF

☐ East Coast
☐ West Coast
☐ Northeast
☐ Mid Atlantic
☐ Gulf States
☐ Northwest
☐ Southeast
☐ Southwest
☐ Midwest
☐ Central
☐ Local to Office
☐ Other Geo Pref

TECHNOLOGY FUNDING INC.

2000 Alameda de las Pulgas
Suite 250
San Mateo CA 94403

Phone (650) 345-2200   Fax (650) 345-1795

PROFESSIONALS

Charles Kokesh
Gregory George

TITLE

Managing General Partner
General Partner

INDUSTRY PREFERENCE

☒ INFORMATION INDUSTRY	☒ BASIC INDUSTRIES
☒ Communications	☐ Consumer
☒ Computer Equipment	☐ Distribution
☒ Computer Services	☐ Manufacturing
☒ Computer Components	☐ Retail
☐ Computer Entertainment	☒ Service
☐ Computer Education	☐ Wholesale
☒ Information Technologies	☐ SPECIFIC INDUSTRIES
☐ Computer Media	☐ Energy
☒ Software	☐ Environmental
☒ Internet	☐ Financial
☒ MEDICAL/HEALTHCARE	☐ Real Estate
☒ Biotechnology	☐ Transportation
☒ Healthcare Services	☐ Publishing
☒ Life Sciences	☐ Food
☒ Medical Products	☐ Franchises
☒ INDUSTRIAL	☒ DIVERSIFIED
☐ Advanced Materials	☐ MISCELLANEOUS
☐ Chemicals	
☒ Instruments & Controls	

STAGE PREFERENCE

☒ EARLY STAGE
☒ Seed
☒ Start-up
☒ 1st Stage
☒ LATER STAGE
☒ 2nd Stage
☒ Mature
☒ Mezzanine
☐ LBO/MBO
☐ Turnaround
☐ INT'L EXPANSION
☐ WILL CONSIDER ALL
☐ VENTURE LEASING

Other Locations:

Affiliation:
Minimum Investment: Less than $1 Million
Capital Under Management: $100 to $500 Million

GEOGRAPHIC PREF

☐ East Coast
☒ West Coast
☐ Northeast
☐ Mid Atlantic
☐ Gulf States
☐ Northwest
☐ Southeast
☐ Southwest
☐ Midwest
☐ Central
☐ Local to Office
☐ Other Geo Pref

TECHNOLOGY PARTNERS

1550 Tiburon Boulevard
Suite A
Belvedere CA 94920

Phone (415) 435-1935   Fax (415) 435-5921

PROFESSIONALS

Ted Ardell III
Roger J. Quy, PhD
William Hart
Ira Ehrenpreis

TITLE

Partner
Partner
Partner
Partner

INDUSTRY PREFERENCE

☒ INFORMATION INDUSTRY	☒ BASIC INDUSTRIES
☒ Communications	☐ Consumer
☐ Computer Equipment	☐ Distribution
☐ Computer Services	☐ Manufacturing
☐ Computer Components	☐ Retail
☐ Computer Entertainment	☒ Service
☐ Computer Education	☐ Wholesale
☒ Information Technologies	☐ SPECIFIC INDUSTRIES
☐ Computer Media	☐ Energy
☐ Software	☐ Environmental
☒ Internet	☐ Financial
☒ MEDICAL/HEALTHCARE	☐ Real Estate
☒ Biotechnology	☐ Transportation
☐ Healthcare Services	☐ Publishing
☒ Life Sciences	☐ Food
☒ Medical Products	☐ Franchises
☐ INDUSTRIAL	☒ DIVERSIFIED
☐ Advanced Materials	☐ MISCELLANEOUS
☐ Chemicals	
☐ Instruments & Controls	

STAGE PREFERENCE

☒ EARLY STAGE
☒ Seed
☒ Start-up
☒ 1st Stage
☐ LATER STAGE
☐ 2nd Stage
☐ Mature
☐ Mezzanine
☐ LBO/MBO
☐ Turnaround
☐ INT'L EXPANSION
☐ WILL CONSIDER ALL
☐ VENTURE LEASING

Other Locations:

Affiliation:
Minimum Investment: Less than $1 Million
Capital Under Management: $100 to $500 Million

GEOGRAPHIC PREF

☐ East Coast
☒ West Coast
☐ Northeast
☐ Mid Atlantic
☐ Gulf States
☐ Northwest
☐ Southeast
☐ Southwest
☐ Midwest
☐ Central
☐ Local to Office
☐ Other Geo Pref

THOMA CRESSEY EQUITY PARTNERS

600 Montgomery Street
27th Floor
San Francisco CA 94111

Phone (415) 263-3660   Fax (415) 392-6480

PROFESSIONALS	TITLE
Robert Manning	Partner
Christian Osborn	Partner
Kenn Lee	Partner

INDUSTRY PREFERENCE

☒ INFORMATION INDUSTRY
☒ Communications
☒ Computer Equipment
☒ Computer Services
☒ Computer Components
☐ Computer Entertainment
☒ Computer Education
☒ Information Technologies
☒ Computer Media
☒ Software
☒ Internet
☒ MEDICAL/HEALTHCARE
☒ Biotechnology
☒ Healthcare Services
☒ Life Sciences
☒ Medical Products
☒ INDUSTRIAL
☒ Advanced Materials
☒ Chemicals
☒ Instruments & Controls

☒ BASIC INDUSTRIES
☒ Consumer
☒ Distribution
☒ Manufacturing
☒ Retail
☒ Service
☒ Wholesale
☒ SPECIFIC INDUSTRIES
☒ Energy
☒ Environmental
☐ Financial
☐ Real Estate
☒ Transportation
☒ Publishing
☐ Food
☐ Franchises
☒ DIVERSIFIED
☐ MISCELLANEOUS

STAGE PREFERENCE

☐ EARLY STAGE
☐ Seed
☐ Start-up
☐ 1st Stage
☒ LATER STAGE
☒ 2nd Stage
☒ Mature
☐ Mezzanine
☒ LBO/MBO
☐ Turnaround
☐ INT'L EXPANSION
☐ WILL CONSIDER ALL
☐ VENTURE LEASING

Other Locations: Chicago IL, Denver CO

Affiliation:
Minimum Investment: $1 Million or more
Capital Under Management: $100 to $500 Million

GEOGRAPHIC PREF

☐ East Coast
☐ West Coast
☐ Northeast
☐ Mid Atlantic
☐ Gulf States
☐ Northwest
☐ Southeast
☐ Southwest
☐ Midwest
☐ Central
☐ Local to Office
☐ Other Geo Pref

THOMPSON CLIVE VENTURE CAPITAL

3000 Sand Hill Road
Building 1, Suite 185
Menlo Park CA 94025

Phone (650) 854-0314   Fax (650) 854-0670

PROFESSIONALS	TITLE
Robert Patterson	Director
Greg Ennis	Director
James Mulford	Director
Michelle Stecklein	Director

INDUSTRY PREFERENCE

☒ INFORMATION INDUSTRY
☒ Communications
☒ Computer Equipment
☒ Computer Services
☒ Computer Components
☐ Computer Entertainment
☒ Computer Education
☒ Information Technologies
☒ Computer Media
☒ Software
☒ Internet
☒ MEDICAL/HEALTHCARE
☒ Biotechnology
☐ Healthcare Services
☒ Life Sciences
☒ Medical Products
☒ INDUSTRIAL
☐ Advanced Materials
☒ Chemicals
☒ Instruments & Controls

☒ BASIC INDUSTRIES
☐ Consumer
☐ Distribution
☐ Manufacturing
☐ Retail
☒ Service
☐ Wholesale
☒ SPECIFIC INDUSTRIES
☐ Energy
☒ Environmental
☐ Financial
☐ Real Estate
☐ Transportation
☐ Publishing
☐ Food
☐ Franchises
☒ DIVERSIFIED
☐ MISCELLANEOUS

STAGE PREFERENCE

☒ EARLY STAGE
☒ Seed
☒ Start-up
☒ 1st Stage
☒ LATER STAGE
☒ 2nd Stage
☒ Mature
☒ Mezzanine
☒ LBO/MBO
☐ Turnaround
☐ INT'L EXPANSION
☐ WILL CONSIDER ALL
☐ VENTURE LEASING

Other Locations:

Affiliation:
Minimum Investment: Less than $1 Million
Capital Under Management: $100 to $500 Million

GEOGRAPHIC PREF

☐ East Coast
☐ West Coast
☐ Northeast
☐ Mid Atlantic
☐ Gulf States
☐ Northwest
☐ Southeast
☐ Southwest
☐ Midwest
☐ Central
☐ Local to Office
☐ Other Geo Pref

THREE ARCH PARTNERS

2800 Sand Hill Road
Suite 270
Menlo Park CA 94025

Phone (650) 854-5550   Fax (650) 854-9880

PROFESSIONALS	TITLE
Mark A. Wan	Partner
Wilfred E. Jaeger	Partner
Thomas J. Fogarty	Partner

INDUSTRY PREFERENCE

☐ INFORMATION INDUSTRY
☐ Communications
☐ Computer Equipment
☐ Computer Services
☐ Computer Components
☐ Computer Entertainment
☐ Computer Education
☐ Information Technologies
☐ Computer Media
☐ Software
☐ Internet
☒ MEDICAL/HEALTHCARE
☒ Biotechnology
☒ Healthcare Services
☒ Life Sciences
☒ Medical Products
☐ INDUSTRIAL
☐ Advanced Materials
☐ Chemicals
☐ Instruments & Controls

☐ BASIC INDUSTRIES
☐ Consumer
☐ Distribution
☐ Manufacturing
☐ Retail
☐ Service
☐ Wholesale
☐ SPECIFIC INDUSTRIES
☐ Energy
☐ Environmental
☐ Financial
☐ Real Estate
☐ Transportation
☐ Publishing
☐ Food
☐ Franchises
☐ DIVERSIFIED
☐ MISCELLANEOUS

STAGE PREFERENCE

☒ EARLY STAGE
☒ Seed
☒ Start-up
☒ 1st Stage
☐ LATER STAGE
☐ 2nd Stage
☐ Mature
☐ Mezzanine
☐ LBO/MBO
☐ Turnaround
☐ INT'L EXPANSION
☐ WILL CONSIDER ALL
☐ VENTURE LEASING

Other Locations:

Affiliation:
Minimum Investment: Less than $1 Million
Capital Under Management: Less than $100 Million

GEOGRAPHIC PREF

☐ East Coast
☐ West Coast
☐ Northeast
☐ Mid Atlantic
☐ Gulf States
☐ Northwest
☐ Southeast
☐ Southwest
☐ Midwest
☐ Central
☐ Local to Office
☐ Other Geo Pref

THRESHOLD VENTURES

55 Pepper Drive
Los Altos CA 94022

Phone (650) 941-6765   Fax (650) 947-9165

PROFESSIONALS	TITLE
Jonathan Baer	General Partner

INDUSTRY PREFERENCE

☒ INFORMATION INDUSTRY
☒ Communications
☒ Computer Equipment
☒ Computer Services
☒ Computer Components
☐ Computer Entertainment
☒ Computer Education
☒ Information Technologies
☐ Computer Media
☒ Software
☒ Internet
☒ MEDICAL/HEALTHCARE
☒ Biotechnology
☒ Healthcare Services
☒ Life Sciences
☒ Medical Products
☒ INDUSTRIAL
☒ Advanced Materials
☒ Chemicals
☒ Instruments & Controls

☒ BASIC INDUSTRIES
☐ Consumer
☐ Distribution
☐ Manufacturing
☐ Retail
☒ Service
☐ Wholesale
☒ SPECIFIC INDUSTRIES
☒ Energy
☒ Environmental
☐ Financial
☐ Real Estate
☒ Transportation
☐ Publishing
☐ Food
☐ Franchises
☒ DIVERSIFIED
☐ MISCELLANEOUS

STAGE PREFERENCE

☒ EARLY STAGE
☐ Seed
☒ Start-up
☒ 1st Stage
☒ LATER STAGE
☒ 2nd Stage
☐ Mature
☐ Mezzanine
☐ LBO/MBO
☐ Turnaround
☐ INT'L EXPANSION
☐ WILL CONSIDER ALL
☐ VENTURE LEASING

Other Locations:

Affiliation:
Minimum Investment: Less than $1 Million
Capital Under Management: Less than $100 Million

GEOGRAPHIC PREF

☐ East Coast
☒ West Coast
☐ Northeast
☐ Mid Atlantic
☐ Gulf States
☐ Northwest
☐ Southeast
☐ Southwest
☐ Midwest
☐ Central
☐ Local to Office
☐ Other Geo Pref

TICONDEROGA CAPITAL INC.

One Post Street
Suite 2525
San Francisco CA 94104

Phone (415) 296-6343   Fax (415) 296-1363

PROFESSIONALS	TITLE
Dr. Graham Crooke	Partner

INDUSTRY PREFERENCE

- ☒ INFORMATION INDUSTRY
- ☐ Communications
- ☐ Computer Equipment
- ☒ Computer Services
- ☐ Computer Components
- ☐ Computer Entertainment
- ☐ Computer Education
- ☒ Information Technologies
- ☐ Computer Media
- ☐ Software
- ☐ Internet
- ☒ MEDICAL/HEALTHCARE
- ☐ Biotechnology
- ☒ Healthcare Services
- ☐ Life Sciences
- ☐ Medical Products
- ☐ INDUSTRIAL
- ☐ Advanced Materials
- ☐ Chemicals
- ☐ Instruments & Controls

- ☒ BASIC INDUSTRIES
- ☐ Consumer
- ☐ Distribution
- ☐ Manufacturing
- ☐ Retail
- ☒ Service
- ☐ Wholesale
- ☒ SPECIFIC INDUSTRIES
- ☒ Energy
- ☐ Environmental
- ☒ Financial
- ☐ Real Estate
- ☐ Transportation
- ☐ Publishing
- ☐ Food
- ☐ Franchises
- ☒ DIVERSIFIED
- ☒ MISCELLANEOUS

STAGE PREFERENCE

- ☐ EARLY STAGE
- ☐ Seed
- ☐ Start-up
- ☐ 1st Stage
- ☒ LATER STAGE
- ☒ 2nd Stage
- ☐ Mature
- ☒ Mezzanine
- ☒ LBO/MBO
- ☐ Turnaround
- ☐ INT'L EXPANSION
- ☐ WILL CONSIDER ALL
- ☐ VENTURE LEASING

Other Locations: Wellesley MA , New York NY

Affiliation:
Minimum Investment: $1 Million or more
Capital Under Management: $100 to $500 Million

GEOGRAPHIC PREF

- ☐ East Coast
- ☐ West Coast
- ☐ Northeast
- ☐ Mid Atlantic
- ☐ Gulf States
- ☐ Northwest
- ☐ Southeast
- ☐ Southwest
- ☐ Midwest
- ☐ Central
- ☐ Local to Office
- ☐ Other Geo Pref

TRANSCAP ASSOCIATES, INC.

1104 Highland
Suite D
Manhattan Beach CA 90266

Phone (310) 374-8320   Fax (310) 374-8329

PROFESSIONALS	TITLE
Jeff Bartlett	

INDUSTRY PREFERENCE

- ☒ INFORMATION INDUSTRY
- ☒ Communications
- ☒ Computer Equipment
- ☒ Computer Services
- ☒ Computer Components
- ☒ Computer Entertainment
- ☐ Computer Education
- ☐ Information Technologies
- ☐ Computer Media
- ☐ Software
- ☐ Internet
- ☒ MEDICAL/HEALTHCARE
- ☐ Biotechnology
- ☐ Healthcare Services
- ☐ Life Sciences
- ☒ Medical Products
- ☒ INDUSTRIAL
- ☐ Advanced Materials
- ☐ Chemicals
- ☒ Instruments & Controls

- ☒ BASIC INDUSTRIES
- ☐ Consumer
- ☒ Distribution
- ☐ Manufacturing
- ☐ Retail
- ☐ Service
- ☒ Wholesale
- ☒ SPECIFIC INDUSTRIES
- ☐ Energy
- ☐ Environmental
- ☐ Financial
- ☐ Real Estate
- ☐ Transportation
- ☐ Publishing
- ☐ Food
- ☐ Franchises
- ☒ DIVERSIFIED
- ☒ MISCELLANEOUS
  Apparal, Electronic
  Games, Toys

STAGE PREFERENCE

- ☐ EARLY STAGE
- ☐ Seed
- ☐ Start-up
- ☐ 1st Stage
- ☒ LATER STAGE
- ☒ 2nd Stage
- ☐ Mature
- ☒ Mezzanine
- ☐ LBO/MBO
- ☐ Turnaround
- ☐ INT'L EXPANSION
- ☐ WILL CONSIDER ALL
- ☐ VENTURE LEASING

Other Locations: New York NY, Northbrook IL

Affiliation:
Minimum Investment: $1 Million or more
Capital Under Management: Less than $100 Million

GEOGRAPHIC PREF

- ☐ East Coast
- ☐ West Coast
- ☐ Northeast
- ☐ Mid Atlantic
- ☐ Gulf States
- ☐ Northwest
- ☐ Southeast
- ☐ Southwest
- ☐ Midwest
- ☐ Central
- ☐ Local to Office
- ☐ Other Geo Pref

TRIDENT CAPITAL

2480 Sand Hill Road
Suite 100
Menlo Park CA 94025

Phone (650) 233-4300   Fax (650) 233-4333

PROFESSIONALS	TITLE
John Moragne	Partner
Donald R. Dixon	Partner
Christopher P. Marshall	Partner
Stephen M. Hall	Partner

INDUSTRY PREFERENCE

- ☒ INFORMATION INDUSTRY
- ☒ Communications
- ☒ Computer Equipment
- ☒ Computer Services
- ☒ Computer Components
- ☐ Computer Entertainment
- ☐ Computer Education
- ☒ Information Technologies
- ☐ Computer Media
- ☒ Software
- ☒ Internet
- ☐ MEDICAL/HEALTHCARE
- ☐ Biotechnology
- ☐ Healthcare Services
- ☐ Life Sciences
- ☐ Medical Products
- ☐ INDUSTRIAL
- ☐ Advanced Materials
- ☐ Chemicals
- ☐ Instruments & Controls

- ☒ BASIC INDUSTRIES
- ☐ Consumer
- ☐ Distribution
- ☐ Manufacturing
- ☐ Retail
- ☒ Service
- ☐ Wholesale
- ☒ SPECIFIC INDUSTRIES
- ☐ Energy
- ☐ Environmental
- ☒ Financial
- ☐ Real Estate
- ☐ Transportation
- ☐ Publishing
- ☐ Food
- ☐ Franchises
- ☒ DIVERSIFIED
- ☐ MISCELLANEOUS

STAGE PREFERENCE

- ☒ EARLY STAGE
- ☐ Seed
- ☐ Start-up
- ☒ 1st Stage
- ☒ LATER STAGE
- ☒ 2nd Stage
- ☒ Mature
- ☐ Mezzanine
- ☒ LBO/MBO
- ☐ Turnaround
- ☐ INT'L EXPANSION
- ☐ WILL CONSIDER ALL
- ☐ VENTURE LEASING

Other Locations: Los Angeles CA, Washington D.C., Lake Forest IL, Westport CT

Affiliation:
Minimum Investment: $1 Million or more
Capital Under Management: $100 to $500 Million

GEOGRAPHIC PREF

- ☐ East Coast
- ☐ West Coast
- ☐ Northeast
- ☐ Mid Atlantic
- ☐ Gulf States
- ☐ Northwest
- ☐ Southeast
- ☐ Southwest
- ☐ Midwest
- ☐ Central
- ☐ Local to Office
- ☐ Other Geo Pref

TRIDENT CAPITAL

11150 Santa Monica Boulevard
Suite 320
Los Angeles CA 90025

Phone (310) 444-3840   Fax (310) 444-3848

PROFESSIONALS	TITLE
Rockwell A. Schnabel	Partner
Todd A. Springer	Partner

INDUSTRY PREFERENCE

- ☒ INFORMATION INDUSTRY
- ☒ Communications
- ☒ Computer Equipment
- ☒ Computer Services
- ☒ Computer Components
- ☐ Computer Entertainment
- ☒ Computer Education
- ☒ Information Technologies
- ☐ Computer Media
- ☒ Software
- ☒ Internet
- ☐ MEDICAL/HEALTHCARE
- ☐ Biotechnology
- ☐ Healthcare Services
- ☐ Life Sciences
- ☐ Medical Products
- ☐ INDUSTRIAL
- ☐ Advanced Materials
- ☐ Chemicals
- ☐ Instruments & Controls

- ☒ BASIC INDUSTRIES
- ☐ Consumer
- ☐ Distribution
- ☐ Manufacturing
- ☐ Retail
- ☒ Service
- ☐ Wholesale
- ☒ SPECIFIC INDUSTRIES
- ☐ Energy
- ☐ Environmental
- ☒ Financial
- ☐ Real Estate
- ☐ Transportation
- ☐ Publishing
- ☐ Food
- ☐ Franchises
- ☒ DIVERSIFIED
- ☐ MISCELLANEOUS

STAGE PREFERENCE

- ☒ EARLY STAGE
- ☐ Seed
- ☐ Start-up
- ☒ 1st Stage
- ☒ LATER STAGE
- ☒ 2nd Stage
- ☒ Mature
- ☐ Mezzanine
- ☒ LBO/MBO
- ☐ Turnaround
- ☐ INT'L EXPANSION
- ☐ WILL CONSIDER ALL
- ☐ VENTURE LEASING

Other Locations: Menlo Park CA, Washington D.C., Lake Forest IL, Westport CT

Affiliation:
Minimum Investment: $1 Million or more
Capital Under Management: $100 to $500 Million

GEOGRAPHIC PREF

- ☐ East Coast
- ☐ West Coast
- ☐ Northeast
- ☐ Mid Atlantic
- ☐ Gulf States
- ☐ Northwest
- ☐ Southeast
- ☐ Southwest
- ☐ Midwest
- ☐ Central
- ☐ Local to Office
- ☐ Other Geo Pref

TRINITY VENTURES, LTD.

**3000 Sand Hill Road
Building One, Suite 240
Menlo Park CA 94025**

Phone (650) 854-9500   Fax (650) 854-9501

PROFESSIONALS	TITLE
Noel J. Fenton	Managing General Partner
Lawrence K. Orr	General Partner
James G. Shennan, Jr.	General Partner
Tod H. Francis	General Partner
Augustus O'Tai	General Partner
Fred Wang	General Partner

INDUSTRY PREFERENCE

☒ INFORMATION INDUSTRY
☒ Communications
☒ Computer Equipment
☒ Computer Services
☒ Computer Components
☐ Computer Entertainment
☒ Computer Education
☒ Information Technologies
☐ Computer Media
☒ Software
☒ Internet
☐ MEDICAL/HEALTHCARE
☐ Biotechnology
☐ Healthcare Services
☐ Life Sciences
☐ Medical Products
☐ INDUSTRIAL
☐ Advanced Materials
☐ Chemicals
☐ Instruments & Controls

☐ BASIC INDUSTRIES
☐ Consumer
☐ Distribution
☐ Manufacturing
☐ Retail
☐ Service
☐ Wholesale
☐ SPECIFIC INDUSTRIES
☐ Energy
☐ Environmental
☐ Financial
☐ Real Estate
☐ Transportation
☐ Publishing
☐ Food
☐ Franchises
☒ DIVERSIFIED
☐ MISCELLANEOUS

STAGE PREFERENCE

☒ EARLY STAGE
☒ Seed
☒ Start-up
☒ 1st Stage
☒ LATER STAGE
☒ 2nd Stage
☒ Mature
☐ Mezzanine
☒ LBO/MBO
☐ Turnaround
☐ INT'L EXPANSION
☐ WILL CONSIDER ALL
☐ VENTURE LEASING

Other Locations:

Affiliation: Bechtel Investments, Inc.
Minimum Investment: Less than $1 Million
Capital Under Management: $100 to $500 Million

GEOGRAPHIC PREF

☐ East Coast
☐ West Coast
☐ Northeast
☐ Mid Atlantic
☐ Gulf States
☐ Northwest
☐ Southeast
☐ Southwest
☐ Midwest
☐ Central
☐ Local to Office
☐ Other Geo Pref

VANGUARD VENTURE PARTNERS

**525 University Avenue
Suite 600
Palo Alto CA 94301**

Phone (650) 321-2900   Fax (650) 321-2902

PROFESSIONALS	TITLE
Jack M. Gill	General Partner
Robert Urlich	General Partner
Donald Wood	General Partner
Paul A. Slakey	Partner
Laura Gwosden	Chief Financial Officer

INDUSTRY PREFERENCE

☒ INFORMATION INDUSTRY
☒ Communications
☒ Computer Equipment
☒ Computer Services
☒ Computer Components
☐ Computer Entertainment
☐ Computer Education
☒ Information Technologies
☐ Computer Media
☒ Software
☒ Internet
☒ MEDICAL/HEALTHCARE
☒ Biotechnology
☒ Healthcare Services
☒ Life Sciences
☒ Medical Products
☐ INDUSTRIAL
☐ Advanced Materials
☐ Chemicals
☐ Instruments & Controls

☒ BASIC INDUSTRIES
☐ Consumer
☐ Distribution
☐ Manufacturing
☐ Retail
☒ Service
☐ Wholesale
☐ SPECIFIC INDUSTRIES
☐ Energy
☐ Environmental
☐ Financial
☐ Real Estate
☐ Transportation
☐ Publishing
☐ Food
☐ Franchises
☒ DIVERSIFIED
☐ MISCELLANEOUS

STAGE PREFERENCE

☒ EARLY STAGE
☒ Seed
☒ Start-up
☒ 1st Stage
☐ LATER STAGE
☐ 2nd Stage
☐ Mature
☐ Mezzanine
☐ LBO/MBO
☐ Turnaround
☐ INT'L EXPANSION
☐ WILL CONSIDER ALL
☐ VENTURE LEASING

Other Locations:

Affiliation:
Minimum Investment: Less than $1 Million
Capital Under Management: $100 to $500 Million

GEOGRAPHIC PREF

☐ East Coast
☐ West Coast
☐ Northeast
☐ Mid Atlantic
☐ Gulf States
☐ Northwest
☐ Southeast
☐ Southwest
☐ Midwest
☐ Central
☐ Local to Office
☐ Other Geo Pref

VANTAGEPOINT VENTURE PARTNERS

1001 Bayhill Drive
Suite 100
San Bruno CA 94066

Phone (650) 866-3100   Fax (650) 869-6078

PROFESSIONALS	TITLE
W. Jefferson Marshall	Partner
James Marver	Partner
Alan Salzman	Partner

INDUSTRY PREFERENCE

☒ INFORMATION INDUSTRY	☐ BASIC INDUSTRIES
☒ Communications	☐ Consumer
☐ Computer Equipment	☐ Distribution
☒ Computer Services	☐ Manufacturing
☒ Computer Components	☐ Retail
☐ Computer Entertainment	☐ Service
☐ Computer Education	☐ Wholesale
☒ Information Technologies	☐ SPECIFIC INDUSTRIES
☐ Computer Media	☐ Energy
☒ Software	☐ Environmental
☒ Internet	☐ Financial
☐ MEDICAL/HEALTHCARE	☐ Real Estate
☐ Biotechnology	☐ Transportation
☐ Healthcare Services	☐ Publishing
☐ Life Sciences	☐ Food
☐ Medical Products	☐ Franchises
☐ INDUSTRIAL	☐ DIVERSIFIED
☐ Advanced Materials	☒ MISCELLANEOUS
☐ Chemicals	
☐ Instruments & Controls	

STAGE PREFERENCE

☒ EARLY STAGE
☒ Seed
☒ Start-up
☒ 1st Stage
☒ LATER STAGE
☒ 2nd Stage
☒ Mature
☒ Mezzanine
☒ LBO/MBO
☒ Turnaround
☒ INT'L EXPANSION
☐ WILL CONSIDER ALL
☒ VENTURE LEASING

Other Locations: Stamford CT

Affiliation:
Minimum Investment: $1 Million or more
Capital Under Management: Over $500 Million

GEOGRAPHIC PREF

☐ East Coast
☐ West Coast
☐ Northeast
☐ Mid Atlantic
☐ Gulf States
☐ Northwest
☐ Southeast
☐ Southwest
☐ Midwest
☐ Central
☐ Local to Office
☐ Other Geo Pref

VENROCK ASSOCIATES

2494 Sand Hill Road
Suite 200
Menlo Park CA 94025

Phone (650) 561-9580   Fax (650) 561-9180

PROFESSIONALS	TITLE
Patrick F. Latterell	General Partner
Anthony Sun	General Partner
Ray Rothrock	

INDUSTRY PREFERENCE

☒ INFORMATION INDUSTRY	☒ BASIC INDUSTRIES
☒ Communications	☐ Consumer
☒ Computer Equipment	☐ Distribution
☒ Computer Services	☐ Manufacturing
☒ Computer Components	☐ Retail
☒ Computer Entertainment	☒ Service
☒ Computer Education	☐ Wholesale
☒ Information Technologies	☒ SPECIFIC INDUSTRIES
☐ Computer Media	☒ Energy
☒ Software	☐ Environmental
☒ Internet	☐ Financial
☒ MEDICAL/HEALTHCARE	☐ Real Estate
☒ Biotechnology	☐ Transportation
☒ Healthcare Services	☐ Publishing
☒ Life Sciences	☐ Food
☒ Medical Products	☐ Franchises
☒ INDUSTRIAL	☒ DIVERSIFIED
☒ Advanced Materials	☐ MISCELLANEOUS
☐ Chemicals	
☐ Instruments & Controls	

STAGE PREFERENCE

☒ EARLY STAGE
☒ Seed
☒ Start-up
☒ 1st Stage
☐ LATER STAGE
☐ 2nd Stage
☐ Mature
☐ Mezzanine
☐ LBO/MBO
☐ Turnaround
☐ INT'L EXPANSION
☐ WILL CONSIDER ALL
☐ VENTURE LEASING

Other Locations: Boston MA, New York NY

Affiliation: Rockefeller family
Minimum Investment: $1 Million or more
Capital Under Management: $100 to $500 Million

GEOGRAPHIC PREF

☐ East Coast
☐ West Coast
☐ Northeast
☐ Mid Atlantic
☐ Gulf States
☐ Northwest
☐ Southeast
☐ Southwest
☐ Midwest
☐ Central
☐ Local to Office
☐ Other Geo Pref

VENTANA

**18881 Von Karman
Tower 17, Suite 1150
Irvine CA 92612**

Phone (949) 476-2204   Fax (949) 752-0223

PROFESSIONALS	TITLE
Karen Kitridge	Managing Partner

INDUSTRY PREFERENCE

☒ INFORMATION INDUSTRY	☐ BASIC INDUSTRIES
☒ Communications	☐ Consumer
☒ Computer Equipment	☐ Distribution
☒ Computer Services	☐ Manufacturing
☒ Computer Components	☐ Retail
☐ Computer Entertainment	☐ Service
☒ Computer Education	☐ Wholesale
☒ Information Technologies	☒ SPECIFIC INDUSTRIES
☐ Computer Media	☐ Energy
☒ Software	☒ Environmental
☒ Internet	☐ Financial
☒ MEDICAL/HEALTHCARE	☐ Real Estate
☒ Biotechnology	☐ Transportation
☒ Healthcare Services	☐ Publishing
☒ Life Sciences	☐ Food
☐ Medical Products	☐ Franchises
☐ INDUSTRIAL	☒ DIVERSIFIED
☐ Advanced Materials	☐ MISCELLANEOUS
☐ Chemicals	
☐ Instruments & Controls	

STAGE PREFERENCE

☒ EARLY STAGE
☒ Seed
☒ Start-up
☒ 1st Stage
☐ LATER STAGE
☐ 2nd Stage
☐ Mature
☐ Mezzanine
☐ LBO/MBO
☐ Turnaround
☐ INT'L EXPANSION
☐ WILL CONSIDER ALL
☐ VENTURE LEASING

Other Locations: San Diego CA

Affiliation: Ventana Leasing, Inc.
Minimum Investment: Less than $1 Million
Capital Under Management: $100 to $500 Million

GEOGRAPHIC PREF

☐ East Coast
☐ West Coast
☐ Northeast
☐ Mid Atlantic
☐ Gulf States
☐ Northwest
☐ Southeast
☐ Southwest
☐ Midwest
☐ Central
☐ Local to Office
☐ Other Geo Pref

VENTANA

**8880 Rio San Diego Drive
Rio Vista Towers, Suite 500
San Diego CA 92108**

Phone (619) 291-2757   Fax (619) 295-0189

PROFESSIONALS	TITLE
Duwaine Townsen	Managing Partner

INDUSTRY PREFERENCE

☒ INFORMATION INDUSTRY	☐ BASIC INDUSTRIES
☒ Communications	☐ Consumer
☒ Computer Equipment	☐ Distribution
☒ Computer Services	☐ Manufacturing
☒ Computer Components	☐ Retail
☐ Computer Entertainment	☐ Service
☒ Computer Education	☐ Wholesale
☒ Information Technologies	☐ SPECIFIC INDUSTRIES
☐ Computer Media	☐ Energy
☒ Software	☐ Environmental
☒ Internet	☐ Financial
☒ MEDICAL/HEALTHCARE	☐ Real Estate
☒ Biotechnology	☐ Transportation
☒ Healthcare Services	☐ Publishing
☒ Life Sciences	☐ Food
☒ Medical Products	☐ Franchises
☐ INDUSTRIAL	☒ DIVERSIFIED
☐ Advanced Materials	☐ MISCELLANEOUS
☐ Chemicals	
☐ Instruments & Controls	

STAGE PREFERENCE

☒ EARLY STAGE
☒ Seed
☒ Start-up
☒ 1st Stage
☐ LATER STAGE
☐ 2nd Stage
☐ Mature
☐ Mezzanine
☐ LBO/MBO
☐ Turnaround
☐ INT'L EXPANSION
☐ WILL CONSIDER ALL
☐ VENTURE LEASING

Other Locations: Irvine CA

Affiliation: Ventana Leasing, Inc.
Minimum Investment: Less than $1 Million
Capital Under Management: $100 to $500 Million

GEOGRAPHIC PREF

☐ East Coast
☐ West Coast
☐ Northeast
☐ Mid Atlantic
☐ Gulf States
☐ Northwest
☐ Southeast
☐ Southwest
☐ Midwest
☐ Central
☐ Local to Office
☐ Other Geo Pref

VERTEX MANAGEMENT, INC.

Three Lagoon Drive
Suite 220
Redwood City CA 94065

Phone (650) 591-0947   Fax (650) 591-5926

PROFESSIONALS	TITLE
Elise Huang	Associate

INDUSTRY PREFERENCE

☒ INFORMATION INDUSTRY	☐ BASIC INDUSTRIES
☒ Communications	☐ Consumer
☒ Computer Equipment	☐ Distribution
☒ Computer Services	☐ Manufacturing
☒ Computer Components	☐ Retail
☐ Computer Entertainment	☐ Service
☒ Computer Education	☐ Wholesale
☒ Information Technologies	☐ SPECIFIC INDUSTRIES
☐ Computer Media	☐ Energy
☒ Software	☐ Environmental
☒ Internet	☐ Financial
☐ MEDICAL/HEALTHCARE	☐ Real Estate
☐ Biotechnology	☐ Transportation
☐ Healthcare Services	☐ Publishing
☐ Life Sciences	☐ Food
☐ Medical Products	☐ Franchises
☐ INDUSTRIAL	☐ DIVERSIFIED
☐ Advanced Materials	☐ MISCELLANEOUS
☐ Chemicals	
☐ Instruments & Controls	

STAGE PREFERENCE

☒ EARLY STAGE
☒ Seed
☒ Start-up
☒ 1st Stage
☐ LATER STAGE
☐ 2nd Stage
☐ Mature
☐ Mezzanine
☐ LBO/MBO
☐ Turnaround
☐ INT'L EXPANSION
☐ WILL CONSIDER ALL
☐ VENTURE LEASING

Other Locations:

Affiliation: Singapore Technologies
Minimum Investment: Less than $1 Million
Capital Under Management: $100 to $500 Million

GEOGRAPHIC PREF

☐ East Coast
☐ West Coast
☐ Northeast
☐ Mid Atlantic
☐ Gulf States
☐ Northwest
☐ Southeast
☐ Southwest
☐ Midwest
☐ Central
☐ Local to Office
☐ Other Geo Pref

VISION CAPITAL

3000 Sand Hill Road
Building Four Suite 230
Menlo Park CA 94025

Phone (650) 854-8070   Fax (650) 854-4961

PROFESSIONALS	TITLE
Dag Tellefson	Managing Partner
Dag Syrrist	General Partner
John Turner	Venture Partner

INDUSTRY PREFERENCE

☒ INFORMATION INDUSTRY	☐ BASIC INDUSTRIES
☒ Communications	☐ Consumer
☒ Computer Equipment	☐ Distribution
☒ Computer Services	☐ Manufacturing
☒ Computer Components	☐ Retail
☐ Computer Entertainment	☐ Service
☐ Computer Education	☐ Wholesale
☒ Information Technologies	☐ SPECIFIC INDUSTRIES
☒ Computer Media	☐ Energy
☒ Software	☐ Environmental
☒ Internet	☐ Financial
☐ MEDICAL/HEALTHCARE	☐ Real Estate
☐ Biotechnology	☐ Transportation
☐ Healthcare Services	☐ Publishing
☐ Life Sciences	☐ Food
☐ Medical Products	☐ Franchises
☐ INDUSTRIAL	☒ DIVERSIFIED
☐ Advanced Materials	☒ MISCELLANEOUS
☐ Chemicals	
☐ Instruments & Controls	

STAGE PREFERENCE

☒ EARLY STAGE
☐ Seed
☒ Start-up
☒ 1st Stage
☒ LATER STAGE
☒ 2nd Stage
☒ Mature
☒ Mezzanine
☒ LBO/MBO
☒ Turnaround
☒ INT'L EXPANSION
☐ WILL CONSIDER ALL
☒ VENTURE LEASING

Other Locations:

Affiliation:
Minimum Investment: Less than $1 Million
Capital Under Management: $100 to $500 Million

GEOGRAPHIC PREF

☐ East Coast
☐ West Coast
☐ Northeast
☐ Mid Atlantic
☐ Gulf States
☐ Northwest
☐ Southeast
☐ Southwest
☐ Midwest
☐ Central
☐ Local to Office
☐ Other Geo Pref

VK VENTURES

**600 California Street
Suite 1700
San Francisco CA 94111**

Phone (415) 391-5600   Fax (415) 397-2744

PROFESSIONALS	TITLE
F. Van Kasper	President, CEO
Stephen Adams	Vice Chairman/Director
Wayne Scott	Sr. Vice President
John Chung	Sr. Vice President
Bruce Emmeluth	Managing Director
D. Jonathan Merriman	Managing Director

INDUSTRY PREFERENCE

- ☒ INFORMATION INDUSTRY
- ☒ Communications
- ☐ Computer Equipment
- ☐ Computer Services
- ☒ Computer Components
- ☐ Computer Entertainment
- ☐ Computer Education
- ☐ Information Technologies
- ☐ Computer Media
- ☒ Software
- ☒ Internet
- ☒ MEDICAL/HEALTHCARE
- ☐ Biotechnology
- ☐ Healthcare Services
- ☐ Life Sciences
- ☒ Medical Products
- ☐ INDUSTRIAL
- ☐ Advanced Materials
- ☐ Chemicals
- ☐ Instruments & Controls

- ☒ BASIC INDUSTRIES
- ☒ Consumer
- ☒ Distribution
- ☐ Manufacturing
- ☐ Retail
- ☐ Service
- ☐ Wholesale
- ☒ SPECIFIC INDUSTRIES
- ☐ Energy
- ☐ Environmental
- ☐ Financial
- ☐ Real Estate
- ☐ Transportation
- ☐ Publishing
- ☐ Food
- ☐ Franchises
- ☒ DIVERSIFIED
- ☒ MISCELLANEOUS

STAGE PREFERENCE

- ☐ EARLY STAGE
- ☐ Seed
- ☐ Start-up
- ☐ 1st Stage
- ☒ LATER STAGE
- ☒ 2nd Stage
- ☐ Mature
- ☒ Mezzanine
- ☒ LBO/MBO
- ☐ Turnaround
- ☐ INT'L EXPANSION
- ☐ WILL CONSIDER ALL
- ☐ VENTURE LEASING

SBIC
Other Locations:

Affiliation:
Minimum Investment: Less than $1 Million
Capital Under Management: Less than $100 Million

GEOGRAPHIC PREF

- ☐ East Coast
- ☒ West Coast
- ☐ Northeast
- ☐ Mid Atlantic
- ☐ Gulf States
- ☐ Northwest
- ☐ Southeast
- ☐ Southwest
- ☐ Midwest
- ☐ Central
- ☐ Local to Office
- ☐ Other Geo Pref

WALDEN GROUP
OF VENTURE CAPITAL FUNDS

**750 Battery Street
Seventh Floor
San Francisco CA 94111-1523**

Phone (415) 391-7225   Fax (415) 391-7262

PROFESSIONALS	TITLE
George S. Sarlo	General Partner
Arthur S. Berliner	General Partner
Steven L. Eskenazi	General Partner
Lip-Bu Tan	General Partner
Charles Hsu	General Partner

INDUSTRY PREFERENCE

- ☒ INFORMATION INDUSTRY
- ☒ Communications
- ☒ Computer Equipment
- ☒ Computer Services
- ☒ Computer Components
- ☐ Computer Entertainment
- ☒ Computer Education
- ☒ Information Technologies
- ☐ Computer Media
- ☒ Software
- ☒ Internet
- ☒ MEDICAL/HEALTHCARE
- ☒ Biotechnology
- ☒ Healthcare Services
- ☒ Life Sciences
- ☒ Medical Products
- ☐ INDUSTRIAL
- ☐ Advanced Materials
- ☐ Chemicals
- ☐ Instruments & Controls

- ☒ BASIC INDUSTRIES
- ☐ Consumer
- ☐ Distribution
- ☐ Manufacturing
- ☒ Retail
- ☒ Service
- ☐ Wholesale
- ☐ SPECIFIC INDUSTRIES
- ☐ Energy
- ☐ Environmental
- ☐ Financial
- ☐ Real Estate
- ☐ Transportation
- ☐ Publishing
- ☐ Food
- ☐ Franchises
- ☒ DIVERSIFIED
- ☐ MISCELLANEOUS

STAGE PREFERENCE

- ☒ EARLY STAGE
- ☒ Seed
- ☒ Start-up
- ☒ 1st Stage
- ☒ LATER STAGE
- ☒ 2nd Stage
- ☒ Mature
- ☐ Mezzanine
- ☒ LBO/MBO
- ☐ Turnaround
- ☐ INT'L EXPANSION
- ☐ WILL CONSIDER ALL
- ☐ VENTURE LEASING

Other Locations:

Affiliation: Walden Capital Corporation
Minimum Investment: Less than $1 Million
Capital Under Management: $100 to $500 Million

GEOGRAPHIC PREF

- ☐ East Coast
- ☒ West Coast
- ☐ Northeast
- ☐ Mid Atlantic
- ☐ Gulf States
- ☐ Northwest
- ☐ Southeast
- ☐ Southwest
- ☐ Midwest
- ☐ Central
- ☐ Local to Office
- ☐ Other Geo Pref

WALDEN-SBIC, LP

750 Battery Street
Seventh Floor
San Francisco CA 94111

Phone (415) 391-7225   Fax (415) 391-7262

PROFESSIONALS	TITLE
Arthur S. Berliner	General Partner

INDUSTRY PREFERENCE

☐ INFORMATION INDUSTRY	☐ BASIC INDUSTRIES
☐ Communications	☐ Consumer
☐ Computer Equipment	☐ Distribution
☐ Computer Services	☐ Manufacturing
☐ Computer Components	☐ Retail
☐ Computer Entertainment	☐ Service
☐ Computer Education	☐ Wholesale
☐ Information Technologies	☐ SPECIFIC INDUSTRIES
☐ Computer Media	☐ Energy
☐ Software	☐ Environmental
☐ Internet	☐ Financial
☐ MEDICAL/HEALTHCARE	☐ Real Estate
☐ Biotechnology	☐ Transportation
☐ Healthcare Services	☐ Publishing
☐ Life Sciences	☐ Food
☐ Medical Products	☐ Franchises
☐ INDUSTRIAL	☒ DIVERSIFIED
☐ Advanced Materials	☐ MISCELLANEOUS
☐ Chemicals	
☐ Instruments & Controls	

STAGE PREFERENCE

☒ EARLY STAGE
☒ Seed
☒ Start-up
☒ 1st Stage
☒ LATER STAGE
☒ 2nd Stage
☒ Mature
☐ Mezzanine
☒ LBO/MBO
☐ Turnaround
☐ INT'L EXPANSION
☐ WILL CONSIDER ALL
☐ VENTURE LEASING

SBIC
Other Locations:

Affiliation:
Minimum Investment: $1 Million or more
Capital Under Management: $100 to $500 Million

GEOGRAPHIC PREF

☐ East Coast
☒ West Coast
☐ Northeast
☐ Mid Atlantic
☐ Gulf States
☐ Northwest
☐ Southeast
☐ Southwest
☐ Midwest
☐ Central
☐ Local to Office
☐ Other Geo Pref

WEISS PECK AND GREER VENTURE PARTNERS

555 California Street
Suite 3130
San Francisco CA 94104-1502

Phone (415) 622-6864   Fax (415) 989-5108

PROFESSIONALS	TITLE
Chris Schaepe	Principal
Philip Greer	General Partner
Gill Cogan	General Partner
Jeani Delaguidelle	General Partner
Peter Nieh	General Partner
Barry Eggers	General Partner

INDUSTRY PREFERENCE

☒ INFORMATION INDUSTRY	☒ BASIC INDUSTRIES
☒ Communications	☐ Consumer
☐ Computer Equipment	☐ Distribution
☐ Computer Services	☐ Manufacturing
☒ Computer Components	☐ Retail
☐ Computer Entertainment	☒ Service
☐ Computer Education	☐ Wholesale
☐ Information Technologies	☐ SPECIFIC INDUSTRIES
☐ Computer Media	☐ Energy
☒ Software	☐ Environmental
☒ Internet	☐ Financial
☒ MEDICAL/HEALTHCARE	☐ Real Estate
☒ Biotechnology	☐ Transportation
☒ Healthcare Services	☐ Publishing
☒ Life Sciences	☐ Food
☒ Medical Products	☐ Franchises
☐ INDUSTRIAL	☒ DIVERSIFIED
☐ Advanced Materials	☐ MISCELLANEOUS
☐ Chemicals	
☐ Instruments & Controls	

STAGE PREFERENCE

☒ EARLY STAGE
☒ Seed
☒ Start-up
☒ 1st Stage
☒ LATER STAGE
☒ 2nd Stage
☒ Mature
☒ Mezzanine
☒ LBO/MBO
☐ Turnaround
☐ INT'L EXPANSION
☐ WILL CONSIDER ALL
☐ VENTURE LEASING

Other Locations:

Affiliation:
Minimum Investment: Less than $1 Million
Capital Under Management: $100 to $500 Million

GEOGRAPHIC PREF

☐ East Coast
☐ West Coast
☐ Northeast
☐ Mid Atlantic
☐ Gulf States
☐ Northwest
☐ Southeast
☐ Southwest
☐ Midwest
☐ Central
☐ Local to Office
☐ Other Geo Pref

WESTAR CAPITAL

949 South Coast Drive
Suite 650
Costa Mesa CA 92626-1776

Phone (714) 481-5160   Fax (714) 481-5166

PROFESSIONALS	TITLE
Bob Polentz	CEO
John Clark	Partner
Frank Do	Partner
Charles Martin	Parnter

INDUSTRY PREFERENCE

☒ INFORMATION INDUSTRY	☒ BASIC INDUSTRIES
☒ Communications	☒ Consumer
☒ Computer Equipment	☒ Distribution
☒ Computer Services	☐ Manufacturing
☒ Computer Components	☐ Retail
☐ Computer Entertainment	☐ Service
☒ Computer Education	☐ Wholesale
☒ Information Technologies	☒ SPECIFIC INDUSTRIES
☒ Computer Media	☒ Energy
☒ Software	☒ Environmental
☒ Internet	☒ Financial
☒ MEDICAL/HEALTHCARE	☐ Real Estate
☒ Biotechnology	☒ Transportation
☒ Healthcare Services	☐ Publishing
☒ Life Sciences	☐ Food
☒ Medical Products	☐ Franchises
☒ INDUSTRIAL	☒ DIVERSIFIED
☐ Advanced Materials	☐ MISCELLANEOUS
☐ Chemicals	
☒ Instruments & Controls	

STAGE PREFERENCE

☐ EARLY STAGE
☐ Seed
☐ Start-up
☐ 1st Stage
☒ LATER STAGE
☒ 2nd Stage
☒ Mature
☐ Mezzanine
☒ LBO/MBO
☐ Turnaround
☐ INT'L EXPANSION
☐ WILL CONSIDER ALL
☐ VENTURE LEASING

Other Locations:

Affiliation: Enterprise Partners
Minimum Investment: $1 Million or more
Capital Under Management: $100 to $500 Million

GEOGRAPHIC PREF

☐ East Coast
☐ West Coast
☐ Northeast
☐ Mid Atlantic
☐ Gulf States
☐ Northwest
☐ Southeast
☐ Southwest
☐ Midwest
☐ Central
☐ Local to Office
☐ Other Geo Pref

WESTERN TECHNOLOGY INVESTMENTS

2010 North First Street
Suite 310
San Jose CA 95131

Phone (408) 436-8577   Fax (408) 436-8625

PROFESSIONALS	TITLE
Ronald W. Swenson	President & Director

INDUSTRY PREFERENCE

☒ INFORMATION INDUSTRY	☐ BASIC INDUSTRIES
☒ Communications	☐ Consumer
☒ Computer Equipment	☐ Distribution
☒ Computer Services	☐ Manufacturing
☒ Computer Components	☐ Retail
☐ Computer Entertainment	☐ Service
☒ Computer Education	☐ Wholesale
☒ Information Technologies	☐ SPECIFIC INDUSTRIES
☐ Computer Media	☐ Energy
☒ Software	☐ Environmental
☒ Internet	☐ Financial
☒ MEDICAL/HEALTHCARE	☐ Real Estate
☒ Biotechnology	☐ Transportation
☒ Healthcare Services	☐ Publishing
☒ Life Sciences	☐ Food
☒ Medical Products	☐ Franchises
☒ INDUSTRIAL	☒ DIVERSIFIED
☒ Advanced Materials	☐ MISCELLANEOUS
☒ Chemicals	
☒ Instruments & Controls	

STAGE PREFERENCE

☒ EARLY STAGE
☒ Seed
☒ Start-up
☒ 1st Stage
☒ LATER STAGE
☒ 2nd Stage
☒ Mature
☒ Mezzanine
☒ LBO/MBO
☐ Turnaround
☐ INT'L EXPANSION
☐ WILL CONSIDER ALL
☐ VENTURE LEASING

Other Locations:

Affiliation:
Minimum Investment: Less than $1 Million
Capital Under Management: $100 to $500 Million

GEOGRAPHIC PREF

☐ East Coast
☐ West Coast
☐ Northeast
☐ Mid Atlantic
☐ Gulf States
☐ Northwest
☐ Southeast
☐ Southwest
☐ Midwest
☐ Central
☐ Local to Office
☐ Other Geo Pref

WESTON PRESIDIO CAPITAL

343 Sansome Street
Suite 1210
San Francisco CA 94104-1316

Phone (415) 398-0770   Fax (415) 398-0990

PROFESSIONALS	TITLE
Michael Lazarus	Managing Partner
Phillip Halperin	General Partner
James McElwee	General Partner

INDUSTRY PREFERENCE

- ☒ INFORMATION INDUSTRY
- ☒ Communications
- ☒ Computer Equipment
- ☒ Computer Services
- ☒ Computer Components
- ☐ Computer Entertainment
- ☒ Computer Education
- ☒ Information Technologies
- ☐ Computer Media
- ☒ Software
- ☒ Internet
- ☒ MEDICAL/HEALTHCARE
- ☐ Biotechnology
- ☒ Healthcare Services
- ☐ Life Sciences
- ☐ Medical Products
- ☐ INDUSTRIAL
- ☐ Advanced Materials
- ☐ Chemicals
- ☐ Instruments & Controls

- ☒ BASIC INDUSTRIES
- ☒ Consumer
- ☒ Distribution
- ☒ Manufacturing
- ☒ Retail
- ☒ Service
- ☐ Wholesale
- ☐ SPECIFIC INDUSTRIES
- ☐ Energy
- ☐ Environmental
- ☐ Financial
- ☐ Real Estate
- ☐ Transportation
- ☐ Publishing
- ☐ Food
- ☐ Franchises
- ☒ DIVERSIFIED
- ☐ MISCELLANEOUS

STAGE PREFERENCE

- ☐ EARLY STAGE
- ☐ Seed
- ☐ Start-up
- ☐ 1st Stage
- ☒ LATER STAGE
- ☒ 2nd Stage
- ☒ Mature
- ☒ Mezzanine
- ☒ LBO/MBO
- ☒ Turnaround
- ☐ INT'L EXPANSION
- ☐ WILL CONSIDER ALL
- ☒ VENTURE LEASING

Other Locations: Boston MA

Affiliation:
Minimum Investment: $1 Million or more
Capital Under Management: Over $500 Million

GEOGRAPHIC PREF

- ☐ East Coast
- ☐ West Coast
- ☐ Northeast
- ☐ Mid Atlantic
- ☐ Gulf States
- ☐ Northwest
- ☐ Southeast
- ☐ Southwest
- ☐ Midwest
- ☐ Central
- ☐ Local to Office
- ☐ Other Geo Pref

WINDWARD VENTURES

12680 High Bluff Drive
Suite 200
San Diego CA 92130

Phone (858) 259-4590   Fax (858) 259-4541

PROFESSIONALS	TITLE
James Cole	General Partner
M. David Titus	General Partner
C. Richard Kramlich	Special Limted Partner
Frank Bonsal	Special Limted Partner
F. Duwaine Townsen	Special Limted Partner

INDUSTRY PREFERENCE

- ☒ INFORMATION INDUSTRY
- ☒ Communications
- ☒ Computer Equipment
- ☒ Computer Services
- ☒ Computer Components
- ☐ Computer Entertainment
- ☐ Computer Education
- ☐ Information Technologies
- ☐ Computer Media
- ☒ Software
- ☒ Internet
- ☒ MEDICAL/HEALTHCARE
- ☒ Biotechnology
- ☒ Healthcare Services
- ☒ Life Sciences
- ☒ Medical Products
- ☒ INDUSTRIAL
- ☐ Advanced Materials
- ☐ Chemicals
- ☒ Instruments & Controls

- ☐ BASIC INDUSTRIES
- ☐ Consumer
- ☐ Distribution
- ☐ Manufacturing
- ☐ Retail
- ☐ Service
- ☐ Wholesale
- ☐ SPECIFIC INDUSTRIES
- ☐ Energy
- ☐ Environmental
- ☐ Financial
- ☐ Real Estate
- ☐ Transportation
- ☐ Publishing
- ☐ Food
- ☐ Franchises
- ☒ DIVERSIFIED
- ☒ MISCELLANEOUS

STAGE PREFERENCE

- ☒ EARLY STAGE
- ☒ Seed
- ☒ Start-up
- ☒ 1st Stage
- ☒ LATER STAGE
- ☒ 2nd Stage
- ☐ Mature
- ☒ Mezzanine
- ☐ LBO/MBO
- ☐ Turnaround
- ☐ INT'L EXPANSION
- ☐ WILL CONSIDER ALL
- ☐ VENTURE LEASING

Other Locations:

Affiliation:
Minimum Investment: Less than $1 Million
Capital Under Management: Less than $100 Million

GEOGRAPHIC PREF

- ☐ East Coast
- ☒ West Coast
- ☐ Northeast
- ☐ Mid Atlantic
- ☐ Gulf States
- ☐ Northwest
- ☐ Southeast
- ☐ Southwest
- ☐ Midwest
- ☐ Central
- ☐ Local to Office
- ☒ Other Geo Pref
  Southern CA

WOODSIDE FUND

850 Woodside Drive
Woodside CA 94062-2359

Phone (650) 368-5545   Fax (650) 368-2416

PROFESSIONALS	TITLE
Charles E. Greb	General Partner
Vincent M. Occhipinti	General Partner
Dr. Robert E. Larson	General Partner

INDUSTRY PREFERENCE

☒ INFORMATION INDUSTRY	☐ BASIC INDUSTRIES
☒ Communications	☐ Consumer
☒ Computer Equipment	☐ Distribution
☒ Computer Services	☐ Manufacturing
☒ Computer Components	☐ Retail
☒ Computer Entertainment	☐ Service
☒ Computer Education	☐ Wholesale
☒ Information Technologies	☐ SPECIFIC INDUSTRIES
☒ Computer Media	☐ Energy
☒ Software	☐ Environmental
☒ Internet	☐ Financial
☐ MEDICAL/HEALTHCARE	☐ Real Estate
☐ Biotechnology	☐ Transportation
☐ Healthcare Services	☐ Publishing
☐ Life Sciences	☐ Food
☐ Medical Products	☐ Franchises
☐ INDUSTRIAL	☐ DIVERSIFIED
☐ Advanced Materials	☐ MISCELLANEOUS
☐ Chemicals	
☐ Instruments & Controls	

STAGE PREFERENCE

☒ EARLY STAGE
☒ Seed
☒ Start-up
☒ 1st Stage
☒ LATER STAGE
☒ 2nd Stage
☐ Mature
☐ Mezzanine
☐ LBO/MBO
☐ Turnaround
☐ INT'L EXPANSION
☐ WILL CONSIDER ALL
☐ VENTURE LEASING

Other Locations:

Affiliation:
Minimum Investment: $1 Million or more
Capital Under Management: $100 to $500 Million

GEOGRAPHIC PREF

☐ East Coast
☒ West Coast
☐ Northeast
☐ Mid Atlantic
☐ Gulf States
☒ Northwest
☐ Southeast
☒ Southwest
☐ Midwest
☐ Central
☐ Local to Office
☐ Other Geo Pref

WORLDVIEW TECHNOLOGY PARTNERS

435 Tasso Street
Suite 120
Palo Alto CA 94301

Phone (650) 322-3800   Fax (650) 322-3880

PROFESSIONALS	TITLE
Mike Orsak	General Partner
James Wei	General Partner
John Boyle	General Partner

INDUSTRY PREFERENCE

☒ INFORMATION INDUSTRY	☐ BASIC INDUSTRIES
☒ Communications	☐ Consumer
☒ Computer Equipment	☐ Distribution
☒ Computer Services	☐ Manufacturing
☒ Computer Components	☐ Retail
☐ Computer Entertainment	☐ Service
☐ Computer Education	☐ Wholesale
☒ Information Technologies	☐ SPECIFIC INDUSTRIES
☐ Computer Media	☐ Energy
☒ Software	☐ Environmental
☒ Internet	☐ Financial
☐ MEDICAL/HEALTHCARE	☐ Real Estate
☐ Biotechnology	☐ Transportation
☐ Healthcare Services	☐ Publishing
☐ Life Sciences	☐ Food
☐ Medical Products	☐ Franchises
☒ INDUSTRIAL	☒ DIVERSIFIED
☐ Advanced Materials	☒ MISCELLANEOUS
☐ Chemicals	
☒ Instruments & Controls	

STAGE PREFERENCE

☒ EARLY STAGE
☒ Seed
☒ Start-up
☒ 1st Stage
☒ LATER STAGE
☒ 2nd Stage
☐ Mature
☒ Mezzanine
☒ LBO/MBO
☐ Turnaround
☐ INT'L EXPANSION
☐ WILL CONSIDER ALL
☐ VENTURE LEASING

Other Locations:

Affiliation:
Minimum Investment: $1 Million or more
Capital Under Management: $100 to $500 Million

GEOGRAPHIC PREF

☐ East Coast
☐ West Coast
☐ Northeast
☐ Mid Atlantic
☐ Gulf States
☐ Northwest
☐ Southeast
☐ Southwest
☐ Midwest
☐ Central
☐ Local to Office
☐ Other Geo Pref

YASUDA ENTERPRISE DEVELOPMENT CORP.

540 Cowper Street
Suite 200
Palo Alto CA 94301

Phone (650) 854-8760   Fax (650) 462-9379

PROFESSIONALS	TITLE
Akira Minakuchi	

INDUSTRY PREFERENCE

- ☒ INFORMATION INDUSTRY
- ☒ Communications
- ☒ Computer Equipment
- ☒ Computer Services
- ☒ Computer Components
- ☐ Computer Entertainment
- ☒ Computer Education
- ☒ Information Technologies
- ☐ Computer Media
- ☒ Software
- ☒ Internet
- ☒ MEDICAL/HEALTHCARE
- ☒ Biotechnology
- ☒ Healthcare Services
- ☒ Life Sciences
- ☒ Medical Products
- ☐ INDUSTRIAL
- ☐ Advanced Materials
- ☐ Chemicals
- ☐ Instruments & Controls
- ☒ BASIC INDUSTRIES
- ☐ Consumer
- ☐ Distribution
- ☐ Manufacturing
- ☐ Retail
- ☒ Service
- ☐ Wholesale
- ☐ SPECIFIC INDUSTRIES
- ☐ Energy
- ☐ Environmental
- ☐ Financial
- ☐ Real Estate
- ☐ Transportation
- ☐ Publishing
- ☐ Food
- ☐ Franchises
- ☒ DIVERSIFIED
- ☐ MISCELLANEOUS

STAGE PREFERENCE

- ☒ EARLY STAGE
- ☒ Seed
- ☒ Start-up
- ☒ 1st Stage
- ☒ LATER STAGE
- ☒ 2nd Stage
- ☒ Mature
- ☒ Mezzanine
- ☒ LBO/MBO
- ☒ Turnaround
- ☒ INT'L EXPANSION
- ☐ WILL CONSIDER ALL
- ☒ VENTURE LEASING

Other Locations:

Affiliation:
Minimum Investment: Less than $1 Million
Capital Under Management: Less than $100 Million

GEOGRAPHIC PREF

- ☐ East Coast
- ☐ West Coast
- ☐ Northeast
- ☐ Mid Atlantic
- ☐ Gulf States
- ☐ Northwest
- ☐ Southeast
- ☐ Southwest
- ☐ Midwest
- ☐ Central
- ☐ Local to Office
- ☐ Other Geo Pref

ALTIRA GROUP, LLC

World Trade Center
1625 Broadway, Suite 2150
Denver CO 80202-4727

Phone (303) 825-1600   Fax (303) 623-3525

PROFESSIONALS	TITLE
Dirk W. McDermott	President
Peter L. Edwards	Vice President

INDUSTRY PREFERENCE

- ☐ INFORMATION INDUSTRY
- ☐ Communications
- ☐ Computer Equipment
- ☐ Computer Services
- ☐ Computer Components
- ☐ Computer Entertainment
- ☐ Computer Education
- ☐ Information Technologies
- ☐ Computer Media
- ☐ Software
- ☐ Internet
- ☐ MEDICAL/HEALTHCARE
- ☐ Biotechnology
- ☐ Healthcare Services
- ☐ Life Sciences
- ☐ Medical Products
- ☐ INDUSTRIAL
- ☐ Advanced Materials
- ☐ Chemicals
- ☐ Instruments & Controls
- ☐ BASIC INDUSTRIES
- ☐ Consumer
- ☐ Distribution
- ☐ Manufacturing
- ☐ Retail
- ☐ Service
- ☐ Wholesale
- ☒ SPECIFIC INDUSTRIES
- ☒ Energy
- ☐ Environmental
- ☐ Financial
- ☐ Real Estate
- ☐ Transportation
- ☐ Publishing
- ☐ Food
- ☐ Franchises
- ☐ DIVERSIFIED
- ☒ MISCELLANEOUS
  - Oil and Gas Industry

STAGE PREFERENCE

- ☒ EARLY STAGE
- ☒ Seed
- ☒ Start-up
- ☐ 1st Stage
- ☐ LATER STAGE
- ☐ 2nd Stage
- ☐ Mature
- ☐ Mezzanine
- ☐ LBO/MBO
- ☐ Turnaround
- ☐ INT'L EXPANSION
- ☐ WILL CONSIDER ALL
- ☐ VENTURE LEASING

Other Locations:

Affiliation:
Minimum Investment: Less than $1 Million
Capital Under Management: Less than $100 Million

GEOGRAPHIC PREF

- ☐ East Coast
- ☐ West Coast
- ☐ Northeast
- ☐ Mid Atlantic
- ☐ Gulf States
- ☐ Northwest
- ☐ Southeast
- ☐ Southwest
- ☐ Midwest
- ☐ Central
- ☐ Local to Office
- ☐ Other Geo Pref

CENTENNIAL FUNDS

1428 Fifteenth Street
Denver CO 80202-1318

Phone (303) 405-7500　Fax (303) 405-7575

PROFESSIONALS	TITLE
Steven C. Halstedt	Principal
Adam Goldman	Principal
David C. Hull, Jr.	Principal
Jeffrey H. Schutz	Principal
Donald H. Parsons, Jr.	Principal

INDUSTRY PREFERENCE

- ☒ INFORMATION INDUSTRY
- ☒ Communications
- ☒ Computer Equipment
- ☒ Computer Services
- ☒ Computer Components
- ☐ Computer Entertainment
- ☐ Computer Education
- ☐ Information Technologies
- ☒ Computer Media
- ☐ Software
- ☐ Internet
- ☐ MEDICAL/HEALTHCARE
- ☐ Biotechnology
- ☐ Healthcare Services
- ☐ Life Sciences
- ☐ Medical Products
- ☒ INDUSTRIAL
- ☐ Advanced Materials
- ☐ Chemicals
- ☒ Instruments & Controls

- ☒ BASIC INDUSTRIES
- ☒ Consumer
- ☐ Distribution
- ☐ Manufacturing
- ☐ Retail
- ☒ Service
- ☐ Wholesale
- ☐ SPECIFIC INDUSTRIES
- ☐ Energy
- ☐ Environmental
- ☐ Financial
- ☐ Real Estate
- ☐ Transportation
- ☐ Publishing
- ☐ Food
- ☐ Franchises
- ☒ DIVERSIFIED
- ☐ MISCELLANEOUS

STAGE PREFERENCE

- ☒ EARLY STAGE
- ☒ Seed
- ☒ Start-up
- ☒ 1st Stage
- ☒ LATER STAGE
- ☒ 2nd Stage
- ☒ Mature
- ☐ Mezzanine
- ☒ LBO/MBO
- ☐ Turnaround
- ☐ INT'L EXPANSION
- ☐ WILL CONSIDER ALL
- ☐ VENTURE LEASING

Other Locations:

Affiliation:
Minimum Investment: Less than $1 Million
Capital Under Management: Over $500 Million

GEOGRAPHIC PREF

- ☐ East Coast
- ☐ West Coast
- ☐ Northeast
- ☐ Mid Atlantic
- ☐ Gulf States
- ☐ Northwest
- ☐ Southeast
- ☐ Southwest
- ☐ Midwest
- ☐ Central
- ☐ Local to Office
- ☐ Other Geo Pref

CHASE CAPITAL PARTNERS

108 South Frontage Road West
Suite 307
Vail CO 81657

Phone (970) 476-7700　Fax (970) 476-7900

PROFESSIONALS	TITLE
David Ferguson	Partner

INDUSTRY PREFERENCE

- ☒ INFORMATION INDUSTRY
- ☒ Communications
- ☒ Computer Equipment
- ☒ Computer Services
- ☒ Computer Components
- ☐ Computer Entertainment
- ☒ Computer Education
- ☒ Information Technologies
- ☒ Computer Media
- ☒ Software
- ☒ Internet
- ☒ MEDICAL/HEALTHCARE
- ☒ Biotechnology
- ☒ Healthcare Services
- ☒ Life Sciences
- ☒ Medical Products
- ☒ INDUSTRIAL
- ☐ Advanced Materials
- ☒ Chemicals
- ☐ Instruments & Controls

- ☒ BASIC INDUSTRIES
- ☐ Consumer
- ☐ Distribution
- ☐ Manufacturing
- ☒ Retail
- ☐ Service
- ☐ Wholesale
- ☒ SPECIFIC INDUSTRIES
- ☐ Energy
- ☐ Environmental
- ☐ Financial
- ☒ Real Estate
- ☐ Transportation
- ☐ Publishing
- ☐ Food
- ☐ Franchises
- ☒ DIVERSIFIED
- ☒ MISCELLANEOUS

STAGE PREFERENCE

- ☒ EARLY STAGE
- ☐ Seed
- ☒ Start-up
- ☒ 1st Stage
- ☒ LATER STAGE
- ☒ 2nd Stage
- ☒ Mature
- ☒ Mezzanine
- ☒ LBO/MBO
- ☒ Turnaround
- ☒ INT'L EXPANSION
- ☐ WILL CONSIDER ALL
- ☒ VENTURE LEASING

SBIC
Other Locations: New York NY, San Francisco CA

Affiliation:
Minimum Investment: $1 Million or more
Capital Under Management: Over $500 Million

GEOGRAPHIC PREF

- ☐ East Coast
- ☐ West Coast
- ☐ Northeast
- ☐ Mid Atlantic
- ☐ Gulf States
- ☐ Northwest
- ☐ Southeast
- ☐ Southwest
- ☐ Midwest
- ☐ Central
- ☐ Local to Office
- ☐ Other Geo Pref

COLUMBINE VENTURE FUNDS

5460 South Quebec Street
Suite 250
Englewood CO 80111

Phone (303) 694-3222   Fax (303) 694-9007

PROFESSIONALS	TITLE
Sherman J. Muller	General Partner

INDUSTRY PREFERENCE

☒ INFORMATION INDUSTRY	☒ BASIC INDUSTRIES
☒ Communications	☐ Consumer
☒ Computer Equipment	☐ Distribution
☒ Computer Services	☐ Manufacturing
☒ Computer Components	☐ Retail
☐ Computer Entertainment	☒ Service
☐ Computer Education	☐ Wholesale
☒ Information Technologies	☒ SPECIFIC INDUSTRIES
☐ Computer Media	☒ Energy
☒ Software	☐ Environmental
☒ Internet	☐ Financial
☒ MEDICAL/HEALTHCARE	☐ Real Estate
☒ Biotechnology	☐ Transportation
☒ Healthcare Services	☐ Publishing
☒ Life Sciences	☐ Food
☒ Medical Products	☐ Franchises
☒ INDUSTRIAL	☒ DIVERSIFIED
☒ Advanced Materials	☐ MISCELLANEOUS
☒ Chemicals	
☒ Instruments & Controls	

STAGE PREFERENCE

☒ EARLY STAGE
☒ Seed
☒ Start-up
☐ 1st Stage
☐ LATER STAGE
☐ 2nd Stage
☐ Mature
☐ Mezzanine
☐ LBO/MBO
☐ Turnaround
☐ INT'L EXPANSION
☐ WILL CONSIDER ALL
☐ VENTURE LEASING

Other Locations:

Affiliation:
Minimum Investment: Less than $1 Million
Capital Under Management: Less than $100 Million

GEOGRAPHIC PREF

☐ East Coast
☐ West Coast
☐ Northeast
☐ Mid Atlantic
☐ Gulf States
☐ Northwest
☒ Southeast
☒ Southwest
☐ Midwest
☐ Central
☐ Local to Office
☐ Other Geo Pref

HANIFEN IMHOFF MEZZANINE FUND, LP

1125 17th Street
Suite 2260
Denver CO 80202

Phone (303) 291-5209   Fax (303) 291-5327

PROFESSIONALS	TITLE
Edward C. Brown	Manager

INDUSTRY PREFERENCE

☐ INFORMATION INDUSTRY	☐ BASIC INDUSTRIES
☐ Communications	☐ Consumer
☐ Computer Equipment	☐ Distribution
☐ Computer Services	☐ Manufacturing
☐ Computer Components	☐ Retail
☐ Computer Entertainment	☐ Service
☐ Computer Education	☐ Wholesale
☐ Information Technologies	☐ SPECIFIC INDUSTRIES
☐ Computer Media	☐ Energy
☐ Software	☐ Environmental
☐ Internet	☐ Financial
☐ MEDICAL/HEALTHCARE	☐ Real Estate
☐ Biotechnology	☐ Transportation
☐ Healthcare Services	☐ Publishing
☐ Life Sciences	☐ Food
☐ Medical Products	☐ Franchises
☐ INDUSTRIAL	☒ DIVERSIFIED
☐ Advanced Materials	☐ MISCELLANEOUS
☐ Chemicals	
☐ Instruments & Controls	

STAGE PREFERENCE

☐ EARLY STAGE
☐ Seed
☐ Start-up
☐ 1st Stage
☒ LATER STAGE
☒ 2nd Stage
☒ Mature
☒ Mezzanine
☒ LBO/MBO
☐ Turnaround
☐ INT'L EXPANSION
☐ WILL CONSIDER ALL
☐ VENTURE LEASING

SBIC
Other Locations:

Affiliation:
Minimum Investment: $1 Million or more
Capital Under Management: Less than $100 Million

GEOGRAPHIC PREF

☐ East Coast
☐ West Coast
☐ Northeast
☐ Mid Atlantic
☐ Gulf States
☐ Northwest
☐ Southeast
☐ Southwest
☐ Midwest
☐ Central
☐ Local to Office
☐ Other Geo Pref

NEW VENTURE RESOURCES

1377 Linden Drive
Boulder CO 80304

Phone (303) 449-7047

PROFESSIONALS	TITLE
Dexter Francis	Managing Director

INDUSTRY PREFERENCE

☒ INFORMATION INDUSTRY
☒ Communications
☒ Computer Equipment
☒ Computer Services
☒ Computer Components
☐ Computer Entertainment
☒ Computer Education
☒ Information Technologies
☐ Computer Media
☒ Software
☒ Internet
☒ MEDICAL/HEALTHCARE
☒ Biotechnology
☒ Healthcare Services
☒ Life Sciences
☒ Medical Products
☒ INDUSTRIAL
☐ Advanced Materials
☐ Chemicals
☒ Instruments & Controls

☒ BASIC INDUSTRIES
☒ Consumer
☐ Distribution
☐ Manufacturing
☐ Retail
☒ Service
☐ Wholesale
☐ SPECIFIC INDUSTRIES
☐ Energy
☐ Environmental
☐ Financial
☐ Real Estate
☐ Transportation
☐ Publishing
☐ Food
☐ Franchises
☒ DIVERSIFIED
☐ MISCELLANEOUS

STAGE PREFERENCE

☒ EARLY STAGE
☒ Seed
☒ Start-up
☒ 1st Stage
☐ LATER STAGE
☐ 2nd Stage
☐ Mature
☐ Mezzanine
☐ LBO/MBO
☐ Turnaround
☐ INT'L EXPANSION
☐ WILL CONSIDER ALL
☐ VENTURE LEASING

Other Locations:

Affiliation:
Minimum Investment: Less than $1 Million
Capital Under Management: Less than $100 Million

GEOGRAPHIC PREF

☐ East Coast
☐ West Coast
☐ Northeast
☐ Mid Atlantic
☐ Gulf States
☐ Northwest
☐ Southeast
☐ Southwest
☐ Midwest
☐ Central
☐ Local to Office
☐ Other Geo Pref

PHILLIPS-SMITH SPECIALTY RETAIL GROUP

102 South Tejon Street
Suite 1100
Colorado Springs CO 80903

Phone (719) 578-3301   Fax (719) 578-8869

PROFESSIONALS	TITLE
James Rothe	Principal

INDUSTRY PREFERENCE

☒ INFORMATION INDUSTRY
☐ Communications
☐ Computer Equipment
☐ Computer Services
☐ Computer Components
☐ Computer Entertainment
☐ Computer Education
☐ Information Technologies
☐ Computer Media
☐ Software
☒ Internet
☐ MEDICAL/HEALTHCARE
☐ Biotechnology
☐ Healthcare Services
☐ Life Sciences
☐ Medical Products
☐ INDUSTRIAL
☐ Advanced Materials
☐ Chemicals
☐ Instruments & Controls

☒ BASIC INDUSTRIES
☒ Consumer
☐ Distribution
☐ Manufacturing
☒ Retail
☒ Service
☐ Wholesale
☒ SPECIFIC INDUSTRIES
☐ Energy
☐ Environmental
☐ Financial
☐ Real Estate
☐ Transportation
☐ Publishing
☐ Food
☐ Franchises
☒ DIVERSIFIED
☐ MISCELLANEOUS
   e-Commerce

STAGE PREFERENCE

☒ EARLY STAGE
☒ Seed
☒ Start-up
☒ 1st Stage
☒ LATER STAGE
☒ 2nd Stage
☒ Mature
☒ Mezzanine
☒ LBO/MBO
☐ Turnaround
☐ INT'L EXPANSION
☐ WILL CONSIDER ALL
☐ VENTURE LEASING

Other Locations: Addison TX, Bronxville NY

Affiliation:
Minimum Investment: $1 Million or more
Capital Under Management: $100 to $500 Million

GEOGRAPHIC PREF

☐ East Coast
☐ West Coast
☐ Northeast
☐ Mid Atlantic
☐ Gulf States
☐ Northwest
☐ Southeast
☐ Southwest
☐ Midwest
☐ Central
☐ Local to Office
☐ Other Geo Pref

ROSER VENTURES LLC

1105 Spruce Street
Boulder CO 80302

Phone (303) 443-6436   Fax (303) 443-1885

PROFESSIONALS	TITLE
James Roser	Partner
Christopher Roser	Partner
Philip Dignan	Partner

INDUSTRY PREFERENCE

☒ INFORMATION INDUSTRY	☒ BASIC INDUSTRIES
☒ Communications	☐ Consumer
☒ Computer Equipment	☒ Distribution
☒ Computer Services	☐ Manufacturing
☒ Computer Components	☐ Retail
☒ Computer Entertainment	☐ Service
☒ Computer Education	☐ Wholesale
☒ Information Technologies	☐ SPECIFIC INDUSTRIES
☒ Computer Media	☐ Energy
☒ Software	☐ Environmental
☒ Internet	☐ Financial
☒ MEDICAL/HEALTHCARE	☐ Real Estate
☐ Biotechnology	☐ Transportation
☒ Healthcare Services	☐ Publishing
☒ Life Sciences	☐ Food
☒ Medical Products	☐ Franchises
☒ INDUSTRIAL	☒ DIVERSIFIED
☐ Advanced Materials	☒ MISCELLANEOUS
☐ Chemicals	
☒ Instruments & Controls	

STAGE PREFERENCE

☒ EARLY STAGE
☐ Seed
☒ Start-up
☒ 1st Stage
☒ LATER STAGE
☒ 2nd Stage
☐ Mature
☐ Mezzanine
☐ LBO/MBO
☐ Turnaround
☐ INT'L EXPANSION
☐ WILL CONSIDER ALL
☐ VENTURE LEASING

Other Locations:

Affiliation:
Minimum Investment: Less than $1 Million
Capital Under Management: Less than $100 Million

GEOGRAPHIC PREF

☐ East Coast
☐ West Coast
☐ Northeast
☐ Mid Atlantic
☐ Gulf States
☐ Northwest
☐ Southeast
☒ Southwest
☐ Midwest
☐ Central
☐ Local to Office
☒ Other Geo Pref
CO

SEQUEL VENTURE PARTNERS

4430 Arapahoe Avenue
Suite 220
Boulder CO 80303

Phone (303) 546-0400   Fax (303) 546-9728

PROFESSIONALS	TITLE
John Greff	Partner
Kinney Johnson	Partner
Dan Mitchell	Partner
Rick Patch	Partner

INDUSTRY PREFERENCE

☒ INFORMATION INDUSTRY	☐ BASIC INDUSTRIES
☒ Communications	☐ Consumer
☐ Computer Equipment	☐ Distribution
☐ Computer Services	☐ Manufacturing
☐ Computer Components	☐ Retail
☐ Computer Entertainment	☐ Service
☐ Computer Education	☐ Wholesale
☐ Information Technologies	☐ SPECIFIC INDUSTRIES
☐ Computer Media	☐ Energy
☒ Software	☐ Environmental
☒ Internet	☐ Financial
☒ MEDICAL/HEALTHCARE	☐ Real Estate
☒ Biotechnology	☐ Transportation
☐ Healthcare Services	☐ Publishing
☐ Life Sciences	☐ Food
☒ Medical Products	☐ Franchises
☒ INDUSTRIAL	☒ DIVERSIFIED
☐ Advanced Materials	☒ MISCELLANEOUS
☐ Chemicals	
☒ Instruments & Controls	

STAGE PREFERENCE

☒ EARLY STAGE
☒ Seed
☒ Start-up
☒ 1st Stage
☐ LATER STAGE
☐ 2nd Stage
☐ Mature
☐ Mezzanine
☐ LBO/MBO
☐ Turnaround
☐ INT'L EXPANSION
☐ WILL CONSIDER ALL
☐ VENTURE LEASING

Other Locations:

Affiliation:
Minimum Investment: Less than $1 Million
Capital Under Management: Less than $100 Million

GEOGRAPHIC PREF

☐ East Coast
☐ West Coast
☐ Northeast
☐ Mid Atlantic
☐ Gulf States
☐ Northwest
☐ Southeast
☐ Southwest
☐ Midwest
☐ Central
☐ Local to Office
☐ Other Geo Pref

SOFTBANK TECHNOLOGY VENTURES

**P.O. Box E
Eldorado Springs CO 80025**

Phone (303) 494-3242   Fax (303) 494-7642

PROFESSIONALS	TITLE
Bradley Feld	Managing Director

INDUSTRY PREFERENCE

☒ INFORMATION INDUSTRY	☒ BASIC INDUSTRIES
☒ Communications	☐ Consumer
☒ Computer Equipment	☐ Distribution
☐ Computer Services	☐ Manufacturing
☒ Computer Components	☐ Retail
☐ Computer Entertainment	☒ Service
☐ Computer Education	☐ Wholesale
☒ Information Technologies	☐ SPECIFIC INDUSTRIES
☒ Computer Media	☐ Energy
☒ Software	☐ Environmental
☒ Internet	☐ Financial
☐ MEDICAL/HEALTHCARE	☐ Real Estate
☐ Biotechnology	☐ Transportation
☐ Healthcare Services	☐ Publishing
☐ Life Sciences	☐ Food
☐ Medical Products	☐ Franchises
☐ INDUSTRIAL	☒ DIVERSIFIED
☐ Advanced Materials	☒ MISCELLANEOUS
☐ Chemicals	
☐ Instruments & Controls	

STAGE PREFERENCE

☒ EARLY STAGE
☒ Seed
☒ Start-up
☒ 1st Stage
☒ LATER STAGE
☒ 2nd Stage
☒ Mature
☒ Mezzanine
☒ LBO/MBO
☐ Turnaround
☐ INT'L EXPANSION
☐ WILL CONSIDER ALL
☐ VENTURE LEASING

Other Locations: Newton Center MA, Eldorado Springs CO

Affiliation:
Minimum Investment: $1 Million or more
Capital Under Management: Over $500 Million

GEOGRAPHIC PREF

☐ East Coast
☐ West Coast
☐ Northeast
☐ Mid Atlantic
☐ Gulf States
☐ Northwest
☐ Southeast
☐ Southwest
☐ Midwest
☐ Central
☐ Local to Office
☐ Other Geo Pref

THOMA CRESSEY EQUITY PARTNERS

**4050 Republic Plaza
370 17th Street
Denver CO 80202**

Phone (303) 592-4888   Fax (303) 592-4845

PROFESSIONALS	TITLE
Robert Manning	Partner
Christian Osborn	Partner
Kenn Lee	Partner

INDUSTRY PREFERENCE

☒ INFORMATION INDUSTRY	☒ BASIC INDUSTRIES
☒ Communications	☒ Consumer
☒ Computer Equipment	☒ Distribution
☒ Computer Services	☒ Manufacturing
☒ Computer Components	☒ Retail
☐ Computer Entertainment	☒ Service
☒ Computer Education	☒ Wholesale
☒ Information Technologies	☒ SPECIFIC INDUSTRIES
☒ Computer Media	☒ Energy
☒ Software	☒ Environmental
☒ Internet	☒ Financial
☒ MEDICAL/HEALTHCARE	☐ Real Estate
☒ Biotechnology	☒ Transportation
☒ Healthcare Services	☒ Publishing
☒ Life Sciences	☐ Food
☒ Medical Products	☐ Franchises
☒ INDUSTRIAL	☒ DIVERSIFIED
☒ Advanced Materials	☐ MISCELLANEOUS
☒ Chemicals	
☒ Instruments & Controls	

STAGE PREFERENCE

☐ EARLY STAGE
☐ Seed
☐ Start-up
☐ 1st Stage
☒ LATER STAGE
☒ 2nd Stage
☒ Mature
☐ Mezzanine
☒ LBO/MBO
☐ Turnaround
☐ INT'L EXPANSION
☐ WILL CONSIDER ALL
☐ VENTURE LEASING

Other Locations: Chicago IL, San Francisco CA

Affiliation:
Minimum Investment: $1 Million or more
Capital Under Management: $100 to $500 Million

GEOGRAPHIC PREF

☐ East Coast
☐ West Coast
☐ Northeast
☐ Mid Atlantic
☐ Gulf States
☐ Northwest
☐ Southeast
☐ Southwest
☐ Midwest
☐ Central
☐ Local to Office
☐ Other Geo Pref

WOLF VENTURES

50 South Steele Street
Suite 777
Denver CO 80209

Phone (303) 321-4800   Fax (303) 321-4848

PROFESSIONALS	TITLE
David O. Wolf	Managing Partner

INDUSTRY PREFERENCE

☒ INFORMATION INDUSTRY	☒ BASIC INDUSTRIES
☐ Communications	☐ Consumer
☒ Computer Equipment	☐ Distribution
☐ Computer Services	☒ Manufacturing
☒ Computer Components	☐ Retail
☐ Computer Entertainment	☐ Service
☐ Computer Education	☐ Wholesale
☐ Information Technologies	☐ SPECIFIC INDUSTRIES
☐ Computer Media	☐ Energy
☒ Software	☐ Environmental
☐ Internet	☐ Financial
☐ MEDICAL/HEALTHCARE	☐ Real Estate
☐ Biotechnology	☐ Transportation
☐ Healthcare Services	☐ Publishing
☐ Life Sciences	☐ Food
☐ Medical Products	☐ Franchises
☒ INDUSTRIAL	☒ DIVERSIFIED
☐ Advanced Materials	☒ MISCELLANEOUS
☐ Chemicals	
☒ Instruments & Controls	

STAGE PREFERENCE

☐ EARLY STAGE	
☐ Seed	
☐ Start-up	
☐ 1st Stage	
☒ LATER STAGE	
☒ 2nd Stage	
☐ Mature	
☐ Mezzanine	
☐ LBO/MBO	
☐ Turnaround	
☐ INT'L EXPANSION	
☐ WILL CONSIDER ALL	
☐ VENTURE LEASING	

Other Locations:

Affiliation:
Minimum Investment: Less than $1 Million
Capital Under Management: Less than $100 Million

GEOGRAPHIC PREF

☐ East Coast
☐ West Coast
☐ Northeast
☐ Mid Atlantic
☐ Gulf States
☐ Northwest
☐ Southeast
☐ Southwest
☐ Midwest
☐ Central
☐ Local to Office
☒ Other Geo Pref
Rocky Mountain Region

ADVANCED MATERIALS PARTNERS, INC.

45 Pine Street
P.O. Box 1022
New Canaan CT 06840-1022

Phone (203) 966-6415   Fax (203) 966-8448

PROFESSIONALS	TITLE
Warner K. Babcock	Managing Director

INDUSTRY PREFERENCE

☒ INFORMATION INDUSTRY	☒ BASIC INDUSTRIES
☒ Communications	☒ Consumer
☒ Computer Equipment	☒ Distribution
☒ Computer Services	☒ Manufacturing
☒ Computer Components	☐ Retail
☐ Computer Entertainment	☐ Service
☒ Computer Education	☐ Wholesale
☒ Information Technologies	☐ SPECIFIC INDUSTRIES
☐ Computer Media	☐ Energy
☐ Software	☐ Environmental
☐ Internet	☐ Financial
☒ MEDICAL/HEALTHCARE	☐ Real Estate
☒ Biotechnology	☐ Transportation
☒ Healthcare Services	☐ Publishing
☒ Life Sciences	☐ Food
☒ Medical Products	☐ Franchises
☒ INDUSTRIAL	☒ DIVERSIFIED
☒ Advanced Materials	☐ MISCELLANEOUS
☒ Chemicals	
☐ Instruments & Controls	

STAGE PREFERENCE

☒ EARLY STAGE	
☒ Seed	
☒ Start-up	
☒ 1st Stage	
☒ LATER STAGE	
☒ 2nd Stage	
☒ Mature	
☒ Mezzanine	
☒ LBO/MBO	
☒ Turnaround	
☒ INT'L EXPANSION	
☐ WILL CONSIDER ALL	
☒ VENTURE LEASING	

Other Locations:

Affiliation: Grumman and Johnson Wax
Minimum Investment: Less than $1 Million
Capital Under Management: Over $500 Million

GEOGRAPHIC PREF

☐ East Coast
☐ West Coast
☐ Northeast
☐ Mid Atlantic
☐ Gulf States
☐ Northwest
☐ Southeast
☐ Southwest
☐ Midwest
☐ Central
☐ Local to Office
☐ Other Geo Pref

BRAND EQUITY VENTURES

**Three Pickwick Plaza
Greenwich CT 06830**

Phone (203) 862-5500   Fax (203) 629-2019

PROFESSIONALS	TITLE
Christopher Kirchen	Managing
David Yarnell	General Partner
William Meurer	Vice President
Marc Singer	Vice President

INDUSTRY PREFERENCE

☒ INFORMATION INDUSTRY	☒ BASIC INDUSTRIES
☐ Communications	☒ Consumer
☐ Computer Equipment	☒ Distribution
☐ Computer Services	☐ Manufacturing
☐ Computer Components	☐ Retail
☐ Computer Entertainment	☐ Service
☒ Computer Education	☐ Wholesale
☐ Information Technologies	☐ SPECIFIC INDUSTRIES
☐ Computer Media	☐ Energy
☐ Software	☐ Environmental
☒ Internet	☐ Financial
☐ MEDICAL/HEALTHCARE	☐ Real Estate
☐ Biotechnology	☐ Transportation
☐ Healthcare Services	☐ Publishing
☐ Life Sciences	☐ Food
☐ Medical Products	☐ Franchises
☐ INDUSTRIAL	☒ DIVERSIFIED
☐ Advanced Materials	☒ MISCELLANEOUS
☐ Chemicals	
☐ Instruments & Controls	

STAGE PREFERENCE

☒ EARLY STAGE
☐   Seed
☒   Start-up
☒   1st Stage
☒ LATER STAGE
☒   2nd Stage
☐   Mature
☒   Mezzanine
☒   LBO/MBO
☐   Turnaround
☐ INT'L EXPANSION
☐ WILL CONSIDER ALL
☐ VENTURE LEASING

Other Locations:

Affiliation:
Minimum Investment: Less than $1 Million
Capital Under Management: Less than $100 Million

GEOGRAPHIC PREF

☐ East Coast
☐ West Coast
☐ Northeast
☐ Mid Atlantic
☐ Gulf States
☐ Northwest
☐ Southeast
☐ Southwest
☐ Midwest
☐ Central
☐ Local to Office
☐ Other Geo Pref

CANAAN VENTURE PARTNERS

**105 Rowayton Avenue
Rowayton CT 06853**

Phone (203) 855-0400   Fax (203) 854-9117

PROFESSIONALS	TITLE
Stephen L. Green	Partner
Gregory Kopchinsky	Partner
Robert Migliorino	Partner
James Fitzpatrick	Partner
Harry T. Rein	Partner

INDUSTRY PREFERENCE

☒ INFORMATION INDUSTRY	☒ BASIC INDUSTRIES
☒ Communications	☒ Consumer
☒ Computer Equipment	☐ Distribution
☒ Computer Services	☐ Manufacturing
☒ Computer Components	☒ Retail
☐ Computer Entertainment	☒ Service
☒ Computer Education	☐ Wholesale
☒ Information Technologies	☒ SPECIFIC INDUSTRIES
☒ Computer Media	☐ Energy
☒ Software	☒ Environmental
☒ Internet	☒ Financial
☒ MEDICAL/HEALTHCARE	☐ Real Estate
☒ Biotechnology	☐ Transportation
☒ Healthcare Services	☐ Publishing
☒ Life Sciences	☐ Food
☒ Medical Products	☐ Franchises
☒ INDUSTRIAL	☒ DIVERSIFIED
☒ Advanced Materials	☐ MISCELLANEOUS
☒ Chemicals	
☒ Instruments & Controls	

STAGE PREFERENCE

☒ EARLY STAGE
☐   Seed
☐   Start-up
☒   1st Stage
☒ LATER STAGE
☒   2nd Stage
☒   Mature
☒   Mezzanine
☒   LBO/MBO
☒   Turnaround
☐ INT'L EXPANSION
☐ WILL CONSIDER ALL
☒ VENTURE LEASING

SBIC
Other Locations: Menlo Park CA

Affiliation:
Minimum Investment: Less than $1 Million
Capital Under Management: Over $500 Million

GEOGRAPHIC PREF

☐ East Coast
☐ West Coast
☐ Northeast
☐ Mid Atlantic
☐ Gulf States
☐ Northwest
☐ Southeast
☐ Southwest
☐ Midwest
☐ Central
☐ Local to Office
☐ Other Geo Pref

CAPITAL RESOURCE CO. OF CONNECTICUT

**Two Bridgewater Road
Farmington CT 06032**

Phone (860) 677-1113   Fax (860) 677-5414

PROFESSIONALS	TITLE
Morris Morgenstein	General Partner

INDUSTRY PREFERENCE

- ☐ INFORMATION INDUSTRY
- ☐ Communications
- ☐ Computer Equipment
- ☐ Computer Services
- ☐ Computer Components
- ☐ Computer Entertainment
- ☐ Computer Education
- ☐ Information Technologies
- ☐ Computer Media
- ☐ Software
- ☐ Internet
- ☐ MEDICAL/HEALTHCARE
- ☐ Biotechnology
- ☐ Healthcare Services
- ☐ Life Sciences
- ☐ Medical Products
- ☐ INDUSTRIAL
- ☐ Advanced Materials
- ☐ Chemicals
- ☐ Instruments & Controls

- ☒ BASIC INDUSTRIES
- ☐ Consumer
- ☐ Distribution
- ☐ Manufacturing
- ☐ Retail
- ☒ Service
- ☐ Wholesale
- ☒ SPECIFIC INDUSTRIES
- ☐ Energy
- ☐ Environmental
- ☐ Financial
- ☐ Real Estate
- ☒ Transportation
- ☐ Publishing
- ☐ Food
- ☐ Franchises
- ☒ DIVERSIFIED
- ☒ MISCELLANEOUS
  Security Guard, Taxicab

STAGE PREFERENCE

- ☐ EARLY STAGE
- ☐ Seed
- ☐ Start-up
- ☐ 1st Stage
- ☒ LATER STAGE
- ☒ 2nd Stage
- ☒ Mature
- ☒ Mezzanine
- ☒ LBO/MBO
- ☒ Turnaround
- ☐ INT'L EXPANSION
- ☐ WILL CONSIDER ALL
- ☒ VENTURE LEASING

SBIC
Other Locations:

Affiliation:
Minimum Investment: Less than $1 Million
Capital Under Management: Less than $100 Million

GEOGRAPHIC PREF

- ☐ East Coast
- ☐ West Coast
- ☒ Northeast
- ☐ Mid Atlantic
- ☐ Gulf States
- ☐ Northwest
- ☐ Southeast
- ☐ Southwest
- ☐ Midwest
- ☐ Central
- ☐ Local to Office
- ☐ Other Geo Pref

CATTERTON-SIMON PARTNERS LP

**Nine Greenwich Office Park
Greenwich CT 06831-5147**

Phone (203) 629-4901   Fax (203) 629-4903

PROFESSIONALS	TITLE
J. Michael Chu	Managing Director
Craig Sakin	Managing Director
J. P. Bolduc	General Partner

INDUSTRY PREFERENCE

- ☒ INFORMATION INDUSTRY
- ☐ Communications
- ☐ Computer Equipment
- ☐ Computer Services
- ☐ Computer Components
- ☐ Computer Entertainment
- ☒ Computer Education
- ☐ Information Technologies
- ☐ Computer Media
- ☐ Software
- ☒ Internet
- ☐ MEDICAL/HEALTHCARE
- ☐ Biotechnology
- ☐ Healthcare Services
- ☐ Life Sciences
- ☐ Medical Products
- ☐ INDUSTRIAL
- ☐ Advanced Materials
- ☐ Chemicals
- ☐ Instruments & Controls

- ☒ BASIC INDUSTRIES
- ☒ Consumer
- ☐ Distribution
- ☐ Manufacturing
- ☐ Retail
- ☐ Service
- ☐ Wholesale
- ☐ SPECIFIC INDUSTRIES
- ☐ Energy
- ☐ Environmental
- ☐ Financial
- ☐ Real Estate
- ☐ Transportation
- ☐ Publishing
- ☐ Food
- ☐ Franchises
- ☒ DIVERSIFIED
- ☒ MISCELLANEOUS

STAGE PREFERENCE

- ☐ EARLY STAGE
- ☐ Seed
- ☐ Start-up
- ☐ 1st Stage
- ☒ LATER STAGE
- ☒ 2nd Stage
- ☐ Mature
- ☐ Mezzanine
- ☒ LBO/MBO
- ☐ Turnaround
- ☐ INT'L EXPANSION
- ☐ WILL CONSIDER ALL
- ☐ VENTURE LEASING

Other Locations: Charleston WV, Los Angeles CA

Affiliation:
Minimum Investment: $1 Million or more
Capital Under Management: $100 to $500 Million

GEOGRAPHIC PREF

- ☐ East Coast
- ☐ West Coast
- ☐ Northeast
- ☐ Mid Atlantic
- ☐ Gulf States
- ☐ Northwest
- ☐ Southeast
- ☐ Southwest
- ☐ Midwest
- ☐ Central
- ☐ Local to Office
- ☐ Other Geo Pref

CONNECTICUT INNOVATIONS

**999 West Street
Rocky Hill CT 06067**

Phone (860) 563-5851   Fax (860) 563-4877

PROFESSIONALS	TITLE
John Anderson	Managing Director

INDUSTRY PREFERENCE

- ☒ INFORMATION INDUSTRY
- ☒ Communications
- ☒ Computer Equipment
- ☒ Computer Services
- ☒ Computer Components
- ☐ Computer Entertainment
- ☒ Computer Education
- ☒ Information Technologies
- ☒ Computer Media
- ☒ Software
- ☒ Internet
- ☒ MEDICAL/HEALTHCARE
- ☒ Biotechnology
- ☐ Healthcare Services
- ☒ Life Sciences
- ☐ Medical Products
- ☒ INDUSTRIAL
- ☐ Advanced Materials
- ☐ Chemicals
- ☒ Instruments & Controls

- ☐ BASIC INDUSTRIES
- ☐ Consumer
- ☐ Distribution
- ☐ Manufacturing
- ☐ Retail
- ☐ Service
- ☐ Wholesale
- ☒ SPECIFIC INDUSTRIES
- ☒ Energy
- ☐ Environmental
- ☐ Financial
- ☐ Real Estate
- ☐ Transportation
- ☐ Publishing
- ☐ Food
- ☐ Franchises
- ☒ DIVERSIFIED
- ☒ MISCELLANEOUS
- Aerospace

STAGE PREFERENCE

- ☒ EARLY STAGE
- ☒ Seed
- ☒ Start-up
- ☒ 1st Stage
- ☐ LATER STAGE
- ☐ 2nd Stage
- ☐ Mature
- ☐ Mezzanine
- ☐ LBO/MBO
- ☐ Turnaround
- ☐ INT'L EXPANSION
- ☐ WILL CONSIDER ALL
- ☐ VENTURE LEASING

Other Locations:

Affiliation:
Minimum Investment: Less than $1 Million
Capital Under Management: Less than $100 Million

GEOGRAPHIC PREF

- ☐ East Coast
- ☐ West Coast
- ☐ Northeast
- ☐ Mid Atlantic
- ☐ Gulf States
- ☐ Northwest
- ☐ Southeast
- ☐ Southwest
- ☐ Midwest
- ☐ Central
- ☐ Local to Office
- ☒ Other Geo Pref
- CT

CONNING CORPORATION

**City Place II
185 Asylum Street
Hartford CT 06103**

Phone (860) 527-1131   Fax (860) 520-1299

PROFESSIONALS	TITLE
John B. Clinton	Sr. Vice President
Steven F. Paiker	Sr. Vice President

INDUSTRY PREFERENCE

- ☐ INFORMATION INDUSTRY
- ☐ Communications
- ☐ Computer Equipment
- ☐ Computer Services
- ☐ Computer Components
- ☐ Computer Entertainment
- ☐ Computer Education
- ☐ Information Technologies
- ☐ Computer Media
- ☐ Software
- ☐ Internet
- ☐ MEDICAL/HEALTHCARE
- ☐ Biotechnology
- ☐ Healthcare Services
- ☐ Life Sciences
- ☐ Medical Products
- ☐ INDUSTRIAL
- ☐ Advanced Materials
- ☐ Chemicals
- ☐ Instruments & Controls

- ☐ BASIC INDUSTRIES
- ☐ Consumer
- ☐ Distribution
- ☐ Manufacturing
- ☐ Retail
- ☐ Service
- ☐ Wholesale
- ☒ SPECIFIC INDUSTRIES
- ☐ Energy
- ☐ Environmental
- ☒ Financial
- ☐ Real Estate
- ☐ Transportation
- ☐ Publishing
- ☐ Food
- ☐ Franchises
- ☐ DIVERSIFIED
- ☒ MISCELLANEOUS
- Insurance Industry only

STAGE PREFERENCE

- ☒ EARLY STAGE
- ☐ Seed
- ☒ Start-up
- ☒ 1st Stage
- ☒ LATER STAGE
- ☒ 2nd Stage
- ☒ Mature
- ☒ Mezzanine
- ☒ LBO/MBO
- ☒ Turnaround
- ☐ INT'L EXPANSION
- ☐ WILL CONSIDER ALL
- ☒ VENTURE LEASING

Other Locations:

Affiliation:
Minimum Investment: $1 Million or more
Capital Under Management: $100 to $500 Million

GEOGRAPHIC PREF

- ☐ East Coast
- ☐ West Coast
- ☐ Northeast
- ☐ Mid Atlantic
- ☐ Gulf States
- ☐ Northwest
- ☐ Southeast
- ☐ Southwest
- ☐ Midwest
- ☐ Central
- ☐ Local to Office
- ☐ Other Geo Pref

CONSUMER VENTURE PARTNERS

Three Pickwick Plaza
Greenwich CT 06830

Phone (203) 629-8800   Fax (203) 629-2019

PROFESSIONALS
Christopher P. Kirchen
Pearson C. Cummin III
David S. Yarnell

TITLE
Managing General Partner
Managing General Partner
Vice President

INDUSTRY PREFERENCE

- ☒ INFORMATION INDUSTRY
- ☒ Communications
- ☒ Computer Equipment
- ☒ Computer Services
- ☒ Computer Components
- ☐ Computer Entertainment
- ☐ Computer Education
- ☒ Information Technologies
- ☒ Computer Media
- ☒ Software
- ☒ Internet
- ☐ MEDICAL/HEALTHCARE
- ☐ Biotechnology
- ☐ Healthcare Services
- ☐ Life Sciences
- ☐ Medical Products
- ☐ INDUSTRIAL
- ☐ Advanced Materials
- ☐ Chemicals
- ☐ Instruments & Controls

- ☒ BASIC INDUSTRIES
- ☒ Consumer
- ☒ Distribution
- ☐ Manufacturing
- ☒ Retail
- ☐ Service
- ☐ Wholesale
- ☐ SPECIFIC INDUSTRIES
- ☐ Energy
- ☐ Environmental
- ☐ Financial
- ☐ Real Estate
- ☐ Transportation
- ☐ Publishing
- ☐ Food
- ☐ Franchises
- ☒ DIVERSIFIED
- ☐ MISCELLANEOUS

STAGE PREFERENCE

- ☒ EARLY STAGE
- ☐ Seed
- ☒ Start-up
- ☒ 1st Stage
- ☒ LATER STAGE
- ☒ 2nd Stage
- ☒ Mature
- ☐ Mezzanine
- ☒ LBO/MBO
- ☐ Turnaround
- ☐ INT'L EXPANSION
- ☐ WILL CONSIDER ALL
- ☐ VENTURE LEASING

Other Locations:

Affiliation:
Minimum Investment: Less than $1 Million
Capital Under Management: Less than $100 Million

GEOGRAPHIC PREF

- ☐ East Coast
- ☐ West Coast
- ☐ Northeast
- ☐ Mid Atlantic
- ☐ Gulf States
- ☐ Northwest
- ☐ Southeast
- ☐ Southwest
- ☐ Midwest
- ☐ Central
- ☐ Local to Office
- ☐ Other Geo Pref

ENTERPRISE ASSOCIATES

200 Nyala Farms
Westport CT 06880

Phone (203) 222-4594   Fax (203) 222-4592

PROFESSIONALS
Venetia Kontogouris
Peter Meekin

TITLE
President
Vice President

INDUSTRY PREFERENCE

- ☒ INFORMATION INDUSTRY
- ☒ Communications
- ☒ Computer Equipment
- ☒ Computer Services
- ☒ Computer Components
- ☐ Computer Entertainment
- ☒ Computer Education
- ☒ Information Technologies
- ☐ Computer Media
- ☒ Software
- ☒ Internet
- ☒ MEDICAL/HEALTHCARE
- ☐ Biotechnology
- ☐ Healthcare Services
- ☐ Life Sciences
- ☒ Medical Products
- ☒ INDUSTRIAL
- ☐ Advanced Materials
- ☐ Chemicals
- ☒ Instruments & Controls

- ☒ BASIC INDUSTRIES
- ☒ Consumer
- ☐ Distribution
- ☐ Manufacturing
- ☐ Retail
- ☐ Service
- ☐ Wholesale
- ☐ SPECIFIC INDUSTRIES
- ☐ Energy
- ☐ Environmental
- ☐ Financial
- ☐ Real Estate
- ☐ Transportation
- ☐ Publishing
- ☐ Food
- ☐ Franchises
- ☒ DIVERSIFIED
- ☒ MISCELLANEOUS

STAGE PREFERENCE

- ☒ EARLY STAGE
- ☐ Seed
- ☒ Start-up
- ☐ 1st Stage
- ☐ LATER STAGE
- ☐ 2nd Stage
- ☐ Mature
- ☐ Mezzanine
- ☐ LBO/MBO
- ☐ Turnaround
- ☐ INT'L EXPANSION
- ☐ WILL CONSIDER ALL
- ☐ VENTURE LEASING

Other Locations:

Affiliation:
Minimum Investment: Less than $1 Million
Capital Under Management: $100 to $500 Million

GEOGRAPHIC PREF

- ☐ East Coast
- ☐ West Coast
- ☐ Northeast
- ☐ Mid Atlantic
- ☐ Gulf States
- ☐ Northwest
- ☐ Southeast
- ☐ Southwest
- ☐ Midwest
- ☐ Central
- ☐ Local to Office
- ☐ Other Geo Pref

FERRER FREEMAN THOMPSON & CO.

The Mill
10 Glenville Street
Greenwich CT 06831

Phone (203) 532-8011   Fax (203) 532-8016

PROFESSIONALS	TITLE
Carlos Ferrer	General Partner
David Freeman	General Partner
Robert Thompson	General Partner

INDUSTRY PREFERENCE

- ☐ INFORMATION INDUSTRY
- ☐ Communications
- ☐ Computer Equipment
- ☐ Computer Services
- ☐ Computer Components
- ☐ Computer Entertainment
- ☐ Computer Education
- ☐ Information Technologies
- ☐ Computer Media
- ☐ Software
- ☐ Internet
- ☒ MEDICAL/HEALTHCARE
- ☒ Biotechnology
- ☒ Healthcare Services
- ☒ Life Sciences
- ☒ Medical Products
- ☐ INDUSTRIAL
- ☐ Advanced Materials
- ☐ Chemicals
- ☐ Instruments & Controls

- ☐ BASIC INDUSTRIES
- ☐ Consumer
- ☐ Distribution
- ☐ Manufacturing
- ☐ Retail
- ☐ Service
- ☐ Wholesale
- ☐ SPECIFIC INDUSTRIES
- ☐ Energy
- ☐ Environmental
- ☐ Financial
- ☐ Real Estate
- ☐ Transportation
- ☐ Publishing
- ☐ Food
- ☐ Franchises
- ☐ DIVERSIFIED
- ☒ MISCELLANEOUS

STAGE PREFERENCE

- ☐ EARLY STAGE
- ☐ Seed
- ☐ Start-up
- ☐ 1st Stage
- ☒ LATER STAGE
- ☒ 2nd Stage
- ☐ Mature
- ☐ Mezzanine
- ☒ LBO/MBO
- ☐ Turnaround
- ☐ INT'L EXPANSION
- ☐ WILL CONSIDER ALL
- ☐ VENTURE LEASING

Other Locations:

Affiliation:
Minimum Investment: $1 Million or more
Capital Under Management: Less than $100 Million

GEOGRAPHIC PREF

- ☐ East Coast
- ☐ West Coast
- ☐ Northeast
- ☐ Mid Atlantic
- ☐ Gulf States
- ☐ Northwest
- ☐ Southeast
- ☐ Southwest
- ☐ Midwest
- ☐ Central
- ☐ Local to Office
- ☐ Other Geo Pref

GE CAPITAL
GE EQUITY GROUP

120 Long Ridge Road
Stamford CT 06927

Phone (203) 357-3100   Fax (203) 357-4462

PROFESSIONALS	TITLE
Michael Pralle	President
Jeff Coats	Managing Director
Paul Gelburd	Managing Director
John Malfettone	Managing Director
Steven Smith	Managing Director
Sharon Pipe	Managing Director

INDUSTRY PREFERENCE

- ☒ INFORMATION INDUSTRY
- ☒ Communications
- ☒ Computer Equipment
- ☒ Computer Services
- ☐ Computer Components
- ☐ Computer Entertainment
- ☒ Computer Education
- ☒ Information Technologies
- ☐ Computer Media
- ☒ Software
- ☒ Internet
- ☒ MEDICAL/HEALTHCARE
- ☒ Biotechnology
- ☒ Healthcare Services
- ☒ Life Sciences
- ☒ Medical Products
- ☒ INDUSTRIAL
- ☐ Advanced Materials
- ☐ Chemicals
- ☒ Instruments & Controls

- ☒ BASIC INDUSTRIES
- ☒ Consumer
- ☐ Distribution
- ☐ Manufacturing
- ☐ Retail
- ☐ Service
- ☐ Wholesale
- ☒ SPECIFIC INDUSTRIES
- ☐ Energy
- ☐ Environmental
- ☒ Financial
- ☐ Real Estate
- ☒ Transportation
- ☐ Publishing
- ☐ Food
- ☐ Franchises
- ☒ DIVERSIFIED
- ☒ MISCELLANEOUS

STAGE PREFERENCE

- ☐ EARLY STAGE
- ☐ Seed
- ☐ Start-up
- ☐ 1st Stage
- ☒ LATER STAGE
- ☒ 2nd Stage
- ☐ Mature
- ☒ Mezzanine
- ☒ LBO/MBO
- ☐ Turnaround
- ☐ INT'L EXPANSION
- ☐ WILL CONSIDER ALL
- ☐ VENTURE LEASING

Other Locations:

Affiliation:
Minimum Investment: $1 Million or more
Capital Under Management: Over $500 Million

GEOGRAPHIC PREF

- ☐ East Coast
- ☐ West Coast
- ☐ Northeast
- ☐ Mid Atlantic
- ☐ Gulf States
- ☐ Northwest
- ☐ Southeast
- ☐ Southwest
- ☐ Midwest
- ☐ Central
- ☐ Local to Office
- ☐ Other Geo Pref

INTERNATIONAL CAPITAL PARTNERS

300 First Place
Stamford CT 06902

Phone (203) 961-8900   Fax (203) 969-2212

PROFESSIONALS	TITLE
Ajit Hutheesing	Managing Partner
Douglas L. Ayer	Managing Partner
Nicholas E. Sinacori	Managing Partner

INDUSTRY PREFERENCE

☐ INFORMATION INDUSTRY
☐ Communications
☐ Computer Equipment
☐ Computer Services
☐ Computer Components
☐ Computer Entertainment
☐ Computer Education
☐ Information Technologies
☐ Computer Media
☐ Software
☐ Internet
☐ MEDICAL/HEALTHCARE
☐ Biotechnology
☐ Healthcare Services
☐ Life Sciences
☐ Medical Products
☐ INDUSTRIAL
☐ Advanced Materials
☐ Chemicals
☐ Instruments & Controls

☐ BASIC INDUSTRIES
☐ Consumer
☐ Distribution
☐ Manufacturing
☐ Retail
☐ Service
☐ Wholesale
☐ SPECIFIC INDUSTRIES
☐ Energy
☐ Environmental
☐ Financial
☐ Real Estate
☐ Transportation
☐ Publishing
☐ Food
☐ Franchises
☒ DIVERSIFIED
☒ MISCELLANEOUS

STAGE PREFERENCE

☐ EARLY STAGE
☐ Seed
☐ Start-up
☐ 1st Stage
☒ LATER STAGE
☒ 2nd Stage
☒ Mature
☐ Mezzanine
☒ LBO/MBO
☐ Turnaround
☐ INT'L EXPANSION
☐ WILL CONSIDER ALL
☐ VENTURE LEASING

Other Locations:

Affiliation:
Minimum Investment: $1 Million or more
Capital Under Management: Less than $100 Million

GEOGRAPHIC PREF

☐ East Coast
☐ West Coast
☐ Northeast
☐ Mid Atlantic
☐ Gulf States
☐ Northwest
☐ Southeast
☐ Southwest
☐ Midwest
☐ Central
☐ Local to Office
☐ Other Geo Pref

J. H. WHITNEY & CO.

177 Broad Street
15th Floor
Stamford CT 06901

Phone (203) 973-1400   Fax (203) 973-1422

PROFESSIONALS	TITLE
Lori Gonye	General Partner
Tenence Logan	General Partner

INDUSTRY PREFERENCE

☒ INFORMATION INDUSTRY
☒ Communications
☒ Computer Equipment
☐ Computer Services
☐ Computer Components
☐ Computer Entertainment
☐ Computer Education
☐ Information Technologies
☐ Computer Media
☐ Software
☒ Internet
☒ MEDICAL/HEALTHCARE
☒ Biotechnology
☒ Healthcare Services
☒ Life Sciences
☒ Medical Products
☒ INDUSTRIAL
☒ Advanced Materials
☒ Chemicals
☒ Instruments & Controls

☒ BASIC INDUSTRIES
☒ Consumer
☐ Distribution
☐ Manufacturing
☒ Retail
☐ Service
☐ Wholesale
☐ SPECIFIC INDUSTRIES
☐ Energy
☐ Environmental
☐ Financial
☐ Real Estate
☐ Transportation
☐ Publishing
☐ Food
☐ Franchises
☒ DIVERSIFIED
☒ MISCELLANEOUS

STAGE PREFERENCE

☒ EARLY STAGE
☐ Seed
☐ Start-up
☒ 1st Stage
☒ LATER STAGE
☒ 2nd Stage
☐ Mature
☒ Mezzanine
☒ LBO/MBO
☐ Turnaround
☐ INT'L EXPANSION
☐ WILL CONSIDER ALL
☐ VENTURE LEASING

Other Locations: New York NY

Affiliation:
Minimum Investment: $1 Million or more
Capital Under Management: Over $500 Million

GEOGRAPHIC PREF

☐ East Coast
☐ West Coast
☐ Northeast
☐ Mid Atlantic
☐ Gulf States
☐ Northwest
☐ Southeast
☐ Southwest
☐ Midwest
☐ Central
☐ Local to Office
☐ Other Geo Pref

LANDMARK PARTNERS, INC.

760 Hopmeadow Street
Simsbury CT 06070-1825

Phone (860) 651-9760   Fax (860) 651-8890

PROFESSIONALS	TITLE
Stanley F. Alfeld	Managing Partner
John A. Griner III	Managing Partner
Francisco Borges	Managing Partner
Timothy L. Haviland	Managing Partner
Richard W. Maine	Managing Partner

INDUSTRY PREFERENCE

☒ INFORMATION INDUSTRY	☒ BASIC INDUSTRIES
☒ Communications	☐ Consumer
☒ Computer Equipment	☐ Distribution
☒ Computer Services	☐ Manufacturing
☒ Computer Components	☐ Retail
☐ Computer Entertainment	☒ Service
☒ Computer Education	☐ Wholesale
☒ Information Technologies	☐ SPECIFIC INDUSTRIES
☒ Computer Media	☐ Energy
☒ Software	☐ Environmental
☒ Internet	☐ Financial
☒ MEDICAL/HEALTHCARE	☐ Real Estate
☒ Biotechnology	☐ Transportation
☒ Healthcare Services	☐ Publishing
☒ Life Sciences	☐ Food
☒ Medical Products	☐ Franchises
☒ INDUSTRIAL	☒ DIVERSIFIED
☒ Advanced Materials	☐ MISCELLANEOUS
☒ Chemicals	
☒ Instruments & Controls	

STAGE PREFERENCE

☐ EARLY STAGE
☐ Seed
☐ Start-up
☐ 1st Stage
☒ LATER STAGE
☐ 2nd Stage
☐ Mature
☐ Mezzanine
☒ LBO/MBO
☒ Turnaround
☐ INT'L EXPANSION
☐ WILL CONSIDER ALL
☒ VENTURE LEASING

Other Locations:

Affiliation:
Minimum Investment: Less than $1 Million
Capital Under Management: Over $500 Million

GEOGRAPHIC PREF

☐ East Coast
☐ West Coast
☐ Northeast
☐ Mid Atlantic
☐ Gulf States
☐ Northwest
☐ Southeast
☐ Southwest
☐ Midwest
☐ Central
☐ Local to Office
☐ Other Geo Pref

MIDDLEBURY VENTURE PARTNERS

1470 Barnum Avenue
Suite 301
Bridgeport CT 06610

Phone (203) 337-4444   Fax (203) 337-4449

PROFESSIONALS	TITLE
Robert Mahoney	Managing Director
Todd Enright	Managing Director

INDUSTRY PREFERENCE

☐ INFORMATION INDUSTRY	☐ BASIC INDUSTRIES
☐ Communications	☐ Consumer
☐ Computer Equipment	☐ Distribution
☐ Computer Services	☐ Manufacturing
☐ Computer Components	☐ Retail
☐ Computer Entertainment	☐ Service
☐ Computer Education	☐ Wholesale
☐ Information Technologies	☐ SPECIFIC INDUSTRIES
☐ Computer Media	☐ Energy
☐ Software	☐ Environmental
☐ Internet	☐ Financial
☐ MEDICAL/HEALTHCARE	☐ Real Estate
☐ Biotechnology	☐ Transportation
☐ Healthcare Services	☐ Publishing
☐ Life Sciences	☐ Food
☐ Medical Products	☐ Franchises
☐ INDUSTRIAL	☒ DIVERSIFIED
☐ Advanced Materials	☐ MISCELLANEOUS
☐ Chemicals	
☐ Instruments & Controls	

STAGE PREFERENCE

☐ EARLY STAGE
☐ Seed
☐ Start-up
☐ 1st Stage
☒ LATER STAGE
☒ 2nd Stage
☒ Mature
☒ Mezzanine
☒ LBO/MBO
☒ Turnaround
☐ INT'L EXPANSION
☐ WILL CONSIDER ALL
☒ VENTURE LEASING
SBIC
Other Locations:

Affiliation:
Minimum Investment: Less than $1 Million
Capital Under Management: Less than $100 Million

GEOGRAPHIC PREF

☒ East Coast
☐ West Coast
☒ Northeast
☐ Mid Atlantic
☐ Gulf States
☐ Northwest
☐ Southeast
☐ Southwest
☐ Midwest
☐ Central
☐ Local to Office
☐ Other Geo Pref

NATURAL GAS PARTNERS

500 West Putnam
4th Floor
Greenwich CT 06830

Phone (203) 629-2440   Fax (203) 629-3334

PROFESSIONALS	TITLE
R. Gamble Baldwin	Managing Partner
John Foster	Managing Partner

INDUSTRY PREFERENCE

☐ INFORMATION INDUSTRY	☐ BASIC INDUSTRIES
☐ Communications	☐ Consumer
☐ Computer Equipment	☐ Distribution
☐ Computer Services	☐ Manufacturing
☐ Computer Components	☐ Retail
☐ Computer Entertainment	☐ Service
☐ Computer Education	☐ Wholesale
☐ Information Technologies	☒ SPECIFIC INDUSTRIES
☐ Computer Media	☒ Energy
☐ Software	☐ Environmental
☐ Internet	☐ Financial
☐ MEDICAL/HEALTHCARE	☐ Real Estate
☐ Biotechnology	☐ Transportation
☐ Healthcare Services	☐ Publishing
☐ Life Sciences	☐ Food
☐ Medical Products	☐ Franchises
☐ INDUSTRIAL	☐ DIVERSIFIED
☐ Advanced Materials	☒ MISCELLANEOUS
☐ Chemicals	
☐ Instruments & Controls	

STAGE PREFERENCE

☒ EARLY STAGE
☐ Seed
☒ Start-up
☒ 1st Stage
☒ LATER STAGE
☒ 2nd Stage
☐ Mature
☐ Mezzanine
☒ LBO/MBO
☐ Turnaround
☐ INT'L EXPANSION
☐ WILL CONSIDER ALL
☐ VENTURE LEASING

Other Locations: Forth Worth TX, Santa Fe NM

Affiliation:
Minimum Investment: $1 Million or more
Capital Under Management: Over $500 Million

GEOGRAPHIC PREF

☐ East Coast
☐ West Coast
☐ Northeast
☐ Mid Atlantic
☐ Gulf States
☐ Northwest
☐ Southeast
☐ Southwest
☐ Midwest
☐ Central
☐ Local to Office
☐ Other Geo Pref

OXFORD BIOSCIENCE PARTNERS

315 Post Road West
Westport CT 06880

Phone (203) 341-3300   Fax (203) 341-3309

PROFESSIONALS	TITLE
Neil T. Ryan	General Partner
Dr. Alan G. Walton	General Partner

INDUSTRY PREFERENCE

☒ INFORMATION INDUSTRY	☒ BASIC INDUSTRIES
☐ Communications	☐ Consumer
☐ Computer Equipment	☐ Distribution
☐ Computer Services	☐ Manufacturing
☐ Computer Components	☐ Retail
☐ Computer Entertainment	☒ Service
☐ Computer Education	☐ Wholesale
☒ Information Technologies	☐ SPECIFIC INDUSTRIES
☐ Computer Media	☐ Energy
☐ Software	☐ Environmental
☒ Internet	☐ Financial
☒ MEDICAL/HEALTHCARE	☐ Real Estate
☒ Biotechnology	☐ Transportation
☒ Healthcare Services	☐ Publishing
☒ Life Sciences	☐ Food
☒ Medical Products	☐ Franchises
☐ INDUSTRIAL	☒ DIVERSIFIED
☐ Advanced Materials	☐ MISCELLANEOUS
☐ Chemicals	
☐ Instruments & Controls	

STAGE PREFERENCE

☒ EARLY STAGE
☒ Seed
☒ Start-up
☒ 1st Stage
☒ LATER STAGE
☒ 2nd Stage
☐ Mature
☒ Mezzanine
☒ LBO/MBO
☐ Turnaround
☐ INT'L EXPANSION
☐ WILL CONSIDER ALL
☐ VENTURE LEASING

Other Locations: Costa Mesa CA

Affiliation:
Minimum Investment: Less than $1 Million
Capital Under Management: $100 to $500 Million

GEOGRAPHIC PREF

☒ East Coast
☒ West Coast
☐ Northeast
☐ Mid Atlantic
☐ Gulf States
☐ Northwest
☐ Southeast
☐ Southwest
☐ Midwest
☐ Central
☐ Local to Office
☐ Other Geo Pref

PRINCE VENTURES

25 Ford Road
Westport CT 06880

Phone (203) 227-8332   Fax (203) 226-5302

PROFESSIONALS	TITLE
James W. Fordyce	General Partner
Mark J. Gabrielson	General Partner
Gregory F. Zaic	General Partner

INDUSTRY PREFERENCE

☐ INFORMATION INDUSTRY
☐ Communications
☐ Computer Equipment
☐ Computer Services
☐ Computer Components
☐ Computer Entertainment
☐ Computer Education
☐ Information Technologies
☐ Computer Media
☐ Software
☐ Internet
☒ MEDICAL/HEALTHCARE
☒ Biotechnology
☒ Healthcare Services
☒ Life Sciences
☒ Medical Products
☐ INDUSTRIAL
☐ Advanced Materials
☐ Chemicals
☐ Instruments & Controls

☒ BASIC INDUSTRIES
☐ Consumer
☐ Distribution
☐ Manufacturing
☐ Retail
☒ Service
☐ Wholesale
☐ SPECIFIC INDUSTRIES
☐ Energy
☐ Environmental
☐ Financial
☐ Real Estate
☐ Transportation
☐ Publishing
☐ Food
☐ Franchises
☒ DIVERSIFIED
☐ MISCELLANEOUS

STAGE PREFERENCE

☒ EARLY STAGE
☒ Seed
☒ Start-up
☒ 1st Stage
☒ LATER STAGE
☒ 2nd Stage
☒ Mature
☒ Mezzanine
☒ LBO/MBO
☐ Turnaround
☐ INT'L EXPANSION
☐ WILL CONSIDER ALL
☐ VENTURE LEASING

Other Locations:

Affiliation:
Minimum Investment: Less than $1 Million
Capital Under Management: Less than $100 Million

GEOGRAPHIC PREF

☐ East Coast
☐ West Coast
☐ Northeast
☐ Mid Atlantic
☐ Gulf States
☐ Northwest
☐ Southeast
☐ Southwest
☐ Midwest
☐ Central
☐ Local to Office
☐ Other Geo Pref

RFE INVESTMENT PARTNERS

36 Grove Street
New Canaan CT 06840

Phone (203) 966-2800   Fax (203) 966-3109

PROFESSIONALS	TITLE
Robert M. Williams	Managing Partner
Michael J. Foster	General Partner
Howard C. Landis	General Partner
A. Dean Davis	General Partner
James A. Parsons	General Partner

INDUSTRY PREFERENCE

☒ INFORMATION INDUSTRY
☒ Communications
☒ Computer Equipment
☒ Computer Services
☒ Computer Components
☐ Computer Entertainment
☒ Computer Education
☒ Information Technologies
☒ Computer Media
☒ Software
☒ Internet
☒ MEDICAL/HEALTHCARE
☐ Biotechnology
☒ Healthcare Services
☒ Life Sciences
☐ Medical Products
☒ INDUSTRIAL
☐ Advanced Materials
☒ Chemicals
☒ Instruments & Controls

☒ BASIC INDUSTRIES
☒ Consumer
☒ Distribution
☒ Manufacturing
☒ Retail
☒ Service
☐ Wholesale
☐ SPECIFIC INDUSTRIES
☐ Energy
☐ Environmental
☐ Financial
☐ Real Estate
☐ Transportation
☐ Publishing
☐ Food
☐ Franchises
☒ DIVERSIFIED
☐ MISCELLANEOUS

STAGE PREFERENCE

☐ EARLY STAGE
☐ Seed
☐ Start-up
☐ 1st Stage
☒ LATER STAGE
☒ 2nd Stage
☒ Mature
☐ Mezzanine
☒ LBO/MBO
☐ Turnaround
☐ INT'L EXPANSION
☐ WILL CONSIDER ALL
☐ VENTURE LEASING

SBIC
Other Locations:

Affiliation: Also operates SBIC
Minimum Investment: $1 Million or more
Capital Under Management: $100 to $500 Million

GEOGRAPHIC PREF

☐ East Coast
☐ West Coast
☐ Northeast
☐ Mid Atlantic
☐ Gulf States
☐ Northwest
☐ Southeast
☐ Southwest
☐ Midwest
☐ Central
☐ Local to Office
☐ Other Geo Pref

SAUGATUCK CAPITAL CO.

One Canterbury Green
Stamford CT 06901

Phone (203) 348-6669   Fax (203) 324-6995

PROFESSIONALS	TITLE
Thomas J. Berardino	Managing Director
Frank E. Grzelecki	Managing Director
Stuart W. Hawley	Managing Director
Frank J. Hawley, Jr.	Managing Director

INDUSTRY PREFERENCE

☒ INFORMATION INDUSTRY
☒ Communications
☐ Computer Equipment
☐ Computer Services
☐ Computer Components
☐ Computer Entertainment
☐ Computer Education
☐ Information Technologies
☒ Computer Media
☐ Software
☐ Internet
☒ MEDICAL/HEALTHCARE
☐ Biotechnology
☒ Healthcare Services
☐ Life Sciences
☒ Medical Products
☒ INDUSTRIAL
☐ Advanced Materials
☒ Chemicals
☒ Instruments & Controls

☐ BASIC INDUSTRIES
☐ Consumer
☐ Distribution
☐ Manufacturing
☐ Retail
☐ Service
☐ Wholesale
☐ SPECIFIC INDUSTRIES
☐ Energy
☐ Environmental
☐ Financial
☐ Real Estate
☐ Transportation
☐ Publishing
☐ Food
☐ Franchises
☒ DIVERSIFIED
☐ MISCELLANEOUS

STAGE PREFERENCE

☐ EARLY STAGE
☐ Seed
☐ Start-up
☐ 1st Stage
☒ LATER STAGE
☒ 2nd Stage
☒ Mature
☐ Mezzanine
☒ LBO/MBO
☐ Turnaround
☐ INT'L EXPANSION
☐ WILL CONSIDER ALL
☐ VENTURE LEASING

Other Locations:

Affiliation: Saugatuck Associates, Inc.
Minimum Investment: $1 Million or more
Capital Under Management: $100 to $500 Million

GEOGRAPHIC PREF

☒ East Coast
☐ West Coast
☐ Northeast
☐ Mid Atlantic
☐ Gulf States
☐ Northwest
☐ Southeast
☐ Southwest
☐ Midwest
☐ Central
☐ Local to Office
☐ Other Geo Pref

STERLING INVESTMENT PARTNERS, LP

276 Post Road West
Westport CT 06880-5430

Phone (203) 226-8711   Fax (203) 454-5780

PROFESSIONALS	TITLE
Douglas Newhouse	Principal
William Selden	Principal
M. William Macey, Jr.	Principal
Charles W. Santoro	Principal

INDUSTRY PREFERENCE

☐ INFORMATION INDUSTRY
☐ Communications
☐ Computer Equipment
☐ Computer Services
☐ Computer Components
☐ Computer Entertainment
☐ Computer Education
☐ Information Technologies
☐ Computer Media
☐ Software
☐ Internet
☐ MEDICAL/HEALTHCARE
☐ Biotechnology
☐ Healthcare Services
☐ Life Sciences
☐ Medical Products
☐ INDUSTRIAL
☐ Advanced Materials
☐ Chemicals
☐ Instruments & Controls

☐ BASIC INDUSTRIES
☐ Consumer
☐ Distribution
☐ Manufacturing
☐ Retail
☐ Service
☐ Wholesale
☐ SPECIFIC INDUSTRIES
☐ Energy
☐ Environmental
☐ Financial
☐ Real Estate
☐ Transportation
☐ Publishing
☐ Food
☐ Franchises
☒ DIVERSIFIED
☒ MISCELLANEOUS

STAGE PREFERENCE

☐ EARLY STAGE
☐ Seed
☐ Start-up
☐ 1st Stage
☒ LATER STAGE
☐ 2nd Stage
☐ Mature
☐ Mezzanine
☒ LBO/MBO
☐ Turnaround
☐ INT'L EXPANSION
☐ WILL CONSIDER ALL
☐ VENTURE LEASING

Other Locations:

Affiliation:
Minimum Investment: $1 Million or more
Capital Under Management: $100 to $500 Million

GEOGRAPHIC PREF

☐ East Coast
☐ West Coast
☐ Northeast
☐ Mid Atlantic
☐ Gulf States
☐ Northwest
☐ Southeast
☐ Southwest
☐ Midwest
☐ Central
☐ Local to Office
☐ Other Geo Pref

TRIDENT CAPITAL

200 Nyala Farms Road
Westport CT 06880

Phone (203) 222-4590   Fax (203) 222-4592

PROFESSIONALS	TITLE
Venetia Kontogouris	
Peter Meekin	

INDUSTRY PREFERENCE

☒ INFORMATION INDUSTRY	☒ BASIC INDUSTRIES
☒ Communications	☐ Consumer
☒ Computer Equipment	☐ Distribution
☒ Computer Services	☐ Manufacturing
☒ Computer Components	☐ Retail
☒ Computer Entertainment	☐ Service
☒ Computer Education	☐ Wholesale
☒ Information Technologies	☒ SPECIFIC INDUSTRIES
☐ Computer Media	☐ Energy
☒ Software	☐ Environmental
☒ Internet	☒ Financial
☐ MEDICAL/HEALTHCARE	☐ Real Estate
☐ Biotechnology	☐ Transportation
☐ Healthcare Services	☐ Publishing
☐ Life Sciences	☐ Food
☐ Medical Products	☐ Franchises
☐ INDUSTRIAL	☒ DIVERSIFIED
☐ Advanced Materials	☒ MISCELLANEOUS
☐ Chemicals	
☐ Instruments & Controls	

STAGE PREFERENCE

☐ EARLY STAGE
☐ Seed
☐ Start-up
☐ 1st Stage
☒ LATER STAGE
☒ 2nd Stage
☒ Mature
☐ Mezzanine
☒ LBO/MBO
☐ Turnaround
☐ INT'L EXPANSION
☐ WILL CONSIDER ALL
☐ VENTURE LEASING

Other Locations: Menlo Park CA, Los Angeles CA, Lake Forest IL, Washington D.C.

Affiliation:
Minimum Investment: $1 Million or more
Capital Under Management: $100 to $500 Million

GEOGRAPHIC PREF

☐ East Coast
☐ West Coast
☐ Northeast
☐ Mid Atlantic
☐ Gulf States
☐ Northwest
☐ Southeast
☐ Southwest
☐ Midwest
☐ Central
☐ Local to Office
☐ Other Geo Pref

TSG CAPITAL GROUP LLC

177 Broad Street
12th Floor
Stamford CT 06901

Phone (203) 406-1500   Fax (203) 406-1590

PROFESSIONALS	TITLE
Cleveland Christophe	Managing Partner
Lauren Tyler	Partner
Darryl Thompson	Partner
Mark Inglis	Partner

INDUSTRY PREFERENCE

☒ INFORMATION INDUSTRY	☒ BASIC INDUSTRIES
☒ Communications	☒ Consumer
☐ Computer Equipment	☒ Distribution
☐ Computer Services	☒ Manufacturing
☐ Computer Components	☒ Retail
☒ Computer Entertainment	☒ Service
☒ Computer Education	☒ Wholesale
☐ Information Technologies	☒ SPECIFIC INDUSTRIES
☒ Computer Media	☐ Energy
☐ Software	☐ Environmental
☐ Internet	☒ Financial
☐ MEDICAL/HEALTHCARE	☐ Real Estate
☐ Biotechnology	☐ Transportation
☐ Healthcare Services	☒ Publishing
☐ Life Sciences	☐ Food
☐ Medical Products	☐ Franchises
☐ INDUSTRIAL	☒ DIVERSIFIED
☐ Advanced Materials	☐ MISCELLANEOUS
☐ Chemicals	Publishing
☐ Instruments & Controls	

STAGE PREFERENCE

☐ EARLY STAGE
☐ Seed
☐ Start-up
☐ 1st Stage
☒ LATER STAGE
☒ 2nd Stage
☒ Mature
☒ Mezzanine
☒ LBO/MBO
☐ Turnaround
☐ INT'L EXPANSION
☐ WILL CONSIDER ALL
☐ VENTURE LEASING

Other Locations:

Affiliation:
Minimum Investment: $1 Million or more
Capital Under Management: Over $500 Million

GEOGRAPHIC PREF

☐ East Coast
☐ West Coast
☐ Northeast
☐ Mid Atlantic
☐ Gulf States
☐ Northwest
☐ Southeast
☐ Southwest
☐ Midwest
☐ Central
☐ Local to Office
☒ Other Geo Pref
Canada

VANTAGEPOINT VENTURE PARTNERS

1 Stamford Landing
Suite 201
Stamford CT 06902

Phone (203) 969-2000   Fax (203) 969-2009

PROFESSIONALS	TITLE
W. Jefferson Marshall	Managing Partner
James Marver	Managing Partner
Alan Salzman	Managing Partner

INDUSTRY PREFERENCE

- ☒ INFORMATION INDUSTRY
- ☒ Communications
- ☐ Computer Equipment
- ☒ Computer Services
- ☒ Computer Components
- ☐ Computer Entertainment
- ☐ Computer Education
- ☒ Information Technologies
- ☐ Computer Media
- ☒ Software
- ☒ Internet
- ☐ MEDICAL/HEALTHCARE
- ☐ Biotechnology
- ☐ Healthcare Services
- ☐ Life Sciences
- ☐ Medical Products
- ☐ INDUSTRIAL
- ☐ Advanced Materials
- ☐ Chemicals
- ☐ Instruments & Controls

- ☐ BASIC INDUSTRIES
- ☐ Consumer
- ☐ Distribution
- ☐ Manufacturing
- ☐ Retail
- ☐ Service
- ☐ Wholesale
- ☐ SPECIFIC INDUSTRIES
- ☐ Energy
- ☐ Environmental
- ☐ Financial
- ☐ Real Estate
- ☐ Transportation
- ☐ Publishing
- ☐ Food
- ☐ Franchises
- ☐ DIVERSIFIED
- ☒ MISCELLANEOUS

STAGE PREFERENCE

- ☒ EARLY STAGE
- ☒ Seed
- ☒ Start-up
- ☒ 1st Stage
- ☒ LATER STAGE
- ☒ 2nd Stage
- ☒ Mature
- ☒ Mezzanine
- ☒ LBO/MBO
- ☒ Turnaround
- ☒ INT'L EXPANSION
- ☐ WILL CONSIDER ALL
- ☒ VENTURE LEASING

Other Locations: San Bruno CA

Affiliation:
Minimum Investment: $1 Million or more
Capital Under Management: Over $500 Million

GEOGRAPHIC PREF

- ☐ East Coast
- ☐ West Coast
- ☐ Northeast
- ☐ Mid Atlantic
- ☐ Gulf States
- ☐ Northwest
- ☐ Southeast
- ☐ Southwest
- ☐ Midwest
- ☐ Central
- ☐ Local to Office
- ☐ Other Geo Pref

BLUE ROCK CAPITAL

5803 Kennett Pike
Suite A
Wilmington DE 19807-1195

Phone (302) 426-0981   Fax (302) 426-0982

PROFESSIONALS	TITLE
Virginia Bonker	Partner
Terry Collision	Partner
Frank Tower	Partner

INDUSTRY PREFERENCE

- ☒ INFORMATION INDUSTRY
- ☒ Communications
- ☒ Computer Equipment
- ☒ Computer Services
- ☒ Computer Components
- ☐ Computer Entertainment
- ☒ Computer Education
- ☒ Information Technologies
- ☒ Computer Media
- ☒ Software
- ☒ Internet
- ☐ MEDICAL/HEALTHCARE
- ☐ Biotechnology
- ☐ Healthcare Services
- ☐ Life Sciences
- ☐ Medical Products
- ☐ INDUSTRIAL
- ☐ Advanced Materials
- ☐ Chemicals
- ☐ Instruments & Controls

- ☐ BASIC INDUSTRIES
- ☐ Consumer
- ☐ Distribution
- ☐ Manufacturing
- ☐ Retail
- ☐ Service
- ☐ Wholesale
- ☐ SPECIFIC INDUSTRIES
- ☐ Energy
- ☐ Environmental
- ☐ Financial
- ☐ Real Estate
- ☐ Transportation
- ☐ Publishing
- ☐ Food
- ☐ Franchises
- ☐ DIVERSIFIED
- ☒ MISCELLANEOUS

STAGE PREFERENCE

- ☒ EARLY STAGE
- ☒ Seed
- ☒ Start-up
- ☒ 1st Stage
- ☐ LATER STAGE
- ☐ 2nd Stage
- ☐ Mature
- ☐ Mezzanine
- ☐ LBO/MBO
- ☐ Turnaround
- ☐ INT'L EXPANSION
- ☐ WILL CONSIDER ALL
- ☐ VENTURE LEASING

SBIC
Other Locations:

Affiliation:
Minimum Investment: Less than $1 Million
Capital Under Management: Less than $100 Million

GEOGRAPHIC PREF

- ☐ East Coast
- ☐ West Coast
- ☒ Northeast
- ☒ Mid Atlantic
- ☐ Gulf States
- ☐ Northwest
- ☐ Southeast
- ☐ Southwest
- ☐ Midwest
- ☐ Central
- ☐ Local to Office
- ☒ Other Geo Pref
  Mid-Atlantic

ALLIED CAPITAL CORP.

1919 Pennsylvania Avenue, NW
Washington DC 20006-3434

Phone (202) 973-6328   Fax (202) 331-2434

PROFESSIONALS	TITLE
G. Cabell Williams III	Managing Director
Phillip A. McNeill	Managing Director

INDUSTRY PREFERENCE

☒ INFORMATION INDUSTRY
☒   Communications
☒   Computer Equipment
☒   Computer Services
☒   Computer Components
☐   Computer Entertainment
☒   Computer Education
☒   Information Technologies
☒   Computer Media
☒   Software
☒   Internet
☐ MEDICAL/HEALTHCARE
☐   Biotechnology
☐   Healthcare Services
☐   Life Sciences
☐   Medical Products
☒ INDUSTRIAL
☒   Advanced Materials
☒   Chemicals
☒   Instruments & Controls

☒ BASIC INDUSTRIES
☐   Consumer
☐   Distribution
☒   Manufacturing
☒   Retail
☐   Service
☒   Wholesale
☒ SPECIFIC INDUSTRIES
☐   Energy
☐   Environmental
☐   Financial
☐   Real Estate
☐   Transportation
☐   Publishing
☐   Food
☐   Franchises
☒ DIVERSIFIED
☐ MISCELLANEOUS

STAGE PREFERENCE

☐ EARLY STAGE
☐   Seed
☐   Start-up
☐   1st Stage
☒ LATER STAGE
☒   2nd Stage
☒   Mature
☐   Mezzanine
☒   LBO/MBO
☐   Turnaround
☐ INT'L EXPANSION
☐ WILL CONSIDER ALL
☐ VENTURE LEASING

SBIC SSBIC
Other Locations:

Affiliation: Allied Investment Corp.
Minimum Investment: $1 Million or more
Capital Under Management: $100 to $500 Million

GEOGRAPHIC PREF

☐   East Coast
☐   West Coast
☐   Northeast
☐   Mid Atlantic
☐   Gulf States
☐   Northwest
☐   Southeast
☐   Southwest
☐   Midwest
☐   Central
☐   Local to Office
☐   Other Geo Pref

ATLANTIC COASTAL VENTURES LP

3101 South Street NW
Washington DC 20007

Phone (202) 293-1166   Fax (202) 293-1181

PROFESSIONALS	TITLE
Walter Threadgill	General Partner

INDUSTRY PREFERENCE

☒ INFORMATION INDUSTRY
☒   Communications
☒   Computer Equipment
☒   Computer Services
☐   Computer Components
☐   Computer Entertainment
☐   Computer Education
☒   Information Technologies
☐   Computer Media
☐   Software
☐   Internet
☒ MEDICAL/HEALTHCARE
☐   Biotechnology
☒   Healthcare Services
☐   Life Sciences
☐   Medical Products
☒ INDUSTRIAL
☐   Advanced Materials
☐   Chemicals
☒   Instruments & Controls

☒ BASIC INDUSTRIES
☒   Consumer
☐   Distribution
☐   Manufacturing
☐   Retail
☐   Service
☐   Wholesale
☒ SPECIFIC INDUSTRIES
☐   Energy
☐   Environmental
☐   Financial
☐   Real Estate
☐   Transportation
☒   Publishing
☐   Food
☐   Franchises
☒ DIVERSIFIED
☒ MISCELLANEOUS

STAGE PREFERENCE

☒ EARLY STAGE
☐   Seed
☒   Start-up
☐   1st Stage
☒ LATER STAGE
☒   2nd Stage
☐   Mature
☒   Mezzanine
☒   LBO/MBO
☐   Turnaround
☐ INT'L EXPANSION
☐ WILL CONSIDER ALL
☐ VENTURE LEASING

Other Locations:

Affiliation:
Minimum Investment: $1 Million or more
Capital Under Management: Less than $100 Million

GEOGRAPHIC PREF

☒   East Coast
☐   West Coast
☐   Northeast
☐   Mid Atlantic
☐   Gulf States
☐   Northwest
☐   Southeast
☐   Southwest
☐   Midwest
☐   Central
☐   Local to Office
☐   Other Geo Pref

BROADCAST CAPITAL, INC.

1700 K Street, N.W.
Suite 403
Washington DC 20036

Phone (202) 496-9250   Fax (202) 496-9259

PROFESSIONALS	TITLE
John E. Oxendine	President & CEO
Rekha C. Henderson	Vice President

INDUSTRY PREFERENCE

☒ INFORMATION INDUSTRY	☐ BASIC INDUSTRIES
☒ Communications	☐ Consumer
☐ Computer Equipment	☐ Distribution
☐ Computer Services	☐ Manufacturing
☐ Computer Components	☐ Retail
☐ Computer Entertainment	☐ Service
☐ Computer Education	☐ Wholesale
☐ Information Technologies	☒ SPECIFIC INDUSTRIES
☒ Computer Media	☐ Energy
☐ Software	☐ Environmental
☐ Internet	☐ Financial
☐ MEDICAL/HEALTHCARE	☐ Real Estate
☐ Biotechnology	☐ Transportation
☐ Healthcare Services	☐ Publishing
☐ Life Sciences	☐ Food
☐ Medical Products	☐ Franchises
☐ INDUSTRIAL	☒ DIVERSIFIED
☐ Advanced Materials	☒ MISCELLANEOUS
☐ Chemicals	Radio / TV Stations
☐ Instruments & Controls	

STAGE PREFERENCE

☒ EARLY STAGE
☒   Seed
☒   Start-up
☒   1st Stage
☒ LATER STAGE
☒   2nd Stage
☒   Mature
☐   Mezzanine
☒   LBO/MBO
☐   Turnaround
☐ INT'L EXPANSION
☐ WILL CONSIDER ALL
☐ VENTURE LEASING
  SSBIC
Other Locations:

Affiliation:
Minimum Investment: Less than $1 Million
Capital Under Management: Less than $100 Million

GEOGRAPHIC PREF

☐ East Coast
☐ West Coast
☐ Northeast
☐ Mid Atlantic
☐ Gulf States
☐ Northwest
☐ Southeast
☐ Southwest
☐ Midwest
☐ Central
☐ Local to Office
☐ Other Geo Pref

MULTIMEDIA BROADCAST INVESTMENT CORP.

3101 South Street NW
Washington DC 20007

Phone (202) 293-1166   Fax (202) 293-1181

PROFESSIONALS	TITLE
Walter Threadgill	President

INDUSTRY PREFERENCE

☒ INFORMATION INDUSTRY	☐ BASIC INDUSTRIES
☒ Communications	☐ Consumer
☐ Computer Equipment	☐ Distribution
☐ Computer Services	☐ Manufacturing
☐ Computer Components	☐ Retail
☐ Computer Entertainment	☐ Service
☐ Computer Education	☐ Wholesale
☒ Information Technologies	☐ SPECIFIC INDUSTRIES
☒ Computer Media	☐ Energy
☐ Software	☐ Environmental
☐ Internet	☐ Financial
☐ MEDICAL/HEALTHCARE	☐ Real Estate
☐ Biotechnology	☐ Transportation
☐ Healthcare Services	☐ Publishing
☐ Life Sciences	☐ Food
☐ Medical Products	☐ Franchises
☐ INDUSTRIAL	☐ DIVERSIFIED
☐ Advanced Materials	☐ MISCELLANEOUS
☐ Chemicals	
☐ Instruments & Controls	

STAGE PREFERENCE

☒ EARLY STAGE
☐   Seed
☐   Start-up
☒   1st Stage
☒ LATER STAGE
☒   2nd Stage
☐   Mature
☐   Mezzanine
☒   LBO/MBO
☐   Turnaround
☐ INT'L EXPANSION
☐ WILL CONSIDER ALL
☐ VENTURE LEASING
  SSBIC
Other Locations:

Affiliation:
Minimum Investment: Less than $1 Million
Capital Under Management: Less than $100 Million

GEOGRAPHIC PREF

☐ East Coast
☐ West Coast
☐ Northeast
☐ Mid Atlantic
☐ Gulf States
☐ Northwest
☐ Southeast
☐ Southwest
☐ Midwest
☐ Central
☐ Local to Office
☐ Other Geo Pref

TRIDENT CAPITAL
THE CARLYLE GROUP
1001 Pennsylvania Avenue NW
Second Floor
Washington DC 20004-2505

Phone (202) 626-1228   Fax (202) 347-1431

PROFESSIONALS	TITLE
Edward J. Mathias	Limited Partner

INDUSTRY PREFERENCE

- ☒ INFORMATION INDUSTRY
- ☒ Communications
- ☒ Computer Equipment
- ☒ Computer Services
- ☒ Computer Components
- ☒ Computer Entertainment
- ☒ Computer Education
- ☒ Information Technologies
- ☐ Computer Media
- ☒ Software
- ☒ Internet
- ☐ MEDICAL/HEALTHCARE
- ☐ Biotechnology
- ☐ Healthcare Services
- ☐ Life Sciences
- ☐ Medical Products
- ☐ INDUSTRIAL
- ☐ Advanced Materials
- ☐ Chemicals
- ☐ Instruments & Controls

- ☒ BASIC INDUSTRIES
- ☐ Consumer
- ☐ Distribution
- ☐ Manufacturing
- ☐ Retail
- ☒ Service
- ☐ Wholesale
- ☒ SPECIFIC INDUSTRIES
- ☐ Energy
- ☐ Environmental
- ☒ Financial
- ☐ Real Estate
- ☐ Transportation
- ☐ Publishing
- ☐ Food
- ☐ Franchises
- ☒ DIVERSIFIED
- ☐ MISCELLANEOUS

STAGE PREFERENCE

- ☐ EARLY STAGE
- ☐ Seed
- ☐ Start-up
- ☐ 1st Stage
- ☒ LATER STAGE
- ☒ 2nd Stage
- ☒ Mature
- ☐ Mezzanine
- ☒ LBO/MBO
- ☐ Turnaround
- ☐ INT'L EXPANSION
- ☐ WILL CONSIDER ALL
- ☐ VENTURE LEASING

Other Locations: Menlo Park CA, Los Angeles CA, Lake Forest IL, Westport CT

Affiliation:
Minimum Investment: $1 Million or more
Capital Under Management: $100 to $500 Million

GEOGRAPHIC PREF

- ☐ East Coast
- ☐ West Coast
- ☐ Northeast
- ☐ Mid Atlantic
- ☐ Gulf States
- ☐ Northwest
- ☐ Southeast
- ☐ Southwest
- ☐ Midwest
- ☐ Central
- ☐ Local to Office
- ☐ Other Geo Pref

WOMEN'S GROWTH CAPITAL FUND
1054 31st Street NW
Suite 110
Washington DC 20007

Phone (202) 342-1431   Fax (202) 342-1203

PROFESSIONALS	TITLE
Patty Abramson	Director
Wendee Kanarek	Director
Rob Stein	Director

INDUSTRY PREFERENCE

- ☐ INFORMATION INDUSTRY
- ☐ Communications
- ☐ Computer Equipment
- ☐ Computer Services
- ☐ Computer Components
- ☐ Computer Entertainment
- ☐ Computer Education
- ☐ Information Technologies
- ☐ Computer Media
- ☐ Software
- ☐ Internet
- ☐ MEDICAL/HEALTHCARE
- ☐ Biotechnology
- ☐ Healthcare Services
- ☐ Life Sciences
- ☐ Medical Products
- ☐ INDUSTRIAL
- ☐ Advanced Materials
- ☐ Chemicals
- ☐ Instruments & Controls

- ☐ BASIC INDUSTRIES
- ☐ Consumer
- ☐ Distribution
- ☐ Manufacturing
- ☐ Retail
- ☐ Service
- ☐ Wholesale
- ☒ SPECIFIC INDUSTRIES
- ☐ Energy
- ☐ Environmental
- ☐ Financial
- ☐ Real Estate
- ☐ Transportation
- ☐ Publishing
- ☐ Food
- ☐ Franchises
- ☒ DIVERSIFIED
- ☐ MISCELLANEOUS
- Women owned and/or managed businesses

STAGE PREFERENCE

- ☐ EARLY STAGE
- ☐ Seed
- ☐ Start-up
- ☐ 1st Stage
- ☒ LATER STAGE
- ☒ 2nd Stage
- ☒ Mature
- ☒ Mezzanine
- ☒ LBO/MBO
- ☐ Turnaround
- ☐ INT'L EXPANSION
- ☐ WILL CONSIDER ALL
- ☐ VENTURE LEASING

SBIC
Other Locations:

Affiliation:
Minimum Investment: Less than $1 Million
Capital Under Management: Less than $100 Million

GEOGRAPHIC PREF

- ☐ East Coast
- ☐ West Coast
- ☐ Northeast
- ☒ Mid Atlantic
- ☐ Gulf States
- ☐ Northwest
- ☐ Southeast
- ☐ Southwest
- ☐ Midwest
- ☐ Central
- ☐ Local to Office
- ☒ Other Geo Pref
  Mid-Atlantic

ADVANTAGE CAPITAL PARTNERS

100 North Tampa Street
Suite 2410
Tampa FL 33602

Phone (813) 221-8700   Fax (813) 221-1606

PROFESSIONALS	TITLE
Steven Stull	President
David Bergmann	Managing Director
Crichton Brown	Managing Director
Scott Zajac	Managing Director
Maurice Doyle	Managing Director

INDUSTRY PREFERENCE

☒ INFORMATION INDUSTRY
☒ Communications
☒ Computer Equipment
☒ Computer Services
☒ Computer Components
☐ Computer Entertainment
☐ Computer Education
☒ Information Technologies
☐ Computer Media
☒ Software
☐ Internet
☒ MEDICAL/HEALTHCARE
☒ Biotechnology
☒ Healthcare Services
☒ Life Sciences
☒ Medical Products
☒ INDUSTRIAL
☒ Advanced Materials
☒ Chemicals
☒ Instruments & Controls

☒ BASIC INDUSTRIES
☒ Consumer
☒ Distribution
☐ Manufacturing
☐ Retail
☐ Service
☐ Wholesale
☒ SPECIFIC INDUSTRIES
☒ Energy
☐ Environmental
☐ Financial
☐ Real Estate
☐ Transportation
☐ Publishing
☐ Food
☐ Franchises
☒ DIVERSIFIED
☒ MISCELLANEOUS

STAGE PREFERENCE

☒ EARLY STAGE
☐ Seed
☒ Start-up
☒ 1st Stage
☒ LATER STAGE
☐ 2nd Stage
☐ Mature
☒ Mezzanine
☒ LBO/MBO
☐ Turnaround
☐ INT'L EXPANSION
☐ WILL CONSIDER ALL
☐ VENTURE LEASING

Other Locations: New Orleans LA, St Louis MO, New York NY

Affiliation:
Minimum Investment: $1 Million or more
Capital Under Management: $100 to $500 Million

GEOGRAPHIC PREF

☐ East Coast
☐ West Coast
☒ Northeast
☐ Mid Atlantic
☒ Gulf States
☐ Northwest
☒ Southeast
☐ Southwest
☐ Midwest
☐ Central
☐ Local to Office
☒ Other Geo Pref
  Gulf States

ANTARES CAPITAL CORP

P.O. Box 410730
Melbourne FL 32941

Phone (407) 777-4884   Fax (407) 777-5884

PROFESSIONALS	TITLE
Randall Poliner	Partner

INDUSTRY PREFERENCE

☒ INFORMATION INDUSTRY
☒ Communications
☒ Computer Equipment
☒ Computer Services
☐ Computer Components
☐ Computer Entertainment
☐ Computer Education
☐ Information Technologies
☐ Computer Media
☒ Software
☒ Internet
☒ MEDICAL/HEALTHCARE
☐ Biotechnology
☒ Healthcare Services
☒ Life Sciences
☒ Medical Products
☒ INDUSTRIAL
☐ Advanced Materials
☐ Chemicals
☒ Instruments & Controls

☒ BASIC INDUSTRIES
☒ Consumer
☐ Distribution
☐ Manufacturing
☒ Retail
☐ Service
☐ Wholesale
☒ SPECIFIC INDUSTRIES
☐ Energy
☐ Environmental
☐ Financial
☐ Real Estate
☐ Transportation
☐ Publishing
☒ Food
☐ Franchises
☒ DIVERSIFIED
☒ MISCELLANEOUS
  Restaurants

STAGE PREFERENCE

☒ EARLY STAGE
☐ Seed
☐ Start-up
☒ 1st Stage
☒ LATER STAGE
☒ 2nd Stage
☐ Mature
☒ Mezzanine
☒ LBO/MBO
☐ Turnaround
☐ INT'L EXPANSION
☐ WILL CONSIDER ALL
☐ VENTURE LEASING

Other Locations: Miami Lakes FL

Affiliation:
Minimum Investment: Less than $1 Million
Capital Under Management: Less than $100 Million

GEOGRAPHIC PREF

☐ East Coast
☐ West Coast
☐ Northeast
☐ Mid Atlantic
☐ Gulf States
☐ Northwest
☒ Southeast
☐ Southwest
☐ Midwest
☐ Central
☐ Local to Office
☐ Other Geo Pref

ANTARES CAPITAL CORP

7900 Miami Lakes Drive West
Miami Lakes FL 33016

Phone (305) 894-2888   Fax (305) 894-3227

PROFESSIONALS	TITLE
Jon Kislak	Partner

INDUSTRY PREFERENCE

☒ INFORMATION INDUSTRY	☒ BASIC INDUSTRIES
☒ Communications	☒ Consumer
☒ Computer Equipment	☐ Distribution
☒ Computer Services	☐ Manufacturing
☒ Computer Components	☒ Retail
☐ Computer Entertainment	☐ Service
☐ Computer Education	☐ Wholesale
☐ Information Technologies	☒ SPECIFIC INDUSTRIES
☐ Computer Media	☐ Energy
☒ Software	☐ Environmental
☒ Internet	☐ Financial
☒ MEDICAL/HEALTHCARE	☐ Real Estate
☐ Biotechnology	☐ Transportation
☒ Healthcare Services	☐ Publishing
☒ Life Sciences	☒ Food
☒ Medical Products	☐ Franchises
☒ INDUSTRIAL	☒ DIVERSIFIED
☐ Advanced Materials	☒ MISCELLANEOUS
☐ Chemicals	Restaurants
☒ Instruments & Controls	

STAGE PREFERENCE

☒ EARLY STAGE	
☐ Seed	
☐ Start-up	
☒ 1st Stage	
☒ LATER STAGE	
☒ 2nd Stage	
☐ Mature	
☒ Mezzanine	
☒ LBO/MBO	
☐ Turnaround	
☐ INT'L EXPANSION	
☐ WILL CONSIDER ALL	
☐ VENTURE LEASING	

Other Locations: Melbourne FL

Affiliation:
Minimum Investment: Less than $1 Million
Capital Under Management: Less than $100 Million

GEOGRAPHIC PREF

☐ East Coast	
☐ West Coast	
☐ Northeast	
☐ Mid Atlantic	
☐ Gulf States	
☐ Northwest	
☒ Southeast	
☐ Southwest	
☐ Midwest	
☐ Central	
☐ Local to Office	
☐ Other Geo Pref	

FLORIDA CAPITAL PARTNERS

601 N. Ashley Drive
Suite 500
Tampa FL 33602

Phone (813) 222-8000   Fax (813) 222-8001

PROFESSIONALS	TITLE
Glenn B. Oken	Partner
Jay Jester	Partner
David Malizia	Partner

INDUSTRY PREFERENCE

☐ INFORMATION INDUSTRY	☒ BASIC INDUSTRIES
☐ Communications	☐ Consumer
☐ Computer Equipment	☒ Distribution
☐ Computer Services	☒ Manufacturing
☐ Computer Components	☐ Retail
☐ Computer Entertainment	☐ Service
☐ Computer Education	☐ Wholesale
☐ Information Technologies	☐ SPECIFIC INDUSTRIES
☐ Computer Media	☐ Energy
☐ Software	☐ Environmental
☐ Internet	☐ Financial
☒ MEDICAL/HEALTHCARE	☐ Real Estate
☐ Biotechnology	☐ Transportation
☐ Healthcare Services	☐ Publishing
☐ Life Sciences	☐ Food
☐ Medical Products	☐ Franchises
☒ INDUSTRIAL	☒ DIVERSIFIED
☒ Advanced Materials	☐ MISCELLANEOUS
☒ Chemicals	
☒ Instruments & Controls	

STAGE PREFERENCE

☐ EARLY STAGE	
☐ Seed	
☐ Start-up	
☐ 1st Stage	
☒ LATER STAGE	
☐ 2nd Stage	
☐ Mature	
☐ Mezzanine	
☒ LBO/MBO	
☐ Turnaround	
☐ INT'L EXPANSION	
☐ WILL CONSIDER ALL	
☐ VENTURE LEASING	

Other Locations:

Affiliation: FCP Southeast Investors
Minimum Investment: $1 Million or more
Capital Under Management: Less than $100 Million

GEOGRAPHIC PREF

☐ East Coast	
☐ West Coast	
☐ Northeast	
☐ Mid Atlantic	
☐ Gulf States	
☐ Northwest	
☒ Southeast	
☐ Southwest	
☐ Midwest	
☐ Central	
☐ Local to Office	
☐ Other Geo Pref	

LJH ALTERNATIVE INVESTMENT ADVISORS INC.

801 Laurel Oak Drive
Naples FL 34108

Phone (941) 593-5000   Fax (941) 593-5001

PROFESSIONALS	TITLE
James R. Hedges IV	Managing Director

INDUSTRY PREFERENCE

☒ INFORMATION INDUSTRY	☒ BASIC INDUSTRIES
☒ Communications	☐ Consumer
☒ Computer Equipment	☒ Distribution
☒ Computer Services	☐ Manufacturing
☒ Computer Components	☐ Retail
☐ Computer Entertainment	☐ Service
☐ Computer Education	☐ Wholesale
☐ Information Technologies	☒ SPECIFIC INDUSTRIES
☐ Computer Media	☐ Energy
☐ Software	☐ Environmental
☐ Internet	☒ Financial
☐ MEDICAL/HEALTHCARE	☐ Real Estate
☐ Biotechnology	☐ Transportation
☐ Healthcare Services	☐ Publishing
☐ Life Sciences	☐ Food
☐ Medical Products	☐ Franchises
☒ INDUSTRIAL	☒ DIVERSIFIED
☐ Advanced Materials	☒ MISCELLANEOUS
☐ Chemicals	
☒ Instruments & Controls	

STAGE PREFERENCE

☐ EARLY STAGE
☐ Seed
☐ Start-up
☐ 1st Stage
☐ LATER STAGE
☐ 2nd Stage
☐ Mature
☐ Mezzanine
☐ LBO/MBO
☐ Turnaround
☐ INT'L EXPANSION
☐ WILL CONSIDER ALL
☐ VENTURE LEASING

Other Locations:

Affiliation:
Minimum Investment: Less than $1 Million
Capital Under Management: $100 to $500 Million

GEOGRAPHIC PREF

☐ East Coast
☐ West Coast
☐ Northeast
☐ Mid Atlantic
☐ Gulf States
☐ Northwest
☐ Southeast
☐ Southwest
☐ Midwest
☐ Central
☐ Local to Office
☐ Other Geo Pref

NORTH AMERICAN BUSINESS DEVELOPMENT CO.

312 S.E. 17th Street
Suite 300
Fort Lauderdale FL 33316

Phone (954) 463-0681   Fax (954) 527-0904

PROFESSIONALS	TITLE
Charles L. Palmer	CEO
Ray Fleites	Vice President

INDUSTRY PREFERENCE

☐ INFORMATION INDUSTRY	☐ BASIC INDUSTRIES
☐ Communications	☐ Consumer
☐ Computer Equipment	☐ Distribution
☐ Computer Services	☐ Manufacturing
☐ Computer Components	☐ Retail
☐ Computer Entertainment	☐ Service
☐ Computer Education	☐ Wholesale
☐ Information Technologies	☐ SPECIFIC INDUSTRIES
☐ Computer Media	☐ Energy
☐ Software	☐ Environmental
☐ Internet	☐ Financial
☐ MEDICAL/HEALTHCARE	☐ Real Estate
☐ Biotechnology	☐ Transportation
☐ Healthcare Services	☐ Publishing
☐ Life Sciences	☐ Food
☐ Medical Products	☐ Franchises
☐ INDUSTRIAL	☒ DIVERSIFIED
☐ Advanced Materials	☐ MISCELLANEOUS
☐ Chemicals	
☐ Instruments & Controls	

STAGE PREFERENCE

☐ EARLY STAGE
☐ Seed
☐ Start-up
☐ 1st Stage
☒ LATER STAGE
☒ 2nd Stage
☒ Mature
☐ Mezzanine
☒ LBO/MBO
☐ Turnaround
☐ INT'L EXPANSION
☐ WILL CONSIDER ALL
☐ VENTURE LEASING

Other Locations: Chicago IL

Affiliation:
Minimum Investment: $1 Million or more
Capital Under Management: $100 to $500 Million

GEOGRAPHIC PREF

☐ East Coast
☐ West Coast
☐ Northeast
☐ Mid Atlantic
☐ Gulf States
☐ Northwest
☒ Southeast
☐ Southwest
☐ Midwest
☐ Central
☐ Local to Office
☐ Other Geo Pref

SOUTH ATLANTIC VENTURE FUNDS

614 West Bay Street
Suite 200
Tampa FL 33606-2704

Phone (813) 253-2500   Fax (813) 253-2360

PROFESSIONALS	TITLE
Donald W. Burton	Chairman/Founder
Sandra P. Barber	Managing Director

INDUSTRY PREFERENCE

☒ INFORMATION INDUSTRY
☒ Communications
☒ Computer Equipment
☒ Computer Services
☒ Computer Components
☐ Computer Entertainment
☐ Computer Education
☒ Information Technologies
☒ Computer Media
☒ Software
☒ Internet
☒ MEDICAL/HEALTHCARE
☒ Biotechnology
☒ Healthcare Services
☒ Life Sciences
☒ Medical Products
☒ INDUSTRIAL
☐ Advanced Materials
☐ Chemicals
☒ Instruments & Controls

☒ BASIC INDUSTRIES
☒ Consumer
☐ Distribution
☐ Manufacturing
☐ Retail
☒ Service
☐ Wholesale
☒ SPECIFIC INDUSTRIES
☐ Energy
☐ Environmental
☒ Financial
☐ Real Estate
☐ Transportation
☐ Publishing
☐ Food
☐ Franchises
☒ DIVERSIFIED
☐ MISCELLANEOUS

STAGE PREFERENCE

☒ EARLY STAGE
☐ Seed
☒ Start-up
☒ 1st Stage
☒ LATER STAGE
☒ 2nd Stage
☒ Mature
☐ Mezzanine
☒ LBO/MBO
☐ Turnaround
☐ INT'L EXPANSION
☐ WILL CONSIDER ALL
☐ VENTURE LEASING

Other Locations: Miami FL

Affiliation:
Minimum Investment: $1 Million or more
Capital Under Management: $100 to $500 Million

GEOGRAPHIC PREF

☐ East Coast
☐ West Coast
☐ Northeast
☐ Mid Atlantic
☐ Gulf States
☐ Northwest
☐ Southeast
☐ Southwest
☐ Midwest
☐ Central
☐ Local to Office
☒ Other Geo Pref
  South Atlantic States

SOUTH ATLANTIC VENTURE FUNDS

2601 South Bayshore Drive
Miami FL 33133

Phone (305) 250-4681   Fax (305) 250-4682

PROFESSIONALS	TITLE
James Davidson	Managing Director

INDUSTRY PREFERENCE

☒ INFORMATION INDUSTRY
☒ Communications
☒ Computer Equipment
☒ Computer Services
☒ Computer Components
☐ Computer Entertainment
☐ Computer Education
☒ Information Technologies
☒ Computer Media
☒ Software
☒ Internet
☒ MEDICAL/HEALTHCARE
☒ Biotechnology
☒ Healthcare Services
☒ Life Sciences
☒ Medical Products
☒ INDUSTRIAL
☐ Advanced Materials
☐ Chemicals
☒ Instruments & Controls

☒ BASIC INDUSTRIES
☒ Consumer
☐ Distribution
☐ Manufacturing
☐ Retail
☒ Service
☐ Wholesale
☒ SPECIFIC INDUSTRIES
☐ Energy
☐ Environmental
☒ Financial
☐ Real Estate
☐ Transportation
☐ Publishing
☐ Food
☐ Franchises
☒ DIVERSIFIED
☒ MISCELLANEOUS

STAGE PREFERENCE

☒ EARLY STAGE
☐ Seed
☒ Start-up
☒ 1st Stage
☒ LATER STAGE
☒ 2nd Stage
☒ Mature
☐ Mezzanine
☒ LBO/MBO
☐ Turnaround
☐ INT'L EXPANSION
☐ WILL CONSIDER ALL
☐ VENTURE LEASING

Other Locations: Tampa FL

Affiliation:
Minimum Investment: $1 Million or more
Capital Under Management: $100 to $500 Million

GEOGRAPHIC PREF

☐ East Coast
☐ West Coast
☐ Northeast
☐ Mid Atlantic
☐ Gulf States
☐ Northwest
☐ Southeast
☐ Southwest
☐ Midwest
☐ Central
☐ Local to Office
☒ Other Geo Pref
  South Atlantic States

ALLIANCE TECHNOLOGY VENTURES

3343 Peachtree Road NE
Suite 1140 East Tower
Atlanta GA 30326

Phone (404) 816-4891   Fax (404) 816-4891

PROFESSIONALS	TITLE
Michael Henos	Managing General Partner
Stephen Fleming	General Partner
Michael Slawson	General Partner

INDUSTRY PREFERENCE

- ☒ INFORMATION INDUSTRY
- ☒ Communications
- ☒ Computer Equipment
- ☒ Computer Services
- ☒ Computer Components
- ☐ Computer Entertainment
- ☐ Computer Education
- ☒ Information Technologies
- ☐ Computer Media
- ☐ Software
- ☐ Internet
- ☒ MEDICAL/HEALTHCARE
- ☐ Biotechnology
- ☐ Healthcare Services
- ☒ Life Sciences
- ☐ Medical Products
- ☒ INDUSTRIAL
- ☐ Advanced Materials
- ☐ Chemicals
- ☒ Instruments & Controls

- ☐ BASIC INDUSTRIES
- ☐ Consumer
- ☐ Distribution
- ☐ Manufacturing
- ☐ Retail
- ☐ Service
- ☐ Wholesale
- ☐ SPECIFIC INDUSTRIES
- ☐ Energy
- ☐ Environmental
- ☐ Financial
- ☐ Real Estate
- ☐ Transportation
- ☐ Publishing
- ☐ Food
- ☐ Franchises
- ☒ DIVERSIFIED
- ☒ MISCELLANEOUS

STAGE PREFERENCE

- ☒ EARLY STAGE
- ☐ Seed
- ☒ Start-up
- ☒ 1st Stage
- ☐ LATER STAGE
- ☐ 2nd Stage
- ☐ Mature
- ☐ Mezzanine
- ☐ LBO/MBO
- ☐ Turnaround
- ☐ INT'L EXPANSION
- ☐ WILL CONSIDER ALL
- ☐ VENTURE LEASING

Other Locations:

Affiliation:
Minimum Investment: $1 Million or more
Capital Under Management: Less than $100 Million

GEOGRAPHIC PREF

- ☐ East Coast
- ☐ West Coast
- ☐ Northeast
- ☐ Mid Atlantic
- ☐ Gulf States
- ☐ Northwest
- ☒ Southeast
- ☐ Southwest
- ☐ Midwest
- ☐ Central
- ☐ Local to Office
- ☐ Other Geo Pref

CORDOVA CAPITAL PARTNERS, LP

Three NorthWinds Center
2500 NorthWinds Parkway, Suite 475
Alpharetta GA 30004

Phone (678) 942-0300   Fax (678) 942-0301

PROFESSIONALS	TITLE
Jerry F. Schmidt	Partner
Ralph R. Wright, Jr.	Partner
Christopher J. Valianos	Partner
Paul R. DiBella	Partner
Charles E. Adiar	Partner
Don B. Stout	Partner
T. Forcht Dagi	Partner
Frank X. Dalton	Partner

INDUSTRY PREFERENCE

- ☒ INFORMATION INDUSTRY
- ☒ Communications
- ☒ Computer Equipment
- ☒ Computer Services
- ☒ Computer Components
- ☐ Computer Entertainment
- ☒ Computer Education
- ☒ Information Technologies
- ☐ Computer Media
- ☒ Software
- ☒ Internet
- ☒ MEDICAL/HEALTHCARE
- ☐ Biotechnology
- ☒ Healthcare Services
- ☒ Life Sciences
- ☒ Medical Products
- ☐ INDUSTRIAL
- ☐ Advanced Materials
- ☐ Chemicals
- ☐ Instruments & Controls

- ☐ BASIC INDUSTRIES
- ☐ Consumer
- ☐ Distribution
- ☐ Manufacturing
- ☐ Retail
- ☐ Service
- ☐ Wholesale
- ☐ SPECIFIC INDUSTRIES
- ☐ Energy
- ☐ Environmental
- ☐ Financial
- ☐ Real Estate
- ☐ Transportation
- ☐ Publishing
- ☐ Food
- ☐ Franchises
- ☒ DIVERSIFIED
- ☐ MISCELLANEOUS

STAGE PREFERENCE

- ☒ EARLY STAGE
- ☐ Seed
- ☒ Start-up
- ☒ 1st Stage
- ☒ LATER STAGE
- ☒ 2nd Stage
- ☒ Mature
- ☒ Mezzanine
- ☒ LBO/MBO
- ☐ Turnaround
- ☐ INT'L EXPANSION
- ☐ WILL CONSIDER ALL
- ☐ VENTURE LEASING

SBIC
Other Locations:

Affiliation:
Minimum Investment: $1 Million or more
Capital Under Management: Less than $100 Million

GEOGRAPHIC PREF

- ☐ East Coast
- ☐ West Coast
- ☐ Northeast
- ☐ Mid Atlantic
- ☐ Gulf States
- ☐ Northwest
- ☒ Southeast
- ☐ Southwest
- ☐ Midwest
- ☐ Central
- ☐ Local to Office
- ☐ Other Geo Pref

EGL HOLDINGS INC.

**3495 Piedmont Road
Ten Piedmont Center, Suite 412
Atlanta GA 30305**

Phone (404) 949-8300   Fax (404) 949-8311

PROFESSIONALS	TITLE
Sal Massaro	Partner
John Festa	Partner
Ron Wallace	Partner
David Ellis	Partner

INDUSTRY PREFERENCE

☒ INFORMATION INDUSTRY
☒ Communications
☒ Computer Equipment
☒ Computer Services
☒ Computer Components
☐ Computer Entertainment
☐ Computer Education
☒ Information Technologies
☐ Computer Media
☒ Software
☒ Internet
☒ MEDICAL/HEALTHCARE
☐ Biotechnology
☒ Healthcare Services
☒ Life Sciences
☒ Medical Products
☒ INDUSTRIAL
☐ Advanced Materials
☒ Chemicals
☒ Instruments & Controls

☒ BASIC INDUSTRIES
☒ Consumer
☒ Distribution
☐ Manufacturing
☐ Retail
☐ Service
☐ Wholesale
☒ SPECIFIC INDUSTRIES
☐ Energy
☒ Environmental
☐ Financial
☐ Real Estate
☐ Transportation
☒ Publishing
☐ Food
☐ Franchises
☒ DIVERSIFIED
☒ MISCELLANEOUS

STAGE PREFERENCE

☐ EARLY STAGE
☐ Seed
☐ Start-up
☐ 1st Stage
☒ LATER STAGE
☐ 2nd Stage
☐ Mature
☐ Mezzanine
☒ LBO/MBO
☐ Turnaround
☐ INT'L EXPANSION
☐ WILL CONSIDER ALL
☐ VENTURE LEASING

Other Locations:

Affiliation:
Minimum Investment: Less than $1 Million
Capital Under Management: Less than $100 Million

GEOGRAPHIC PREF

☒ East Coast
☐ West Coast
☐ Northeast
☐ Mid Atlantic
☐ Gulf States
☐ Northwest
☐ Southeast
☐ Southwest
☐ Midwest
☐ Central
☐ Local to Office
☐ Other Geo Pref

KINETIC VENTURE CAPITAL CORPORATION

**115 Perimeter Center Place
Suite 640
Atlanta GA 30346**

Phone (770) 399-1660   Fax (770) 399-1664

PROFESSIONALS	TITLE
George W. Levert, Jr.	Vice President

INDUSTRY PREFERENCE

☒ INFORMATION INDUSTRY
☒ Communications
☒ Computer Equipment
☒ Computer Services
☐ Computer Components
☐ Computer Entertainment
☐ Computer Education
☒ Information Technologies
☐ Computer Media
☒ Software
☒ Internet
☐ MEDICAL/HEALTHCARE
☐ Biotechnology
☐ Healthcare Services
☐ Life Sciences
☐ Medical Products
☐ INDUSTRIAL
☐ Advanced Materials
☐ Chemicals
☐ Instruments & Controls

☐ BASIC INDUSTRIES
☐ Consumer
☐ Distribution
☐ Manufacturing
☐ Retail
☐ Service
☐ Wholesale
☐ SPECIFIC INDUSTRIES
☐ Energy
☐ Environmental
☐ Financial
☐ Real Estate
☐ Transportation
☐ Publishing
☐ Food
☐ Franchises
☒ DIVERSIFIED
☐ MISCELLANEOUS

STAGE PREFERENCE

☒ EARLY STAGE
☒ Seed
☒ Start-up
☒ 1st Stage
☒ LATER STAGE
☒ 2nd Stage
☒ Mature
☒ Mezzanine
☒ LBO/MBO
☒ Turnaround
☐ INT'L EXPANSION
☐ WILL CONSIDER ALL
☒ VENTURE LEASING

Other Locations:

Affiliation: Arete Ventures, Inc.
Minimum Investment: Less than $1 Million
Capital Under Management: Less than $100 Million

GEOGRAPHIC PREF

☐ East Coast
☐ West Coast
☐ Northeast
☐ Mid Atlantic
☐ Gulf States
☐ Northwest
☐ Southeast
☒ Southwest
☐ Midwest
☐ Central
☐ Local to Office
☐ Other Geo Pref

MELLON VENTURES, INC.

One Buckhead Plaza
3060 Peachtree Road, Suite 780
Atlanta GA 30305-2240

Phone (404) 264-9180   Fax (404) 264-9305

PROFESSIONALS

John Richardson

TITLE

Managing Director

INDUSTRY PREFERENCE

- ☒ INFORMATION INDUSTRY
- ☒ Communications
- ☒ Computer Equipment
- ☒ Computer Services
- ☒ Computer Components
- ☒ Computer Entertainment
- ☒ Computer Education
- ☒ Information Technologies
- ☒ Computer Media
- ☒ Software
- ☒ Internet
- ☒ MEDICAL/HEALTHCARE
- ☐ Biotechnology
- ☒ Healthcare Services
- ☐ Life Sciences
- ☐ Medical Products
- ☒ INDUSTRIAL
- ☒ Advanced Materials
- ☒ Chemicals
- ☒ Instruments & Controls

- ☒ BASIC INDUSTRIES
- ☒ Consumer
- ☒ Distribution
- ☒ Manufacturing
- ☒ Retail
- ☒ Service
- ☒ Wholesale
- ☒ SPECIFIC INDUSTRIES
- ☐ Energy
- ☐ Environmental
- ☒ Financial
- ☐ Real Estate
- ☒ Transportation
- ☐ Publishing
- ☐ Food
- ☐ Franchises
- ☒ DIVERSIFIED
- ☒ MISCELLANEOUS

STAGE PREFERENCE

- ☐ EARLY STAGE
- ☐ Seed
- ☐ Start-up
- ☐ 1st Stage
- ☒ LATER STAGE
- ☐ 2nd Stage
- ☐ Mature
- ☒ Mezzanine
- ☒ LBO/MBO
- ☒ Turnaround
- ☐ INT'L EXPANSION
- ☐ WILL CONSIDER ALL
- ☒ VENTURE LEASING

SBIC

Other Locations: Los Angeles CA, Pittsburgh PA, Radnor PA

Affiliation: Mellon Bank, NA
Minimum Investment: $1 Million or more
Capital Under Management: Less than $100 Million

GEOGRAPHIC PREF

- ☐ East Coast
- ☐ West Coast
- ☐ Northeast
- ☐ Mid Atlantic
- ☐ Gulf States
- ☐ Northwest
- ☐ Southeast
- ☐ Southwest
- ☐ Midwest
- ☐ Central
- ☐ Local to Office
- ☐ Other Geo Pref

NORO-MOSELEY PARTNERS

9 North Parkway Square
4200 Northside Parkway
Atlanta GA 30327-3054

Phone (404) 233-1966   Fax (404) 239-9280

PROFESSIONALS

Jack R. Kelly, Jr.
Russell R. French
Charles A. Johnson
Charles D. Moseley, Jr.
Alan J. Taetle
Allen S. Moseley

TITLE

General Partner
General Partner
General Partner
General Partner
General Partner
General Parnter

INDUSTRY PREFERENCE

- ☒ INFORMATION INDUSTRY
- ☒ Communications
- ☒ Computer Equipment
- ☒ Computer Services
- ☒ Computer Components
- ☐ Computer Entertainment
- ☒ Computer Education
- ☒ Information Technologies
- ☐ Computer Media
- ☒ Software
- ☒ Internet
- ☒ MEDICAL/HEALTHCARE
- ☒ Biotechnology
- ☒ Healthcare Services
- ☒ Life Sciences
- ☒ Medical Products
- ☐ INDUSTRIAL
- ☐ Advanced Materials
- ☐ Chemicals
- ☐ Instruments & Controls

- ☒ BASIC INDUSTRIES
- ☐ Consumer
- ☐ Distribution
- ☐ Manufacturing
- ☒ Retail
- ☒ Service
- ☐ Wholesale
- ☐ SPECIFIC INDUSTRIES
- ☐ Energy
- ☐ Environmental
- ☐ Financial
- ☐ Real Estate
- ☐ Transportation
- ☐ Publishing
- ☐ Food
- ☐ Franchises
- ☒ DIVERSIFIED
- ☐ MISCELLANEOUS

STAGE PREFERENCE

- ☒ EARLY STAGE
- ☐ Seed
- ☒ Start-up
- ☒ 1st Stage
- ☒ LATER STAGE
- ☒ 2nd Stage
- ☒ Mature
- ☐ Mezzanine
- ☒ LBO/MBO
- ☐ Turnaround
- ☐ INT'L EXPANSION
- ☐ WILL CONSIDER ALL
- ☐ VENTURE LEASING

Other Locations:

Affiliation:
Minimum Investment: Less than $1 Million
Capital Under Management: $100 to $500 Million

GEOGRAPHIC PREF

- ☐ East Coast
- ☐ West Coast
- ☐ Northeast
- ☐ Mid Atlantic
- ☐ Gulf States
- ☐ Northwest
- ☒ Southeast
- ☐ Southwest
- ☐ Midwest
- ☐ Central
- ☐ Local to Office
- ☐ Other Geo Pref

RIVER CAPITAL EQUITY PARTNERS

Two Midtown Plaza
Suite 1430
Atlanta GA 30309

Phone (404) 873-2166   Fax (404) 873-2158

PROFESSIONALS	TITLE
Jerry Wethington	Managing Principal
F. W. Hulse IV	Principal
Denis Brown	Vice President
J. Phillip Falls	Vice President
John Van Tuin	Vice President

INDUSTRY PREFERENCE

☒ INFORMATION INDUSTRY
☒ Communications
☐ Computer Equipment
☐ Computer Services
☒ Computer Components
☐ Computer Entertainment
☐ Computer Education
☐ Information Technologies
☐ Computer Media
☐ Software
☐ Internet
☒ MEDICAL/HEALTHCARE
☐ Biotechnology
☐ Healthcare Services
☐ Life Sciences
☒ Medical Products
☐ INDUSTRIAL
☐ Advanced Materials
☐ Chemicals
☐ Instruments & Controls

☒ BASIC INDUSTRIES
☒ Consumer
☒ Distribution
☒ Manufacturing
☐ Retail
☒ Service
☒ Wholesale
☒ SPECIFIC INDUSTRIES
☐ Energy
☐ Environmental
☐ Financial
☐ Real Estate
☒ Transportation
☒ Publishing
☐ Food
☒ Franchises
☒ DIVERSIFIED
☐ MISCELLANEOUS

STAGE PREFERENCE

☐ EARLY STAGE
☐ Seed
☐ Start-up
☐ 1st Stage
☒ LATER STAGE
☐ 2nd Stage
☐ Mature
☒ Mezzanine
☒ LBO/MBO
☐ Turnaround
☐ INT'L EXPANSION
☐ WILL CONSIDER ALL
☐ VENTURE LEASING

Other Locations:

Affiliation:
Minimum Investment: $1 Million or more
Capital Under Management: Less than $100 Million

GEOGRAPHIC PREF

☐ East Coast
☐ West Coast
☐ Northeast
☒ Mid Atlantic
☒ Gulf States
☐ Northwest
☒ Southeast
☒ Southwest
☐ Midwest
☐ Central
☐ Local to Office
☒ Other Geo Pref
    Mid-Atlantic, Gulf
    States

WACHOVIA CAPITAL ASSOCIATES INC.

191 Peachtree Street NE
26th Floor
Atlanta GA 30303

Phone (404) 332-1437   Fax (404) 332-1392

PROFESSIONALS	TITLE
Matthew J. Sullivan	Managing Director

INDUSTRY PREFERENCE

☐ INFORMATION INDUSTRY
☐ Communications
☐ Computer Equipment
☐ Computer Services
☐ Computer Components
☐ Computer Entertainment
☐ Computer Education
☐ Information Technologies
☐ Computer Media
☐ Software
☐ Internet
☐ MEDICAL/HEALTHCARE
☐ Biotechnology
☐ Healthcare Services
☐ Life Sciences
☐ Medical Products
☐ INDUSTRIAL
☐ Advanced Materials
☐ Chemicals
☐ Instruments & Controls

☐ BASIC INDUSTRIES
☐ Consumer
☐ Distribution
☐ Manufacturing
☐ Retail
☐ Service
☐ Wholesale
☐ SPECIFIC INDUSTRIES
☐ Energy
☐ Environmental
☐ Financial
☐ Real Estate
☐ Transportation
☐ Publishing
☐ Food
☐ Franchises
☒ DIVERSIFIED
☐ MISCELLANEOUS

STAGE PREFERENCE

☒ EARLY STAGE
☐ Seed
☒ Start-up
☒ 1st Stage
☒ LATER STAGE
☒ 2nd Stage
☐ Mature
☐ Mezzanine
☐ LBO/MBO
☐ Turnaround
☐ INT'L EXPANSION
☐ WILL CONSIDER ALL
☐ VENTURE LEASING
SBIC
Other Locations:

Affiliation:
Minimum Investment: $1 Million or more
Capital Under Management: Less than $100 Million

GEOGRAPHIC PREF

☐ East Coast
☐ West Coast
☐ Northeast
☐ Mid Atlantic
☐ Gulf States
☐ Northwest
☒ Southeast
☐ Southwest
☐ Midwest
☐ Central
☐ Local to Office
☐ Other Geo Pref

HMS HAWAII MANAGEMENT PARTNERS

Davies Pacific Center
841 Bishop Street, Suite 860
Honolulu HI 96813

Phone (808) 545-3755   Fax (808) 531-2611

PROFESSIONALS	TITLE
Richard G. Grey	General Partner
William Richardson	General Partner

INDUSTRY PREFERENCE

☒ INFORMATION INDUSTRY
☒ Communications
☒ Computer Equipment
☒ Computer Services
☒ Computer Components
☐ Computer Entertainment
☒ Computer Education
☒ Information Technologies
☒ Computer Media
☒ Software
☒ Internet
☐ MEDICAL/HEALTHCARE
☐ Biotechnology
☐ Healthcare Services
☐ Life Sciences
☐ Medical Products
☒ INDUSTRIAL
☐ Advanced Materials
☐ Chemicals
☒ Instruments & Controls

☒ BASIC INDUSTRIES
☐ Consumer
☐ Distribution
☐ Manufacturing
☐ Retail
☒ Service
☐ Wholesale
☐ SPECIFIC INDUSTRIES
☐ Energy
☐ Environmental
☐ Financial
☐ Real Estate
☐ Transportation
☐ Publishing
☐ Food
☐ Franchises
☒ DIVERSIFIED
☐ MISCELLANEOUS

STAGE PREFERENCE

☒ EARLY STAGE
☒ Seed
☒ Start-up
☒ 1st Stage
☐ LATER STAGE
☐ 2nd Stage
☐ Mature
☐ Mezzanine
☐ LBO/MBO
☐ Turnaround
☐ INT'L EXPANSION
☐ WILL CONSIDER ALL
☐ VENTURE LEASING

Other Locations:

Affiliation:
Minimum Investment: Less than $1 Million
Capital Under Management: Less than $100 Million

GEOGRAPHIC PREF

☐ East Coast
☐ West Coast
☐ Northeast
☐ Mid Atlantic
☐ Gulf States
☐ Northwest
☐ Southeast
☐ Southwest
☐ Midwest
☐ Central
☐ Local to Office
☒ Other Geo Pref
  HI

PACIFIC VENTURE CAPITAL LTD.

222 South Vineyard Street
PH.1
Honolulu HI 96813

Phone (808) 521-6502   Fax (808) 521-6541

PROFESSIONALS	TITLE
Dexter J. Taniguchi	President

INDUSTRY PREFERENCE

☐ INFORMATION INDUSTRY
☐ Communications
☐ Computer Equipment
☐ Computer Services
☐ Computer Components
☐ Computer Entertainment
☐ Computer Education
☐ Information Technologies
☐ Computer Media
☐ Software
☐ Internet
☐ MEDICAL/HEALTHCARE
☐ Biotechnology
☐ Healthcare Services
☐ Life Sciences
☐ Medical Products
☐ INDUSTRIAL
☐ Advanced Materials
☐ Chemicals
☐ Instruments & Controls

☐ BASIC INDUSTRIES
☐ Consumer
☐ Distribution
☐ Manufacturing
☐ Retail
☐ Service
☐ Wholesale
☐ SPECIFIC INDUSTRIES
☐ Energy
☐ Environmental
☐ Financial
☐ Real Estate
☐ Transportation
☐ Publishing
☐ Food
☐ Franchises
☒ DIVERSIFIED
☐ MISCELLANEOUS

STAGE PREFERENCE

☒ EARLY STAGE
☐ Seed
☐ Start-up
☒ 1st Stage
☒ LATER STAGE
☒ 2nd Stage
☐ Mature
☒ Mezzanine
☒ LBO/MBO
☐ Turnaround
☐ INT'L EXPANSION
☐ WILL CONSIDER ALL
☐ VENTURE LEASING

SBIC
Other Locations:

Affiliation:
Minimum Investment: Less than $1 Million
Capital Under Management: Less than $100 Million

GEOGRAPHIC PREF

☐ East Coast
☐ West Coast
☐ Northeast
☐ Mid Atlantic
☐ Gulf States
☐ Northwest
☐ Southeast
☐ Southwest
☐ Midwest
☐ Central
☐ Local to Office
☐ Other Geo Pref

ABN AMRO PRIVATE EQUITY

208 South LaSalle Street
10th Floor
Chicago IL 60604

Phone (312) 855-7079   Fax (312) 553-6648

PROFESSIONALS	TITLE
David Bogetz	

INDUSTRY PREFERENCE

- ☒ INFORMATION INDUSTRY
- ☐ Communications
- ☒ Computer Equipment
- ☒ Computer Services
- ☒ Computer Components
- ☐ Computer Entertainment
- ☐ Computer Education
- ☐ Information Technologies
- ☐ Computer Media
- ☒ Software
- ☐ Internet
- ☒ MEDICAL/HEALTHCARE
- ☐ Biotechnology
- ☒ Healthcare Services
- ☒ Life Sciences
- ☒ Medical Products
- ☐ INDUSTRIAL
- ☐ Advanced Materials
- ☐ Chemicals
- ☐ Instruments & Controls

- ☒ BASIC INDUSTRIES
- ☒ Consumer
- ☐ Distribution
- ☐ Manufacturing
- ☒ Retail
- ☐ Service
- ☐ Wholesale
- ☒ SPECIFIC INDUSTRIES
- ☐ Energy
- ☐ Environmental
- ☐ Financial
- ☐ Real Estate
- ☐ Transportation
- ☒ Publishing
- ☒ Food
- ☐ Franchises
- ☒ DIVERSIFIED
- ☒ MISCELLANEOUS
  - Restaurants

STAGE PREFERENCE

- ☒ EARLY STAGE
- ☐ Seed
- ☐ Start-up
- ☒ 1st Stage
- ☒ LATER STAGE
- ☒ 2nd Stage
- ☐ Mature
- ☒ Mezzanine
- ☒ LBO/MBO
- ☐ Turnaround
- ☐ INT'L EXPANSION
- ☐ WILL CONSIDER ALL
- ☐ VENTURE LEASING

Other Locations:

Affiliation:
Minimum Investment: $1 Million or more
Capital Under Management: $100 to $500 Million

GEOGRAPHIC PREF

- ☐ East Coast
- ☐ West Coast
- ☐ Northeast
- ☐ Mid Atlantic
- ☐ Gulf States
- ☐ Northwest
- ☐ Southeast
- ☐ Southwest
- ☐ Midwest
- ☐ Central
- ☐ Local to Office
- ☒ Other Geo Pref
  - IL

ALPHA CAPITAL PARTNERS LTD.

122 South Michigan Avenue
Suite 1700
Chicago IL 60603

Phone (312) 322-9800   Fax (312) 322-9808

PROFESSIONALS	TITLE
Andrew H. Kalnow	President
W. Oberholtzer	Vice President

INDUSTRY PREFERENCE

- ☒ INFORMATION INDUSTRY
- ☒ Communications
- ☒ Computer Equipment
- ☒ Computer Services
- ☒ Computer Components
- ☐ Computer Entertainment
- ☒ Computer Education
- ☒ Information Technologies
- ☐ Computer Media
- ☒ Software
- ☒ Internet
- ☒ MEDICAL/HEALTHCARE
- ☒ Biotechnology
- ☒ Healthcare Services
- ☒ Life Sciences
- ☒ Medical Products
- ☒ INDUSTRIAL
- ☒ Advanced Materials
- ☒ Chemicals
- ☒ Instruments & Controls

- ☒ BASIC INDUSTRIES
- ☒ Consumer
- ☒ Distribution
- ☒ Manufacturing
- ☒ Retail
- ☒ Service
- ☐ Wholesale
- ☐ SPECIFIC INDUSTRIES
- ☐ Energy
- ☐ Environmental
- ☐ Financial
- ☐ Real Estate
- ☐ Transportation
- ☐ Publishing
- ☐ Food
- ☐ Franchises
- ☒ DIVERSIFIED
- ☐ MISCELLANEOUS

STAGE PREFERENCE

- ☒ EARLY STAGE
- ☐ Seed
- ☐ Start-up
- ☒ 1st Stage
- ☒ LATER STAGE
- ☒ 2nd Stage
- ☒ Mature
- ☐ Mezzanine
- ☒ LBO/MBO
- ☐ Turnaround
- ☐ INT'L EXPANSION
- ☐ WILL CONSIDER ALL
- ☐ VENTURE LEASING

Other Locations: Dayton OH

Affiliation:
Minimum Investment: Less than $1 Million
Capital Under Management: Less than $100 Million

GEOGRAPHIC PREF

- ☐ East Coast
- ☐ West Coast
- ☐ Northeast
- ☐ Mid Atlantic
- ☐ Gulf States
- ☐ Northwest
- ☐ Southeast
- ☐ Southwest
- ☐ Midwest
- ☐ Central
- ☐ Local to Office
- ☐ Other Geo Pref

APEX INVESTMENT PARTNERS

225 West Washington
Suite 1450
Chicago IL 60606

Phone (312) 857-2800   Fax (312) 857-1800

PROFESSIONALS	TITLE
George Middlemas	General Partner
James A. Johnson	General Partner

INDUSTRY PREFERENCE

☒ INFORMATION INDUSTRY	☒ BASIC INDUSTRIES	
☒ Communications	☐ Consumer	
☐ Computer Equipment	☐ Distribution	
☐ Computer Services	☐ Manufacturing	
☐ Computer Components	☒ Retail	
☐ Computer Entertainment	☒ Service	
☐ Computer Education	☐ Wholesale	
☒ Information Technologies	☒ SPECIFIC INDUSTRIES	
☐ Computer Media	☐ Energy	
☒ Software	☒ Environmental	
☐ Internet	☒ Financial	
☒ MEDICAL/HEALTHCARE	☐ Real Estate	
☐ Biotechnology	☐ Transportation	
☒ Healthcare Services	☐ Publishing	
☐ Life Sciences	☐ Food	
☒ Medical Products	☐ Franchises	
☐ INDUSTRIAL	☒ DIVERSIFIED	
☐ Advanced Materials	☐ MISCELLANEOUS	
☐ Chemicals		
☐ Instruments & Controls		

STAGE PREFERENCE

☒ EARLY STAGE
☒ Seed
☒ Start-up
☒ 1st Stage
☒ LATER STAGE
☒ 2nd Stage
☒ Mature
☒ Mezzanine
☒ LBO/MBO
☒ Turnaround
☒ INT'L EXPANSION
☐ WILL CONSIDER ALL
☒ VENTURE LEASING

Other Locations:

Affiliation:
Minimum Investment: $1 Million or more
Capital Under Management: Over $500 Million

GEOGRAPHIC PREF

☐ East Coast
☐ West Coast
☐ Northeast
☐ Mid Atlantic
☐ Gulf States
☐ Northwest
☐ Southeast
☐ Southwest
☐ Midwest
☐ Central
☐ Local to Office
☐ Other Geo Pref

ARCH VENTURE PARTNERS

8725 W. Higgins Road
Suite 290
Chicago IL 60631

Phone (773) 380-6600   Fax (773) 380-6606

PROFESSIONALS	TITLE
Steven Lazarus	Managing Director
Keith Crandell	Managing Director
Robert Nelsen	Managing Director
Alex Knight	Managing Director
Karen Kerr	Managing Director

INDUSTRY PREFERENCE

☒ INFORMATION INDUSTRY	☐ BASIC INDUSTRIES	
☒ Communications	☐ Consumer	
☒ Computer Equipment	☐ Distribution	
☒ Computer Services	☐ Manufacturing	
☐ Computer Components	☐ Retail	
☐ Computer Entertainment	☐ Service	
☐ Computer Education	☐ Wholesale	
☐ Information Technologies	☒ SPECIFIC INDUSTRIES	
☐ Computer Media	☒ Energy	
☐ Software	☒ Environmental	
☐ Internet	☐ Financial	
☒ MEDICAL/HEALTHCARE	☐ Real Estate	
☒ Biotechnology	☐ Transportation	
☒ Healthcare Services	☒ Publishing	
☒ Life Sciences	☐ Food	
☒ Medical Products	☐ Franchises	
☒ INDUSTRIAL	☒ DIVERSIFIED	
☐ Advanced Materials	☒ MISCELLANEOUS	
☐ Chemicals	Agriculture	
☒ Instruments & Controls		

STAGE PREFERENCE

☒ EARLY STAGE
☒ Seed
☒ Start-up
☐ 1st Stage
☐ LATER STAGE
☐ 2nd Stage
☐ Mature
☐ Mezzanine
☐ LBO/MBO
☐ Turnaround
☐ INT'L EXPANSION
☐ WILL CONSIDER ALL
☐ VENTURE LEASING

Other Locations: Albuquerque NM, New York NY,
Seattle WA

Affiliation:
Minimum Investment: $1 Million or more
Capital Under Management: $100 to $500 Million

GEOGRAPHIC PREF

☐ East Coast
☐ West Coast
☐ Northeast
☐ Mid Atlantic
☐ Gulf States
☐ Northwest
☐ Southeast
☐ Southwest
☐ Midwest
☐ Central
☐ Local to Office
☐ Other Geo Pref

ARGENTUM GROUP

233 South Wacker Drive
Suite 9500
Chicago IL 60606

Phone (312) 258-1400   Fax (312) 258-0334

PROFESSIONALS	TITLE
Daniel Raynor	General Partner
Walter Barandiaran	General Partner

INDUSTRY PREFERENCE

⊠ INFORMATION INDUSTRY	⊠ BASIC INDUSTRIES	
⊠ Communications	☐ Consumer	
⊠ Computer Equipment	☐ Distribution	
⊠ Computer Services	☐ Manufacturing	
⊠ Computer Components	☐ Retail	
☐ Computer Entertainment	⊠ Service	
⊠ Computer Education	☐ Wholesale	
⊠ Information Technologies	⊠ SPECIFIC INDUSTRIES	
⊠ Computer Media	⊠ Energy	
⊠ Software	⊠ Environmental	
⊠ Internet	☐ Financial	
☐ MEDICAL/HEALTHCARE	☐ Real Estate	
☐ Biotechnology	☐ Transportation	
☐ Healthcare Services	☐ Publishing	
☐ Life Sciences	☐ Food	
☐ Medical Products	☐ Franchises	
⊠ INDUSTRIAL	⊠ DIVERSIFIED	
⊠ Advanced Materials	☐ MISCELLANEOUS	
⊠ Chemicals		
⊠ Instruments & Controls		

STAGE PREFERENCE

⊠ EARLY STAGE
☐ Seed
☐ Start-up
⊠ 1st Stage
⊠ LATER STAGE
⊠ 2nd Stage
⊠ Mature
⊠ Mezzanine
⊠ LBO/MBO
☐ Turnaround
☐ INT'L EXPANSION
☐ WILL CONSIDER ALL
☐ VENTURE LEASING
SBIC
Other Locations:

Affiliation:
Minimum Investment: Less than $1 Million
Capital Under Management: $100 to $500 Million

GEOGRAPHIC PREF

☐ East Coast
☐ West Coast
☐ Northeast
☐ Mid Atlantic
☐ Gulf States
☐ Northwest
☐ Southeast
☐ Southwest
☐ Midwest
☐ Central
☐ Local to Office
☐ Other Geo Pref

BAIRD CAPITAL PARTNERS

227 West Monroe Street
Suite 2100
Chicago IL 60606

Phone (312) 609-4700   Fax (312) 609-4707

PROFESSIONALS	TITLE
Paul Carbone	Managing Director

INDUSTRY PREFERENCE

⊠ INFORMATION INDUSTRY	⊠ BASIC INDUSTRIES	
⊠ Communications	⊠ Consumer	
☐ Computer Equipment	⊠ Distribution	
☐ Computer Services	☐ Manufacturing	
☐ Computer Components	☐ Retail	
☐ Computer Entertainment	☐ Service	
☐ Computer Education	☐ Wholesale	
☐ Information Technologies	☐ SPECIFIC INDUSTRIES	
☐ Computer Media	☐ Energy	
☐ Software	☐ Environmental	
☐ Internet	☐ Financial	
⊠ MEDICAL/HEALTHCARE	☐ Real Estate	
☐ Biotechnology	☐ Transportation	
⊠ Healthcare Services	☐ Publishing	
☐ Life Sciences	☐ Food	
⊠ Medical Products	☐ Franchises	
⊠ INDUSTRIAL	⊠ DIVERSIFIED	
☐ Advanced Materials	⊠ MISCELLANEOUS	
☐ Chemicals		
⊠ Instruments & Controls		

STAGE PREFERENCE

☐ EARLY STAGE
☐ Seed
☐ Start-up
☐ 1st Stage
⊠ LATER STAGE
⊠ 2nd Stage
⊠ Mature
⊠ Mezzanine
⊠ LBO/MBO
☐ Turnaround
☐ INT'L EXPANSION
☐ WILL CONSIDER ALL
☐ VENTURE LEASING

Other Locations:

Affiliation:
Minimum Investment: $1 Million or more
Capital Under Management: Less than $100 Million

GEOGRAPHIC PREF

☐ East Coast
☐ West Coast
☐ Northeast
☐ Mid Atlantic
☐ Gulf States
☐ Northwest
☐ Southeast
☐ Southwest
☐ Midwest
☐ Central
☐ Local to Office
☐ Other Geo Pref

BATTERSON VENTURE PARTNERS, LLC

303 West Madison
Suite 1110
Chicago IL 60606

Phone (312) 269-0300 Fax (312) 269-0021

PROFESSIONALS	TITLE
Donald R. Johnson	Sr. General Partner
Leonard A. Batterson	Managing General Partner
Tom Zimmerman	Associate

INDUSTRY PREFERENCE

☒ INFORMATION INDUSTRY	☐ BASIC INDUSTRIES
☒ Communications	☐ Consumer
☐ Computer Equipment	☐ Distribution
☐ Computer Services	☐ Manufacturing
☐ Computer Components	☐ Retail
☐ Computer Entertainment	☐ Service
☐ Computer Education	☐ Wholesale
☒ Information Technologies	☐ SPECIFIC INDUSTRIES
☐ Computer Media	☐ Energy
☒ Software	☐ Environmental
☒ Internet	☐ Financial
☒ MEDICAL/HEALTHCARE	☐ Real Estate
☒ Biotechnology	☐ Transportation
☒ Healthcare Services	☐ Publishing
☒ Life Sciences	☐ Food
☒ Medical Products	☐ Franchises
☒ INDUSTRIAL	☒ DIVERSIFIED
☒ Advanced Materials	☐ MISCELLANEOUS
☒ Chemicals	
☒ Instruments & Controls	

STAGE PREFERENCE

☒ EARLY STAGE
☒ Seed
☒ Start-up
☒ 1st Stage
☐ LATER STAGE
☐ 2nd Stage
☐ Mature
☐ Mezzanine
☐ LBO/MBO
☐ Turnaround
☐ INT'L EXPANSION
☐ WILL CONSIDER ALL
☐ VENTURE LEASING

Other Locations:

Affiliation:
Minimum Investment: Less than $1 Million
Capital Under Management: Less than $100 Million

GEOGRAPHIC PREF

☐ East Coast
☐ West Coast
☐ Northeast
☐ Mid Atlantic
☐ Gulf States
☐ Northwest
☐ Southeast
☐ Southwest
☐ Midwest
☐ Central
☐ Local to Office
☐ Other Geo Pref

BEECKEN PETTY & CO. LLC

901 Warrenville Road
Suite 205
Lisle IL 60532

Phone (630) 435-0300 Fax (630) 435-0370

PROFESSIONALS	TITLE
David Beecken	Managing Director
William Petty, Jr	Managing Director
Kenneth O'Keefe	Managing Director
Gregory Moerschel	Managing Director

INDUSTRY PREFERENCE

☐ INFORMATION INDUSTRY	☐ BASIC INDUSTRIES
☐ Communications	☐ Consumer
☐ Computer Equipment	☐ Distribution
☐ Computer Services	☐ Manufacturing
☐ Computer Components	☐ Retail
☐ Computer Entertainment	☐ Service
☐ Computer Education	☐ Wholesale
☐ Information Technologies	☐ SPECIFIC INDUSTRIES
☐ Computer Media	☐ Energy
☐ Software	☐ Environmental
☐ Internet	☐ Financial
☒ MEDICAL/HEALTHCARE	☐ Real Estate
☐ Biotechnology	☐ Transportation
☐ Healthcare Services	☐ Publishing
☐ Life Sciences	☐ Food
☐ Medical Products	☐ Franchises
☐ INDUSTRIAL	☐ DIVERSIFIED
☐ Advanced Materials	☒ MISCELLANEOUS
☐ Chemicals	
☐ Instruments & Controls	

STAGE PREFERENCE

☒ EARLY STAGE
☐ Seed
☐ Start-up
☒ 1st Stage
☒ LATER STAGE
☒ 2nd Stage
☐ Mature
☐ Mezzanine
☒ LBO/MBO
☐ Turnaround
☐ INT'L EXPANSION
☐ WILL CONSIDER ALL
☐ VENTURE LEASING

Other Locations:

Affiliation:
Minimum Investment: $1 Million or more
Capital Under Management: $100 to $500 Million

GEOGRAPHIC PREF

☐ East Coast
☐ West Coast
☐ Northeast
☐ Mid Atlantic
☐ Gulf States
☐ Northwest
☐ Southeast
☐ Southwest
☐ Midwest
☐ Central
☐ Local to Office
☒ Other Geo Pref
Canada

CODE, HENNESSY & SIMONS, INC.

**10 South Wacker Drive
Suite 3175
Chicago IL 60606**

Phone (312) 876-1840   Fax (312) 876-3854

PROFESSIONALS	TITLE
Andrew Code	Partner
Thomas Formolo	Partner
Peter Gotsch	Partner
Daniel Hennessey	Partner
Brian Simmons	Partner
Jon Vesely	Partner

INDUSTRY PREFERENCE

☐ INFORMATION INDUSTRY
☐ Communications
☐ Computer Equipment
☐ Computer Services
☐ Computer Components
☐ Computer Entertainment
☐ Computer Education
☐ Information Technologies
☐ Computer Media
☐ Software
☐ Internet
☐ MEDICAL/HEALTHCARE
☐ Biotechnology
☐ Healthcare Services
☐ Life Sciences
☐ Medical Products
☐ INDUSTRIAL
☐ Advanced Materials
☐ Chemicals
☐ Instruments & Controls

☒ BASIC INDUSTRIES
☒ Consumer
☒ Distribution
☒ Manufacturing
☐ Retail
☐ Service
☐ Wholesale
☒ SPECIFIC INDUSTRIES
☐ Energy
☐ Environmental
☐ Financial
☒ Real Estate
☐ Transportation
☐ Publishing
☐ Food
☐ Franchises
☒ DIVERSIFIED
☒ MISCELLANEOUS
Equipment and Machinery

STAGE PREFERENCE

☐ EARLY STAGE
☐ Seed
☐ Start-up
☐ 1st Stage
☒ LATER STAGE
☐ 2nd Stage
☐ Mature
☐ Mezzanine
☒ LBO/MBO
☐ Turnaround
☐ INT'L EXPANSION
☐ WILL CONSIDER ALL
☐ VENTURE LEASING

Other Locations:

Affiliation:
Minimum Investment: $1 Million or more
Capital Under Management: Over $500 Million

GEOGRAPHIC PREF

☐ East Coast
☐ West Coast
☐ Northeast
☐ Mid Atlantic
☐ Gulf States
☐ Northwest
☐ Southeast
☐ Southwest
☐ Midwest
☐ Central
☐ Local to Office
☐ Other Geo Pref

COMDISCO VENTURES

**6111 North River Road
Rosemont IL 60018**

Phone (847) 698-3000   Fax (847) 518-5465

PROFESSIONALS	TITLE
James Labe	Managing Partner

INDUSTRY PREFERENCE

☒ INFORMATION INDUSTRY
☒ Communications
☒ Computer Equipment
☒ Computer Services
☒ Computer Components
☐ Computer Entertainment
☒ Computer Education
☒ Information Technologies
☒ Computer Media
☒ Software
☒ Internet
☒ MEDICAL/HEALTHCARE
☒ Biotechnology
☒ Healthcare Services
☒ Life Sciences
☒ Medical Products
☒ INDUSTRIAL
☒ Advanced Materials
☒ Chemicals
☒ Instruments & Controls

☒ BASIC INDUSTRIES
☒ Consumer
☐ Distribution
☐ Manufacturing
☐ Retail
☒ Service
☐ Wholesale
☐ SPECIFIC INDUSTRIES
☐ Energy
☐ Environmental
☐ Financial
☐ Real Estate
☐ Transportation
☐ Publishing
☐ Food
☐ Franchises
☒ DIVERSIFIED
☐ MISCELLANEOUS

STAGE PREFERENCE

☒ EARLY STAGE
☒ Seed
☒ Start-up
☒ 1st Stage
☒ LATER STAGE
☒ 2nd Stage
☒ Mature
☒ Mezzanine
☒ LBO/MBO
☐ Turnaround
☐ INT'L EXPANSION
☐ WILL CONSIDER ALL
☐ VENTURE LEASING

Other Locations: Menlo Park CA, Waltham MA

Affiliation: Comdisco, Inc.
Minimum Investment: Less than $1 Million
Capital Under Management: Over $500 Million

GEOGRAPHIC PREF

☐ East Coast
☐ West Coast
☐ Northeast
☐ Mid Atlantic
☐ Gulf States
☐ Northwest
☐ Southeast
☐ Southwest
☐ Midwest
☐ Central
☐ Local to Office
☐ Other Geo Pref

CONTINENTAL ILLINOIS VENTURE CORP.

209 South LaSalle Street
Suite 11C
Chicago IL 60697

Phone (312) 828-8023   Fax (312) 987-0887

PROFESSIONALS	TITLE
Christopher J. Perry	

INDUSTRY PREFERENCE

☐ INFORMATION INDUSTRY
☐ Communications
☐ Computer Equipment
☐ Computer Services
☐ Computer Components
☐ Computer Entertainment
☐ Computer Education
☐ Information Technologies
☐ Computer Media
☐ Software
☐ Internet
☐ MEDICAL/HEALTHCARE
☐ Biotechnology
☐ Healthcare Services
☐ Life Sciences
☐ Medical Products
☐ INDUSTRIAL
☐ Advanced Materials
☐ Chemicals
☐ Instruments & Controls

☐ BASIC INDUSTRIES
☐ Consumer
☐ Distribution
☐ Manufacturing
☐ Retail
☐ Service
☐ Wholesale
☐ SPECIFIC INDUSTRIES
☐ Energy
☐ Environmental
☐ Financial
☐ Real Estate
☐ Transportation
☐ Publishing
☐ Food
☐ Franchises
☒ DIVERSIFIED
☐ MISCELLANEOUS

STAGE PREFERENCE

☐ EARLY STAGE
☐ Seed
☐ Start-up
☐ 1st Stage
☒ LATER STAGE
☐ 2nd Stage
☐ Mature
☐ Mezzanine
☒ LBO/MBO
☐ Turnaround
☐ INT'L EXPANSION
☐ WILL CONSIDER ALL
☐ VENTURE LEASING

SBIC
Other Locations:

Affiliation:
Minimum Investment: $1 Million or more
Capital Under Management: $100 to $500 Million

GEOGRAPHIC PREF

☐ East Coast
☐ West Coast
☐ Northeast
☐ Mid Atlantic
☐ Gulf States
☐ Northwest
☐ Southeast
☐ Southwest
☐ Midwest
☐ Central
☐ Local to Office
☐ Other Geo Pref

ESSEX WOODLANDS HEALTH VENTURES

190 South LaSalle Street
Suite 2800
Chicago IL 60603-3410

Phone (312) 444-6040   Fax (312) 444-6034

PROFESSIONALS	TITLE
James L. Currie	Managing General Partner
Marc Sandroff	General Partner
Martin Sutter	General Partner

INDUSTRY PREFERENCE

☐ INFORMATION INDUSTRY
☐ Communications
☐ Computer Equipment
☐ Computer Services
☐ Computer Components
☐ Computer Entertainment
☐ Computer Education
☐ Information Technologies
☐ Computer Media
☐ Software
☐ Internet
☒ MEDICAL/HEALTHCARE
☒ Biotechnology
☒ Healthcare Services
☒ Life Sciences
☒ Medical Products
☐ INDUSTRIAL
☐ Advanced Materials
☐ Chemicals
☐ Instruments & Controls

☐ BASIC INDUSTRIES
☐ Consumer
☐ Distribution
☐ Manufacturing
☐ Retail
☐ Service
☐ Wholesale
☐ SPECIFIC INDUSTRIES
☐ Energy
☐ Environmental
☐ Financial
☐ Real Estate
☐ Transportation
☐ Publishing
☐ Food
☐ Franchises
☐ DIVERSIFIED
☐ MISCELLANEOUS

STAGE PREFERENCE

☒ EARLY STAGE
☒ Seed
☒ Start-up
☒ 1st Stage
☒ LATER STAGE
☒ 2nd Stage
☐ Mature
☐ Mezzanine
☒ LBO/MBO
☐ Turnaround
☐ INT'L EXPANSION
☐ WILL CONSIDER ALL
☐ VENTURE LEASING

Other Locations:

Affiliation: The Woodlands
Minimum Investment: $1 Million or more
Capital Under Management: $100 to $500 Million

GEOGRAPHIC PREF

☐ East Coast
☐ West Coast
☐ Northeast
☐ Mid Atlantic
☐ Gulf States
☐ Northwest
☐ Southeast
☐ Southwest
☐ Midwest
☐ Central
☐ Local to Office
☐ Other Geo Pref

FIRST ANALYSIS CORP

233 South Wacker Drive
The Sears Tower, Suite 9500
Chicago IL 60606

Phone (312) 258-1400   Fax (312) 258-0334

PROFESSIONALS	TITLE
F. Oliver Nicklin	President
Bret Maxwell	Managing Director
Mark Koulogeorge	Executive Vice President

INDUSTRY PREFERENCE

☒ INFORMATION INDUSTRY	☐ BASIC INDUSTRIES
☒ Communications	☐ Consumer
☒ Computer Equipment	☐ Distribution
☒ Computer Services	☐ Manufacturing
☒ Computer Components	☐ Retail
☐ Computer Entertainment	☐ Service
☐ Computer Education	☐ Wholesale
☒ Information Technologies	☒ SPECIFIC INDUSTRIES
☐ Computer Media	☐ Energy
☒ Software	☒ Environmental
☒ Internet	☐ Financial
☐ MEDICAL/HEALTHCARE	☐ Real Estate
☐ Biotechnology	☐ Transportation
☐ Healthcare Services	☐ Publishing
☐ Life Sciences	☐ Food
☐ Medical Products	☐ Franchises
☒ INDUSTRIAL	☒ DIVERSIFIED
☐ Advanced Materials	☐ MISCELLANEOUS
☒ Chemicals	
☐ Instruments & Controls	

STAGE PREFERENCE

☒ EARLY STAGE
☐ Seed
☒ Start-up
☒ 1st Stage
☒ LATER STAGE
☒ 2nd Stage
☒ Mature
☒ Mezzanine
☒ LBO/MBO
☐ Turnaround
☐ INT'L EXPANSION
☐ WILL CONSIDER ALL
☐ VENTURE LEASING

Other Locations:

Affiliation:
Minimum Investment: $1 Million or more
Capital Under Management: Less than $100 Million

GEOGRAPHIC PREF

☐ East Coast
☐ West Coast
☐ Northeast
☐ Mid Atlantic
☐ Gulf States
☐ Northwest
☐ Southeast
☐ Southwest
☐ Midwest
☐ Central
☐ Local to Office
☐ Other Geo Pref

FIRST CHICAGO EQUITY CAPITAL

Three First National Plaza
Suite 1210
Chicago IL 60670-0610

Phone (312) 732-6281   Fax (312) 732-7483

PROFESSIONALS	TITLE
Eric Larson	Managing General Partner
Carol Bramson	General Partner
Timothy Dugan	General Partner
Jefferey Holway	General Partner
Burton McGillivray	General Partner

INDUSTRY PREFERENCE

☒ INFORMATION INDUSTRY	☒ BASIC INDUSTRIES
☐ Communications	☐ Consumer
☐ Computer Equipment	☒ Distribution
☒ Computer Services	☒ Manufacturing
☒ Computer Components	☐ Retail
☐ Computer Entertainment	☐ Service
☒ Computer Education	☐ Wholesale
☐ Information Technologies	☒ SPECIFIC INDUSTRIES
☐ Computer Media	☐ Energy
☐ Software	☐ Environmental
☐ Internet	☐ Financial
☒ MEDICAL/HEALTHCARE	☐ Real Estate
☐ Biotechnology	☒ Transportation
☐ Healthcare Services	☐ Publishing
☒ Life Sciences	☐ Food
☒ Medical Products	☐ Franchises
☒ INDUSTRIAL	☒ DIVERSIFIED
☐ Advanced Materials	☐ MISCELLANEOUS
☐ Chemicals	
☒ Instruments & Controls	

STAGE PREFERENCE

☐ EARLY STAGE
☐ Seed
☐ Start-up
☐ 1st Stage
☒ LATER STAGE
☒ 2nd Stage
☐ Mature
☐ Mezzanine
☒ LBO/MBO
☐ Turnaround
☐ INT'L EXPANSION
☐ WILL CONSIDER ALL
☐ VENTURE LEASING

Other Locations:

Affiliation:
Minimum Investment: $1 Million or more
Capital Under Management: $100 to $500 Million

GEOGRAPHIC PREF

☐ East Coast
☐ West Coast
☐ Northeast
☐ Mid Atlantic
☐ Gulf States
☐ Northwest
☐ Southeast
☐ Southwest
☐ Midwest
☐ Central
☐ Local to Office
☐ Other Geo Pref

FRONTENAC CO.

135 South La Salle Street
Suite 3800
Chicago IL 60603

Phone (312) 368-0044   Fax (312) 368-9520

PROFESSIONALS	TITLE
Rodney L. Goldstein	General Partner
Roger S. McEniry	General Partner
Peter Carbery	General Partner
M. Laird Koldyke	General Partner
James E. Crawford III	General Partner
James E. Cowie	General Partner
Martin J. Koldyke	General Partner
Laura P. Pearl	General Partner

INDUSTRY PREFERENCE

☒ INFORMATION INDUSTRY
☐ Communications
☐ Computer Equipment
☐ Computer Services
☐ Computer Components
☐ Computer Entertainment
☐ Computer Education
☒ Information Technologies
☐ Computer Media
☐ Software
☐ Internet
☒ MEDICAL/HEALTHCARE
☐ Biotechnology
☒ Healthcare Services
☐ Life Sciences
☒ Medical Products
☐ INDUSTRIAL
☐ Advanced Materials
☐ Chemicals
☐ Instruments & Controls

☒ BASIC INDUSTRIES
☒ Consumer
☐ Distribution
☐ Manufacturing
☒ Retail
☒ Service
☐ Wholesale
☐ SPECIFIC INDUSTRIES
☐ Energy
☐ Environmental
☐ Financial
☐ Real Estate
☐ Transportation
☐ Publishing
☐ Food
☐ Franchises
☒ DIVERSIFIED
☐ MISCELLANEOUS

STAGE PREFERENCE

☒ EARLY STAGE
☒ Seed
☒ Start-up
☒ 1st Stage
☒ LATER STAGE
☒ 2nd Stage
☒ Mature
☒ Mezzanine
☒ LBO/MBO
☒ Turnaround
☐ INT'L EXPANSION
☐ WILL CONSIDER ALL
☒ VENTURE LEASING

Other Locations:

Affiliation:
Minimum Investment: $1 Million or more
Capital Under Management: Over $500 Million

GEOGRAPHIC PREF

☐ East Coast
☐ West Coast
☐ Northeast
☐ Mid Atlantic
☐ Gulf States
☐ Northwest
☐ Southeast
☐ Southwest
☐ Midwest
☐ Central
☐ Local to Office
☐ Other Geo Pref

GTCR GOLDER RAUNER LLC

6100 Sears Tower
Chicago IL 60606-6402

Phone (312) 382-2200   Fax (312) 382-2201

PROFESSIONALS	TITLE
Philip A. Canfield	Principal
Edgar D. Jannotta, Jr.	Principal
Joseph P. Nolan	Principal
David A. Donnini	Principal
William C. Kessinger	Principal
Bruce V. Rauner	Principal
Donald J. Edwards	Principal

INDUSTRY PREFERENCE

☒ INFORMATION INDUSTRY
☒ Communications
☒ Computer Equipment
☒ Computer Services
☐ Computer Components
☐ Computer Entertainment
☒ Computer Education
☒ Information Technologies
☐ Computer Media
☒ Software
☒ Internet
☒ MEDICAL/HEALTHCARE
☐ Biotechnology
☒ Healthcare Services
☐ Life Sciences
☐ Medical Products
☐ INDUSTRIAL
☐ Advanced Materials
☐ Chemicals
☐ Instruments & Controls

☒ BASIC INDUSTRIES
☐ Consumer
☒ Distribution
☐ Manufacturing
☒ Retail
☒ Service
☐ Wholesale
☒ SPECIFIC INDUSTRIES
☐ Energy
☐ Environmental
☒ Financial
☐ Real Estate
☐ Transportation
☐ Publishing
☐ Food
☐ Franchises
☒ DIVERSIFIED
☒ MISCELLANEOUS
   Outsourcing

STAGE PREFERENCE

☐ EARLY STAGE
☐ Seed
☐ Start-up
☐ 1st Stage
☒ LATER STAGE
☐ 2nd Stage
☒ Mature
☐ Mezzanine
☒ LBO/MBO
☐ Turnaround
☐ INT'L EXPANSION
☐ WILL CONSIDER ALL
☐ VENTURE LEASING

Other Locations:

Affiliation:
Minimum Investment: $1 Million or more
Capital Under Management: Over $500 Million

GEOGRAPHIC PREF

☐ East Coast
☐ West Coast
☐ Northeast
☐ Mid Atlantic
☐ Gulf States
☐ Northwest
☐ Southeast
☐ Southwest
☐ Midwest
☐ Central
☐ Local to Office
☐ Other Geo Pref

INROADS CAPITAL PARTNERS

1603 Orrington Avenue
Suite 2050
Evanston IL 60201

Phone (847) 864-2000   Fax (847) 864-9692

PROFESSIONALS	TITLE
Sona Wang	General Partner
Jerrold Carrington	General Partner

INDUSTRY PREFERENCE

☐ INFORMATION INDUSTRY	☒ BASIC INDUSTRIES
☐ Communications	☒ Consumer
☐ Computer Equipment	☐ Distribution
☐ Computer Services	☐ Manufacturing
☐ Computer Components	☒ Retail
☐ Computer Entertainment	☐ Service
☐ Computer Education	☐ Wholesale
☐ Information Technologies	☒ SPECIFIC INDUSTRIES
☐ Computer Media	☐ Energy
☐ Software	☐ Environmental
☐ Internet	☐ Financial
☒ MEDICAL/HEALTHCARE	☐ Real Estate
☐ Biotechnology	☐ Transportation
☐ Healthcare Services	☒ Publishing
☐ Life Sciences	☐ Food
☒ Medical Products	☐ Franchises
☐ INDUSTRIAL	☒ DIVERSIFIED
☐ Advanced Materials	☐ MISCELLANEOUS
☐ Chemicals	Publishing
☐ Instruments & Controls	

STAGE PREFERENCE

☐ EARLY STAGE
☐ Seed
☐ Start-up
☐ 1st Stage
☒ LATER STAGE
☒ 2nd Stage
☐ Mature
☐ Mezzanine
☒ LBO/MBO
☐ Turnaround
☐ INT'L EXPANSION
☐ WILL CONSIDER ALL
☐ VENTURE LEASING

Other Locations:

Affiliation:
Minimum Investment: Less than $1 Million
Capital Under Management: Less than $100 Million

GEOGRAPHIC PREF

☐ East Coast
☐ West Coast
☐ Northeast
☐ Mid Atlantic
☐ Gulf States
☐ Northwest
☐ Southeast
☐ Southwest
☐ Midwest
☐ Central
☐ Local to Office
☐ Other Geo Pref

JK&B CAPITAL

205 North Michigan
Suite 808
Chicago IL 60601

Phone (312) 946-1200   Fax (312) 946-1103

PROFESSIONALS	TITLE
David Kronfeld	Chairman
Tasha Seitz	Principal Member
Thomas M. Neustaetter	Executive Member
Constance Capone	Principal Member
Nancy O'Leary	Member
Robert Humes	Executive Member
Richard Finkelstein	Executive Member

INDUSTRY PREFERENCE

☒ INFORMATION INDUSTRY	☒ BASIC INDUSTRIES
☒ Communications	☐ Consumer
☒ Computer Equipment	☒ Distribution
☒ Computer Services	☐ Manufacturing
☒ Computer Components	☐ Retail
☐ Computer Entertainment	☐ Service
☐ Computer Education	☐ Wholesale
☐ Information Technologies	☒ SPECIFIC INDUSTRIES
☐ Computer Media	☐ Energy
☐ Software	☐ Environmental
☐ Internet	☒ Financial
☐ MEDICAL/HEALTHCARE	☐ Real Estate
☐ Biotechnology	☐ Transportation
☐ Healthcare Services	☐ Publishing
☐ Life Sciences	☐ Food
☐ Medical Products	☐ Franchises
☒ INDUSTRIAL	☒ DIVERSIFIED
☐ Advanced Materials	☒ MISCELLANEOUS
☐ Chemicals	
☒ Instruments & Controls	

STAGE PREFERENCE

☒ EARLY STAGE
☐ Seed
☐ Start-up
☒ 1st Stage
☒ LATER STAGE
☒ 2nd Stage
☐ Mature
☒ Mezzanine
☐ LBO/MBO
☐ Turnaround
☐ INT'L EXPANSION
☐ WILL CONSIDER ALL
☐ VENTURE LEASING

Other Locations:

Affiliation:
Minimum Investment: Less than $1 Million
Capital Under Management: $100 to $500 Million

GEOGRAPHIC PREF

☐ East Coast
☐ West Coast
☐ Northeast
☐ Mid Atlantic
☐ Gulf States
☐ Northwest
☐ Southeast
☐ Southwest
☐ Midwest
☐ Central
☐ Local to Office
☐ Other Geo Pref

LASALLE CAPITAL GROUP INC.

70 West Madison Street
Chicago IL 60602

Phone (312) 236-7041   Fax (312) 236-0720

PROFESSIONALS	TITLE
Charles S. Meyer	Chairman
Rocco J. Martino	Partner
Anthony R. Pesavento	Partner

INDUSTRY PREFERENCE

☒ INFORMATION INDUSTRY	☒ BASIC INDUSTRIES
☐ Communications	☒ Consumer
☐ Computer Equipment	☒ Distribution
☐ Computer Services	☒ Manufacturing
☐ Computer Components	☒ Retail
☐ Computer Entertainment	☐ Service
☒ Computer Education	☐ Wholesale
☐ Information Technologies	☐ SPECIFIC INDUSTRIES
☐ Computer Media	☐ Energy
☐ Software	☐ Environmental
☐ Internet	☐ Financial
☐ MEDICAL/HEALTHCARE	☐ Real Estate
☐ Biotechnology	☐ Transportation
☐ Healthcare Services	☐ Publishing
☐ Life Sciences	☐ Food
☐ Medical Products	☐ Franchises
☐ INDUSTRIAL	☒ DIVERSIFIED
☐ Advanced Materials	☐ MISCELLANEOUS
☐ Chemicals	
☐ Instruments & Controls	

STAGE PREFERENCE

☐ EARLY STAGE	
☐ Seed	
☐ Start-up	
☐ 1st Stage	
☒ LATER STAGE	
☐ 2nd Stage	
☐ Mature	
☐ Mezzanine	
☒ LBO/MBO	
☐ Turnaround	
☐ INT'L EXPANSION	
☐ WILL CONSIDER ALL	
☐ VENTURE LEASING	

Other Locations:

Affiliation:
Minimum Investment: Less than $1 Million
Capital Under Management: Less than $100 Million

GEOGRAPHIC PREF

☐ East Coast	
☐ West Coast	
☐ Northeast	
☐ Mid Atlantic	
☐ Gulf States	
☐ Northwest	
☐ Southeast	
☐ Southwest	
☐ Midwest	
☐ Central	
☐ Local to Office	
☐ Other Geo Pref	

MADISON DEARBORN PARTNERS, INC.

Three First National Plaza
Suite 3800
Chicago IL 60602

Phone (312) 895-1000   Fax (312) 895-1111

PROFESSIONALS	TITLE
John Canning, Jr.	President
Nicholas W. Alexox	Managing Director
Benjamin Chereskin	Managing Director
Paul J. Finnegan	Managing Director
William Hunckler	Managing Director
Justin S. Huscher	Managing Director
Gary Little	Managing Director
Samuel M. Mencoff	Managing Director

INDUSTRY PREFERENCE

☒ INFORMATION INDUSTRY	☒ BASIC INDUSTRIES
☒ Communications	☒ Consumer
☒ Computer Equipment	☒ Distribution
☒ Computer Services	☒ Manufacturing
☒ Computer Components	☒ Retail
☐ Computer Entertainment	☒ Service
☒ Computer Education	☐ Wholesale
☒ Information Technologies	☒ SPECIFIC INDUSTRIES
☒ Computer Media	☒ Energy
☒ Software	☒ Environmental
☒ Internet	☐ Financial
☒ MEDICAL/HEALTHCARE	☐ Real Estate
☒ Biotechnology	☒ Transportation
☒ Healthcare Services	☐ Publishing
☒ Life Sciences	☐ Food
☒ Medical Products	☐ Franchises
☒ INDUSTRIAL	☒ DIVERSIFIED
☐ Advanced Materials	☐ MISCELLANEOUS
☒ Chemicals	
☐ Instruments & Controls	

STAGE PREFERENCE

☐ EARLY STAGE	
☐ Seed	
☐ Start-up	
☐ 1st Stage	
☒ LATER STAGE	
☒ 2nd Stage	
☒ Mature	
☒ Mezzanine	
☒ LBO/MBO	
☒ Turnaround	
☐ INT'L EXPANSION	
☐ WILL CONSIDER ALL	
☒ VENTURE LEASING	

Other Locations:

Affiliation:
Minimum Investment: $1 Million or more
Capital Under Management: Over $500 Million

GEOGRAPHIC PREF

☐ East Coast	
☐ West Coast	
☐ Northeast	
☐ Mid Atlantic	
☐ Gulf States	
☐ Northwest	
☐ Southeast	
☐ Southwest	
☐ Midwest	
☐ Central	
☐ Local to Office	
☐ Other Geo Pref	

MARQUETTE VENTURE PARTNERS

520 Lake Cook Road
Suite 450
Deerfield IL 60015

Phone (847) 940-1700   Fax (847) 940-1724

PROFESSIONALS	TITLE
James E. Daverman	General Partner
Lloyd D. Ruth	General Partner

INDUSTRY PREFERENCE

☒ INFORMATION INDUSTRY	☒ BASIC INDUSTRIES
☒ Communications	☒ Consumer
☒ Computer Equipment	☒ Distribution
☒ Computer Services	☐ Manufacturing
☒ Computer Components	☐ Retail
☐ Computer Entertainment	☒ Service
☒ Computer Education	☐ Wholesale
☒ Information Technologies	☐ SPECIFIC INDUSTRIES
☒ Computer Media	☐ Energy
☒ Software	☐ Environmental
☒ Internet	☐ Financial
☒ MEDICAL/HEALTHCARE	☐ Real Estate
☒ Biotechnology	☐ Transportation
☒ Healthcare Services	☐ Publishing
☒ Life Sciences	☐ Food
☒ Medical Products	☐ Franchises
☐ INDUSTRIAL	☒ DIVERSIFIED
☐ Advanced Materials	☐ MISCELLANEOUS
☐ Chemicals	
☐ Instruments & Controls	

STAGE PREFERENCE

☒ EARLY STAGE
☒ Seed
☒ Start-up
☒ 1st Stage
☒ LATER STAGE
☒ 2nd Stage
☐ Mature
☐ Mezzanine
☐ LBO/MBO
☐ Turnaround
☐ INT'L EXPANSION
☐ WILL CONSIDER ALL
☐ VENTURE LEASING

Other Locations:

Affiliation:
Minimum Investment: Less than $1 Million
Capital Under Management: $100 to $500 Million

GEOGRAPHIC PREF

☒ East Coast
☐ West Coast
☐ Northeast
☐ Mid Atlantic
☐ Gulf States
☐ Northwest
☐ Southeast
☐ Southwest
☐ Midwest
☐ Central
☐ Local to Office
☒ Other Geo Pref
    East Coast, Rocky
    Mountian States

MESIROW FINANCIAL PRIVATE EQUITY

350 North Clark Street
Chicago IL 60610

Phone (312) 595-6099   Fax (312) 595-6211

PROFESSIONALS	TITLE
James C. Tyree	Chairman & CEO
William P. Sutter, Jr.	Sr. Managing Director
Daniel P. Howell	Sr. Managing Director
Thomas E. Galuhn	Sr. Managing Director

INDUSTRY PREFERENCE

☒ INFORMATION INDUSTRY	☒ BASIC INDUSTRIES
☐ Communications	☒ Consumer
☐ Computer Equipment	☒ Distribution
☐ Computer Services	☒ Manufacturing
☐ Computer Components	☐ Retail
☐ Computer Entertainment	☒ Service
☒ Computer Education	☐ Wholesale
☐ Information Technologies	☒ SPECIFIC INDUSTRIES
☐ Computer Media	☐ Energy
☐ Software	☐ Environmental
☐ Internet	☒ Financial
☐ MEDICAL/HEALTHCARE	☐ Real Estate
☐ Biotechnology	☐ Transportation
☐ Healthcare Services	☐ Publishing
☐ Life Sciences	☐ Food
☐ Medical Products	☐ Franchises
☐ INDUSTRIAL	☒ DIVERSIFIED
☐ Advanced Materials	☐ MISCELLANEOUS
☐ Chemicals	
☐ Instruments & Controls	

STAGE PREFERENCE

☐ EARLY STAGE
☐ Seed
☐ Start-up
☐ 1st Stage
☒ LATER STAGE
☒ 2nd Stage
☒ Mature
☐ Mezzanine
☒ LBO/MBO
☐ Turnaround
☐ INT'L EXPANSION
☐ WILL CONSIDER ALL
☐ VENTURE LEASING

Other Locations:

Affiliation: Mesirow Capital Markets, Inc.
Minimum Investment: $1 Million or more
Capital Under Management: $100 to $500 Million

GEOGRAPHIC PREF

☐ East Coast
☐ West Coast
☐ Northeast
☐ Mid Atlantic
☐ Gulf States
☐ Northwest
☐ Southeast
☐ Southwest
☐ Midwest
☐ Central
☐ Local to Office
☐ Other Geo Pref

NORTH AMERICAN BUSINESS DEVELOPMENT CO.

135 South LaSalle Street
Suite 4000
Chicago IL 60603

Phone (312) 332-4950   Fax (312) 332-1540

PROFESSIONALS	TITLE
Robert L. Underwood	Executive Vice President
R. David Bergonia	Executive Vice President
Charles Palmer	President
Samir D. Desai	Vice President
Craig Dougherty	Principal
Raymond A. Fleites	Vice President

INDUSTRY PREFERENCE

- ☐ INFORMATION INDUSTRY
- ☐ Communications
- ☐ Computer Equipment
- ☐ Computer Services
- ☐ Computer Components
- ☐ Computer Entertainment
- ☐ Computer Education
- ☐ Information Technologies
- ☐ Computer Media
- ☐ Software
- ☐ Internet
- ☐ MEDICAL/HEALTHCARE
- ☐ Biotechnology
- ☐ Healthcare Services
- ☐ Life Sciences
- ☐ Medical Products
- ☐ INDUSTRIAL
- ☐ Advanced Materials
- ☐ Chemicals
- ☐ Instruments & Controls

- ☐ BASIC INDUSTRIES
- ☐ Consumer
- ☐ Distribution
- ☐ Manufacturing
- ☐ Retail
- ☐ Service
- ☐ Wholesale
- ☐ SPECIFIC INDUSTRIES
- ☐ Energy
- ☐ Environmental
- ☐ Financial
- ☐ Real Estate
- ☐ Transportation
- ☐ Publishing
- ☐ Food
- ☐ Franchises
- ☒ DIVERSIFIED
- ☐ MISCELLANEOUS

STAGE PREFERENCE

- ☐ EARLY STAGE
- ☐ Seed
- ☐ Start-up
- ☐ 1st Stage
- ☒ LATER STAGE
- ☒ 2nd Stage
- ☒ Mature
- ☐ Mezzanine
- ☒ LBO/MBO
- ☐ Turnaround
- ☐ INT'L EXPANSION
- ☐ WILL CONSIDER ALL
- ☐ VENTURE LEASING

Other Locations: Ft. Lauderdale FL

Affiliation:
Minimum Investment: $1 Million or more
Capital Under Management: $100 to $500 Million

GEOGRAPHIC PREF

- ☐ East Coast
- ☐ West Coast
- ☐ Northeast
- ☐ Mid Atlantic
- ☐ Gulf States
- ☐ Northwest
- ☐ Southeast
- ☐ Southwest
- ☐ Midwest
- ☐ Central
- ☐ Local to Office
- ☒ Other Geo Pref
- IL, FL

OPEN PRAIRIE VENTURES

115 North Neil Street
Suite 209
Champaign IL 61820

Phone (217) 351-7000   Fax (217) 351-7051

PROFESSIONALS	TITLE
Dennis Spice	Managing Member
Andrew Jones	Managaing Member
James Schultz	Managing Member

INDUSTRY PREFERENCE

- ☒ INFORMATION INDUSTRY
- ☒ Communications
- ☒ Computer Equipment
- ☒ Computer Services
- ☒ Computer Components
- ☐ Computer Entertainment
- ☐ Computer Education
- ☐ Information Technologies
- ☐ Computer Media
- ☒ Software
- ☒ Internet
- ☒ MEDICAL/HEALTHCARE
- ☐ Biotechnology
- ☐ Healthcare Services
- ☐ Life Sciences
- ☒ Medical Products
- ☐ INDUSTRIAL
- ☐ Advanced Materials
- ☐ Chemicals
- ☐ Instruments & Controls

- ☐ BASIC INDUSTRIES
- ☐ Consumer
- ☐ Distribution
- ☐ Manufacturing
- ☐ Retail
- ☐ Service
- ☐ Wholesale
- ☐ SPECIFIC INDUSTRIES
- ☐ Energy
- ☐ Environmental
- ☐ Financial
- ☐ Real Estate
- ☐ Transportation
- ☐ Publishing
- ☐ Food
- ☐ Franchises
- ☒ DIVERSIFIED
- ☒ MISCELLANEOUS

STAGE PREFERENCE

- ☒ EARLY STAGE
- ☒ Seed
- ☒ Start-up
- ☐ 1st Stage
- ☐ LATER STAGE
- ☐ 2nd Stage
- ☐ Mature
- ☐ Mezzanine
- ☐ LBO/MBO
- ☐ Turnaround
- ☐ INT'L EXPANSION
- ☐ WILL CONSIDER ALL
- ☐ VENTURE LEASING

Other Locations:

Affiliation:
Minimum Investment: Less than $1 Million
Capital Under Management: Less than $100 Million

GEOGRAPHIC PREF

- ☐ East Coast
- ☐ West Coast
- ☐ Northeast
- ☐ Mid Atlantic
- ☐ Gulf States
- ☐ Northwest
- ☐ Southeast
- ☐ Southwest
- ☐ Midwest
- ☐ Central
- ☐ Local to Office
- ☐ Other Geo Pref

PENMAN PARTNERS

333 West Wacker Drive
Suite 1450
Chicago IL 60606

Phone (312) 845-9055   Fax (312) 845-9056

PROFESSIONALS	TITLE
Lawrence Manson	General Partner

INDUSTRY PREFERENCE

☒ INFORMATION INDUSTRY   ☒ BASIC INDUSTRIES
☒ Communications   ☒ Consumer
☒ Computer Equipment   ☐ Distribution
☒ Computer Services   ☐ Manufacturing
☒ Computer Components   ☐ Retail
☐ Computer Entertainment ☐ Service
☒ Computer Education   ☐ Wholesale
☐ Information Technologies ☒ SPECIFIC INDUSTRIES
☐ Computer Media   ☐ Energy
☒ Software   ☐ Environmental
☒ Internet   ☐ Financial
☒ MEDICAL/HEALTHCARE   ☐ Real Estate
☐ Biotechnology   ☒ Transportation
☒ Healthcare Services   ☒ Publishing
☐ Life Sciences   ☐ Food
☒ Medical Products   ☐ Franchises
☐ INDUSTRIAL   ☒ DIVERSIFIED
☐ Advanced Materials   ☐ MISCELLANEOUS
☐ Chemicals
☐ Instruments & Controls

STAGE PREFERENCE

☐ EARLY STAGE
☐ Seed
☐ Start-up
☐ 1st Stage
☒ LATER STAGE
☐ 2nd Stage
☐ Mature
☐ Mezzanine
☒ LBO/MBO
☐ Turnaround
☐ INT'L EXPANSION
☐ WILL CONSIDER ALL
☐ VENTURE LEASING

Other Locations:

Affiliation:
Minimum Investment: $1 Million or more
Capital Under Management: Less than $100 Million

GEOGRAPHIC PREF

☐ East Coast
☐ West Coast
☐ Northeast
☐ Mid Atlantic
☐ Gulf States
☐ Northwest
☐ Southeast
☐ Southwest
☐ Midwest
☐ Central
☐ Local to Office
☐ Other Geo Pref

PFINGSTEN PARTNERS, LP

520 Lake Cook Road
Suite 375
Deerfield IL 60015-5291

Phone (847) 374-9140   Fax (847) 374-9150

PROFESSIONALS	TITLE
Thomas S. Bagley	Sr. Managing Director
Richard W. Manning	Managing Director
John Underwood	Managing Director

INDUSTRY PREFERENCE

☒ INFORMATION INDUSTRY   ☒ BASIC INDUSTRIES
☐ Communications   ☐ Consumer
☐ Computer Equipment   ☒ Distribution
☐ Computer Services   ☒ Manufacturing
☐ Computer Components   ☐ Retail
☐ Computer Entertainment ☒ Service
☐ Computer Education   ☐ Wholesale
☒ Information Technologies ☐ SPECIFIC INDUSTRIES
☒ Computer Media   ☐ Energy
☒ Software   ☐ Environmental
☒ Internet   ☐ Financial
☐ MEDICAL/HEALTHCARE   ☐ Real Estate
☐ Biotechnology   ☐ Transportation
☐ Healthcare Services   ☐ Publishing
☐ Life Sciences   ☐ Food
☐ Medical Products   ☐ Franchises
☐ INDUSTRIAL   ☒ DIVERSIFIED
☐ Advanced Materials   ☐ MISCELLANEOUS
☐ Chemicals
☐ Instruments & Controls

STAGE PREFERENCE

☐ EARLY STAGE
☐ Seed
☐ Start-up
☐ 1st Stage
☒ LATER STAGE
☒ 2nd Stage
☒ Mature
☒ Mezzanine
☒ LBO/MBO
☒ Turnaround
☐ INT'L EXPANSION
☐ WILL CONSIDER ALL
☒ VENTURE LEASING

Other Locations:

Affiliation:
Minimum Investment: $1 Million or more
Capital Under Management: $100 to $500 Million

GEOGRAPHIC PREF

☐ East Coast
☐ West Coast
☐ Northeast
☐ Mid Atlantic
☐ Gulf States
☐ Northwest
☐ Southeast
☐ Southwest
☐ Midwest
☐ Central
☐ Local to Office
☐ Other Geo Pref

PLATINUM VENTURE PARTNERS

1815 S. Meyers Road
Oakbrook Terrace IL 60181

Phone (630) 691-9174   Fax (630) 691-9134

PROFESSIONALS	TITLE
Andrew Filipowski	Chairman/Founder
Michael Santer	Cofounder

INDUSTRY PREFERENCE

- ☒ INFORMATION INDUSTRY
- ☒ Communications
- ☒ Computer Equipment
- ☒ Computer Services
- ☒ Computer Components
- ☒ Computer Entertainment
- ☒ Computer Education
- ☒ Information Technologies
- ☒ Computer Media
- ☒ Software
- ☒ Internet
- ☐ MEDICAL/HEALTHCARE
- ☐ Biotechnology
- ☐ Healthcare Services
- ☐ Life Sciences
- ☐ Medical Products
- ☒ INDUSTRIAL
- ☐ Advanced Materials
- ☐ Chemicals
- ☒ Instruments & Controls

- ☒ BASIC INDUSTRIES
- ☒ Consumer
- ☐ Distribution
- ☐ Manufacturing
- ☐ Retail
- ☐ Service
- ☐ Wholesale
- ☒ SPECIFIC INDUSTRIES
- ☐ Energy
- ☐ Environmental
- ☐ Financial
- ☐ Real Estate
- ☐ Transportation
- ☐ Publishing
- ☒ Food
- ☐ Franchises
- ☒ DIVERSIFIED
- ☒ MISCELLANEOUS
- Restaurants

STAGE PREFERENCE

- ☒ EARLY STAGE
- ☐ Seed
- ☒ Start-up
- ☒ 1st Stage
- ☒ LATER STAGE
- ☒ 2nd Stage
- ☐ Mature
- ☐ Mezzanine
- ☐ LBO/MBO
- ☐ Turnaround
- ☐ INT'L EXPANSION
- ☐ WILL CONSIDER ALL
- ☐ VENTURE LEASING

Other Locations:

Affiliation:
Minimum Investment: Less than $1 Million
Capital Under Management: Less than $100 Million

GEOGRAPHIC PREF

- ☐ East Coast
- ☐ West Coast
- ☐ Northeast
- ☐ Mid Atlantic
- ☐ Gulf States
- ☐ Northwest
- ☐ Southeast
- ☐ Southwest
- ☐ Midwest
- ☐ Central
- ☐ Local to Office
- ☐ Other Geo Pref

PORTAGE VENTURE PARTNERS, LLC

One Northfield Plaza
Suite 530
Northfield IL 60093

Phone (847) 446-9460   Fax (847) 446-9470

PROFESSIONALS	TITLE
David Horn	Chairman
Edward Chandler	Managing Director
Judith Bultman Meyer	Managing Director
Matthew B. McCall	Partner

INDUSTRY PREFERENCE

- ☒ INFORMATION INDUSTRY
- ☒ Communications
- ☒ Computer Equipment
- ☒ Computer Services
- ☒ Computer Components
- ☒ Computer Entertainment
- ☒ Computer Education
- ☒ Information Technologies
- ☒ Computer Media
- ☒ Software
- ☒ Internet
- ☒ MEDICAL/HEALTHCARE
- ☒ Biotechnology
- ☒ Healthcare Services
- ☒ Life Sciences
- ☒ Medical Products
- ☒ INDUSTRIAL
- ☒ Advanced Materials
- ☒ Chemicals
- ☒ Instruments & Controls

- ☒ BASIC INDUSTRIES
- ☒ Consumer
- ☒ Distribution
- ☐ Manufacturing
- ☒ Retail
- ☒ Service
- ☐ Wholesale
- ☐ SPECIFIC INDUSTRIES
- ☐ Energy
- ☐ Environmental
- ☐ Financial
- ☐ Real Estate
- ☐ Transportation
- ☐ Publishing
- ☐ Food
- ☐ Franchises
- ☒ DIVERSIFIED
- ☒ MISCELLANEOUS

STAGE PREFERENCE

- ☒ EARLY STAGE
- ☐ Seed
- ☒ Start-up
- ☒ 1st Stage
- ☒ LATER STAGE
- ☒ 2nd Stage
- ☐ Mature
- ☐ Mezzanine
- ☐ LBO/MBO
- ☐ Turnaround
- ☐ INT'L EXPANSION
- ☐ WILL CONSIDER ALL
- ☐ VENTURE LEASING

Other Locations:

Affiliation:
Minimum Investment: Less than $1 Million
Capital Under Management: $100 to $500 Million

GEOGRAPHIC PREF

- ☐ East Coast
- ☐ West Coast
- ☐ Northeast
- ☐ Mid Atlantic
- ☐ Gulf States
- ☐ Northwest
- ☐ Southeast
- ☐ Southwest
- ☐ Midwest
- ☐ Central
- ☐ Local to Office
- ☐ Other Geo Pref

RIDGE CAPITAL PARTNERS, LLC

257 E. Main Street
Suite 300
Barrington IL 60010

Phone (847) 381-2510   Fax (847) 381-2599

PROFESSIONALS	TITLE
J. Bradley Davis	Partner
D. Taylor Mayoras	Partner
Ross Posner	Partner
Clark Davis	Partner

INDUSTRY PREFERENCE

☒ INFORMATION INDUSTRY
☒ Communications
☐ Computer Equipment
☐ Computer Services
☒ Computer Components
☐ Computer Entertainment
☐ Computer Education
☒ Information Technologies
☐ Computer Media
☐ Software
☐ Internet
☒ MEDICAL/HEALTHCARE
☐ Biotechnology
☐ Healthcare Services
☐ Life Sciences
☒ Medical Products
☒ INDUSTRIAL
☒ Advanced Materials
☒ Chemicals
☒ Instruments & Controls

☒ BASIC INDUSTRIES
☒ Consumer
☒ Distribution
☒ Manufacturing
☐ Retail
☒ Service
☐ Wholesale
☒ SPECIFIC INDUSTRIES
☐ Energy
☐ Environmental
☒ Financial
☐ Real Estate
☒ Transportation
☒ Publishing
☐ Food
☐ Franchises
☒ DIVERSIFIED
☐ MISCELLANEOUS

STAGE PREFERENCE

☐ EARLY STAGE
☐ Seed
☐ Start-up
☐ 1st Stage
☒ LATER STAGE
☐ 2nd Stage
☒ Mature
☐ Mezzanine
☒ LBO/MBO
☐ Turnaround
☐ INT'L EXPANSION
☐ WILL CONSIDER ALL
☐ VENTURE LEASING

Other Locations:

Affiliation:
Minimum Investment: $1 Million or more
Capital Under Management: Less than $100 Million

GEOGRAPHIC PREF

☐ East Coast
☐ West Coast
☐ Northeast
☐ Mid Atlantic
☐ Gulf States
☐ Northwest
☐ Southeast
☐ Southwest
☐ Midwest
☐ Central
☐ Local to Office
☐ Other Geo Pref

SB PARTNERS

7936 S. Cottage Grove Avenue
Chicago IL 60619

Phone (773) 371-7030   Fax (773) 371-7035

PROFESSIONALS	TITLE
David Shryock	CEO

INDUSTRY PREFERENCE

☐ INFORMATION INDUSTRY
☐ Communications
☐ Computer Equipment
☐ Computer Services
☐ Computer Components
☐ Computer Entertainment
☐ Computer Education
☐ Information Technologies
☐ Computer Media
☐ Software
☐ Internet
☐ MEDICAL/HEALTHCARE
☐ Biotechnology
☐ Healthcare Services
☐ Life Sciences
☐ Medical Products
☐ INDUSTRIAL
☐ Advanced Materials
☐ Chemicals
☐ Instruments & Controls

☐ BASIC INDUSTRIES
☐ Consumer
☐ Distribution
☐ Manufacturing
☐ Retail
☐ Service
☐ Wholesale
☐ SPECIFIC INDUSTRIES
☐ Energy
☐ Environmental
☐ Financial
☐ Real Estate
☐ Transportation
☐ Publishing
☐ Food
☐ Franchises
☒ DIVERSIFIED
☐ MISCELLANEOUS

STAGE PREFERENCE

☒ EARLY STAGE
☐ Seed
☐ Start-up
☒ 1st Stage
☒ LATER STAGE
☒ 2nd Stage
☐ Mature
☐ Mezzanine
☒ LBO/MBO
☐ Turnaround
☐ INT'L EXPANSION
☐ WILL CONSIDER ALL
☐ VENTURE LEASING
SBIC
Other Locations:

Affiliation:
Minimum Investment: Less than $1 Million
Capital Under Management: Less than $100 Million

GEOGRAPHIC PREF

☐ East Coast
☐ West Coast
☐ Northeast
☐ Mid Atlantic
☐ Gulf States
☐ Northwest
☐ Southeast
☐ Southwest
☐ Midwest
☐ Central
☐ Local to Office
☐ Other Geo Pref

THOMA CRESSEY EQUITY PARTNERS

233 South Wacker Drive
Sears Tower, 44th Floor
Chicago IL 60603-3402

Phone (312) 777-4444   Fax (312) 777-4445

PROFESSIONALS	TITLE
Carl D. Thoma	Partner/Founder
Bryan C. Cressey	Partner/Founder
Lee M. Mitchell	Partner
David Mayer	Partner
Robert Levin	Partner
Daniel Richards	Partner
David Schuppan	Partner

INDUSTRY PREFERENCE

- ☒ INFORMATION INDUSTRY
- ☒ Communications
- ☒ Computer Equipment
- ☒ Computer Services
- ☒ Computer Components
- ☐ Computer Entertainment
- ☒ Computer Education
- ☒ Information Technologies
- ☒ Computer Media
- ☒ Software
- ☒ Internet
- ☒ MEDICAL/HEALTHCARE
- ☒ Biotechnology
- ☒ Healthcare Services
- ☒ Life Sciences
- ☒ Medical Products
- ☒ INDUSTRIAL
- ☒ Advanced Materials
- ☒ Chemicals
- ☒ Instruments & Controls

- ☒ BASIC INDUSTRIES
- ☒ Consumer
- ☒ Distribution
- ☒ Manufacturing
- ☒ Retail
- ☒ Service
- ☒ Wholesale
- ☒ SPECIFIC INDUSTRIES
- ☒ Energy
- ☒ Environmental
- ☒ Financial
- ☐ Real Estate
- ☒ Transportation
- ☒ Publishing
- ☐ Food
- ☐ Franchises
- ☒ DIVERSIFIED
- ☐ MISCELLANEOUS

STAGE PREFERENCE

- ☐ EARLY STAGE
- ☐ Seed
- ☐ Start-up
- ☐ 1st Stage
- ☒ LATER STAGE
- ☒ 2nd Stage
- ☒ Mature
- ☐ Mezzanine
- ☒ LBO/MBO
- ☐ Turnaround
- ☐ INT'L EXPANSION
- ☐ WILL CONSIDER ALL
- ☐ VENTURE LEASING

Other Locations: Denver CO, San Francisco CA

Affiliation:
Minimum Investment: $1 Million or more
Capital Under Management: $100 to $500 Million

GEOGRAPHIC PREF

- ☐ East Coast
- ☐ West Coast
- ☐ Northeast
- ☐ Mid Atlantic
- ☐ Gulf States
- ☐ Northwest
- ☐ Southeast
- ☐ Southwest
- ☐ Midwest
- ☐ Central
- ☐ Local to Office
- ☐ Other Geo Pref

TRANSCAP ASSOCIATES, INC.

900 Skokie Boulevard
Suite 210
Northbrook IL 60062

Phone (847) 753-9600   Fax (847) 753-9090

PROFESSIONALS	TITLE
Ira Edelson	President
Michael Epton	Vice President
Michael Sear	Executive Vice President
Thomas O'Hare	Managing Director

INDUSTRY PREFERENCE

- ☒ INFORMATION INDUSTRY
- ☒ Communications
- ☒ Computer Equipment
- ☒ Computer Services
- ☒ Computer Components
- ☒ Computer Entertainment
- ☐ Computer Education
- ☐ Information Technologies
- ☐ Computer Media
- ☐ Software
- ☐ Internet
- ☒ MEDICAL/HEALTHCARE
- ☐ Biotechnology
- ☐ Healthcare Services
- ☒ Life Sciences
- ☒ Medical Products
- ☒ INDUSTRIAL
- ☐ Advanced Materials
- ☒ Chemicals
- ☒ Instruments & Controls

- ☒ BASIC INDUSTRIES
- ☐ Consumer
- ☒ Distribution
- ☐ Manufacturing
- ☐ Retail
- ☐ Service
- ☒ Wholesale
- ☒ SPECIFIC INDUSTRIES
- ☐ Energy
- ☐ Environmental
- ☐ Financial
- ☐ Real Estate
- ☐ Transportation
- ☒ Publishing
- ☐ Food
- ☐ Franchises
- ☒ DIVERSIFIED
- ☒ MISCELLANEOUS
  Apparel, Electronic Games, Toys

STAGE PREFERENCE

- ☐ EARLY STAGE
- ☐ Seed
- ☐ Start-up
- ☐ 1st Stage
- ☒ LATER STAGE
- ☒ 2nd Stage
- ☐ Mature
- ☒ Mezzanine
- ☐ LBO/MBO
- ☐ Turnaround
- ☐ INT'L EXPANSION
- ☐ WILL CONSIDER ALL
- ☐ VENTURE LEASING

Other Locations: New York NY, Manhattan Beach CA

Affiliation:
Minimum Investment: Less than $1 Million
Capital Under Management: Less than $100 Million

GEOGRAPHIC PREF

- ☐ East Coast
- ☐ West Coast
- ☐ Northeast
- ☐ Mid Atlantic
- ☐ Gulf States
- ☐ Northwest
- ☐ Southeast
- ☐ Southwest
- ☐ Midwest
- ☐ Central
- ☐ Local to Office
- ☐ Other Geo Pref

TRIBUNE VENTURES

435 N. Michigan Avenue
Chicago IL 60611

Phone (312) 222-3893   Fax (312) 222-5993

PROFESSIONALS	TITLE
Andrew Oleszczuk	President
David Kniffin	Director
Shawn Luetchens	Manager

INDUSTRY PREFERENCE

☒ INFORMATION INDUSTRY
☒ Communications
☐ Computer Equipment
☐ Computer Services
☐ Computer Components
☐ Computer Entertainment
☒ Computer Education
☐ Information Technologies
☒ Computer Media
☒ Software
☒ Internet
☐ MEDICAL/HEALTHCARE
☐ Biotechnology
☐ Healthcare Services
☐ Life Sciences
☐ Medical Products
☐ INDUSTRIAL
☐ Advanced Materials
☐ Chemicals
☐ Instruments & Controls

☒ BASIC INDUSTRIES
☒ Consumer
☐ Distribution
☐ Manufacturing
☐ Retail
☐ Service
☐ Wholesale
☒ SPECIFIC INDUSTRIES
☐ Energy
☐ Environmental
☐ Financial
☐ Real Estate
☐ Transportation
☒ Publishing
☐ Food
☐ Franchises
☒ DIVERSIFIED
☐ MISCELLANEOUS

STAGE PREFERENCE

☐ EARLY STAGE
☐ Seed
☐ Start-up
☐ 1st Stage
☒ LATER STAGE
☒ 2nd Stage
☐ Mature
☐ Mezzanine
☐ LBO/MBO
☐ Turnaround
☐ INT'L EXPANSION
☐ WILL CONSIDER ALL
☐ VENTURE LEASING

Other Locations:

Affiliation:
Minimum Investment: $1 Million or more
Capital Under Management: $100 to $500 Million

GEOGRAPHIC PREF

☐ East Coast
☐ West Coast
☐ Northeast
☐ Mid Atlantic
☐ Gulf States
☐ Northwest
☐ Southeast
☐ Southwest
☐ Midwest
☐ Central
☐ Local to Office
☐ Other Geo Pref

TRIDENT CAPITAL

272 East Deerpath
Suite 304
Lake Forest IL 60045

Phone (847) 283-9890   Fax (847) 283-9901

PROFESSIONALS	TITLE
Robert C. McCormack	
Stephen S. Beitler	

INDUSTRY PREFERENCE

☒ INFORMATION INDUSTRY
☒ Communications
☒ Computer Equipment
☒ Computer Services
☒ Computer Components
☒ Computer Entertainment
☒ Computer Education
☒ Information Technologies
☐ Computer Media
☒ Software
☒ Internet
☐ MEDICAL/HEALTHCARE
☐ Biotechnology
☐ Healthcare Services
☐ Life Sciences
☐ Medical Products
☐ INDUSTRIAL
☐ Advanced Materials
☐ Chemicals
☐ Instruments & Controls

☒ BASIC INDUSTRIES
☐ Consumer
☐ Distribution
☐ Manufacturing
☐ Retail
☒ Service
☐ Wholesale
☒ SPECIFIC INDUSTRIES
☐ Energy
☐ Environmental
☒ Financial
☐ Real Estate
☐ Transportation
☐ Publishing
☐ Food
☐ Franchises
☒ DIVERSIFIED
☒ MISCELLANEOUS

STAGE PREFERENCE

☐ EARLY STAGE
☐ Seed
☐ Start-up
☐ 1st Stage
☒ LATER STAGE
☒ 2nd Stage
☒ Mature
☐ Mezzanine
☒ LBO/MBO
☐ Turnaround
☐ INT'L EXPANSION
☐ WILL CONSIDER ALL
☐ VENTURE LEASING

Other Locations: Menlo Park CA, Los Angeles CA, Westport CT, Washington D.C.

Affiliation:
Minimum Investment: $1 Million or more
Capital Under Management: $100 to $500 Million

GEOGRAPHIC PREF

☐ East Coast
☐ West Coast
☐ Northeast
☐ Mid Atlantic
☐ Gulf States
☐ Northwest
☐ Southeast
☐ Southwest
☐ Midwest
☐ Central
☐ Local to Office
☐ Other Geo Pref

VECTOR FUND MANAGEMENT

1751 Lake Cook Road
Suite 350
Deerfield IL 60015

Phone (847) 374-3862 Fax (847) 374-3899

PROFESSIONALS	TITLE
Ranjan Lal	Managing Director
K. Flynn McDonald	Managing Director
Peter Drake	Partner
D. Theodore Berghorst	Partner
James Foght	Partner

INDUSTRY PREFERENCE

☐ INFORMATION INDUSTRY	☐ BASIC INDUSTRIES
☐ Communications	☐ Consumer
☐ Computer Equipment	☐ Distribution
☐ Computer Services	☐ Manufacturing
☐ Computer Components	☐ Retail
☐ Computer Entertainment	☐ Service
☐ Computer Education	☐ Wholesale
☐ Information Technologies	☐ SPECIFIC INDUSTRIES
☐ Computer Media	☐ Energy
☐ Software	☐ Environmental
☐ Internet	☐ Financial
☒ MEDICAL/HEALTHCARE	☐ Real Estate
☒ Biotechnology	☐ Transportation
☒ Healthcare Services	☐ Publishing
☒ Life Sciences	☐ Food
☒ Medical Products	☐ Franchises
☐ INDUSTRIAL	☐ DIVERSIFIED
☐ Advanced Materials	☒ MISCELLANEOUS
☐ Chemicals	
☐ Instruments & Controls	

STAGE PREFERENCE

☐ EARLY STAGE
☐ Seed
☐ Start-up
☐ 1st Stage
☒ LATER STAGE
☒ 2nd Stage
☐ Mature
☒ Mezzanine
☐ LBO/MBO
☐ Turnaround
☐ INT'L EXPANSION
☐ WILL CONSIDER ALL
☐ VENTURE LEASING

Other Locations:

Affiliation:
Minimum Investment: $1 Million or more
Capital Under Management: $100 to $500 Million

GEOGRAPHIC PREF

☐ East Coast
☐ West Coast
☐ Northeast
☐ Mid Atlantic
☐ Gulf States
☐ Northwest
☐ Southeast
☐ Southwest
☐ Midwest
☐ Central
☐ Local to Office
☐ Other Geo Pref

WILLIAM BLAIR CAPITAL PARTNERS

222 West Adams Street
Chicago IL 60606-5312

Phone (312) 336-1600 Fax (312) 236-1042

PROFESSIONALS	TITLE
Gregg S. Newmark	Sr. Managing Director
Robert Blank	Managing Director
Ellen Carnahan	Managing Director
David Chandler	Managing Director
Ian Larkin	Managing Director
Arda Minocherhomjee	Managing Director
Tomothy M. Murray	Managing Director
Lawrence Shagrin	Managing Director

INDUSTRY PREFERENCE

☒ INFORMATION INDUSTRY	☒ BASIC INDUSTRIES
☒ Communications	☒ Consumer
☒ Computer Equipment	☒ Distribution
☒ Computer Services	☐ Manufacturing
☒ Computer Components	☐ Retail
☐ Computer Entertainment	☒ Service
☒ Computer Education	☐ Wholesale
☒ Information Technologies	☐ SPECIFIC INDUSTRIES
☐ Computer Media	☐ Energy
☒ Software	☐ Environmental
☒ Internet	☐ Financial
☒ MEDICAL/HEALTHCARE	☐ Real Estate
☐ Biotechnology	☐ Transportation
☒ Healthcare Services	☐ Publishing
☐ Life Sciences	☐ Food
☒ Medical Products	☐ Franchises
☐ INDUSTRIAL	☒ DIVERSIFIED
☐ Advanced Materials	☐ MISCELLANEOUS
☐ Chemicals	
☐ Instruments & Controls	

STAGE PREFERENCE

☒ EARLY STAGE
☐ Seed
☐ Start-up
☒ 1st Stage
☒ LATER STAGE
☒ 2nd Stage
☒ Mature
☒ Mezzanine
☒ LBO/MBO
☒ Turnaround
☐ INT'L EXPANSION
☐ WILL CONSIDER ALL
☒ VENTURE LEASING

Other Locations:

Affiliation: William Blair & Co.
Minimum Investment: $1 Million or more
Capital Under Management: $100 to $500 Million

GEOGRAPHIC PREF

☐ East Coast
☐ West Coast
☐ Northeast
☐ Mid Atlantic
☐ Gulf States
☐ Northwest
☐ Southeast
☐ Southwest
☐ Midwest
☐ Central
☐ Local to Office
☐ Other Geo Pref

WIND POINT PARTNERS

676 North Michigan Avenue
Suite 3300
Chicago IL 60611

Phone (312) 649-4000   Fax (312) 649-9644

PROFESSIONALS	TITLE
Robert L. Cummings	General Partner
James E. Forrest	General Partner

INDUSTRY PREFERENCE

☒ INFORMATION INDUSTRY	☒ BASIC INDUSTRIES
☒ Communications	☐ Consumer
☐ Computer Equipment	☐ Distribution
☐ Computer Services	☒ Manufacturing
☐ Computer Components	☐ Retail
☐ Computer Entertainment	☒ Service
☐ Computer Education	☐ Wholesale
☐ Information Technologies	☐ SPECIFIC INDUSTRIES
☐ Computer Media	☐ Energy
☐ Software	☐ Environmental
☐ Internet	☐ Financial
☒ MEDICAL/HEALTHCARE	☐ Real Estate
☒ Biotechnology	☐ Transportation
☐ Healthcare Services	☐ Publishing
☒ Life Sciences	☐ Food
☒ Medical Products	☐ Franchises
☐ INDUSTRIAL	☒ DIVERSIFIED
☐ Advanced Materials	☐ MISCELLANEOUS
☐ Chemicals	
☐ Instruments & Controls	

STAGE PREFERENCE

☒ EARLY STAGE
☐   Seed
☒   Start-up
☒   1st Stage
☒ LATER STAGE
☐   2nd Stage
☐   Mature
☐   Mezzanine
☒   LBO/MBO
☐   Turnaround
☐ INT'L EXPANSION
☐ WILL CONSIDER ALL
☐ VENTURE LEASING

Other Locations:

Affiliation:
Minimum Investment: $1 Million or more
Capital Under Management: $100 to $500 Million

GEOGRAPHIC PREF

☐   East Coast
☐   West Coast
☐   Northeast
☐   Mid Atlantic
☐   Gulf States
☐   Northwest
☐   Southeast
☐   Southwest
☐   Midwest
☐   Central
☐   Local to Office
☒   Other Geo Pref
      Great Lakes States

CAMBRIDGE VENTURES, LP

8440 Woodfield Crossing
Suite 315
Indianapolis IN 46240

Phone (317) 469-9704   Fax (317) 469-3926

PROFESSIONALS	TITLE
Jean Wojtowicz	President

INDUSTRY PREFERENCE

☐ INFORMATION INDUSTRY	☒ BASIC INDUSTRIES
☐ Communications	☐ Consumer
☐ Computer Equipment	☐ Distribution
☐ Computer Services	☒ Manufacturing
☐ Computer Components	☐ Retail
☐ Computer Entertainment	☐ Service
☐ Computer Education	☐ Wholesale
☐ Information Technologies	☐ SPECIFIC INDUSTRIES
☐ Computer Media	☐ Energy
☐ Software	☐ Environmental
☐ Internet	☐ Financial
☐ MEDICAL/HEALTHCARE	☐ Real Estate
☐ Biotechnology	☐ Transportation
☐ Healthcare Services	☐ Publishing
☐ Life Sciences	☐ Food
☐ Medical Products	☐ Franchises
☐ INDUSTRIAL	☐ DIVERSIFIED
☐ Advanced Materials	☐ MISCELLANEOUS
☐ Chemicals	
☐ Instruments & Controls	

STAGE PREFERENCE

☐ EARLY STAGE
☐   Seed
☐   Start-up
☐   1st Stage
☒ LATER STAGE
☒   2nd Stage
☒   Mature
☐   Mezzanine
☒   LBO/MBO
☐   Turnaround
☐ INT'L EXPANSION
☐ WILL CONSIDER ALL
☐ VENTURE LEASING
SBIC
Other Locations:

Affiliation:
Minimum Investment: Less than $1 Million
Capital Under Management: Less than $100 Million

GEOGRAPHIC PREF

☐   East Coast
☐   West Coast
☐   Northeast
☐   Mid Atlantic
☐   Gulf States
☐   Northwest
☐   Southeast
☐   Southwest
☐   Midwest
☐   Central
☐   Local to Office
☒   Other Geo Pref
      IN

CID EQUITY PARTNERS

One American Square
Suite 2850, Box 82074
Indianapolis IN 46282

Phone (317) 269-2350   Fax (317) 269-2355

PROFESSIONALS	TITLE
John T. Hackett	Managing General Partner
John G. Aplin	General Partner
G. Cook Jordan	General Partner
Kevin Sheehan	General Partner
James Philipkosky	General Partner

INDUSTRY PREFERENCE

☒ INFORMATION INDUSTRY
☒ Communications
☒ Computer Equipment
☒ Computer Services
☒ Computer Components
☐ Computer Entertainment
☒ Computer Education
☒ Information Technologies
☒ Computer Media
☒ Software
☒ Internet
☒ MEDICAL/HEALTHCARE
☐ Biotechnology
☒ Healthcare Services
☐ Life Sciences
☒ Medical Products
☐ INDUSTRIAL
☐ Advanced Materials
☐ Chemicals
☐ Instruments & Controls

☒ BASIC INDUSTRIES
☐ Consumer
☐ Distribution
☒ Manufacturing
☐ Retail
☒ Service
☐ Wholesale
☒ SPECIFIC INDUSTRIES
☐ Energy
☐ Environmental
☒ Financial
☐ Real Estate
☐ Transportation
☐ Publishing
☐ Food
☐ Franchises
☒ DIVERSIFIED
☐ MISCELLANEOUS

STAGE PREFERENCE

☒ EARLY STAGE
☐ Seed
☒ Start-up
☒ 1st Stage
☒ LATER STAGE
☒ 2nd Stage
☒ Mature
☐ Mezzanine
☒ LBO/MBO
☐ Turnaround
☐ INT'L EXPANSION
☐ WILL CONSIDER ALL
☐ VENTURE LEASING

Other Locations:

Affiliation:
Minimum Investment: $1 Million or more
Capital Under Management: $100 to $500 Million

GEOGRAPHIC PREF

☐ East Coast
☐ West Coast
☐ Northeast
☐ Mid Atlantic
☐ Gulf States
☐ Northwest
☐ Southeast
☐ Southwest
☐ Midwest
☐ Central
☐ Local to Office
☐ Other Geo Pref

MVW

201 N. Meridian Street
Suite 300
Indianapolis IN 46204

Phone (317) 237-2323   Fax (317) 237-2325

PROFESSIONALS	TITLE
Thomas Hiatt	Managing Partner
Garth Dickey	Managing Partner
Scott Lutzke	Managing Director

INDUSTRY PREFERENCE

☒ INFORMATION INDUSTRY
☒ Communications
☒ Computer Equipment
☒ Computer Services
☒ Computer Components
☐ Computer Entertainment
☒ Computer Education
☒ Information Technologies
☐ Computer Media
☒ Software
☒ Internet
☒ MEDICAL/HEALTHCARE
☒ Biotechnology
☒ Healthcare Services
☒ Life Sciences
☒ Medical Products
☒ INDUSTRIAL
☒ Advanced Materials
☒ Chemicals
☒ Instruments & Controls

☒ BASIC INDUSTRIES
☒ Consumer
☐ Distribution
☐ Manufacturing
☐ Retail
☒ Service
☐ Wholesale
☒ SPECIFIC INDUSTRIES
☐ Energy
☐ Environmental
☒ Financial
☐ Real Estate
☐ Transportation
☐ Publishing
☐ Food
☐ Franchises
☒ DIVERSIFIED
☐ MISCELLANEOUS

STAGE PREFERENCE

☒ EARLY STAGE
☐ Seed
☐ Start-up
☒ 1st Stage
☒ LATER STAGE
☒ 2nd Stage
☒ Mature
☒ Mezzanine
☒ LBO/MBO
☐ Turnaround
☐ INT'L EXPANSION
☐ WILL CONSIDER ALL
☐ VENTURE LEASING

Other Locations:

Affiliation:
Minimum Investment: Less than $1 Million
Capital Under Management: Less than $100 Million

GEOGRAPHIC PREF

☐ East Coast
☐ West Coast
☐ Northeast
☐ Mid Atlantic
☐ Gulf States
☐ Northwest
☐ Southeast
☐ Southwest
☐ Midwest
☐ Central
☐ Local to Office
☐ Other Geo Pref

INVESTAMERICA INVESTMENT ADVISORS, INC.

101 Second Street SE
Suite 800
Cedar Rapids IA 52401

Phone (319) 363-8249   Fax (319) 363-9683

PROFESSIONALS	TITLE
David Schroder	President
Robert Comey	Executive Vice President

INDUSTRY PREFERENCE

☒ INFORMATION INDUSTRY	☒ BASIC INDUSTRIES
☒ Communications	☒ Consumer
☒ Computer Equipment	☒ Distribution
☒ Computer Services	☒ Manufacturing
☒ Computer Components	☒ Retail
☐ Computer Entertainment	☒ Service
☐ Computer Education	☐ Wholesale
☐ Information Technologies	☒ SPECIFIC INDUSTRIES
☒ Computer Media	☒ Energy
☒ Software	☐ Environmental
☐ Internet	☐ Financial
☒ MEDICAL/HEALTHCARE	☐ Real Estate
☒ Biotechnology	☐ Transportation
☒ Healthcare Services	☒ Publishing
☒ Life Sciences	☐ Food
☒ Medical Products	☐ Franchises
☒ INDUSTRIAL	☒ DIVERSIFIED
☐ Advanced Materials	☒ MISCELLANEOUS
☐ Chemicals	Agriculture, Forestry, Fishing
☒ Instruments & Controls	

STAGE PREFERENCE

☐ EARLY STAGE
☐　 Seed
☐　 Start-up
☐　 1st Stage
☒ LATER STAGE
☐　 2nd Stage
☐　 Mature
☐　 Mezzanine
☒　 LBO/MBO
☐　 Turnaround
☐ INT'L EXPANSION
☐ WILL CONSIDER ALL
☐ VENTURE LEASING

Other Locations: Kansas City MO

Affiliation:
Minimum Investment: $1 Million or more
Capital Under Management: Less than $100 Million

GEOGRAPHIC PREF

☐ East Coast
☐ West Coast
☐ Northeast
☐ Mid Atlantic
☐ Gulf States
☐ Northwest
☐ Southeast
☐ Southwest
☐ Midwest
☐ Central
☐ Local to Office
☐ Other Geo Pref

MORAMERICA CAPITAL CORPORATION

101 Second Street SE
Suite 800
Cedar Rapids IA 52401

Phone (319) 363-8249   Fax (319) 363-9683

PROFESSIONALS	TITLE
David R. Schroder	President
Robert A. Comey	Executive Vice President

INDUSTRY PREFERENCE

☒ INFORMATION INDUSTRY	☒ BASIC INDUSTRIES
☒ Communications	☒ Consumer
☒ Computer Equipment	☒ Distribution
☒ Computer Services	☒ Manufacturing
☒ Computer Components	☒ Retail
☐ Computer Entertainment	☒ Service
☐ Computer Education	☐ Wholesale
☐ Information Technologies	☒ SPECIFIC INDUSTRIES
☒ Computer Media	☒ Energy
☒ Software	☐ Environmental
☐ Internet	☐ Financial
☒ MEDICAL/HEALTHCARE	☐ Real Estate
☒ Biotechnology	☐ Transportation
☒ Healthcare Services	☒ Publishing
☒ Life Sciences	☐ Food
☒ Medical Products	☐ Franchises
☒ INDUSTRIAL	☒ DIVERSIFIED
☐ Advanced Materials	☐ MISCELLANEOUS
☐ Chemicals	
☒ Instruments & Controls	

STAGE PREFERENCE

☐ EARLY STAGE
☐　 Seed
☐　 Start-up
☐　 1st Stage
☒ LATER STAGE
☐　 2nd Stage
☐　 Mature
☐　 Mezzanine
☒　 LBO/MBO
☐　 Turnaround
☐ INT'L EXPANSION
☐ WILL CONSIDER ALL
☐ VENTURE LEASING
SBIC
Other Locations: Kansas City MO

Affiliation:
Minimum Investment: $1 Million or more
Capital Under Management: Less than $100 Million

GEOGRAPHIC PREF

☐ East Coast
☐ West Coast
☐ Northeast
☐ Mid Atlantic
☐ Gulf States
☐ Northwest
☐ Southeast
☐ Southwest
☐ Midwest
☐ Central
☐ Local to Office
☐ Other Geo Pref

PAPPAJOHN CAPITAL RESOURCES

2116 Financial Center
Des Moines IA 50309

Phone (515) 244-5746   Fax (515) 244-2346

PROFESSIONALS	TITLE
John Pappajohn	President
Joseph Dunham	Vice President
Matt Kinley	Vice President / CFO

INDUSTRY PREFERENCE

☒ INFORMATION INDUSTRY
☒ Communications
☒ Computer Equipment
☒ Computer Services
☐ Computer Components
☐ Computer Entertainment
☐ Computer Education
☒ Information Technologies
☐ Computer Media
☒ Software
☒ Internet
☒ MEDICAL/HEALTHCARE
☐ Biotechnology
☒ Healthcare Services
☒ Life Sciences
☒ Medical Products
☐ INDUSTRIAL
☐ Advanced Materials
☐ Chemicals
☐ Instruments & Controls

☐ BASIC INDUSTRIES
☐ Consumer
☐ Distribution
☐ Manufacturing
☐ Retail
☐ Service
☐ Wholesale
☐ SPECIFIC INDUSTRIES
☐ Energy
☐ Environmental
☐ Financial
☐ Real Estate
☐ Transportation
☐ Publishing
☐ Food
☐ Franchises
☒ DIVERSIFIED
☒ MISCELLANEOUS

STAGE PREFERENCE

☒ EARLY STAGE
☒ Seed
☒ Start-up
☒ 1st Stage
☒ LATER STAGE
☒ 2nd Stage
☐ Mature
☐ Mezzanine
☒ LBO/MBO
☐ Turnaround
☐ INT'L EXPANSION
☐ WILL CONSIDER ALL
☐ VENTURE LEASING

Other Locations:

Affiliation:
Minimum Investment: Less than $1 Million
Capital Under Management: $100 to $500 Million

GEOGRAPHIC PREF

☐ East Coast
☐ West Coast
☐ Northeast
☐ Mid Atlantic
☐ Gulf States
☐ Northwest
☐ Southeast
☐ Southwest
☐ Midwest
☐ Central
☐ Local to Office
☐ Other Geo Pref

KANSAS VENTURE CAPITAL, INC.

6700 Antioch Plaza
Suite 460
Overland Park KS 66204

Phone (913) 262-7117   Fax (913) 262-3509

PROFESSIONALS	TITLE
John D. Dalton	President
Thomas C. Blackburn	Exec. Vice President
Marshall D. Parker	Exec. Vice President

INDUSTRY PREFERENCE

☒ INFORMATION INDUSTRY
☒ Communications
☐ Computer Equipment
☐ Computer Services
☐ Computer Components
☐ Computer Entertainment
☐ Computer Education
☐ Information Technologies
☒ Computer Media
☒ Software
☐ Internet
☐ MEDICAL/HEALTHCARE
☐ Biotechnology
☐ Healthcare Services
☐ Life Sciences
☐ Medical Products
☐ INDUSTRIAL
☐ Advanced Materials
☐ Chemicals
☐ Instruments & Controls

☒ BASIC INDUSTRIES
☐ Consumer
☐ Distribution
☒ Manufacturing
☐ Retail
☐ Service
☐ Wholesale
☐ SPECIFIC INDUSTRIES
☐ Energy
☐ Environmental
☐ Financial
☐ Real Estate
☐ Transportation
☐ Publishing
☐ Food
☐ Franchises
☒ DIVERSIFIED
☐ MISCELLANEOUS

STAGE PREFERENCE

☒ EARLY STAGE
☐ Seed
☒ Start-up
☒ 1st Stage
☒ LATER STAGE
☒ 2nd Stage
☒ Mature
☒ Mezzanine
☒ LBO/MBO
☒ Turnaround
☐ INT'L EXPANSION
☐ WILL CONSIDER ALL
☒ VENTURE LEASING

SBIC
Other Locations:

Affiliation:
Minimum Investment: Less than $1 Million
Capital Under Management: Less than $100 Million

GEOGRAPHIC PREF

☐ East Coast
☐ West Coast
☐ Northeast
☐ Mid Atlantic
☐ Gulf States
☐ Northwest
☐ Southeast
☐ Southwest
☐ Midwest
☐ Central
☐ Local to Office
☐ Other Geo Pref

CHRYSALIS VENTURES, INC.

101 South 5th Street
Suite 11850
Louisville KY 40202

Phone (502) 583-7644   Fax (502) 583-7648

PROFESSIONALS	TITLE
David A. Jones, Jr.	Chairman
Robert Saunders	Sr. Managing Partner

INDUSTRY PREFERENCE

☒ INFORMATION INDUSTRY
☒   Communications
☐   Computer Equipment
☐   Computer Services
☐   Computer Components
☐   Computer Entertainment
☐   Computer Education
☒   Information Technologies
☒   Computer Media
☐   Software
☐   Internet
☒ MEDICAL/HEALTHCARE
☐   Biotechnology
☒   Healthcare Services
☐   Life Sciences
☐   Medical Products
☐ INDUSTRIAL
☐   Advanced Materials
☐   Chemicals
☐   Instruments & Controls

☒ BASIC INDUSTRIES
☐   Consumer
☐   Distribution
☐   Manufacturing
☐   Retail
☒   Service
☐   Wholesale
☒ SPECIFIC INDUSTRIES
☐   Energy
☐   Environmental
☒   Financial
☐   Real Estate
☐   Transportation
☐   Publishing
☐   Food
☐   Franchises
☒ DIVERSIFIED
☐ MISCELLANEOUS

STAGE PREFERENCE

☒ EARLY STAGE
☐   Seed
☒   Start-up
☒   1st Stage
☒ LATER STAGE
☒   2nd Stage
☐   Mature
☐   Mezzanine
☐   LBO/MBO
☐   Turnaround
☐ INT'L EXPANSION
☐ WILL CONSIDER ALL
☐ VENTURE LEASING

Other Locations:

Affiliation:
Minimum Investment: Less than $1 Million
Capital Under Management: Less than $100 Million

GEOGRAPHIC PREF

☐ East Coast
☐ West Coast
☐ Northeast
☐ Mid Atlantic
☐ Gulf States
☐ Northwest
☒ Southeast
☐ Southwest
☐ Midwest
☐ Central
☐ Local to Office
☐ Other Geo Pref

EQUAL OPPORTUNITY FINANCE, INC.

420 S. Hurstbourne Parkway
Suite 201
Louisville KY 40222

Phone (502) 423-1943   Fax (502) 423-1945

PROFESSIONALS	TITLE
David A. Sattich	President

INDUSTRY PREFERENCE

☐ INFORMATION INDUSTRY
☐   Communications
☐   Computer Equipment
☐   Computer Services
☐   Computer Components
☐   Computer Entertainment
☐   Computer Education
☐   Information Technologies
☐   Computer Media
☐   Software
☐   Internet
☐ MEDICAL/HEALTHCARE
☐   Biotechnology
☐   Healthcare Services
☐   Life Sciences
☐   Medical Products
☐ INDUSTRIAL
☐   Advanced Materials
☐   Chemicals
☐   Instruments & Controls

☐ BASIC INDUSTRIES
☐   Consumer
☐   Distribution
☐   Manufacturing
☐   Retail
☐   Service
☐   Wholesale
☐ SPECIFIC INDUSTRIES
☐   Energy
☐   Environmental
☐   Financial
☐   Real Estate
☐   Transportation
☐   Publishing
☐   Food
☐   Franchises
☒ DIVERSIFIED
☐ MISCELLANEOUS

STAGE PREFERENCE

☒ EARLY STAGE
☐   Seed
☐   Start-up
☒   1st Stage
☒ LATER STAGE
☒   2nd Stage
☒   Mature
☒   Mezzanine
☒   LBO/MBO
☐   Turnaround
☐ INT'L EXPANSION
☐ WILL CONSIDER ALL
☐ VENTURE LEASING
SSBIC
Other Locations:

Affiliation:
Minimum Investment: Less than $1 Million
Capital Under Management: Less than $100 Million

GEOGRAPHIC PREF

☐ East Coast
☐ West Coast
☐ Northeast
☐ Mid Atlantic
☐ Gulf States
☐ Northwest
☐ Southeast
☐ Southwest
☐ Midwest
☐ Central
☐ Local to Office
☒ Other Geo Pref
  OH, KY, WV, IN

HUMANA VENTURE CAPITAL

500 West Main Street
Louisville KY 40202

Phone (502) 580-3022   Fax (502) 580-2051

PROFESSIONALS	TITLE
Tom Liston	Vice President

INDUSTRY PREFERENCE

- ☐ INFORMATION INDUSTRY
- ☐ Communications
- ☐ Computer Equipment
- ☐ Computer Services
- ☐ Computer Components
- ☐ Computer Entertainment
- ☐ Computer Education
- ☐ Information Technologies
- ☐ Computer Media
- ☐ Software
- ☐ Internet
- ☒ MEDICAL/HEALTHCARE
- ☐ Biotechnology
- ☒ Healthcare Services
- ☐ Life Sciences
- ☐ Medical Products
- ☐ INDUSTRIAL
- ☐ Advanced Materials
- ☐ Chemicals
- ☐ Instruments & Controls

- ☐ BASIC INDUSTRIES
- ☐ Consumer
- ☐ Distribution
- ☐ Manufacturing
- ☐ Retail
- ☐ Service
- ☐ Wholesale
- ☐ SPECIFIC INDUSTRIES
- ☐ Energy
- ☐ Environmental
- ☐ Financial
- ☐ Real Estate
- ☐ Transportation
- ☐ Publishing
- ☐ Food
- ☐ Franchises
- ☐ DIVERSIFIED
- ☐ MISCELLANEOUS

STAGE PREFERENCE

- ☒ EARLY STAGE
- ☐ Seed
- ☒ Start-up
- ☒ 1st Stage
- ☒ LATER STAGE
- ☒ 2nd Stage
- ☒ Mature
- ☐ Mezzanine
- ☒ LBO/MBO
- ☐ Turnaround
- ☐ INT'L EXPANSION
- ☐ WILL CONSIDER ALL
- ☐ VENTURE LEASING

Other Locations:

Affiliation: Humana, Inc.
Minimum Investment: Less than $1 Million
Capital Under Management: $100 to $500 Million

GEOGRAPHIC PREF

- ☐ East Coast
- ☐ West Coast
- ☐ Northeast
- ☐ Mid Atlantic
- ☐ Gulf States
- ☐ Northwest
- ☐ Southeast
- ☐ Southwest
- ☐ Midwest
- ☐ Central
- ☐ Local to Office
- ☐ Other Geo Pref

MOUNTAIN VENTURES, INC.

362 Old Whitley Road
P.O. Box 1738
London KY 40743

Phone (606) 864-5175   Fax (606) 864-5194

PROFESSIONALS	TITLE
L. Ray Moncrief	Executive Vice President

INDUSTRY PREFERENCE

- ☐ INFORMATION INDUSTRY
- ☐ Communications
- ☐ Computer Equipment
- ☐ Computer Services
- ☐ Computer Components
- ☐ Computer Entertainment
- ☐ Computer Education
- ☐ Information Technologies
- ☐ Computer Media
- ☐ Software
- ☐ Internet
- ☐ MEDICAL/HEALTHCARE
- ☐ Biotechnology
- ☐ Healthcare Services
- ☐ Life Sciences
- ☐ Medical Products
- ☐ INDUSTRIAL
- ☐ Advanced Materials
- ☐ Chemicals
- ☐ Instruments & Controls

- ☐ BASIC INDUSTRIES
- ☐ Consumer
- ☐ Distribution
- ☐ Manufacturing
- ☐ Retail
- ☐ Service
- ☐ Wholesale
- ☐ SPECIFIC INDUSTRIES
- ☐ Energy
- ☐ Environmental
- ☐ Financial
- ☐ Real Estate
- ☐ Transportation
- ☐ Publishing
- ☐ Food
- ☐ Franchises
- ☒ DIVERSIFIED
- ☐ MISCELLANEOUS

STAGE PREFERENCE

- ☒ EARLY STAGE
- ☒ Seed
- ☒ Start-up
- ☒ 1st Stage
- ☒ LATER STAGE
- ☒ 2nd Stage
- ☐ Mature
- ☒ Mezzanine
- ☒ LBO/MBO
- ☐ Turnaround
- ☐ INT'L EXPANSION
- ☐ WILL CONSIDER ALL
- ☐ VENTURE LEASING

SBIC
Other Locations:

Affiliation:
Minimum Investment: Less than $1 Million
Capital Under Management: Less than $100 Million

GEOGRAPHIC PREF

- ☐ East Coast
- ☐ West Coast
- ☐ Northeast
- ☐ Mid Atlantic
- ☐ Gulf States
- ☐ Northwest
- ☒ Southeast
- ☐ Southwest
- ☐ Midwest
- ☐ Central
- ☐ Local to Office
- ☐ Other Geo Pref

ADVANTAGE CAPITAL PARTNERS

909 Poydras Street
Suite 2230
New Orleans LA 70112

Phone (504) 522-4850   Fax (504) 522-4950

PROFESSIONALS	TITLE
Steven Stull	President
David Bergmann	Managing Director
Crichton Brown	Managing Director
Scott Zajac	Managing Director
Maurice Doyle	Managing Director

INDUSTRY PREFERENCE

☒ INFORMATION INDUSTRY
☒ Communications
☒ Computer Equipment
☒ Computer Services
☒ Computer Components
☐ Computer Entertainment
☐ Computer Education
☒ Information Technologies
☐ Computer Media
☒ Software
☐ Internet
☒ MEDICAL/HEALTHCARE
☒ Biotechnology
☒ Healthcare Services
☒ Life Sciences
☒ Medical Products
☒ INDUSTRIAL
☒ Advanced Materials
☒ Chemicals
☒ Instruments & Controls

☒ BASIC INDUSTRIES
☒ Consumer
☒ Distribution
☐ Manufacturing
☐ Retail
☐ Service
☐ Wholesale
☒ SPECIFIC INDUSTRIES
☒ Energy
☐ Environmental
☐ Financial
☐ Real Estate
☐ Transportation
☐ Publishing
☐ Food
☐ Franchises
☒ DIVERSIFIED
☒ MISCELLANEOUS

STAGE PREFERENCE

☒ EARLY STAGE
☐ Seed
☒ Start-up
☒ 1st Stage
☒ LATER STAGE
☐ 2nd Stage
☐ Mature
☒ Mezzanine
☒ LBO/MBO
☐ Turnaround
☐ INT'L EXPANSION
☐ WILL CONSIDER ALL
☐ VENTURE LEASING

Other Locations: St Louis MO, New York NY, Tampa FL

Affiliation:
Minimum Investment: $1 Million or more
Capital Under Management: $100 to $500 Million

GEOGRAPHIC PREF

☐ East Coast
☐ West Coast
☒ Northeast
☐ Mid Atlantic
☒ Gulf States
☐ Northwest
☒ Southeast
☐ Southwest
☐ Midwest
☐ Central
☐ Local to Office
☒ Other Geo Pref
  Gulf States

HIBERNIA CAPITAL CORP.

313 Carondelet Street
New Orleans LA 70130

Phone (504) 533-5988   Fax (504) 533-3873

PROFESSIONALS	TITLE
Thomas Hoyt	President
John Driscoll	
Chris Nines	

INDUSTRY PREFERENCE

☒ INFORMATION INDUSTRY
☒ Communications
☐ Computer Equipment
☐ Computer Services
☐ Computer Components
☐ Computer Entertainment
☐ Computer Education
☒ Information Technologies
☐ Computer Media
☐ Software
☐ Internet
☐ MEDICAL/HEALTHCARE
☐ Biotechnology
☐ Healthcare Services
☐ Life Sciences
☐ Medical Products
☒ INDUSTRIAL
☒ Advanced Materials
☒ Chemicals
☒ Instruments & Controls

☒ BASIC INDUSTRIES
☒ Consumer
☒ Distribution
☒ Manufacturing
☒ Retail
☒ Service
☒ Wholesale
☐ SPECIFIC INDUSTRIES
☐ Energy
☐ Environmental
☐ Financial
☐ Real Estate
☐ Transportation
☐ Publishing
☐ Food
☐ Franchises
☒ DIVERSIFIED
☐ MISCELLANEOUS

STAGE PREFERENCE

☐ EARLY STAGE
☐ Seed
☐ Start-up
☐ 1st Stage
☒ LATER STAGE
☒ 2nd Stage
☐ Mature
☐ Mezzanine
☒ LBO/MBO
☐ Turnaround
☐ INT'L EXPANSION
☐ WILL CONSIDER ALL
☐ VENTURE LEASING
SBIC
Other Locations:

Affiliation:
Minimum Investment: $1 Million or more
Capital Under Management: Less than $100 Million

GEOGRAPHIC PREF

☐ East Coast
☐ West Coast
☐ Northeast
☐ Mid Atlantic
☐ Gulf States
☐ Northwest
☐ Southeast
☐ Southwest
☐ Midwest
☐ Central
☐ Local to Office
☒ Other Geo Pref
  TX, LA

NORTH ATLANTIC
VENTURE FUND II LP
70 Center Street
Portland ME 04101

Two City Center

Phone (207) 772-1001   Fax (207) 772-3257

PROFESSIONALS	TITLE
David M. Coit	President

INDUSTRY PREFERENCE

☐ INFORMATION INDUSTRY	☐ BASIC INDUSTRIES
☐ Communications	☐ Consumer
☐ Computer Equipment	☐ Distribution
☐ Computer Services	☐ Manufacturing
☐ Computer Components	☐ Retail
☐ Computer Entertainment	☐ Service
☐ Computer Education	☐ Wholesale
☐ Information Technologies	☐ SPECIFIC INDUSTRIES
☐ Computer Media	☐ Energy
☐ Software	☐ Environmental
☐ Internet	☐ Financial
☐ MEDICAL/HEALTHCARE	☐ Real Estate
☐ Biotechnology	☐ Transportation
☐ Healthcare Services	☐ Publishing
☐ Life Sciences	☐ Food
☐ Medical Products	☐ Franchises
☐ INDUSTRIAL	☒ DIVERSIFIED
☐ Advanced Materials	☐ MISCELLANEOUS
☐ Chemicals	
☐ Instruments & Controls	

STAGE PREFERENCE

☐ EARLY STAGE
☐ Seed
☐ Start-up
☐ 1st Stage
☒ LATER STAGE
☒ 2nd Stage
☒ Mature
☐ Mezzanine
☒ LBO/MBO
☐ Turnaround
☐ INT'L EXPANSION
☐ WILL CONSIDER ALL
☐ VENTURE LEASING
SBIC
Other Locations:

Affiliation:
Minimum Investment: $1 Million or more
Capital Under Management: Less than $100 Million

GEOGRAPHIC PREF

☐ East Coast
☐ West Coast
☒ Northeast
☐ Mid Atlantic
☐ Gulf States
☐ Northwest
☐ Southeast
☐ Southwest
☐ Midwest
☐ Central
☐ Local to Office
☒ Other Geo Pref
　 New England

ABS CAPITAL PARTNERS

1 South Street
25th Floor
Baltimore MD 21202

Phone (410) 895-4400   Fax (410) 895-4380

PROFESSIONALS	TITLE
Fredrick Bryant	General Partner
Donald Hebb	Managing General Partner
Timothy Weglicki	General Partner

INDUSTRY PREFERENCE

☒ INFORMATION INDUSTRY	☒ BASIC INDUSTRIES
☒ Communications	☐ Consumer
☒ Computer Equipment	☐ Distribution
☒ Computer Services	☐ Manufacturing
☐ Computer Components	☐ Retail
☐ Computer Entertainment	☒ Service
☒ Computer Education	☐ Wholesale
☒ Information Technologies	☒ SPECIFIC INDUSTRIES
☒ Computer Media	☒ Energy
☒ Software	☐ Environmental
☒ Internet	☐ Financial
☒ MEDICAL/HEALTHCARE	☐ Real Estate
☒ Biotechnology	☐ Transportation
☒ Healthcare Services	☒ Publishing
☒ Life Sciences	☐ Food
☒ Medical Products	☐ Franchises
☒ INDUSTRIAL	☒ DIVERSIFIED
☒ Advanced Materials	☐ MISCELLANEOUS
☒ Chemicals	
☒ Instruments & Controls	

STAGE PREFERENCE

☐ EARLY STAGE
☐ Seed
☐ Start-up
☐ 1st Stage
☒ LATER STAGE
☒ 2nd Stage
☐ Mature
☒ Mezzanine
☒ LBO/MBO
☐ Turnaround
☐ INT'L EXPANSION
☐ WILL CONSIDER ALL
☐ VENTURE LEASING

Other Locations: San Francisco CA

Affiliation:
Minimum Investment: $1 Million or more
Capital Under Management: Over $500 Million

GEOGRAPHIC PREF

☐ East Coast
☐ West Coast
☐ Northeast
☐ Mid Atlantic
☐ Gulf States
☐ Northwest
☐ Southeast
☐ Southwest
☐ Midwest
☐ Central
☐ Local to Office
☐ Other Geo Pref

ANTHEM CAPITAL, LP

16 S. Calvert Street
Suite 800
Baltimore MD 21202

Phone (410) 625-1510   Fax (410) 625-1735

PROFESSIONALS	TITLE
William M. Gust	Managing General Partner
C Edward Spiva	General Partner
Geral Schaafsma	General Partner
Alexander Perry	Associate

INDUSTRY PREFERENCE

- ☐ INFORMATION INDUSTRY
- ☐ Communications
- ☐ Computer Equipment
- ☐ Computer Services
- ☐ Computer Components
- ☐ Computer Entertainment
- ☐ Computer Education
- ☐ Information Technologies
- ☐ Computer Media
- ☐ Software
- ☐ Internet
- ☐ MEDICAL/HEALTHCARE
- ☐ Biotechnology
- ☐ Healthcare Services
- ☐ Life Sciences
- ☐ Medical Products
- ☐ INDUSTRIAL
- ☐ Advanced Materials
- ☐ Chemicals
- ☐ Instruments & Controls
- ☐ BASIC INDUSTRIES
- ☐ Consumer
- ☐ Distribution
- ☐ Manufacturing
- ☐ Retail
- ☐ Service
- ☐ Wholesale
- ☐ SPECIFIC INDUSTRIES
- ☐ Energy
- ☐ Environmental
- ☐ Financial
- ☐ Real Estate
- ☐ Transportation
- ☐ Publishing
- ☐ Food
- ☐ Franchises
- ☒ DIVERSIFIED
- ☐ MISCELLANEOUS

STAGE PREFERENCE

- ☒ EARLY STAGE
- ☐ Seed
- ☐ Start-up
- ☒ 1st Stage
- ☒ LATER STAGE
- ☒ 2nd Stage
- ☒ Mature
- ☒ Mezzanine
- ☒ LBO/MBO
- ☐ Turnaround
- ☐ INT'L EXPANSION
- ☐ WILL CONSIDER ALL
- ☐ VENTURE LEASING

SBIC
Other Locations:

Affiliation:
Minimum Investment: $1 Million or more
Capital Under Management: Less than $100 Million

GEOGRAPHIC PREF

- ☐ East Coast
- ☐ West Coast
- ☐ Northeast
- ☐ Mid Atlantic
- ☐ Gulf States
- ☐ Northwest
- ☒ Southeast
- ☐ Southwest
- ☐ Midwest
- ☐ Central
- ☐ Local to Office
- ☐ Other Geo Pref

AT&T VENTURES

Two Wisconsin Circle
Suite 610
Chevy Chase MD 20815

Phone (301) 652-5225   Fax (301) 664-8590

PROFESSIONALS	TITLE
Richard S. Bodman	Managing General Partner
James J. Pastoriza	Partner

INDUSTRY PREFERENCE

- ☒ INFORMATION INDUSTRY
- ☒ Communications
- ☐ Computer Equipment
- ☐ Computer Services
- ☐ Computer Components
- ☐ Computer Entertainment
- ☐ Computer Education
- ☒ Information Technologies
- ☐ Computer Media
- ☒ Software
- ☒ Internet
- ☐ MEDICAL/HEALTHCARE
- ☐ Biotechnology
- ☐ Healthcare Services
- ☐ Life Sciences
- ☐ Medical Products
- ☐ INDUSTRIAL
- ☐ Advanced Materials
- ☐ Chemicals
- ☐ Instruments & Controls
- ☐ BASIC INDUSTRIES
- ☐ Consumer
- ☐ Distribution
- ☐ Manufacturing
- ☐ Retail
- ☐ Service
- ☐ Wholesale
- ☐ SPECIFIC INDUSTRIES
- ☐ Energy
- ☐ Environmental
- ☐ Financial
- ☐ Real Estate
- ☐ Transportation
- ☐ Publishing
- ☐ Food
- ☐ Franchises
- ☐ DIVERSIFIED
- ☒ MISCELLANEOUS

STAGE PREFERENCE

- ☒ EARLY STAGE
- ☒ Seed
- ☒ Start-up
- ☒ 1st Stage
- ☒ LATER STAGE
- ☒ 2nd Stage
- ☐ Mature
- ☐ Mezzanine
- ☐ LBO/MBO
- ☐ Turnaround
- ☐ INT'L EXPANSION
- ☐ WILL CONSIDER ALL
- ☐ VENTURE LEASING

Other Locations: Menlo Park CA, Basking Ridge NJ

Affiliation: AT&T
Minimum Investment: Less than $1 Million
Capital Under Management: $100 to $500 Million

GEOGRAPHIC PREF

- ☐ East Coast
- ☐ West Coast
- ☐ Northeast
- ☐ Mid Atlantic
- ☐ Gulf States
- ☐ Northwest
- ☐ Southeast
- ☐ Southwest
- ☐ Midwest
- ☐ Central
- ☐ Local to Office
- ☐ Other Geo Pref

GROTECH CAPITAL GROUP

9690 Deereco Road
Suite 800
Timonium MD 21093

Phone (410) 560-2000   Fax (410) 560-1910

PROFESSIONALS	TITLE
Frank A. Adams	Managing Director
David G. Bannister	Managing Director
Stuart D. Frankel	Managing Director
Dennis Shaughnessy	Managing Director
Hugh A. Woltzch	Manging Director

INDUSTRY PREFERENCE

- ☒ INFORMATION INDUSTRY
- ☒ Communications
- ☒ Computer Equipment
- ☒ Computer Services
- ☒ Computer Components
- ☒ Computer Entertainment
- ☒ Computer Education
- ☒ Information Technologies
- ☒ Computer Media
- ☒ Software
- ☒ Internet
- ☒ MEDICAL/HEALTHCARE
- ☐ Biotechnology
- ☒ Healthcare Services
- ☐ Life Sciences
- ☒ Medical Products
- ☐ INDUSTRIAL
- ☐ Advanced Materials
- ☐ Chemicals
- ☐ Instruments & Controls

- ☒ BASIC INDUSTRIES
- ☒ Consumer
- ☒ Distribution
- ☐ Manufacturing
- ☐ Retail
- ☒ Service
- ☐ Wholesale
- ☐ SPECIFIC INDUSTRIES
- ☐ Energy
- ☐ Environmental
- ☐ Financial
- ☐ Real Estate
- ☐ Transportation
- ☐ Publishing
- ☐ Food
- ☐ Franchises
- ☒ DIVERSIFIED
- ☐ MISCELLANEOUS

STAGE PREFERENCE

- ☒ EARLY STAGE
- ☐ Seed
- ☐ Start-up
- ☒ 1st Stage
- ☒ LATER STAGE
- ☒ 2nd Stage
- ☒ Mature
- ☐ Mezzanine
- ☒ LBO/MBO
- ☐ Turnaround
- ☐ INT'L EXPANSION
- ☐ WILL CONSIDER ALL
- ☐ VENTURE LEASING

Other Locations:

Affiliation:
Minimum Investment: Less than $1 Million
Capital Under Management: $100 to $500 Million

GEOGRAPHIC PREF

- ☒ East Coast
- ☐ West Coast
- ☐ Northeast
- ☐ Mid Atlantic
- ☐ Gulf States
- ☐ Northwest
- ☐ Southeast
- ☐ Southwest
- ☐ Midwest
- ☐ Central
- ☐ Local to Office
- ☐ Other Geo Pref

MMG VENTURES LP (SSBIC)

826 E. Baltimore Street
Baltimore MD 21202

Phone (410) 659-7851   Fax (410) 333-2552

PROFESSIONALS	TITLE
Stanley W. Tucker	Manager

INDUSTRY PREFERENCE

- ☒ INFORMATION INDUSTRY
- ☒ Communications
- ☒ Computer Equipment
- ☒ Computer Services
- ☒ Computer Components
- ☐ Computer Entertainment
- ☒ Computer Education
- ☒ Information Technologies
- ☒ Computer Media
- ☒ Software
- ☒ Internet
- ☒ MEDICAL/HEALTHCARE
- ☐ Biotechnology
- ☒ Healthcare Services
- ☐ Life Sciences
- ☒ Medical Products
- ☐ INDUSTRIAL
- ☐ Advanced Materials
- ☐ Chemicals
- ☐ Instruments & Controls

- ☐ BASIC INDUSTRIES
- ☐ Consumer
- ☐ Distribution
- ☐ Manufacturing
- ☐ Retail
- ☐ Service
- ☐ Wholesale
- ☐ SPECIFIC INDUSTRIES
- ☐ Energy
- ☐ Environmental
- ☐ Financial
- ☐ Real Estate
- ☐ Transportation
- ☐ Publishing
- ☐ Food
- ☐ Franchises
- ☒ DIVERSIFIED
- ☐ MISCELLANEOUS

STAGE PREFERENCE

- ☒ EARLY STAGE
- ☐ Seed
- ☒ Start-up
- ☒ 1st Stage
- ☒ LATER STAGE
- ☒ 2nd Stage
- ☒ Mature
- ☐ Mezzanine
- ☒ LBO/MBO
- ☐ Turnaround
- ☐ INT'L EXPANSION
- ☐ WILL CONSIDER ALL
- ☐ VENTURE LEASING

SSBIC
Other Locations:

Affiliation:
Minimum Investment: Less than $1 Million
Capital Under Management: Less than $100 Million

GEOGRAPHIC PREF

- ☒ East Coast
- ☐ West Coast
- ☐ Northeast
- ☒ Mid Atlantic
- ☐ Gulf States
- ☐ Northwest
- ☐ Southeast
- ☐ Southwest
- ☐ Midwest
- ☐ Central
- ☐ Local to Office
- ☒ Other Geo Pref
  Mid-Atlantic

NEW ENTERPRISE ASSOCIATES

1119 St. Paul Street
Baltimore MD 21202

Phone (410) 244-0115   Fax (410) 752-7721

PROFESSIONALS	TITLE
Frank A. Bonsal, Jr.	General Partner
John M. Nehra	General Partner
Howie Wolfe	General Partner
Chuck W. Newhall III	General Partner
Nancy Dorman	General Partner

INDUSTRY PREFERENCE

☒ INFORMATION INDUSTRY
☒ Communications
☒ Computer Equipment
☒ Computer Services
☒ Computer Components
☒ Computer Entertainment
☒ Computer Education
☒ Information Technologies
☒ Computer Media
☒ Software
☒ Internet
☒ MEDICAL/HEALTHCARE
☒ Biotechnology
☒ Healthcare Services
☒ Life Sciences
☒ Medical Products
☒ INDUSTRIAL
☒ Advanced Materials
☒ Chemicals
☐ Instruments & Controls

☒ BASIC INDUSTRIES
☐ Consumer
☐ Distribution
☐ Manufacturing
☐ Retail
☒ Service
☐ Wholesale
☐ SPECIFIC INDUSTRIES
☐ Energy
☐ Environmental
☐ Financial
☐ Real Estate
☐ Transportation
☐ Publishing
☐ Food
☐ Franchises
☒ DIVERSIFIED
☐ MISCELLANEOUS

STAGE PREFERENCE

☒ EARLY STAGE
☒ Seed
☒ Start-up
☒ 1st Stage
☐ LATER STAGE
☐ 2nd Stage
☐ Mature
☐ Mezzanine
☐ LBO/MBO
☐ Turnaround
☐ INT'L EXPANSION
☐ WILL CONSIDER ALL
☐ VENTURE LEASING

Other Locations: Menlo Park CA, Reston VA

Affiliation:
Minimum Investment: Less than $1 Million
Capital Under Management: Over $500 Million

GEOGRAPHIC PREF

☐ East Coast
☐ West Coast
☐ Northeast
☐ Mid Atlantic
☐ Gulf States
☐ Northwest
☐ Southeast
☐ Southwest
☐ Midwest
☐ Central
☐ Local to Office
☐ Other Geo Pref

T. ROWE PRICE INVESTMENT SERVICES, INC.

100 East Pratt Street
Baltimore MD 21202

Phone (410) 345-2000   Fax (410) 345-6853

PROFESSIONALS	TITLE
Terral M. Jordan	Managing Director

INDUSTRY PREFERENCE

☐ INFORMATION INDUSTRY
☐ Communications
☐ Computer Equipment
☐ Computer Services
☐ Computer Components
☐ Computer Entertainment
☐ Computer Education
☐ Information Technologies
☐ Computer Media
☐ Software
☐ Internet
☐ MEDICAL/HEALTHCARE
☐ Biotechnology
☐ Healthcare Services
☐ Life Sciences
☐ Medical Products
☐ INDUSTRIAL
☐ Advanced Materials
☐ Chemicals
☐ Instruments & Controls

☐ BASIC INDUSTRIES
☐ Consumer
☐ Distribution
☐ Manufacturing
☐ Retail
☐ Service
☐ Wholesale
☐ SPECIFIC INDUSTRIES
☐ Energy
☐ Environmental
☐ Financial
☐ Real Estate
☐ Transportation
☐ Publishing
☐ Food
☐ Franchises
☒ DIVERSIFIED
☐ MISCELLANEOUS

STAGE PREFERENCE

☐ EARLY STAGE
☐ Seed
☐ Start-up
☐ 1st Stage
☒ LATER STAGE
☒ 2nd Stage
☒ Mature
☒ Mezzanine
☒ LBO/MBO
☒ Turnaround
☐ INT'L EXPANSION
☐ WILL CONSIDER ALL
☒ VENTURE LEASING

Other Locations:

Affiliation: T. Rowe Price Associates, Inc.
Minimum Investment: $1 Million or more
Capital Under Management: $100 to $500 Million

GEOGRAPHIC PREF

☐ East Coast
☐ West Coast
☐ Northeast
☐ Mid Atlantic
☐ Gulf States
☐ Northwest
☐ Southeast
☐ Southwest
☐ Midwest
☐ Central
☐ Local to Office
☐ Other Geo Pref

ADVANCED TECHNOLOGY VENTURES

281 White Street
Suite 350
Waltham MA 02451

Phone (781) 290-0707   Fax (781) 684-0045

PROFESSIONALS	TITLE
Albert E. Paladino	Partner
Pieter J. Schiller	Partner

INDUSTRY PREFERENCE

☒ INFORMATION INDUSTRY	☒ BASIC INDUSTRIES
☒ Communications	☐ Consumer
☒ Computer Equipment	☐ Distribution
☒ Computer Services	☐ Manufacturing
☒ Computer Components	☐ Retail
☐ Computer Entertainment	☒ Service
☒ Computer Education	☐ Wholesale
☒ Information Technologies	☒ SPECIFIC INDUSTRIES
☒ Computer Media	☒ Energy
☒ Software	☐ Environmental
☒ Internet	☐ Financial
☒ MEDICAL/HEALTHCARE	☐ Real Estate
☒ Biotechnology	☐ Transportation
☒ Healthcare Services	☐ Publishing
☒ Life Sciences	☐ Food
☒ Medical Products	☐ Franchises
☒ INDUSTRIAL	☒ DIVERSIFIED
☒ Advanced Materials	☐ MISCELLANEOUS
☒ Chemicals	
☒ Instruments & Controls	

STAGE PREFERENCE

☒ EARLY STAGE
☒ Seed
☒ Start-up
☒ 1st Stage
☒ LATER STAGE
☒ 2nd Stage
☐ Mature
☒ Mezzanine
☐ LBO/MBO
☐ Turnaround
☐ INT'L EXPANSION
☐ WILL CONSIDER ALL
☐ VENTURE LEASING

Other Locations: Palo Alto CA

Affiliation:
Minimum Investment: $1 Million or more
Capital Under Management: Over $500 Million

GEOGRAPHIC PREF

☒ East Coast
☐ West Coast
☐ Northeast
☐ Mid Atlantic
☐ Gulf States
☐ Northwest
☐ Southeast
☐ Southwest
☐ Midwest
☐ Central
☐ Local to Office
☐ Other Geo Pref

ADVENT INTERNATIONAL CORP.

75 State Street
29th floor
Boston MA 02109

Phone (617) 951-9400   Fax (617) 951-0566

PROFESSIONALS	TITLE
Dennis Costello	Managing Director
Nicholas Callinan	Managing Director
Jason Fisherman MD	Partner
Stephen Kahn	Managing Director
Douglas Kingsley	Managing Director
Olaf Krohg	Partner
Lawrence McKenna PhD	Partner
Gerard Moufflet	Managing Director

INDUSTRY PREFERENCE

☒ INFORMATION INDUSTRY	☒ BASIC INDUSTRIES
☒ Communications	☒ Consumer
☒ Computer Equipment	☐ Distribution
☒ Computer Services	☐ Manufacturing
☒ Computer Components	☒ Retail
☐ Computer Entertainment	☒ Service
☒ Computer Education	☐ Wholesale
☒ Information Technologies	☐ SPECIFIC INDUSTRIES
☐ Computer Media	☐ Energy
☒ Software	☐ Environmental
☒ Internet	☐ Financial
☒ MEDICAL/HEALTHCARE	☐ Real Estate
☒ Biotechnology	☐ Transportation
☒ Healthcare Services	☐ Publishing
☒ Life Sciences	☐ Food
☒ Medical Products	☐ Franchises
☒ INDUSTRIAL	☒ DIVERSIFIED
☒ Advanced Materials	☐ MISCELLANEOUS
☒ Chemicals	
☒ Instruments & Controls	

STAGE PREFERENCE

☒ EARLY STAGE
☒ Seed
☒ Start-up
☒ 1st Stage
☒ LATER STAGE
☒ 2nd Stage
☒ Mature
☒ Mezzanine
☒ LBO/MBO
☒ Turnaround
☒ INT'L EXPANSION
☐ WILL CONSIDER ALL
☒ VENTURE LEASING

Other Locations: Menlo Park CA

Affiliation:
Minimum Investment: Less than $1 Million
Capital Under Management: Over $500 Million

GEOGRAPHIC PREF

☐ East Coast
☐ West Coast
☐ Northeast
☐ Mid Atlantic
☐ Gulf States
☐ Northwest
☐ Southeast
☐ Southwest
☐ Midwest
☐ Central
☐ Local to Office
☐ Other Geo Pref

AMERICAN RESEARCH AND DEVELOPMENT (ARD)

30 Federal Street
3rd Floor
Boston MA 02110

Phone (617) 423-7500   Fax (617) 423-9655

PROFESSIONALS	TITLE
Harold L. Finelt	General Partner

INDUSTRY PREFERENCE

☒ INFORMATION INDUSTRY	☒ BASIC INDUSTRIES
☒ Communications	☒ Consumer
☒ Computer Equipment	☐ Distribution
☒ Computer Services	☐ Manufacturing
☒ Computer Components	☐ Retail
☐ Computer Entertainment	☒ Service
☒ Computer Education	☐ Wholesale
☒ Information Technologies	☒ SPECIFIC INDUSTRIES
☒ Computer Media	☒ Energy
☒ Software	☐ Environmental
☒ Internet	☐ Financial
☒ MEDICAL/HEALTHCARE	☐ Real Estate
☐ Biotechnology	☐ Transportation
☒ Healthcare Services	☐ Publishing
☒ Life Sciences	☐ Food
☒ Medical Products	☐ Franchises
☒ INDUSTRIAL	☒ DIVERSIFIED
☒ Advanced Materials	☐ MISCELLANEOUS
☒ Chemicals	
☒ Instruments & Controls	

STAGE PREFERENCE

☒ EARLY STAGE
☒ Seed
☒ Start-up
☒ 1st Stage
☒ LATER STAGE
☒ 2nd Stage
☒ Mature
☒ Mezzanine
☒ LBO/MBO
☒ Turnaround
☐ INT'L EXPANSION
☐ WILL CONSIDER ALL
☒ VENTURE LEASING

Other Locations:

Affiliation:
Minimum Investment: Less than $1 Million
Capital Under Management: Less than $100 Million

GEOGRAPHIC PREF

☐ East Coast
☐ West Coast
☒ Northeast
☐ Mid Atlantic
☐ Gulf States
☐ Northwest
☐ Southeast
☐ Southwest
☐ Midwest
☐ Central
☐ Local to Office
☐ Other Geo Pref

AMPERSAND VENTURES

55 William Street
Suite 240
Wellesley MA 02181-4003

Phone (781) 239-0700   Fax (781) 239-0824

PROFESSIONALS	TITLE
Richard A. Charpie	Managing General Partner
Peter D. Parker	General Partner
Charles D. Yie	General Partner
Stuart Auerbach	General Partner
K. Kachadurian	General Partner
Robert A. Charpie	General Partner
David Parker	General Partner

INDUSTRY PREFERENCE

☒ INFORMATION INDUSTRY	☐ BASIC INDUSTRIES
☒ Communications	☐ Consumer
☐ Computer Equipment	☐ Distribution
☐ Computer Services	☐ Manufacturing
☒ Computer Components	☐ Retail
☐ Computer Entertainment	☐ Service
☐ Computer Education	☐ Wholesale
☐ Information Technologies	☐ SPECIFIC INDUSTRIES
☐ Computer Media	☐ Energy
☐ Software	☐ Environmental
☐ Internet	☐ Financial
☒ MEDICAL/HEALTHCARE	☐ Real Estate
☐ Biotechnology	☐ Transportation
☐ Healthcare Services	☐ Publishing
☐ Life Sciences	☐ Food
☒ Medical Products	☐ Franchises
☒ INDUSTRIAL	☒ DIVERSIFIED
☒ Advanced Materials	☐ MISCELLANEOUS
☒ Chemicals	
☒ Instruments & Controls	

STAGE PREFERENCE

☒ EARLY STAGE
☒ Seed
☒ Start-up
☒ 1st Stage
☒ LATER STAGE
☒ 2nd Stage
☒ Mature
☒ Mezzanine
☒ LBO/MBO
☒ Turnaround
☐ INT'L EXPANSION
☐ WILL CONSIDER ALL
☒ VENTURE LEASING

Other Locations:

Affiliation: PaineWebber Venture Management
Minimum Investment: $1 Million or more
Capital Under Management: $100 to $500 Million

GEOGRAPHIC PREF

☐ East Coast
☐ West Coast
☐ Northeast
☐ Mid Atlantic
☐ Gulf States
☐ Northwest
☐ Southeast
☐ Southwest
☐ Midwest
☐ Central
☐ Local to Office
☐ Other Geo Pref

APPLIED TECHNOLOGY

One Cranberry Hill
Lexington MA 02173

Phone (781) 862-8622   Fax (781) 862-8367

PROFESSIONALS

Frederick Bamber
Thomas Grant
Nicholas Negroponte

TITLE

Managing General Partner
Managing General Partner
Special General Partner

INDUSTRY PREFERENCE

☒ INFORMATION INDUSTRY
☒ Communications
☒ Computer Equipment
☒ Computer Services
☒ Computer Components
☐ Computer Entertainment
☒ Computer Education
☒ Information Technologies
☒ Computer Media
☒ Software
☒ Internet
☐ MEDICAL/HEALTHCARE
☐ Biotechnology
☐ Healthcare Services
☐ Life Sciences
☐ Medical Products
☐ INDUSTRIAL
☐ Advanced Materials
☐ Chemicals
☐ Instruments & Controls

☐ BASIC INDUSTRIES
☐ Consumer
☐ Distribution
☐ Manufacturing
☐ Retail
☐ Service
☐ Wholesale
☐ SPECIFIC INDUSTRIES
☐ Energy
☐ Environmental
☐ Financial
☐ Real Estate
☐ Transportation
☐ Publishing
☐ Food
☐ Franchises
☐ DIVERSIFIED
☐ MISCELLANEOUS

STAGE PREFERENCE

☒ EARLY STAGE
☒ Seed
☒ Start-up
☒ 1st Stage
☐ LATER STAGE
☐ 2nd Stage
☐ Mature
☐ Mezzanine
☐ LBO/MBO
☐ Turnaround
☐ INT'L EXPANSION
☐ WILL CONSIDER ALL
☐ VENTURE LEASING

Other Locations:

Affiliation:
Minimum Investment: Less than $1 Million
Capital Under Management: Less than $100 Million

GEOGRAPHIC PREF

☐ East Coast
☐ West Coast
☐ Northeast
☐ Mid Atlantic
☐ Gulf States
☐ Northwest
☐ Southeast
☐ Southwest
☐ Midwest
☐ Central
☐ Local to Office
☐ Other Geo Pref

ARGO GLOBAL CAPITAL, INC

210 Broadway
Suite 101
Lynnfield MA 01940

Phone (781) 592-5250   Fax (781) 592-5230

PROFESSIONALS

H. H. Haight
Bernice Bradin
Ronald White
Thomas Wooters, Jr.

TITLE

President
Partner
Partner
Partner

INDUSTRY PREFERENCE

☒ INFORMATION INDUSTRY
☒ Communications
☐ Computer Equipment
☐ Computer Services
☐ Computer Components
☐ Computer Entertainment
☐ Computer Education
☐ Information Technologies
☐ Computer Media
☐ Software
☐ Internet
☐ MEDICAL/HEALTHCARE
☐ Biotechnology
☐ Healthcare Services
☐ Life Sciences
☐ Medical Products
☐ INDUSTRIAL
☐ Advanced Materials
☐ Chemicals
☐ Instruments & Controls

☐ BASIC INDUSTRIES
☐ Consumer
☐ Distribution
☐ Manufacturing
☐ Retail
☐ Service
☐ Wholesale
☒ SPECIFIC INDUSTRIES
☐ Energy
☐ Environmental
☐ Financial
☐ Real Estate
☐ Transportation
☐ Publishing
☐ Food
☐ Franchises
☒ DIVERSIFIED
☒ MISCELLANEOUS
Wireless
Communications Only

STAGE PREFERENCE

☒ EARLY STAGE
☐ Seed
☒ Start-up
☒ 1st Stage
☒ LATER STAGE
☒ 2nd Stage
☐ Mature
☒ Mezzanine
☒ LBO/MBO
☐ Turnaround
☐ INT'L EXPANSION
☐ WILL CONSIDER ALL
☐ VENTURE LEASING

Other Locations:

Affiliation:
Minimum Investment: $1 Million or more
Capital Under Management: $100 to $500 Million

GEOGRAPHIC PREF

☐ East Coast
☐ West Coast
☐ Northeast
☐ Mid Atlantic
☐ Gulf States
☐ Northwest
☐ Southeast
☐ Southwest
☐ Midwest
☐ Central
☐ Local to Office
☐ Other Geo Pref

ASCENT VENTURE MANAGEMENT, INC.

60 State Street
19th Floor
Boston MA 02109

Phone (617) 422-4947   Fax (617) 742-7315

PROFESSIONALS	TITLE
Frank M. Polestra	General Partner
Christopher W. Lynch	General Partner
C. W. Dick	General Partner
Leigh E. Michl	General Partner

INDUSTRY PREFERENCE

☒ INFORMATION INDUSTRY	☒ BASIC INDUSTRIES
☒ Communications	☐ Consumer
☒ Computer Equipment	☐ Distribution
☒ Computer Services	☒ Manufacturing
☒ Computer Components	☒ Retail
☐ Computer Entertainment	☒ Service
☒ Computer Education	☐ Wholesale
☒ Information Technologies	☐ SPECIFIC INDUSTRIES
☐ Computer Media	☐ Energy
☒ Software	☐ Environmental
☒ Internet	☐ Financial
☐ MEDICAL/HEALTHCARE	☐ Real Estate
☐ Biotechnology	☐ Transportation
☐ Healthcare Services	☐ Publishing
☐ Life Sciences	☐ Food
☐ Medical Products	☐ Franchises
☐ INDUSTRIAL	☒ DIVERSIFIED
☐ Advanced Materials	☐ MISCELLANEOUS
☐ Chemicals	
☐ Instruments & Controls	

STAGE PREFERENCE

☒ EARLY STAGE
☒   Seed
☒   Start-up
☒   1st Stage
☒ LATER STAGE
☒   2nd Stage
☒   Mature
☒   Mezzanine
☒   LBO/MBO
☐   Turnaround
☐ INT'L EXPANSION
☐ WILL CONSIDER ALL
☐ VENTURE LEASING
SBIC
Other Locations:

Affiliation: The Pioneer Group, Inc.
Minimum Investment: Less than $1 Million
Capital Under Management: $100 to $500 Million

GEOGRAPHIC PREF

☒   East Coast
☐   West Coast
☐   Northeast
☐   Mid Atlantic
☐   Gulf States
☐   Northwest
☐   Southeast
☐   Southwest
☐   Midwest
☐   Central
☐   Local to Office
☐   Other Geo Pref

ATLAS VENTURE

222 Berkeley Street
Boston MA 02116

Phone (617) 859-9290   Fax (617) 859-9292

PROFESSIONALS	TITLE
Allan R. Ferguson	General Partner
Christopher Spray	General Partner
Barry Fidelman	General Partner
Jean-Francois Formela	General Partner
Michael DuCros	Partner

INDUSTRY PREFERENCE

☒ INFORMATION INDUSTRY	☒ BASIC INDUSTRIES
☒ Communications	☐ Consumer
☒ Computer Equipment	☐ Distribution
☒ Computer Services	☐ Manufacturing
☒ Computer Components	☐ Retail
☒ Computer Entertainment	☒ Service
☒ Computer Education	☐ Wholesale
☒ Information Technologies	☐ SPECIFIC INDUSTRIES
☒ Computer Media	☐ Energy
☒ Software	☐ Environmental
☒ Internet	☐ Financial
☒ MEDICAL/HEALTHCARE	☐ Real Estate
☒ Biotechnology	☐ Transportation
☒ Healthcare Services	☐ Publishing
☒ Life Sciences	☐ Food
☒ Medical Products	☐ Franchises
☒ INDUSTRIAL	☒ DIVERSIFIED
☒ Advanced Materials	☐ MISCELLANEOUS
☒ Chemicals	
☒ Instruments & Controls	

STAGE PREFERENCE

☒ EARLY STAGE
☒   Seed
☒   Start-up
☒   1st Stage
☒ LATER STAGE
☒   2nd Stage
☒   Mature
☒   Mezzanine
☒   LBO/MBO
☒   Turnaround
☒ INT'L EXPANSION
☐ WILL CONSIDER ALL
☒ VENTURE LEASING

Other Locations:

Affiliation: Atlas Venture-Amsterdam
Minimum Investment: Less than $1 Million
Capital Under Management: $100 to $500 Million

GEOGRAPHIC PREF

☐   East Coast
☐   West Coast
☐   Northeast
☐   Mid Atlantic
☐   Gulf States
☐   Northwest
☐   Southeast
☐   Southwest
☐   Midwest
☐   Central
☐   Local to Office
☐   Other Geo Pref

BANCBOSTON VENTURES, INC.

175 Federal Street
10th Floor
Boston MA 02110

Phone (617) 434-2509   Fax (617) 434-1153

PROFESSIONALS	TITLE
John Cullinane	Managing Director
Marcia Bates	Managing Director
Jeanne McGovern	

INDUSTRY PREFERENCE

☒ INFORMATION INDUSTRY	☐ BASIC INDUSTRIES
☒ Communications	☐ Consumer
☒ Computer Equipment	☐ Distribution
☒ Computer Services	☐ Manufacturing
☒ Computer Components	☐ Retail
☐ Computer Entertainment	☐ Service
☒ Computer Education	☐ Wholesale
☒ Information Technologies	☐ SPECIFIC INDUSTRIES
☒ Computer Media	☐ Energy
☒ Software	☐ Environmental
☒ Internet	☐ Financial
☒ MEDICAL/HEALTHCARE	☐ Real Estate
☐ Biotechnology	☐ Transportation
☒ Healthcare Services	☐ Publishing
☐ Life Sciences	☐ Food
☐ Medical Products	☐ Franchises
☐ INDUSTRIAL	☒ DIVERSIFIED
☐ Advanced Materials	☐ MISCELLANEOUS
☐ Chemicals	
☐ Instruments & Controls	

STAGE PREFERENCE

☒ EARLY STAGE
☒ Seed
☒ Start-up
☒ 1st Stage
☒ LATER STAGE
☒ 2nd Stage
☒ Mature
☒ Mezzanine
☒ LBO/MBO
☐ Turnaround
☐ INT'L EXPANSION
☐ WILL CONSIDER ALL
☐ VENTURE LEASING
SBIC
Other Locations: Palo Alto CA

Affiliation: Bank of Boston
Minimum Investment: Less than $1 Million
Capital Under Management: Over $500 Million

GEOGRAPHIC PREF

☐ East Coast
☐ West Coast
☐ Northeast
☐ Mid Atlantic
☐ Gulf States
☐ Northwest
☐ Southeast
☐ Southwest
☐ Midwest
☐ Central
☐ Local to Office
☐ Other Geo Pref

BATTERY VENTURES, LP

20 William Street
Suite 200
Boston MA 02481

Phone (781) 996-1000   Fax (781) 996-1001

PROFESSIONALS	TITLE
Morgan Jones	
Scott Tobin	
Sunil Dhaliwal	
Michael Brown	

INDUSTRY PREFERENCE

☒ INFORMATION INDUSTRY	☐ BASIC INDUSTRIES
☐ Communications	☐ Consumer
☒ Computer Equipment	☐ Distribution
☒ Computer Services	☐ Manufacturing
☒ Computer Components	☐ Retail
☐ Computer Entertainment	☐ Service
☒ Computer Education	☐ Wholesale
☒ Information Technologies	☐ SPECIFIC INDUSTRIES
☒ Computer Media	☐ Energy
☒ Software	☐ Environmental
☒ Internet	☐ Financial
☐ MEDICAL/HEALTHCARE	☐ Real Estate
☐ Biotechnology	☐ Transportation
☐ Healthcare Services	☐ Publishing
☐ Life Sciences	☐ Food
☐ Medical Products	☐ Franchises
☐ INDUSTRIAL	☐ DIVERSIFIED
☐ Advanced Materials	☐ MISCELLANEOUS
☐ Chemicals	
☐ Instruments & Controls	

STAGE PREFERENCE

☒ EARLY STAGE
☒ Seed
☒ Start-up
☒ 1st Stage
☒ LATER STAGE
☒ 2nd Stage
☒ Mature
☒ Mezzanine
☒ LBO/MBO
☒ Turnaround
☐ INT'L EXPANSION
☐ WILL CONSIDER ALL
☒ VENTURE LEASING

Other Locations: San Mateo CA

Affiliation: The Yankee Group
Minimum Investment: Less than $1 Million
Capital Under Management: Over $500 Million

GEOGRAPHIC PREF

☐ East Coast
☐ West Coast
☐ Northeast
☐ Mid Atlantic
☐ Gulf States
☐ Northwest
☐ Southeast
☐ Southwest
☐ Midwest
☐ Central
☐ Local to Office
☐ Other Geo Pref

BERKSHIRE PARTNERS, LLC

**One Boston Place
Suite 3300
Boston MA 02108**

Phone (617) 227-0050   Fax (617) 227-6105

PROFESSIONALS	TITLE
Bradley M. Bloom	Managing Director
Jane Brock-Wilson	Managing Director
Kevin T. Callaghan	Managing Director
Chris Clifford	Managing Director
Russell L. Epker	Managing Director
Carl Ferenbach	Managing Director
Garth H. Greimann	Managing Director
Richard K. Lubin	Managing Director

INDUSTRY PREFERENCE

☒ INFORMATION INDUSTRY	☒ BASIC INDUSTRIES		
☒ Communications	☐ Consumer		
☐ Computer Equipment	☐ Distribution		
☐ Computer Services	☒ Manufacturing		
☐ Computer Components	☒ Retail		
☐ Computer Entertainment	☒ Service		
☐ Computer Education	☐ Wholesale		
☐ Information Technologies	☒ SPECIFIC INDUSTRIES		
☐ Computer Media	☐ Energy		
☐ Software	☐ Environmental		
☐ Internet	☐ Financial		
☐ MEDICAL/HEALTHCARE	☐ Real Estate		
☐ Biotechnology	☒ Transportation		
☐ Healthcare Services	☐ Publishing		
☐ Life Sciences	☐ Food		
☐ Medical Products	☐ Franchises		
☐ INDUSTRIAL	☒ DIVERSIFIED		
☐ Advanced Materials	☒ MISCELLANEOUS		
☐ Chemicals			
☐ Instruments & Controls			

STAGE PREFERENCE

☐ EARLY STAGE
☐ Seed
☐ Start-up
☐ 1st Stage
☒ LATER STAGE
☐ 2nd Stage
☒ Mature
☒ Mezzanine
☒ LBO/MBO
☐ Turnaround
☐ INT'L EXPANSION
☐ WILL CONSIDER ALL
☐ VENTURE LEASING

Other Locations:

Affiliation:
Minimum Investment: $1 Million or more
Capital Under Management: Over $500 Million

GEOGRAPHIC PREF

☐ East Coast
☐ West Coast
☐ Northeast
☐ Mid Atlantic
☐ Gulf States
☐ Northwest
☐ Southeast
☐ Southwest
☐ Midwest
☐ Central
☐ Local to Office
☐ Other Geo Pref

BESSEMER VENTURE PARTNERS

**83 Walnut Street
Wellesley Hills MA 02481**

Phone (781) 237-6050   Fax (781) 237-7576

PROFESSIONALS	TITLE
G. Felda Hardymon	General Partner
Christopher F.O. Gabrieli	General Partner
William T. Burgin	General Partner

INDUSTRY PREFERENCE

☒ INFORMATION INDUSTRY	☒ BASIC INDUSTRIES
☒ Communications	☒ Consumer
☒ Computer Equipment	☐ Distribution
☒ Computer Services	☐ Manufacturing
☒ Computer Components	☒ Retail
☐ Computer Entertainment	☒ Service
☒ Computer Education	☐ Wholesale
☒ Information Technologies	☒ SPECIFIC INDUSTRIES
☒ Computer Media	☒ Energy
☒ Software	☒ Environmental
☒ Internet	☐ Financial
☒ MEDICAL/HEALTHCARE	☐ Real Estate
☒ Biotechnology	☐ Transportation
☒ Healthcare Services	☐ Publishing
☒ Life Sciences	☐ Food
☒ Medical Products	☐ Franchises
☒ INDUSTRIAL	☒ DIVERSIFIED
☒ Advanced Materials	☐ MISCELLANEOUS
☒ Chemicals	
☒ Instruments & Controls	

STAGE PREFERENCE

☒ EARLY STAGE
☒ Seed
☒ Start-up
☒ 1st Stage
☒ LATER STAGE
☒ 2nd Stage
☒ Mature
☒ Mezzanine
☒ LBO/MBO
☐ Turnaround
☐ INT'L EXPANSION
☐ WILL CONSIDER ALL
☐ VENTURE LEASING

Other Locations: Westbury NY, Menlo Park CA

Affiliation: Bessemer Securities Corp.
Minimum Investment: Less than $1 Million
Capital Under Management: $100 to $500 Million

GEOGRAPHIC PREF

☐ East Coast
☐ West Coast
☐ Northeast
☐ Mid Atlantic
☐ Gulf States
☐ Northwest
☐ Southeast
☐ Southwest
☐ Midwest
☐ Central
☐ Local to Office
☐ Other Geo Pref

BOSTON CAPITAL VENTURES

Old City Hall
45 School Street
Boston MA 02108-3204

Phone (617) 227-6550   Fax (617) 227-3847

PROFESSIONALS	TITLE
H. J. von der Goltz	General Partner
J. J. Shields	General Partner

INDUSTRY PREFERENCE

- ☒ INFORMATION INDUSTRY
- ☒ Communications
- ☒ Computer Equipment
- ☒ Computer Services
- ☒ Computer Components
- ☐ Computer Entertainment
- ☒ Computer Education
- ☒ Information Technologies
- ☒ Computer Media
- ☒ Software
- ☒ Internet
- ☒ MEDICAL/HEALTHCARE
- ☐ Biotechnology
- ☒ Healthcare Services
- ☐ Life Sciences
- ☒ Medical Products
- ☒ INDUSTRIAL
- ☒ Advanced Materials
- ☒ Chemicals
- ☒ Instruments & Controls

- ☐ BASIC INDUSTRIES
- ☐ Consumer
- ☐ Distribution
- ☐ Manufacturing
- ☐ Retail
- ☐ Service
- ☐ Wholesale
- ☐ SPECIFIC INDUSTRIES
- ☐ Energy
- ☐ Environmental
- ☐ Financial
- ☐ Real Estate
- ☐ Transportation
- ☐ Publishing
- ☐ Food
- ☐ Franchises
- ☒ DIVERSIFIED
- ☐ MISCELLANEOUS

STAGE PREFERENCE

- ☒ EARLY STAGE
- ☐ Seed
- ☐ Start-up
- ☒ 1st Stage
- ☒ LATER STAGE
- ☒ 2nd Stage
- ☒ Mature
- ☐ Mezzanine
- ☐ LBO/MBO
- ☐ Turnaround
- ☐ INT'L EXPANSION
- ☐ WILL CONSIDER ALL
- ☐ VENTURE LEASING

Other Locations:

Affiliation:
Minimum Investment: Less than $1 Million
Capital Under Management: $100 to $500 Million

GEOGRAPHIC PREF

- ☐ East Coast
- ☐ West Coast
- ☒ Northeast
- ☐ Mid Atlantic
- ☐ Gulf States
- ☐ Northwest
- ☐ Southeast
- ☐ Southwest
- ☐ Midwest
- ☐ Central
- ☐ Local to Office
- ☐ Other Geo Pref

BOSTON MILLENNIA PARTNERS

30 Rowes Wharf
Boston MA 02110

Phone (617) 428-5150   Fax (617) 428-5160

PROFESSIONALS	TITLE
A. Dana Callow, Jr.	Managing General Partner
Robert S. Sherman	General Partner
Marty Hernon	General Partner

INDUSTRY PREFERENCE

- ☒ INFORMATION INDUSTRY
- ☒ Communications
- ☒ Computer Equipment
- ☒ Computer Services
- ☒ Computer Components
- ☐ Computer Entertainment
- ☒ Computer Education
- ☒ Information Technologies
- ☒ Computer Media
- ☒ Software
- ☒ Internet
- ☒ MEDICAL/HEALTHCARE
- ☒ Biotechnology
- ☒ Healthcare Services
- ☒ Life Sciences
- ☒ Medical Products
- ☐ INDUSTRIAL
- ☐ Advanced Materials
- ☐ Chemicals
- ☐ Instruments & Controls

- ☐ BASIC INDUSTRIES
- ☐ Consumer
- ☐ Distribution
- ☐ Manufacturing
- ☐ Retail
- ☐ Service
- ☐ Wholesale
- ☒ SPECIFIC INDUSTRIES
- ☐ Energy
- ☐ Environmental
- ☐ Financial
- ☐ Real Estate
- ☐ Transportation
- ☐ Publishing
- ☐ Food
- ☐ Franchises
- ☒ DIVERSIFIED
- ☒ MISCELLANEOUS
-    e-Commerce

STAGE PREFERENCE

- ☒ EARLY STAGE
- ☒ Seed
- ☒ Start-up
- ☒ 1st Stage
- ☒ LATER STAGE
- ☒ 2nd Stage
- ☐ Mature
- ☐ Mezzanine
- ☒ LBO/MBO
- ☐ Turnaround
- ☐ INT'L EXPANSION
- ☐ WILL CONSIDER ALL
- ☐ VENTURE LEASING

Other Locations:

Affiliation:
Minimum Investment: $1 Million or more
Capital Under Management: $100 to $500 Million

GEOGRAPHIC PREF

- ☐ East Coast
- ☐ West Coast
- ☐ Northeast
- ☐ Mid Atlantic
- ☐ Gulf States
- ☐ Northwest
- ☐ Southeast
- ☐ Southwest
- ☐ Midwest
- ☐ Central
- ☐ Local to Office
- ☐ Other Geo Pref

BURR, EGAN, DELEAGE & CO. INC.
ALTA COMMUNICATIONS
One Post Office Square
Suite 3800
Boston MA 02109

Phone (617) 482-8020   Fax (617) 482-1944

PROFESSIONALS	TITLE
William P. Egan	Founding Partner

INDUSTRY PREFERENCE

- ☒ INFORMATION INDUSTRY
- ☒ Communications
- ☒ Computer Equipment
- ☒ Computer Services
- ☒ Computer Components
- ☒ Computer Entertainment
- ☒ Computer Education
- ☒ Information Technologies
- ☒ Computer Media
- ☐ Software
- ☒ Internet
- ☒ MEDICAL/HEALTHCARE
- ☒ Biotechnology
- ☒ Healthcare Services
- ☐ Life Sciences
- ☒ Medical Products
- ☒ INDUSTRIAL
- ☒ Advanced Materials
- ☒ Chemicals
- ☒ Instruments & Controls

- ☒ BASIC INDUSTRIES
- ☐ Consumer
- ☐ Distribution
- ☐ Manufacturing
- ☐ Retail
- ☒ Service
- ☐ Wholesale
- ☐ SPECIFIC INDUSTRIES
- ☐ Energy
- ☐ Environmental
- ☐ Financial
- ☐ Real Estate
- ☐ Transportation
- ☐ Publishing
- ☐ Food
- ☐ Franchises
- ☒ DIVERSIFIED
- ☐ MISCELLANEOUS

STAGE PREFERENCE

- ☒ EARLY STAGE
- ☒ Seed
- ☒ Start-up
- ☒ 1st Stage
- ☒ LATER STAGE
- ☒ 2nd Stage
- ☒ Mature
- ☒ Mezzanine
- ☒ LBO/MBO
- ☒ Turnaround
- ☐ INT'L EXPANSION
- ☐ WILL CONSIDER ALL
- ☒ VENTURE LEASING

Other Locations: San Francisco CA

Affiliation:
Minimum Investment: Less than $1 Million
Capital Under Management: Over $500 Million

GEOGRAPHIC PREF

- ☐ East Coast
- ☒ West Coast
- ☒ Northeast
- ☐ Mid Atlantic
- ☐ Gulf States
- ☐ Northwest
- ☐ Southeast
- ☐ Southwest
- ☐ Midwest
- ☐ Central
- ☐ Local to Office
- ☐ Other Geo Pref

CAPITAL RESOURCE PARTNERS

85 Merrimac Street
Suite 200
Boston MA 02114

Phone (617) 723-9000   Fax (617) 723-9819

PROFESSIONALS	TITLE
Robert C. Ammerman	Managing Partner
Fred C. Danforth	Managing Partner
Stephen M. Jenks	Partner
Alexander S. McGrath	Partner

INDUSTRY PREFERENCE

- ☒ INFORMATION INDUSTRY
- ☒ Communications
- ☐ Computer Equipment
- ☒ Computer Services
- ☐ Computer Components
- ☐ Computer Entertainment
- ☒ Computer Education
- ☐ Information Technologies
- ☐ Computer Media
- ☐ Software
- ☐ Internet
- ☒ MEDICAL/HEALTHCARE
- ☒ Biotechnology
- ☒ Healthcare Services
- ☒ Life Sciences
- ☒ Medical Products
- ☒ INDUSTRIAL
- ☐ Advanced Materials
- ☐ Chemicals
- ☐ Instruments & Controls

- ☒ BASIC INDUSTRIES
- ☒ Consumer
- ☒ Distribution
- ☐ Manufacturing
- ☐ Retail
- ☒ Service
- ☐ Wholesale
- ☒ SPECIFIC INDUSTRIES
- ☐ Energy
- ☐ Environmental
- ☒ Financial
- ☐ Real Estate
- ☒ Transportation
- ☒ Publishing
- ☐ Food
- ☐ Franchises
- ☒ DIVERSIFIED
- ☒ MISCELLANEOUS
- Agriculture

STAGE PREFERENCE

- ☐ EARLY STAGE
- ☐ Seed
- ☐ Start-up
- ☐ 1st Stage
- ☒ LATER STAGE
- ☒ 2nd Stage
- ☐ Mature
- ☒ Mezzanine
- ☒ LBO/MBO
- ☐ Turnaround
- ☐ INT'L EXPANSION
- ☐ WILL CONSIDER ALL
- ☐ VENTURE LEASING

Other Locations:

Affiliation:
Minimum Investment: $1 Million or more
Capital Under Management: Over $500 Million

GEOGRAPHIC PREF

- ☐ East Coast
- ☐ West Coast
- ☐ Northeast
- ☐ Mid Atlantic
- ☐ Gulf States
- ☐ Northwest
- ☐ Southeast
- ☐ Southwest
- ☐ Midwest
- ☐ Central
- ☐ Local to Office
- ☐ Other Geo Pref

CHARLES RIVER VENTURES

Bay Colony Corporate Center
1000 Winter Street, Suite 3300
Waltham MA 02451

Phone (781) 487-7060   Fax (781) 487-7065

PROFESSIONALS	TITLE
Michael J. Zak	General Partner
Richard M. Burnes, Jr.	General Partner
Ted Dintersmith	
Jonathan M. Guerster	
Iahar Armony	

INDUSTRY PREFERENCE

- ☒ INFORMATION INDUSTRY
- ☒ Communications
- ☒ Computer Equipment
- ☒ Computer Services
- ☒ Computer Components
- ☐ Computer Entertainment
- ☒ Computer Education
- ☒ Information Technologies
- ☒ Computer Media
- ☒ Software
- ☒ Internet
- ☐ MEDICAL/HEALTHCARE
- ☐ Biotechnology
- ☐ Healthcare Services
- ☐ Life Sciences
- ☐ Medical Products
- ☐ INDUSTRIAL
- ☐ Advanced Materials
- ☐ Chemicals
- ☐ Instruments & Controls

- ☐ BASIC INDUSTRIES
- ☐ Consumer
- ☐ Distribution
- ☐ Manufacturing
- ☐ Retail
- ☐ Service
- ☐ Wholesale
- ☐ SPECIFIC INDUSTRIES
- ☐ Energy
- ☐ Environmental
- ☐ Financial
- ☐ Real Estate
- ☐ Transportation
- ☐ Publishing
- ☐ Food
- ☐ Franchises
- ☐ DIVERSIFIED
- ☐ MISCELLANEOUS

STAGE PREFERENCE

- ☒ EARLY STAGE
- ☒ Seed
- ☒ Start-up
- ☒ 1st Stage
- ☒ LATER STAGE
- ☒ 2nd Stage
- ☐ Mature
- ☐ Mezzanine
- ☐ LBO/MBO
- ☐ Turnaround
- ☐ INT'L EXPANSION
- ☐ WILL CONSIDER ALL
- ☐ VENTURE LEASING

Other Locations:

Affiliation:
Minimum Investment: Less than $1 Million
Capital Under Management: $100 to $500 Million

GEOGRAPHIC PREF

- ☐ East Coast
- ☐ West Coast
- ☒ Northeast
- ☐ Mid Atlantic
- ☐ Gulf States
- ☐ Northwest
- ☐ Southeast
- ☐ Southwest
- ☐ Midwest
- ☐ Central
- ☐ Local to Office
- ☐ Other Geo Pref

CLAFLIN CAPITAL MANAGEMENT, INC.

10 Liberty Square, Suite 300
Boston MA 02109

Phone (617) 426-6505   Fax (617) 482-0016

PROFESSIONALS	TITLE
Frederick Zhang	General Partner
Joseph Stavenhagen	General Partner
Thomas M. Claflin II	General Partner
John O. Flender	General Partner
Walter Bird	General Partner
Rolf Stutz	General Partner

INDUSTRY PREFERENCE

- ☒ INFORMATION INDUSTRY
- ☒ Communications
- ☒ Computer Equipment
- ☒ Computer Services
- ☒ Computer Components
- ☐ Computer Entertainment
- ☒ Computer Education
- ☒ Information Technologies
- ☐ Computer Media
- ☒ Software
- ☒ Internet
- ☒ MEDICAL/HEALTHCARE
- ☒ Biotechnology
- ☐ Healthcare Services
- ☒ Life Sciences
- ☐ Medical Products
- ☒ INDUSTRIAL
- ☒ Advanced Materials
- ☒ Chemicals
- ☒ Instruments & Controls

- ☒ BASIC INDUSTRIES
- ☐ Consumer
- ☐ Distribution
- ☐ Manufacturing
- ☐ Retail
- ☒ Service
- ☐ Wholesale
- ☐ SPECIFIC INDUSTRIES
- ☐ Energy
- ☐ Environmental
- ☐ Financial
- ☐ Real Estate
- ☐ Transportation
- ☐ Publishing
- ☐ Food
- ☐ Franchises
- ☒ DIVERSIFIED
- ☐ MISCELLANEOUS

STAGE PREFERENCE

- ☒ EARLY STAGE
- ☒ Seed
- ☒ Start-up
- ☒ 1st Stage
- ☐ LATER STAGE
- ☐ 2nd Stage
- ☐ Mature
- ☐ Mezzanine
- ☐ LBO/MBO
- ☐ Turnaround
- ☐ INT'L EXPANSION
- ☐ WILL CONSIDER ALL
- ☐ VENTURE LEASING

Other Locations:

Affiliation:
Minimum Investment: Less than $1 Million
Capital Under Management: Less than $100 Million

GEOGRAPHIC PREF

- ☐ East Coast
- ☐ West Coast
- ☒ Northeast
- ☐ Mid Atlantic
- ☐ Gulf States
- ☐ Northwest
- ☐ Southeast
- ☐ Southwest
- ☐ Midwest
- ☐ Central
- ☐ Local to Office
- ☐ Other Geo Pref

COMDISCO VENTURES

Totten Pond Office Center
400-1 Totten Pond Road #5
Waltham MA 02451

Phone (781) 672-0250   Fax (781) 398-8099

PROFESSIONALS	TITLE
Geoffrey L. Tickner, Jr.	

INDUSTRY PREFERENCE

- ☒ INFORMATION INDUSTRY
- ☒ Communications
- ☒ Computer Equipment
- ☒ Computer Services
- ☒ Computer Components
- ☐ Computer Entertainment
- ☒ Computer Education
- ☒ Information Technologies
- ☒ Computer Media
- ☒ Software
- ☒ Internet
- ☒ MEDICAL/HEALTHCARE
- ☒ Biotechnology
- ☒ Healthcare Services
- ☒ Life Sciences
- ☒ Medical Products
- ☒ INDUSTRIAL
- ☒ Advanced Materials
- ☒ Chemicals
- ☒ Instruments & Controls

- ☒ BASIC INDUSTRIES
- ☒ Consumer
- ☐ Distribution
- ☐ Manufacturing
- ☐ Retail
- ☒ Service
- ☐ Wholesale
- ☐ SPECIFIC INDUSTRIES
- ☐ Energy
- ☐ Environmental
- ☐ Financial
- ☐ Real Estate
- ☐ Transportation
- ☐ Publishing
- ☐ Food
- ☐ Franchises
- ☒ DIVERSIFIED
- ☐ MISCELLANEOUS

STAGE PREFERENCE

- ☒ EARLY STAGE
- ☒ Seed
- ☒ Start-up
- ☒ 1st Stage
- ☒ LATER STAGE
- ☒ 2nd Stage
- ☒ Mature
- ☒ Mezzanine
- ☐ LBO/MBO
- ☐ Turnaround
- ☐ INT'L EXPANSION
- ☐ WILL CONSIDER ALL
- ☐ VENTURE LEASING

Other Locations: Rosemont IL, Menlo Park CA

Affiliation: Comdisco, Inc.
Minimum Investment: Less than $1 Million
Capital Under Management: $100 to $500 Million

GEOGRAPHIC PREF

- ☐ East Coast
- ☐ West Coast
- ☐ Northeast
- ☐ Mid Atlantic
- ☐ Gulf States
- ☐ Northwest
- ☐ Southeast
- ☐ Southwest
- ☐ Midwest
- ☐ Central
- ☐ Local to Office
- ☐ Other Geo Pref

COMMONWEALTH CAPITAL VENTURES

20 William Street
Suite 225
Wellesley MA 02481

Phone (781) 237-7373   Fax (781) 235-8627

PROFESSIONALS	TITLE
Rob Chandra	General Partner
Michael Fitzgerald	General Partner
Jeffrey Hurst	General Partner
Stephen McCormack	General Partner

INDUSTRY PREFERENCE

- ☒ INFORMATION INDUSTRY
- ☒ Communications
- ☒ Computer Equipment
- ☒ Computer Services
- ☒ Computer Components
- ☐ Computer Entertainment
- ☒ Computer Education
- ☒ Information Technologies
- ☐ Computer Media
- ☒ Software
- ☒ Internet
- ☒ MEDICAL/HEALTHCARE
- ☐ Biotechnology
- ☒ Healthcare Services
- ☐ Life Sciences
- ☒ Medical Products
- ☒ INDUSTRIAL
- ☒ Advanced Materials
- ☒ Chemicals
- ☒ Instruments & Controls

- ☒ BASIC INDUSTRIES
- ☒ Consumer
- ☒ Distribution
- ☐ Manufacturing
- ☐ Retail
- ☐ Service
- ☐ Wholesale
- ☐ SPECIFIC INDUSTRIES
- ☐ Energy
- ☐ Environmental
- ☐ Financial
- ☐ Real Estate
- ☐ Transportation
- ☐ Publishing
- ☐ Food
- ☐ Franchises
- ☒ DIVERSIFIED
- ☒ MISCELLANEOUS

STAGE PREFERENCE

- ☒ EARLY STAGE
- ☒ Seed
- ☒ Start-up
- ☒ 1st Stage
- ☒ LATER STAGE
- ☒ 2nd Stage
- ☐ Mature
- ☒ Mezzanine
- ☒ LBO/MBO
- ☒ Turnaround
- ☐ INT'L EXPANSION
- ☐ WILL CONSIDER ALL
- ☒ VENTURE LEASING

Other Locations:

Affiliation:
Minimum Investment: Less than $1 Million
Capital Under Management: $100 to $500 Million

GEOGRAPHIC PREF

- ☐ East Coast
- ☐ West Coast
- ☒ Northeast
- ☐ Mid Atlantic
- ☐ Gulf States
- ☐ Northwest
- ☐ Southeast
- ☐ Southwest
- ☐ Midwest
- ☐ Central
- ☐ Local to Office
- ☒ Other Geo Pref
  New England Region

COMMONWEALTH ENTERPRISE FUND INC.

10 Post Office Square
Suite 1090
Boston MA 02109

Phone (617) 482-9141   Fax (617) 482-7129

PROFESSIONALS	TITLE
Kamal M. Quadir	Portfolio Manager

INDUSTRY PREFERENCE

- ☐ INFORMATION INDUSTRY
- ☐ Communications
- ☐ Computer Equipment
- ☐ Computer Services
- ☐ Computer Components
- ☐ Computer Entertainment
- ☐ Computer Education
- ☐ Information Technologies
- ☐ Computer Media
- ☐ Software
- ☐ Internet
- ☐ MEDICAL/HEALTHCARE
- ☐ Biotechnology
- ☐ Healthcare Services
- ☐ Life Sciences
- ☐ Medical Products
- ☐ INDUSTRIAL
- ☐ Advanced Materials
- ☐ Chemicals
- ☐ Instruments & Controls

- ☐ BASIC INDUSTRIES
- ☐ Consumer
- ☐ Distribution
- ☐ Manufacturing
- ☐ Retail
- ☐ Service
- ☐ Wholesale
- ☐ SPECIFIC INDUSTRIES
- ☐ Energy
- ☐ Environmental
- ☐ Financial
- ☐ Real Estate
- ☐ Transportation
- ☐ Publishing
- ☐ Food
- ☐ Franchises
- ☒ DIVERSIFIED
- ☐ MISCELLANEOUS

STAGE PREFERENCE

- ☒ EARLY STAGE
- ☐ Seed
- ☒ Start-up
- ☒ 1st Stage
- ☒ LATER STAGE
- ☒ 2nd Stage
- ☒ Mature
- ☐ Mezzanine
- ☒ LBO/MBO
- ☐ Turnaround
- ☐ INT'L EXPANSION
- ☐ WILL CONSIDER ALL
- ☐ VENTURE LEASING

SSBIC
Other Locations:

Affiliation:
Minimum Investment: Less than $1 Million
Capital Under Management: Less than $100 Million

GEOGRAPHIC PREF

- ☐ East Coast
- ☐ West Coast
- ☒ Northeast
- ☐ Mid Atlantic
- ☐ Gulf States
- ☒ Northwest
- ☐ Southeast
- ☐ Southwest
- ☐ Midwest
- ☐ Central
- ☐ Local to Office
- ☐ Other Geo Pref

COMMUNITY TECHNOLOGY FUND

108 Bay State Road
Boston MA 02215

Phone (617) 353-4550   Fax (617) 353-6141

PROFESSIONALS	TITLE
Randall C. Crawford	Director
Matthew J. Burns	Managing Director

INDUSTRY PREFERENCE

- ☒ INFORMATION INDUSTRY
- ☒ Communications
- ☒ Computer Equipment
- ☒ Computer Services
- ☒ Computer Components
- ☐ Computer Entertainment
- ☒ Computer Education
- ☒ Information Technologies
- ☒ Computer Media
- ☒ Software
- ☒ Internet
- ☒ MEDICAL/HEALTHCARE
- ☒ Biotechnology
- ☒ Healthcare Services
- ☒ Life Sciences
- ☒ Medical Products
- ☐ INDUSTRIAL
- ☐ Advanced Materials
- ☐ Chemicals
- ☐ Instruments & Controls

- ☐ BASIC INDUSTRIES
- ☐ Consumer
- ☐ Distribution
- ☐ Manufacturing
- ☐ Retail
- ☐ Service
- ☐ Wholesale
- ☐ SPECIFIC INDUSTRIES
- ☐ Energy
- ☐ Environmental
- ☐ Financial
- ☐ Real Estate
- ☐ Transportation
- ☐ Publishing
- ☐ Food
- ☐ Franchises
- ☒ DIVERSIFIED
- ☐ MISCELLANEOUS

STAGE PREFERENCE

- ☒ EARLY STAGE
- ☒ Seed
- ☒ Start-up
- ☒ 1st Stage
- ☒ LATER STAGE
- ☒ 2nd Stage
- ☐ Mature
- ☐ Mezzanine
- ☐ LBO/MBO
- ☐ Turnaround
- ☐ INT'L EXPANSION
- ☐ WILL CONSIDER ALL
- ☐ VENTURE LEASING

Other Locations:

Affiliation: Boston University
Minimum Investment: Less than $1 Million
Capital Under Management: Less than $100 Million

GEOGRAPHIC PREF

- ☐ East Coast
- ☐ West Coast
- ☐ Northeast
- ☐ Mid Atlantic
- ☐ Gulf States
- ☐ Northwest
- ☐ Southeast
- ☐ Southwest
- ☐ Midwest
- ☐ Central
- ☐ Local to Office
- ☐ Other Geo Pref

CORNING TECHNOLOGY VENTURES, LLP

121 High Street
Suite 400
Boston MA 02110-2416

Phone (617) 338-2656   Fax (617) 261-3864

PROFESSIONALS	TITLE
Dwight "Barney" Corning	General Partner
J. Samborne Foster, Jr.	General Partner

INDUSTRY PREFERENCE

☒ INFORMATION INDUSTRY
☒ Communications
☒ Computer Equipment
☒ Computer Services
☒ Computer Components
☐ Computer Entertainment
☒ Computer Education
☒ Information Technologies
☒ Computer Media
☒ Software
☒ Internet
☒ MEDICAL/HEALTHCARE
☒ Biotechnology
☒ Healthcare Services
☒ Life Sciences
☒ Medical Products
☒ INDUSTRIAL
☒ Advanced Materials
☒ Chemicals
☒ Instruments & Controls

☒ BASIC INDUSTRIES
☐ Consumer
☐ Distribution
☒ Manufacturing
☐ Retail
☒ Service
☐ Wholesale
☐ SPECIFIC INDUSTRIES
☐ Energy
☐ Environmental
☐ Financial
☐ Real Estate
☐ Transportation
☐ Publishing
☐ Food
☐ Franchises
☒ DIVERSIFIED
☐ MISCELLANEOUS

STAGE PREFERENCE

☒ EARLY STAGE
☐ Seed
☒ Start-up
☒ 1st Stage
☒ LATER STAGE
☒ 2nd Stage
☒ Mature
☒ Mezzanine
☒ LBO/MBO
☐ Turnaround
☐ INT'L EXPANSION
☐ WILL CONSIDER ALL
☐ VENTURE LEASING

Other Locations:

Affiliation:
Minimum Investment: Less than $1 Million
Capital Under Management: Less than $100 Million

GEOGRAPHIC PREF

☐ East Coast
☐ West Coast
☒ Northeast
☐ Mid Atlantic
☐ Gulf States
☐ Northwest
☐ Southeast
☐ Southwest
☐ Midwest
☐ Central
☐ Local to Office
☐ Other Geo Pref

DOMINION VENTURES, INC.

One Post Office Square
38th Floor Suite 3820
Boston MA 02109

Phone (617) 367-8575   Fax (617) 367-0323

PROFESSIONALS	TITLE
Randolph Werner	General Partner
James Bratton	Managing Director

INDUSTRY PREFERENCE

☒ INFORMATION INDUSTRY
☒ Communications
☒ Computer Equipment
☒ Computer Services
☒ Computer Components
☐ Computer Entertainment
☒ Computer Education
☒ Information Technologies
☒ Computer Media
☒ Software
☒ Internet
☐ MEDICAL/HEALTHCARE
☐ Biotechnology
☐ Healthcare Services
☐ Life Sciences
☐ Medical Products
☒ INDUSTRIAL
☐ Advanced Materials
☐ Chemicals
☒ Instruments & Controls

☒ BASIC INDUSTRIES
☒ Consumer
☐ Distribution
☒ Manufacturing
☒ Retail
☐ Service
☐ Wholesale
☒ SPECIFIC INDUSTRIES
☐ Energy
☐ Environmental
☒ Financial
☐ Real Estate
☐ Transportation
☐ Publishing
☐ Food
☐ Franchises
☒ DIVERSIFIED
☒ MISCELLANEOUS

STAGE PREFERENCE

☒ EARLY STAGE
☐ Seed
☐ Start-up
☒ 1st Stage
☒ LATER STAGE
☒ 2nd Stage
☒ Mature
☒ Mezzanine
☒ LBO/MBO
☐ Turnaround
☐ INT'L EXPANSION
☐ WILL CONSIDER ALL
☐ VENTURE LEASING

Other Locations: San Francisco CA, Menlo Park CA

Affiliation:
Minimum Investment: $1 Million or more
Capital Under Management: $100 to $500 Million

GEOGRAPHIC PREF

☐ East Coast
☐ West Coast
☐ Northeast
☐ Mid Atlantic
☐ Gulf States
☐ Northwest
☐ Southeast
☐ Southwest
☐ Midwest
☐ Central
☐ Local to Office
☐ Other Geo Pref

EGAN MANAGED CAPITAL

30 Federal Street
Boston MA 02110

Phone (617) 695-2600   Fax (617) 695-2699

PROFESSIONALS	TITLE
Michael Shanahan	General Partner
John Egan	General Partner
Francis J. Hughes	
Robert Creeden	

INDUSTRY PREFERENCE

☒ INFORMATION INDUSTRY
☒ Communications
☒ Computer Equipment
☒ Computer Services
☒ Computer Components
☐ Computer Entertainment
☒ Computer Education
☒ Information Technologies
☒ Computer Media
☒ Software
☒ Internet
☐ MEDICAL/HEALTHCARE
☐ Biotechnology
☐ Healthcare Services
☐ Life Sciences
☐ Medical Products
☒ INDUSTRIAL
☒ Advanced Materials
☒ Chemicals
☒ Instruments & Controls

☐ BASIC INDUSTRIES
☐ Consumer
☐ Distribution
☐ Manufacturing
☐ Retail
☐ Service
☐ Wholesale
☐ SPECIFIC INDUSTRIES
☐ Energy
☐ Environmental
☐ Financial
☐ Real Estate
☐ Transportation
☐ Publishing
☐ Food
☐ Franchises
☒ DIVERSIFIED
☒ MISCELLANEOUS

STAGE PREFERENCE

☒ EARLY STAGE
☒ Seed
☒ Start-up
☒ 1st Stage
☐ LATER STAGE
☐ 2nd Stage
☐ Mature
☐ Mezzanine
☐ LBO/MBO
☐ Turnaround
☐ INT'L EXPANSION
☐ WILL CONSIDER ALL
☐ VENTURE LEASING

Other Locations:

Affiliation:
Minimum Investment: $1 Million or more
Capital Under Management: Less than $100 Million

GEOGRAPHIC PREF

☐ East Coast
☐ West Coast
☐ Northeast
☐ Mid Atlantic
☐ Gulf States
☐ Northwest
☐ Southeast
☐ Southwest
☐ Midwest
☐ Central
☐ Local to Office
☐ Other Geo Pref

GCC INVESTMENTS

1300 Boylston Street
Chestnut HIII MA 02467

Phone (617) 975-3201   Fax (617) 975-3201

PROFESSIONALS	TITLE
John Berylson	President
Michael Greeley	Sr. Vice President
David Cohen	Vice President
Demos Kouvaris	Vice President

INDUSTRY PREFERENCE

☒ INFORMATION INDUSTRY
☐ Communications
☐ Computer Equipment
☐ Computer Services
☐ Computer Components
☒ Computer Entertainment
☐ Computer Education
☐ Information Technologies
☒ Computer Media
☐ Software
☒ Internet
☐ MEDICAL/HEALTHCARE
☐ Biotechnology
☐ Healthcare Services
☐ Life Sciences
☐ Medical Products
☐ INDUSTRIAL
☐ Advanced Materials
☐ Chemicals
☐ Instruments & Controls

☒ BASIC INDUSTRIES
☒ Consumer
☐ Distribution
☐ Manufacturing
☐ Retail
☒ Service
☐ Wholesale
☐ SPECIFIC INDUSTRIES
☐ Energy
☐ Environmental
☐ Financial
☐ Real Estate
☐ Transportation
☐ Publishing
☐ Food
☐ Franchises
☒ DIVERSIFIED
☒ MISCELLANEOUS

STAGE PREFERENCE

☒ EARLY STAGE
☐ Seed
☐ Start-up
☒ 1st Stage
☒ LATER STAGE
☒ 2nd Stage
☒ Mature
☒ Mezzanine
☒ LBO/MBO
☒ Turnaround
☐ INT'L EXPANSION
☐ WILL CONSIDER ALL
☒ VENTURE LEASING

Other Locations:

Affiliation:
Minimum Investment: $1 Million or more
Capital Under Management: $100 to $500 Million

GEOGRAPHIC PREF

☐ East Coast
☐ West Coast
☐ Northeast
☐ Mid Atlantic
☐ Gulf States
☐ Northwest
☐ Southeast
☐ Southwest
☐ Midwest
☐ Central
☐ Local to Office
☐ Other Geo Pref

GREYLOCK MANAGEMENT

One Federal Street
Boston MA 02110-2003

Phone (617) 423-5525   Fax (617) 482-0059

PROFESSIONALS	TITLE
Bill Helman	General Partner
Henry F. McCance	General Partner
Robert P. Henderson	General Partner
William S. Kaiser	General Partner
Howard E. Cox	General Partner
David Aronoff	General Partner

INDUSTRY PREFERENCE

☒ INFORMATION INDUSTRY	☒ BASIC INDUSTRIES
☒ Communications	☒ Consumer
☐ Computer Equipment	☐ Distribution
☐ Computer Services	☐ Manufacturing
☐ Computer Components	☒ Retail
☐ Computer Entertainment	☒ Service
☐ Computer Education	☐ Wholesale
☐ Information Technologies	☒ SPECIFIC INDUSTRIES
☐ Computer Media	☐ Energy
☒ Software	☐ Environmental
☐ Internet	☒ Financial
☒ MEDICAL/HEALTHCARE	☐ Real Estate
☐ Biotechnology	☐ Transportation
☒ Healthcare Services	☐ Publishing
☐ Life Sciences	☐ Food
☒ Medical Products	☐ Franchises
☒ INDUSTRIAL	☒ DIVERSIFIED
☐ Advanced Materials	☐ MISCELLANEOUS
☐ Chemicals	
☒ Instruments & Controls	

STAGE PREFERENCE

☒ EARLY STAGE
☒ Seed
☒ Start-up
☒ 1st Stage
☒ LATER STAGE
☒ 2nd Stage
☒ Mature
☒ Mezzanine
☒ LBO/MBO
☐ Turnaround
☐ INT'L EXPANSION
☐ WILL CONSIDER ALL
☐ VENTURE LEASING

Other Locations: Palo Alto CA

Affiliation:
Minimum Investment: Less than $1 Million
Capital Under Management: Over $500 Million

GEOGRAPHIC PREF

☐ East Coast
☐ West Coast
☐ Northeast
☐ Mid Atlantic
☐ Gulf States
☐ Northwest
☐ Southeast
☐ Southwest
☐ Midwest
☐ Central
☐ Local to Office
☐ Other Geo Pref

GRYPHON VENTURES

222 Berkeley Street
Suite 1600
Boston MA 02116-3748

Phone (617) 267-9191   Fax (617) 267-4293

PROFESSIONALS	TITLE
Edward B. Lurier	General Partner
William F. Aikman	Managing General Partner

INDUSTRY PREFERENCE

☒ INFORMATION INDUSTRY	☐ BASIC INDUSTRIES
☒ Communications	☐ Consumer
☒ Computer Equipment	☐ Distribution
☐ Computer Services	☐ Manufacturing
☐ Computer Components	☐ Retail
☐ Computer Entertainment	☐ Service
☐ Computer Education	☐ Wholesale
☐ Information Technologies	☒ SPECIFIC INDUSTRIES
☐ Computer Media	☒ Energy
☐ Software	☒ Environmental
☐ Internet	☐ Financial
☒ MEDICAL/HEALTHCARE	☐ Real Estate
☒ Biotechnology	☐ Transportation
☐ Healthcare Services	☐ Publishing
☒ Life Sciences	☐ Food
☒ Medical Products	☐ Franchises
☒ INDUSTRIAL	☒ DIVERSIFIED
☐ Advanced Materials	☐ MISCELLANEOUS
☒ Chemicals	
☒ Instruments & Controls	

STAGE PREFERENCE

☒ EARLY STAGE
☒ Seed
☒ Start-up
☒ 1st Stage
☐ LATER STAGE
☐ 2nd Stage
☐ Mature
☐ Mezzanine
☐ LBO/MBO
☐ Turnaround
☐ INT'L EXPANSION
☐ WILL CONSIDER ALL
☐ VENTURE LEASING

Other Locations:

Affiliation:
Minimum Investment: Less than $1 Million
Capital Under Management: Less than $100 Million

GEOGRAPHIC PREF

☐ East Coast
☐ West Coast
☐ Northeast
☐ Mid Atlantic
☐ Gulf States
☐ Northwest
☐ Southeast
☐ Southwest
☐ Midwest
☐ Central
☐ Local to Office
☐ Other Geo Pref

HALPERN, DENNY & CO.

500 Boylston Street
Boston MA 02116

Phone (617) 536-6602   Fax (617) 536-8535

PROFESSIONALS	TITLE
John Halpern	Partner
George Denny III	Parnter
William LaPoint	Partner
David Malm	Partner
William Nimmo	Partner

INDUSTRY PREFERENCE

☒ INFORMATION INDUSTRY	☐ BASIC INDUSTRIES
☒ Communications	☐ Consumer
☐ Computer Equipment	☐ Distribution
☐ Computer Services	☐ Manufacturing
☐ Computer Components	☐ Retail
☐ Computer Entertainment	☐ Service
☒ Computer Education	☐ Wholesale
☐ Information Technologies	☐ SPECIFIC INDUSTRIES
☐ Computer Media	☐ Energy
☐ Software	☐ Environmental
☒ Internet	☐ Financial
☒ MEDICAL/HEALTHCARE	☐ Real Estate
☐ Biotechnology	☐ Transportation
☒ Healthcare Services	☐ Publishing
☐ Life Sciences	☐ Food
☐ Medical Products	☐ Franchises
☐ INDUSTRIAL	☒ DIVERSIFIED
☐ Advanced Materials	☒ MISCELLANEOUS
☐ Chemicals	
☐ Instruments & Controls	

STAGE PREFERENCE

☒ EARLY STAGE
☐ Seed
☐ Start-up
☒ 1st Stage
☒ LATER STAGE
☒ 2nd Stage
☒ Mature
☐ Mezzanine
☒ LBO/MBO
☐ Turnaround
☐ INT'L EXPANSION
☐ WILL CONSIDER ALL
☐ VENTURE LEASING

Other Locations:

Affiliation:
Minimum Investment: $1 Million or more
Capital Under Management: Less than $100 Million

GEOGRAPHIC PREF

☐ East Coast
☐ West Coast
☐ Northeast
☐ Mid Atlantic
☐ Gulf States
☐ Northwest
☐ Southeast
☐ Southwest
☐ Midwest
☐ Central
☐ Local to Office
☐ Other Geo Pref

HARBOURVEST PARTNERS LLC

One Financial Center
44th Floor
Boston MA 02111

Phone (617) 348-3707   Fax (617) 350-0305

PROFESSIONALS	TITLE
Edward Kane	Sr. Managing Director
Brooks Zug	Sr. Managing Director
John Begg	Managing Director
Theodore Clark	Managing Director
Kevin Delbridge	Managing Director
William Johnson	Managing Director

INDUSTRY PREFERENCE

☒ INFORMATION INDUSTRY	☒ BASIC INDUSTRIES
☒ Communications	☒ Consumer
☒ Computer Equipment	☒ Distribution
☒ Computer Services	☐ Manufacturing
☒ Computer Components	☐ Retail
☐ Computer Entertainment	☒ Service
☒ Computer Education	☐ Wholesale
☒ Information Technologies	☒ SPECIFIC INDUSTRIES
☒ Computer Media	☐ Energy
☒ Software	☐ Environmental
☒ Internet	☒ Financial
☒ MEDICAL/HEALTHCARE	☐ Real Estate
☐ Biotechnology	☐ Transportation
☐ Healthcare Services	☐ Publishing
☐ Life Sciences	☐ Food
☒ Medical Products	☐ Franchises
☒ INDUSTRIAL	☒ DIVERSIFIED
☒ Advanced Materials	☒ MISCELLANEOUS
☒ Chemicals	
☒ Instruments & Controls	

STAGE PREFERENCE

☐ EARLY STAGE
☐ Seed
☐ Start-up
☐ 1st Stage
☒ LATER STAGE
☒ 2nd Stage
☐ Mature
☒ Mezzanine
☒ LBO/MBO
☐ Turnaround
☐ INT'L EXPANSION
☐ WILL CONSIDER ALL
☐ VENTURE LEASING

Other Locations:

Affiliation:
Minimum Investment: $1 Million or more
Capital Under Management: Over $500 Million

GEOGRAPHIC PREF

☐ East Coast
☐ West Coast
☐ Northeast
☐ Mid Atlantic
☐ Gulf States
☐ Northwest
☐ Southeast
☐ Southwest
☐ Midwest
☐ Central
☐ Local to Office
☐ Other Geo Pref

HEALTHCARE VENTURES, LLC

**One Kendall Square
Building 300, Suite 329
Cambridge MA 02193-1562**

Phone (617) 252-4343   Fax (617) 252-4342

PROFESSIONALS	TITLE
John W. Littlechild	Managing Director

INDUSTRY PREFERENCE

☐ INFORMATION INDUSTRY		☐ BASIC INDUSTRIES	
☐ Communications		☐ Consumer	
☐ Computer Equipment		☐ Distribution	
☐ Computer Services		☐ Manufacturing	
☐ Computer Components		☐ Retail	
☐ Computer Entertainment		☐ Service	
☐ Computer Education		☐ Wholesale	
☐ Information Technologies		☐ SPECIFIC INDUSTRIES	
☐ Computer Media		☐ Energy	
☐ Software		☐ Environmental	
☐ Internet		☐ Financial	
☒ MEDICAL/HEALTHCARE		☐ Real Estate	
☒ Biotechnology		☐ Transportation	
☒ Healthcare Services		☐ Publishing	
☒ Life Sciences		☐ Food	
☒ Medical Products		☐ Franchises	
☐ INDUSTRIAL		☐ DIVERSIFIED	
☐ Advanced Materials		☐ MISCELLANEOUS	
☐ Chemicals			
☐ Instruments & Controls			

STAGE PREFERENCE

☒ EARLY STAGE
☐ Seed
☐ Start-up
☒ 1st Stage
☒ LATER STAGE
☒ 2nd Stage
☒ Mature
☒ Mezzanine
☒ LBO/MBO
☐ Turnaround
☐ INT'L EXPANSION
☐ WILL CONSIDER ALL
☐ VENTURE LEASING

Other Locations: Princeton NJ

Affiliation: HealthCare Ventures
Minimum Investment: Less than $1 Million
Capital Under Management: $100 to $500 Million

GEOGRAPHIC PREF

☐ East Coast
☐ West Coast
☐ Northeast
☐ Mid Atlantic
☐ Gulf States
☐ Northwest
☐ Southeast
☐ Southwest
☐ Midwest
☐ Central
☐ Local to Office
☐ Other Geo Pref

HIGHLAND CAPITAL PARTNERS

**Two International Place
Boston MA 02110**

Phone (617) 531-1500   Fax (617) 531-1550

PROFESSIONALS	TITLE
Robert Higgins	Managing General Partner
Paul Maeder	Managing General Partner
Wycliffe Grousbeck	Managing General Partner
Daniel Nova	Managing General Partner
Sean Dalton	Principal
Steve Dalton	Principal
Jo Tango	Principal
LeeWrubel	Principal

INDUSTRY PREFERENCE

☒ INFORMATION INDUSTRY		☐ BASIC INDUSTRIES	
☒ Communications		☐ Consumer	
☒ Computer Equipment		☐ Distribution	
☒ Computer Services		☐ Manufacturing	
☒ Computer Components		☐ Retail	
☐ Computer Entertainment		☐ Service	
☒ Computer Education		☐ Wholesale	
☒ Information Technologies		☐ SPECIFIC INDUSTRIES	
☒ Computer Media		☐ Energy	
☒ Software		☐ Environmental	
☒ Internet		☐ Financial	
☒ MEDICAL/HEALTHCARE		☐ Real Estate	
☒ Biotechnology		☐ Transportation	
☒ Healthcare Services		☐ Publishing	
☒ Life Sciences		☐ Food	
☒ Medical Products		☐ Franchises	
☐ INDUSTRIAL		☒ DIVERSIFIED	
☐ Advanced Materials		☒ MISCELLANEOUS	
☐ Chemicals			
☐ Instruments & Controls			

STAGE PREFERENCE

☒ EARLY STAGE
☒ Seed
☒ Start-up
☒ 1st Stage
☒ LATER STAGE
☒ 2nd Stage
☐ Mature
☒ Mezzanine
☒ LBO/MBO
☒ Turnaround
☐ INT'L EXPANSION
☐ WILL CONSIDER ALL
☒ VENTURE LEASING

Other Locations:

Affiliation:
Minimum Investment: $1 Million or more
Capital Under Management: Over $500 Million

GEOGRAPHIC PREF

☐ East Coast
☐ West Coast
☐ Northeast
☐ Mid Atlantic
☐ Gulf States
☐ Northwest
☐ Southeast
☐ Southwest
☐ Midwest
☐ Central
☐ Local to Office
☐ Other Geo Pref

INTERNET CAPITAL GROUP

45 Milk Street
7th Floor
Boston MA 02109

Phone (617) 338-7171   Fax (617) 338-7117

PROFESSIONALS

Walter Buckley
Ken Fox

TITLE

Founding Partner
Founding Partner

INDUSTRY PREFERENCE

- ☒ INFORMATION INDUSTRY
- ☐ Communications
- ☐ Computer Equipment
- ☐ Computer Services
- ☐ Computer Components
- ☐ Computer Entertainment
- ☐ Computer Education
- ☐ Information Technologies
- ☐ Computer Media
- ☐ Software
- ☒ Internet
- ☐ MEDICAL/HEALTHCARE
- ☐ Biotechnology
- ☐ Healthcare Services
- ☐ Life Sciences
- ☐ Medical Products
- ☐ INDUSTRIAL
- ☐ Advanced Materials
- ☐ Chemicals
- ☐ Instruments & Controls

- ☐ BASIC INDUSTRIES
- ☐ Consumer
- ☐ Distribution
- ☐ Manufacturing
- ☐ Retail
- ☐ Service
- ☐ Wholesale
- ☐ SPECIFIC INDUSTRIES
- ☐ Energy
- ☐ Environmental
- ☐ Financial
- ☐ Real Estate
- ☐ Transportation
- ☐ Publishing
- ☐ Food
- ☐ Franchises
- ☒ DIVERSIFIED
- ☒ MISCELLANEOUS

STAGE PREFERENCE

- ☒ EARLY STAGE
- ☐ Seed
- ☐ Start-up
- ☒ 1st Stage
- ☒ LATER STAGE
- ☒ 2nd Stage
- ☐ Mature
- ☐ Mezzanine
- ☐ LBO/MBO
- ☐ Turnaround
- ☐ INT'L EXPANSION
- ☐ WILL CONSIDER ALL
- ☐ VENTURE LEASING

Other Locations: San Francisco CA, Wayne PA

Affiliation:
Minimum Investment: Less than $1 Million
Capital Under Management: $100 to $500 Million

GEOGRAPHIC PREF

- ☐ East Coast
- ☐ West Coast
- ☐ Northeast
- ☐ Mid Atlantic
- ☐ Gulf States
- ☐ Northwest
- ☐ Southeast
- ☐ Southwest
- ☐ Midwest
- ☐ Central
- ☐ Local to Office
- ☐ Other Geo Pref

KESTREL VENTURE MANAGEMENT

31 Milk Street
Boston MA 02109

Phone (617) 451-6722   Fax (617) 261-3322

PROFESSIONALS

Edward Stewart III
Greg G. Stone
Nuri Wissa

TITLE

General Partner
General Partner
General Partner

INDUSTRY PREFERENCE

- ☒ INFORMATION INDUSTRY
- ☒ Communications
- ☒ Computer Equipment
- ☒ Computer Services
- ☒ Computer Components
- ☐ Computer Entertainment
- ☒ Computer Education
- ☒ Information Technologies
- ☒ Computer Media
- ☒ Software
- ☒ Internet
- ☒ MEDICAL/HEALTHCARE
- ☐ Biotechnology
- ☒ Healthcare Services
- ☐ Life Sciences
- ☒ Medical Products
- ☐ INDUSTRIAL
- ☐ Advanced Materials
- ☐ Chemicals
- ☐ Instruments & Controls

- ☒ BASIC INDUSTRIES
- ☒ Consumer
- ☐ Distribution
- ☐ Manufacturing
- ☒ Retail
- ☐ Service
- ☐ Wholesale
- ☐ SPECIFIC INDUSTRIES
- ☐ Energy
- ☐ Environmental
- ☐ Financial
- ☐ Real Estate
- ☐ Transportation
- ☐ Publishing
- ☐ Food
- ☐ Franchises
- ☒ DIVERSIFIED
- ☒ MISCELLANEOUS

STAGE PREFERENCE

- ☒ EARLY STAGE
- ☒ Seed
- ☒ Start-up
- ☒ 1st Stage
- ☒ LATER STAGE
- ☒ 2nd Stage
- ☐ Mature
- ☒ Mezzanine
- ☒ LBO/MBO
- ☐ Turnaround
- ☐ INT'L EXPANSION
- ☐ WILL CONSIDER ALL
- ☐ VENTURE LEASING

Other Locations:

Affiliation:
Minimum Investment: $1 Million or more
Capital Under Management: Less than $100 Million

GEOGRAPHIC PREF

- ☐ East Coast
- ☐ West Coast
- ☐ Northeast
- ☐ Mid Atlantic
- ☐ Gulf States
- ☒ Northwest
- ☐ Southeast
- ☐ Southwest
- ☐ Midwest
- ☐ Central
- ☐ Local to Office
- ☐ Other Geo Pref

MASSACHUSETTS CAPITAL RESOURCE CO.

The Berkeley
420 Boylston Street
Boston MA 02116

Phone (617) 536-3900   Fax (617) 536-7930

PROFESSIONALS	TITLE
William J. Torpey, Jr.	President
Richard W. Anderson	Sr. Vice President
Ben Bailey III	Vice President
Joan Creamer McArdle	Vice President
Kenneth J. Lavery	Vice President

INDUSTRY PREFERENCE

☒ INFORMATION INDUSTRY
☐ Communications
☐ Computer Equipment
☐ Computer Services
☐ Computer Components
☐ Computer Entertainment
☐ Computer Education
☐ Information Technologies
☐ Computer Media
☒ Software
☒ Internet
☒ MEDICAL/HEALTHCARE
☐ Biotechnology
☒ Healthcare Services
☐ Life Sciences
☐ Medical Products
☐ INDUSTRIAL
☐ Advanced Materials
☐ Chemicals
☐ Instruments & Controls

☒ BASIC INDUSTRIES
☐ Consumer
☒ Distribution
☒ Manufacturing
☐ Retail
☒ Service
☐ Wholesale
☐ SPECIFIC INDUSTRIES
☐ Energy
☐ Environmental
☐ Financial
☐ Real Estate
☐ Transportation
☐ Publishing
☐ Food
☐ Franchises
☒ DIVERSIFIED
☐ MISCELLANEOUS

STAGE PREFERENCE

☐ EARLY STAGE
☐ Seed
☐ Start-up
☐ 1st Stage
☒ LATER STAGE
☒ 2nd Stage
☒ Mature
☒ Mezzanine
☒ LBO/MBO
☐ Turnaround
☐ INT'L EXPANSION
☐ WILL CONSIDER ALL
☐ VENTURE LEASING

Other Locations:

Affiliation: John Hancock Mutual Life
Minimum Investment: Less than $1 Million
Capital Under Management: $100 to $500 Million

GEOGRAPHIC PREF

☐ East Coast
☐ West Coast
☐ Northeast
☐ Mid Atlantic
☐ Gulf States
☐ Northwest
☐ Southeast
☐ Southwest
☐ Midwest
☐ Central
☐ Local to Office
☒ Other Geo Pref
  MA

MASSACHUSETTS TECHNOLOGY DEVELOPMENT CORPORATION

148 State Street
Boston MA 02109

Phone (617) 723-4920   Fax (617) 723-5983

PROFESSIONALS	TITLE
John Hodgman	President
Robert J. Crowley	Executive Vice President
Robert Creeden	Vice President

INDUSTRY PREFERENCE

☒ INFORMATION INDUSTRY
☒ Communications
☒ Computer Equipment
☒ Computer Services
☒ Computer Components
☐ Computer Entertainment
☒ Computer Education
☒ Information Technologies
☐ Computer Media
☒ Software
☒ Internet
☒ MEDICAL/HEALTHCARE
☒ Biotechnology
☒ Healthcare Services
☒ Life Sciences
☒ Medical Products
☒ INDUSTRIAL
☒ Advanced Materials
☒ Chemicals
☒ Instruments & Controls

☒ BASIC INDUSTRIES
☐ Consumer
☐ Distribution
☐ Manufacturing
☐ Retail
☒ Service
☐ Wholesale
☒ SPECIFIC INDUSTRIES
☒ Energy
☒ Environmental
☐ Financial
☐ Real Estate
☐ Transportation
☐ Publishing
☐ Food
☐ Franchises
☒ DIVERSIFIED
☐ MISCELLANEOUS

STAGE PREFERENCE

☒ EARLY STAGE
☒ Seed
☒ Start-up
☒ 1st Stage
☒ LATER STAGE
☒ 2nd Stage
☐ Mature
☐ Mezzanine
☐ LBO/MBO
☐ Turnaround
☐ INT'L EXPANSION
☐ WILL CONSIDER ALL
☐ VENTURE LEASING

Other Locations:

Affiliation:
Minimum Investment: Less than $1 Million
Capital Under Management: Less than $100 Million

GEOGRAPHIC PREF

☐ East Coast
☐ West Coast
☐ Northeast
☐ Mid Atlantic
☐ Gulf States
☐ Northwest
☐ Southeast
☐ Southwest
☐ Midwest
☐ Central
☐ Local to Office
☒ Other Geo Pref
  MA

MATRIX PARTNERS

Bay Colony Corporate Center
1000 Winter Street, Suite 4500
Waltham MA 02451

Phone (781) 890-2244   Fax (781) 890-2288

PROFESSIONALS	TITLE
Paul J. Ferri	General Partner
Timothy A. Barrows	General Partner
W. Michael Humphreys	General Partner
Andrew Marcuvitz	General Partner
David Schantz	General Partner

INDUSTRY PREFERENCE

☒ INFORMATION INDUSTRY	☐ BASIC INDUSTRIES	
☒ Communications	☐ Consumer	
☒ Computer Equipment	☐ Distribution	
☒ Computer Services	☐ Manufacturing	
☒ Computer Components	☐ Retail	
☐ Computer Entertainment	☐ Service	
☒ Computer Education	☐ Wholesale	
☒ Information Technologies	☐ SPECIFIC INDUSTRIES	
☐ Computer Media	☐ Energy	
☒ Software	☐ Environmental	
☒ Internet	☐ Financial	
☐ MEDICAL/HEALTHCARE	☐ Real Estate	
☐ Biotechnology	☐ Transportation	
☐ Healthcare Services	☐ Publishing	
☐ Life Sciences	☐ Food	
☐ Medical Products	☐ Franchises	
☐ INDUSTRIAL	☐ DIVERSIFIED	
☐ Advanced Materials	☐ MISCELLANEOUS	
☐ Chemicals		
☐ Instruments & Controls		

STAGE PREFERENCE

☒ EARLY STAGE
☒ Seed
☒ Start-up
☒ 1st Stage
☒ LATER STAGE
☒ 2nd Stage
☒ Mature
☒ Mezzanine
☒ LBO/MBO
☐ Turnaround
☐ INT'L EXPANSION
☐ WILL CONSIDER ALL
☐ VENTURE LEASING

Other Locations: Menlo Park CA

Affiliation:
Minimum Investment: Less than $1 Million
Capital Under Management: $100 to $500 Million

GEOGRAPHIC PREF

☐ East Coast
☐ West Coast
☐ Northeast
☐ Mid Atlantic
☐ Gulf States
☐ Northwest
☐ Southeast
☐ Southwest
☐ Midwest
☐ Central
☐ Local to Office
☐ Other Geo Pref

METAPOINT PARTNERS

Three Centennial Drive
Peabody MA 01960

Phone (978) 531-4444   Fax (978) 531-6662

PROFESSIONALS	TITLE
Palu Casey	Chairman
Keith Shaughnessy	President
Stuart Matthews	Sr. Vice President
Erik Dukema	Principal
Luke McInnis	Vice President

INDUSTRY PREFERENCE

☐ INFORMATION INDUSTRY	☒ BASIC INDUSTRIES	
☐ Communications	☐ Consumer	
☐ Computer Equipment	☐ Distribution	
☐ Computer Services	☒ Manufacturing	
☐ Computer Components	☐ Retail	
☐ Computer Entertainment	☐ Service	
☐ Computer Education	☐ Wholesale	
☐ Information Technologies	☒ SPECIFIC INDUSTRIES	
☐ Computer Media	☐ Energy	
☐ Software	☐ Environmental	
☐ Internet	☐ Financial	
☐ MEDICAL/HEALTHCARE	☐ Real Estate	
☐ Biotechnology	☒ Transportation	
☐ Healthcare Services	☐ Publishing	
☐ Life Sciences	☐ Food	
☐ Medical Products	☐ Franchises	
☒ INDUSTRIAL	☒ DIVERSIFIED	
☒ Advanced Materials	☒ MISCELLANEOUS	
☒ Chemicals	Aerospace	
☒ Instruments & Controls		

STAGE PREFERENCE

☐ EARLY STAGE
☐ Seed
☐ Start-up
☐ 1st Stage
☒ LATER STAGE
☐ 2nd Stage
☐ Mature
☐ Mezzanine
☒ LBO/MBO
☐ Turnaround
☐ INT'L EXPANSION
☐ WILL CONSIDER ALL
☐ VENTURE LEASING

Other Locations:

Affiliation:
Minimum Investment: $1 Million or more
Capital Under Management: Less than $100 Million

GEOGRAPHIC PREF

☐ East Coast
☐ West Coast
☐ Northeast
☐ Mid Atlantic
☐ Gulf States
☐ Northwest
☐ Southeast
☐ Southwest
☐ Midwest
☐ Central
☐ Local to Office
☐ Other Geo Pref

MPM ASSET MANAGEMENT LLC

**One Cambridge Center
9th Floor
Cambridge MA 02142**

Phone (617) 225-7054   Fax (617) 225-2210

PROFESSIONALS	TITLE
Ansbert Gadicke	Managing Director
Luke Evnin	Managing Director
Michael Setinmetz	Managing Director

INDUSTRY PREFERENCE

- ☐ INFORMATION INDUSTRY
- ☐ Communications
- ☐ Computer Equipment
- ☐ Computer Services
- ☐ Computer Components
- ☐ Computer Entertainment
- ☐ Computer Education
- ☐ Information Technologies
- ☐ Computer Media
- ☐ Software
- ☐ Internet
- ☒ MEDICAL/HEALTHCARE
- ☒ Biotechnology
- ☐ Healthcare Services
- ☒ Life Sciences
- ☒ Medical Products
- ☐ INDUSTRIAL
- ☐ Advanced Materials
- ☐ Chemicals
- ☐ Instruments & Controls

- ☐ BASIC INDUSTRIES
- ☐ Consumer
- ☐ Distribution
- ☐ Manufacturing
- ☐ Retail
- ☐ Service
- ☐ Wholesale
- ☐ SPECIFIC INDUSTRIES
- ☐ Energy
- ☐ Environmental
- ☐ Financial
- ☐ Real Estate
- ☐ Transportation
- ☐ Publishing
- ☐ Food
- ☐ Franchises
- ☐ DIVERSIFIED
- ☒ MISCELLANEOUS

STAGE PREFERENCE

- ☐ EARLY STAGE
- ☐ Seed
- ☐ Start-up
- ☐ 1st Stage
- ☒ LATER STAGE
- ☒ 2nd Stage
- ☐ Mature
- ☐ Mezzanine
- ☐ LBO/MBO
- ☐ Turnaround
- ☐ INT'L EXPANSION
- ☐ WILL CONSIDER ALL
- ☐ VENTURE LEASING

Other Locations:

Affiliation:
Minimum Investment: $1 Million or more
Capital Under Management: $100 to $500 Million

GEOGRAPHIC PREF

- ☐ East Coast
- ☐ West Coast
- ☐ Northeast
- ☐ Mid Atlantic
- ☐ Gulf States
- ☐ Northwest
- ☐ Southeast
- ☐ Southwest
- ☐ Midwest
- ☐ Central
- ☐ Local to Office
- ☐ Other Geo Pref

NEW ENGLAND PARTNERS

**One Boston Place
Suite 2100
Boston MA 02109**

Phone (617) 624-8400   Fax (617) 624-8416

PROFESSIONALS	TITLE
John Rousseau, Jr.	Principal
Robert J. Hanks	Principal
Edwin Snape	Principal
David Dullum	Principal

INDUSTRY PREFERENCE

- ☒ INFORMATION INDUSTRY
- ☒ Communications
- ☐ Computer Equipment
- ☐ Computer Services
- ☐ Computer Components
- ☐ Computer Entertainment
- ☐ Computer Education
- ☒ Information Technologies
- ☐ Computer Media
- ☐ Software
- ☐ Internet
- ☒ MEDICAL/HEALTHCARE
- ☒ Biotechnology
- ☐ Healthcare Services
- ☐ Life Sciences
- ☒ Medical Products
- ☐ INDUSTRIAL
- ☐ Advanced Materials
- ☐ Chemicals
- ☐ Instruments & Controls

- ☒ BASIC INDUSTRIES
- ☒ Consumer
- ☐ Distribution
- ☐ Manufacturing
- ☐ Retail
- ☐ Service
- ☐ Wholesale
- ☐ SPECIFIC INDUSTRIES
- ☐ Energy
- ☐ Environmental
- ☐ Financial
- ☐ Real Estate
- ☐ Transportation
- ☐ Publishing
- ☐ Food
- ☐ Franchises
- ☒ DIVERSIFIED
- ☒ MISCELLANEOUS

STAGE PREFERENCE

- ☐ EARLY STAGE
- ☐ Seed
- ☐ Start-up
- ☐ 1st Stage
- ☒ LATER STAGE
- ☒ 2nd Stage
- ☐ Mature
- ☒ Mezzanine
- ☒ LBO/MBO
- ☐ Turnaround
- ☐ INT'L EXPANSION
- ☐ WILL CONSIDER ALL
- ☐ VENTURE LEASING

Other Locations:

Affiliation:
Minimum Investment: $1 Million or more
Capital Under Management: $100 to $500 Million

GEOGRAPHIC PREF

- ☐ East Coast
- ☐ West Coast
- ☐ Northeast
- ☐ Mid Atlantic
- ☐ Gulf States
- ☐ Northwest
- ☐ Southeast
- ☐ Southwest
- ☐ Midwest
- ☐ Central
- ☐ Local to Office
- ☐ Other Geo Pref

NORTHBRIDGE VENTURE PARTNERS

950 Winter Street
Suite 4600
Waltham MA 02451

Phone (781) 290-0004   Fax (781) 290-0999

PROFESSIONALS

PROFESSIONALS	TITLE
Edward Andersen	General Partner
Richard D'Amore	General Partner
William Geary	General Partner
Jeffrey McCarthy	General Partner
Angelo Santinelli	General Partner

INDUSTRY PREFERENCE

☒ INFORMATION INDUSTRY
☒ Communications
☒ Computer Equipment
☒ Computer Services
☒ Computer Components
☐ Computer Entertainment
☐ Computer Education
☒ Information Technologies
☒ Computer Media
☒ Software
☒ Internet
☒ MEDICAL/HEALTHCARE
☐ Biotechnology
☒ Healthcare Services
☐ Life Sciences
☒ Medical Products
☒ INDUSTRIAL
☒ Advanced Materials
☒ Chemicals
☒ Instruments & Controls

☐ BASIC INDUSTRIES
☐ Consumer
☐ Distribution
☐ Manufacturing
☐ Retail
☐ Service
☐ Wholesale
☐ SPECIFIC INDUSTRIES
☐ Energy
☐ Environmental
☐ Financial
☐ Real Estate
☐ Transportation
☐ Publishing
☐ Food
☐ Franchises
☒ DIVERSIFIED
☒ MISCELLANEOUS

STAGE PREFERENCE

☒ EARLY STAGE
☒ Seed
☒ Start-up
☒ 1st Stage
☒ LATER STAGE
☒ 2nd Stage
☐ Mature
☐ Mezzanine
☐ LBO/MBO
☐ Turnaround
☐ INT'L EXPANSION
☐ WILL CONSIDER ALL
☐ VENTURE LEASING

Other Locations:

Affiliation:
Minimum Investment: Less than $1 Million
Capital Under Management: $100 to $500 Million

GEOGRAPHIC PREF

☐ East Coast
☐ West Coast
☐ Northeast
☐ Mid Atlantic
☐ Gulf States
☐ Northwest
☐ Southeast
☐ Southwest
☐ Midwest
☐ Central
☐ Local to Office
☐ Other Geo Pref

NORWEST VENTURE CAPITAL

40 William Street
Suite 305
Wellesley MA 02181

Phone (781) 237-5870   Fax (781) 237-6270

PROFESSIONALS

PROFESSIONALS	TITLE
Ernest C. Parizeau	General Partner
Blair Whitaker	General Partner

INDUSTRY PREFERENCE

☒ INFORMATION INDUSTRY
☒ Communications
☒ Computer Equipment
☐ Computer Services
☐ Computer Components
☐ Computer Entertainment
☐ Computer Education
☒ Information Technologies
☐ Computer Media
☒ Software
☒ Internet
☐ MEDICAL/HEALTHCARE
☐ Biotechnology
☐ Healthcare Services
☐ Life Sciences
☐ Medical Products
☐ INDUSTRIAL
☐ Advanced Materials
☐ Chemicals
☐ Instruments & Controls

☐ BASIC INDUSTRIES
☐ Consumer
☐ Distribution
☐ Manufacturing
☐ Retail
☐ Service
☐ Wholesale
☐ SPECIFIC INDUSTRIES
☐ Energy
☐ Environmental
☐ Financial
☐ Real Estate
☐ Transportation
☐ Publishing
☐ Food
☐ Franchises
☐ DIVERSIFIED
☐ MISCELLANEOUS

STAGE PREFERENCE

☒ EARLY STAGE
☒ Seed
☒ Start-up
☒ 1st Stage
☒ LATER STAGE
☒ 2nd Stage
☒ Mature
☒ Mezzanine
☒ LBO/MBO
☒ Turnaround
☐ INT'L EXPANSION
☐ WILL CONSIDER ALL
☒ VENTURE LEASING
SBIC
Other Locations: Minneapolis MN, Palo Alto CA

Affiliation: Norwest Corp.
Minimum Investment: Less than $1 Million
Capital Under Management: Over $500 Million

GEOGRAPHIC PREF

☐ East Coast
☐ West Coast
☐ Northeast
☐ Mid Atlantic
☐ Gulf States
☐ Northwest
☐ Southeast
☐ Southwest
☐ Midwest
☐ Central
☐ Local to Office
☐ Other Geo Pref

ONE LIBERTY VENTURES

One Liberty Square
Boston MA 02109

Phone (617) 423-1765   Fax (617) 338-4362

PROFESSIONALS	TITLE
Edwin M. Kania, Jr.	Partner
Duncan C. McCallum	Partner
Stephen J. Ricci	Partner
Langley Steinert	Partner
Daniel J. Holland	Partner

INDUSTRY PREFERENCE

☒ INFORMATION INDUSTRY	☐ BASIC INDUSTRIES
☒ Communications	☐ Consumer
☒ Computer Equipment	☐ Distribution
☒ Computer Services	☐ Manufacturing
☒ Computer Components	☐ Retail
☐ Computer Entertainment	☐ Service
☒ Computer Education	☐ Wholesale
☒ Information Technologies	☐ SPECIFIC INDUSTRIES
☐ Computer Media	☐ Energy
☒ Software	☐ Environmental
☒ Internet	☐ Financial
☒ MEDICAL/HEALTHCARE	☐ Real Estate
☐ Biotechnology	☐ Transportation
☐ Healthcare Services	☐ Publishing
☒ Life Sciences	☐ Food
☒ Medical Products	☐ Franchises
☐ INDUSTRIAL	☒ DIVERSIFIED
☐ Advanced Materials	☒ MISCELLANEOUS
☐ Chemicals	
☐ Instruments & Controls	

STAGE PREFERENCE

☒ EARLY STAGE
☒   Seed
☒   Start-up
☐   1st Stage
☐ LATER STAGE
☐   2nd Stage
☐   Mature
☐   Mezzanine
☐   LBO/MBO
☐   Turnaround
☐ INT'L EXPANSION
☐ WILL CONSIDER ALL
☐ VENTURE LEASING

Other Locations:

Affiliation:
Minimum Investment: $1 Million or more
Capital Under Management: Less than $100 Million

GEOGRAPHIC PREF

☐ East Coast
☐ West Coast
☐ Northeast
☐ Mid Atlantic
☐ Gulf States
☐ Northwest
☐ Southeast
☐ Southwest
☐ Midwest
☐ Central
☐ Local to Office
☐ Other Geo Pref

ORION PARTNERS

20 William Street
Suite 145
Wellesley MA 02481

Phone (781) 235-1904   Fax (781) 235-8822

PROFESSIONALS	TITLE
Steven A. Kandarian	Managing Director
Jeffrey R. Ackerman	Vice President

INDUSTRY PREFERENCE

☒ INFORMATION INDUSTRY	☒ BASIC INDUSTRIES
☒ Communications	☒ Consumer
☒ Computer Equipment	☒ Distribution
☒ Computer Services	☒ Manufacturing
☒ Computer Components	☒ Retail
☐ Computer Entertainment	☒ Service
☒ Computer Education	☒ Wholesale
☒ Information Technologies	☒ SPECIFIC INDUSTRIES
☒ Computer Media	☐ Energy
☒ Software	☐ Environmental
☒ Internet	☒ Financial
☒ MEDICAL/HEALTHCARE	☐ Real Estate
☐ Biotechnology	☐ Transportation
☒ Healthcare Services	☐ Publishing
☒ Life Sciences	☐ Food
☒ Medical Products	☐ Franchises
☒ INDUSTRIAL	☒ DIVERSIFIED
☒ Advanced Materials	☒ MISCELLANEOUS
☒ Chemicals	
☒ Instruments & Controls	

STAGE PREFERENCE

☐ EARLY STAGE
☐   Seed
☐   Start-up
☐   1st Stage
☒ LATER STAGE
☒   2nd Stage
☐   Mature
☐   Mezzanine
☒   LBO/MBO
☐   Turnaround
☐ INT'L EXPANSION
☐ WILL CONSIDER ALL
☐ VENTURE LEASING

Other Locations:

Affiliation:
Minimum Investment: $1 Million or more
Capital Under Management: Less than $100 Million

GEOGRAPHIC PREF

☒ East Coast
☐ West Coast
☐ Northeast
☐ Mid Atlantic
☐ Gulf States
☐ Northwest
☐ Southeast
☐ Southwest
☐ Midwest
☐ Central
☐ Local to Office
☐ Other Geo Pref

POLARIS VENTURE PARTNERS

Bay Colony Corporate Center
1000 Winter Street, Suite 3350
Waltham MA 02451

Phone (781) 290-0770   Fax (781) 290-0880

PROFESSIONALS	TITLE
Jonathan Flint	General Partner
Terrance McGuire	General Partner
John Gannon	CFO / Partner
George Conrades	Venture Partner
Thomas Herring	Venture Partner
James Brown	Associate
Michael Hirshland	Associate

INDUSTRY PREFERENCE

- ☒ INFORMATION INDUSTRY
- ☒ Communications
- ☒ Computer Equipment
- ☒ Computer Services
- ☒ Computer Components
- ☒ Computer Entertainment
- ☒ Computer Education
- ☐ Information Technologies
- ☒ Computer Media
- ☒ Software
- ☒ Internet
- ☒ MEDICAL/HEALTHCARE
- ☒ Biotechnology
- ☒ Healthcare Services
- ☒ Life Sciences
- ☒ Medical Products
- ☐ INDUSTRIAL
- ☐ Advanced Materials
- ☐ Chemicals
- ☐ Instruments & Controls

- ☐ BASIC INDUSTRIES
- ☐ Consumer
- ☐ Distribution
- ☐ Manufacturing
- ☐ Retail
- ☐ Service
- ☐ Wholesale
- ☐ SPECIFIC INDUSTRIES
- ☐ Energy
- ☐ Environmental
- ☐ Financial
- ☐ Real Estate
- ☐ Transportation
- ☐ Publishing
- ☐ Food
- ☐ Franchises
- ☒ DIVERSIFIED
- ☒ MISCELLANEOUS

STAGE PREFERENCE

- ☒ EARLY STAGE
- ☒ Seed
- ☒ Start-up
- ☒ 1st Stage
- ☒ LATER STAGE
- ☒ 2nd Stage
- ☐ Mature
- ☐ Mezzanine
- ☐ LBO/MBO
- ☐ Turnaround
- ☐ INT'L EXPANSION
- ☐ WILL CONSIDER ALL
- ☐ VENTURE LEASING

Other Locations: Seattle WA

Affiliation:
Minimum Investment: Less than $1 Million
Capital Under Management: $100 to $500 Million

GEOGRAPHIC PREF

- ☐ East Coast
- ☐ West Coast
- ☐ Northeast
- ☐ Mid Atlantic
- ☐ Gulf States
- ☐ Northwest
- ☐ Southeast
- ☐ Southwest
- ☐ Midwest
- ☐ Central
- ☐ Local to Office
- ☐ Other Geo Pref

PRISM VENTURE PARTNERS

100 Lowder Brook Lane
Suite 2500
Westwood MA 02090

Phone (781) 302-4000   Fax (781) 302-4040

PROFESSIONALS	TITLE
John Brooks	General Partner
Robert Fleming	General Partner
Duane Mason	General Partner
Laurie Thompson	General Partner
Bill Seifert	General Partner
David Baum	Principal

INDUSTRY PREFERENCE

- ☒ INFORMATION INDUSTRY
- ☒ Communications
- ☒ Computer Equipment
- ☒ Computer Services
- ☒ Computer Components
- ☐ Computer Entertainment
- ☐ Computer Education
- ☒ Information Technologies
- ☒ Computer Media
- ☒ Software
- ☒ Internet
- ☒ MEDICAL/HEALTHCARE
- ☐ Biotechnology
- ☒ Healthcare Services
- ☐ Life Sciences
- ☒ Medical Products
- ☐ INDUSTRIAL
- ☐ Advanced Materials
- ☐ Chemicals
- ☐ Instruments & Controls

- ☐ BASIC INDUSTRIES
- ☐ Consumer
- ☐ Distribution
- ☐ Manufacturing
- ☐ Retail
- ☐ Service
- ☐ Wholesale
- ☐ SPECIFIC INDUSTRIES
- ☐ Energy
- ☐ Environmental
- ☐ Financial
- ☐ Real Estate
- ☐ Transportation
- ☐ Publishing
- ☐ Food
- ☐ Franchises
- ☒ DIVERSIFIED
- ☒ MISCELLANEOUS

STAGE PREFERENCE

- ☒ EARLY STAGE
- ☐ Seed
- ☒ Start-up
- ☒ 1st Stage
- ☒ LATER STAGE
- ☒ 2nd Stage
- ☐ Mature
- ☐ Mezzanine
- ☐ LBO/MBO
- ☐ Turnaround
- ☐ INT'L EXPANSION
- ☐ WILL CONSIDER ALL
- ☐ VENTURE LEASING

Other Locations:

Affiliation:
Minimum Investment: $1 Million or more
Capital Under Management: $100 to $500 Million

GEOGRAPHIC PREF

- ☒ East Coast
- ☐ West Coast
- ☐ Northeast
- ☐ Mid Atlantic
- ☐ Gulf States
- ☐ Northwest
- ☐ Southeast
- ☐ Southwest
- ☐ Midwest
- ☐ Central
- ☐ Local to Office
- ☒ Other Geo Pref
- Eastern U.S.

SCHRODER VENTURES LIFE SCIENCES

**60 State Street, Suite 3650
Boston MA 02109**

Phone (617) 367-8100　Fax (617) 367-1590

PROFESSIONALS	TITLE
James Garvey	Managing Partner
Eugene Hill	Partner
Charles Warden	Principal
Ningge Hsu	Principal
Donald Nelson	Chief Financial Officer
Jeffrey Ferrell	Associate
Jonathan Gertler	Venture Partner

INDUSTRY PREFERENCE

☐ INFORMATION INDUSTRY
☐　Communications
☐　Computer Equipment
☐　Computer Services
☐　Computer Components
☐　Computer Entertainment
☐　Computer Education
☐　Information Technologies
☐　Computer Media
☐　Software
☐　Internet
☒ MEDICAL/HEALTHCARE
☒　Biotechnology
☒　Healthcare Services
☒　Life Sciences
☒　Medical Products
☐ INDUSTRIAL
☐　Advanced Materials
☐　Chemicals
☐　Instruments & Controls

☐ BASIC INDUSTRIES
☐　Consumer
☐　Distribution
☐　Manufacturing
☐　Retail
☐　Service
☐　Wholesale
☐ SPECIFIC INDUSTRIES
☐　Energy
☐　Environmental
☐　Financial
☐　Real Estate
☐　Transportation
☐　Publishing
☐　Food
☐　Franchises
☐ DIVERSIFIED
☒ MISCELLANEOUS

STAGE PREFERENCE

☒ EARLY STAGE
☐　Seed
☒　Start-up
☒　1st Stage
☒ LATER STAGE
☒　2nd Stage
☐　Mature
☒　Mezzanine
☒　LBO/MBO
☐　Turnaround
☐ INT'L EXPANSION
☐ WILL CONSIDER ALL
☐ VENTURE LEASING

Other Locations:

Affiliation:
Minimum Investment: $1 Million or more
Capital Under Management: $100 to $500 Million

GEOGRAPHIC PREF

☐　East Coast
☐　West Coast
☐　Northeast
☐　Mid Atlantic
☐　Gulf States
☐　Northwest
☐　Southeast
☐　Southwest
☐　Midwest
☐　Central
☐　Local to Office
☐　Other Geo Pref

SEACOAST CAPITAL PARTNERS, LP

**55 Ferncroft Road
Danvers MA 01923**

Phone (978) 750-1300　Fax (978) 750-1301

PROFESSIONALS	TITLE
Paul Giovacchini	Managing Director
Thomas Gorman	Managing Director
Gregory Hulecki	Managing Director

INDUSTRY PREFERENCE

☐ INFORMATION INDUSTRY
☐　Communications
☐　Computer Equipment
☐　Computer Services
☐　Computer Components
☐　Computer Entertainment
☐　Computer Education
☐　Information Technologies
☐　Computer Media
☐　Software
☐　Internet
☐ MEDICAL/HEALTHCARE
☐　Biotechnology
☐　Healthcare Services
☐　Life Sciences
☐　Medical Products
☐ INDUSTRIAL
☐　Advanced Materials
☐　Chemicals
☐　Instruments & Controls

☐ BASIC INDUSTRIES
☐　Consumer
☐　Distribution
☐　Manufacturing
☐　Retail
☐　Service
☐　Wholesale
☐ SPECIFIC INDUSTRIES
☐　Energy
☐　Environmental
☐　Financial
☐　Real Estate
☐　Transportation
☐　Publishing
☐　Food
☐　Franchises
☒ DIVERSIFIED
☐ MISCELLANEOUS

STAGE PREFERENCE

☐ EARLY STAGE
☐　Seed
☐　Start-up
☐　1st Stage
☒ LATER STAGE
☒　2nd Stage
☒　Mature
☒　Mezzanine
☒　LBO/MBO
☐　Turnaround
☐ INT'L EXPANSION
☐ WILL CONSIDER ALL
☐ VENTURE LEASING
SBIC
Other Locations: San Francisco CA

Affiliation:
Minimum Investment: $1 Million or more
Capital Under Management: $100 to $500 Million

GEOGRAPHIC PREF

☐　East Coast
☐　West Coast
☐　Northeast
☐　Mid Atlantic
☐　Gulf States
☐　Northwest
☐　Southeast
☐　Southwest
☐　Midwest
☐　Central
☐　Local to Office
☐　Other Geo Pref

SIGMA PARTNERS

**300 Commercial Street
Suite 705
Boston MA 02109-1185**

Phone (617) 227-0303   Fax (617) 367-0478

PROFESSIONALS	TITLE
Robert Davoli	General Partner
John Mandile	General Partner
Gardner C. Hendrie	General Partner

INDUSTRY PREFERENCE

- ☒ INFORMATION INDUSTRY
- ☒ Communications
- ☒ Computer Equipment
- ☒ Computer Services
- ☒ Computer Components
- ☐ Computer Entertainment
- ☒ Computer Education
- ☒ Information Technologies
- ☐ Computer Media
- ☒ Software
- ☒ Internet
- ☒ MEDICAL/HEALTHCARE
- ☐ Biotechnology
- ☒ Healthcare Services
- ☐ Life Sciences
- ☒ Medical Products
- ☐ INDUSTRIAL
- ☐ Advanced Materials
- ☐ Chemicals
- ☐ Instruments & Controls

- ☒ BASIC INDUSTRIES
- ☐ Consumer
- ☐ Distribution
- ☐ Manufacturing
- ☒ Retail
- ☒ Service
- ☐ Wholesale
- ☐ SPECIFIC INDUSTRIES
- ☐ Energy
- ☐ Environmental
- ☐ Financial
- ☐ Real Estate
- ☐ Transportation
- ☐ Publishing
- ☐ Food
- ☐ Franchises
- ☒ DIVERSIFIED
- ☐ MISCELLANEOUS

STAGE PREFERENCE

- ☒ EARLY STAGE
- ☒ Seed
- ☒ Start-up
- ☒ 1st Stage
- ☒ LATER STAGE
- ☒ 2nd Stage
- ☐ Mature
- ☐ Mezzanine
- ☒ LBO/MBO
- ☐ Turnaround
- ☐ INT'L EXPANSION
- ☐ WILL CONSIDER ALL
- ☐ VENTURE LEASING

Other Locations: Menlo Park CA

Affiliation: SIGMA PARTNERS
Minimum Investment: Less than $1 Million
Capital Under Management: $100 to $500 Million

GEOGRAPHIC PREF

- ☐ East Coast
- ☐ West Coast
- ☐ Northeast
- ☐ Mid Atlantic
- ☐ Gulf States
- ☐ Northwest
- ☐ Southeast
- ☐ Southwest
- ☐ Midwest
- ☐ Central
- ☐ Local to Office
- ☐ Other Geo Pref

SOFTBANK TECHNOLOGY VENTURES

**10 Langley Road
Suite 202
Newton Center MA 02159**

Phone (617) 928-9300   Fax (617) 928-9305

PROFESSIONALS	TITLE
Charles Lax	

INDUSTRY PREFERENCE

- ☒ INFORMATION INDUSTRY
- ☒ Communications
- ☒ Computer Equipment
- ☐ Computer Services
- ☒ Computer Components
- ☐ Computer Entertainment
- ☐ Computer Education
- ☒ Information Technologies
- ☒ Computer Media
- ☒ Software
- ☒ Internet
- ☐ MEDICAL/HEALTHCARE
- ☐ Biotechnology
- ☐ Healthcare Services
- ☐ Life Sciences
- ☐ Medical Products
- ☐ INDUSTRIAL
- ☐ Advanced Materials
- ☐ Chemicals
- ☐ Instruments & Controls

- ☒ BASIC INDUSTRIES
- ☐ Consumer
- ☐ Distribution
- ☐ Manufacturing
- ☐ Retail
- ☒ Service
- ☐ Wholesale
- ☐ SPECIFIC INDUSTRIES
- ☐ Energy
- ☐ Environmental
- ☐ Financial
- ☐ Real Estate
- ☐ Transportation
- ☐ Publishing
- ☐ Food
- ☐ Franchises
- ☒ DIVERSIFIED
- ☒ MISCELLANEOUS

STAGE PREFERENCE

- ☒ EARLY STAGE
- ☒ Seed
- ☒ Start-up
- ☒ 1st Stage
- ☒ LATER STAGE
- ☒ 2nd Stage
- ☒ Mature
- ☒ Mezzanine
- ☒ LBO/MBO
- ☐ Turnaround
- ☐ INT'L EXPANSION
- ☐ WILL CONSIDER ALL
- ☐ VENTURE LEASING

Other Locations: San Jose CA, Eldorado Springs CO

Affiliation:
Minimum Investment: $1 Million or more
Capital Under Management: Over $500 Million

GEOGRAPHIC PREF

- ☐ East Coast
- ☐ West Coast
- ☐ Northeast
- ☐ Mid Atlantic
- ☐ Gulf States
- ☐ Northwest
- ☐ Southeast
- ☐ Southwest
- ☐ Midwest
- ☐ Central
- ☐ Local to Office
- ☐ Other Geo Pref

SOLSTICE CAPITAL

33 Broad Street
Third Floor
Boston MA 02109

Phone (617) 523-7733   Fax (617) 523-5827

PROFESSIONALS	TITLE
Henry Newman	General Partner
Harry George	Managing General Partner

INDUSTRY PREFERENCE

☒ INFORMATION INDUSTRY	☐ BASIC INDUSTRIES
☒ Communications	☐ Consumer
☒ Computer Equipment	☐ Distribution
☒ Computer Services	☐ Manufacturing
☒ Computer Components	☐ Retail
☐ Computer Entertainment	☐ Service
☒ Computer Education	☐ Wholesale
☒ Information Technologies	☒ SPECIFIC INDUSTRIES
☒ Computer Media	☒ Energy
☒ Software	☒ Environmental
☒ Internet	☐ Financial
☒ MEDICAL/HEALTHCARE	☐ Real Estate
☐ Biotechnology	☐ Transportation
☐ Healthcare Services	☐ Publishing
☐ Life Sciences	☐ Food
☒ Medical Products	☐ Franchises
☐ INDUSTRIAL	☒ DIVERSIFIED
☐ Advanced Materials	☒ MISCELLANEOUS
☐ Chemicals	
☐ Instruments & Controls	

STAGE PREFERENCE

☒ EARLY STAGE
☐ Seed
☒ Start-up
☒ 1st Stage
☒ LATER STAGE
☒ 2nd Stage
☐ Mature
☐ Mezzanine
☐ LBO/MBO
☐ Turnaround
☐ INT'L EXPANSION
☐ WILL CONSIDER ALL
☐ VENTURE LEASING

Other Locations:

Affiliation:
Minimum Investment: Less than $1 Million
Capital Under Management: Less than $100 Million

GEOGRAPHIC PREF

☒ East Coast
☐ West Coast
☐ Northeast
☐ Mid Atlantic
☐ Gulf States
☐ Northwest
☐ Southeast
☒ Southwest
☐ Midwest
☐ Central
☐ Local to Office
☐ Other Geo Pref

SPECTRUM EQUITY INVESTORS

One International Place
29th Floor
Boston MA 02110

Phone (617) 464-4600   Fax (617) 464-4601

PROFESSIONALS	TITLE
William Collatos	Managing General Partner
Kevin Maroni	General Partner
Michael Kennealy	Partner
Robert Nicholson	Partner

INDUSTRY PREFERENCE

☒ INFORMATION INDUSTRY	☐ BASIC INDUSTRIES
☒ Communications	☐ Consumer
☒ Computer Equipment	☐ Distribution
☒ Computer Services	☐ Manufacturing
☒ Computer Components	☐ Retail
☐ Computer Entertainment	☐ Service
☐ Computer Education	☐ Wholesale
☒ Information Technologies	☐ SPECIFIC INDUSTRIES
☒ Computer Media	☐ Energy
☒ Software	☐ Environmental
☒ Internet	☐ Financial
☐ MEDICAL/HEALTHCARE	☐ Real Estate
☐ Biotechnology	☐ Transportation
☐ Healthcare Services	☐ Publishing
☐ Life Sciences	☐ Food
☐ Medical Products	☐ Franchises
☐ INDUSTRIAL	☒ DIVERSIFIED
☐ Advanced Materials	☒ MISCELLANEOUS
☐ Chemicals	
☐ Instruments & Controls	

STAGE PREFERENCE

☒ EARLY STAGE
☒ Seed
☒ Start-up
☒ 1st Stage
☒ LATER STAGE
☒ 2nd Stage
☒ Mature
☒ Mezzanine
☒ LBO/MBO
☐ Turnaround
☐ INT'L EXPANSION
☐ WILL CONSIDER ALL
☐ VENTURE LEASING

Other Locations: Palo Alto CA

Affiliation:
Minimum Investment: $1 Million or more
Capital Under Management: $100 to $500 Million

GEOGRAPHIC PREF

☐ East Coast
☐ West Coast
☐ Northeast
☐ Mid Atlantic
☐ Gulf States
☐ Northwest
☐ Southeast
☐ Southwest
☐ Midwest
☐ Central
☐ Local to Office
☐ Other Geo Pref

SPRAY VENTURE PARTNERS

One Walnut Street
Boston MA 02108

Phone (617) 305-4140   Fax (617) 305-4144

PROFESSIONALS	TITLE
Kevin Connors	General Partner
Daniel Cole	General Partner
Dan Sachs, MD	Principal

INDUSTRY PREFERENCE

☐ INFORMATION INDUSTRY	☐ BASIC INDUSTRIES
☐ Communications	☐ Consumer
☐ Computer Equipment	☐ Distribution
☐ Computer Services	☐ Manufacturing
☐ Computer Components	☐ Retail
☐ Computer Entertainment	☐ Service
☐ Computer Education	☐ Wholesale
☐ Information Technologies	☐ SPECIFIC INDUSTRIES
☐ Computer Media	☐ Energy
☐ Software	☐ Environmental
☐ Internet	☐ Financial
☒ MEDICAL/HEALTHCARE	☐ Real Estate
☒ Biotechnology	☐ Transportation
☐ Healthcare Services	☐ Publishing
☒ Life Sciences	☐ Food
☒ Medical Products	☐ Franchises
☐ INDUSTRIAL	☐ DIVERSIFIED
☐ Advanced Materials	☒ MISCELLANEOUS
☐ Chemicals	
☐ Instruments & Controls	

STAGE PREFERENCE

☒ EARLY STAGE
☒ Seed
☒ Start-up
☒ 1st Stage
☒ LATER STAGE
☒ 2nd Stage
☐ Mature
☐ Mezzanine
☐ LBO/MBO
☐ Turnaround
☐ INT'L EXPANSION
☐ WILL CONSIDER ALL
☐ VENTURE LEASING

Other Locations:

Affiliation:
Minimum Investment: Less than $1 Million
Capital Under Management: Less than $100 Million

GEOGRAPHIC PREF

☐ East Coast
☐ West Coast
☐ Northeast
☐ Mid Atlantic
☐ Gulf States
☐ Northwest
☐ Southeast
☐ Southwest
☐ Midwest
☐ Central
☐ Local to Office
☐ Other Geo Pref

ST. PAUL VENTURE CAPITAL, INC.

138 River Road
Andover MA 01810

Phone (978) 837-3198   Fax (978) 837-3199

PROFESSIONALS	TITLE
Rick Boswell	General Partner

INDUSTRY PREFERENCE

☒ INFORMATION INDUSTRY	☒ BASIC INDUSTRIES
☒ Communications	☒ Consumer
☒ Computer Equipment	☐ Distribution
☒ Computer Services	☐ Manufacturing
☒ Computer Components	☐ Retail
☐ Computer Entertainment	☐ Service
☒ Computer Education	☐ Wholesale
☒ Information Technologies	☒ SPECIFIC INDUSTRIES
☐ Computer Media	☐ Energy
☒ Software	☐ Environmental
☒ Internet	☐ Financial
☒ MEDICAL/HEALTHCARE	☐ Real Estate
☒ Biotechnology	☐ Transportation
☒ Healthcare Services	☐ Publishing
☒ Life Sciences	☐ Food
☒ Medical Products	☐ Franchises
☒ INDUSTRIAL	☒ DIVERSIFIED
☐ Advanced Materials	☒ MISCELLANEOUS
☐ Chemicals	
☒ Instruments & Controls	

STAGE PREFERENCE

☒ EARLY STAGE
☒ Seed
☒ Start-up
☒ 1st Stage
☒ LATER STAGE
☒ 2nd Stage
☒ Mature
☒ Mezzanine
☒ LBO/MBO
☐ Turnaround
☐ INT'L EXPANSION
☐ WILL CONSIDER ALL
☐ VENTURE LEASING

Other Locations: Redwood City CA, Eden Prairie MN

Affiliation:
Minimum Investment: $1 Million or more
Capital Under Management: Over $500 Million

GEOGRAPHIC PREF

☐ East Coast
☐ West Coast
☐ Northeast
☐ Mid Atlantic
☐ Gulf States
☐ Northwest
☐ Southeast
☐ Southwest
☐ Midwest
☐ Central
☐ Local to Office
☐ Other Geo Pref

STILL RIVER FUND

**100 Federal Street
29th Floor
Boston MA 02110**

Phone (617) 348-2327   Fax (617) 348-2371

PROFESSIONALS	TITLE
James Saalfield	Partner
Joseph Tischler	Partner

INDUSTRY PREFERENCE

- ☒ INFORMATION INDUSTRY
- ☒ Communications
- ☒ Computer Equipment
- ☒ Computer Services
- ☒ Computer Components
- ☐ Computer Entertainment
- ☒ Computer Education
- ☒ Information Technologies
- ☐ Computer Media
- ☒ Software
- ☒ Internet
- ☒ MEDICAL/HEALTHCARE
- ☐ Biotechnology
- ☐ Healthcare Services
- ☐ Life Sciences
- ☒ Medical Products
- ☒ INDUSTRIAL
- ☐ Advanced Materials
- ☐ Chemicals
- ☒ Instruments & Controls

- ☒ BASIC INDUSTRIES
- ☒ Consumer
- ☐ Distribution
- ☐ Manufacturing
- ☒ Retail
- ☒ Service
- ☐ Wholesale
- ☒ SPECIFIC INDUSTRIES
- ☐ Energy
- ☐ Environmental
- ☒ Financial
- ☐ Real Estate
- ☐ Transportation
- ☐ Publishing
- ☐ Food
- ☐ Franchises
- ☒ DIVERSIFIED
- ☒ MISCELLANEOUS

STAGE PREFERENCE

- ☒ EARLY STAGE
- ☐ Seed
- ☐ Start-up
- ☒ 1st Stage
- ☒ LATER STAGE
- ☒ 2nd Stage
- ☐ Mature
- ☐ Mezzanine
- ☒ LBO/MBO
- ☐ Turnaround
- ☐ INT'L EXPANSION
- ☐ WILL CONSIDER ALL
- ☐ VENTURE LEASING

Other Locations:

Affiliation:

Minimum Investment: Less than $1 Million
Capital Under Management: Less than $100 Million

GEOGRAPHIC PREF

- ☐ East Coast
- ☐ West Coast
- ☒ Northeast
- ☐ Mid Atlantic
- ☐ Gulf States
- ☐ Northwest
- ☐ Southeast
- ☐ Southwest
- ☐ Midwest
- ☐ Central
- ☐ Local to Office
- ☐ Other Geo Pref

SUMMIT PARTNERS

**600 Atlantic Avenue
Suite 2800
Boston MA 02210-2227**

Phone (617) 824-1000   Fax (617) 824-1100

PROFESSIONALS	TITLE
E. Roe Stamps IV	Managing Partner
Stephen G. Woodsum	Managing Partner
Bruce R. Evans	Managing Partner
Lawrence D. Greenberg	General Partner
Martin J. Mannion	General Partner

INDUSTRY PREFERENCE

- ☒ INFORMATION INDUSTRY
- ☒ Communications
- ☒ Computer Equipment
- ☒ Computer Services
- ☒ Computer Components
- ☐ Computer Entertainment
- ☒ Computer Education
- ☒ Information Technologies
- ☐ Computer Media
- ☒ Software
- ☒ Internet
- ☒ MEDICAL/HEALTHCARE
- ☐ Biotechnology
- ☒ Healthcare Services
- ☐ Life Sciences
- ☐ Medical Products
- ☐ INDUSTRIAL
- ☐ Advanced Materials
- ☐ Chemicals
- ☐ Instruments & Controls

- ☒ BASIC INDUSTRIES
- ☐ Consumer
- ☐ Distribution
- ☐ Manufacturing
- ☐ Retail
- ☒ Service
- ☐ Wholesale
- ☐ SPECIFIC INDUSTRIES
- ☐ Energy
- ☐ Environmental
- ☐ Financial
- ☐ Real Estate
- ☐ Transportation
- ☐ Publishing
- ☐ Food
- ☐ Franchises
- ☒ DIVERSIFIED
- ☐ MISCELLANEOUS

STAGE PREFERENCE

- ☒ EARLY STAGE
- ☐ Seed
- ☐ Start-up
- ☒ 1st Stage
- ☒ LATER STAGE
- ☒ 2nd Stage
- ☒ Mature
- ☒ Mezzanine
- ☒ LBO/MBO
- ☐ Turnaround
- ☐ INT'L EXPANSION
- ☐ WILL CONSIDER ALL
- ☐ VENTURE LEASING

Other Locations: Palo Alto CA

Affiliation:

Minimum Investment: $1 Million or more
Capital Under Management: Over $500 Million

GEOGRAPHIC PREF

- ☐ East Coast
- ☐ West Coast
- ☐ Northeast
- ☐ Mid Atlantic
- ☐ Gulf States
- ☐ Northwest
- ☐ Southeast
- ☐ Southwest
- ☐ Midwest
- ☐ Central
- ☐ Local to Office
- ☐ Other Geo Pref

TA ASSOCIATES, INC.

High Street Tower
125 High Street, Suite 2500
Boston MA 02110-2720

Phone (617) 574-6700   Fax (617) 574-6728

PROFESSIONALS	TITLE
C. Kevin Landry	Managing Director & CEO
Roger B. Kafker	Managing Director
P. Andrews McLane	Sr. Managing Director
Richard D. Tadler	Managing Director
Kurt R. Jaggers	Managing Director
Brian J. Conway	Managing Director

INDUSTRY PREFERENCE

- ☒ INFORMATION INDUSTRY
- ☒ Communications
- ☒ Computer Equipment
- ☒ Computer Services
- ☒ Computer Components
- ☐ Computer Entertainment
- ☒ Computer Education
- ☒ Information Technologies
- ☒ Computer Media
- ☒ Software
- ☒ Internet
- ☒ MEDICAL/HEALTHCARE
- ☐ Biotechnology
- ☒ Healthcare Services
- ☐ Life Sciences
- ☐ Medical Products
- ☒ INDUSTRIAL
- ☐ Advanced Materials
- ☐ Chemicals
- ☒ Instruments & Controls

- ☒ BASIC INDUSTRIES
- ☒ Consumer
- ☒ Distribution
- ☐ Manufacturing
- ☒ Retail
- ☒ Service
- ☐ Wholesale
- ☒ SPECIFIC INDUSTRIES
- ☒ Energy
- ☒ Environmental
- ☒ Financial
- ☐ Real Estate
- ☐ Transportation
- ☐ Publishing
- ☐ Food
- ☐ Franchises
- ☒ DIVERSIFIED
- ☐ MISCELLANEOUS

STAGE PREFERENCE

- ☐ EARLY STAGE
- ☐ Seed
- ☐ Start-up
- ☐ 1st Stage
- ☒ LATER STAGE
- ☒ 2nd Stage
- ☒ Mature
- ☒ Mezzanine
- ☒ LBO/MBO
- ☐ Turnaround
- ☐ INT'L EXPANSION
- ☐ WILL CONSIDER ALL
- ☐ VENTURE LEASING

Other Locations: Palo Alto CA , Pittsburgh PA

Affiliation:
Minimum Investment: $1 Million or more
Capital Under Management: Over $500 Million

GEOGRAPHIC PREF

- ☐ East Coast
- ☐ West Coast
- ☐ Northeast
- ☐ Mid Atlantic
- ☐ Gulf States
- ☐ Northwest
- ☐ Southeast
- ☐ Southwest
- ☐ Midwest
- ☐ Central
- ☐ Local to Office
- ☐ Other Geo Pref

TECHNO VENTURE MANAGEMENT

101 Arch Street
Suite 1950
Boston MA 02110

Phone (617) 345-9320   Fax (617) 345-9377

PROFESSIONALS	TITLE
Peter Levin	Investment Manager

INDUSTRY PREFERENCE

- ☒ INFORMATION INDUSTRY
- ☒ Communications
- ☐ Computer Equipment
- ☐ Computer Services
- ☐ Computer Components
- ☐ Computer Entertainment
- ☐ Computer Education
- ☒ Information Technologies
- ☐ Computer Media
- ☒ Software
- ☒ Internet
- ☒ MEDICAL/HEALTHCARE
- ☒ Biotechnology
- ☐ Healthcare Services
- ☐ Life Sciences
- ☐ Medical Products
- ☐ INDUSTRIAL
- ☐ Advanced Materials
- ☐ Chemicals
- ☐ Instruments & Controls

- ☐ BASIC INDUSTRIES
- ☐ Consumer
- ☐ Distribution
- ☐ Manufacturing
- ☐ Retail
- ☐ Service
- ☐ Wholesale
- ☐ SPECIFIC INDUSTRIES
- ☐ Energy
- ☐ Environmental
- ☐ Financial
- ☐ Real Estate
- ☐ Transportation
- ☐ Publishing
- ☐ Food
- ☐ Franchises
- ☒ DIVERSIFIED
- ☐ MISCELLANEOUS

STAGE PREFERENCE

- ☒ EARLY STAGE
- ☐ Seed
- ☒ Start-up
- ☒ 1st Stage
- ☐ LATER STAGE
- ☐ 2nd Stage
- ☐ Mature
- ☐ Mezzanine
- ☐ LBO/MBO
- ☐ Turnaround
- ☐ INT'L EXPANSION
- ☐ WILL CONSIDER ALL
- ☐ VENTURE LEASING

Other Locations:

Affiliation:
Minimum Investment: Less than $1 Million
Capital Under Management: $100 to $500 Million

GEOGRAPHIC PREF

- ☐ East Coast
- ☐ West Coast
- ☐ Northeast
- ☐ Mid Atlantic
- ☐ Gulf States
- ☐ Northwest
- ☐ Southeast
- ☐ Southwest
- ☐ Midwest
- ☐ Central
- ☐ Local to Office
- ☐ Other Geo Pref

TICONDEROGA CAPITAL, INC.

20 William Street
Suite G40
Wellesley MA 02481-4102

Phone (781) 416-3400   Fax (781) 416-9868

PROFESSIONALS	TITLE
Craig A. T. Jones	Managing Director
James Vandervelden	Principal
Tyler Wick	Vice President

INDUSTRY PREFERENCE

☒ INFORMATION INDUSTRY	☒ BASIC INDUSTRIES
☐ Communications	☐ Consumer
☐ Computer Equipment	☐ Distribution
☒ Computer Services	☐ Manufacturing
☐ Computer Components	☐ Retail
☐ Computer Entertainment	☒ Service
☐ Computer Education	☐ Wholesale
☒ Information Technologies	☒ SPECIFIC INDUSTRIES
☐ Computer Media	☒ Energy
☐ Software	☐ Environmental
☐ Internet	☒ Financial
☒ MEDICAL/HEALTHCARE	☐ Real Estate
☐ Biotechnology	☐ Transportation
☒ Healthcare Services	☐ Publishing
☐ Life Sciences	☐ Food
☐ Medical Products	☐ Franchises
☐ INDUSTRIAL	☒ DIVERSIFIED
☐ Advanced Materials	☒ MISCELLANEOUS
☐ Chemicals	
☐ Instruments & Controls	

STAGE PREFERENCE

☐ EARLY STAGE
☐ Seed
☐ Start-up
☐ 1st Stage
☒ LATER STAGE
☒ 2nd Stage
☐ Mature
☒ Mezzanine
☒ LBO/MBO
☐ Turnaround
☐ INT'L EXPANSION
☐ WILL CONSIDER ALL
☐ VENTURE LEASING

Other Locations: San Francisco CA, New York NY

Affiliation:
Minimum Investment: $1 Million or more
Capital Under Management: $100 to $500 Million

GEOGRAPHIC PREF

☐ East Coast
☐ West Coast
☐ Northeast
☐ Mid Atlantic
☐ Gulf States
☐ Northwest
☐ Southeast
☐ Southwest
☐ Midwest
☐ Central
☐ Local to Office
☐ Other Geo Pref

TTC VENTURES

One Main Street
6th Floor
Cambridge MA 02142

Phone (617) 528-3137   Fax (617) 577-1715

PROFESSIONALS	TITLE
Jarrett Collins	Director

INDUSTRY PREFERENCE

☒ INFORMATION INDUSTRY	☒ BASIC INDUSTRIES
☒ Communications	☒ Consumer
☐ Computer Equipment	☐ Distribution
☒ Computer Services	☐ Manufacturing
☐ Computer Components	☐ Retail
☐ Computer Entertainment	☐ Service
☒ Computer Education	☐ Wholesale
☒ Information Technologies	☐ SPECIFIC INDUSTRIES
☒ Computer Media	☐ Energy
☒ Software	☐ Environmental
☒ Internet	☐ Financial
☐ MEDICAL/HEALTHCARE	☐ Real Estate
☐ Biotechnology	☐ Transportation
☐ Healthcare Services	☐ Publishing
☐ Life Sciences	☐ Food
☐ Medical Products	☐ Franchises
☐ INDUSTRIAL	☒ DIVERSIFIED
☐ Advanced Materials	☒ MISCELLANEOUS
☐ Chemicals	
☐ Instruments & Controls	

STAGE PREFERENCE

☒ EARLY STAGE
☒ Seed
☒ Start-up
☒ 1st Stage
☒ LATER STAGE
☒ 2nd Stage
☐ Mature
☒ Mezzanine
☐ LBO/MBO
☐ Turnaround
☐ INT'L EXPANSION
☐ WILL CONSIDER ALL
☐ VENTURE LEASING

Other Locations:

Affiliation:
Minimum Investment: Less than $1 Million
Capital Under Management: Less than $100 Million

GEOGRAPHIC PREF

☐ East Coast
☐ West Coast
☐ Northeast
☐ Mid Atlantic
☐ Gulf States
☐ Northwest
☐ Southeast
☐ Southwest
☐ Midwest
☐ Central
☐ Local to Office
☐ Other Geo Pref

UST CAPITAL CORP.

40 Court Street
Boston MA 02108

Phone (617) 726-7196   Fax (617) 695-4185

PROFESSIONALS	TITLE
Arthur F. Snyder	Chairman
Kathie S. Stevens	President
Kenneth F. Daley	Vice President

INDUSTRY PREFERENCE

☐ INFORMATION INDUSTRY	☐ BASIC INDUSTRIES
☐ Communications	☐ Consumer
☐ Computer Equipment	☐ Distribution
☐ Computer Services	☐ Manufacturing
☐ Computer Components	☐ Retail
☐ Computer Entertainment	☐ Service
☐ Computer Education	☐ Wholesale
☐ Information Technologies	☐ SPECIFIC INDUSTRIES
☐ Computer Media	☐ Energy
☐ Software	☐ Environmental
☐ Internet	☐ Financial
☐ MEDICAL/HEALTHCARE	☐ Real Estate
☐ Biotechnology	☐ Transportation
☐ Healthcare Services	☐ Publishing
☐ Life Sciences	☐ Food
☐ Medical Products	☐ Franchises
☐ INDUSTRIAL	☒ DIVERSIFIED
☐ Advanced Materials	☐ MISCELLANEOUS
☐ Chemicals	
☐ Instruments & Controls	

STAGE PREFERENCE

☒ EARLY STAGE	
☒ Seed	
☒ Start-up	
☒ 1st Stage	
☐ LATER STAGE	
☐ 2nd Stage	
☐ Mature	
☐ Mezzanine	
☐ LBO/MBO	
☐ Turnaround	
☐ INT'L EXPANSION	
☐ WILL CONSIDER ALL	
☐ VENTURE LEASING	

SBIC
Other Locations:

Affiliation:
Minimum Investment: Less than $1 Million
Capital Under Management: Less than $100 Million

GEOGRAPHIC PREF

☐ East Coast	
☐ West Coast	
☒ Northeast	
☐ Mid Atlantic	
☐ Gulf States	
☐ Northwest	
☐ Southeast	
☐ Southwest	
☐ Midwest	
☐ Central	
☐ Local to Office	
☐ Other Geo Pref	

VENROCK ASSOCIATES

101 Federal Street
Suite 1900
Boston MA 02110

Phone (617) 204-5710   Fax (617) 204-6190

PROFESSIONALS	TITLE
Michael F. Tyrell	Venture Partner

INDUSTRY PREFERENCE

☒ INFORMATION INDUSTRY	☒ BASIC INDUSTRIES
☒ Communications	☐ Consumer
☒ Computer Equipment	☐ Distribution
☒ Computer Services	☐ Manufacturing
☒ Computer Components	☐ Retail
☒ Computer Entertainment	☒ Service
☒ Computer Education	☐ Wholesale
☒ Information Technologies	☒ SPECIFIC INDUSTRIES
☐ Computer Media	☒ Energy
☒ Software	☐ Environmental
☒ Internet	☐ Financial
☒ MEDICAL/HEALTHCARE	☐ Real Estate
☒ Biotechnology	☐ Transportation
☒ Healthcare Services	☐ Publishing
☒ Life Sciences	☐ Food
☒ Medical Products	☐ Franchises
☒ INDUSTRIAL	☒ DIVERSIFIED
☒ Advanced Materials	☒ MISCELLANEOUS
☐ Chemicals	
☐ Instruments & Controls	

STAGE PREFERENCE

☒ EARLY STAGE	
☒ Seed	
☒ Start-up	
☒ 1st Stage	
☐ LATER STAGE	
☐ 2nd Stage	
☐ Mature	
☐ Mezzanine	
☐ LBO/MBO	
☐ Turnaround	
☐ INT'L EXPANSION	
☐ WILL CONSIDER ALL	
☐ VENTURE LEASING	

Other Locations: Menlo Park CA, New York NY

Affiliation: Rockefeller family
Minimum Investment: $1 Million or more
Capital Under Management: $100 to $500 Million

GEOGRAPHIC PREF

☐ East Coast	
☐ West Coast	
☐ Northeast	
☐ Mid Atlantic	
☐ Gulf States	
☐ Northwest	
☐ Southeast	
☐ Southwest	
☐ Midwest	
☐ Central	
☐ Local to Office	
☐ Other Geo Pref	

VENTURE CAPITAL FUND OF NEW ENGLAND

70 Walnut Street
Suite 120
Wellesley Hills MA 02481-2175

Phone (781) 239-8262   Fax (781) 239-8263

PROFESSIONALS	TITLE
Richard A. Farrell	General Partner
Harry J. Healer, Jr.	General Partner
Kevin J. Dougherty	General Partner

INDUSTRY PREFERENCE

- ☒ INFORMATION INDUSTRY
- ☒ Communications
- ☒ Computer Equipment
- ☒ Computer Services
- ☒ Computer Components
- ☐ Computer Entertainment
- ☐ Computer Education
- ☒ Information Technologies
- ☒ Computer Media
- ☒ Software
- ☒ Internet
- ☐ MEDICAL/HEALTHCARE
- ☐ Biotechnology
- ☐ Healthcare Services
- ☐ Life Sciences
- ☐ Medical Products
- ☒ INDUSTRIAL
- ☐ Advanced Materials
- ☐ Chemicals
- ☒ Instruments & Controls

- ☒ BASIC INDUSTRIES
- ☐ Consumer
- ☐ Distribution
- ☐ Manufacturing
- ☐ Retail
- ☒ Service
- ☐ Wholesale
- ☐ SPECIFIC INDUSTRIES
- ☐ Energy
- ☐ Environmental
- ☐ Financial
- ☐ Real Estate
- ☐ Transportation
- ☐ Publishing
- ☐ Food
- ☐ Franchises
- ☒ DIVERSIFIED
- ☐ MISCELLANEOUS

STAGE PREFERENCE

- ☒ EARLY STAGE
- ☐ Seed
- ☒ Start-up
- ☒ 1st Stage
- ☒ LATER STAGE
- ☒ 2nd Stage
- ☐ Mature
- ☐ Mezzanine
- ☐ LBO/MBO
- ☐ Turnaround
- ☐ INT'L EXPANSION
- ☐ WILL CONSIDER ALL
- ☐ VENTURE LEASING

Other Locations:

Affiliation: Farrell, Healer & Co.
Minimum Investment: Less than $1 Million
Capital Under Management: Less than $100 Million

GEOGRAPHIC PREF

- ☐ East Coast
- ☐ West Coast
- ☒ Northeast
- ☐ Mid Atlantic
- ☐ Gulf States
- ☐ Northwest
- ☐ Southeast
- ☐ Southwest
- ☐ Midwest
- ☐ Central
- ☐ Local to Office
- ☐ Other Geo Pref

WESTON PRESIDIO CAPITAL

One Federal Street
21st Floor
Boston MA 02110-2004

Phone (617) 988-2500   Fax (617) 988-2515

PROFESSIONALS	TITLE
Michael F. Cronin	Managing Partner
Carlo A. von Schroeter	General Partner

INDUSTRY PREFERENCE

- ☒ INFORMATION INDUSTRY
- ☒ Communications
- ☒ Computer Equipment
- ☒ Computer Services
- ☒ Computer Components
- ☐ Computer Entertainment
- ☒ Computer Education
- ☒ Information Technologies
- ☐ Computer Media
- ☒ Software
- ☒ Internet
- ☒ MEDICAL/HEALTHCARE
- ☐ Biotechnology
- ☒ Healthcare Services
- ☐ Life Sciences
- ☐ Medical Products
- ☐ INDUSTRIAL
- ☐ Advanced Materials
- ☐ Chemicals
- ☐ Instruments & Controls

- ☒ BASIC INDUSTRIES
- ☒ Consumer
- ☒ Distribution
- ☒ Manufacturing
- ☒ Retail
- ☒ Service
- ☐ Wholesale
- ☐ SPECIFIC INDUSTRIES
- ☐ Energy
- ☐ Environmental
- ☐ Financial
- ☐ Real Estate
- ☐ Transportation
- ☐ Publishing
- ☐ Food
- ☐ Franchises
- ☒ DIVERSIFIED
- ☐ MISCELLANEOUS

STAGE PREFERENCE

- ☐ EARLY STAGE
- ☐ Seed
- ☐ Start-up
- ☐ 1st Stage
- ☒ LATER STAGE
- ☒ 2nd Stage
- ☒ Mature
- ☒ Mezzanine
- ☒ LBO/MBO
- ☐ Turnaround
- ☐ INT'L EXPANSION
- ☐ WILL CONSIDER ALL
- ☐ VENTURE LEASING

Other Locations: San Francisco CA

Affiliation:
Minimum Investment: $1 Million or more
Capital Under Management: Over $500 Million

GEOGRAPHIC PREF

- ☐ East Coast
- ☐ West Coast
- ☐ Northeast
- ☐ Mid Atlantic
- ☐ Gulf States
- ☐ Northwest
- ☐ Southeast
- ☐ Southwest
- ☐ Midwest
- ☐ Central
- ☐ Local to Office
- ☐ Other Geo Pref

ZERO STAGE CAPITAL CO., INC.

101 Main Street
17th Floor
Cambridge MA 02142-1519

Phone (617) 876-5355   Fax (617) 876-1248

PROFESSIONALS	TITLE
Paul M. Kelley	Managing General Parnter
Gordon B. Baty	Managing General Partner
Stanley L. Fung	Managing Director
Nancy C. McDonald	Investment Officer
Inder Soni	Vice President
G. Bickley Stevens II	Managing Director
Mark C. Thaller	Vice President

INDUSTRY PREFERENCE

☒ INFORMATION INDUSTRY
☒ Communications
☒ Computer Equipment
☒ Computer Services
☒ Computer Components
☐ Computer Entertainment
☒ Computer Education
☒ Information Technologies
☐ Computer Media
☒ Software
☒ Internet
☒ MEDICAL/HEALTHCARE
☒ Biotechnology
☒ Healthcare Services
☒ Life Sciences
☒ Medical Products
☒ INDUSTRIAL
☐ Advanced Materials
☐ Chemicals
☐ Instruments & Controls

☐ BASIC INDUSTRIES
☐ Consumer
☐ Distribution
☐ Manufacturing
☐ Retail
☐ Service
☐ Wholesale
☒ SPECIFIC INDUSTRIES
☐ Energy
☒ Environmental
☐ Financial
☐ Real Estate
☐ Transportation
☐ Publishing
☐ Food
☐ Franchises
☒ DIVERSIFIED
☐ MISCELLANEOUS

STAGE PREFERENCE

☒ EARLY STAGE
☒ Seed
☒ Start-up
☒ 1st Stage
☒ LATER STAGE
☒ 2nd Stage
☐ Mature
☒ Mezzanine
☐ LBO/MBO
☐ Turnaround
☐ INT'L EXPANSION
☐ WILL CONSIDER ALL
☐ VENTURE LEASING

SBIC
Other Locations:

Affiliation:
Minimum Investment: Less than $1 Million
Capital Under Management: Less than $100 Million

GEOGRAPHIC PREF

☐ East Coast
☐ West Coast
☒ Northeast
☐ Mid Atlantic
☐ Gulf States
☐ Northwest
☐ Southeast
☐ Southwest
☐ Midwest
☐ Central
☐ Local to Office
☐ Other Geo Pref

BLUE WATER CAPITAL LLC

260 East Brown Street
Suite 310
Birmingham MI 48009

Phone (248) 647-2010

PROFESSIONALS	TITLE
Michael Acheson	Managing Director

INDUSTRY PREFERENCE

☒ INFORMATION INDUSTRY
☒ Communications
☒ Computer Equipment
☒ Computer Services
☒ Computer Components
☐ Computer Entertainment
☒ Computer Education
☒ Information Technologies
☒ Computer Media
☒ Software
☒ Internet
☐ MEDICAL/HEALTHCARE
☐ Biotechnology
☐ Healthcare Services
☐ Life Sciences
☐ Medical Products
☐ INDUSTRIAL
☐ Advanced Materials
☐ Chemicals
☐ Instruments & Controls

☐ BASIC INDUSTRIES
☐ Consumer
☐ Distribution
☐ Manufacturing
☐ Retail
☐ Service
☐ Wholesale
☐ SPECIFIC INDUSTRIES
☐ Energy
☐ Environmental
☐ Financial
☐ Real Estate
☐ Transportation
☐ Publishing
☐ Food
☐ Franchises
☐ DIVERSIFIED
☒ MISCELLANEOUS

STAGE PREFERENCE

☐ EARLY STAGE
☐ Seed
☐ Start-up
☐ 1st Stage
☒ LATER STAGE
☒ 2nd Stage
☒ Mature
☒ Mezzanine
☒ LBO/MBO
☐ Turnaround
☐ INT'L EXPANSION
☐ WILL CONSIDER ALL
☐ VENTURE LEASING

Other Locations: McLean VA

Affiliation:
Minimum Investment: $1 Million or more
Capital Under Management: Less than $100 Million

GEOGRAPHIC PREF

☐ East Coast
☐ West Coast
☐ Northeast
☐ Mid Atlantic
☐ Gulf States
☐ Northwest
☐ Southeast
☐ Southwest
☐ Midwest
☐ Central
☐ Local to Office
☐ Other Geo Pref

DETROIT INVESTMENT FUND

600 Renaissance Center
Suite 1710
Detroit MI 48423

Phone (313) 259-6368   Fax (313) 259-6393

PROFESSIONALS	TITLE
Peter Weipert	President

INDUSTRY PREFERENCE

- ☐ INFORMATION INDUSTRY
- ☐ Communications
- ☐ Computer Equipment
- ☐ Computer Services
- ☐ Computer Components
- ☐ Computer Entertainment
- ☐ Computer Education
- ☐ Information Technologies
- ☐ Computer Media
- ☐ Software
- ☐ Internet
- ☐ MEDICAL/HEALTHCARE
- ☐ Biotechnology
- ☐ Healthcare Services
- ☐ Life Sciences
- ☐ Medical Products
- ☐ INDUSTRIAL
- ☐ Advanced Materials
- ☐ Chemicals
- ☐ Instruments & Controls

- ☐ BASIC INDUSTRIES
- ☐ Consumer
- ☐ Distribution
- ☐ Manufacturing
- ☐ Retail
- ☐ Service
- ☐ Wholesale
- ☐ SPECIFIC INDUSTRIES
- ☐ Energy
- ☐ Environmental
- ☐ Financial
- ☐ Real Estate
- ☐ Transportation
- ☐ Publishing
- ☐ Food
- ☐ Franchises
- ☒ DIVERSIFIED
- ☒ MISCELLANEOUS

STAGE PREFERENCE

- ☐ EARLY STAGE
- ☐ Seed
- ☐ Start-up
- ☐ 1st Stage
- ☒ LATER STAGE
- ☒ 2nd Stage
- ☐ Mature
- ☒ Mezzanine
- ☒ LBO/MBO
- ☐ Turnaround
- ☐ INT'L EXPANSION
- ☐ WILL CONSIDER ALL
- ☐ VENTURE LEASING

Other Locations:

Affiliation:
Minimum Investment: $1 Million or more
Capital Under Management: Less than $100 Million

GEOGRAPHIC PREF

- ☐ East Coast
- ☐ West Coast
- ☐ Northeast
- ☐ Mid Atlantic
- ☐ Gulf States
- ☐ Northwest
- ☐ Southeast
- ☐ Southwest
- ☐ Midwest
- ☐ Central
- ☐ Local to Office
- ☒ Other Geo Pref
  Detroit

DOW CHEMICAL

2030 Dow Center
Midland MI 48674

Phone (517) 636-5692   Fax (517) 636-8127

PROFESSIONALS	TITLE
Dennis Merens	Director

INDUSTRY PREFERENCE

- ☒ INFORMATION INDUSTRY
- ☒ Communications
- ☐ Computer Equipment
- ☒ Computer Services
- ☒ Computer Components
- ☐ Computer Entertainment
- ☐ Computer Education
- ☒ Information Technologies
- ☐ Computer Media
- ☒ Software
- ☒ Internet
- ☒ MEDICAL/HEALTHCARE
- ☒ Biotechnology
- ☐ Healthcare Services
- ☐ Life Sciences
- ☐ Medical Products
- ☒ INDUSTRIAL
- ☒ Advanced Materials
- ☒ Chemicals
- ☐ Instruments & Controls

- ☐ BASIC INDUSTRIES
- ☐ Consumer
- ☐ Distribution
- ☐ Manufacturing
- ☐ Retail
- ☐ Service
- ☐ Wholesale
- ☐ SPECIFIC INDUSTRIES
- ☐ Energy
- ☐ Environmental
- ☐ Financial
- ☐ Real Estate
- ☐ Transportation
- ☐ Publishing
- ☐ Food
- ☐ Franchises
- ☒ DIVERSIFIED
- ☒ MISCELLANEOUS

STAGE PREFERENCE

- ☒ EARLY STAGE
- ☐ Seed
- ☐ Start-up
- ☒ 1st Stage
- ☒ LATER STAGE
- ☒ 2nd Stage
- ☐ Mature
- ☒ Mezzanine
- ☒ LBO/MBO
- ☐ Turnaround
- ☒ INT'L EXPANSION
- ☐ WILL CONSIDER ALL
- ☐ VENTURE LEASING

Other Locations:

Affiliation:
Minimum Investment: Less than $1 Million
Capital Under Management: Less than $100 Million

GEOGRAPHIC PREF

- ☐ East Coast
- ☐ West Coast
- ☐ Northeast
- ☐ Mid Atlantic
- ☐ Gulf States
- ☐ Northwest
- ☐ Southeast
- ☐ Southwest
- ☐ Midwest
- ☐ Central
- ☐ Local to Office
- ☐ Other Geo Pref

INVESTCARE PARTNERS LP

31500 Northwest Highway
Suite 120
Farmington Hills MI 48334

Phone (248) 851-9200   Fax (248) 851-9208

PROFESSIONALS	TITLE
Malcolm Moss	Managing Director
Rajegh Kothari	Director
Charles Rothstein	Managing Director
David Eberly	Director

INDUSTRY PREFERENCE

☐ INFORMATION INDUSTRY
☐ Communications
☐ Computer Equipment
☐ Computer Services
☐ Computer Components
☐ Computer Entertainment
☐ Computer Education
☐ Information Technologies
☐ Computer Media
☐ Software
☐ Internet
☒ MEDICAL/HEALTHCARE
☐ Biotechnology
☒ Healthcare Services
☒ Life Sciences
☒ Medical Products
☐ INDUSTRIAL
☐ Advanced Materials
☐ Chemicals
☐ Instruments & Controls

☐ BASIC INDUSTRIES
☐ Consumer
☐ Distribution
☐ Manufacturing
☐ Retail
☐ Service
☐ Wholesale
☐ SPECIFIC INDUSTRIES
☐ Energy
☐ Environmental
☐ Financial
☐ Real Estate
☐ Transportation
☐ Publishing
☐ Food
☐ Franchises
☐ DIVERSIFIED
☐ MISCELLANEOUS

STAGE PREFERENCE

☐ EARLY STAGE
☐ Seed
☐ Start-up
☐ 1st Stage
☒ LATER STAGE
☒ 2nd Stage
☒ Mature
☐ Mezzanine
☒ LBO/MBO
☐ Turnaround
☐ INT'L EXPANSION
☐ WILL CONSIDER ALL
☐ VENTURE LEASING

SBIC
Other Locations:

Affiliation:
Minimum Investment: $1 Million or more
Capital Under Management: Less than $100 Million

GEOGRAPHIC PREF

☐ East Coast
☐ West Coast
☐ Northeast
☐ Mid Atlantic
☐ Gulf States
☐ Northwest
☐ Southeast
☐ Southwest
☐ Midwest
☐ Central
☐ Local to Office
☐ Other Geo Pref

PACIFIC CAPITAL LP

2401 Plymouth Road
Suite B
Ann Arbor MI 48105

Phone (734) 747-9401   Fax (734) 747-9704

PROFESSIONALS	TITLE
Frederick L Yocum	Chairman
Daniel Boyle	Vice President
Lois Marler	Vice President

INDUSTRY PREFERENCE

☒ INFORMATION INDUSTRY
☒ Communications
☒ Computer Equipment
☒ Computer Services
☒ Computer Components
☐ Computer Entertainment
☒ Computer Education
☒ Information Technologies
☒ Computer Media
☒ Software
☒ Internet
☒ MEDICAL/HEALTHCARE
☒ Biotechnology
☒ Healthcare Services
☒ Life Sciences
☒ Medical Products
☒ INDUSTRIAL
☒ Advanced Materials
☒ Chemicals
☒ Instruments & Controls

☒ BASIC INDUSTRIES
☒ Consumer
☒ Distribution
☒ Manufacturing
☒ Retail
☒ Service
☐ Wholesale
☒ SPECIFIC INDUSTRIES
☐ Energy
☒ Environmental
☒ Financial
☐ Real Estate
☐ Transportation
☐ Publishing
☐ Food
☐ Franchises
☒ DIVERSIFIED
☐ MISCELLANEOUS

STAGE PREFERENCE

☐ EARLY STAGE
☐ Seed
☐ Start-up
☐ 1st Stage
☒ LATER STAGE
☒ 2nd Stage
☒ Mature
☒ Mezzanine
☒ LBO/MBO
☐ Turnaround
☐ INT'L EXPANSION
☐ WILL CONSIDER ALL
☐ VENTURE LEASING

SBIC
Other Locations:

Affiliation:
Minimum Investment: $1 Million or more
Capital Under Management: Less than $100 Million

GEOGRAPHIC PREF

☐ East Coast
☐ West Coast
☐ Northeast
☐ Mid Atlantic
☐ Gulf States
☐ Northwest
☒ Southeast
☐ Southwest
☐ Midwest
☐ Central
☐ Local to Office
☐ Other Geo Pref

PENINSULA CAPITAL PARTNERS

**The Buhl Building
535 Griswold, Suite 2050
Detroit MI 48226**

Phone (313) 237-5100   Fax (313) 237-5111

PROFESSIONALS	TITLE
William Campbell	Chairman
Scott Reilly	President
William McKinley	Executive Vice President
Karl LaPeer	Senior Vice President
Steven Beckett	Senior Vice President

INDUSTRY PREFERENCE

☒ INFORMATION INDUSTRY
☒ Communications
☒ Computer Equipment
☒ Computer Services
☒ Computer Components
☐ Computer Entertainment
☒ Computer Education
☒ Information Technologies
☒ Computer Media
☒ Software
☒ Internet
☒ MEDICAL/HEALTHCARE
☒ Biotechnology
☒ Healthcare Services
☒ Life Sciences
☒ Medical Products
☒ INDUSTRIAL
☒ Advanced Materials
☒ Chemicals
☒ Instruments & Controls

☒ BASIC INDUSTRIES
☒ Consumer
☒ Distribution
☒ Manufacturing
☒ Retail
☒ Service
☒ Wholesale
☒ SPECIFIC INDUSTRIES
☐ Energy
☐ Environmental
☒ Financial
☐ Real Estate
☒ Transportation
☐ Publishing
☐ Food
☐ Franchises
☒ DIVERSIFIED
☒ MISCELLANEOUS

STAGE PREFERENCE

☐ EARLY STAGE
☐ Seed
☐ Start-up
☐ 1st Stage
☒ LATER STAGE
☒ 2nd Stage
☒ Mature
☒ Mezzanine
☒ LBO/MBO
☒ Turnaround
☐ INT'L EXPANSION
☐ WILL CONSIDER ALL
☒ VENTURE LEASING

Other Locations:

Affiliation:
Minimum Investment: $1 Million or more
Capital Under Management: Less than $100 Million

GEOGRAPHIC PREF

☐ East Coast
☐ West Coast
☐ Northeast
☐ Mid Atlantic
☐ Gulf States
☐ Northwest
☐ Southeast
☐ Southwest
☐ Midwest
☐ Central
☐ Local to Office
☐ Other Geo Pref

WHITE PINES LIMITED PARTNERSHIP I

**2401 Plymouth Road
Suite B
Ann Arbor MI 48105**

Phone (734) 747-9401   Fax (734) 747-9704

PROFESSIONALS	TITLE
Ian R.N. Bund	President
Ronald Kalish	Partner

INDUSTRY PREFERENCE

☒ INFORMATION INDUSTRY
☒ Communications
☒ Computer Equipment
☒ Computer Services
☒ Computer Components
☐ Computer Entertainment
☒ Computer Education
☒ Information Technologies
☒ Computer Media
☒ Software
☒ Internet
☒ MEDICAL/HEALTHCARE
☒ Biotechnology
☒ Healthcare Services
☒ Life Sciences
☒ Medical Products
☒ INDUSTRIAL
☒ Advanced Materials
☒ Chemicals
☒ Instruments & Controls

☒ BASIC INDUSTRIES
☒ Consumer
☒ Distribution
☒ Manufacturing
☒ Retail
☒ Service
☐ Wholesale
☒ SPECIFIC INDUSTRIES
☐ Energy
☒ Environmental
☒ Financial
☐ Real Estate
☐ Transportation
☐ Publishing
☐ Food
☐ Franchises
☒ DIVERSIFIED
☐ MISCELLANEOUS

STAGE PREFERENCE

☐ EARLY STAGE
☐ Seed
☐ Start-up
☐ 1st Stage
☒ LATER STAGE
☒ 2nd Stage
☒ Mature
☒ Mezzanine
☒ LBO/MBO
☐ Turnaround
☐ INT'L EXPANSION
☐ WILL CONSIDER ALL
☐ VENTURE LEASING
SBIC
Other Locations:

Affiliation:
Minimum Investment: Less than $1 Million
Capital Under Management: Less than $100 Million

GEOGRAPHIC PREF

☐ East Coast
☐ West Coast
☐ Northeast
☐ Mid Atlantic
☐ Gulf States
☐ Northwest
☒ Southeast
☐ Southwest
☐ Midwest
☐ Central
☐ Local to Office
☐ Other Geo Pref

WIND POINT PARTNERS

One Town Square
Suite 780
Southfield MI 48076

Phone (248) 354-7000   Fax (248) 945-7220

PROFESSIONALS	TITLE
Robert L. Cummings	Managing Director
James E. Forrest	Managing Director
Jeffrey Gonya	Managing Director
Richard Kracum	Managing Director
James TenBroek	Managing Director
Thomas Darden	Vice President

INDUSTRY PREFERENCE

☒ INFORMATION INDUSTRY	☒ BASIC INDUSTRIES
☒ Communications	☐ Consumer
☐ Computer Equipment	☒ Distribution
☐ Computer Services	☒ Manufacturing
☐ Computer Components	☒ Retail
☐ Computer Entertainment	☒ Service
☐ Computer Education	☐ Wholesale
☒ Information Technologies	☐ SPECIFIC INDUSTRIES
☐ Computer Media	☐ Energy
☐ Software	☐ Environmental
☐ Internet	☐ Financial
☒ MEDICAL/HEALTHCARE	☐ Real Estate
☐ Biotechnology	☐ Transportation
☒ Healthcare Services	☐ Publishing
☐ Life Sciences	☐ Food
☒ Medical Products	☐ Franchises
☒ INDUSTRIAL	☒ DIVERSIFIED
☒ Advanced Materials	☒ MISCELLANEOUS
☐ Chemicals	
☐ Instruments & Controls	

STAGE PREFERENCE

☒ EARLY STAGE
☐ Seed
☒ Start-up
☒ 1st Stage
☒ LATER STAGE
☐ 2nd Stage
☐ Mature
☐ Mezzanine
☒ LBO/MBO
☐ Turnaround
☐ INT'L EXPANSION
☐ WILL CONSIDER ALL
☐ VENTURE LEASING

Other Locations:

Affiliation:
Minimum Investment: $1 Million or more
Capital Under Management: $100 to $500 Million

GEOGRAPHIC PREF

☐ East Coast
☐ West Coast
☐ Northeast
☐ Mid Atlantic
☐ Gulf States
☐ Northwest
☐ Southeast
☐ Southwest
☐ Midwest
☐ Central
☐ Local to Office
☒ Other Geo Pref
Great Lakes States

AGIO CAPITAL PARTNERS I LP

First Bank Place Suite 4600
601 Second Avenue South
Minneapolis MN 55402

Phone (612) 339-8408   Fax (612) 349-4232

PROFESSIONALS	TITLE
Kenneth F. Gudorf	President

INDUSTRY PREFERENCE

☐ INFORMATION INDUSTRY	☐ BASIC INDUSTRIES
☐ Communications	☐ Consumer
☐ Computer Equipment	☐ Distribution
☐ Computer Services	☐ Manufacturing
☐ Computer Components	☐ Retail
☐ Computer Entertainment	☐ Service
☐ Computer Education	☐ Wholesale
☐ Information Technologies	☐ SPECIFIC INDUSTRIES
☐ Computer Media	☐ Energy
☐ Software	☐ Environmental
☐ Internet	☐ Financial
☐ MEDICAL/HEALTHCARE	☐ Real Estate
☐ Biotechnology	☐ Transportation
☐ Healthcare Services	☐ Publishing
☐ Life Sciences	☐ Food
☐ Medical Products	☐ Franchises
☐ INDUSTRIAL	☒ DIVERSIFIED
☐ Advanced Materials	☐ MISCELLANEOUS
☐ Chemicals	
☐ Instruments & Controls	

STAGE PREFERENCE

☐ EARLY STAGE
☐ Seed
☐ Start-up
☐ 1st Stage
☒ LATER STAGE
☒ 2nd Stage
☒ Mature
☐ Mezzanine
☒ LBO/MBO
☐ Turnaround
☐ INT'L EXPANSION
☐ WILL CONSIDER ALL
☐ VENTURE LEASING

SBIC
Other Locations:

Affiliation:
Minimum Investment: $1 Million or more
Capital Under Management: Less than $100 Million

GEOGRAPHIC PREF

☐ East Coast
☐ West Coast
☐ Northeast
☐ Mid Atlantic
☐ Gulf States
☐ Northwest
☐ Southeast
☐ Southwest
☐ Midwest
☐ Central
☐ Local to Office
☐ Other Geo Pref

CAPSTONE VENTURES

60 South Sixth Street
Dain Bosworth Plaza
Minneapolis MN 55402

Phone (612) 371-7733   Fax (612) 371-2837

PROFESSIONALS	TITLE
Brian Johnson	Managing Member

INDUSTRY PREFERENCE

☒	INFORMATION INDUSTRY	☐	BASIC INDUSTRIES
☐	Communications	☐	Consumer
☐	Computer Equipment	☐	Distribution
☐	Computer Services	☐	Manufacturing
☐	Computer Components	☐	Retail
☐	Computer Entertainment	☐	Service
☐	Computer Education	☐	Wholesale
☐	Information Technologies	☒	SPECIFIC INDUSTRIES
☐	Computer Media	☐	Energy
☒	Software	☐	Environmental
☒	Internet	☐	Financial
☒	MEDICAL/HEALTHCARE	☐	Real Estate
☐	Biotechnology	☐	Transportation
☒	Healthcare Services	☐	Publishing
☐	Life Sciences	☐	Food
☒	Medical Products	☐	Franchises
☐	INDUSTRIAL	☒	DIVERSIFIED
☐	Advanced Materials	☒	MISCELLANEOUS
☐	Chemicals		Outsourcing
☐	Instruments & Controls		

STAGE PREFERENCE

☒	EARLY STAGE
☒	Seed
☒	Start-up
☒	1st Stage
☐	LATER STAGE
☐	2nd Stage
☐	Mature
☐	Mezzanine
☐	LBO/MBO
☐	Turnaround
☐	INT'L EXPANSION
☐	WILL CONSIDER ALL
☐	VENTURE LEASING

SBIC
Other Locations: Menlo Park CA

Affiliation:
Minimum Investment: Less than $1 Million
Capital Under Management: Less than $100 Million

GEOGRAPHIC PREF

☐	East Coast
☒	West Coast
☐	Northeast
☐	Mid Atlantic
☐	Gulf States
☐	Northwest
☐	Southeast
☒	Southwest
☐	Midwest
☐	Central
☐	Local to Office
☐	Other Geo Pref

CHERRY TREE INVESTMENT CO.

7601 France Avenue South
Suite 225
Edina MN 55435

Phone (612) 893-9012   Fax (612) 893-9036

PROFESSIONALS	TITLE
David Henderson	Managing Director

INDUSTRY PREFERENCE

☒	INFORMATION INDUSTRY	☒	BASIC INDUSTRIES
☐	Communications	☐	Consumer
☐	Computer Equipment	☐	Distribution
☒	Computer Services	☐	Manufacturing
☐	Computer Components	☐	Retail
☐	Computer Entertainment	☒	Service
☐	Computer Education	☐	Wholesale
☒	Information Technologies	☒	SPECIFIC INDUSTRIES
☐	Computer Media	☐	Energy
☐	Software	☐	Environmental
☐	Internet	☒	Financial
☐	MEDICAL/HEALTHCARE	☐	Real Estate
☐	Biotechnology	☐	Transportation
☐	Healthcare Services	☐	Publishing
☐	Life Sciences	☐	Food
☐	Medical Products	☐	Franchises
☐	INDUSTRIAL	☒	DIVERSIFIED
☐	Advanced Materials	☒	MISCELLANEOUS
☐	Chemicals		Outsourcing
☐	Instruments & Controls		

STAGE PREFERENCE

☒	EARLY STAGE
☐	Seed
☐	Start-up
☒	1st Stage
☒	LATER STAGE
☒	2nd Stage
☒	Mature
☒	Mezzanine
☒	LBO/MBO
☐	Turnaround
☐	INT'L EXPANSION
☐	WILL CONSIDER ALL
☐	VENTURE LEASING

Other Locations:

Affiliation: Founding Partners
Minimum Investment: $1 Million or more
Capital Under Management: $100 to $500 Million

GEOGRAPHIC PREF

☐	East Coast
☐	West Coast
☐	Northeast
☐	Mid Atlantic
☐	Gulf States
☐	Northwest
☐	Southeast
☐	Southwest
☐	Midwest
☐	Central
☐	Local to Office
☐	Other Geo Pref

CHURCHILL CAPITAL INC.

2400 Lincoln Center
333 S. Seventh Street, Suite 2400
Minneapolis MN 55402

Phone (612) 832-3300   Fax (612) 673-6630

PROFESSIONALS	TITLE
Russ Peppet	Principal
Charles R. Carson	Principal
John Quirk	Principal
Melissa White	Principal

INDUSTRY PREFERENCE

☐ INFORMATION INDUSTRY
☐ Communications
☐ Computer Equipment
☐ Computer Services
☐ Computer Components
☐ Computer Entertainment
☐ Computer Education
☐ Information Technologies
☐ Computer Media
☐ Software
☐ Internet
☐ MEDICAL/HEALTHCARE
☐ Biotechnology
☐ Healthcare Services
☐ Life Sciences
☐ Medical Products
☐ INDUSTRIAL
☐ Advanced Materials
☐ Chemicals
☐ Instruments & Controls

☐ BASIC INDUSTRIES
☐ Consumer
☐ Distribution
☐ Manufacturing
☐ Retail
☐ Service
☐ Wholesale
☒ SPECIFIC INDUSTRIES
☐ Energy
☒ Environmental
☐ Financial
☐ Real Estate
☐ Transportation
☐ Publishing
☐ Food
☐ Franchises
☐ DIVERSIFIED
☐ MISCELLANEOUS

STAGE PREFERENCE

☐ EARLY STAGE
☐ Seed
☐ Start-up
☐ 1st Stage
☒ LATER STAGE
☒ 2nd Stage
☒ Mature
☒ Mezzanine
☒ LBO/MBO
☒ Turnaround
☐ INT'L EXPANSION
☐ WILL CONSIDER ALL
☒ VENTURE LEASING

Other Locations:

Affiliation: Churchill Capital Partners
Minimum Investment: $1 Million or more
Capital Under Management: $100 to $500 Million

GEOGRAPHIC PREF

☐ East Coast
☐ West Coast
☐ Northeast
☐ Mid Atlantic
☐ Gulf States
☐ Northwest
☐ Southeast
☐ Southwest
☐ Midwest
☐ Central
☐ Local to Office
☐ Other Geo Pref

CORAL VENTURES

60 South Sixth Street
Suite 3510
Minneapolis MN 55402

Phone (612) 335-8666   Fax (612) 335-8668

PROFESSIONALS	TITLE
Yuval Almog	Managing Partner
Peter McNerney	Managing Partner
William R. Baumel	Venture Partner

INDUSTRY PREFERENCE

☒ INFORMATION INDUSTRY
☒ Communications
☒ Computer Equipment
☒ Computer Services
☒ Computer Components
☐ Computer Entertainment
☒ Computer Education
☒ Information Technologies
☒ Computer Media
☒ Software
☒ Internet
☒ MEDICAL/HEALTHCARE
☒ Biotechnology
☒ Healthcare Services
☒ Life Sciences
☒ Medical Products
☐ INDUSTRIAL
☐ Advanced Materials
☐ Chemicals
☐ Instruments & Controls

☒ BASIC INDUSTRIES
☐ Consumer
☐ Distribution
☐ Manufacturing
☐ Retail
☒ Service
☐ Wholesale
☐ SPECIFIC INDUSTRIES
☐ Energy
☐ Environmental
☐ Financial
☐ Real Estate
☐ Transportation
☐ Publishing
☐ Food
☐ Franchises
☒ DIVERSIFIED
☐ MISCELLANEOUS

STAGE PREFERENCE

☒ EARLY STAGE
☒ Seed
☒ Start-up
☒ 1st Stage
☒ LATER STAGE
☒ 2nd Stage
☒ Mature
☒ Mezzanine
☐ LBO/MBO
☐ Turnaround
☐ INT'L EXPANSION
☐ WILL CONSIDER ALL
☐ VENTURE LEASING

Other Locations:

Affiliation:
Minimum Investment: Less than $1 Million
Capital Under Management: $100 to $500 Million

GEOGRAPHIC PREF

☐ East Coast
☐ West Coast
☐ Northeast
☐ Mid Atlantic
☐ Gulf States
☐ Northwest
☐ Southeast
☐ Southwest
☐ Midwest
☐ Central
☐ Local to Office
☐ Other Geo Pref

MEDICAL INNOVATION PARTNERS

6450 City West Parkway
Eden Prarie MN 55344-3245

Phone (612) 828-9616   Fax (612) 828-9596

PROFESSIONALS	TITLE
Timothy I. Maudlin	General Partner
Mark B. Knudson, PhD	General Partner
Robert S. Nickoloff	General Partner

INDUSTRY PREFERENCE

☐ INFORMATION INDUSTRY
☐ Communications
☐ Computer Equipment
☐ Computer Services
☐ Computer Components
☐ Computer Entertainment
☐ Computer Education
☐ Information Technologies
☐ Computer Media
☐ Software
☐ Internet
☒ MEDICAL/HEALTHCARE
☒ Biotechnology
☒ Healthcare Services
☒ Life Sciences
☒ Medical Products
☐ INDUSTRIAL
☐ Advanced Materials
☐ Chemicals
☐ Instruments & Controls

☒ BASIC INDUSTRIES
☐ Consumer
☐ Distribution
☐ Manufacturing
☐ Retail
☒ Service
☐ Wholesale
☐ SPECIFIC INDUSTRIES
☐ Energy
☐ Environmental
☐ Financial
☐ Real Estate
☐ Transportation
☐ Publishing
☐ Food
☐ Franchises
☒ DIVERSIFIED
☐ MISCELLANEOUS

STAGE PREFERENCE

☒ EARLY STAGE
☒ Seed
☒ Start-up
☐ 1st Stage
☐ LATER STAGE
☐ 2nd Stage
☐ Mature
☐ Mezzanine
☐ LBO/MBO
☐ Turnaround
☐ INT'L EXPANSION
☐ WILL CONSIDER ALL
☐ VENTURE LEASING

Other Locations:

Affiliation:
Minimum Investment: Less than $1 Million
Capital Under Management: Less than $100 Million

GEOGRAPHIC PREF

☐ East Coast
☐ West Coast
☐ Northeast
☐ Mid Atlantic
☐ Gulf States
☒ Northwest
☐ Southeast
☐ Southwest
☐ Midwest
☐ Central
☐ Local to Office
☐ Other Geo Pref

NORWEST VENTURE CAPITAL

2800 Piper Jaffray Tower
222 South Ninth Street
Minneapolis MN 55402-3388

Phone (612) 667-1650   Fax (612) 667-1660

PROFESSIONALS	TITLE
John Whaley	

INDUSTRY PREFERENCE

☒ INFORMATION INDUSTRY
☒ Communications
☒ Computer Equipment
☐ Computer Services
☐ Computer Components
☐ Computer Entertainment
☐ Computer Education
☒ Information Technologies
☐ Computer Media
☒ Software
☒ Internet
☐ MEDICAL/HEALTHCARE
☐ Biotechnology
☐ Healthcare Services
☐ Life Sciences
☐ Medical Products
☐ INDUSTRIAL
☐ Advanced Materials
☐ Chemicals
☐ Instruments & Controls

☐ BASIC INDUSTRIES
☐ Consumer
☐ Distribution
☐ Manufacturing
☐ Retail
☐ Service
☐ Wholesale
☐ SPECIFIC INDUSTRIES
☐ Energy
☐ Environmental
☐ Financial
☐ Real Estate
☐ Transportation
☐ Publishing
☐ Food
☐ Franchises
☐ DIVERSIFIED
☐ MISCELLANEOUS

STAGE PREFERENCE

☒ EARLY STAGE
☒ Seed
☒ Start-up
☒ 1st Stage
☒ LATER STAGE
☒ 2nd Stage
☒ Mature
☒ Mezzanine
☒ LBO/MBO
☒ Turnaround
☐ INT'L EXPANSION
☐ WILL CONSIDER ALL
☒ VENTURE LEASING
SBIC
Other Locations: Wellesley MA, Palo Alto CA

Affiliation: Norwest Corp.
Minimum Investment: Less than $1 Million
Capital Under Management: Over $500 Million

GEOGRAPHIC PREF

☐ East Coast
☐ West Coast
☐ Northeast
☐ Mid Atlantic
☐ Gulf States
☐ Northwest
☐ Southeast
☐ Southwest
☐ Midwest
☐ Central
☐ Local to Office
☐ Other Geo Pref

OAK INVESTMENT PARTNERS

**4550 Norwest Center
90 South Seventh Street
Minneapolis MN 55402**

Phone (612) 339-9322   Fax (612) 337-8017

PROFESSIONALS	TITLE
Gerald R. Gallagher	General Partner
Catherine L. Agee	Vice President

INDUSTRY PREFERENCE

- ☒ INFORMATION INDUSTRY
- ☒ Communications
- ☒ Computer Equipment
- ☒ Computer Services
- ☒ Computer Components
- ☐ Computer Entertainment
- ☒ Computer Education
- ☒ Information Technologies
- ☐ Computer Media
- ☒ Software
- ☒ Internet
- ☒ MEDICAL/HEALTHCARE
- ☒ Biotechnology
- ☒ Healthcare Services
- ☒ Life Sciences
- ☒ Medical Products
- ☐ INDUSTRIAL
- ☐ Advanced Materials
- ☐ Chemicals
- ☐ Instruments & Controls

- ☒ BASIC INDUSTRIES
- ☐ Consumer
- ☐ Distribution
- ☐ Manufacturing
- ☒ Retail
- ☒ Service
- ☐ Wholesale
- ☐ SPECIFIC INDUSTRIES
- ☐ Energy
- ☐ Environmental
- ☐ Financial
- ☐ Real Estate
- ☐ Transportation
- ☐ Publishing
- ☐ Food
- ☐ Franchises
- ☒ DIVERSIFIED
- ☐ MISCELLANEOUS

STAGE PREFERENCE

- ☒ EARLY STAGE
- ☒ Seed
- ☒ Start-up
- ☒ 1st Stage
- ☒ LATER STAGE
- ☒ 2nd Stage
- ☒ Mature
- ☐ Mezzanine
- ☒ LBO/MBO
- ☐ Turnaround
- ☐ INT'L EXPANSION
- ☐ WILL CONSIDER ALL
- ☐ VENTURE LEASING

Other Locations: Palo Alto CA

Affiliation:
Minimum Investment: Less than $1 Million
Capital Under Management: Over $500 Million

GEOGRAPHIC PREF

- ☐ East Coast
- ☐ West Coast
- ☐ Northeast
- ☐ Mid Atlantic
- ☐ Gulf States
- ☐ Northwest
- ☐ Southeast
- ☐ Southwest
- ☐ Midwest
- ☐ Central
- ☐ Local to Office
- ☐ Other Geo Pref

PIPER JAFFRAY VENTURES, INC.

**222 South 9th Street
Minneapolis MN 55402**

Phone (612) 342-6368   Fax (612) 342-8514

PROFESSIONALS	TITLE
Buzz Benson	Managing Director
Gary Blauer	Managing Director

INDUSTRY PREFERENCE

- ☒ INFORMATION INDUSTRY
- ☒ Communications
- ☒ Computer Equipment
- ☒ Computer Services
- ☒ Computer Components
- ☐ Computer Entertainment
- ☐ Computer Education
- ☒ Information Technologies
- ☐ Computer Media
- ☒ Software
- ☒ Internet
- ☒ MEDICAL/HEALTHCARE
- ☒ Biotechnology
- ☐ Healthcare Services
- ☒ Life Sciences
- ☒ Medical Products
- ☐ INDUSTRIAL
- ☐ Advanced Materials
- ☐ Chemicals
- ☐ Instruments & Controls

- ☐ BASIC INDUSTRIES
- ☐ Consumer
- ☐ Distribution
- ☐ Manufacturing
- ☐ Retail
- ☐ Service
- ☐ Wholesale
- ☐ SPECIFIC INDUSTRIES
- ☐ Energy
- ☐ Environmental
- ☐ Financial
- ☐ Real Estate
- ☐ Transportation
- ☐ Publishing
- ☐ Food
- ☐ Franchises
- ☒ DIVERSIFIED
- ☐ MISCELLANEOUS

STAGE PREFERENCE

- ☒ EARLY STAGE
- ☐ Seed
- ☐ Start-up
- ☒ 1st Stage
- ☒ LATER STAGE
- ☒ 2nd Stage
- ☒ Mature
- ☐ Mezzanine
- ☒ LBO/MBO
- ☐ Turnaround
- ☐ INT'L EXPANSION
- ☐ WILL CONSIDER ALL
- ☐ VENTURE LEASING

SBIC
Other Locations:

Affiliation:
Minimum Investment: Less than $1 Million
Capital Under Management: Less than $100 Million

GEOGRAPHIC PREF

- ☐ East Coast
- ☐ West Coast
- ☐ Northeast
- ☐ Mid Atlantic
- ☐ Gulf States
- ☐ Northwest
- ☐ Southeast
- ☐ Southwest
- ☐ Midwest
- ☐ Central
- ☐ Local to Office
- ☒ Other Geo Pref
- MN

ST. PAUL VENTURE CAPITAL, INC.

10400 Viking Drive
Suite 550
Eden Prairie MN 55344

Phone (612) 995-7474   Fax (612) 995-7475

PROFESSIONALS	TITLE
Patrick A. Hopf	General Partner
Everett V. Cox	General Partner
Brian D. Jacobs	General Partner

INDUSTRY PREFERENCE

☒ INFORMATION INDUSTRY
☒ Communications
☒ Computer Equipment
☒ Computer Services
☒ Computer Components
☐ Computer Entertainment
☒ Computer Education
☒ Information Technologies
☐ Computer Media
☒ Software
☒ Internet
☒ MEDICAL/HEALTHCARE
☒ Biotechnology
☒ Healthcare Services
☒ Life Sciences
☒ Medical Products
☒ INDUSTRIAL
☐ Advanced Materials
☐ Chemicals
☒ Instruments & Controls

☒ BASIC INDUSTRIES
☒ Consumer
☐ Distribution
☐ Manufacturing
☐ Retail
☐ Service
☐ Wholesale
☐ SPECIFIC INDUSTRIES
☐ Energy
☐ Environmental
☐ Financial
☐ Real Estate
☐ Transportation
☐ Publishing
☐ Food
☐ Franchises
☒ DIVERSIFIED
☐ MISCELLANEOUS

STAGE PREFERENCE

☒ EARLY STAGE
☒ Seed
☒ Start-up
☒ 1st Stage
☒ LATER STAGE
☒ 2nd Stage
☒ Mature
☒ Mezzanine
☒ LBO/MBO
☐ Turnaround
☐ INT'L EXPANSION
☐ WILL CONSIDER ALL
☐ VENTURE LEASING

Other Locations: Andover MA, Redwood City CA

Affiliation:
Minimum Investment: $1 Million or more
Capital Under Management: Over $500 Million

GEOGRAPHIC PREF

☐ East Coast
☐ West Coast
☐ Northeast
☐ Mid Atlantic
☐ Gulf States
☐ Northwest
☐ Southeast
☐ Southwest
☐ Midwest
☐ Central
☐ Local to Office
☐ Other Geo Pref

ADVANTAGE CAPITAL PARTNERS

7733 Forsyth Boulevard
Suite 1850
St. Louis MO 63105

Phone (314) 725-0800   Fax (314) 725-4265

PROFESSIONALS	TITLE
Steven Stull	President
David Bergmann	Managing Director
Crichton Brown	Managing Director
Scott Zajac	Managing Director
Maurice Doyle	Managing Director

INDUSTRY PREFERENCE

☒ INFORMATION INDUSTRY
☒ Communications
☒ Computer Equipment
☒ Computer Services
☒ Computer Components
☐ Computer Entertainment
☐ Computer Education
☒ Information Technologies
☐ Computer Media
☒ Software
☐ Internet
☒ MEDICAL/HEALTHCARE
☒ Biotechnology
☒ Healthcare Services
☒ Life Sciences
☒ Medical Products
☒ INDUSTRIAL
☒ Advanced Materials
☒ Chemicals
☒ Instruments & Controls

☒ BASIC INDUSTRIES
☒ Consumer
☒ Distribution
☐ Manufacturing
☐ Retail
☐ Service
☐ Wholesale
☒ SPECIFIC INDUSTRIES
☒ Energy
☐ Environmental
☐ Financial
☐ Real Estate
☐ Transportation
☐ Publishing
☐ Food
☐ Franchises
☒ DIVERSIFIED
☒ MISCELLANEOUS

STAGE PREFERENCE

☒ EARLY STAGE
☐ Seed
☒ Start-up
☒ 1st Stage
☒ LATER STAGE
☐ 2nd Stage
☐ Mature
☒ Mezzanine
☒ LBO/MBO
☐ Turnaround
☐ INT'L EXPANSION
☐ WILL CONSIDER ALL
☐ VENTURE LEASING

Other Locations: New Orleans LA, New York NY, Tampa FL

Affiliation:
Minimum Investment: $1 Million or more
Capital Under Management: $100 to $500 Million

GEOGRAPHIC PREF

☐ East Coast
☐ West Coast
☒ Northeast
☐ Mid Atlantic
☒ Gulf States
☐ Northwest
☒ Southeast
☐ Southwest
☐ Midwest
☐ Central
☐ Local to Office
☒ Other Geo Pref
  Gulf States

BANKERS CAPITAL CORP.

**3100 Gillham Road
Kansas City MO 64109**

Phone (816) 531-1600   Fax (816) 531-1334

PROFESSIONALS	TITLE
Raymond E. Glasnapp	President

INDUSTRY PREFERENCE

☐ INFORMATION INDUSTRY	☐ BASIC INDUSTRIES
☐ Communications	☐ Consumer
☐ Computer Equipment	☐ Distribution
☐ Computer Services	☐ Manufacturing
☐ Computer Components	☐ Retail
☐ Computer Entertainment	☐ Service
☐ Computer Education	☐ Wholesale
☐ Information Technologies	☐ SPECIFIC INDUSTRIES
☐ Computer Media	☐ Energy
☐ Software	☐ Environmental
☐ Internet	☐ Financial
☐ MEDICAL/HEALTHCARE	☐ Real Estate
☐ Biotechnology	☐ Transportation
☐ Healthcare Services	☐ Publishing
☐ Life Sciences	☐ Food
☐ Medical Products	☐ Franchises
☐ INDUSTRIAL	☒ DIVERSIFIED
☐ Advanced Materials	☐ MISCELLANEOUS
☐ Chemicals	
☐ Instruments & Controls	

STAGE PREFERENCE

☐ EARLY STAGE
☐ Seed
☐ Start-up
☐ 1st Stage
☒ LATER STAGE
☒ 2nd Stage
☒ Mature
☐ Mezzanine
☒ LBO/MBO
☐ Turnaround
☐ INT'L EXPANSION
☐ WILL CONSIDER ALL
☐ VENTURE LEASING

SBIC
Other Locations:

Affiliation:
Minimum Investment: Less than $1 Million
Capital Under Management: Less than $100 Million

GEOGRAPHIC PREF

☐ East Coast
☐ West Coast
☐ Northeast
☐ Mid Atlantic
☐ Gulf States
☐ Northwest
☐ Southeast
☐ Southwest
☐ Midwest
☐ Central
☐ Local to Office
☐ Other Geo Pref

INVESTAMERICA INVESTMENT ADVISORS, INC.

**Commerce Tower Suite 2424
911 Main Street
Kansas City MO 64105**

Phone (816) 842-0114   Fax (816) 471-7339

PROFESSIONALS	TITLE
Kevin F. Mullane	Sr. Vice President

INDUSTRY PREFERENCE

☒ INFORMATION INDUSTRY	☒ BASIC INDUSTRIES
☒ Communications	☒ Consumer
☒ Computer Equipment	☒ Distribution
☒ Computer Services	☒ Manufacturing
☒ Computer Components	☒ Retail
☐ Computer Entertainment	☒ Service
☐ Computer Education	☐ Wholesale
☐ Information Technologies	☒ SPECIFIC INDUSTRIES
☒ Computer Media	☒ Energy
☒ Software	☐ Environmental
☐ Internet	☐ Financial
☒ MEDICAL/HEALTHCARE	☐ Real Estate
☒ Biotechnology	☐ Transportation
☒ Healthcare Services	☒ Publishing
☒ Life Sciences	☐ Food
☒ Medical Products	☐ Franchises
☒ INDUSTRIAL	☒ DIVERSIFIED
☐ Advanced Materials	☒ MISCELLANEOUS
☐ Chemicals	Agriculture, forestry, fishing
☒ Instruments & Controls	

STAGE PREFERENCE

☐ EARLY STAGE
☐ Seed
☐ Start-up
☐ 1st Stage
☒ LATER STAGE
☐ 2nd Stage
☐ Mature
☐ Mezzanine
☒ LBO/MBO
☐ Turnaround
☐ INT'L EXPANSION
☐ WILL CONSIDER ALL
☐ VENTURE LEASING

Other Locations: Cedar Rapids IA

Affiliation:
Minimum Investment: $1 Million or more
Capital Under Management: Less than $100 Million

GEOGRAPHIC PREF

☐ East Coast
☐ West Coast
☐ Northeast
☐ Mid Atlantic
☐ Gulf States
☐ Northwest
☐ Southeast
☐ Southwest
☐ Midwest
☐ Central
☐ Local to Office
☐ Other Geo Pref

KANSAS CITY CAPITAL PARTNERS

233 West 47th Street
Kansas City MO 64112

Phone (816) 960-1771   Fax (816) 960-1777

PROFESSIONALS	TITLE
William Reisler	Managing Partner

INDUSTRY PREFERENCE

☒ INFORMATION INDUSTRY	☒ BASIC INDUSTRIES
☒ Communications	☒ Consumer
☒ Computer Equipment	☒ Distribution
☒ Computer Services	☒ Manufacturing
☐ Computer Components	☒ Retail
☐ Computer Entertainment	☐ Service
☐ Computer Education	☒ Wholesale
☒ Information Technologies	☐ SPECIFIC INDUSTRIES
☐ Computer Media	☐ Energy
☐ Software	☐ Environmental
☒ Internet	☐ Financial
☒ MEDICAL/HEALTHCARE	☐ Real Estate
☐ Biotechnology	☐ Transportation
☒ Healthcare Services	☐ Publishing
☐ Life Sciences	☐ Food
☒ Medical Products	☐ Franchises
☐ INDUSTRIAL	☒ DIVERSIFIED
☐ Advanced Materials	☐ MISCELLANEOUS
☐ Chemicals	
☐ Instruments & Controls	

STAGE PREFERENCE

☒ EARLY STAGE	
☐ Seed	
☒ Start-up	
☒ 1st Stage	
☒ LATER STAGE	
☒ 2nd Stage	
☒ Mature	
☒ Mezzanine	
☒ LBO/MBO	
☐ Turnaround	
☐ INT'L EXPANSION	
☐ WILL CONSIDER ALL	
☐ VENTURE LEASING	

SBIC
Other Locations:

Affiliation:
Minimum Investment: $1 Million or more
Capital Under Management: Less than $100 Million

GEOGRAPHIC PREF

☐ East Coast	
☐ West Coast	
☐ Northeast	
☐ Mid Atlantic	
☐ Gulf States	
☐ Northwest	
☐ Southeast	
☐ Southwest	
☐ Midwest	
☐ Central	
☐ Local to Office	
☐ Other Geo Pref	

MORAMERICA CAPITAL CORP.

Commerce Tower Suite 2424
911 Main Street
Kansas City MO 64105

Phone (816) 842-0114   Fax (816) 471-7339

PROFESSIONALS	TITLE
Kevin F. Mullane	Sr. Vice President

INDUSTRY PREFERENCE

☒ INFORMATION INDUSTRY	☒ BASIC INDUSTRIES
☒ Communications	☒ Consumer
☒ Computer Equipment	☒ Distribution
☒ Computer Services	☒ Manufacturing
☒ Computer Components	☒ Retail
☐ Computer Entertainment	☒ Service
☐ Computer Education	☐ Wholesale
☐ Information Technologies	☒ SPECIFIC INDUSTRIES
☒ Computer Media	☒ Energy
☒ Software	☐ Environmental
☐ Internet	☐ Financial
☒ MEDICAL/HEALTHCARE	☐ Real Estate
☒ Biotechnology	☐ Transportation
☒ Healthcare Services	☒ Publishing
☒ Life Sciences	☐ Food
☒ Medical Products	☐ Franchises
☒ INDUSTRIAL	☒ DIVERSIFIED
☐ Advanced Materials	☐ MISCELLANEOUS
☐ Chemicals	
☒ Instruments & Controls	

STAGE PREFERENCE

☐ EARLY STAGE	
☐ Seed	
☐ Start-up	
☐ 1st Stage	
☒ LATER STAGE	
☐ 2nd Stage	
☐ Mature	
☐ Mezzanine	
☒ LBO/MBO	
☐ Turnaround	
☐ INT'L EXPANSION	
☐ WILL CONSIDER ALL	
☐ VENTURE LEASING	

SBIC
Other Locations: Cedar Rapids IA

Affiliation: InvestAmerica
Minimum Investment: $1 Million or more
Capital Under Management: Less than $100 Million

GEOGRAPHIC PREF

☐ East Coast	
☐ West Coast	
☐ Northeast	
☐ Mid Atlantic	
☐ Gulf States	
☐ Northwest	
☐ Southeast	
☐ Southwest	
☐ Midwest	
☐ Central	
☐ Local to Office	
☐ Other Geo Pref	

UNITED MISSOURI CAPITAL CORPORATION

1010 Grand Avenue
P.O. Box 419226
Kansas City MO 64141

Phone (816) 860-7914   Fax (816) 860-7143

PROFESSIONALS	TITLE
Noel Shull	Manager

INDUSTRY PREFERENCE

- ☐ INFORMATION INDUSTRY
- ☐ Communications
- ☐ Computer Equipment
- ☐ Computer Services
- ☐ Computer Components
- ☐ Computer Entertainment
- ☐ Computer Education
- ☐ Information Technologies
- ☐ Computer Media
- ☐ Software
- ☐ Internet
- ☐ MEDICAL/HEALTHCARE
- ☐ Biotechnology
- ☐ Healthcare Services
- ☐ Life Sciences
- ☐ Medical Products
- ☐ INDUSTRIAL
- ☐ Advanced Materials
- ☐ Chemicals
- ☐ Instruments & Controls
- ☒ BASIC INDUSTRIES
- ☐ Consumer
- ☐ Distribution
- ☒ Manufacturing
- ☐ Retail
- ☐ Service
- ☐ Wholesale
- ☐ SPECIFIC INDUSTRIES
- ☐ Energy
- ☐ Environmental
- ☐ Financial
- ☐ Real Estate
- ☐ Transportation
- ☐ Publishing
- ☐ Food
- ☐ Franchises
- ☐ DIVERSIFIED
- ☐ MISCELLANEOUS

STAGE PREFERENCE

- ☐ EARLY STAGE
- ☐ Seed
- ☐ Start-up
- ☐ 1st Stage
- ☒ LATER STAGE
- ☒ 2nd Stage
- ☒ Mature
- ☒ Mezzanine
- ☒ LBO/MBO
- ☐ Turnaround
- ☐ INT'L EXPANSION
- ☐ WILL CONSIDER ALL
- ☐ VENTURE LEASING

SBIC
Other Locations:

Affiliation:
Minimum Investment: Less than $1 Million
Capital Under Management: Less than $100 Million

GEOGRAPHIC PREF

- ☐ East Coast
- ☐ West Coast
- ☐ Northeast
- ☐ Mid Atlantic
- ☐ Gulf States
- ☐ Northwest
- ☐ Southeast
- ☐ Southwest
- ☐ Midwest
- ☐ Central
- ☐ Local to Office
- ☐ Other Geo Pref

ATALANTA INVESTMENT COMPANY, INC.

601 Fairview Boulevard
Call Box 10,001
Incline Village NV 89450

Phone (775) 833-1836   Fax (775) 833-1890

PROFESSIONALS	TITLE
L. Mark Newman	Chairman

INDUSTRY PREFERENCE

- ☒ INFORMATION INDUSTRY
- ☒ Communications
- ☒ Computer Equipment
- ☒ Computer Services
- ☒ Computer Components
- ☐ Computer Entertainment
- ☒ Computer Education
- ☒ Information Technologies
- ☒ Computer Media
- ☒ Software
- ☒ Internet
- ☐ MEDICAL/HEALTHCARE
- ☐ Biotechnology
- ☐ Healthcare Services
- ☐ Life Sciences
- ☐ Medical Products
- ☐ INDUSTRIAL
- ☐ Advanced Materials
- ☐ Chemicals
- ☐ Instruments & Controls
- ☐ BASIC INDUSTRIES
- ☐ Consumer
- ☐ Distribution
- ☐ Manufacturing
- ☐ Retail
- ☐ Service
- ☐ Wholesale
- ☒ SPECIFIC INDUSTRIES
- ☐ Energy
- ☐ Environmental
- ☐ Financial
- ☐ Real Estate
- ☐ Transportation
- ☐ Publishing
- ☐ Food
- ☐ Franchises
- ☒ DIVERSIFIED
- ☐ MISCELLANEOUS

STAGE PREFERENCE

- ☐ EARLY STAGE
- ☐ Seed
- ☐ Start-up
- ☐ 1st Stage
- ☒ LATER STAGE
- ☒ 2nd Stage
- ☒ Mature
- ☒ Mezzanine
- ☒ LBO/MBO
- ☐ Turnaround
- ☐ INT'L EXPANSION
- ☐ WILL CONSIDER ALL
- ☐ VENTURE LEASING

SBIC
Other Locations:

Affiliation:
Minimum Investment: $1 Million or more
Capital Under Management: Less than $100 Million

GEOGRAPHIC PREF

- ☐ East Coast
- ☐ West Coast
- ☐ Northeast
- ☐ Mid Atlantic
- ☐ Gulf States
- ☐ Northwest
- ☐ Southeast
- ☐ Southwest
- ☐ Midwest
- ☐ Central
- ☐ Local to Office
- ☐ Other Geo Pref

INCORPORATED INVESTORS

P.O. Box 1336
Crystal Bay NV 89402

Phone (775) 832-9798   Fax (775) 832-9031

PROFESSIONALS	TITLE
J. A. Barry	Director
M. A. Cassin	Director
C. A. Baumann	Director
R. G. Bahr	Director

INDUSTRY PREFERENCE

- ☒ INFORMATION INDUSTRY
- ☒ Communications
- ☒ Computer Equipment
- ☒ Computer Services
- ☒ Computer Components
- ☒ Computer Entertainment
- ☒ Computer Education
- ☒ Information Technologies
- ☒ Computer Media
- ☒ Software
- ☒ Internet
- ☐ MEDICAL/HEALTHCARE
- ☐ Biotechnology
- ☐ Healthcare Services
- ☐ Life Sciences
- ☐ Medical Products
- ☒ INDUSTRIAL
- ☒ Advanced Materials
- ☒ Chemicals
- ☒ Instruments & Controls

- ☐ BASIC INDUSTRIES
- ☐ Consumer
- ☐ Distribution
- ☐ Manufacturing
- ☐ Retail
- ☐ Service
- ☐ Wholesale
- ☒ SPECIFIC INDUSTRIES
- ☒ Energy
- ☐ Environmental
- ☐ Financial
- ☐ Real Estate
- ☐ Transportation
- ☐ Publishing
- ☐ Food
- ☐ Franchises
- ☒ DIVERSIFIED
- ☒ MISCELLANEOUS

STAGE PREFERENCE

- ☒ EARLY STAGE
- ☐ Seed
- ☐ Start-up
- ☒ 1st Stage
- ☒ LATER STAGE
- ☒ 2nd Stage
- ☐ Mature
- ☒ Mezzanine
- ☒ LBO/MBO
- ☒ Turnaround
- ☒ INT'L EXPANSION
- ☐ WILL CONSIDER ALL
- ☒ VENTURE LEASING

Other Locations:

Affiliation:
Minimum Investment: $1 Million or more
Capital Under Management: $100 to $500 Million

GEOGRAPHIC PREF

- ☐ East Coast
- ☐ West Coast
- ☐ Northeast
- ☐ Mid Atlantic
- ☐ Gulf States
- ☐ Northwest
- ☐ Southeast
- ☐ Southwest
- ☐ Midwest
- ☐ Central
- ☐ Local to Office
- ☐ Other Geo Pref

ACCEL PARTNERS

One Palmer Square
Princeton NJ 08542

Phone (609) 683-4500   Fax (609) 683-0384

PROFESSIONALS	TITLE
Carter Sednaoui	Chief Financial Officer

INDUSTRY PREFERENCE

- ☒ INFORMATION INDUSTRY
- ☒ Communications
- ☒ Computer Equipment
- ☒ Computer Services
- ☒ Computer Components
- ☐ Computer Entertainment
- ☒ Computer Education
- ☒ Information Technologies
- ☒ Computer Media
- ☒ Software
- ☒ Internet
- ☐ MEDICAL/HEALTHCARE
- ☐ Biotechnology
- ☐ Healthcare Services
- ☐ Life Sciences
- ☐ Medical Products
- ☐ INDUSTRIAL
- ☐ Advanced Materials
- ☐ Chemicals
- ☐ Instruments & Controls

- ☒ BASIC INDUSTRIES
- ☐ Consumer
- ☐ Distribution
- ☐ Manufacturing
- ☐ Retail
- ☒ Service
- ☐ Wholesale
- ☐ SPECIFIC INDUSTRIES
- ☐ Energy
- ☐ Environmental
- ☐ Financial
- ☐ Real Estate
- ☐ Transportation
- ☐ Publishing
- ☐ Food
- ☐ Franchises
- ☒ DIVERSIFIED
- ☐ MISCELLANEOUS

STAGE PREFERENCE

- ☒ EARLY STAGE
- ☒ Seed
- ☒ Start-up
- ☒ 1st Stage
- ☒ LATER STAGE
- ☒ 2nd Stage
- ☒ Mature
- ☒ Mezzanine
- ☒ LBO/MBO
- ☐ Turnaround
- ☐ INT'L EXPANSION
- ☐ WILL CONSIDER ALL
- ☐ VENTURE LEASING

Other Locations: Palo Alto CA

Affiliation:
Minimum Investment: Less than $1 Million
Capital Under Management: $100 to $500 Million

GEOGRAPHIC PREF

- ☐ East Coast
- ☐ West Coast
- ☐ Northeast
- ☐ Mid Atlantic
- ☐ Gulf States
- ☐ Northwest
- ☐ Southeast
- ☐ Southwest
- ☐ Midwest
- ☐ Central
- ☐ Local to Office
- ☐ Other Geo Pref

AMERICAN ACQUISITION PARTNERS

**175 South Street
Morristown NJ 07960**

Phone (973) 267-7800   Fax (973) 267-7695

PROFESSIONALS	TITLE
Ted Bustany, PhD	Managing Partner

INDUSTRY PREFERENCE

☐ INFORMATION INDUSTRY
☐ Communications
☐ Computer Equipment
☐ Computer Services
☐ Computer Components
☐ Computer Entertainment
☐ Computer Education
☐ Information Technologies
☐ Computer Media
☐ Software
☐ Internet
☐ MEDICAL/HEALTHCARE
☐ Biotechnology
☐ Healthcare Services
☐ Life Sciences
☐ Medical Products
☒ INDUSTRIAL
☐ Advanced Materials
☒ Chemicals
☒ Instruments & Controls

☒ BASIC INDUSTRIES
☒ Consumer
☒ Distribution
☒ Manufacturing
☐ Retail
☐ Service
☐ Wholesale
☐ SPECIFIC INDUSTRIES
☐ Energy
☐ Environmental
☐ Financial
☐ Real Estate
☐ Transportation
☐ Publishing
☐ Food
☐ Franchises
☒ DIVERSIFIED
☐ MISCELLANEOUS

STAGE PREFERENCE

☐ EARLY STAGE
☐ Seed
☐ Start-up
☐ 1st Stage
☒ LATER STAGE
☐ 2nd Stage
☐ Mature
☐ Mezzanine
☒ LBO/MBO
☒ Turnaround
☐ INT'L EXPANSION
☐ WILL CONSIDER ALL
☒ VENTURE LEASING

Other Locations:

Affiliation:
Minimum Investment: $1 Million or more
Capital Under Management: Less than $100 Million

GEOGRAPHIC PREF

☒ East Coast
☐ West Coast
☒ Northeast
☐ Mid Atlantic
☐ Gulf States
☐ Northwest
☐ Southeast
☐ Southwest
☐ Midwest
☐ Central
☐ Local to Office
☐ Other Geo Pref

AT&T VENTURES

**295 North Maple Avenue
Room 3354 – B3
Basking Ridge NJ 07920**

Phone (908) 221-3893   Fax (908) 630-1455

PROFESSIONALS	TITLE
Bradford Burnham	General Partner

INDUSTRY PREFERENCE

☒ INFORMATION INDUSTRY
☒ Communications
☐ Computer Equipment
☐ Computer Services
☐ Computer Components
☐ Computer Entertainment
☐ Computer Education
☒ Information Technologies
☐ Computer Media
☒ Software
☒ Internet
☐ MEDICAL/HEALTHCARE
☐ Biotechnology
☐ Healthcare Services
☐ Life Sciences
☐ Medical Products
☐ INDUSTRIAL
☐ Advanced Materials
☐ Chemicals
☐ Instruments & Controls

☐ BASIC INDUSTRIES
☐ Consumer
☐ Distribution
☐ Manufacturing
☐ Retail
☐ Service
☐ Wholesale
☐ SPECIFIC INDUSTRIES
☐ Energy
☐ Environmental
☐ Financial
☐ Real Estate
☐ Transportation
☐ Publishing
☐ Food
☐ Franchises
☐ DIVERSIFIED
☒ MISCELLANEOUS

STAGE PREFERENCE

☒ EARLY STAGE
☒ Seed
☒ Start-up
☒ 1st Stage
☒ LATER STAGE
☒ 2nd Stage
☐ Mature
☐ Mezzanine
☐ LBO/MBO
☐ Turnaround
☐ INT'L EXPANSION
☐ WILL CONSIDER ALL
☐ VENTURE LEASING

Other Locations: Chevy Chase MD, Menlo Park CA

Affiliation: AT&T
Minimum Investment: Less than $1 Million
Capital Under Management: $100 to $500 Million

GEOGRAPHIC PREF

☐ East Coast
☐ West Coast
☐ Northeast
☐ Mid Atlantic
☐ Gulf States
☐ Northwest
☐ Southeast
☐ Southwest
☐ Midwest
☐ Central
☐ Local to Office
☐ Other Geo Pref

BCI ADVISORS INC.

**Glenpointe Centre West
2nd Floor
Teaneck NJ 07666-6883**

Phone (201) 836-3900   Fax (201) 836-6368

PROFESSIONALS	TITLE
Donald P. Remey	General Partner
Hoyt J. Goodrich	General Partner
J. Barton Goodwin	General Partner
Theodore T. Horton, Jr.	General Partner

INDUSTRY PREFERENCE

☒ INFORMATION INDUSTRY
☒ Communications
☐ Computer Equipment
☐ Computer Services
☒ Computer Components
☐ Computer Entertainment
☐ Computer Education
☒ Information Technologies
☐ Computer Media
☐ Software
☒ Internet
☒ MEDICAL/HEALTHCARE
☐ Biotechnology
☒ Healthcare Services
☒ Life Sciences
☒ Medical Products
☐ INDUSTRIAL
☐ Advanced Materials
☐ Chemicals
☐ Instruments & Controls

☐ BASIC INDUSTRIES
☐ Consumer
☐ Distribution
☐ Manufacturing
☐ Retail
☐ Service
☐ Wholesale
☐ SPECIFIC INDUSTRIES
☐ Energy
☐ Environmental
☐ Financial
☐ Real Estate
☐ Transportation
☐ Publishing
☐ Food
☐ Franchises
☒ DIVERSIFIED
☐ MISCELLANEOUS

STAGE PREFERENCE

☐ EARLY STAGE
☐ Seed
☐ Start-up
☐ 1st Stage
☒ LATER STAGE
☒ 2nd Stage
☒ Mature
☒ Mezzanine
☐ LBO/MBO
☐ Turnaround
☐ INT'L EXPANSION
☐ WILL CONSIDER ALL
☐ VENTURE LEASING

Other Locations:

Affiliation:
Minimum Investment: $1 Million or more
Capital Under Management: $100 to $500 Million

GEOGRAPHIC PREF

☐ East Coast
☐ West Coast
☐ Northeast
☐ Mid Atlantic
☐ Gulf States
☐ Northwest
☐ Southeast
☐ Southwest
☐ Midwest
☐ Central
☐ Local to Office
☐ Other Geo Pref

CARDINAL HEALTH PARTNERS

**221 Nassau Street
Princeton NJ 08542**

Phone (609) 924-6452   Fax (609) 683-0174

PROFESSIONALS	TITLE
John Clarke	Managing General Partner
Brandon Hull	General Partner

INDUSTRY PREFERENCE

☐ INFORMATION INDUSTRY
☐ Communications
☐ Computer Equipment
☐ Computer Services
☐ Computer Components
☐ Computer Entertainment
☐ Computer Education
☐ Information Technologies
☐ Computer Media
☐ Software
☐ Internet
☒ MEDICAL/HEALTHCARE
☒ Biotechnology
☒ Healthcare Services
☒ Life Sciences
☒ Medical Products
☐ INDUSTRIAL
☐ Advanced Materials
☐ Chemicals
☐ Instruments & Controls

☐ BASIC INDUSTRIES
☐ Consumer
☐ Distribution
☐ Manufacturing
☐ Retail
☐ Service
☐ Wholesale
☐ SPECIFIC INDUSTRIES
☐ Energy
☐ Environmental
☐ Financial
☐ Real Estate
☐ Transportation
☐ Publishing
☐ Food
☐ Franchises
☐ DIVERSIFIED
☒ MISCELLANEOUS

STAGE PREFERENCE

☒ EARLY STAGE
☒ Seed
☒ Start-up
☒ 1st Stage
☒ LATER STAGE
☒ 2nd Stage
☐ Mature
☐ Mezzanine
☐ LBO/MBO
☐ Turnaround
☐ INT'L EXPANSION
☐ WILL CONSIDER ALL
☐ VENTURE LEASING

Other Locations:

Affiliation:
Minimum Investment: Less than $1 Million
Capital Under Management: Less than $100 Million

GEOGRAPHIC PREF

☐ East Coast
☐ West Coast
☐ Northeast
☐ Mid Atlantic
☐ Gulf States
☐ Northwest
☐ Southeast
☐ Southwest
☐ Midwest
☐ Central
☐ Local to Office
☐ Other Geo Pref

CIT GROUP/VENTURE CAPITAL, INC.

650 CIT Drive
Livingston NJ 07039

Phone (973) 740-5429   Fax (973) 740-5555

PROFESSIONALS	TITLE
Colby W. Collier	Managing Director

INDUSTRY PREFERENCE

☐ INFORMATION INDUSTRY	☐ BASIC INDUSTRIES
☐ Communications	☐ Consumer
☐ Computer Equipment	☐ Distribution
☐ Computer Services	☐ Manufacturing
☐ Computer Components	☐ Retail
☐ Computer Entertainment	☐ Service
☐ Computer Education	☐ Wholesale
☐ Information Technologies	☐ SPECIFIC INDUSTRIES
☐ Computer Media	☐ Energy
☐ Software	☐ Environmental
☐ Internet	☐ Financial
☐ MEDICAL/HEALTHCARE	☐ Real Estate
☐ Biotechnology	☐ Transportation
☐ Healthcare Services	☐ Publishing
☐ Life Sciences	☐ Food
☐ Medical Products	☐ Franchises
☐ INDUSTRIAL	☒ DIVERSIFIED
☐ Advanced Materials	☐ MISCELLANEOUS
☐ Chemicals	
☐ Instruments & Controls	

STAGE PREFERENCE

☐ EARLY STAGE
☐ Seed
☐ Start-up
☐ 1st Stage
☒ LATER STAGE
☒ 2nd Stage
☒ Mature
☐ Mezzanine
☒ LBO/MBO
☐ Turnaround
☐ INT'L EXPANSION
☐ WILL CONSIDER ALL
☐ VENTURE LEASING

SBIC
Other Locations:

Affiliation:
Minimum Investment: $1 Million or more
Capital Under Management: Less than $100 Million

GEOGRAPHIC PREF

☐ East Coast
☐ West Coast
☐ Northeast
☐ Mid Atlantic
☐ Gulf States
☐ Northwest
☐ Southeast
☐ Southwest
☐ Midwest
☐ Central
☐ Local to Office
☐ Other Geo Pref

DEMUTH, FOLGER & WETHERILL

Glenpointe Center East, 5th Floor
300 Frank W. Burr Boulevard
Teaneck NJ 07666

Phone (201) 836-6000   Fax (201) 836-5666

PROFESSIONALS	TITLE
Thomas W. Folger	General Partner
David C. Wetherill	General Partner
Donald F. DeMuth	General Partner
Lisa Roumell	General Partner
Keith Pennell	General Partner

INDUSTRY PREFERENCE

☒ INFORMATION INDUSTRY	☒ BASIC INDUSTRIES
☒ Communications	☒ Consumer
☒ Computer Equipment	☒ Distribution
☒ Computer Services	☒ Manufacturing
☒ Computer Components	☐ Retail
☐ Computer Entertainment	☒ Service
☒ Computer Education	☐ Wholesale
☒ Information Technologies	☒ SPECIFIC INDUSTRIES
☒ Computer Media	☐ Energy
☒ Software	☒ Environmental
☒ Internet	☐ Financial
☒ MEDICAL/HEALTHCARE	☐ Real Estate
☐ Biotechnology	☒ Transportation
☒ Healthcare Services	☐ Publishing
☐ Life Sciences	☐ Food
☒ Medical Products	☐ Franchises
☒ INDUSTRIAL	☒ DIVERSIFIED
☐ Advanced Materials	☐ MISCELLANEOUS
☐ Chemicals	
☒ Instruments & Controls	

STAGE PREFERENCE

☐ EARLY STAGE
☐ Seed
☐ Start-up
☒ 1st Stage
☒ LATER STAGE
☐ 2nd Stage
☐ Mature
☐ Mezzanine
☐ LBO/MBO
☒ Turnaround
☐ INT'L EXPANSION
☐ WILL CONSIDER ALL
☒ VENTURE LEASING

Other Locations:

Affiliation:
Minimum Investment: $1 Million or more
Capital Under Management: $100 to $500 Million

GEOGRAPHIC PREF

☐ East Coast
☐ West Coast
☐ Northeast
☐ Mid Atlantic
☐ Gulf States
☐ Northwest
☐ Southeast
☐ Southwest
☐ Midwest
☐ Central
☐ Local to Office
☐ Other Geo Pref

DFW CAPITAL PARTNERS, L.P.

Glenpointe Center East, 5th Floor
300 Frank W. Burr Boulevard
Teaneck NJ 07666

Phone (201) 836-2233   Fax (201) 836-5666

PROFESSIONALS	TITLE
Donald F. DeMuth	Manager
Thomas W. Folger	General Partner
Keith W. Penwell	General Partner
Lisa Roumell	General Partner
David C. Wetherill	General Partner

INDUSTRY PREFERENCE

☒ INFORMATION INDUSTRY
☒ Communications
☐ Computer Equipment
☒ Computer Services
☐ Computer Components
☐ Computer Entertainment
☐ Computer Education
☒ Information Technologies
☒ Computer Media
☒ Software
☒ Internet
☒ MEDICAL/HEALTHCARE
☐ Biotechnology
☒ Healthcare Services
☐ Life Sciences
☐ Medical Products
☐ INDUSTRIAL
☐ Advanced Materials
☐ Chemicals
☐ Instruments & Controls

☒ BASIC INDUSTRIES
☒ Consumer
☒ Distribution
☒ Manufacturing
☐ Retail
☐ Service
☐ Wholesale
☒ SPECIFIC INDUSTRIES
☐ Energy
☐ Environmental
☒ Financial
☐ Real Estate
☐ Transportation
☐ Publishing
☐ Food
☐ Franchises
☒ DIVERSIFIED
☐ MISCELLANEOUS

STAGE PREFERENCE

☐ EARLY STAGE
☐ Seed
☐ Start-up
☐ 1st Stage
☒ LATER STAGE
☒ 2nd Stage
☒ Mature
☒ Mezzanine
☒ LBO/MBO
☐ Turnaround
☐ INT'L EXPANSION
☐ WILL CONSIDER ALL
☐ VENTURE LEASING
SBIC
Other Locations:

Affiliation:
Minimum Investment: $1 Million or more
Capital Under Management: $100 to $500 Million

GEOGRAPHIC PREF

☐ East Coast
☐ West Coast
☐ Northeast
☐ Mid Atlantic
☐ Gulf States
☐ Northwest
☐ Southeast
☐ Southwest
☐ Midwest
☐ Central
☐ Local to Office
☐ Other Geo Pref

DOMAIN ASSOCIATES

One Palmer Square
Princeton NJ 08542

Phone (609) 683-5656   Fax (609) 683-9789

PROFESSIONALS	TITLE
Brian Dovey	General Partner
James C. Blair	General Partner
Jesse I. Treu	General Partner

INDUSTRY PREFERENCE

☐ INFORMATION INDUSTRY
☐ Communications
☐ Computer Equipment
☐ Computer Services
☐ Computer Components
☐ Computer Entertainment
☐ Computer Education
☐ Information Technologies
☐ Computer Media
☐ Software
☐ Internet
☒ MEDICAL/HEALTHCARE
☒ Biotechnology
☒ Healthcare Services
☒ Life Sciences
☒ Medical Products
☒ INDUSTRIAL
☒ Advanced Materials
☐ Chemicals
☒ Instruments & Controls

☒ BASIC INDUSTRIES
☐ Consumer
☐ Distribution
☐ Manufacturing
☐ Retail
☒ Service
☐ Wholesale
☐ SPECIFIC INDUSTRIES
☐ Energy
☐ Environmental
☐ Financial
☐ Real Estate
☐ Transportation
☐ Publishing
☐ Food
☐ Franchises
☒ DIVERSIFIED
☐ MISCELLANEOUS

STAGE PREFERENCE

☒ EARLY STAGE
☒ Seed
☒ Start-up
☒ 1st Stage
☒ LATER STAGE
☒ 2nd Stage
☐ Mature
☐ Mezzanine
☐ LBO/MBO
☐ Turnaround
☐ INT'L EXPANSION
☐ WILL CONSIDER ALL
☐ VENTURE LEASING

Other Locations: Laguna Niguel CA

Affiliation:
Minimum Investment: Less than $1 Million
Capital Under Management: $100 to $500 Million

GEOGRAPHIC PREF

☐ East Coast
☐ West Coast
☐ Northeast
☐ Mid Atlantic
☐ Gulf States
☐ Northwest
☐ Southeast
☐ Southwest
☐ Midwest
☐ Central
☐ Local to Office
☐ Other Geo Pref

DSV PARTNERS

221 Nassau Street
Princeton NJ 08542

Phone (609) 924-6420   Fax (609) 683-0174

PROFESSIONALS
Morton Collins

TITLE
Partner

INDUSTRY PREFERENCE

☒ INFORMATION INDUSTRY	☒ BASIC INDUSTRIES
☒ Communications	☐ Consumer
☒ Computer Equipment	☐ Distribution
☒ Computer Services	☐ Manufacturing
☒ Computer Components	☐ Retail
☐ Computer Entertainment	☒ Service
☒ Computer Education	☐ Wholesale
☒ Information Technologies	☒ SPECIFIC INDUSTRIES
☒ Computer Media	☒ Energy
☒ Software	☒ Environmental
☒ Internet	☐ Financial
☒ MEDICAL/HEALTHCARE	☐ Real Estate
☒ Biotechnology	☐ Transportation
☒ Healthcare Services	☐ Publishing
☒ Life Sciences	☐ Food
☒ Medical Products	☐ Franchises
☒ INDUSTRIAL	☒ DIVERSIFIED
☒ Advanced Materials	☐ MISCELLANEOUS
☒ Chemicals	
☒ Instruments & Controls	

STAGE PREFERENCE

☒ EARLY STAGE
☒ Seed
☒ Start-up
☒ 1st Stage
☐ LATER STAGE
☐ 2nd Stage
☐ Mature
☐ Mezzanine
☐ LBO/MBO
☐ Turnaround
☐ INT'L EXPANSION
☐ WILL CONSIDER ALL
☐ VENTURE LEASING

Other Locations: Irvine CA

Affiliation:
Minimum Investment: Less than $1 Million
Capital Under Management: $100 to $500 Million

GEOGRAPHIC PREF

☐ East Coast
☐ West Coast
☐ Northeast
☐ Mid Atlantic
☐ Gulf States
☐ Northwest
☐ Southeast
☐ Southwest
☐ Midwest
☐ Central
☐ Local to Office
☐ Other Geo Pref

EARLY STAGE ENTERPRISES LP

995 Route 518
Skillman NJ 08558

Phone (609) 921-8896   Fax (609) 921-8703

PROFESSIONALS
Ronald Hahn
James Millar

TITLE
Manager
Manager

INDUSTRY PREFERENCE

☐ INFORMATION INDUSTRY	☐ BASIC INDUSTRIES
☐ Communications	☐ Consumer
☐ Computer Equipment	☐ Distribution
☐ Computer Services	☐ Manufacturing
☐ Computer Components	☐ Retail
☐ Computer Entertainment	☐ Service
☐ Computer Education	☐ Wholesale
☐ Information Technologies	☐ SPECIFIC INDUSTRIES
☐ Computer Media	☐ Energy
☐ Software	☐ Environmental
☐ Internet	☐ Financial
☐ MEDICAL/HEALTHCARE	☐ Real Estate
☐ Biotechnology	☐ Transportation
☐ Healthcare Services	☐ Publishing
☐ Life Sciences	☐ Food
☐ Medical Products	☐ Franchises
☐ INDUSTRIAL	☒ DIVERSIFIED
☐ Advanced Materials	☐ MISCELLANEOUS
☐ Chemicals	
☐ Instruments & Controls	

STAGE PREFERENCE

☒ EARLY STAGE
☒ Seed
☒ Start-up
☒ 1st Stage
☐ LATER STAGE
☐ 2nd Stage
☐ Mature
☐ Mezzanine
☐ LBO/MBO
☐ Turnaround
☐ INT'L EXPANSION
☐ WILL CONSIDER ALL
☐ VENTURE LEASING

SBIC
Other Locations:

Affiliation:
Minimum Investment: Less than $1 Million
Capital Under Management: Less than $100 Million

GEOGRAPHIC PREF

☐ East Coast
☐ West Coast
☒ Northeast
☒ Mid Atlantic
☐ Gulf States
☐ Northwest
☐ Southeast
☐ Southwest
☐ Midwest
☐ Central
☐ Local to Office
☒ Other Geo Pref
   Mid-Atlantic

EDELSON TECHNOLOGY PARTNERS

300 Tice Boulevard
Woodcliff Lake NJ 07675

Phone (201) 930-9898   Fax (201) 930-8899

PROFESSIONALS	TITLE
Nicholas Purd	Partner
Harry Edelson	Partner

INDUSTRY PREFERENCE

- ☒ INFORMATION INDUSTRY
- ☒ Communications
- ☒ Computer Equipment
- ☒ Computer Services
- ☒ Computer Components
- ☐ Computer Entertainment
- ☒ Computer Education
- ☒ Information Technologies
- ☒ Computer Media
- ☒ Software
- ☒ Internet
- ☐ MEDICAL/HEALTHCARE
- ☐ Biotechnology
- ☐ Healthcare Services
- ☐ Life Sciences
- ☐ Medical Products
- ☒ INDUSTRIAL
- ☒ Advanced Materials
- ☒ Chemicals
- ☒ Instruments & Controls

- ☒ BASIC INDUSTRIES
- ☒ Consumer
- ☐ Distribution
- ☐ Manufacturing
- ☐ Retail
- ☐ Service
- ☐ Wholesale
- ☐ SPECIFIC INDUSTRIES
- ☐ Energy
- ☐ Environmental
- ☐ Financial
- ☐ Real Estate
- ☐ Transportation
- ☐ Publishing
- ☐ Food
- ☐ Franchises
- ☒ DIVERSIFIED
- ☐ MISCELLANEOUS

STAGE PREFERENCE

- ☒ EARLY STAGE
- ☒ Seed
- ☒ Start-up
- ☒ 1st Stage
- ☒ LATER STAGE
- ☒ 2nd Stage
- ☒ Mature
- ☐ Mezzanine
- ☒ LBO/MBO
- ☐ Turnaround
- ☐ INT'L EXPANSION
- ☐ WILL CONSIDER ALL
- ☐ VENTURE LEASING

Other Locations:

Affiliation:
Minimum Investment: Less than $1 Million
Capital Under Management: Less than $100 Million

GEOGRAPHIC PREF

- ☐ East Coast
- ☐ West Coast
- ☐ Northeast
- ☐ Mid Atlantic
- ☐ Gulf States
- ☐ Northwest
- ☐ Southeast
- ☐ Southwest
- ☐ Midwest
- ☐ Central
- ☐ Local to Office
- ☐ Other Geo Pref

EDISON VENTURE FUND

1009 Lenox Drive, # 4
Lawrenceville NJ 08648

Phone (609) 896-1900   Fax (609) 896-0066

PROFESSIONALS	TITLE
John H. Martinson	General Partner
Bruce Luehrs	General Partner
Ross T. Martinson	General Partner
James T. Gunton	Vice President

INDUSTRY PREFERENCE

- ☒ INFORMATION INDUSTRY
- ☒ Communications
- ☐ Computer Equipment
- ☒ Computer Services
- ☒ Computer Components
- ☐ Computer Entertainment
- ☒ Computer Education
- ☒ Information Technologies
- ☒ Computer Media
- ☒ Software
- ☒ Internet
- ☐ MEDICAL/HEALTHCARE
- ☐ Biotechnology
- ☐ Healthcare Services
- ☐ Life Sciences
- ☐ Medical Products
- ☒ INDUSTRIAL
- ☒ Advanced Materials
- ☒ Chemicals
- ☒ Instruments & Controls

- ☒ BASIC INDUSTRIES
- ☐ Consumer
- ☐ Distribution
- ☐ Manufacturing
- ☐ Retail
- ☒ Service
- ☐ Wholesale
- ☒ SPECIFIC INDUSTRIES
- ☐ Energy
- ☐ Environmental
- ☒ Financial
- ☐ Real Estate
- ☐ Transportation
- ☐ Publishing
- ☐ Food
- ☐ Franchises
- ☒ DIVERSIFIED
- ☐ MISCELLANEOUS

STAGE PREFERENCE

- ☒ EARLY STAGE
- ☐ Seed
- ☐ Start-up
- ☒ 1st Stage
- ☒ LATER STAGE
- ☒ 2nd Stage
- ☒ Mature
- ☒ Mezzanine
- ☒ LBO/MBO
- ☐ Turnaround
- ☐ INT'L EXPANSION
- ☐ WILL CONSIDER ALL
- ☐ VENTURE LEASING

Other Locations: McClean VA

Affiliation:
Minimum Investment: $1 Million or more
Capital Under Management: $100 to $500 Million

GEOGRAPHIC PREF

- ☒ East Coast
- ☐ West Coast
- ☐ Northeast
- ☐ Mid Atlantic
- ☐ Gulf States
- ☐ Northwest
- ☐ Southeast
- ☐ Southwest
- ☐ Midwest
- ☐ Central
- ☐ Local to Office
- ☐ Other Geo Pref

FIREMARK GROUP

67 Park Place
Morristown NJ 07960

Phone (973) 538-5102   Fax (973) 538-0484

PROFESSIONALS	TITLE
Joshua Landau	
Bart Zanelli	
Michael Morrisey	
Phillip Tuberg	
Allen Rork	

INDUSTRY PREFERENCE

- ☒ INFORMATION INDUSTRY
- ☐ Communications
- ☐ Computer Equipment
- ☐ Computer Services
- ☐ Computer Components
- ☐ Computer Entertainment
- ☐ Computer Education
- ☐ Information Technologies
- ☐ Computer Media
- ☒ Software
- ☒ Internet
- ☒ MEDICAL/HEALTHCARE
- ☐ Biotechnology
- ☐ Healthcare Services
- ☐ Life Sciences
- ☒ Medical Products
- ☐ INDUSTRIAL
- ☐ Advanced Materials
- ☐ Chemicals
- ☐ Instruments & Controls

- ☐ BASIC INDUSTRIES
- ☐ Consumer
- ☐ Distribution
- ☐ Manufacturing
- ☐ Retail
- ☐ Service
- ☐ Wholesale
- ☒ SPECIFIC INDUSTRIES
- ☐ Energy
- ☐ Environmental
- ☒ Financial
- ☐ Real Estate
- ☐ Transportation
- ☐ Publishing
- ☐ Food
- ☐ Franchises
- ☒ DIVERSIFIED
- ☒ MISCELLANEOUS

STAGE PREFERENCE

- ☒ EARLY STAGE
- ☐ Seed
- ☐ Start-up
- ☒ 1st Stage
- ☒ LATER STAGE
- ☒ 2nd Stage
- ☐ Mature
- ☐ Mezzanine
- ☐ LBO/MBO
- ☐ Turnaround
- ☐ INT'L EXPANSION
- ☐ WILL CONSIDER ALL
- ☐ VENTURE LEASING

Other Locations:

Affiliation:
Minimum Investment: $1 Million or more
Capital Under Management: $100 to $500 Million

GEOGRAPHIC PREF

- ☐ East Coast
- ☐ West Coast
- ☐ Northeast
- ☐ Mid Atlantic
- ☐ Gulf States
- ☐ Northwest
- ☐ Southeast
- ☐ Southwest
- ☐ Midwest
- ☐ Central
- ☐ Local to Office
- ☐ Other Geo Pref

GEOCAPITAL PARTNERS

2 Executive Drive, Suite 820
Fort Lee NJ 07024

Phone (201) 461-9292   Fax (201) 461-7793

PROFESSIONALS	TITLE
Stephen J. Clearman	General Partner
Lawrence Lepard	General Partner
Richard Vines	General Partner
Colin Amies	General Partner
Mark Diker	General Partner
Nic Humphries	General Partner

INDUSTRY PREFERENCE

- ☒ INFORMATION INDUSTRY
- ☒ Communications
- ☒ Computer Equipment
- ☒ Computer Services
- ☒ Computer Components
- ☐ Computer Entertainment
- ☒ Computer Education
- ☒ Information Technologies
- ☒ Computer Media
- ☒ Software
- ☒ Internet
- ☐ MEDICAL/HEALTHCARE
- ☐ Biotechnology
- ☐ Healthcare Services
- ☐ Life Sciences
- ☐ Medical Products
- ☐ INDUSTRIAL
- ☐ Advanced Materials
- ☐ Chemicals
- ☐ Instruments & Controls

- ☒ BASIC INDUSTRIES
- ☐ Consumer
- ☐ Distribution
- ☐ Manufacturing
- ☐ Retail
- ☒ Service
- ☐ Wholesale
- ☐ SPECIFIC INDUSTRIES
- ☐ Energy
- ☐ Environmental
- ☐ Financial
- ☐ Real Estate
- ☐ Transportation
- ☐ Publishing
- ☐ Food
- ☐ Franchises
- ☒ DIVERSIFIED
- ☐ MISCELLANEOUS

STAGE PREFERENCE

- ☒ EARLY STAGE
- ☐ Seed
- ☐ Start-up
- ☒ 1st Stage
- ☒ LATER STAGE
- ☒ 2nd Stage
- ☒ Mature
- ☐ Mezzanine
- ☒ LBO/MBO
- ☐ Turnaround
- ☐ INT'L EXPANSION
- ☐ WILL CONSIDER ALL
- ☐ VENTURE LEASING

Other Locations:

Affiliation:
Minimum Investment: $1 Million or more
Capital Under Management: Over $500 Million

GEOGRAPHIC PREF

- ☐ East Coast
- ☐ West Coast
- ☐ Northeast
- ☐ Mid Atlantic
- ☐ Gulf States
- ☐ Northwest
- ☐ Southeast
- ☐ Southwest
- ☐ Midwest
- ☐ Central
- ☐ Local to Office
- ☐ Other Geo Pref

HEALTHCARE VENTURES LLC

44 Nassau Street
Princeton NJ 08542-4506

Phone (609) 430-3900   Fax (609) 430-9525

PROFESSIONALS	TITLE
William Crouse	Managing Director
Harold R. Werner	Managing Director
Dr. James H. Cavanaugh	Managing Director

INDUSTRY PREFERENCE

- ☐ INFORMATION INDUSTRY
- ☐ Communications
- ☐ Computer Equipment
- ☐ Computer Services
- ☐ Computer Components
- ☐ Computer Entertainment
- ☐ Computer Education
- ☐ Information Technologies
- ☐ Computer Media
- ☐ Software
- ☐ Internet
- ☒ MEDICAL/HEALTHCARE
- ☒ Biotechnology
- ☒ Healthcare Services
- ☒ Life Sciences
- ☒ Medical Products
- ☐ INDUSTRIAL
- ☐ Advanced Materials
- ☐ Chemicals
- ☐ Instruments & Controls

- ☐ BASIC INDUSTRIES
- ☐ Consumer
- ☐ Distribution
- ☐ Manufacturing
- ☐ Retail
- ☐ Service
- ☐ Wholesale
- ☐ SPECIFIC INDUSTRIES
- ☐ Energy
- ☐ Environmental
- ☐ Financial
- ☐ Real Estate
- ☐ Transportation
- ☐ Publishing
- ☐ Food
- ☐ Franchises
- ☐ DIVERSIFIED
- ☐ MISCELLANEOUS

STAGE PREFERENCE

- ☒ EARLY STAGE
- ☐ Seed
- ☐ Start-up
- ☒ 1st Stage
- ☒ LATER STAGE
- ☒ 2nd Stage
- ☒ Mature
- ☒ Mezzanine
- ☒ LBO/MBO
- ☐ Turnaround
- ☐ INT'L EXPANSION
- ☐ WILL CONSIDER ALL
- ☐ VENTURE LEASING

Other Locations: Cambridge MA

Affiliation: HealthCare Ventures
Minimum Investment: Less than $1 Million
Capital Under Management: $100 to $500 Million

GEOGRAPHIC PREF

- ☐ East Coast
- ☐ West Coast
- ☐ Northeast
- ☐ Mid Atlantic
- ☐ Gulf States
- ☐ Northwest
- ☐ Southeast
- ☐ Southwest
- ☐ Midwest
- ☐ Central
- ☐ Local to Office
- ☐ Other Geo Pref

JOHNSON & JOHNSON DEVELOPMENT

One Johnson & Johnson Plaza
New Brunswick NJ 08933

Phone (732) 524-3218   Fax (732) 247-5309

PROFESSIONALS	TITLE
James Utaski	

INDUSTRY PREFERENCE

- ☐ INFORMATION INDUSTRY
- ☐ Communications
- ☐ Computer Equipment
- ☐ Computer Services
- ☐ Computer Components
- ☐ Computer Entertainment
- ☐ Computer Education
- ☐ Information Technologies
- ☐ Computer Media
- ☐ Software
- ☐ Internet
- ☒ MEDICAL/HEALTHCARE
- ☒ Biotechnology
- ☒ Healthcare Services
- ☒ Life Sciences
- ☒ Medical Products
- ☐ INDUSTRIAL
- ☐ Advanced Materials
- ☐ Chemicals
- ☐ Instruments & Controls

- ☐ BASIC INDUSTRIES
- ☐ Consumer
- ☐ Distribution
- ☐ Manufacturing
- ☐ Retail
- ☐ Service
- ☐ Wholesale
- ☐ SPECIFIC INDUSTRIES
- ☐ Energy
- ☐ Environmental
- ☐ Financial
- ☐ Real Estate
- ☐ Transportation
- ☐ Publishing
- ☐ Food
- ☐ Franchises
- ☐ DIVERSIFIED
- ☒ MISCELLANEOUS

STAGE PREFERENCE

- ☒ EARLY STAGE
- ☒ Seed
- ☒ Start-up
- ☒ 1st Stage
- ☒ LATER STAGE
- ☒ 2nd Stage
- ☐ Mature
- ☐ Mezzanine
- ☐ LBO/MBO
- ☐ Turnaround
- ☐ INT'L EXPANSION
- ☐ WILL CONSIDER ALL
- ☐ VENTURE LEASING

Other Locations:

Affiliation: Johnson & Johnson
Minimum Investment: Less than $1 Million
Capital Under Management: $100 to $500 Million

GEOGRAPHIC PREF

- ☐ East Coast
- ☐ West Coast
- ☐ Northeast
- ☐ Mid Atlantic
- ☐ Gulf States
- ☐ Northwest
- ☐ Southeast
- ☐ Southwest
- ☐ Midwest
- ☐ Central
- ☐ Local to Office
- ☐ Other Geo Pref

JOHNSTON ASSOCIATES INC.

181 Cherry Valley Road
Princeton NJ 08540

Phone (609) 924-3131   Fax (609) 683-7524

PROFESSIONALS	TITLE
Robert F. Johnston	President
Robert B. Stockman	Vice President

INDUSTRY PREFERENCE

- ☐ INFORMATION INDUSTRY
- ☐ Communications
- ☐ Computer Equipment
- ☐ Computer Services
- ☐ Computer Components
- ☐ Computer Entertainment
- ☐ Computer Education
- ☐ Information Technologies
- ☐ Computer Media
- ☐ Software
- ☐ Internet
- ☒ MEDICAL/HEALTHCARE
- ☒ Biotechnology
- ☒ Healthcare Services
- ☒ Life Sciences
- ☒ Medical Products
- ☐ INDUSTRIAL
- ☐ Advanced Materials
- ☐ Chemicals
- ☐ Instruments & Controls

- ☐ BASIC INDUSTRIES
- ☐ Consumer
- ☐ Distribution
- ☐ Manufacturing
- ☐ Retail
- ☐ Service
- ☐ Wholesale
- ☒ SPECIFIC INDUSTRIES
- ☐ Energy
- ☒ Environmental
- ☐ Financial
- ☐ Real Estate
- ☐ Transportation
- ☐ Publishing
- ☐ Food
- ☐ Franchises
- ☒ DIVERSIFIED
- ☐ MISCELLANEOUS

STAGE PREFERENCE

- ☒ EARLY STAGE
- ☒ Seed
- ☒ Start-up
- ☒ 1st Stage
- ☒ LATER STAGE
- ☒ 2nd Stage
- ☐ Mature
- ☐ Mezzanine
- ☐ LBO/MBO
- ☐ Turnaround
- ☐ INT'L EXPANSION
- ☐ WILL CONSIDER ALL
- ☐ VENTURE LEASING

Other Locations:

Affiliation:
Minimum Investment: Less than $1 Million
Capital Under Management: Less than $100 Million

GEOGRAPHIC PREF

- ☐ East Coast
- ☐ West Coast
- ☐ Northeast
- ☐ Mid Atlantic
- ☐ Gulf States
- ☐ Northwest
- ☐ Southeast
- ☐ Southwest
- ☐ Midwest
- ☐ Central
- ☐ Local to Office
- ☐ Other Geo Pref

MIDMARK CAPITAL, LP

466 Southern Boulevard
Chatham NJ 07928

Phone (973) 822-2999   Fax (973) 822-8911

PROFESSIONALS	TITLE
Denis Newman	Managing Director

INDUSTRY PREFERENCE

- ☒ INFORMATION INDUSTRY
- ☒ Communications
- ☐ Computer Equipment
- ☐ Computer Services
- ☐ Computer Components
- ☐ Computer Entertainment
- ☐ Computer Education
- ☐ Information Technologies
- ☐ Computer Media
- ☐ Software
- ☐ Internet
- ☐ MEDICAL/HEALTHCARE
- ☐ Biotechnology
- ☐ Healthcare Services
- ☐ Life Sciences
- ☐ Medical Products
- ☐ INDUSTRIAL
- ☐ Advanced Materials
- ☐ Chemicals
- ☐ Instruments & Controls

- ☒ BASIC INDUSTRIES
- ☐ Consumer
- ☐ Distribution
- ☒ Manufacturing
- ☐ Retail
- ☐ Service
- ☐ Wholesale
- ☐ SPECIFIC INDUSTRIES
- ☐ Energy
- ☐ Environmental
- ☐ Financial
- ☐ Real Estate
- ☐ Transportation
- ☐ Publishing
- ☐ Food
- ☐ Franchises
- ☒ DIVERSIFIED
- ☐ MISCELLANEOUS

STAGE PREFERENCE

- ☐ EARLY STAGE
- ☐ Seed
- ☐ Start-up
- ☐ 1st Stage
- ☐ LATER STAGE
- ☒ 2nd Stage
- ☐ Mature
- ☐ Mezzanine
- ☐ LBO/MBO
- ☐ Turnaround
- ☐ INT'L EXPANSION
- ☐ WILL CONSIDER ALL
- ☐ VENTURE LEASING

SBIC
Other Locations:

Affiliation:
Minimum Investment: $1 Million or more
Capital Under Management: Less than $100 Million

GEOGRAPHIC PREF

- ☒ East Coast
- ☐ West Coast
- ☐ Northeast
- ☐ Mid Atlantic
- ☐ Gulf States
- ☐ Northwest
- ☐ Southeast
- ☐ Southwest
- ☐ Midwest
- ☐ Central
- ☐ Local to Office
- ☐ Other Geo Pref

NASSAU CAPITAL

22 Chambers Street
Princeton NJ 08452

Phone (609) 924-3555   Fax (609) 924-8887

PROFESSIONALS	TITLE
Curtis Glovier	Managing Director

INDUSTRY PREFERENCE

☒ INFORMATION INDUSTRY
☒ Communications
☐ Computer Equipment
☐ Computer Services
☐ Computer Components
☐ Computer Entertainment
☒ Computer Education
☒ Information Technologies
☒ Computer Media
☐ Software
☒ Internet
☒ MEDICAL/HEALTHCARE
☐ Biotechnology
☒ Healthcare Services
☐ Life Sciences
☒ Medical Products
☐ INDUSTRIAL
☐ Advanced Materials
☐ Chemicals
☐ Instruments & Controls

☒ BASIC INDUSTRIES
☐ Consumer
☐ Distribution
☐ Manufacturing
☒ Retail
☐ Service
☐ Wholesale
☒ SPECIFIC INDUSTRIES
☐ Energy
☐ Environmental
☐ Financial
☐ Real Estate
☐ Transportation
☐ Publishing
☐ Food
☐ Franchises
☒ DIVERSIFIED
☒ MISCELLANEOUS

STAGE PREFERENCE

☐ EARLY STAGE
☐ Seed
☐ Start-up
☐ 1st Stage
☒ LATER STAGE
☒ 2nd Stage
☐ Mature
☒ Mezzanine
☒ LBO/MBO
☐ Turnaround
☐ INT'L EXPANSION
☐ WILL CONSIDER ALL
☐ VENTURE LEASING

Other Locations:

Affiliation: Princeton University
Minimum Investment: $1 Million or more
Capital Under Management: $100 to $500 Million

GEOGRAPHIC PREF

☐ East Coast
☐ West Coast
☐ Northeast
☐ Mid Atlantic
☐ Gulf States
☐ Northwest
☐ Southeast
☐ Southwest
☐ Midwest
☐ Central
☐ Local to Office
☐ Other Geo Pref

PENNY LANE PARTNERS LP

One Palmer Square
Suite 309
Princeton NJ 08542

Phone (609) 497-4646   Fax (609) 497-0611

PROFESSIONALS	TITLE
Stephen H. Shaffer	Manager

INDUSTRY PREFERENCE

☐ INFORMATION INDUSTRY
☐ Communications
☐ Computer Equipment
☐ Computer Services
☐ Computer Components
☐ Computer Entertainment
☐ Computer Education
☐ Information Technologies
☐ Computer Media
☐ Software
☐ Internet
☐ MEDICAL/HEALTHCARE
☐ Biotechnology
☐ Healthcare Services
☐ Life Sciences
☐ Medical Products
☐ INDUSTRIAL
☐ Advanced Materials
☐ Chemicals
☐ Instruments & Controls

☐ BASIC INDUSTRIES
☐ Consumer
☐ Distribution
☐ Manufacturing
☐ Retail
☐ Service
☐ Wholesale
☐ SPECIFIC INDUSTRIES
☐ Energy
☐ Environmental
☐ Financial
☐ Real Estate
☐ Transportation
☐ Publishing
☐ Food
☐ Franchises
☒ DIVERSIFIED
☐ MISCELLANEOUS

STAGE PREFERENCE

☐ EARLY STAGE
☐ Seed
☐ Start-up
☐ 1st Stage
☒ LATER STAGE
☒ 2nd Stage
☒ Mature
☒ Mezzanine
☒ LBO/MBO
☐ Turnaround
☐ INT'L EXPANSION
☐ WILL CONSIDER ALL
☐ VENTURE LEASING
SBIC
Other Locations:

Affiliation:
Minimum Investment: $1 Million or more
Capital Under Management: Less than $100 Million

GEOGRAPHIC PREF

☐ East Coast
☐ West Coast
☐ Northeast
☐ Mid Atlantic
☐ Gulf States
☐ Northwest
☐ Southeast
☐ Southwest
☐ Midwest
☐ Central
☐ Local to Office
☐ Other Geo Pref

RUTGERS MINORITY INVESTMENT COMPANY

180 University Avenue
Third Floor
Newark NJ 07102

Phone (973) 353-5627

PROFESSIONALS	TITLE
Oscar Figueroa	President

INDUSTRY PREFERENCE

- ☐ INFORMATION INDUSTRY
- ☐ Communications
- ☐ Computer Equipment
- ☐ Computer Services
- ☐ Computer Components
- ☐ Computer Entertainment
- ☐ Computer Education
- ☐ Information Technologies
- ☐ Computer Media
- ☐ Software
- ☐ Internet
- ☐ MEDICAL/HEALTHCARE
- ☐ Biotechnology
- ☐ Healthcare Services
- ☐ Life Sciences
- ☐ Medical Products
- ☐ INDUSTRIAL
- ☐ Advanced Materials
- ☐ Chemicals
- ☐ Instruments & Controls

- ☐ BASIC INDUSTRIES
- ☐ Consumer
- ☐ Distribution
- ☐ Manufacturing
- ☐ Retail
- ☐ Service
- ☐ Wholesale
- ☐ SPECIFIC INDUSTRIES
- ☐ Energy
- ☐ Environmental
- ☐ Financial
- ☐ Real Estate
- ☐ Transportation
- ☐ Publishing
- ☐ Food
- ☐ Franchises
- ☒ DIVERSIFIED
- ☐ MISCELLANEOUS

STAGE PREFERENCE

- ☒ EARLY STAGE
- ☐ Seed
- ☒ Start-up
- ☒ 1st Stage
- ☒ LATER STAGE
- ☒ 2nd Stage
- ☐ Mature
- ☐ Mezzanine
- ☐ LBO/MBO
- ☐ Turnaround
- ☐ INT'L EXPANSION
- ☐ WILL CONSIDER ALL
- ☐ VENTURE LEASING

SSBIC

Other Locations:

Affiliation:
Minimum Investment: Less than $1 Million
Capital Under Management: Less than $100 Million

GEOGRAPHIC PREF

- ☐ East Coast
- ☐ West Coast
- ☒ Northeast
- ☐ Mid Atlantic
- ☐ Gulf States
- ☒ Northwest
- ☐ Southeast
- ☐ Southwest
- ☐ Midwest
- ☐ Central
- ☐ Local to Office
- ☐ Other Geo Pref

SYCAMORE VENTURES

989 Lenox Drive
Suite 208
Lawrenceville NJ 08648

Phone (609) 219-0100   Fax (609) 219-0101

PROFESSIONALS	TITLE
Kilin To	Partner
John Whitman	Partner
Peter Gerry	Partner
Kit Wong	Partner
Simon Wong	Partner
Rich Chong	Partner

INDUSTRY PREFERENCE

- ☒ INFORMATION INDUSTRY
- ☒ Communications
- ☒ Computer Equipment
- ☒ Computer Services
- ☒ Computer Components
- ☐ Computer Entertainment
- ☒ Computer Education
- ☒ Information Technologies
- ☒ Computer Media
- ☒ Software
- ☒ Internet
- ☒ MEDICAL/HEALTHCARE
- ☐ Biotechnology
- ☒ Healthcare Services
- ☒ Life Sciences
- ☒ Medical Products
- ☒ INDUSTRIAL
- ☒ Advanced Materials
- ☒ Chemicals
- ☒ Instruments & Controls

- ☒ BASIC INDUSTRIES
- ☒ Consumer
- ☐ Distribution
- ☐ Manufacturing
- ☐ Retail
- ☐ Service
- ☐ Wholesale
- ☐ SPECIFIC INDUSTRIES
- ☐ Energy
- ☐ Environmental
- ☐ Financial
- ☐ Real Estate
- ☐ Transportation
- ☐ Publishing
- ☐ Food
- ☐ Franchises
- ☒ DIVERSIFIED
- ☒ MISCELLANEOUS

STAGE PREFERENCE

- ☒ EARLY STAGE
- ☐ Seed
- ☐ Start-up
- ☒ 1st Stage
- ☒ LATER STAGE
- ☒ 2nd Stage
- ☐ Mature
- ☒ Mezzanine
- ☒ LBO/MBO
- ☐ Turnaround
- ☐ INT'L EXPANSION
- ☐ WILL CONSIDER ALL
- ☐ VENTURE LEASING

Other Locations:

Affiliation:
Minimum Investment: Less than $1 Million
Capital Under Management: $100 to $500 Million

GEOGRAPHIC PREF

- ☐ East Coast
- ☐ West Coast
- ☐ Northeast
- ☐ Mid Atlantic
- ☐ Gulf States
- ☐ Northwest
- ☐ Southeast
- ☐ Southwest
- ☐ Midwest
- ☐ Central
- ☐ Local to Office
- ☒ Other Geo Pref
  Asia

TAPPAN ZEE CAPITAL CORPORATION

201 Lower Notch Road
P.O. Box 416
Little Falls NJ 07424

Phone (973) 256-8280   Fax (973) 256-2841

PROFESSIONALS	TITLE
Jeffrey Birnberg	President

INDUSTRY PREFERENCE

☐ INFORMATION INDUSTRY	☒ BASIC INDUSTRIES
☐ Communications	☐ Consumer
☐ Computer Equipment	☐ Distribution
☐ Computer Services	☒ Manufacturing
☐ Computer Components	☒ Retail
☐ Computer Entertainment	☐ Service
☐ Computer Education	☐ Wholesale
☐ Information Technologies	☐ SPECIFIC INDUSTRIES
☐ Computer Media	☐ Energy
☐ Software	☐ Environmental
☐ Internet	☐ Financial
☐ MEDICAL/HEALTHCARE	☐ Real Estate
☐ Biotechnology	☐ Transportation
☐ Healthcare Services	☐ Publishing
☐ Life Sciences	☐ Food
☐ Medical Products	☐ Franchises
☐ INDUSTRIAL	☒ DIVERSIFIED
☐ Advanced Materials	☐ MISCELLANEOUS
☐ Chemicals	
☐ Instruments & Controls	

STAGE PREFERENCE

☐ EARLY STAGE
  ☐ Seed
  ☐ Start-up
  ☐ 1st Stage
☒ LATER STAGE
  ☒ 2nd Stage
  ☒ Mature
  ☒ Mezzanine
  ☒ LBO/MBO
  ☐ Turnaround
☐ INT'L EXPANSION
☐ WILL CONSIDER ALL
☐ VENTURE LEASING
SBIC
Other Locations:

Affiliation:
Minimum Investment: Less than $1 Million
Capital Under Management: Less than $100 Million

GEOGRAPHIC PREF

☐ East Coast
☐ West Coast
☒ Northeast
☐ Mid Atlantic
☐ Gulf States
☐ Northwest
☐ Southeast
☐ Southwest
☐ Midwest
☐ Central
☐ Local to Office
☐ Other Geo Pref

ARCH VENTURE PARTNERS

1155 University NE
Albuquerque NM 87106

Phone (505) 843-4293   Fax (505) 843-4294

PROFESSIONALS	TITLE
Clinton W. Bybee	Managing Director

INDUSTRY PREFERENCE

☒ INFORMATION INDUSTRY	☐ BASIC INDUSTRIES
☒ Communications	☐ Consumer
☒ Computer Equipment	☐ Distribution
☒ Computer Services	☐ Manufacturing
☐ Computer Components	☐ Retail
☐ Computer Entertainment	☐ Service
☐ Computer Education	☐ Wholesale
☐ Information Technologies	☒ SPECIFIC INDUSTRIES
☐ Computer Media	☒ Energy
☐ Software	☒ Environmental
☐ Internet	☐ Financial
☒ MEDICAL/HEALTHCARE	☐ Real Estate
☒ Biotechnology	☐ Transportation
☒ Healthcare Services	☒ Publishing
☒ Life Sciences	☐ Food
☒ Medical Products	☐ Franchises
☒ INDUSTRIAL	☒ DIVERSIFIED
☐ Advanced Materials	☒ MISCELLANEOUS
☐ Chemicals	Agriculture
☒ Instruments & Controls	

STAGE PREFERENCE

☒ EARLY STAGE
  ☒ Seed
  ☒ Start-up
  ☐ 1st Stage
☐ LATER STAGE
  ☐ 2nd Stage
  ☐ Mature
  ☐ Mezzanine
  ☐ LBO/MBO
  ☐ Turnaround
☐ INT'L EXPANSION
☐ WILL CONSIDER ALL
☐ VENTURE LEASING

Other Locations: New York NY, Seattle WA, Chicago IL

Affiliation:
Minimum Investment: $1 Million or more
Capital Under Management: $100 to $500 Million

GEOGRAPHIC PREF

☐ East Coast
☐ West Coast
☐ Northeast
☐ Mid Atlantic
☐ Gulf States
☐ Northwest
☐ Southeast
☐ Southwest
☐ Midwest
☐ Central
☐ Local to Office
☐ Other Geo Pref

NATURAL GAS PARTNERS

100 N Guadalupe Street
Suite 205
Santa Fe NM 87501

Phone (505) 983-8400   Fax (505) 983-8120

PROFESSIONALS	TITLE
David R. Albin	Managing Partner
John Foster	Managing Partner

INDUSTRY PREFERENCE

☐ INFORMATION INDUSTRY
☐ Communications
☐ Computer Equipment
☐ Computer Services
☐ Computer Components
☐ Computer Entertainment
☐ Computer Education
☐ Information Technologies
☐ Computer Media
☐ Software
☐ Internet
☐ MEDICAL/HEALTHCARE
☐ Biotechnology
☐ Healthcare Services
☐ Life Sciences
☐ Medical Products
☐ INDUSTRIAL
☐ Advanced Materials
☐ Chemicals
☐ Instruments & Controls

☐ BASIC INDUSTRIES
☐ Consumer
☐ Distribution
☐ Manufacturing
☐ Retail
☐ Service
☐ Wholesale
☒ SPECIFIC INDUSTRIES
☒ Energy
☐ Environmental
☐ Financial
☐ Real Estate
☐ Transportation
☐ Publishing
☐ Food
☐ Franchises
☐ DIVERSIFIED
☒ MISCELLANEOUS

STAGE PREFERENCE

☒ EARLY STAGE
☐ Seed
☒ Start-up
☒ 1st Stage
☒ LATER STAGE
☒ 2nd Stage
☐ Mature
☐ Mezzanine
☒ LBO/MBO
☐ Turnaround
☐ INT'L EXPANSION
☐ WILL CONSIDER ALL
☐ VENTURE LEASING

Other Locations: Greenwich CT, Forth Worth TX

Affiliation:
Minimum Investment: $1 Million or more
Capital Under Management: Over $500 Million

GEOGRAPHIC PREF

☐ East Coast
☐ West Coast
☐ Northeast
☐ Mid Atlantic
☐ Gulf States
☐ Northwest
☐ Southeast
☐ Southwest
☐ Midwest
☐ Central
☐ Local to Office
☐ Other Geo Pref

ADVANTA PARTNERS LP

712 Fifth Avenue
New York NY 10019-4102

Phone (212) 649-6900   Fax (212) 956-3301

PROFESSIONALS	TITLE
Gary Neems	Managing Director

INDUSTRY PREFERENCE

☒ INFORMATION INDUSTRY
☒ Communications
☒ Computer Equipment
☒ Computer Services
☒ Computer Components
☒ Computer Entertainment
☒ Computer Education
☒ Information Technologies
☒ Computer Media
☒ Software
☒ Internet
☐ MEDICAL/HEALTHCARE
☐ Biotechnology
☐ Healthcare Services
☐ Life Sciences
☐ Medical Products
☐ INDUSTRIAL
☐ Advanced Materials
☐ Chemicals
☐ Instruments & Controls

☐ BASIC INDUSTRIES
☐ Consumer
☐ Distribution
☐ Manufacturing
☐ Retail
☐ Service
☐ Wholesale
☐ SPECIFIC INDUSTRIES
☐ Energy
☐ Environmental
☐ Financial
☐ Real Estate
☐ Transportation
☐ Publishing
☐ Food
☐ Franchises
☐ DIVERSIFIED
☒ MISCELLANEOUS

STAGE PREFERENCE

☐ EARLY STAGE
☐ Seed
☐ Start-up
☐ 1st Stage
☒ LATER STAGE
☒ 2nd Stage
☐ Mature
☒ Mezzanine
☒ LBO/MBO
☐ Turnaround
☐ INT'L EXPANSION
☐ WILL CONSIDER ALL
☐ VENTURE LEASING

Other Locations: Spring House PA

Affiliation:
Minimum Investment: $1 Million or more
Capital Under Management: $100 to $500 Million

GEOGRAPHIC PREF

☐ East Coast
☐ West Coast
☐ Northeast
☐ Mid Atlantic
☐ Gulf States
☐ Northwest
☐ Southeast
☐ Southwest
☐ Midwest
☐ Central
☐ Local to Office
☐ Other Geo Pref

ADVANTAGE CAPITAL PARTNERS

521 Madison Avenue
Seventh Floor
New York NY 10022

Phone (212) 893-8600   Fax (212) 893-8700

PROFESSIONALS	TITLE
Steven Stull	President
David Bergmann	Managing Director
Crichton Brown	Managing Director
Scott Zajac	Managing Director
Maurice Doyle	Managing Director

INDUSTRY PREFERENCE

- ☒ INFORMATION INDUSTRY
- ☒ Communications
- ☒ Computer Equipment
- ☒ Computer Services
- ☒ Computer Components
- ☐ Computer Entertainment
- ☐ Computer Education
- ☒ Information Technologies
- ☐ Computer Media
- ☒ Software
- ☐ Internet
- ☒ MEDICAL/HEALTHCARE
- ☒ Biotechnology
- ☒ Healthcare Services
- ☒ Life Sciences
- ☒ Medical Products
- ☒ INDUSTRIAL
- ☒ Advanced Materials
- ☒ Chemicals
- ☒ Instruments & Controls

- ☒ BASIC INDUSTRIES
- ☒ Consumer
- ☒ Distribution
- ☐ Manufacturing
- ☐ Retail
- ☐ Service
- ☐ Wholesale
- ☒ SPECIFIC INDUSTRIES
- ☒ Energy
- ☐ Environmental
- ☐ Financial
- ☐ Real Estate
- ☐ Transportation
- ☐ Publishing
- ☐ Food
- ☐ Franchises
- ☒ DIVERSIFIED
- ☒ MISCELLANEOUS

STAGE PREFERENCE

- ☒ EARLY STAGE
- ☐ Seed
- ☒ Start-up
- ☒ 1st Stage
- ☒ LATER STAGE
- ☐ 2nd Stage
- ☐ Mature
- ☒ Mezzanine
- ☒ LBO/MBO
- ☐ Turnaround
- ☐ INT'L EXPANSION
- ☐ WILL CONSIDER ALL
- ☐ VENTURE LEASING

Other Locations: New Orleans LA, St Louis MO, Tampa FL

Affiliation:
Minimum Investment: $1 Million or more
Capital Under Management: $100 to $500 Million

GEOGRAPHIC PREF

- ☐ East Coast
- ☐ West Coast
- ☒ Northeast
- ☐ Mid Atlantic
- ☒ Gulf States
- ☐ Northwest
- ☒ Southeast
- ☐ Southwest
- ☐ Midwest
- ☐ Central
- ☐ Local to Office
- ☒ Other Geo Pref
     Gulf States

ALLEGRA PARTNERS

515 Madison Avenue
29th Floor
New York NY 10022

Phone (212) 826-9080   Fax (212) 759-2561

PROFESSIONALS	TITLE
Larry Lawrence	General Partner
Richard W. Smith	General Partner

INDUSTRY PREFERENCE

- ☒ INFORMATION INDUSTRY
- ☒ Communications
- ☐ Computer Equipment
- ☒ Computer Services
- ☐ Computer Components
- ☐ Computer Entertainment
- ☒ Computer Education
- ☒ Information Technologies
- ☒ Computer Media
- ☒ Software
- ☒ Internet
- ☒ MEDICAL/HEALTHCARE
- ☐ Biotechnology
- ☒ Healthcare Services
- ☐ Life Sciences
- ☐ Medical Products
- ☐ INDUSTRIAL
- ☐ Advanced Materials
- ☐ Chemicals
- ☐ Instruments & Controls

- ☐ BASIC INDUSTRIES
- ☐ Consumer
- ☐ Distribution
- ☐ Manufacturing
- ☐ Retail
- ☐ Service
- ☐ Wholesale
- ☐ SPECIFIC INDUSTRIES
- ☐ Energy
- ☐ Environmental
- ☐ Financial
- ☐ Real Estate
- ☐ Transportation
- ☐ Publishing
- ☐ Food
- ☐ Franchises
- ☒ DIVERSIFIED
- ☒ MISCELLANEOUS

STAGE PREFERENCE

- ☒ EARLY STAGE
- ☐ Seed
- ☐ Start-up
- ☒ 1st Stage
- ☒ LATER STAGE
- ☒ 2nd Stage
- ☒ Mature
- ☐ Mezzanine
- ☐ LBO/MBO
- ☐ Turnaround
- ☐ INT'L EXPANSION
- ☐ WILL CONSIDER ALL
- ☐ VENTURE LEASING

Other Locations:

Affiliation:
Minimum Investment: Less than $1 Million
Capital Under Management: $100 to $500 Million

GEOGRAPHIC PREF

- ☒ East Coast
- ☐ West Coast
- ☐ Northeast
- ☐ Mid Atlantic
- ☐ Gulf States
- ☐ Northwest
- ☐ Southeast
- ☐ Southwest
- ☐ Midwest
- ☐ Central
- ☐ Local to Office
- ☐ Other Geo Pref

AMERINDO INVESTMENT ADVISORS

**399 Park Avenue
22nd Floor
New York NY 10022**

Phone (212) 371-6360   Fax (212) 371-6988

PROFESSIONALS	TITLE
Alberto W. Vilar	
Gary A. Tanaka, PhD	
Ralph Cechettini	

INDUSTRY PREFERENCE

☒ INFORMATION INDUSTRY	☐ BASIC INDUSTRIES
☒ Communications	☐ Consumer
☒ Computer Equipment	☐ Distribution
☒ Computer Services	☐ Manufacturing
☒ Computer Components	☐ Retail
☐ Computer Entertainment	☐ Service
☒ Computer Education	☐ Wholesale
☒ Information Technologies	☒ SPECIFIC INDUSTRIES
☒ Computer Media	☒ Energy
☒ Software	☒ Environmental
☒ Internet	☒ Financial
☒ MEDICAL/HEALTHCARE	☐ Real Estate
☐ Biotechnology	☐ Transportation
☒ Healthcare Services	☐ Publishing
☐ Life Sciences	☐ Food
☐ Medical Products	☐ Franchises
☐ INDUSTRIAL	☒ DIVERSIFIED
☐ Advanced Materials	☒ MISCELLANEOUS
☐ Chemicals	
☐ Instruments & Controls	

STAGE PREFERENCE

☐ EARLY STAGE	
☐ Seed	
☐ Start-up	
☐ 1st Stage	
☒ LATER STAGE	
☒ 2nd Stage	
☒ Mature	
☒ Mezzanine	
☐ LBO/MBO	
☐ Turnaround	
☐ INT'L EXPANSION	
☐ WILL CONSIDER ALL	
☐ VENTURE LEASING	

Other Locations:

Affiliation:
Minimum Investment: $1 Million or more
Capital Under Management: Less than $100 Million

GEOGRAPHIC PREF

☐ East Coast
☐ West Coast
☐ Northeast
☐ Mid Atlantic
☐ Gulf States
☐ Northwest
☐ Southeast
☐ Southwest
☐ Midwest
☐ Central
☐ Local to Office
☐ Other Geo Pref

ARCH VENTURE PARTNERS

**45 Rockefeller Plaza
Suite 2000
New York NY 10020**

Phone (212) 262-7260   Fax (212) 332-5054

PROFESSIONALS	TITLE
Steven Lazarus	Managing Director
Keith Crandell	Managing Director
Robert Nelsen	Managing Director
Alex Knight	Managing Director
Karen Kerr	Managing Director

INDUSTRY PREFERENCE

☒ INFORMATION INDUSTRY	☐ BASIC INDUSTRIES
☒ Communications	☐ Consumer
☒ Computer Equipment	☐ Distribution
☒ Computer Services	☐ Manufacturing
☐ Computer Components	☐ Retail
☐ Computer Entertainment	☐ Service
☐ Computer Education	☐ Wholesale
☐ Information Technologies	☒ SPECIFIC INDUSTRIES
☐ Computer Media	☒ Energy
☐ Software	☒ Environmental
☐ Internet	☐ Financial
☒ MEDICAL/HEALTHCARE	☐ Real Estate
☒ Biotechnology	☐ Transportation
☒ Healthcare Services	☒ Publishing
☒ Life Sciences	☐ Food
☒ Medical Products	☐ Franchises
☒ INDUSTRIAL	☒ DIVERSIFIED
☐ Advanced Materials	☒ MISCELLANEOUS
☐ Chemicals	Agriculture
☒ Instruments & Controls	

STAGE PREFERENCE

☒ EARLY STAGE	
☒ Seed	
☒ Start-up	
☐ 1st Stage	
☐ LATER STAGE	
☐ 2nd Stage	
☐ Mature	
☐ Mezzanine	
☐ LBO/MBO	
☐ Turnaround	
☐ INT'L EXPANSION	
☐ WILL CONSIDER ALL	
☐ VENTURE LEASING	

Other Locations: Albuquerque NM, Seattle WA, Chicago IL

Affiliation:
Minimum Investment: $1 Million or more
Capital Under Management: $100 to $500 Million

GEOGRAPHIC PREF

☐ East Coast
☐ West Coast
☐ Northeast
☐ Mid Atlantic
☐ Gulf States
☐ Northwest
☐ Southeast
☐ Southwest
☐ Midwest
☐ Central
☐ Local to Office
☐ Other Geo Pref

ARDSHIEL INC

230 Park Avenue
Suite 2527
New York NY 10169

Phone (212) 697-8570   Fax (212) 972-1809

PROFESSIONALS

Dennis McCormick
Daniel Morley

TITLE

Managing Partner
Managing Partner

INDUSTRY PREFERENCE

☒ INFORMATION INDUSTRY	☒ BASIC INDUSTRIES
☒ Communications	☒ Consumer
☒ Computer Equipment	☒ Distribution
☒ Computer Services	☐ Manufacturing
☒ Computer Components	☐ Retail
☐ Computer Entertainment	☐ Service
☒ Computer Education	☐ Wholesale
☒ Information Technologies	☒ SPECIFIC INDUSTRIES
☒ Computer Media	☐ Energy
☒ Software	☐ Environmental
☒ Internet	☒ Financial
☒ MEDICAL/HEALTHCARE	☐ Real Estate
☒ Biotechnology	☐ Transportation
☒ Healthcare Services	☐ Publishing
☒ Life Sciences	☐ Food
☒ Medical Products	☐ Franchises
☒ INDUSTRIAL	☒ DIVERSIFIED
☒ Advanced Materials	☒ MISCELLANEOUS
☒ Chemicals	
☒ Instruments & Controls	

STAGE PREFERENCE

☐ EARLY STAGE
☐ Seed
☐ Start-up
☐ 1st Stage
☒ LATER STAGE
☐ 2nd Stage
☐ Mature
☐ Mezzanine
☒ LBO/MBO
☐ Turnaround
☐ INT'L EXPANSION
☐ WILL CONSIDER ALL
☐ VENTURE LEASING

Other Locations:

Affiliation:
Minimum Investment: $1 Million or more
Capital Under Management: $100 to $500 Million

GEOGRAPHIC PREF

☐ East Coast
☐ West Coast
☐ Northeast
☐ Mid Atlantic
☐ Gulf States
☐ Northwest
☐ Southeast
☐ Southwest
☐ Midwest
☐ Central
☐ Local to Office
☐ Other Geo Pref

ATLANTIC MEDICAL CAPITAL

156 West 56th Street
Suite 1605
New York NY 10019

Phone (212) 307-3580   Fax (212) 957-1586

PROFESSIONALS

Matthew Hermann
Tom O'Connor
Andy Cowherd
Michael Sinclair

TITLE

Vice President
Managing Director
Managing Director
Managing Director

INDUSTRY PREFERENCE

☐ INFORMATION INDUSTRY	☐ BASIC INDUSTRIES
☐ Communications	☐ Consumer
☐ Computer Equipment	☐ Distribution
☐ Computer Services	☐ Manufacturing
☐ Computer Components	☐ Retail
☐ Computer Entertainment	☐ Service
☐ Computer Education	☐ Wholesale
☐ Information Technologies	☐ SPECIFIC INDUSTRIES
☐ Computer Media	☐ Energy
☐ Software	☐ Environmental
☐ Internet	☐ Financial
☒ MEDICAL/HEALTHCARE	☐ Real Estate
☐ Biotechnology	☐ Transportation
☒ Healthcare Services	☐ Publishing
☐ Life Sciences	☐ Food
☒ Medical Products	☐ Franchises
☐ INDUSTRIAL	☐ DIVERSIFIED
☐ Advanced Materials	☒ MISCELLANEOUS
☐ Chemicals	
☐ Instruments & Controls	

STAGE PREFERENCE

☐ EARLY STAGE
☐ Seed
☐ Start-up
☐ 1st Stage
☒ LATER STAGE
☒ 2nd Stage
☒ Mature
☒ Mezzanine
☒ LBO/MBO
☒ Turnaround
☐ INT'L EXPANSION
☐ WILL CONSIDER ALL
☒ VENTURE LEASING

Other Locations:

Affiliation:
Minimum Investment: $1 Million or more
Capital Under Management: Less than $100 Million

GEOGRAPHIC PREF

☐ East Coast
☐ West Coast
☐ Northeast
☐ Mid Atlantic
☐ Gulf States
☐ Northwest
☐ Southeast
☐ Southwest
☐ Midwest
☐ Central
☐ Local to Office
☒ Other Geo Pref
   United Kingdom,
   Europe

BARCLAYS CAPITAL INVESTORS CORP.

**222 Broadway, 11th Floor
New York NY 10038**

Phone (212) 412-3583   Fax (212) 412-7600

PROFESSIONALS	TITLE
Lorrie Stapleton	President

INDUSTRY PREFERENCE

☒ INFORMATION INDUSTRY
☒ Communications
☒ Computer Equipment
☒ Computer Services
☒ Computer Components
☐ Computer Entertainment
☒ Computer Education
☒ Information Technologies
☒ Computer Media
☒ Software
☒ Internet
☒ MEDICAL/HEALTHCARE
☒ Biotechnology
☒ Healthcare Services
☒ Life Sciences
☒ Medical Products
☒ INDUSTRIAL
☒ Advanced Materials
☐ Chemicals
☒ Instruments & Controls

☒ BASIC INDUSTRIES
☒ Consumer
☐ Distribution
☒ Manufacturing
☒ Retail
☒ Service
☒ Wholesale
☐ SPECIFIC INDUSTRIES
☐ Energy
☐ Environmental
☐ Financial
☐ Real Estate
☐ Transportation
☐ Publishing
☐ Food
☐ Franchises
☒ DIVERSIFIED
☐ MISCELLANEOUS

STAGE PREFERENCE

☐ EARLY STAGE
☐ Seed
☐ Start-up
☐ 1st Stage
☒ LATER STAGE
☒ 2nd Stage
☒ Mature
☐ Mezzanine
☒ LBO/MBO
☐ Turnaround
☐ INT'L EXPANSION
☐ WILL CONSIDER ALL
☐ VENTURE LEASING

SBIC
Other Locations:

Affiliation:
Minimum Investment: Less than $1 Million
Capital Under Management: Less than $100 Million

GEOGRAPHIC PREF

☐ East Coast
☐ West Coast
☐ Northeast
☐ Mid Atlantic
☐ Gulf States
☐ Northwest
☐ Southeast
☐ Southwest
☐ Midwest
☐ Central
☐ Local to Office
☒ Other Geo Pref
  Eastern U.S.

BAUSCH & LOMB INC.

**One Bausch Place
Rochester NY 14604**

Phone (716) 338-5830   Fax (716) 338-5043

PROFESSIONALS	TITLE
Alan Farnsworth	Vice President

INDUSTRY PREFERENCE

☐ INFORMATION INDUSTRY
☐ Communications
☐ Computer Equipment
☐ Computer Services
☐ Computer Components
☐ Computer Entertainment
☐ Computer Education
☐ Information Technologies
☐ Computer Media
☐ Software
☐ Internet
☒ MEDICAL/HEALTHCARE
☒ Biotechnology
☒ Healthcare Services
☒ Life Sciences
☒ Medical Products
☐ INDUSTRIAL
☐ Advanced Materials
☐ Chemicals
☐ Instruments & Controls

☐ BASIC INDUSTRIES
☐ Consumer
☐ Distribution
☐ Manufacturing
☐ Retail
☐ Service
☐ Wholesale
☐ SPECIFIC INDUSTRIES
☐ Energy
☐ Environmental
☐ Financial
☐ Real Estate
☐ Transportation
☐ Publishing
☐ Food
☐ Franchises
☐ DIVERSIFIED
☒ MISCELLANEOUS

STAGE PREFERENCE

☒ EARLY STAGE
☒ Seed
☒ Start-up
☐ 1st Stage
☒ LATER STAGE
☐ 2nd Stage
☒ Mature
☐ Mezzanine
☒ LBO/MBO
☐ Turnaround
☐ INT'L EXPANSION
☐ WILL CONSIDER ALL
☐ VENTURE LEASING

Other Locations:

Affiliation:
Minimum Investment: Less than $1 Million
Capital Under Management: $100 to $500 Million

GEOGRAPHIC PREF

☐ East Coast
☐ West Coast
☐ Northeast
☐ Mid Atlantic
☐ Gulf States
☐ Northwest
☐ Southeast
☐ Southwest
☐ Midwest
☐ Central
☐ Local to Office
☐ Other Geo Pref

BEHRMAN CAPITAL

126 East 56th Street
New York NY 10022

Phone (212) 980-6500   Fax (212) 980-7024

PROFESSIONALS	TITLE
Darryl G. Behrman	Managing Partner
Grant Behrman	Managing Partner
William Matthes	Managing Partner
Dennis Sisco	Partner
Neil J. Sandler	Partner

INDUSTRY PREFERENCE

☒ INFORMATION INDUSTRY
☒ Communications
☒ Computer Equipment
☒ Computer Services
☒ Computer Components
☐ Computer Entertainment
☒ Computer Education
☒ Information Technologies
☒ Computer Media
☒ Software
☒ Internet
☒ MEDICAL/HEALTHCARE
☒ Biotechnology
☒ Healthcare Services
☒ Life Sciences
☒ Medical Products
☐ INDUSTRIAL
☐ Advanced Materials
☐ Chemicals
☐ Instruments & Controls

☒ BASIC INDUSTRIES
☐ Consumer
☐ Distribution
☒ Manufacturing
☐ Retail
☒ Service
☐ Wholesale
☐ SPECIFIC INDUSTRIES
☐ Energy
☐ Environmental
☐ Financial
☐ Real Estate
☐ Transportation
☐ Publishing
☐ Food
☐ Franchises
☒ DIVERSIFIED
☐ MISCELLANEOUS

STAGE PREFERENCE

☐ EARLY STAGE
☐ Seed
☐ Start-up
☐ 1st Stage
☒ LATER STAGE
☒ 2nd Stage
☒ Mature
☒ Mezzanine
☒ LBO/MBO
☐ Turnaround
☐ INT'L EXPANSION
☐ WILL CONSIDER ALL
☐ VENTURE LEASING

Other Locations:

Affiliation:
Minimum Investment: $1 Million or more
Capital Under Management: Over $500 Million

GEOGRAPHIC PREF

☐ East Coast
☐ West Coast
☐ Northeast
☐ Mid Atlantic
☐ Gulf States
☐ Northwest
☐ Southeast
☐ Southwest
☐ Midwest
☐ Central
☐ Local to Office
☐ Other Geo Pref

BESSEMER VENTURE PARTNERS

1400 Old Country Road
Suite 407
Westbury NY 11590

Phone (516) 997-2300   Fax (516) 997-2371

PROFESSIONALS	TITLE
Bob Buescher	General Partner

INDUSTRY PREFERENCE

☒ INFORMATION INDUSTRY
☒ Communications
☒ Computer Equipment
☒ Computer Services
☒ Computer Components
☐ Computer Entertainment
☒ Computer Education
☒ Information Technologies
☒ Computer Media
☒ Software
☒ Internet
☒ MEDICAL/HEALTHCARE
☒ Biotechnology
☒ Healthcare Services
☒ Life Sciences
☒ Medical Products
☒ INDUSTRIAL
☒ Advanced Materials
☒ Chemicals
☒ Instruments & Controls

☒ BASIC INDUSTRIES
☒ Consumer
☐ Distribution
☐ Manufacturing
☒ Retail
☒ Service
☐ Wholesale
☒ SPECIFIC INDUSTRIES
☒ Energy
☒ Environmental
☐ Financial
☐ Real Estate
☐ Transportation
☐ Publishing
☐ Food
☐ Franchises
☒ DIVERSIFIED
☐ MISCELLANEOUS

STAGE PREFERENCE

☒ EARLY STAGE
☒ Seed
☒ Start-up
☒ 1st Stage
☒ LATER STAGE
☒ 2nd Stage
☒ Mature
☒ Mezzanine
☒ LBO/MBO
☐ Turnaround
☐ INT'L EXPANSION
☐ WILL CONSIDER ALL
☐ VENTURE LEASING

Other Locations: Menlo Park CA, Wellesley Hills MA

Affiliation: Bessemer Securities Corp.
Minimum Investment: Less than $1 Million
Capital Under Management: $100 to $500 Million

GEOGRAPHIC PREF

☐ East Coast
☐ West Coast
☐ Northeast
☐ Mid Atlantic
☐ Gulf States
☐ Northwest
☐ Southeast
☐ Southwest
☐ Midwest
☐ Central
☐ Local to Office
☐ Other Geo Pref

BT CAPITAL CORP.

130 Liberty Street
25th Floor
New York NY 10006

Phone (212) 250-4648   Fax (212) 250-7651

PROFESSIONALS	TITLE
Charlie Ayers	Managing Director
Joseph T. Wood	Managing Director

INDUSTRY PREFERENCE

☒ INFORMATION INDUSTRY	☒ BASIC INDUSTRIES
☒ Communications	☒ Consumer
☒ Computer Equipment	☐ Distribution
☒ Computer Services	☒ Manufacturing
☒ Computer Components	☒ Retail
☐ Computer Entertainment	☒ Service
☒ Computer Education	☐ Wholesale
☒ Information Technologies	☒ SPECIFIC INDUSTRIES
☒ Computer Media	☒ Energy
☒ Software	☒ Environmental
☒ Internet	☒ Financial
☒ MEDICAL/HEALTHCARE	☐ Real Estate
☐ Biotechnology	☐ Transportation
☒ Healthcare Services	☐ Publishing
☐ Life Sciences	☐ Food
☒ Medical Products	☐ Franchises
☒ INDUSTRIAL	☒ DIVERSIFIED
☐ Advanced Materials	☐ MISCELLANEOUS
☐ Chemicals	
☒ Instruments & Controls	

STAGE PREFERENCE

☐ EARLY STAGE
☐   Seed
☐   Start-up
☐   1st Stage
☒ LATER STAGE
☒   2nd Stage
☒   Mature
☒   Mezzanine
☒   LBO/MBO
☐   Turnaround
☐ INT'L EXPANSION
☐ WILL CONSIDER ALL
☐ VENTURE LEASING
SBIC
Other Locations:

Affiliation: Bankers Trust New York Corp.
Minimum Investment: $1 Million or more
Capital Under Management: Over $500 Million

GEOGRAPHIC PREF

☐ East Coast
☐ West Coast
☐ Northeast
☐ Mid Atlantic
☐ Gulf States
☐ Northwest
☐ Southeast
☐ Southwest
☐ Midwest
☐ Central
☐ Local to Office
☐ Other Geo Pref

CANTERBURY MEZZANINE CAPITAL

600 5th Avenue
23rd Floor
New York NY 10020

Phone (212) 332-1565   Fax (212) 332-1584

PROFESSIONALS	TITLE
Nicholas Dunphy	Partner

INDUSTRY PREFERENCE

☒ INFORMATION INDUSTRY	☒ BASIC INDUSTRIES
☐ Communications	☒ Consumer
☒ Computer Equipment	☒ Distribution
☐ Computer Services	☐ Manufacturing
☐ Computer Components	☒ Retail
☐ Computer Entertainment	☐ Service
☐ Computer Education	☐ Wholesale
☐ Information Technologies	☐ SPECIFIC INDUSTRIES
☐ Computer Media	☐ Energy
☐ Software	☐ Environmental
☐ Internet	☐ Financial
☒ MEDICAL/HEALTHCARE	☐ Real Estate
☐ Biotechnology	☐ Transportation
☐ Healthcare Services	☐ Publishing
☐ Life Sciences	☐ Food
☒ Medical Products	☐ Franchises
☒ INDUSTRIAL	☒ DIVERSIFIED
☒ Advanced Materials	☒ MISCELLANEOUS
☒ Chemicals	
☒ Instruments & Controls	

STAGE PREFERENCE

☐ EARLY STAGE
☐   Seed
☐   Start-up
☐   1st Stage
☒ LATER STAGE
☐   2nd Stage
☐   Mature
☒   Mezzanine
☒   LBO/MBO
☐   Turnaround
☐ INT'L EXPANSION
☐ WILL CONSIDER ALL
☐ VENTURE LEASING

Other Locations:

Affiliation:
Minimum Investment: $1 Million or more
Capital Under Management: $100 to $500 Million

GEOGRAPHIC PREF

☐ East Coast
☐ West Coast
☐ Northeast
☐ Mid Atlantic
☐ Gulf States
☐ Northwest
☐ Southeast
☐ Southwest
☐ Midwest
☐ Central
☐ Local to Office
☐ Other Geo Pref

CEA CAPITAL PARTNERS

17 State Street
35th Floor
New York NY 10004

Phone (212) 425-1400   Fax (212) 425-1420

PROFESSIONALS	TITLE
William Luby	Partner
James Collis	Partner
Alison Mulhern	Managing Director

INDUSTRY PREFERENCE

☒ INFORMATION INDUSTRY	☐ BASIC INDUSTRIES
☒ Communications	☐ Consumer
☐ Computer Equipment	☐ Distribution
☐ Computer Services	☐ Manufacturing
☐ Computer Components	☐ Retail
☒ Computer Entertainment	☐ Service
☐ Computer Education	☐ Wholesale
☐ Information Technologies	☐ SPECIFIC INDUSTRIES
☒ Computer Media	☐ Energy
☐ Software	☐ Environmental
☒ Internet	☐ Financial
☐ MEDICAL/HEALTHCARE	☐ Real Estate
☐ Biotechnology	☐ Transportation
☐ Healthcare Services	☐ Publishing
☐ Life Sciences	☐ Food
☐ Medical Products	☐ Franchises
☐ INDUSTRIAL	☐ DIVERSIFIED
☐ Advanced Materials	☒ MISCELLANEOUS
☐ Chemicals	
☐ Instruments & Controls	

STAGE PREFERENCE

☐ EARLY STAGE
☐ Seed
☐ Start-up
☐ 1st Stage
☒ LATER STAGE
☒ 2nd Stage
☒ Mature
☐ Mezzanine
☒ LBO/MBO
☐ Turnaround
☐ INT'L EXPANSION
☐ WILL CONSIDER ALL
☐ VENTURE LEASING

Other Locations:

Affiliation:
Minimum Investment: $1 Million or more
Capital Under Management: Less than $100 Million

GEOGRAPHIC PREF

☐ East Coast
☐ West Coast
☐ Northeast
☐ Mid Atlantic
☐ Gulf States
☐ Northwest
☐ Southeast
☐ Southwest
☐ Midwest
☐ Central
☐ Local to Office
☐ Other Geo Pref

CHASE CAPITAL PARTNERS

380 Madison Avenue
12th Floor
New York NY 10017

Phone (212) 622-3100   Fax (212) 622-3101

PROFESSIONALS	TITLE
Jeffery C. Walker	Managing General Partner
Arnold L. Chavkin	General Partner
John Baron	General Partner

INDUSTRY PREFERENCE

☒ INFORMATION INDUSTRY	☒ BASIC INDUSTRIES
☒ Communications	☐ Consumer
☒ Computer Equipment	☐ Distribution
☒ Computer Services	☐ Manufacturing
☒ Computer Components	☒ Retail
☐ Computer Entertainment	☐ Service
☒ Computer Education	☐ Wholesale
☒ Information Technologies	☒ SPECIFIC INDUSTRIES
☒ Computer Media	☐ Energy
☒ Software	☐ Environmental
☒ Internet	☐ Financial
☒ MEDICAL/HEALTHCARE	☒ Real Estate
☒ Biotechnology	☐ Transportation
☒ Healthcare Services	☐ Publishing
☒ Life Sciences	☐ Food
☒ Medical Products	☐ Franchises
☒ INDUSTRIAL	☒ DIVERSIFIED
☐ Advanced Materials	☐ MISCELLANEOUS
☒ Chemicals	
☐ Instruments & Controls	

STAGE PREFERENCE

☒ EARLY STAGE
☐ Seed
☒ Start-up
☒ 1st Stage
☒ LATER STAGE
☒ 2nd Stage
☒ Mature
☒ Mezzanine
☒ LBO/MBO
☒ Turnaround
☒ INT'L EXPANSION
☐ WILL CONSIDER ALL
☒ VENTURE LEASING

SBIC
Other Locations: San Francisco CA, Vail CO

Affiliation:
Minimum Investment: $1 Million or more
Capital Under Management: Over $500 Million

GEOGRAPHIC PREF

☐ East Coast
☐ West Coast
☐ Northeast
☐ Mid Atlantic
☐ Gulf States
☐ Northwest
☐ Southeast
☐ Southwest
☐ Midwest
☐ Central
☐ Local to Office
☐ Other Geo Pref

CIBC WOOD GUNDY VENTURES, INC.

**425 Lexington Avenue
Ninth Floor
New York NY 10017**

Phone (212) 856-3713   Fax (212) 697-1554

PROFESSIONALS	TITLE
Robi Blumenstein	Managing Director

INDUSTRY PREFERENCE

- ☐ INFORMATION INDUSTRY
- ☐ Communications
- ☐ Computer Equipment
- ☐ Computer Services
- ☐ Computer Components
- ☐ Computer Entertainment
- ☐ Computer Education
- ☐ Information Technologies
- ☐ Computer Media
- ☐ Software
- ☐ Internet
- ☐ MEDICAL/HEALTHCARE
- ☐ Biotechnology
- ☐ Healthcare Services
- ☐ Life Sciences
- ☐ Medical Products
- ☐ INDUSTRIAL
- ☐ Advanced Materials
- ☐ Chemicals
- ☐ Instruments & Controls

- ☐ BASIC INDUSTRIES
- ☐ Consumer
- ☐ Distribution
- ☐ Manufacturing
- ☐ Retail
- ☐ Service
- ☐ Wholesale
- ☐ SPECIFIC INDUSTRIES
- ☐ Energy
- ☐ Environmental
- ☐ Financial
- ☐ Real Estate
- ☐ Transportation
- ☐ Publishing
- ☐ Food
- ☐ Franchises
- ☒ DIVERSIFIED
- ☐ MISCELLANEOUS

STAGE PREFERENCE

- ☐ EARLY STAGE
- ☐ Seed
- ☐ Start-up
- ☐ 1st Stage
- ☒ LATER STAGE
- ☒ 2nd Stage
- ☒ Mature
- ☐ Mezzanine
- ☒ LBO/MBO
- ☐ Turnaround
- ☐ INT'L EXPANSION
- ☐ WILL CONSIDER ALL
- ☐ VENTURE LEASING

SBIC
Other Locations:

Affiliation:
Minimum Investment: $1 Million or more
Capital Under Management: Less than $100 Million

GEOGRAPHIC PREF

- ☐ East Coast
- ☐ West Coast
- ☐ Northeast
- ☐ Mid Atlantic
- ☐ Gulf States
- ☐ Northwest
- ☐ Southeast
- ☐ Southwest
- ☐ Midwest
- ☐ Central
- ☐ Local to Office
- ☐ Other Geo Pref

CITICORP VENTURE CAPITAL, LTD.

**399 Park Avenue
14th Floor, Zone 4
New York NY 10043**

Phone (212) 559-1127   Fax (212) 793-6164

PROFESSIONALS	TITLE
William Comfort	Chairman
Michael Bradley	Vice President

INDUSTRY PREFERENCE

- ☐ INFORMATION INDUSTRY
- ☐ Communications
- ☐ Computer Equipment
- ☐ Computer Services
- ☐ Computer Components
- ☐ Computer Entertainment
- ☐ Computer Education
- ☐ Information Technologies
- ☐ Computer Media
- ☐ Software
- ☐ Internet
- ☐ MEDICAL/HEALTHCARE
- ☐ Biotechnology
- ☐ Healthcare Services
- ☐ Life Sciences
- ☐ Medical Products
- ☐ INDUSTRIAL
- ☐ Advanced Materials
- ☐ Chemicals
- ☐ Instruments & Controls

- ☐ BASIC INDUSTRIES
- ☐ Consumer
- ☐ Distribution
- ☐ Manufacturing
- ☐ Retail
- ☐ Service
- ☐ Wholesale
- ☐ SPECIFIC INDUSTRIES
- ☐ Energy
- ☐ Environmental
- ☐ Financial
- ☐ Real Estate
- ☐ Transportation
- ☐ Publishing
- ☐ Food
- ☐ Franchises
- ☒ DIVERSIFIED
- ☐ MISCELLANEOUS

STAGE PREFERENCE

- ☐ EARLY STAGE
- ☐ Seed
- ☐ Start-up
- ☐ 1st Stage
- ☒ LATER STAGE
- ☒ 2nd Stage
- ☒ Mature
- ☒ Mezzanine
- ☒ LBO/MBO
- ☐ Turnaround
- ☐ INT'L EXPANSION
- ☐ WILL CONSIDER ALL
- ☐ VENTURE LEASING

SBIC
Other Locations:

Affiliation:
Minimum Investment: $1 Million or more
Capital Under Management: Less than $100 Million

GEOGRAPHIC PREF

- ☐ East Coast
- ☐ West Coast
- ☐ Northeast
- ☐ Mid Atlantic
- ☐ Gulf States
- ☐ Northwest
- ☐ Southeast
- ☐ Southwest
- ☐ Midwest
- ☐ Central
- ☐ Local to Office
- ☐ Other Geo Pref

CMNY CAPITAL II, LP

135 East 57th Street
26th Floor
New York NY 10022

Phone (212) 909-8428   Fax (212) 980-2630

PROFESSIONALS	TITLE
Robert G. Davidoff	General Partner

INDUSTRY PREFERENCE

☐ INFORMATION INDUSTRY
☐ Communications
☐ Computer Equipment
☐ Computer Services
☐ Computer Components
☐ Computer Entertainment
☐ Computer Education
☐ Information Technologies
☐ Computer Media
☐ Software
☐ Internet
☐ MEDICAL/HEALTHCARE
☐ Biotechnology
☐ Healthcare Services
☐ Life Sciences
☐ Medical Products
☐ INDUSTRIAL
☐ Advanced Materials
☐ Chemicals
☐ Instruments & Controls

☐ BASIC INDUSTRIES
☐ Consumer
☐ Distribution
☐ Manufacturing
☐ Retail
☐ Service
☐ Wholesale
☐ SPECIFIC INDUSTRIES
☐ Energy
☐ Environmental
☐ Financial
☐ Real Estate
☐ Transportation
☐ Publishing
☐ Food
☐ Franchises
☒ DIVERSIFIED
☐ MISCELLANEOUS

STAGE PREFERENCE

☐ EARLY STAGE
☐ Seed
☐ Start-up
☐ 1st Stage
☒ LATER STAGE
☒ 2nd Stage
☒ Mature
☒ Mezzanine
☒ LBO/MBO
☐ Turnaround
☐ INT'L EXPANSION
☐ WILL CONSIDER ALL
☐ VENTURE LEASING

SBIC
Other Locations:

Affiliation:
Minimum Investment: Less than $1 Million
Capital Under Management: Less than $100 Million

GEOGRAPHIC PREF

☐ East Coast
☐ West Coast
☐ Northeast
☐ Mid Atlantic
☐ Gulf States
☐ Northwest
☐ Southeast
☐ Southwest
☐ Midwest
☐ Central
☐ Local to Office
☐ Other Geo Pref

CORNERSTONE EQUITY INVESTORS, LLC

717 Fifth Avenue
Suite 1100
New York NY 10022

Phone (212) 753-0901   Fax (212) 826-6798

PROFESSIONALS	TITLE
Dana O'Brien	Sr. Managing Partner
Robert Knox	Sr. Managing Partner

INDUSTRY PREFERENCE

☒ INFORMATION INDUSTRY
☒ Communications
☒ Computer Equipment
☒ Computer Services
☒ Computer Components
☐ Computer Entertainment
☒ Computer Education
☒ Information Technologies
☒ Computer Media
☒ Software
☒ Internet
☒ MEDICAL/HEALTHCARE
☒ Biotechnology
☒ Healthcare Services
☒ Life Sciences
☒ Medical Products
☒ INDUSTRIAL
☐ Advanced Materials
☐ Chemicals
☒ Instruments & Controls

☒ BASIC INDUSTRIES
☒ Consumer
☐ Distribution
☐ Manufacturing
☐ Retail
☐ Service
☐ Wholesale
☐ SPECIFIC INDUSTRIES
☐ Energy
☐ Environmental
☐ Financial
☐ Real Estate
☐ Transportation
☐ Publishing
☐ Food
☐ Franchises
☒ DIVERSIFIED
☒ MISCELLANEOUS

STAGE PREFERENCE

☐ EARLY STAGE
☐ Seed
☐ Start-up
☐ 1st Stage
☒ LATER STAGE
☐ 2nd Stage
☐ Mature
☒ Mezzanine
☒ LBO/MBO
☒ Turnaround
☐ INT'L EXPANSION
☐ WILL CONSIDER ALL
☒ VENTURE LEASING

Other Locations:

Affiliation:
Minimum Investment: $1 Million or more
Capital Under Management: Over $500 Million

GEOGRAPHIC PREF

☐ East Coast
☐ West Coast
☐ Northeast
☐ Mid Atlantic
☐ Gulf States
☐ Northwest
☐ Southeast
☐ Southwest
☐ Midwest
☐ Central
☐ Local to Office
☐ Other Geo Pref

CREST COMMUNICATIONS HOLDINGS

320 Park Avenue
17th Floor
New York NY 10022

Phone (212) 317-2700   Fax (212) 317-2710

PROFESSIONALS	TITLE
William Sprague	Managing Director
Jim Kuster	Managing Director
Michael Fitzgerald	Managing Director
Gregg Mockenhaupt	Managing Director
Matt O'Connell	General Counsel

INDUSTRY PREFERENCE

☒ INFORMATION INDUSTRY	☐ BASIC INDUSTRIES
☒ Communications	☐ Consumer
☒ Computer Equipment	☐ Distribution
☒ Computer Services	☐ Manufacturing
☒ Computer Components	☐ Retail
☐ Computer Entertainment	☐ Service
☒ Computer Education	☐ Wholesale
☒ Information Technologies	☐ SPECIFIC INDUSTRIES
☒ Computer Media	☐ Energy
☒ Software	☐ Environmental
☒ Internet	☐ Financial
☐ MEDICAL/HEALTHCARE	☐ Real Estate
☐ Biotechnology	☐ Transportation
☐ Healthcare Services	☐ Publishing
☐ Life Sciences	☐ Food
☐ Medical Products	☐ Franchises
☐ INDUSTRIAL	☐ DIVERSIFIED
☐ Advanced Materials	☒ MISCELLANEOUS
☐ Chemicals	
☐ Instruments & Controls	

STAGE PREFERENCE

☒ EARLY STAGE
☐ Seed
☐ Start-up
☒ 1st Stage
☒ LATER STAGE
☒ 2nd Stage
☒ Mature
☒ Mezzanine
☒ LBO/MBO
☒ Turnaround
☐ INT'L EXPANSION
☐ WILL CONSIDER ALL
☒ VENTURE LEASING

SBIC
Other Locations:

Affiliation:
Minimum Investment: $1 Million or more
Capital Under Management: Less than $100 Million

GEOGRAPHIC PREF

☐ East Coast
☐ West Coast
☐ Northeast
☐ Mid Atlantic
☐ Gulf States
☐ Northwest
☐ Southeast
☐ Southwest
☐ Midwest
☐ Central
☐ Local to Office
☐ Other Geo Pref

CROWN ADVISORS, LTD.

60 East 42nd Street
Suite 3405
New York NY 10165

Phone (212) 808-5278   Fax (212) 808-9073

PROFESSIONALS	TITLE
Geoffrey Block	Partner
David Bellet	Chairman

INDUSTRY PREFERENCE

☒ INFORMATION INDUSTRY	☐ BASIC INDUSTRIES
☒ Communications	☐ Consumer
☒ Computer Equipment	☐ Distribution
☒ Computer Services	☐ Manufacturing
☒ Computer Components	☐ Retail
☐ Computer Entertainment	☐ Service
☒ Computer Education	☐ Wholesale
☒ Information Technologies	☐ SPECIFIC INDUSTRIES
☒ Computer Media	☐ Energy
☒ Software	☐ Environmental
☒ Internet	☐ Financial
☒ MEDICAL/HEALTHCARE	☐ Real Estate
☒ Biotechnology	☐ Transportation
☒ Healthcare Services	☐ Publishing
☒ Life Sciences	☐ Food
☒ Medical Products	☐ Franchises
☐ INDUSTRIAL	☒ DIVERSIFIED
☐ Advanced Materials	☒ MISCELLANEOUS
☐ Chemicals	
☐ Instruments & Controls	

STAGE PREFERENCE

☐ EARLY STAGE
☐ Seed
☐ Start-up
☐ 1st Stage
☒ LATER STAGE
☒ 2nd Stage
☐ Mature
☐ Mezzanine
☐ LBO/MBO
☐ Turnaround
☐ INT'L EXPANSION
☐ WILL CONSIDER ALL
☐ VENTURE LEASING

SBIC
Other Locations:

Affiliation:
Minimum Investment: $1 Million or more
Capital Under Management: Less than $100 Million

GEOGRAPHIC PREF

☐ East Coast
☐ West Coast
☐ Northeast
☐ Mid Atlantic
☐ Gulf States
☐ Northwest
☐ Southeast
☐ Southwest
☐ Midwest
☐ Central
☐ Local to Office
☐ Other Geo Pref

CW GROUP, INC.

1041 Third Avenue
Second Floor
New York NY 10021

Phone (212) 308-5266   Fax (212) 644-0354

PROFESSIONALS	TITLE
Charles M. Hartman	General Partner
Barry Weinberg	General Partner
Walter Channing, Jr.	General Partner

INDUSTRY PREFERENCE

- ☐ INFORMATION INDUSTRY
- ☐ Communications
- ☐ Computer Equipment
- ☐ Computer Services
- ☐ Computer Components
- ☐ Computer Entertainment
- ☐ Computer Education
- ☐ Information Technologies
- ☐ Computer Media
- ☐ Software
- ☐ Internet
- ☒ MEDICAL/HEALTHCARE
- ☒ Biotechnology
- ☒ Healthcare Services
- ☒ Life Sciences
- ☒ Medical Products
- ☐ INDUSTRIAL
- ☐ Advanced Materials
- ☐ Chemicals
- ☐ Instruments & Controls

- ☐ BASIC INDUSTRIES
- ☐ Consumer
- ☐ Distribution
- ☐ Manufacturing
- ☐ Retail
- ☐ Service
- ☐ Wholesale
- ☐ SPECIFIC INDUSTRIES
- ☐ Energy
- ☐ Environmental
- ☐ Financial
- ☐ Real Estate
- ☐ Transportation
- ☐ Publishing
- ☐ Food
- ☐ Franchises
- ☐ DIVERSIFIED
- ☐ MISCELLANEOUS

STAGE PREFERENCE

- ☒ EARLY STAGE
- ☒ Seed
- ☒ Start-up
- ☒ 1st Stage
- ☒ LATER STAGE
- ☒ 2nd Stage
- ☐ Mature
- ☐ Mezzanine
- ☐ LBO/MBO
- ☐ Turnaround
- ☐ INT'L EXPANSION
- ☐ WILL CONSIDER ALL
- ☐ VENTURE LEASING

Other Locations: San Diego CA

Affiliation:
Minimum Investment: Less than $1 Million
Capital Under Management: $100 to $500 Million

GEOGRAPHIC PREF

- ☐ East Coast
- ☐ West Coast
- ☐ Northeast
- ☐ Mid Atlantic
- ☐ Gulf States
- ☐ Northwest
- ☐ Southeast
- ☐ Southwest
- ☐ Midwest
- ☐ Central
- ☐ Local to Office
- ☐ Other Geo Pref

DH BLAIR INVESTMENT BANKING GROUP

44 Wall Street
2nd Floor
New York NY 10005

Phone (212) 495-5000   Fax (212) 269-1438

PROFESSIONALS	TITLE
J. Morton Davis	Chairman / CEO
Andrew Plevin	Vice President
Leonard Katz	Vice President

INDUSTRY PREFERENCE

- ☒ INFORMATION INDUSTRY
- ☒ Communications
- ☒ Computer Equipment
- ☒ Computer Services
- ☒ Computer Components
- ☐ Computer Entertainment
- ☒ Computer Education
- ☒ Information Technologies
- ☒ Computer Media
- ☒ Software
- ☒ Internet
- ☒ MEDICAL/HEALTHCARE
- ☒ Biotechnology
- ☒ Healthcare Services
- ☒ Life Sciences
- ☒ Medical Products
- ☒ INDUSTRIAL
- ☒ Advanced Materials
- ☒ Chemicals
- ☒ Instruments & Controls

- ☒ BASIC INDUSTRIES
- ☒ Consumer
- ☐ Distribution
- ☐ Manufacturing
- ☐ Retail
- ☐ Service
- ☐ Wholesale
- ☐ SPECIFIC INDUSTRIES
- ☐ Energy
- ☐ Environmental
- ☐ Financial
- ☐ Real Estate
- ☐ Transportation
- ☐ Publishing
- ☐ Food
- ☐ Franchises
- ☒ DIVERSIFIED
- ☒ MISCELLANEOUS

STAGE PREFERENCE

- ☒ EARLY STAGE
- ☒ Seed
- ☒ Start-up
- ☒ 1st Stage
- ☒ LATER STAGE
- ☐ 2nd Stage
- ☐ Mature
- ☐ Mezzanine
- ☒ LBO/MBO
- ☐ Turnaround
- ☐ INT'L EXPANSION
- ☐ WILL CONSIDER ALL
- ☐ VENTURE LEASING

Other Locations:

Affiliation:
Minimum Investment: Less than $1 Million
Capital Under Management: Less than $100 Million

GEOGRAPHIC PREF

- ☐ East Coast
- ☐ West Coast
- ☐ Northeast
- ☐ Mid Atlantic
- ☐ Gulf States
- ☐ Northwest
- ☐ Southeast
- ☐ Southwest
- ☐ Midwest
- ☐ Central
- ☐ Local to Office
- ☐ Other Geo Pref

DRESDNER KLEINWORT BENSON PRIVATE EQUITY

75 Wall Street
24th Floor
New York NY 10005

Phone (212) 429-3131   Fax (212) 429-3139

PROFESSIONALS	TITLE
Christopher Wright	Partner

INDUSTRY PREFERENCE

☒ INFORMATION INDUSTRY	☐ BASIC INDUSTRIES
☒ Communications	☐ Consumer
☒ Computer Equipment	☐ Distribution
☒ Computer Services	☐ Manufacturing
☒ Computer Components	☐ Retail
☐ Computer Entertainment	☐ Service
☒ Computer Education	☐ Wholesale
☒ Information Technologies	☐ SPECIFIC INDUSTRIES
☒ Computer Media	☐ Energy
☒ Software	☐ Environmental
☒ Internet	☐ Financial
☒ MEDICAL/HEALTHCARE	☐ Real Estate
☒ Biotechnology	☐ Transportation
☒ Healthcare Services	☐ Publishing
☒ Life Sciences	☐ Food
☒ Medical Products	☐ Franchises
☒ INDUSTRIAL	☒ DIVERSIFIED
☒ Advanced Materials	☒ MISCELLANEOUS
☒ Chemicals	
☒ Instruments & Controls	

STAGE PREFERENCE

☐ EARLY STAGE	
☐ Seed	
☐ Start-up	
☐ 1st Stage	
☒ LATER STAGE	
☒ 2nd Stage	
☒ Mature	
☒ Mezzanine	
☒ LBO/MBO	
☐ Turnaround	
☐ INT'L EXPANSION	
☐ WILL CONSIDER ALL	
☐ VENTURE LEASING	

SBIC
Other Locations:

Affiliation:
Minimum Investment: $1 Million or more
Capital Under Management: Less than $100 Million

GEOGRAPHIC PREF

☐ East Coast	
☐ West Coast	
☐ Northeast	
☐ Mid Atlantic	
☐ Gulf States	
☐ Northwest	
☐ Southeast	
☐ Southwest	
☐ Midwest	
☐ Central	
☐ Local to Office	
☐ Other Geo Pref	

EAST COAST VENTURE CAPITAL, INC.

570 Seventh Avenue
Suite 1802
New York NY 10018

Phone (212) 869-7778   Fax (212) 869-3892

PROFESSIONALS	TITLE
Zindel Zelmanovitch	President

INDUSTRY PREFERENCE

☐ INFORMATION INDUSTRY	☐ BASIC INDUSTRIES
☐ Communications	☐ Consumer
☐ Computer Equipment	☐ Distribution
☐ Computer Services	☐ Manufacturing
☐ Computer Components	☐ Retail
☐ Computer Entertainment	☐ Service
☐ Computer Education	☐ Wholesale
☐ Information Technologies	☐ SPECIFIC INDUSTRIES
☐ Computer Media	☐ Energy
☐ Software	☐ Environmental
☐ Internet	☐ Financial
☐ MEDICAL/HEALTHCARE	☐ Real Estate
☐ Biotechnology	☐ Transportation
☐ Healthcare Services	☐ Publishing
☐ Life Sciences	☐ Food
☐ Medical Products	☐ Franchises
☐ INDUSTRIAL	☒ DIVERSIFIED
☐ Advanced Materials	☐ MISCELLANEOUS
☐ Chemicals	
☐ Instruments & Controls	

STAGE PREFERENCE

☒ EARLY STAGE	
☒ Seed	
☒ Start-up	
☒ 1st Stage	
☒ LATER STAGE	
☒ 2nd Stage	
☐ Mature	
☒ Mezzanine	
☒ LBO/MBO	
☐ Turnaround	
☐ INT'L EXPANSION	
☐ WILL CONSIDER ALL	
☐ VENTURE LEASING	

SSBIC
Other Locations:

Affiliation:
Minimum Investment: Less than $1 Million
Capital Under Management: Less than $100 Million

GEOGRAPHIC PREF

☐ East Coast	
☐ West Coast	
☒ Northeast	
☐ Mid Atlantic	
☐ Gulf States	
☐ Northwest	
☐ Southeast	
☐ Southwest	
☐ Midwest	
☐ Central	
☐ Local to Office	
☐ Other Geo Pref	

EAST RIVER VENTURES LP

**645 Madison Avenue
22th Floor
New York NY 10022**

Phone (212) 644-6211   Fax (212) 644-5498

PROFESSIONALS	TITLE
Alexander Paluch	Co-President
Walter Carozza	Co-President

INDUSTRY PREFERENCE

- ☒ INFORMATION INDUSTRY
- ☒ Communications
- ☒ Computer Equipment
- ☒ Computer Services
- ☒ Computer Components
- ☐ Computer Entertainment
- ☒ Computer Education
- ☒ Information Technologies
- ☒ Computer Media
- ☒ Software
- ☒ Internet
- ☒ MEDICAL/HEALTHCARE
- ☒ Biotechnology
- ☒ Healthcare Services
- ☒ Life Sciences
- ☒ Medical Products
- ☐ INDUSTRIAL
- ☐ Advanced Materials
- ☐ Chemicals
- ☐ Instruments & Controls

- ☐ BASIC INDUSTRIES
- ☐ Consumer
- ☐ Distribution
- ☐ Manufacturing
- ☐ Retail
- ☐ Service
- ☐ Wholesale
- ☐ SPECIFIC INDUSTRIES
- ☐ Energy
- ☐ Environmental
- ☐ Financial
- ☐ Real Estate
- ☐ Transportation
- ☐ Publishing
- ☐ Food
- ☐ Franchises
- ☒ DIVERSIFIED
- ☒ MISCELLANEOUS

STAGE PREFERENCE

- ☒ EARLY STAGE
- ☐ Seed
- ☐ Start-up
- ☒ 1st Stage
- ☒ LATER STAGE
- ☒ 2nd Stage
- ☐ Mature
- ☒ Mezzanine
- ☐ LBO/MBO
- ☐ Turnaround
- ☐ INT'L EXPANSION
- ☐ WILL CONSIDER ALL
- ☐ VENTURE LEASING

Other Locations:

Affiliation:
Minimum Investment: $1 Million or more
Capital Under Management: Less than $100 Million

GEOGRAPHIC PREF

- ☐ East Coast
- ☐ West Coast
- ☐ Northeast
- ☐ Mid Atlantic
- ☐ Gulf States
- ☐ Northwest
- ☐ Southeast
- ☐ Southwest
- ☐ Midwest
- ☐ Central
- ☐ Local to Office
- ☐ Other Geo Pref

EASTON CAPITAL CORP.

**415 Madison Avenue
20th Floor
New York NY 10017**

Phone (212) 702-0950   Fax (212) 702-0952

PROFESSIONALS	TITLE
John Friedman	Managing Director
Richard Schneider	Managing Director

INDUSTRY PREFERENCE

- ☒ INFORMATION INDUSTRY
- ☒ Communications
- ☒ Computer Equipment
- ☒ Computer Services
- ☒ Computer Components
- ☒ Computer Entertainment
- ☒ Computer Education
- ☒ Information Technologies
- ☒ Computer Media
- ☒ Software
- ☒ Internet
- ☒ MEDICAL/HEALTHCARE
- ☐ Biotechnology
- ☐ Healthcare Services
- ☐ Life Sciences
- ☒ Medical Products
- ☐ INDUSTRIAL
- ☐ Advanced Materials
- ☐ Chemicals
- ☐ Instruments & Controls

- ☒ BASIC INDUSTRIES
- ☐ Consumer
- ☐ Distribution
- ☒ Manufacturing
- ☒ Retail
- ☒ Service
- ☐ Wholesale
- ☒ SPECIFIC INDUSTRIES
- ☐ Energy
- ☐ Environmental
- ☒ Financial
- ☐ Real Estate
- ☐ Transportation
- ☐ Publishing
- ☐ Food
- ☐ Franchises
- ☒ DIVERSIFIED
- ☒ MISCELLANEOUS

STAGE PREFERENCE

- ☒ EARLY STAGE
- ☒ Seed
- ☒ Start-up
- ☒ 1st Stage
- ☒ LATER STAGE
- ☒ 2nd Stage
- ☐ Mature
- ☐ Mezzanine
- ☒ LBO/MBO
- ☐ Turnaround
- ☐ INT'L EXPANSION
- ☐ WILL CONSIDER ALL
- ☐ VENTURE LEASING

Other Locations:

Affiliation:
Minimum Investment: Less than $1 Million
Capital Under Management: Less than $100 Million

GEOGRAPHIC PREF

- ☐ East Coast
- ☐ West Coast
- ☐ Northeast
- ☐ Mid Atlantic
- ☐ Gulf States
- ☐ Northwest
- ☐ Southeast
- ☐ Southwest
- ☐ Midwest
- ☐ Central
- ☐ Local to Office
- ☐ Other Geo Pref

ELECTRA INC.

320 Park Avenue
28th Floor
New York NY 10022

Phone (212) 319-0081   Fax (212) 319-3069

PROFESSIONALS	TITLE
Peter A. Carnwath	Managing Director

INDUSTRY PREFERENCE

☒ INFORMATION INDUSTRY	☒ BASIC INDUSTRIES
☒ Communications	☒ Consumer
☒ Computer Equipment	☒ Distribution
☒ Computer Services	☐ Manufacturing
☒ Computer Components	☒ Retail
☐ Computer Entertainment	☒ Service
☒ Computer Education	☐ Wholesale
☒ Information Technologies	☐ SPECIFIC INDUSTRIES
☒ Computer Media	☐ Energy
☒ Software	☐ Environmental
☒ Internet	☐ Financial
☒ MEDICAL/HEALTHCARE	☐ Real Estate
☒ Biotechnology	☐ Transportation
☒ Healthcare Services	☐ Publishing
☒ Life Sciences	☐ Food
☒ Medical Products	☐ Franchises
☒ INDUSTRIAL	☒ DIVERSIFIED
☒ Advanced Materials	☐ MISCELLANEOUS
☒ Chemicals	
☒ Instruments & Controls	

STAGE PREFERENCE

☐ EARLY STAGE
☐ Seed
☐ Start-up
☐ 1st Stage
☒ LATER STAGE
☒ 2nd Stage
☒ Mature
☒ Mezzanine
☒ LBO/MBO
☐ Turnaround
☐ INT'L EXPANSION
☐ WILL CONSIDER ALL
☐ VENTURE LEASING

Other Locations:

Affiliation: Electra Investment Trust
Minimum Investment: $1 Million or more
Capital Under Management: $100 to $500 Million

GEOGRAPHIC PREF

☐ East Coast
☐ West Coast
☐ Northeast
☐ Mid Atlantic
☐ Gulf States
☐ Northwest
☐ Southeast
☐ Southwest
☐ Midwest
☐ Central
☐ Local to Office
☐ Other Geo Pref

ELK ASSOCIATES FUNDING CORPORATION

747 Third Avenue
New York NY 10017

Phone (212) 355-2449   Fax (212) 759-3338

PROFESSIONALS	TITLE
Gary C. Granoff	President

INDUSTRY PREFERENCE

☐ INFORMATION INDUSTRY	☐ BASIC INDUSTRIES
☐ Communications	☐ Consumer
☐ Computer Equipment	☐ Distribution
☐ Computer Services	☐ Manufacturing
☐ Computer Components	☐ Retail
☐ Computer Entertainment	☐ Service
☐ Computer Education	☐ Wholesale
☐ Information Technologies	☒ SPECIFIC INDUSTRIES
☐ Computer Media	☐ Energy
☐ Software	☐ Environmental
☐ Internet	☐ Financial
☐ MEDICAL/HEALTHCARE	☐ Real Estate
☐ Biotechnology	☒ Transportation
☐ Healthcare Services	☐ Publishing
☐ Life Sciences	☐ Food
☐ Medical Products	☐ Franchises
☐ INDUSTRIAL	☒ DIVERSIFIED
☐ Advanced Materials	☐ MISCELLANEOUS
☐ Chemicals	
☐ Instruments & Controls	

STAGE PREFERENCE

☐ EARLY STAGE
☐ Seed
☐ Start-up
☐ 1st Stage
☒ LATER STAGE
☒ 2nd Stage
☒ Mature
☒ Mezzanine
☒ LBO/MBO
☐ Turnaround
☐ INT'L EXPANSION
☐ WILL CONSIDER ALL
☐ VENTURE LEASING

SSBIC
Other Locations:

Affiliation:
Minimum Investment: Less than $1 Million
Capital Under Management: Less than $100 Million

GEOGRAPHIC PREF

☐ East Coast
☐ West Coast
☒ Northeast
☐ Mid Atlantic
☐ Gulf States
☐ Northwest
☒ Southeast
☐ Southwest
☐ Midwest
☐ Central
☐ Local to Office
☐ Other Geo Pref

EMPIRE STATE CAPITAL CORPORATION

170 Broadway
Suite 1200
New York NY 10038

Phone (212) 513-1799   Fax (212) 513-1892

PROFESSIONALS	TITLE
Dr. Joseph Wu	President

INDUSTRY PREFERENCE

- ☐ INFORMATION INDUSTRY
- ☐ Communications
- ☐ Computer Equipment
- ☐ Computer Services
- ☐ Computer Components
- ☐ Computer Entertainment
- ☐ Computer Education
- ☐ Information Technologies
- ☐ Computer Media
- ☐ Software
- ☐ Internet
- ☐ MEDICAL/HEALTHCARE
- ☐ Biotechnology
- ☐ Healthcare Services
- ☐ Life Sciences
- ☐ Medical Products
- ☐ INDUSTRIAL
- ☐ Advanced Materials
- ☐ Chemicals
- ☐ Instruments & Controls

- ☐ BASIC INDUSTRIES
- ☐ Consumer
- ☐ Distribution
- ☐ Manufacturing
- ☐ Retail
- ☐ Service
- ☐ Wholesale
- ☐ SPECIFIC INDUSTRIES
- ☐ Energy
- ☐ Environmental
- ☐ Financial
- ☐ Real Estate
- ☐ Transportation
- ☐ Publishing
- ☐ Food
- ☐ Franchises
- ☒ DIVERSIFIED
- ☐ MISCELLANEOUS

STAGE PREFERENCE

- ☒ EARLY STAGE
- ☐ Seed
- ☒ Start-up
- ☒ 1st Stage
- ☒ LATER STAGE
- ☒ 2nd Stage
- ☒ Mature
- ☒ Mezzanine
- ☒ LBO/MBO
- ☐ Turnaround
- ☐ INT'L EXPANSION
- ☐ WILL CONSIDER ALL
- ☐ VENTURE LEASING

SSBIC
Other Locations:

Affiliation:
Minimum Investment: Less than $1 Million
Capital Under Management: Less than $100 Million

GEOGRAPHIC PREF

- ☒ East Coast
- ☐ West Coast
- ☐ Northeast
- ☐ Mid Atlantic
- ☐ Gulf States
- ☐ Northwest
- ☐ Southeast
- ☐ Southwest
- ☐ Midwest
- ☐ Central
- ☐ Local to Office
- ☐ Other Geo Pref

EOS PARTNERS, LP

320 Park Avenue
22nd Floor
New York NY 10022

Phone (212) 832-5800   Fax (212) 832-5815

PROFESSIONALS	TITLE
Steven M. Friedman	General Partner
Brian D. Young	General Partner
Douglas R. Korn	Managing Director
Mark L. First	Managing Director

INDUSTRY PREFERENCE

- ☒ INFORMATION INDUSTRY
- ☒ Communications
- ☒ Computer Equipment
- ☒ Computer Services
- ☒ Computer Components
- ☐ Computer Entertainment
- ☒ Computer Education
- ☒ Information Technologies
- ☒ Computer Media
- ☒ Software
- ☒ Internet
- ☒ MEDICAL/HEALTHCARE
- ☒ Biotechnology
- ☒ Healthcare Services
- ☒ Life Sciences
- ☒ Medical Products
- ☐ INDUSTRIAL
- ☐ Advanced Materials
- ☐ Chemicals
- ☐ Instruments & Controls

- ☒ BASIC INDUSTRIES
- ☐ Consumer
- ☐ Distribution
- ☐ Manufacturing
- ☒ Retail
- ☒ Service
- ☐ Wholesale
- ☒ SPECIFIC INDUSTRIES
- ☒ Energy
- ☐ Environmental
- ☐ Financial
- ☐ Real Estate
- ☒ Transportation
- ☐ Publishing
- ☐ Food
- ☐ Franchises
- ☒ DIVERSIFIED
- ☒ MISCELLANEOUS
- Outsourcing

STAGE PREFERENCE

- ☐ EARLY STAGE
- ☐ Seed
- ☐ Start-up
- ☐ 1st Stage
- ☒ LATER STAGE
- ☒ 2nd Stage
- ☒ Mature
- ☒ Mezzanine
- ☒ LBO/MBO
- ☐ Turnaround
- ☐ INT'L EXPANSION
- ☐ WILL CONSIDER ALL
- ☐ VENTURE LEASING

SBIC
Other Locations:

Affiliation:
Minimum Investment: $1 Million or more
Capital Under Management: Less than $100 Million

GEOGRAPHIC PREF

- ☐ East Coast
- ☐ West Coast
- ☐ Northeast
- ☐ Mid Atlantic
- ☐ Gulf States
- ☐ Northwest
- ☐ Southeast
- ☐ Southwest
- ☐ Midwest
- ☐ Central
- ☐ Local to Office
- ☐ Other Geo Pref

EQUINOX INVESTMENT PARTNERS

405 Lexington Avenue
21st Floor
New York NY 10174

Phone (212) 883-4600   Fax (212) 883-4615

PROFESSIONALS	TITLE
Robert Wickey	Managing Director
Caroline Merison	Director

INDUSTRY PREFERENCE

☒ INFORMATION INDUSTRY	☒ BASIC INDUSTRIES
☒ Communications	☒ Consumer
☒ Computer Equipment	☒ Distribution
☒ Computer Services	☐ Manufacturing
☒ Computer Components	☐ Retail
☐ Computer Entertainment	☐ Service
☒ Computer Education	☐ Wholesale
☒ Information Technologies	☒ SPECIFIC INDUSTRIES
☒ Computer Media	☐ Energy
☒ Software	☐ Environmental
☒ Internet	☒ Financial
☒ MEDICAL/HEALTHCARE	☐ Real Estate
☒ Biotechnology	☐ Transportation
☒ Healthcare Services	☐ Publishing
☒ Life Sciences	☐ Food
☒ Medical Products	☐ Franchises
☐ INDUSTRIAL	☒ DIVERSIFIED
☐ Advanced Materials	☒ MISCELLANEOUS
☐ Chemicals	
☐ Instruments & Controls	

STAGE PREFERENCE

☐ EARLY STAGE
☐ Seed
☐ Start-up
☐ 1st Stage
☒ LATER STAGE
☐ 2nd Stage
☐ Mature
☒ Mezzanine
☒ LBO/MBO
☒ Turnaround
☐ INT'L EXPANSION
☐ WILL CONSIDER ALL
☒ VENTURE LEASING

Other Locations:

Affiliation:
Minimum Investment: $1 Million or more
Capital Under Management: $100 to $500 Million

GEOGRAPHIC PREF

☐ East Coast
☐ West Coast
☐ Northeast
☐ Mid Atlantic
☐ Gulf States
☐ Northwest
☐ Southeast
☐ Southwest
☐ Midwest
☐ Central
☐ Local to Office
☐ Other Geo Pref

ESQUIRE CAPITAL CORP.

69 Veterans Memorial Highway
Commack NY 11725

Phone (516) 462-6946   Fax (516) 864-8152

PROFESSIONALS	TITLE
C. C. Chou	President
F. Eliassen	Manager

INDUSTRY PREFERENCE

☐ INFORMATION INDUSTRY	☐ BASIC INDUSTRIES
☐ Communications	☐ Consumer
☐ Computer Equipment	☐ Distribution
☐ Computer Services	☐ Manufacturing
☐ Computer Components	☐ Retail
☐ Computer Entertainment	☐ Service
☐ Computer Education	☐ Wholesale
☐ Information Technologies	☐ SPECIFIC INDUSTRIES
☐ Computer Media	☐ Energy
☐ Software	☐ Environmental
☐ Internet	☐ Financial
☐ MEDICAL/HEALTHCARE	☐ Real Estate
☐ Biotechnology	☐ Transportation
☐ Healthcare Services	☐ Publishing
☐ Life Sciences	☐ Food
☐ Medical Products	☐ Franchises
☐ INDUSTRIAL	☒ DIVERSIFIED
☐ Advanced Materials	☐ MISCELLANEOUS
☐ Chemicals	
☐ Instruments & Controls	

STAGE PREFERENCE

☒ EARLY STAGE
☒ Seed
☒ Start-up
☒ 1st Stage
☒ LATER STAGE
☒ 2nd Stage
☐ Mature
☐ Mezzanine
☐ LBO/MBO
☐ Turnaround
☐ INT'L EXPANSION
☐ WILL CONSIDER ALL
☐ VENTURE LEASING

SSBIC
Other Locations:

Affiliation:
Minimum Investment: Less than $1 Million
Capital Under Management: Less than $100 Million

GEOGRAPHIC PREF

☐ East Coast
☐ West Coast
☒ Northeast
☐ Mid Atlantic
☐ Gulf States
☐ Northwest
☐ Southeast
☐ Southwest
☐ Midwest
☐ Central
☐ Local to Office
☐ Other Geo Pref

EXETER CAPITAL PARTNERS

10 East 53rd Street
32nd Floor
New York NY 10022

Phone (212) 872-1172   Fax (212) 872-1198

PROFESSIONALS	TITLE
Keith R. Fox	Managing General Partner

INDUSTRY PREFERENCE

☒ INFORMATION INDUSTRY
☒ Communications
☒ Computer Equipment
☐ Computer Services
☐ Computer Components
☐ Computer Entertainment
☐ Computer Education
☒ Information Technologies
☐ Computer Media
☐ Software
☒ Internet
☒ MEDICAL/HEALTHCARE
☒ Biotechnology
☒ Healthcare Services
☒ Life Sciences
☒ Medical Products
☒ INDUSTRIAL
☒ Advanced Materials
☐ Chemicals
☒ Instruments & Controls

☒ BASIC INDUSTRIES
☒ Consumer
☒ Distribution
☒ Manufacturing
☐ Retail
☐ Service
☐ Wholesale
☐ SPECIFIC INDUSTRIES
☐ Energy
☐ Environmental
☐ Financial
☐ Real Estate
☐ Transportation
☐ Publishing
☐ Food
☐ Franchises
☒ DIVERSIFIED
☐ MISCELLANEOUS

STAGE PREFERENCE

☐ EARLY STAGE
☐ Seed
☐ Start-up
☐ 1st Stage
☒ LATER STAGE
☒ 2nd Stage
☒ Mature
☒ Mezzanine
☒ LBO/MBO
☐ Turnaround
☐ INT'L EXPANSION
☐ WILL CONSIDER ALL
☐ VENTURE LEASING
SBIC
Other Locations:

Affiliation: The Exeter Group of Funds
Minimum Investment: $1 Million or more
Capital Under Management: $100 to $500 Million

GEOGRAPHIC PREF

☐ East Coast
☐ West Coast
☐ Northeast
☐ Mid Atlantic
☐ Gulf States
☐ Northwest
☐ Southeast
☐ Southwest
☐ Midwest
☐ Central
☐ Local to Office
☐ Other Geo Pref

FIRST COUNTY CAPITAL, INC.

135-14 Northern Boulevard
Second Floor
Flushing NY 11354

Phone (718) 461-1778   Fax (718) 461-1835

PROFESSIONALS	TITLE
Orest Glut	Manager

INDUSTRY PREFERENCE

☐ INFORMATION INDUSTRY
☐ Communications
☐ Computer Equipment
☐ Computer Services
☐ Computer Components
☐ Computer Entertainment
☐ Computer Education
☐ Information Technologies
☐ Computer Media
☐ Software
☐ Internet
☐ MEDICAL/HEALTHCARE
☐ Biotechnology
☐ Healthcare Services
☐ Life Sciences
☐ Medical Products
☐ INDUSTRIAL
☐ Advanced Materials
☐ Chemicals
☐ Instruments & Controls

☒ BASIC INDUSTRIES
☐ Consumer
☐ Distribution
☒ Manufacturing
☒ Retail
☐ Service
☒ Wholesale
☒ SPECIFIC INDUSTRIES
☐ Energy
☐ Environmental
☐ Financial
☐ Real Estate
☐ Transportation
☐ Publishing
☒ Food
☐ Franchises
☒ DIVERSIFIED
☐ MISCELLANEOUS
Food Service

STAGE PREFERENCE

☒ EARLY STAGE
☒ Seed
☒ Start-up
☒ 1st Stage
☒ LATER STAGE
☒ 2nd Stage
☒ Mature
☒ Mezzanine
☒ LBO/MBO
☐ Turnaround
☐ INT'L EXPANSION
☐ WILL CONSIDER ALL
☐ VENTURE LEASING
SSBIC
Other Locations:

Affiliation:
Minimum Investment: Less than $1 Million
Capital Under Management: Less than $100 Million

GEOGRAPHIC PREF

☐ East Coast
☐ West Coast
☒ Northeast
☐ Mid Atlantic
☐ Gulf States
☐ Northwest
☐ Southeast
☐ Southwest
☐ Midwest
☐ Central
☐ Local to Office
☐ Other Geo Pref

FLATIRON PARNTERS

257 Park Avenue South
12th Floor
New York NY 10010

Phone (212) 228-3800 Fax (212) 228-0552

PROFESSIONALS	TITLE
Jerry Colonna	Managing Partner
Fred Wilson	Managing Partner
Robert Greene	Managing Partner

INDUSTRY PREFERENCE

☒ INFORMATION INDUSTRY	☐ BASIC INDUSTRIES
☒ Communications	☐ Consumer
☒ Computer Equipment	☐ Distribution
☐ Computer Services	☐ Manufacturing
☒ Computer Components	☐ Retail
☐ Computer Entertainment	☐ Service
☐ Computer Education	☐ Wholesale
☒ Information Technologies	☐ SPECIFIC INDUSTRIES
☐ Computer Media	☐ Energy
☒ Software	☐ Environmental
☒ Internet	☐ Financial
☐ MEDICAL/HEALTHCARE	☐ Real Estate
☐ Biotechnology	☐ Transportation
☐ Healthcare Services	☐ Publishing
☐ Life Sciences	☐ Food
☐ Medical Products	☐ Franchises
☐ INDUSTRIAL	☐ DIVERSIFIED
☐ Advanced Materials	☒ MISCELLANEOUS
☐ Chemicals	
☐ Instruments & Controls	

STAGE PREFERENCE

☒ EARLY STAGE
☐ Seed
☒ Start-up
☒ 1st Stage
☒ LATER STAGE
☒ 2nd Stage
☐ Mature
☐ Mezzanine
☐ LBO/MBO
☐ Turnaround
☐ INT'L EXPANSION
☐ WILL CONSIDER ALL
☐ VENTURE LEASING

Other Locations:

Affiliation:
Minimum Investment: Less than $1 Million
Capital Under Management: Less than $100 Million

GEOGRAPHIC PREF

☐ East Coast
☐ West Coast
☐ Northeast
☐ Mid Atlantic
☐ Gulf States
☐ Northwest
☐ Southeast
☐ Southwest
☐ Midwest
☐ Central
☐ Local to Office
☐ Other Geo Pref

FRESHSTART VENTURE CAPITAL CORPORATION

24-29 Jackson Avenue
Long Island City NY 11101

Phone (718) 361-9595 Fax (718) 361-8295

PROFESSIONALS	TITLE
Zindel Zelmanovitch	President

INDUSTRY PREFERENCE

☐ INFORMATION INDUSTRY	☐ BASIC INDUSTRIES
☐ Communications	☐ Consumer
☐ Computer Equipment	☐ Distribution
☐ Computer Services	☐ Manufacturing
☐ Computer Components	☐ Retail
☐ Computer Entertainment	☐ Service
☐ Computer Education	☐ Wholesale
☐ Information Technologies	☐ SPECIFIC INDUSTRIES
☐ Computer Media	☐ Energy
☐ Software	☐ Environmental
☐ Internet	☐ Financial
☐ MEDICAL/HEALTHCARE	☐ Real Estate
☐ Biotechnology	☐ Transportation
☐ Healthcare Services	☐ Publishing
☐ Life Sciences	☐ Food
☐ Medical Products	☐ Franchises
☐ INDUSTRIAL	☒ DIVERSIFIED
☐ Advanced Materials	☐ MISCELLANEOUS
☐ Chemicals	
☐ Instruments & Controls	

STAGE PREFERENCE

☒ EARLY STAGE
☒ Seed
☒ Start-up
☒ 1st Stage
☒ LATER STAGE
☒ 2nd Stage
☐ Mature
☐ Mezzanine
☐ LBO/MBO
☐ Turnaround
☐ INT'L EXPANSION
☐ WILL CONSIDER ALL
☐ VENTURE LEASING
SSBIC
Other Locations:

Affiliation:
Minimum Investment: Less than $1 Million
Capital Under Management: Less than $100 Million

GEOGRAPHIC PREF

☐ East Coast
☐ West Coast
☒ Northeast
☐ Mid Atlantic
☐ Gulf States
☐ Northwest
☐ Southeast
☐ Southwest
☐ Midwest
☐ Central
☐ Local to Office
☐ Other Geo Pref

FUNDEX CAPITAL CORP.

**780 Third Avenue
48th Floor
New York NY 10017**

Phone (212) 527-7135   Fax (212) 527-7134

PROFESSIONALS	TITLE
Lawrence Lintesman	President

INDUSTRY PREFERENCE

☐ INFORMATION INDUSTRY	☒ BASIC INDUSTRIES	
☐ Communications	☒ Consumer	
☐ Computer Equipment	☐ Distribution	
☐ Computer Services	☐ Manufacturing	
☐ Computer Components	☐ Retail	
☐ Computer Entertainment	☐ Service	
☐ Computer Education	☐ Wholesale	
☐ Information Technologies	☒ SPECIFIC INDUSTRIES	
☐ Computer Media	☐ Energy	
☐ Software	☐ Environmental	
☐ Internet	☐ Financial	
☐ MEDICAL/HEALTHCARE	☐ Real Estate	
☐ Biotechnology	☐ Transportation	
☐ Healthcare Services	☐ Publishing	
☐ Life Sciences	☐ Food	
☐ Medical Products	☐ Franchises	
☐ INDUSTRIAL	☐ DIVERSIFIED	
☐ Advanced Materials	☐ MISCELLANEOUS	
☐ Chemicals		
☐ Instruments & Controls		

STAGE PREFERENCE

☒ EARLY STAGE
☒ Seed
☒ Start-up
☒ 1st Stage
☒ LATER STAGE
☒ 2nd Stage
☒ Mature
☒ Mezzanine
☒ LBO/MBO
☐ Turnaround
☐ INT'L EXPANSION
☐ WILL CONSIDER ALL
☐ VENTURE LEASING
SBIC
Other Locations:

Affiliation:
Minimum Investment: $1 Million or more
Capital Under Management: Less than $100 Million

GEOGRAPHIC PREF

☐ East Coast
☐ West Coast
☒ Northeast
☐ Mid Atlantic
☐ Gulf States
☐ Northwest
☐ Southeast
☐ Southwest
☐ Midwest
☐ Central
☐ Local to Office
☒ Other Geo Pref
  NY, NJ, CT

GALEN ASSOCIATES

**610 Fifth Avenue
Rockefeller Center, 5th Floor
New York NY 10020**

Phone (212) 218-4990   Fax (212) 218-4999

PROFESSIONALS	TITLE
Srini Conjeevaram	General Partner
Zubeen Schroff	General Partner
Bruce F. Wesson	General Partner
David Jahns	General Partner
William R. Grant	General Partner
L. John Wilkerson	General Partner

INDUSTRY PREFERENCE

☐ INFORMATION INDUSTRY	☐ BASIC INDUSTRIES	
☐ Communications	☐ Consumer	
☐ Computer Equipment	☐ Distribution	
☐ Computer Services	☐ Manufacturing	
☐ Computer Components	☐ Retail	
☐ Computer Entertainment	☐ Service	
☐ Computer Education	☐ Wholesale	
☐ Information Technologies	☐ SPECIFIC INDUSTRIES	
☐ Computer Media	☐ Energy	
☐ Software	☐ Environmental	
☐ Internet	☐ Financial	
☒ MEDICAL/HEALTHCARE	☐ Real Estate	
☒ Biotechnology	☐ Transportation	
☒ Healthcare Services	☐ Publishing	
☒ Life Sciences	☐ Food	
☒ Medical Products	☐ Franchises	
☐ INDUSTRIAL	☐ DIVERSIFIED	
☐ Advanced Materials	☒ MISCELLANEOUS	
☐ Chemicals		
☐ Instruments & Controls		

STAGE PREFERENCE

☐ EARLY STAGE
☐ Seed
☐ Start-up
☐ 1st Stage
☒ LATER STAGE
☒ 2nd Stage
☐ Mature
☐ Mezzanine
☐ LBO/MBO
☐ Turnaround
☐ INT'L EXPANSION
☐ WILL CONSIDER ALL
☐ VENTURE LEASING

Other Locations:

Affiliation:
Minimum Investment: $1 Million or more
Capital Under Management: $100 to $500 Million

GEOGRAPHIC PREF

☐ East Coast
☐ West Coast
☐ Northeast
☐ Mid Atlantic
☐ Gulf States
☐ Northwest
☐ Southeast
☐ Southwest
☐ Midwest
☐ Central
☐ Local to Office
☐ Other Geo Pref

GENERATION PARTNERS

**551 Fifth Avenue
Suite 3100
New York NY 10176**

Phone (212) 450-8500   Fax (212) 450-8550

PROFESSIONALS	TITLE
John Hawkins	Managing Partner
Mark Jennings	Managing Partner
Paul Baker	Managing Partner

INDUSTRY PREFERENCE

☒ INFORMATION INDUSTRY	☒ BASIC INDUSTRIES
☒ Communications	☒ Consumer
☐ Computer Equipment	☐ Distribution
☐ Computer Services	☐ Manufacturing
☐ Computer Components	☐ Retail
☐ Computer Entertainment	☐ Service
☐ Computer Education	☐ Wholesale
☒ Information Technologies	☐ SPECIFIC INDUSTRIES
☐ Computer Media	☐ Energy
☐ Software	☐ Environmental
☒ Internet	☐ Financial
☒ MEDICAL/HEALTHCARE	☐ Real Estate
☒ Biotechnology	☐ Transportation
☒ Healthcare Services	☐ Publishing
☒ Life Sciences	☐ Food
☒ Medical Products	☐ Franchises
☐ INDUSTRIAL	☒ DIVERSIFIED
☐ Advanced Materials	☒ MISCELLANEOUS
☐ Chemicals	
☐ Instruments & Controls	

STAGE PREFERENCE

☒ EARLY STAGE
☐ Seed
☒ Start-up
☒ 1st Stage
☒ LATER STAGE
☒ 2nd Stage
☐ Mature
☐ Mezzanine
☒ LBO/MBO
☐ Turnaround
☐ INT'L EXPANSION
☐ WILL CONSIDER ALL
☐ VENTURE LEASING

Other Locations:

Affiliation:
Minimum Investment: $1 Million or more
Capital Under Management: $100 to $500 Million

GEOGRAPHIC PREF

☐ East Coast
☐ West Coast
☐ Northeast
☐ Mid Atlantic
☐ Gulf States
☐ Northwest
☐ Southeast
☐ Southwest
☐ Midwest
☐ Central
☐ Local to Office
☐ Other Geo Pref

GENESEE FUNDING, INC.

**70 Linden Oaks
3rd Floor
Rochester NY 14625**

Phone (716) 383-5550   Fax (716) 272-9466

PROFESSIONALS	TITLE
Stuart W. Marsh	President

INDUSTRY PREFERENCE

☐ INFORMATION INDUSTRY	☐ BASIC INDUSTRIES
☐ Communications	☐ Consumer
☐ Computer Equipment	☐ Distribution
☐ Computer Services	☐ Manufacturing
☐ Computer Components	☐ Retail
☐ Computer Entertainment	☐ Service
☐ Computer Education	☐ Wholesale
☐ Information Technologies	☐ SPECIFIC INDUSTRIES
☐ Computer Media	☐ Energy
☐ Software	☐ Environmental
☐ Internet	☐ Financial
☐ MEDICAL/HEALTHCARE	☐ Real Estate
☐ Biotechnology	☐ Transportation
☐ Healthcare Services	☐ Publishing
☐ Life Sciences	☐ Food
☐ Medical Products	☐ Franchises
☐ INDUSTRIAL	☒ DIVERSIFIED
☐ Advanced Materials	☐ MISCELLANEOUS
☐ Chemicals	
☐ Instruments & Controls	

STAGE PREFERENCE

☐ EARLY STAGE
☐ Seed
☐ Start-up
☐ 1st Stage
☒ LATER STAGE
☒ 2nd Stage
☒ Mature
☒ Mezzanine
☒ LBO/MBO
☐ Turnaround
☐ INT'L EXPANSION
☐ WILL CONSIDER ALL
☐ VENTURE LEASING

SBIC
Other Locations:

Affiliation:
Minimum Investment: Less than $1 Million
Capital Under Management: Less than $100 Million

GEOGRAPHIC PREF

☐ East Coast
☐ West Coast
☒ Northeast
☐ Mid Atlantic
☐ Gulf States
☐ Northwest
☐ Southeast
☐ Southwest
☐ Midwest
☐ Central
☐ Local to Office
☐ Other Geo Pref

GOLUB ASSOCIATES, INCORPORATED

**230 Park Avenue
19th Floor
New York NY 10169**

Phone (212) 207-1575   Fax (212) 207-1579

PROFESSIONALS	TITLE
Lawrence E. Golub	President
Evelyn Mordechai	Vice President
Greg W. Cashman	Vice President

INDUSTRY PREFERENCE

- ☒ INFORMATION INDUSTRY
- ☒ Communications
- ☐ Computer Equipment
- ☐ Computer Services
- ☐ Computer Components
- ☐ Computer Entertainment
- ☐ Computer Education
- ☐ Information Technologies
- ☒ Computer Media
- ☐ Software
- ☐ Internet
- ☒ MEDICAL/HEALTHCARE
- ☐ Biotechnology
- ☒ Healthcare Services
- ☐ Life Sciences
- ☒ Medical Products
- ☐ INDUSTRIAL
- ☐ Advanced Materials
- ☐ Chemicals
- ☐ Instruments & Controls

- ☒ BASIC INDUSTRIES
- ☒ Consumer
- ☒ Distribution
- ☒ Manufacturing
- ☒ Retail
- ☐ Service
- ☐ Wholesale
- ☐ SPECIFIC INDUSTRIES
- ☐ Energy
- ☐ Environmental
- ☐ Financial
- ☐ Real Estate
- ☐ Transportation
- ☐ Publishing
- ☐ Food
- ☐ Franchises
- ☒ DIVERSIFIED
- ☐ MISCELLANEOUS

STAGE PREFERENCE

- ☐ EARLY STAGE
- ☐ Seed
- ☐ Start-up
- ☐ 1st Stage
- ☒ LATER STAGE
- ☒ 2nd Stage
- ☒ Mature
- ☒ Mezzanine
- ☒ LBO/MBO
- ☐ Turnaround
- ☐ INT'L EXPANSION
- ☐ WILL CONSIDER ALL
- ☐ VENTURE LEASING

SBIC
Other Locations:

Affiliation:
Minimum Investment: $1 Million or more
Capital Under Management: $100 to $500 Million

GEOGRAPHIC PREF

- ☐ East Coast
- ☐ West Coast
- ☐ Northeast
- ☒ Mid Atlantic
- ☐ Gulf States
- ☐ Northwest
- ☐ Southeast
- ☐ Southwest
- ☐ Midwest
- ☐ Central
- ☐ Local to Office
- ☒ Other Geo Pref
      Mid-Atlantic

HANAM CAPITAL CORP.

**38 West 32nd Street
Suite 1512
New York NY 10001**

Phone (212) 564-5225   Fax (212) 564-5307

PROFESSIONALS	TITLE
Robert Schairer	President

INDUSTRY PREFERENCE

- ☐ INFORMATION INDUSTRY
- ☐ Communications
- ☐ Computer Equipment
- ☐ Computer Services
- ☐ Computer Components
- ☐ Computer Entertainment
- ☐ Computer Education
- ☐ Information Technologies
- ☐ Computer Media
- ☐ Software
- ☐ Internet
- ☐ MEDICAL/HEALTHCARE
- ☐ Biotechnology
- ☐ Healthcare Services
- ☐ Life Sciences
- ☐ Medical Products
- ☐ INDUSTRIAL
- ☐ Advanced Materials
- ☐ Chemicals
- ☐ Instruments & Controls

- ☐ BASIC INDUSTRIES
- ☐ Consumer
- ☐ Distribution
- ☐ Manufacturing
- ☐ Retail
- ☐ Service
- ☐ Wholesale
- ☐ SPECIFIC INDUSTRIES
- ☐ Energy
- ☐ Environmental
- ☐ Financial
- ☐ Real Estate
- ☐ Transportation
- ☐ Publishing
- ☐ Food
- ☐ Franchises
- ☒ DIVERSIFIED
- ☐ MISCELLANEOUS

STAGE PREFERENCE

- ☒ EARLY STAGE
- ☐ Seed
- ☐ Start-up
- ☒ 1st Stage
- ☒ LATER STAGE
- ☒ 2nd Stage
- ☒ Mature
- ☒ Mezzanine
- ☒ LBO/MBO
- ☐ Turnaround
- ☐ INT'L EXPANSION
- ☐ WILL CONSIDER ALL
- ☐ VENTURE LEASING

SSBIC
Other Locations:

Affiliation:
Minimum Investment: Less than $1 Million
Capital Under Management: Less than $100 Million

GEOGRAPHIC PREF

- ☐ East Coast
- ☐ West Coast
- ☒ Northeast
- ☐ Mid Atlantic
- ☐ Gulf States
- ☐ Northwest
- ☐ Southeast
- ☐ Southwest
- ☐ Midwest
- ☐ Central
- ☐ Local to Office
- ☐ Other Geo Pref

HARVEST PARTNERS, INC.

280 Park Avenue, 33rd Floor
New York NY 10017

Phone (212) 599-6300   Fax (212) 812-0100

PROFESSIONALS	TITLE
Harvey J. Wertheim	Managing General Partner
Harvey P. Mallement	Managing General Partner
William J. Kane	General Partner
Ira D. Kleinman	General Partner
Thomas W. Arenz	General Partner

INDUSTRY PREFERENCE

☒ INFORMATION INDUSTRY
☐ Communications
☐ Computer Equipment
☒ Computer Services
☐ Computer Components
☐ Computer Entertainment
☒ Computer Education
☐ Information Technologies
☐ Computer Media
☐ Software
☐ Internet
☒ MEDICAL/HEALTHCARE
☐ Biotechnology
☒ Healthcare Services
☒ Life Sciences
☒ Medical Products
☐ INDUSTRIAL
☐ Advanced Materials
☐ Chemicals
☐ Instruments & Controls

☒ BASIC INDUSTRIES
☐ Consumer
☒ Distribution
☒ Manufacturing
☐ Retail
☒ Service
☒ Wholesale
☐ SPECIFIC INDUSTRIES
☐ Energy
☐ Environmental
☐ Financial
☐ Real Estate
☐ Transportation
☐ Publishing
☐ Food
☐ Franchises
☒ DIVERSIFIED
☐ MISCELLANEOUS

STAGE PREFERENCE

☐ EARLY STAGE
☐ Seed
☐ Start-up
☐ 1st Stage
☒ LATER STAGE
☒ 2nd Stage
☐ Mature
☐ Mezzanine
☒ LBO/MBO
☐ Turnaround
☐ INT'L EXPANSION
☐ WILL CONSIDER ALL
☐ VENTURE LEASING

Other Locations:

Affiliation:
Minimum Investment: $1 Million or more
Capital Under Management: Over $500 Million

GEOGRAPHIC PREF

☐ East Coast
☐ West Coast
☐ Northeast
☐ Mid Atlantic
☐ Gulf States
☐ Northwest
☐ Southeast
☐ Southwest
☐ Midwest
☐ Central
☐ Local to Office
☐ Other Geo Pref

IBERO AMERICAN INVESTORS CORP.

104 Scio Street
Rochester NY 14604

Phone (716) 262-3440   Fax (716) 262-3441

PROFESSIONALS	TITLE
Domingo Garcia	President

INDUSTRY PREFERENCE

☐ INFORMATION INDUSTRY
☐ Communications
☐ Computer Equipment
☐ Computer Services
☐ Computer Components
☐ Computer Entertainment
☐ Computer Education
☐ Information Technologies
☐ Computer Media
☐ Software
☐ Internet
☐ MEDICAL/HEALTHCARE
☐ Biotechnology
☐ Healthcare Services
☐ Life Sciences
☐ Medical Products
☐ INDUSTRIAL
☐ Advanced Materials
☐ Chemicals
☐ Instruments & Controls

☐ BASIC INDUSTRIES
☐ Consumer
☐ Distribution
☐ Manufacturing
☐ Retail
☐ Service
☐ Wholesale
☐ SPECIFIC INDUSTRIES
☐ Energy
☐ Environmental
☐ Financial
☐ Real Estate
☐ Transportation
☐ Publishing
☐ Food
☐ Franchises
☒ DIVERSIFIED
☐ MISCELLANEOUS

STAGE PREFERENCE

☒ EARLY STAGE
☐ Seed
☐ Start-up
☒ 1st Stage
☒ LATER STAGE
☒ 2nd Stage
☒ Mature
☒ Mezzanine
☒ LBO/MBO
☐ Turnaround
☐ INT'L EXPANSION
☐ WILL CONSIDER ALL
☐ VENTURE LEASING
SSBIC
Other Locations:

Affiliation:
Minimum Investment: Less than $1 Million
Capital Under Management: Less than $100 Million

GEOGRAPHIC PREF

☐ East Coast
☐ West Coast
☒ Northeast
☐ Mid Atlantic
☐ Gulf States
☐ Northwest
☐ Southeast
☐ Southwest
☐ Midwest
☐ Central
☐ Local to Office
☐ Other Geo Pref

IBJ WHITEHALL CAPITAL CORP.

One State Street
Eighth Floor
New York NY 10004

Phone (212) 858-2000   Fax (212) 952-1629

PROFESSIONALS	TITLE
JoAnne Dillon	

INDUSTRY PREFERENCE

☐ INFORMATION INDUSTRY	☒ BASIC INDUSTRIES
☐ Communications	☒ Consumer
☐ Computer Equipment	☒ Distribution
☐ Computer Services	☒ Manufacturing
☐ Computer Components	☐ Retail
☐ Computer Entertainment	☒ Service
☐ Computer Education	☐ Wholesale
☐ Information Technologies	☐ SPECIFIC INDUSTRIES
☐ Computer Media	☐ Energy
☐ Software	☐ Environmental
☐ Internet	☐ Financial
☐ MEDICAL/HEALTHCARE	☐ Real Estate
☐ Biotechnology	☐ Transportation
☐ Healthcare Services	☐ Publishing
☐ Life Sciences	☐ Food
☐ Medical Products	☐ Franchises
☐ INDUSTRIAL	☒ DIVERSIFIED
☐ Advanced Materials	☐ MISCELLANEOUS
☐ Chemicals	
☐ Instruments & Controls	

STAGE PREFERENCE

☐ EARLY STAGE
☐ Seed
☐ Start-up
☐ 1st Stage
☒ LATER STAGE
☒ 2nd Stage
☒ Mature
☐ Mezzanine
☒ LBO/MBO
☒ Turnaround
☐ INT'L EXPANSION
☐ WILL CONSIDER ALL
☒ VENTURE LEASING

SBIC
Other Locations:

Affiliation:
Minimum Investment: $1 Million or more
Capital Under Management: Less than $100 Million

GEOGRAPHIC PREF

☐ East Coast
☐ West Coast
☐ Northeast
☐ Mid Atlantic
☐ Gulf States
☐ Northwest
☐ Southeast
☐ Southwest
☐ Midwest
☐ Central
☐ Local to Office
☐ Other Geo Pref

ING FURMAN SELZ INVESTMENTS

55 East 52nd
37th Floor
New York NY 10055

Phone (212) 409-6518   Fax (212) 409-5874

PROFESSIONALS	TITLE
Brian Friedman	President

INDUSTRY PREFERENCE

☐ INFORMATION INDUSTRY	☐ BASIC INDUSTRIES
☐ Communications	☐ Consumer
☐ Computer Equipment	☐ Distribution
☐ Computer Services	☐ Manufacturing
☐ Computer Components	☐ Retail
☐ Computer Entertainment	☐ Service
☐ Computer Education	☐ Wholesale
☐ Information Technologies	☐ SPECIFIC INDUSTRIES
☐ Computer Media	☐ Energy
☐ Software	☐ Environmental
☐ Internet	☐ Financial
☐ MEDICAL/HEALTHCARE	☐ Real Estate
☐ Biotechnology	☐ Transportation
☐ Healthcare Services	☐ Publishing
☐ Life Sciences	☐ Food
☐ Medical Products	☐ Franchises
☐ INDUSTRIAL	☒ DIVERSIFIED
☐ Advanced Materials	☐ MISCELLANEOUS
☐ Chemicals	
☐ Instruments & Controls	

STAGE PREFERENCE

☐ EARLY STAGE
☐ Seed
☐ Start-up
☐ 1st Stage
☒ LATER STAGE
☒ 2nd Stage
☒ Mature
☒ Mezzanine
☒ LBO/MBO
☐ Turnaround
☐ INT'L EXPANSION
☐ WILL CONSIDER ALL
☐ VENTURE LEASING

SBIC
Other Locations:

Affiliation:
Minimum Investment: $1 Million or more
Capital Under Management: Less than $100 Million

GEOGRAPHIC PREF

☐ East Coast
☐ West Coast
☐ Northeast
☐ Mid Atlantic
☐ Gulf States
☐ Northwest
☐ Southeast
☐ Southwest
☐ Midwest
☐ Central
☐ Local to Office
☐ Other Geo Pref

INTEREQUITY CAPITAL PARTNERS, LP

220 Fifth Avenue
12th Floor
New York NY 10001

Phone (212) 779-2022   Fax (212) 779-2103

PROFESSIONALS	TITLE
Irwin Schlass	President
Abraham Goldstein	Managing Director

INDUSTRY PREFERENCE

☒ INFORMATION INDUSTRY
☒ Communications
☒ Computer Equipment
☒ Computer Services
☒ Computer Components
☐ Computer Entertainment
☒ Computer Education
☒ Information Technologies
☒ Computer Media
☒ Software
☒ Internet
☒ MEDICAL/HEALTHCARE
☒ Biotechnology
☒ Healthcare Services
☒ Life Sciences
☒ Medical Products
☒ INDUSTRIAL
☒ Advanced Materials
☒ Chemicals
☒ Instruments & Controls

☒ BASIC INDUSTRIES
☒ Consumer
☒ Distribution
☐ Manufacturing
☐ Retail
☐ Service
☐ Wholesale
☐ SPECIFIC INDUSTRIES
☐ Energy
☐ Environmental
☐ Financial
☐ Real Estate
☐ Transportation
☐ Publishing
☐ Food
☐ Franchises
☒ DIVERSIFIED
☐ MISCELLANEOUS

STAGE PREFERENCE

☒ EARLY STAGE
☐ Seed
☒ Start-up
☒ 1st Stage
☒ LATER STAGE
☒ 2nd Stage
☒ Mature
☒ Mezzanine
☒ LBO/MBO
☐ Turnaround
☐ INT'L EXPANSION
☐ WILL CONSIDER ALL
☐ VENTURE LEASING

SBIC
Other Locations:

Affiliation:
Minimum Investment: Less than $1 Million
Capital Under Management: Less than $100 Million

GEOGRAPHIC PREF

☐ East Coast
☐ West Coast
☐ Northeast
☐ Mid Atlantic
☐ Gulf States
☐ Northwest
☐ Southeast
☐ Southwest
☐ Midwest
☐ Central
☐ Local to Office
☐ Other Geo Pref

INTERNATIONAL PAPER CAPITAL FORMATION, INC.

Two Manhattanville Road
Purchase NY 10577

Phone (914) 397-1578   Fax (914) 397-1909

PROFESSIONALS	TITLE
Jules Weiss	President

INDUSTRY PREFERENCE

☐ INFORMATION INDUSTRY
☐ Communications
☐ Computer Equipment
☐ Computer Services
☐ Computer Components
☐ Computer Entertainment
☐ Computer Education
☐ Information Technologies
☐ Computer Media
☐ Software
☐ Internet
☐ MEDICAL/HEALTHCARE
☐ Biotechnology
☐ Healthcare Services
☐ Life Sciences
☐ Medical Products
☒ INDUSTRIAL
☒ Advanced Materials
☐ Chemicals
☐ Instruments & Controls

☐ BASIC INDUSTRIES
☐ Consumer
☐ Distribution
☐ Manufacturing
☐ Retail
☐ Service
☐ Wholesale
☒ SPECIFIC INDUSTRIES
☐ Energy
☒ Environmental
☐ Financial
☐ Real Estate
☐ Transportation
☐ Publishing
☐ Food
☐ Franchises
☒ DIVERSIFIED
☐ MISCELLANEOUS

STAGE PREFERENCE

☐ EARLY STAGE
☐ Seed
☐ Start-up
☐ 1st Stage
☒ LATER STAGE
☒ 2nd Stage
☒ Mature
☒ Mezzanine
☒ LBO/MBO
☐ Turnaround
☐ INT'L EXPANSION
☐ WILL CONSIDER ALL
☐ VENTURE LEASING

SSBIC
Other Locations: Memphis TN

Affiliation:
Minimum Investment: Less than $1 Million
Capital Under Management: Less than $100 Million

GEOGRAPHIC PREF

☐ East Coast
☐ West Coast
☐ Northeast
☐ Mid Atlantic
☐ Gulf States
☐ Northwest
☐ Southeast
☐ Southwest
☐ Midwest
☐ Central
☐ Local to Office
☐ Other Geo Pref

J.H. WHITNEY & COMPANY

630 Fifth Avenue
32nd Floor
New York NY 10111

Phone (212) 332-2400   Fax (212) 332-2422

PROFESSIONALS	TITLE
Peter Castleman	Managing Partner

INDUSTRY PREFERENCE

☒ INFORMATION INDUSTRY
☒ Communications
☒ Computer Equipment
☐ Computer Services
☐ Computer Components
☐ Computer Entertainment
☐ Computer Education
☐ Information Technologies
☐ Computer Media
☐ Software
☒ Internet
☒ MEDICAL/HEALTHCARE
☒ Biotechnology
☒ Healthcare Services
☒ Life Sciences
☒ Medical Products
☒ INDUSTRIAL
☒ Advanced Materials
☒ Chemicals
☒ Instruments & Controls

☒ BASIC INDUSTRIES
☒ Consumer
☐ Distribution
☐ Manufacturing
☒ Retail
☐ Service
☐ Wholesale
☒ SPECIFIC INDUSTRIES
☐ Energy
☐ Environmental
☐ Financial
☐ Real Estate
☐ Transportation
☐ Publishing
☐ Food
☐ Franchises
☒ DIVERSIFIED
☐ MISCELLANEOUS

STAGE PREFERENCE

☒ EARLY STAGE
☐ Seed
☐ Start-up
☒ 1st Stage
☒ LATER STAGE
☒ 2nd Stage
☒ Mature
☒ Mezzanine
☒ LBO/MBO
☐ Turnaround
☐ INT'L EXPANSION
☐ WILL CONSIDER ALL
☐ VENTURE LEASING

Other Locations: Stamford CT

Affiliation:
Minimum Investment: $1 Million or more
Capital Under Management: Over $500 Million

GEOGRAPHIC PREF

☐ East Coast
☐ West Coast
☐ Northeast
☐ Mid Atlantic
☐ Gulf States
☐ Northwest
☐ Southeast
☐ Southwest
☐ Midwest
☐ Central
☐ Local to Office
☐ Other Geo Pref

J.P. MORGAN INVESTMENT CORPORATION

60 Wall Street
New York NY 10260

Phone (212) 648-9000   Fax (212) 648-5032

PROFESSIONALS	TITLE
Steve Skoczylas	Managing Director

INDUSTRY PREFERENCE

☒ INFORMATION INDUSTRY
☒ Communications
☒ Computer Equipment
☒ Computer Services
☒ Computer Components
☐ Computer Entertainment
☒ Computer Education
☒ Information Technologies
☒ Computer Media
☒ Software
☒ Internet
☒ MEDICAL/HEALTHCARE
☒ Biotechnology
☒ Healthcare Services
☒ Life Sciences
☒ Medical Products
☒ INDUSTRIAL
☒ Advanced Materials
☒ Chemicals
☒ Instruments & Controls

☒ BASIC INDUSTRIES
☒ Consumer
☒ Distribution
☐ Manufacturing
☒ Retail
☐ Service
☐ Wholesale
☐ SPECIFIC INDUSTRIES
☐ Energy
☐ Environmental
☐ Financial
☐ Real Estate
☐ Transportation
☐ Publishing
☐ Food
☐ Franchises
☒ DIVERSIFIED
☐ MISCELLANEOUS

STAGE PREFERENCE

☐ EARLY STAGE
☐ Seed
☐ Start-up
☐ 1st Stage
☒ LATER STAGE
☒ 2nd Stage
☒ Mature
☒ Mezzanine
☒ LBO/MBO
☐ Turnaround
☐ INT'L EXPANSION
☐ WILL CONSIDER ALL
☐ VENTURE LEASING
SBIC
Other Locations:

Affiliation:
Minimum Investment: $1 Million or more
Capital Under Management: Over $500 Million

GEOGRAPHIC PREF

☐ East Coast
☐ West Coast
☐ Northeast
☐ Mid Atlantic
☐ Gulf States
☐ Northwest
☐ Southeast
☐ Southwest
☐ Midwest
☐ Central
☐ Local to Office
☐ Other Geo Pref

KBL HEALTHCARE VENTURES

645 Madison Avenue
14th Floor
New York NY 10022

Phone (212) 319-5555   Fax (212) 319-5591

PROFESSIONALS	TITLE
Dr. Marlene R. Krauss	Managing Director
Dr. Zachary C. Berk	Managing Director

INDUSTRY PREFERENCE

☐ INFORMATION INDUSTRY
☐ Communications
☐ Computer Equipment
☐ Computer Services
☐ Computer Components
☐ Computer Entertainment
☐ Computer Education
☐ Information Technologies
☐ Computer Media
☐ Software
☐ Internet
☒ MEDICAL/HEALTHCARE
☐ Biotechnology
☒ Healthcare Services
☒ Life Sciences
☒ Medical Products
☐ INDUSTRIAL
☐ Advanced Materials
☐ Chemicals
☐ Instruments & Controls

☐ BASIC INDUSTRIES
☐ Consumer
☐ Distribution
☐ Manufacturing
☐ Retail
☐ Service
☐ Wholesale
☐ SPECIFIC INDUSTRIES
☐ Energy
☐ Environmental
☐ Financial
☐ Real Estate
☐ Transportation
☐ Publishing
☐ Food
☐ Franchises
☐ DIVERSIFIED
☒ MISCELLANEOUS

STAGE PREFERENCE

☒ EARLY STAGE
☐ Seed
☒ Start-up
☒ 1st Stage
☒ LATER STAGE
☒ 2nd Stage
☒ Mature
☐ Mezzanine
☐ LBO/MBO
☐ Turnaround
☐ INT'L EXPANSION
☐ WILL CONSIDER ALL
☐ VENTURE LEASING

Other Locations:

Affiliation:
Minimum Investment: Less than $1 Million
Capital Under Management: Less than $100 Million

GEOGRAPHIC PREF

☐ East Coast
☐ West Coast
☐ Northeast
☐ Mid Atlantic
☐ Gulf States
☐ Northwest
☐ Southeast
☐ Southwest
☐ Midwest
☐ Central
☐ Local to Office
☐ Other Geo Pref

KOCO CAPITAL COMPANY, LP

111 Radio Circle
Mount Kisco NY 10549

Phone (914) 242-2324   Fax (914) 244-3985

PROFESSIONALS	TITLE
Evan Wildstein	Principal

INDUSTRY PREFERENCE

☐ INFORMATION INDUSTRY
☐ Communications
☐ Computer Equipment
☐ Computer Services
☐ Computer Components
☐ Computer Entertainment
☐ Computer Education
☐ Information Technologies
☐ Computer Media
☐ Software
☐ Internet
☐ MEDICAL/HEALTHCARE
☐ Biotechnology
☐ Healthcare Services
☐ Life Sciences
☐ Medical Products
☐ INDUSTRIAL
☐ Advanced Materials
☐ Chemicals
☐ Instruments & Controls

☐ BASIC INDUSTRIES
☐ Consumer
☐ Distribution
☐ Manufacturing
☐ Retail
☐ Service
☐ Wholesale
☐ SPECIFIC INDUSTRIES
☐ Energy
☐ Environmental
☐ Financial
☐ Real Estate
☐ Transportation
☐ Publishing
☐ Food
☐ Franchises
☒ DIVERSIFIED
☐ MISCELLANEOUS

STAGE PREFERENCE

☒ EARLY STAGE
☐ Seed
☐ Start-up
☒ 1st Stage
☒ LATER STAGE
☒ 2nd Stage
☒ Mature
☒ Mezzanine
☒ LBO/MBO
☐ Turnaround
☐ INT'L EXPANSION
☐ WILL CONSIDER ALL
☐ VENTURE LEASING

SBIC
Other Locations:

Affiliation:
Minimum Investment: $1 Million or more
Capital Under Management: Less than $100 Million

GEOGRAPHIC PREF

☐ East Coast
☐ West Coast
☐ Northeast
☐ Mid Atlantic
☐ Gulf States
☐ Northwest
☐ Southeast
☐ Southwest
☐ Midwest
☐ Central
☐ Local to Office
☐ Other Geo Pref

MCCOWN DE LEEUW AND COMPANY

65 East 55th Street
New York NY 10022

Phone (212) 355-5500   Fax (212) 355-6283

PROFESSIONALS	TITLE
David De Leeuw	Managing Director
David E. King	Managing Director

INDUSTRY PREFERENCE

- ☐ INFORMATION INDUSTRY
- ☐ Communications
- ☐ Computer Equipment
- ☐ Computer Services
- ☐ Computer Components
- ☐ Computer Entertainment
- ☐ Computer Education
- ☐ Information Technologies
- ☐ Computer Media
- ☐ Software
- ☐ Internet
- ☐ MEDICAL/HEALTHCARE
- ☐ Biotechnology
- ☐ Healthcare Services
- ☐ Life Sciences
- ☐ Medical Products
- ☐ INDUSTRIAL
- ☐ Advanced Materials
- ☐ Chemicals
- ☐ Instruments & Controls

- ☒ BASIC INDUSTRIES
- ☒ Consumer
- ☒ Distribution
- ☒ Manufacturing
- ☒ Retail
- ☒ Service
- ☐ Wholesale
- ☐ SPECIFIC INDUSTRIES
- ☐ Energy
- ☐ Environmental
- ☐ Financial
- ☐ Real Estate
- ☐ Transportation
- ☐ Publishing
- ☐ Food
- ☐ Franchises
- ☒ DIVERSIFIED
- ☐ MISCELLANEOUS

STAGE PREFERENCE

- ☐ EARLY STAGE
- ☐ Seed
- ☐ Start-up
- ☐ 1st Stage
- ☒ LATER STAGE
- ☒ 2nd Stage
- ☒ Mature
- ☐ Mezzanine
- ☒ LBO/MBO
- ☒ Turnaround
- ☐ INT'L EXPANSION
- ☐ WILL CONSIDER ALL
- ☒ VENTURE LEASING

Other Locations: Menlo Park CA

Affiliation:
Minimum Investment: $1 Million or more
Capital Under Management: Over $500 Million

GEOGRAPHIC PREF

- ☐ East Coast
- ☐ West Coast
- ☐ Northeast
- ☐ Mid Atlantic
- ☐ Gulf States
- ☐ Northwest
- ☐ Southeast
- ☐ Southwest
- ☐ Midwest
- ☐ Central
- ☐ Local to Office
- ☐ Other Geo Pref

MEDALLION FUNDING CORPORATION

437 Madison Avenue
New York NY 10022

Phone (212) 328-2100   Fax (212) 328-2125

PROFESSIONALS	TITLE
Alvin Murstein	President

INDUSTRY PREFERENCE

- ☐ INFORMATION INDUSTRY
- ☐ Communications
- ☐ Computer Equipment
- ☐ Computer Services
- ☐ Computer Components
- ☐ Computer Entertainment
- ☐ Computer Education
- ☐ Information Technologies
- ☐ Computer Media
- ☐ Software
- ☐ Internet
- ☐ MEDICAL/HEALTHCARE
- ☐ Biotechnology
- ☐ Healthcare Services
- ☐ Life Sciences
- ☐ Medical Products
- ☐ INDUSTRIAL
- ☐ Advanced Materials
- ☐ Chemicals
- ☐ Instruments & Controls

- ☒ BASIC INDUSTRIES
- ☐ Consumer
- ☐ Distribution
- ☐ Manufacturing
- ☒ Retail
- ☒ Service
- ☐ Wholesale
- ☐ SPECIFIC INDUSTRIES
- ☐ Energy
- ☐ Environmental
- ☐ Financial
- ☐ Real Estate
- ☐ Transportation
- ☐ Publishing
- ☐ Food
- ☐ Franchises
- ☒ DIVERSIFIED
- ☐ MISCELLANEOUS

STAGE PREFERENCE

- ☐ EARLY STAGE
- ☐ Seed
- ☐ Start-up
- ☐ 1st Stage
- ☒ LATER STAGE
- ☒ 2nd Stage
- ☒ Mature
- ☒ Mezzanine
- ☒ LBO/MBO
- ☐ Turnaround
- ☐ INT'L EXPANSION
- ☐ WILL CONSIDER ALL
- ☐ VENTURE LEASING

SSBIC
Other Locations:

Affiliation:
Minimum Investment: $1 Million or more
Capital Under Management: Less than $100 Million

GEOGRAPHIC PREF

- ☐ East Coast
- ☐ West Coast
- ☒ Northeast
- ☐ Mid Atlantic
- ☐ Gulf States
- ☐ Northwest
- ☐ Southeast
- ☐ Southwest
- ☐ Midwest
- ☐ Central
- ☐ Local to Office
- ☐ Other Geo Pref

MERCURY CAPITAL, LP

153 East 53rd
49th Floor
New York NY 10022

Phone (212) 838-0888   Fax (212) 759-3897

PROFESSIONALS	TITLE
David W. Elenowitz	Manager

INDUSTRY PREFERENCE

- ☐ INFORMATION INDUSTRY
- ☐ Communications
- ☐ Computer Equipment
- ☐ Computer Services
- ☐ Computer Components
- ☐ Computer Entertainment
- ☐ Computer Education
- ☐ Information Technologies
- ☐ Computer Media
- ☐ Software
- ☐ Internet
- ☐ MEDICAL/HEALTHCARE
- ☐ Biotechnology
- ☐ Healthcare Services
- ☐ Life Sciences
- ☐ Medical Products
- ☐ INDUSTRIAL
- ☐ Advanced Materials
- ☐ Chemicals
- ☐ Instruments & Controls

- ☒ BASIC INDUSTRIES
- ☐ Consumer
- ☒ Distribution
- ☒ Manufacturing
- ☐ Retail
- ☒ Service
- ☐ Wholesale
- ☐ SPECIFIC INDUSTRIES
- ☐ Energy
- ☐ Environmental
- ☐ Financial
- ☐ Real Estate
- ☐ Transportation
- ☐ Publishing
- ☐ Food
- ☐ Franchises
- ☒ DIVERSIFIED
- ☐ MISCELLANEOUS

STAGE PREFERENCE

- ☐ EARLY STAGE
- ☐ Seed
- ☐ Start-up
- ☐ 1st Stage
- ☒ LATER STAGE
- ☒ 2nd Stage
- ☒ Mature
- ☒ Mezzanine
- ☒ LBO/MBO
- ☐ Turnaround
- ☐ INT'L EXPANSION
- ☐ WILL CONSIDER ALL
- ☐ VENTURE LEASING

SBIC
Other Locations:

Affiliation:
Minimum Investment: $1 Million or more
Capital Under Management: Less than $100 Million

GEOGRAPHIC PREF

- ☐ East Coast
- ☐ West Coast
- ☐ Northeast
- ☐ Mid Atlantic
- ☐ Gulf States
- ☐ Northwest
- ☐ Southeast
- ☐ Southwest
- ☐ Midwest
- ☐ Central
- ☐ Local to Office
- ☐ Other Geo Pref

MORGAN STANLEY DEAN WITTER VENTURE PARTNERS

1221 Avenue of the Americas
33th Floor
New York NY 10020-1104

Phone (212) 762-7900   Fax (212) 762-8424

PROFESSIONALS	TITLE
Guy L. de Chazal	General Partner
M. Fazle Husain	Vice President

INDUSTRY PREFERENCE

- ☒ INFORMATION INDUSTRY
- ☒ Communications
- ☒ Computer Equipment
- ☒ Computer Services
- ☒ Computer Components
- ☐ Computer Entertainment
- ☒ Computer Education
- ☒ Information Technologies
- ☒ Computer Media
- ☒ Software
- ☒ Internet
- ☒ MEDICAL/HEALTHCARE
- ☒ Biotechnology
- ☒ Healthcare Services
- ☒ Life Sciences
- ☒ Medical Products
- ☒ INDUSTRIAL
- ☐ Advanced Materials
- ☐ Chemicals
- ☒ Instruments & Controls

- ☒ BASIC INDUSTRIES
- ☒ Consumer
- ☐ Distribution
- ☐ Manufacturing
- ☒ Retail
- ☒ Service
- ☐ Wholesale
- ☐ SPECIFIC INDUSTRIES
- ☐ Energy
- ☐ Environmental
- ☐ Financial
- ☐ Real Estate
- ☐ Transportation
- ☐ Publishing
- ☐ Food
- ☐ Franchises
- ☒ DIVERSIFIED
- ☐ MISCELLANEOUS

STAGE PREFERENCE

- ☐ EARLY STAGE
- ☐ Seed
- ☐ Start-up
- ☐ 1st Stage
- ☒ LATER STAGE
- ☒ 2nd Stage
- ☒ Mature
- ☒ Mezzanine
- ☒ LBO/MBO
- ☐ Turnaround
- ☐ INT'L EXPANSION
- ☐ WILL CONSIDER ALL
- ☐ VENTURE LEASING

Other Locations: Menlo Park CA

Affiliation: Morgan Stanley & Co.
Minimum Investment: $1 Million or more
Capital Under Management: $100 to $500 Million

GEOGRAPHIC PREF

- ☐ East Coast
- ☐ West Coast
- ☐ Northeast
- ☐ Mid Atlantic
- ☐ Gulf States
- ☐ Northwest
- ☐ Southeast
- ☐ Southwest
- ☐ Midwest
- ☐ Central
- ☐ Local to Office
- ☐ Other Geo Pref

NATIONAL BANK OF KUWAIT

299 Park Avenue
17th Floor
New York NY 10171

Phone (212) 303-9800   Fax (212) 688-1362

PROFESSIONALS	TITLE
Jason Bross	Managing Director

INDUSTRY PREFERENCE

☒	INFORMATION INDUSTRY	☒	BASIC INDUSTRIES
☒	Communications	☒	Consumer
☒	Computer Equipment	☒	Distribution
☒	Computer Services	☐	Manufacturing
☒	Computer Components	☐	Retail
☐	Computer Entertainment	☐	Service
☒	Computer Education	☐	Wholesale
☒	Information Technologies	☐	SPECIFIC INDUSTRIES
☒	Computer Media	☐	Energy
☒	Software	☐	Environmental
☒	Internet	☐	Financial
☒	MEDICAL/HEALTHCARE	☐	Real Estate
☐	Biotechnology	☐	Transportation
☒	Healthcare Services	☐	Publishing
☐	Life Sciences	☐	Food
☒	Medical Products	☐	Franchises
☒	INDUSTRIAL	☒	DIVERSIFIED
☒	Advanced Materials	☒	MISCELLANEOUS
☒	Chemicals		
☒	Instruments & Controls		

STAGE PREFERENCE

☐	EARLY STAGE
☐	Seed
☐	Start-up
☐	1st Stage
☒	LATER STAGE
☒	2nd Stage
☒	Mature
☒	Mezzanine
☒	LBO/MBO
☒	Turnaround
☐	INT'L EXPANSION
☐	WILL CONSIDER ALL
☒	VENTURE LEASING

Other Locations:

Affiliation:
Minimum Investment: $1 Million or more
Capital Under Management: $100 to $500 Million

GEOGRAPHIC PREF

☐	East Coast
☐	West Coast
☐	Northeast
☐	Mid Atlantic
☐	Gulf States
☐	Northwest
☐	Southeast
☐	Southwest
☐	Midwest
☐	Central
☐	Local to Office
☐	Other Geo Pref

NAZEM AND COMPANY

645 Madison Avenue
12th Floor
New York NY 10022

Phone (212) 371-7900   Fax (212) 371-2150

PROFESSIONALS	TITLE
Fred F. Nazem	Managing Partner
Jeffrey M. Krauss	General Partner
Richard J. Racine	General Partner
Phillip E. Barek	General Partner

INDUSTRY PREFERENCE

☒	INFORMATION INDUSTRY	☐	BASIC INDUSTRIES
☒	Communications	☐	Consumer
☒	Computer Equipment	☐	Distribution
☒	Computer Services	☐	Manufacturing
☒	Computer Components	☐	Retail
☒	Computer Entertainment	☐	Service
☐	Computer Education	☐	Wholesale
☒	Information Technologies	☐	SPECIFIC INDUSTRIES
☒	Computer Media	☐	Energy
☒	Software	☐	Environmental
☒	Internet	☐	Financial
☒	MEDICAL/HEALTHCARE	☐	Real Estate
☒	Biotechnology	☐	Transportation
☒	Healthcare Services	☐	Publishing
☒	Life Sciences	☐	Food
☒	Medical Products	☐	Franchises
☒	INDUSTRIAL	☒	DIVERSIFIED
☒	Advanced Materials	☐	MISCELLANEOUS
☒	Chemicals		
☒	Instruments & Controls		

STAGE PREFERENCE

☒	EARLY STAGE
☒	Seed
☒	Start-up
☒	1st Stage
☒	LATER STAGE
☒	2nd Stage
☒	Mature
☒	Mezzanine
☒	LBO/MBO
☒	Turnaround
☐	INT'L EXPANSION
☐	WILL CONSIDER ALL
☒	VENTURE LEASING

Other Locations:

Affiliation:
Minimum Investment: Less than $1 Million
Capital Under Management: $100 to $500 Million

GEOGRAPHIC PREF

☐	East Coast
☐	West Coast
☐	Northeast
☐	Mid Atlantic
☐	Gulf States
☐	Northwest
☐	Southeast
☐	Southwest
☐	Midwest
☐	Central
☐	Local to Office
☐	Other Geo Pref

NEEDHAM CAPITAL SBIC II, LP

445 Park Avenue
New York NY 10022

Phone (212) 705-0297 Fax (212) 751-1450

PROFESSIONALS	TITLE
John Michaelson	General Partner
George A. Needham	General Partner
John J. Prior, Jr.	General Partner
Glen W. Albanese	Chief Financial Officer

INDUSTRY PREFERENCE

☒ INFORMATION INDUSTRY	☒ BASIC INDUSTRIES
☒ Communications	☒ Consumer
☐ Computer Equipment	☐ Distribution
☐ Computer Services	☐ Manufacturing
☐ Computer Components	☐ Retail
☐ Computer Entertainment	☐ Service
☐ Computer Education	☐ Wholesale
☒ Information Technologies	☒ SPECIFIC INDUSTRIES
☐ Computer Media	☐ Energy
☒ Software	☐ Environmental
☒ Internet	☐ Financial
☐ MEDICAL/HEALTHCARE	☐ Real Estate
☐ Biotechnology	☐ Transportation
☐ Healthcare Services	☐ Publishing
☐ Life Sciences	☐ Food
☐ Medical Products	☐ Franchises
☐ INDUSTRIAL	☒ DIVERSIFIED
☐ Advanced Materials	☒ MISCELLANEOUS
☐ Chemicals	Technology
☐ Instruments & Controls	

STAGE PREFERENCE

☐ EARLY STAGE
☐ Seed
☐ Start-up
☐ 1st Stage
☒ LATER STAGE
☒ 2nd Stage
☒ Mature
☒ Mezzanine
☒ LBO/MBO
☐ Turnaround
☐ INT'L EXPANSION
☐ WILL CONSIDER ALL
☐ VENTURE LEASING

SBIC
Other Locations:

Affiliation:
Minimum Investment: $1 Million or more
Capital Under Management: $100 to $500 Million

GEOGRAPHIC PREF

☐ East Coast
☐ West Coast
☐ Northeast
☐ Mid Atlantic
☐ Gulf States
☐ Northwest
☐ Southeast
☐ Southwest
☐ Midwest
☐ Central
☐ Local to Office
☐ Other Geo Pref

NEW YORK STATE SCIENCE & TECHNOLOGY FOUNDATION

30 South Pearl Street
Albany NY 12245

Phone (518) 292-5700 Fax (518) 292-5813

PROFESSIONALS	TITLE
Robert Malone	Program Manager

INDUSTRY PREFERENCE

☒ INFORMATION INDUSTRY	☐ BASIC INDUSTRIES
☒ Communications	☐ Consumer
☒ Computer Equipment	☐ Distribution
☒ Computer Services	☐ Manufacturing
☒ Computer Components	☐ Retail
☐ Computer Entertainment	☐ Service
☒ Computer Education	☐ Wholesale
☒ Information Technologies	☐ SPECIFIC INDUSTRIES
☒ Computer Media	☐ Energy
☒ Software	☐ Environmental
☒ Internet	☐ Financial
☒ MEDICAL/HEALTHCARE	☐ Real Estate
☒ Biotechnology	☐ Transportation
☒ Healthcare Services	☐ Publishing
☒ Life Sciences	☐ Food
☒ Medical Products	☐ Franchises
☒ INDUSTRIAL	☒ DIVERSIFIED
☒ Advanced Materials	☐ MISCELLANEOUS
☒ Chemicals	
☒ Instruments & Controls	

STAGE PREFERENCE

☒ EARLY STAGE
☒ Seed
☒ Start-up
☒ 1st Stage
☒ LATER STAGE
☒ 2nd Stage
☐ Mature
☐ Mezzanine
☐ LBO/MBO
☐ Turnaround
☐ INT'L EXPANSION
☐ WILL CONSIDER ALL
☐ VENTURE LEASING

Other Locations:

Affiliation: Corp. of Innovation & Development Prog.
Minimum Investment: Less than $1 Million
Capital Under Management: Less than $100 Million

GEOGRAPHIC PREF

☐ East Coast
☐ West Coast
☐ Northeast
☐ Mid Atlantic
☐ Gulf States
☐ Northwest
☐ Southeast
☐ Southwest
☐ Midwest
☐ Central
☐ Local to Office
☒ Other Geo Pref
NY

NORTHWOOD VENTURES

485 Underhill Boulevard
Suite 205
Syosset NY 11791

Phone (516) 364-5544   Fax (516) 364-0879

PROFESSIONALS	TITLE
Henry T. Wilson	Managing Director
Peter G. Schiff	President

INDUSTRY PREFERENCE

☒ INFORMATION INDUSTRY	☒ BASIC INDUSTRIES
☒ Communications	☒ Consumer
☐ Computer Equipment	☒ Distribution
☐ Computer Services	☒ Manufacturing
☐ Computer Components	☒ Retail
☐ Computer Entertainment	☒ Service
☒ Computer Education	☒ Wholesale
☐ Information Technologies	☒ SPECIFIC INDUSTRIES
☒ Computer Media	☐ Energy
☐ Software	☐ Environmental
☒ Internet	☒ Financial
☒ MEDICAL/HEALTHCARE	☐ Real Estate
☒ Biotechnology	☐ Transportation
☒ Healthcare Services	☐ Publishing
☒ Life Sciences	☐ Food
☒ Medical Products	☐ Franchises
☒ INDUSTRIAL	☒ DIVERSIFIED
☒ Advanced Materials	☐ MISCELLANEOUS
☒ Chemicals	
☒ Instruments & Controls	

STAGE PREFERENCE

☒ EARLY STAGE	
☐ Seed	
☐ Start-up	
☒ 1st Stage	
☒ LATER STAGE	
☒ 2nd Stage	
☒ Mature	
☒ Mezzanine	
☒ LBO/MBO	
☐ Turnaround	
☐ INT'L EXPANSION	
☐ WILL CONSIDER ALL	
☐ VENTURE LEASING	

Other Locations:

Affiliation:
Minimum Investment: $1 Million or more
Capital Under Management: $100 to $500 Million

GEOGRAPHIC PREF

☐ East Coast	
☐ West Coast	
☐ Northeast	
☐ Mid Atlantic	
☐ Gulf States	
☐ Northwest	
☐ Southeast	
☐ Southwest	
☐ Midwest	
☐ Central	
☐ Local to Office	
☐ Other Geo Pref	

NORWOOD VENTURE CORP.

1430 Broadway
Suite 1607
New York NY 10018

Phone (212) 869-5075   Fax (212) 869-5331

PROFESSIONALS	TITLE
Mark R. Littell	President
Robert E. LaBlanc	Director
Mark B. Anderson	Director

INDUSTRY PREFERENCE

☐ INFORMATION INDUSTRY	☐ BASIC INDUSTRIES
☐ Communications	☐ Consumer
☐ Computer Equipment	☐ Distribution
☐ Computer Services	☐ Manufacturing
☐ Computer Components	☐ Retail
☐ Computer Entertainment	☐ Service
☐ Computer Education	☐ Wholesale
☐ Information Technologies	☐ SPECIFIC INDUSTRIES
☐ Computer Media	☐ Energy
☐ Software	☐ Environmental
☐ Internet	☐ Financial
☐ MEDICAL/HEALTHCARE	☐ Real Estate
☐ Biotechnology	☐ Transportation
☐ Healthcare Services	☐ Publishing
☐ Life Sciences	☐ Food
☐ Medical Products	☐ Franchises
☐ INDUSTRIAL	☒ DIVERSIFIED
☐ Advanced Materials	☐ MISCELLANEOUS
☐ Chemicals	
☐ Instruments & Controls	

STAGE PREFERENCE

☐ EARLY STAGE	
☐ Seed	
☐ Start-up	
☒ 1st Stage	
☒ LATER STAGE	
☒ 2nd Stage	
☒ Mature	
☒ Mezzanine	
☒ LBO/MBO	
☐ Turnaround	
☐ INT'L EXPANSION	
☐ WILL CONSIDER ALL	
☐ VENTURE LEASING	

SBIC
Other Locations:

Affiliation:
Minimum Investment: $1 Million or more
Capital Under Management: Less than $100 Million

GEOGRAPHIC PREF

☐ East Coast	
☐ West Coast	
☐ Northeast	
☐ Mid Atlantic	
☐ Gulf States	
☐ Northwest	
☐ Southeast	
☐ Southwest	
☐ Midwest	
☐ Central	
☐ Local to Office	
☐ Other Geo Pref	

NYBDC CAPITAL CORP.

41 State Street
P.O. Box 738
Albany NY 12207

Phone (518) 463-2268   Fax (518) 463-0240

PROFESSIONALS	TITLE
Robert W. Lazar	President

INDUSTRY PREFERENCE

☐ INFORMATION INDUSTRY
☐ Communications
☐ Computer Equipment
☐ Computer Services
☐ Computer Components
☐ Computer Entertainment
☐ Computer Education
☐ Information Technologies
☐ Computer Media
☐ Software
☐ Internet
☐ MEDICAL/HEALTHCARE
☐ Biotechnology
☐ Healthcare Services
☐ Life Sciences
☐ Medical Products
☐ INDUSTRIAL
☐ Advanced Materials
☐ Chemicals
☐ Instruments & Controls

☐ BASIC INDUSTRIES
☐ Consumer
☐ Distribution
☐ Manufacturing
☐ Retail
☐ Service
☐ Wholesale
☐ SPECIFIC INDUSTRIES
☐ Energy
☐ Environmental
☐ Financial
☐ Real Estate
☐ Transportation
☐ Publishing
☐ Food
☐ Franchises
☒ DIVERSIFIED
☐ MISCELLANEOUS

STAGE PREFERENCE

☒ EARLY STAGE
☒ Seed
☒ Start-up
☒ 1st Stage
☒ LATER STAGE
☐ 2nd Stage
☒ Mature
☒ Mezzanine
☒ LBO/MBO
☐ Turnaround
☐ INT'L EXPANSION
☐ WILL CONSIDER ALL
☐ VENTURE LEASING

SBIC
Other Locations:

Affiliation:
Minimum Investment: Less than $1 Million
Capital Under Management: Less than $100 Million

GEOGRAPHIC PREF

☐ East Coast
☐ West Coast
☐ Northeast
☐ Mid Atlantic
☐ Gulf States
☐ Northwest
☐ Southeast
☐ Southwest
☐ Midwest
☐ Central
☐ Local to Office
☒ Other Geo Pref
NY

PARIBAS PRINCIPAL INCORPORATED

787 Seventh Avenue
33rd Floor
New York NY 10019

Phone (212) 841-2000   Fax (212) 841-3558

PROFESSIONALS	TITLE
Steven Alexander	President

INDUSTRY PREFERENCE

☒ INFORMATION INDUSTRY
☒ Communications
☐ Computer Equipment
☐ Computer Services
☐ Computer Components
☐ Computer Entertainment
☐ Computer Education
☐ Information Technologies
☒ Computer Media
☐ Software
☐ Internet
☒ MEDICAL/HEALTHCARE
☐ Biotechnology
☒ Healthcare Services
☐ Life Sciences
☐ Medical Products
☐ INDUSTRIAL
☐ Advanced Materials
☐ Chemicals
☐ Instruments & Controls

☒ BASIC INDUSTRIES
☐ Consumer
☐ Distribution
☒ Manufacturing
☐ Retail
☒ Service
☐ Wholesale
☐ SPECIFIC INDUSTRIES
☐ Energy
☐ Environmental
☐ Financial
☐ Real Estate
☐ Transportation
☐ Publishing
☐ Food
☐ Franchises
☒ DIVERSIFIED
☐ MISCELLANEOUS

STAGE PREFERENCE

☐ EARLY STAGE
☐ Seed
☐ Start-up
☐ 1st Stage
☒ LATER STAGE
☒ 2nd Stage
☒ Mature
☒ Mezzanine
☒ LBO/MBO
☐ Turnaround
☐ INT'L EXPANSION
☐ WILL CONSIDER ALL
☐ VENTURE LEASING

SBIC
Other Locations:

Affiliation:
Minimum Investment: $1 Million or more
Capital Under Management: Less than $100 Million

GEOGRAPHIC PREF

☐ East Coast
☐ West Coast
☐ Northeast
☐ Mid Atlantic
☐ Gulf States
☐ Northwest
☐ Southeast
☐ Southwest
☐ Midwest
☐ Central
☐ Local to Office
☐ Other Geo Pref

PATRICOF AND COMPANY

445 Park Avenue
New York NY 10022

Phone (212) 753-6300   Fax (212) 319-6155

PROFESSIONALS	TITLE
Alan J. Patricof	Co-Chairman
Patricia M. Cloherty	Co-Chairman
Robert Chefitz	Managing Director
David Landau	Managing Director

INDUSTRY PREFERENCE

- ☒ INFORMATION INDUSTRY
- ☒ Communications
- ☒ Computer Equipment
- ☒ Computer Services
- ☒ Computer Components
- ☐ Computer Entertainment
- ☒ Computer Education
- ☒ Information Technologies
- ☒ Computer Media
- ☒ Software
- ☒ Internet
- ☒ MEDICAL/HEALTHCARE
- ☒ Biotechnology
- ☒ Healthcare Services
- ☒ Life Sciences
- ☒ Medical Products
- ☒ INDUSTRIAL
- ☒ Advanced Materials
- ☒ Chemicals
- ☒ Instruments & Controls

- ☒ BASIC INDUSTRIES
- ☒ Consumer
- ☐ Distribution
- ☒ Manufacturing
- ☒ Retail
- ☒ Service
- ☐ Wholesale
- ☒ SPECIFIC INDUSTRIES
- ☒ Energy
- ☒ Environmental
- ☒ Financial
- ☐ Real Estate
- ☐ Transportation
- ☐ Publishing
- ☐ Food
- ☐ Franchises
- ☒ DIVERSIFIED
- ☐ MISCELLANEOUS

STAGE PREFERENCE

- ☒ EARLY STAGE
- ☒ Seed
- ☒ Start-up
- ☒ 1st Stage
- ☒ LATER STAGE
- ☒ 2nd Stage
- ☒ Mature
- ☒ Mezzanine
- ☒ LBO/MBO
- ☒ Turnaround
- ☐ INT'L EXPANSION
- ☐ WILL CONSIDER ALL
- ☒ VENTURE LEASING

Other Locations: Palo Alto CA, Radnor PA

Affiliation: MMG Patricof & Co., Inc.
Minimum Investment: Less than $1 Million
Capital Under Management: Over $500 Million

GEOGRAPHIC PREF

- ☐ East Coast
- ☐ West Coast
- ☐ Northeast
- ☐ Mid Atlantic
- ☐ Gulf States
- ☐ Northwest
- ☐ Southeast
- ☐ Southwest
- ☐ Midwest
- ☐ Central
- ☐ Local to Office
- ☐ Other Geo Pref

PHILLIPS-SMITH SPECIALTY RETAIL GROUP

7 Locust Lane
Bronxville NY 10708

Phone (914) 961-0407   Fax (914) 961-6169

PROFESSIONALS	TITLE
Craig Foley	Principal

INDUSTRY PREFERENCE

- ☒ INFORMATION INDUSTRY
- ☐ Communications
- ☐ Computer Equipment
- ☐ Computer Services
- ☐ Computer Components
- ☐ Computer Entertainment
- ☐ Computer Education
- ☐ Information Technologies
- ☐ Computer Media
- ☐ Software
- ☒ Internet
- ☐ MEDICAL/HEALTHCARE
- ☐ Biotechnology
- ☐ Healthcare Services
- ☐ Life Sciences
- ☐ Medical Products
- ☐ INDUSTRIAL
- ☐ Advanced Materials
- ☐ Chemicals
- ☐ Instruments & Controls

- ☒ BASIC INDUSTRIES
- ☐ Consumer
- ☐ Distribution
- ☐ Manufacturing
- ☒ Retail
- ☐ Service
- ☐ Wholesale
- ☒ SPECIFIC INDUSTRIES
- ☐ Energy
- ☐ Environmental
- ☐ Financial
- ☐ Real Estate
- ☐ Transportation
- ☐ Publishing
- ☐ Food
- ☐ Franchises
- ☒ DIVERSIFIED
- ☐ MISCELLANEOUS
  - e-Commerce

STAGE PREFERENCE

- ☒ EARLY STAGE
- ☒ Seed
- ☒ Start-up
- ☒ 1st Stage
- ☒ LATER STAGE
- ☒ 2nd Stage
- ☒ Mature
- ☒ Mezzanine
- ☒ LBO/MBO
- ☐ Turnaround
- ☐ INT'L EXPANSION
- ☐ WILL CONSIDER ALL
- ☐ VENTURE LEASING

Other Locations: Addison TX, Colorado Springs CO

Affiliation:
Minimum Investment: $1 Million or more
Capital Under Management: $100 to $500 Million

GEOGRAPHIC PREF

- ☐ East Coast
- ☐ West Coast
- ☐ Northeast
- ☐ Mid Atlantic
- ☐ Gulf States
- ☐ Northwest
- ☐ Southeast
- ☐ Southwest
- ☐ Midwest
- ☐ Central
- ☐ Local to Office
- ☐ Other Geo Pref

PROSPECT STREET VENTURES

10 East 40th Street
44th Floor
New York NY 10016

Phone (212) 448-0702   Fax (212) 448-9652

PROFESSIONALS	TITLE
John Barry	Managing Partner

INDUSTRY PREFERENCE

- ☒ INFORMATION INDUSTRY
- ☒ Communications
- ☒ Computer Equipment
- ☒ Computer Services
- ☒ Computer Components
- ☒ Computer Entertainment
- ☒ Computer Education
- ☒ Information Technologies
- ☒ Computer Media
- ☒ Software
- ☒ Internet
- ☐ MEDICAL/HEALTHCARE
- ☐ Biotechnology
- ☐ Healthcare Services
- ☐ Life Sciences
- ☐ Medical Products
- ☒ INDUSTRIAL
- ☒ Advanced Materials
- ☐ Chemicals
- ☒ Instruments & Controls

- ☒ BASIC INDUSTRIES
- ☒ Consumer
- ☒ Distribution
- ☒ Manufacturing
- ☒ Retail
- ☒ Service
- ☒ Wholesale
- ☒ SPECIFIC INDUSTRIES
- ☒ Energy
- ☒ Environmental
- ☒ Financial
- ☐ Real Estate
- ☒ Transportation
- ☐ Publishing
- ☐ Food
- ☐ Franchises
- ☒ DIVERSIFIED
- ☐ MISCELLANEOUS

STAGE PREFERENCE

- ☒ EARLY STAGE
- ☒ Seed
- ☒ Start-up
- ☒ 1st Stage
- ☒ LATER STAGE
- ☒ 2nd Stage
- ☒ Mature
- ☒ Mezzanine
- ☒ LBO/MBO
- ☒ Turnaround
- ☐ INT'L EXPANSION
- ☐ WILL CONSIDER ALL
- ☒ VENTURE LEASING

SBIC
Other Locations:

Affiliation:
Minimum Investment: $1 Million or more
Capital Under Management: $100 to $500 Million

GEOGRAPHIC PREF

- ☐ East Coast
- ☐ West Coast
- ☐ Northeast
- ☐ Mid Atlantic
- ☐ Gulf States
- ☐ Northwest
- ☐ Southeast
- ☐ Southwest
- ☐ Midwest
- ☐ Central
- ☐ Local to Office
- ☐ Other Geo Pref

RADIUS VENTURES, LLC

1 Rockefeller Plaza
Suite 920
New York NY 10020

Phone (212) 897-7778   Fax (212) 397-2656

PROFESSIONALS	TITLE
Jordan S. Davis	Managing Partner
Daniel C. Lubin	Managing Partner

INDUSTRY PREFERENCE

- ☒ INFORMATION INDUSTRY
- ☐ Communications
- ☐ Computer Equipment
- ☐ Computer Services
- ☐ Computer Components
- ☐ Computer Entertainment
- ☐ Computer Education
- ☒ Information Technologies
- ☐ Computer Media
- ☒ Software
- ☒ Internet
- ☒ MEDICAL/HEALTHCARE
- ☒ Biotechnology
- ☒ Healthcare Services
- ☒ Life Sciences
- ☒ Medical Products
- ☒ INDUSTRIAL
- ☐ Advanced Materials
- ☒ Chemicals
- ☐ Instruments & Controls

- ☐ BASIC INDUSTRIES
- ☐ Consumer
- ☐ Distribution
- ☐ Manufacturing
- ☐ Retail
- ☐ Service
- ☐ Wholesale
- ☐ SPECIFIC INDUSTRIES
- ☐ Energy
- ☐ Environmental
- ☐ Financial
- ☐ Real Estate
- ☐ Transportation
- ☐ Publishing
- ☐ Food
- ☐ Franchises
- ☒ DIVERSIFIED
- ☒ MISCELLANEOUS

STAGE PREFERENCE

- ☒ EARLY STAGE
- ☒ Seed
- ☒ Start-up
- ☒ 1st Stage
- ☒ LATER STAGE
- ☒ 2nd Stage
- ☐ Mature
- ☐ Mezzanine
- ☐ LBO/MBO
- ☐ Turnaround
- ☐ INT'L EXPANSION
- ☐ WILL CONSIDER ALL
- ☐ VENTURE LEASING

Other Locations:

Affiliation:
Minimum Investment: Less than $1 Million
Capital Under Management: Less than $100 Million

GEOGRAPHIC PREF

- ☐ East Coast
- ☐ West Coast
- ☐ Northeast
- ☐ Mid Atlantic
- ☐ Gulf States
- ☐ Northwest
- ☐ Southeast
- ☐ Southwest
- ☐ Midwest
- ☐ Central
- ☐ Local to Office
- ☐ Other Geo Pref

RAND CAPITAL CORP.

**2200 Rand Building
Buffalo NY 14203**

Phone (716) 853-0802   Fax (716) 854-8480

PROFESSIONALS	TITLE
Allen F. Grum	President

INDUSTRY PREFERENCE

- ☒ INFORMATION INDUSTRY
- ☒ Communications
- ☒ Computer Equipment
- ☒ Computer Services
- ☒ Computer Components
- ☐ Computer Entertainment
- ☒ Computer Education
- ☒ Information Technologies
- ☒ Computer Media
- ☒ Software
- ☒ Internet
- ☒ MEDICAL/HEALTHCARE
- ☒ Biotechnology
- ☒ Healthcare Services
- ☒ Life Sciences
- ☒ Medical Products
- ☒ INDUSTRIAL
- ☒ Advanced Materials
- ☒ Chemicals
- ☒ Instruments & Controls

- ☐ BASIC INDUSTRIES
- ☐ Consumer
- ☐ Distribution
- ☐ Manufacturing
- ☐ Retail
- ☐ Service
- ☐ Wholesale
- ☒ SPECIFIC INDUSTRIES
- ☐ Energy
- ☐ Environmental
- ☒ Financial
- ☐ Real Estate
- ☐ Transportation
- ☐ Publishing
- ☐ Food
- ☐ Franchises
- ☒ DIVERSIFIED
- ☐ MISCELLANEOUS

STAGE PREFERENCE

- ☒ EARLY STAGE
- ☐ Seed
- ☐ Start-up
- ☒ 1st Stage
- ☒ LATER STAGE
- ☒ 2nd Stage
- ☐ Mature
- ☒ Mezzanine
- ☒ LBO/MBO
- ☐ Turnaround
- ☐ INT'L EXPANSION
- ☐ WILL CONSIDER ALL
- ☐ VENTURE LEASING

Other Locations:

Affiliation:
Minimum Investment: Less than $1 Million
Capital Under Management: Less than $100 Million

GEOGRAPHIC PREF

- ☐ East Coast
- ☐ West Coast
- ☒ Northeast
- ☐ Mid Atlantic
- ☐ Gulf States
- ☐ Northwest
- ☐ Southeast
- ☐ Southwest
- ☐ Midwest
- ☐ Central
- ☐ Local to Office
- ☐ Other Geo Pref

REGENT CAPITAL PARTNERS

**505 Park Avenue
Suite 1700
New York NY 10022**

Phone (212) 735-9900   Fax (212) 735-9908

PROFESSIONALS	TITLE
Richard Hochman	
Nina McLemore	
J. Oliver Maggard	
Douglas Parker	

INDUSTRY PREFERENCE

- ☒ INFORMATION INDUSTRY
- ☒ Communications
- ☐ Computer Equipment
- ☐ Computer Services
- ☐ Computer Components
- ☒ Computer Entertainment
- ☐ Computer Education
- ☐ Information Technologies
- ☒ Computer Media
- ☐ Software
- ☐ Internet
- ☐ MEDICAL/HEALTHCARE
- ☐ Biotechnology
- ☐ Healthcare Services
- ☐ Life Sciences
- ☐ Medical Products
- ☐ INDUSTRIAL
- ☐ Advanced Materials
- ☐ Chemicals
- ☐ Instruments & Controls

- ☒ BASIC INDUSTRIES
- ☒ Consumer
- ☐ Distribution
- ☐ Manufacturing
- ☐ Retail
- ☐ Service
- ☐ Wholesale
- ☐ SPECIFIC INDUSTRIES
- ☐ Energy
- ☐ Environmental
- ☐ Financial
- ☐ Real Estate
- ☐ Transportation
- ☐ Publishing
- ☐ Food
- ☐ Franchises
- ☒ DIVERSIFIED
- ☒ MISCELLANEOUS

STAGE PREFERENCE

- ☐ EARLY STAGE
- ☐ Seed
- ☐ Start-up
- ☐ 1st Stage
- ☒ LATER STAGE
- ☒ 2nd Stage
- ☒ Mature
- ☒ Mezzanine
- ☒ LBO/MBO
- ☐ Turnaround
- ☐ INT'L EXPANSION
- ☐ WILL CONSIDER ALL
- ☐ VENTURE LEASING

SBIC
Other Locations:

Affiliation:
Minimum Investment: $1 Million or more
Capital Under Management: Less than $100 Million

GEOGRAPHIC PREF

- ☐ East Coast
- ☐ West Coast
- ☐ Northeast
- ☐ Mid Atlantic
- ☐ Gulf States
- ☐ Northwest
- ☐ Southeast
- ☐ Southwest
- ☐ Midwest
- ☐ Central
- ☐ Local to Office
- ☐ Other Geo Pref

REPRISE CAPITAL CORP.

400 Post Avenue
Westbury NY 11590

Phone (516) 997-2400   Fax (516) 338-2808

PROFESSIONALS	TITLE
Stanley Tulchin	Chairman
Norman Tulchin	President

INDUSTRY PREFERENCE

- ☐ INFORMATION INDUSTRY
- ☐ Communications
- ☐ Computer Equipment
- ☐ Computer Services
- ☐ Computer Components
- ☐ Computer Entertainment
- ☐ Computer Education
- ☐ Information Technologies
- ☐ Computer Media
- ☐ Software
- ☐ Internet
- ☐ MEDICAL/HEALTHCARE
- ☐ Biotechnology
- ☐ Healthcare Services
- ☐ Life Sciences
- ☐ Medical Products
- ☒ INDUSTRIAL
- ☒ Advanced Materials
- ☒ Chemicals
- ☒ Instruments & Controls

- ☒ BASIC INDUSTRIES
- ☒ Consumer
- ☐ Distribution
- ☒ Manufacturing
- ☒ Retail
- ☒ Service
- ☐ Wholesale
- ☒ SPECIFIC INDUSTRIES
- ☒ Energy
- ☒ Environmental
- ☒ Financial
- ☐ Real Estate
- ☐ Transportation
- ☐ Publishing
- ☐ Food
- ☐ Franchises
- ☒ DIVERSIFIED
- ☒ MISCELLANEOUS

STAGE PREFERENCE

- ☐ EARLY STAGE
- ☐ Seed
- ☐ Start-up
- ☐ 1st Stage
- ☒ LATER STAGE
- ☐ 2nd Stage
- ☐ Mature
- ☐ Mezzanine
- ☐ LBO/MBO
- ☒ Turnaround
- ☐ INT'L EXPANSION
- ☐ WILL CONSIDER ALL
- ☒ VENTURE LEASING

Other Locations:

Affiliation:
Minimum Investment: $1 Million or more
Capital Under Management: Less than $100 Million

GEOGRAPHIC PREF

- ☐ East Coast
- ☐ West Coast
- ☐ Northeast
- ☐ Mid Atlantic
- ☐ Gulf States
- ☐ Northwest
- ☐ Southeast
- ☐ Southwest
- ☐ Midwest
- ☐ Central
- ☐ Local to Office
- ☐ Other Geo Pref

ROTHSCHILD VENTURES

1251 Avenue of the Americas
51st Floor
New York NY 10020

Phone (212) 403-3500   Fax (212) 403-3652

PROFESSIONALS	TITLE
Sherri A. Croasdale	Partner

INDUSTRY PREFERENCE

- ☒ INFORMATION INDUSTRY
- ☒ Communications
- ☒ Computer Equipment
- ☒ Computer Services
- ☒ Computer Components
- ☐ Computer Entertainment
- ☒ Computer Education
- ☒ Information Technologies
- ☒ Computer Media
- ☒ Software
- ☒ Internet
- ☒ MEDICAL/HEALTHCARE
- ☒ Biotechnology
- ☒ Healthcare Services
- ☒ Life Sciences
- ☒ Medical Products
- ☒ INDUSTRIAL
- ☒ Advanced Materials
- ☒ Chemicals
- ☒ Instruments & Controls

- ☒ BASIC INDUSTRIES
- ☒ Consumer
- ☒ Distribution
- ☐ Manufacturing
- ☐ Retail
- ☐ Service
- ☐ Wholesale
- ☒ SPECIFIC INDUSTRIES
- ☒ Energy
- ☒ Environmental
- ☐ Financial
- ☐ Real Estate
- ☐ Transportation
- ☐ Publishing
- ☐ Food
- ☐ Franchises
- ☒ DIVERSIFIED
- ☐ MISCELLANEOUS

STAGE PREFERENCE

- ☒ EARLY STAGE
- ☒ Seed
- ☒ Start-up
- ☒ 1st Stage
- ☒ LATER STAGE
- ☒ 2nd Stage
- ☒ Mature
- ☒ Mezzanine
- ☒ LBO/MBO
- ☒ Turnaround
- ☐ INT'L EXPANSION
- ☐ WILL CONSIDER ALL
- ☒ VENTURE LEASING

Other Locations:

Affiliation: Rothschild Inc
Minimum Investment: Less than $1 Million
Capital Under Management: Less than $100 Million

GEOGRAPHIC PREF

- ☐ East Coast
- ☐ West Coast
- ☐ Northeast
- ☐ Mid Atlantic
- ☐ Gulf States
- ☐ Northwest
- ☐ Southeast
- ☐ Southwest
- ☐ Midwest
- ☐ Central
- ☐ Local to Office
- ☐ Other Geo Pref

SANDLER CAPITAL MANAGEMENT

767 5th Avenue, 45th Floor
New York NY 10153

Phone (212) 754-8100   Fax (212) 826-0280

PROFESSIONALS	TITLE
Harvey Sandler	Principal
Michael Morrocco	Principal

INDUSTRY PREFERENCE

☒ INFORMATION INDUSTRY	☒ BASIC INDUSTRIES
☒ Communications	☒ Consumer
☒ Computer Equipment	☐ Distribution
☒ Computer Services	☐ Manufacturing
☒ Computer Components	☐ Retail
☐ Computer Entertainment	☐ Service
☒ Computer Education	☐ Wholesale
☒ Information Technologies	☐ SPECIFIC INDUSTRIES
☒ Computer Media	☐ Energy
☒ Software	☐ Environmental
☒ Internet	☐ Financial
☐ MEDICAL/HEALTHCARE	☐ Real Estate
☐ Biotechnology	☐ Transportation
☐ Healthcare Services	☐ Publishing
☐ Life Sciences	☐ Food
☐ Medical Products	☐ Franchises
☐ INDUSTRIAL	☒ DIVERSIFIED
☐ Advanced Materials	☒ MISCELLANEOUS
☐ Chemicals	
☐ Instruments & Controls	

STAGE PREFERENCE

☒ EARLY STAGE
☒ Seed
☒ Start-up
☒ 1st Stage
☒ LATER STAGE
☒ 2nd Stage
☒ Mature
☒ Mezzanine
☒ LBO/MBO
☒ Turnaround
☐ INT'L EXPANSION
☐ WILL CONSIDER ALL
☒ VENTURE LEASING

Other Locations:

Affiliation:
Minimum Investment: Less than $1 Million
Capital Under Management: Over $500 Million

GEOGRAPHIC PREF

☐ East Coast
☐ West Coast
☐ Northeast
☐ Mid Atlantic
☐ Gulf States
☐ Northwest
☐ Southeast
☐ Southwest
☐ Midwest
☐ Central
☐ Local to Office
☐ Other Geo Pref

SENTINEL CAPITAL PARTNERS

777 Third Avenue
32nd Floor
New York NY 10017

Phone (212) 688-3100   Fax (212) 688-6513

PROFESSIONALS	TITLE
David Lobel	Founder
John McCormack	Co-founder
Eric Bommer	Vice President

INDUSTRY PREFERENCE

☒ INFORMATION INDUSTRY	☒ BASIC INDUSTRIES
☐ Communications	☒ Consumer
☐ Computer Equipment	☒ Distribution
☐ Computer Services	☒ Manufacturing
☐ Computer Components	☒ Retail
☐ Computer Entertainment	☒ Service
☐ Computer Education	☒ Wholesale
☐ Information Technologies	☐ SPECIFIC INDUSTRIES
☒ Computer Media	☐ Energy
☐ Software '	☐ Environmental
☐ Internet	☐ Financial
☐ MEDICAL/HEALTHCARE	☐ Real Estate
☐ Biotechnology	☐ Transportation
☐ Healthcare Services	☐ Publishing
☐ Life Sciences	☐ Food
☐ Medical Products	☐ Franchises
☐ INDUSTRIAL	☒ DIVERSIFIED
☐ Advanced Materials	☒ MISCELLANEOUS
☐ Chemicals	
☐ Instruments & Controls	

STAGE PREFERENCE

☐ EARLY STAGE
☐ Seed
☐ Start-up
☐ 1st Stage
☒ LATER STAGE
☐ 2nd Stage
☐ Mature
☒ Mezzanine
☒ LBO/MBO
☒ Turnaround
☐ INT'L EXPANSION
☐ WILL CONSIDER ALL
☒ VENTURE LEASING

Other Locations:

Affiliation:
Minimum Investment: $1 Million or more
Capital Under Management: $100 to $500 Million

GEOGRAPHIC PREF

☐ East Coast
☐ West Coast
☐ Northeast
☐ Mid Atlantic
☐ Gulf States
☐ Northwest
☐ Southeast
☐ Southwest
☐ Midwest
☐ Central
☐ Local to Office
☒ Other Geo Pref
   Canada

SITUATION VENTURES CORPORATION

56-20 59th Street
Maspeth NY 11378

Phone (718) 894-2000   Fax (718) 326-4642

PROFESSIONALS

Sam Hollander

TITLE

President

INDUSTRY PREFERENCE

- ☐ INFORMATION INDUSTRY
- ☐ Communications
- ☐ Computer Equipment
- ☐ Computer Services
- ☐ Computer Components
- ☐ Computer Entertainment
- ☐ Computer Education
- ☐ Information Technologies
- ☐ Computer Media
- ☐ Software
- ☐ Internet
- ☐ MEDICAL/HEALTHCARE
- ☐ Biotechnology
- ☐ Healthcare Services
- ☐ Life Sciences
- ☐ Medical Products
- ☐ INDUSTRIAL
- ☐ Advanced Materials
- ☐ Chemicals
- ☐ Instruments & Controls

- ☒ BASIC INDUSTRIES
- ☐ Consumer
- ☐ Distribution
- ☒ Manufacturing
- ☒ Retail
- ☒ Service
- ☐ Wholesale
- ☐ SPECIFIC INDUSTRIES
- ☐ Energy
- ☐ Environmental
- ☐ Financial
- ☐ Real Estate
- ☐ Transportation
- ☐ Publishing
- ☐ Food
- ☐ Franchises
- ☒ DIVERSIFIED
- ☐ MISCELLANEOUS

STAGE PREFERENCE

- ☒ EARLY STAGE
- ☐ Seed
- ☐ Start-up
- ☒ 1st Stage
- ☒ LATER STAGE
- ☒ 2nd Stage
- ☒ Mature
- ☒ Mezzanine
- ☒ LBO/MBO
- ☐ Turnaround
- ☐ INT'L EXPANSION
- ☐ WILL CONSIDER ALL
- ☐ VENTURE LEASING

SSBIC

Other Locations:

Affiliation:
Minimum Investment: Less than $1 Million
Capital Under Management: Less than $100 Million

GEOGRAPHIC PREF

- ☐ East Coast
- ☐ West Coast
- ☐ Northeast
- ☐ Mid Atlantic
- ☐ Gulf States
- ☐ Northwest
- ☐ Southeast
- ☐ Southwest
- ☐ Midwest
- ☐ Central
- ☐ Local to Office
- ☒ Other Geo Pref
  NY

SPROUT GROUP

277 Park Avenue
21st Floor
New York NY 10172

Phone (212) 892-3600   Fax (212) 892-3444

PROFESSIONALS

Janet A. Hickey

TITLE

General Partner

INDUSTRY PREFERENCE

- ☒ INFORMATION INDUSTRY
- ☒ Communications
- ☒ Computer Equipment
- ☒ Computer Services
- ☒ Computer Components
- ☐ Computer Entertainment
- ☒ Computer Education
- ☒ Information Technologies
- ☐ Computer Media
- ☒ Software
- ☒ Internet
- ☒ MEDICAL/HEALTHCARE
- ☒ Biotechnology
- ☒ Healthcare Services
- ☐ Life Sciences
- ☒ Medical Products
- ☒ INDUSTRIAL
- ☐ Advanced Materials
- ☒ Chemicals
- ☐ Instruments & Controls

- ☒ BASIC INDUSTRIES
- ☒ Consumer
- ☒ Distribution
- ☐ Manufacturing
- ☐ Retail
- ☒ Service
- ☒ Wholesale
- ☒ SPECIFIC INDUSTRIES
- ☐ Energy
- ☐ Environmental
- ☒ Financial
- ☐ Real Estate
- ☐ Transportation
- ☐ Publishing
- ☐ Food
- ☐ Franchises
- ☒ DIVERSIFIED
- ☐ MISCELLANEOUS

STAGE PREFERENCE

- ☒ EARLY STAGE
- ☒ Seed
- ☒ Start-up
- ☒ 1st Stage
- ☒ LATER STAGE
- ☒ 2nd Stage
- ☒ Mature
- ☒ Mezzanine
- ☒ LBO/MBO
- ☒ Turnaround
- ☐ INT'L EXPANSION
- ☐ WILL CONSIDER ALL
- ☒ VENTURE LEASING

Other Locations: Menlo Park CA

Affiliation: Donaldson, Lufkin & Jenrette, Inc.
Minimum Investment: $1 Million or more
Capital Under Management: Over $500 Million

GEOGRAPHIC PREF

- ☐ East Coast
- ☐ West Coast
- ☐ Northeast
- ☐ Mid Atlantic
- ☐ Gulf States
- ☐ Northwest
- ☐ Southeast
- ☐ Southwest
- ☐ Midwest
- ☐ Central
- ☐ Local to Office
- ☐ Other Geo Pref

STERLING / CARL MARKS CAPITAL, INC.

175 Great Neck Road
Suite 408
Great Neck NY 11021

Phone (516) 482-7374   Fax (516) 487-0781

PROFESSIONALS	TITLE
Harvey L. Granat	President

INDUSTRY PREFERENCE

☐	INFORMATION INDUSTRY	☒	BASIC INDUSTRIES
☐	Communications	☒	Consumer
☐	Computer Equipment	☒	Distribution
☐	Computer Services	☒	Manufacturing
☐	Computer Components	☒	Retail
☐	Computer Entertainment	☐	Service
☐	Computer Education	☐	Wholesale
☐	Information Technologies	☐	SPECIFIC INDUSTRIES
☐	Computer Media	☐	Energy
☐	Software	☐	Environmental
☐	Internet	☐	Financial
☐	MEDICAL/HEALTHCARE	☐	Real Estate
☐	Biotechnology	☐	Transportation
☐	Healthcare Services	☐	Publishing
☐	Life Sciences	☐	Food
☐	Medical Products	☐	Franchises
☐	INDUSTRIAL	☒	DIVERSIFIED
☐	Advanced Materials	☐	MISCELLANEOUS
☐	Chemicals		
☐	Instruments & Controls		

STAGE PREFERENCE

☐	EARLY STAGE
☐	Seed
☐	Start-up
☐	1st Stage
☒	LATER STAGE
☒	2nd Stage
☒	Mature
☒	Mezzanine
☒	LBO/MBO
☐	Turnaround
☐	INT'L EXPANSION
☐	WILL CONSIDER ALL
☐	VENTURE LEASING

SBIC
Other Locations:

Affiliation:
Minimum Investment: Less than $1 Million
Capital Under Management: Less than $100 Million

GEOGRAPHIC PREF

☐	East Coast
☐	West Coast
☒	Northeast
☐	Mid Atlantic
☐	Gulf States
☐	Northwest
☐	Southeast
☐	Southwest
☐	Midwest
☐	Central
☐	Local to Office
☐	Other Geo Pref

STOLBERG, MEEHAN & SCANO

767 Third Avenue
32nd Floor
New York NY 10017

Phone (212) 826-1110   Fax (212) 826-0371

PROFESSIONALS	TITLE
Mark Naylor	Partner
Matthew Meehan	Partner

INDUSTRY PREFERENCE

☒	INFORMATION INDUSTRY	☒	BASIC INDUSTRIES
☒	Communications	☒	Consumer
☒	Computer Equipment	☐	Distribution
☒	Computer Services	☐	Manufacturing
☒	Computer Components	☒	Retail
☐	Computer Entertainment	☐	Service
☒	Computer Education	☐	Wholesale
☒	Information Technologies	☐	SPECIFIC INDUSTRIES
☒	Computer Media	☐	Energy
☒	Software	☐	Environmental
☒	Internet	☐	Financial
☐	MEDICAL/HEALTHCARE	☐	Real Estate
☐	Biotechnology	☐	Transportation
☐	Healthcare Services	☐	Publishing
☐	Life Sciences	☐	Food
☐	Medical Products	☐	Franchises
☒	INDUSTRIAL	☒	DIVERSIFIED
☒	Advanced Materials	☒	MISCELLANEOUS
☒	Chemicals		
☒	Instruments & Controls		

STAGE PREFERENCE

☐	EARLY STAGE
☐	Seed
☐	Start-up
☐	1st Stage
☒	LATER STAGE
☒	2nd Stage
☐	Mature
☐	Mezzanine
☒	LBO/MBO
☒	Turnaround
☐	INT'L EXPANSION
☐	WILL CONSIDER ALL
☒	VENTURE LEASING

Other Locations:

Affiliation:
Minimum Investment: $1 Million or more
Capital Under Management: Less than $100 Million

GEOGRAPHIC PREF

☐	East Coast
☐	West Coast
☐	Northeast
☐	Mid Atlantic
☐	Gulf States
☐	Northwest
☐	Southeast
☐	Southwest
☐	Midwest
☐	Central
☐	Local to Office
☐	Other Geo Pref

STONEBRIDGE PARTNERS

50 Main Street, 9th Floor
White Plains NY 10606

Phone (914) 682-2285   Fax (914) 682-0834

PROFESSIONALS	TITLE
Michael Bruno	Partner
Harrison Wilson	Partner

INDUSTRY PREFERENCE

- ☐ INFORMATION INDUSTRY
- ☐ Communications
- ☐ Computer Equipment
- ☐ Computer Services
- ☐ Computer Components
- ☐ Computer Entertainment
- ☐ Computer Education
- ☐ Information Technologies
- ☐ Computer Media
- ☐ Software
- ☐ Internet
- ☒ MEDICAL/HEALTHCARE
- ☐ Biotechnology
- ☐ Healthcare Services
- ☐ Life Sciences
- ☒ Medical Products
- ☒ INDUSTRIAL
- ☒ Advanced Materials
- ☒ Chemicals
- ☒ Instruments & Controls

- ☒ BASIC INDUSTRIES
- ☒ Consumer
- ☐ Distribution
- ☐ Manufacturing
- ☐ Retail
- ☐ Service
- ☐ Wholesale
- ☐ SPECIFIC INDUSTRIES
- ☐ Energy
- ☐ Environmental
- ☐ Financial
- ☐ Real Estate
- ☐ Transportation
- ☐ Publishing
- ☐ Food
- ☐ Franchises
- ☒ DIVERSIFIED
- ☒ MISCELLANEOUS

STAGE PREFERENCE

- ☐ EARLY STAGE
- ☐ Seed
- ☐ Start-up
- ☐ 1st Stage
- ☒ LATER STAGE
- ☐ 2nd Stage
- ☐ Mature
- ☐ Mezzanine
- ☒ LBO/MBO
- ☐ Turnaround
- ☐ INT'L EXPANSION
- ☐ WILL CONSIDER ALL
- ☐ VENTURE LEASING

Other Locations:

Affiliation:
Minimum Investment: $1 Million or more
Capital Under Management: $100 to $500 Million

GEOGRAPHIC PREF

- ☐ East Coast
- ☐ West Coast
- ☐ Northeast
- ☐ Mid Atlantic
- ☐ Gulf States
- ☐ Northwest
- ☐ Southeast
- ☐ Southwest
- ☐ Midwest
- ☐ Central
- ☐ Local to Office
- ☐ Other Geo Pref

TICONDEROGA CAPITAL INC

410 Park Avenue
19th Floor
New York NY 10022

Phone (212) 515-2117   Fax (212) 515-2105

PROFESSIONALS	TITLE
Peter Leidel	Partner

INDUSTRY PREFERENCE

- ☐ INFORMATION INDUSTRY
- ☐ Communications
- ☐ Computer Equipment
- ☐ Computer Services
- ☐ Computer Components
- ☐ Computer Entertainment
- ☐ Computer Education
- ☐ Information Technologies
- ☐ Computer Media
- ☐ Software
- ☐ Internet
- ☐ MEDICAL/HEALTHCARE
- ☐ Biotechnology
- ☐ Healthcare Services
- ☐ Life Sciences
- ☐ Medical Products
- ☐ INDUSTRIAL
- ☐ Advanced Materials
- ☐ Chemicals
- ☐ Instruments & Controls

- ☐ BASIC INDUSTRIES
- ☐ Consumer
- ☐ Distribution
- ☐ Manufacturing
- ☐ Retail
- ☐ Service
- ☐ Wholesale
- ☒ SPECIFIC INDUSTRIES
- ☒ Energy
- ☐ Environmental
- ☐ Financial
- ☐ Real Estate
- ☐ Transportation
- ☐ Publishing
- ☐ Food
- ☐ Franchises
- ☐ DIVERSIFIED
- ☒ MISCELLANEOUS

STAGE PREFERENCE

- ☐ EARLY STAGE
- ☐ Seed
- ☐ Start-up
- ☐ 1st Stage
- ☒ LATER STAGE
- ☒ 2nd Stage
- ☐ Mature
- ☒ Mezzanine
- ☒ LBO/MBO
- ☐ Turnaround
- ☐ INT'L EXPANSION
- ☐ WILL CONSIDER ALL
- ☐ VENTURE LEASING

Other Locations: Wellesley MA , San Francisco CA

Affiliation:
Minimum Investment: $1 Million or more
Capital Under Management: $100 to $500 Million

GEOGRAPHIC PREF

- ☐ East Coast
- ☐ West Coast
- ☐ Northeast
- ☐ Mid Atlantic
- ☐ Gulf States
- ☐ Northwest
- ☐ Southeast
- ☐ Southwest
- ☐ Midwest
- ☐ Central
- ☐ Local to Office
- ☐ Other Geo Pref

TRANSCAP ASSOCIATES, INC.

11 Penn Plaza
Fifth Floor
New York NY 10001

Phone (212) 946-2888

PROFESSIONALS	TITLE
Paul Schuldiner	Managing Director

INDUSTRY PREFERENCE

☒ INFORMATION INDUSTRY	☒ BASIC INDUSTRIES
☒ Communications	☐ Consumer
☒ Computer Equipment	☒ Distribution
☒ Computer Services	☐ Manufacturing
☒ Computer Components	☐ Retail
☒ Computer Entertainment	☐ Service
☐ Computer Education	☒ Wholesale
☐ Information Technologies	☒ SPECIFIC INDUSTRIES
☐ Computer Media	☐ Energy
☐ Software	☐ Environmental
☐ Internet	☐ Financial
☒ MEDICAL/HEALTHCARE	☐ Real Estate
☐ Biotechology	☐ Transportation
☐ Healthcare Services	☐ Publishing
☐ Life Sciences	☐ Food
☒ Medical Products	☐ Franchises
☒ INDUSTRIAL	☒ DIVERSIFIED
☐ Advanced Materials	☒ MISCELLANEOUS
☐ Chemicals	Apparal, Electronic
☒ Instruments & Controls	Games, Toys

STAGE PREFERENCE

☐ EARLY STAGE
☐ Seed
☐ Start-up
☐ 1st Stage
☒ LATER STAGE
☒ 2nd Stage
☐ Mature
☒ Mezzanine
☐ LBO/MBO
☐ Turnaround
☐ INT'L EXPANSION
☐ WILL CONSIDER ALL
☐ VENTURE LEASING

Other Locations: Manhattan Beach CA, Northbrook IL

Affiliation:
Minimum Investment: $1 Million or more
Capital Under Management: Less than $100 Million

GEOGRAPHIC PREF

☐ East Coast
☐ West Coast
☐ Northeast
☐ Mid Atlantic
☐ Gulf States
☐ Northwest
☐ Southeast
☐ Southwest
☐ Midwest
☐ Central
☐ Local to Office
☐ Other Geo Pref

TRIAD CAPITAL CORP. OF NEW YORK

305 Seventh Avenue
20th Floor
New York NY 10001

Phone (212) 243-7360   Fax (212) 243-7647

PROFESSIONALS	TITLE
Marcial Robiou	President
Oscar Figueroa	Investment Manager

INDUSTRY PREFERENCE

☐ INFORMATION INDUSTRY	☐ BASIC INDUSTRIES
☐ Communications	☐ Consumer
☐ Computer Equipment	☐ Distribution
☐ Computer Services	☐ Manufacturing
☐ Computer Components	☐ Retail
☐ Computer Entertainment	☐ Service
☐ Computer Education	☐ Wholesale
☐ Information Technologies	☐ SPECIFIC INDUSTRIES
☐ Computer Media	☐ Energy
☐ Software	☐ Environmental
☐ Internet	☐ Financial
☐ MEDICAL/HEALTHCARE	☐ Real Estate
☐ Biotechnology	☐ Transportation
☐ Healthcare Services	☐ Publishing
☐ Life Sciences	☐ Food
☐ Medical Products	☐ Franchises
☐ INDUSTRIAL	☒ DIVERSIFIED
☐ Advanced Materials	☐ MISCELLANEOUS
☐ Chemicals	
☐ Instruments & Controls	

STAGE PREFERENCE

☐ EARLY STAGE
☐ Seed
☐ Start-up
☐ 1st Stage
☒ LATER STAGE
☒ 2nd Stage
☒ Mature
☒ Mezzanine
☒ LBO/MBO
☐ Turnaround
☐ INT'L EXPANSION
☐ WILL CONSIDER ALL
☐ VENTURE LEASING

SSBIC
Other Locations:

Affiliation:
Minimum Investment: Less than $1 Million
Capital Under Management: Less than $100 Million

GEOGRAPHIC PREF

☐ East Coast
☐ West Coast
☐ Northeast
☐ Mid Atlantic
☐ Gulf States
☐ Northwest
☐ Southeast
☐ Southwest
☐ Midwest
☐ Central
☐ Local to Office
☐ Other Geo Pref

TRUSTY CAPITAL INC.

350 Fifth Avenue
Suite 2026
New York NY 10118

Phone (212) 736-7653   Fax (212) 629-3019

PROFESSIONALS	TITLE
Yungduk Hahn	President

INDUSTRY PREFERENCE

☐ INFORMATION INDUSTRY
☐ Communications
☐ Computer Equipment
☐ Computer Services
☐ Computer Components
☐ Computer Entertainment
☐ Computer Education
☐ Information Technologies
☐ Computer Media
☐ Software
☐ Internet
☐ MEDICAL/HEALTHCARE
☐ Biotechnology
☐ Healthcare Services
☐ Life Sciences
☐ Medical Products
☐ INDUSTRIAL
☐ Advanced Materials
☐ Chemicals
☐ Instruments & Controls

☐ BASIC INDUSTRIES
☐ Consumer
☐ Distribution
☐ Manufacturing
☐ Retail
☐ Service
☐ Wholesale
☐ SPECIFIC INDUSTRIES
☐ Energy
☐ Environmental
☐ Financial
☐ Real Estate
☐ Transportation
☐ Publishing
☐ Food
☐ Franchises
☒ DIVERSIFIED
☐ MISCELLANEOUS

STAGE PREFERENCE

☒ EARLY STAGE
☒ Seed
☒ Start-up
☒ 1st Stage
☒ LATER STAGE
☒ 2nd Stage
☐ Mature
☐ Mezzanine
☐ LBO/MBO
☐ Turnaround
☐ INT'L EXPANSION
☐ WILL CONSIDER ALL
☐ VENTURE LEASING
SSBIC
Other Locations:

Affiliation:
Minimum Investment: Less than $1 Million
Capital Under Management: Less than $100 Million

GEOGRAPHIC PREF

☐ East Coast
☐ West Coast
☒ Northeast
☐ Mid Atlantic
☐ Gulf States
☐ Northwest
☐ Southeast
☐ Southwest
☐ Midwest
☐ Central
☐ Local to Office
☐ Other Geo Pref

VENROCK ASSOCIATES

30 Rockefeller Plaza
Suite 5508
New York NY 10112

Phone (212) 649-5600   Fax (212) 649-5788

PROFESSIONALS	TITLE
David R. Hathaway	General Partner
Ted H. McCourtney, Jr.	General Partner
Dr. Anthony B. Evnin	General Partner

INDUSTRY PREFERENCE

☒ INFORMATION INDUSTRY
☒ Communications
☒ Computer Equipment
☒ Computer Services
☒ Computer Components
☐ Computer Entertainment
☒ Computer Education
☒ Information Technologies
☐ Computer Media
☒ Software
☒ Internet
☒ MEDICAL/HEALTHCARE
☒ Biotechnology
☒ Healthcare Services
☒ Life Sciences
☒ Medical Products
☒ INDUSTRIAL
☒ Advanced Materials
☐ Chemicals
☐ Instruments & Controls

☒ BASIC INDUSTRIES
☐ Consumer
☐ Distribution
☐ Manufacturing
☐ Retail
☒ Service
☐ Wholesale
☒ SPECIFIC INDUSTRIES
☒ Energy
☐ Environmental
☐ Financial
☐ Real Estate
☐ Transportation
☐ Publishing
☐ Food
☐ Franchises
☒ DIVERSIFIED
☐ MISCELLANEOUS

STAGE PREFERENCE

☒ EARLY STAGE
☒ Seed
☒ Start-up
☒ 1st Stage
☐ LATER STAGE
☐ 2nd Stage
☐ Mature
☐ Mezzanine
☐ LBO/MBO
☐ Turnaround
☐ INT'L EXPANSION
☐ WILL CONSIDER ALL
☐ VENTURE LEASING

Other Locations: Boston MA, Menlo Park CA

Affiliation: Rockefeller family
Minimum Investment: $1 Million or more
Capital Under Management: $100 to $500 Million

GEOGRAPHIC PREF

☐ East Coast
☐ West Coast
☐ Northeast
☐ Mid Atlantic
☐ Gulf States
☐ Northwest
☐ Southeast
☐ Southwest
☐ Midwest
☐ Central
☐ Local to Office
☐ Other Geo Pref

WALDEN CAPITAL PARTNERS

150 East 58th Street
34th Floor
New York NY 10155

Phone (212) 355-0090

PROFESSIONALS

Martin Boorstein
John R. Constantino
Allen Greenbert

TITLE

Principal
Principal
Principal

INDUSTRY PREFERENCE

☒ INFORMATION INDUSTRY	☒ BASIC INDUSTRIES
☐ Communications	☐ Consumer
☐ Computer Equipment	☐ Distribution
☐ Computer Services	☒ Manufacturing
☐ Computer Components	☐ Retail
☐ Computer Entertainment	☐ Service
☐ Computer Education	☐ Wholesale
☐ Information Technologies	☒ SPECIFIC INDUSTRIES
☐ Computer Media	☐ Energy
☐ Software	☐ Environmental
☒ Internet	☐ Financial
☒ MEDICAL/HEALTHCARE	☐ Real Estate
☐ Biotechnology	☐ Transportation
☒ Healthcare Services	☐ Publishing
☒ Life Sciences	☐ Food
☒ Medical Products	☐ Franchises
☒ INDUSTRIAL	☒ DIVERSIFIED
☐ Advanced Materials	☒ MISCELLANEOUS
☐ Chemicals	
☒ Instruments & Controls	

STAGE PREFERENCE

☐ EARLY STAGE
☐ Seed
☐ Start-up
☐ 1st Stage
☒ LATER STAGE
☒ 2nd Stage
☒ Mature
☒ Mezzanine
☒ LBO/MBO
☐ Turnaround
☐ INT'L EXPANSION
☐ WILL CONSIDER ALL
☐ VENTURE LEASING

SBIC
Other Locations:

Affiliation:
Minimum Investment: $1 Million or more
Capital Under Management: Less than $100 Million

GEOGRAPHIC PREF

☐ East Coast
☐ West Coast
☐ Northeast
☐ Mid Atlantic
☐ Gulf States
☐ Northwest
☐ Southeast
☐ Southwest
☐ Midwest
☐ Central
☐ Local to Office
☐ Other Geo Pref

WARBURG DILLON READ LLC

299 Park Avenue
New York NY 10171

Phone (212) 821-6490   Fax (212) 821-4138

PROFESSIONALS

Jeft Wald
Jason S. Marconi

TITLE

Executive Director
Associate Director

INDUSTRY PREFERENCE

☐ INFORMATION INDUSTRY	☐ BASIC INDUSTRIES
☐ Communications	☐ Consumer
☐ Computer Equipment	☐ Distribution
☐ Computer Services	☐ Manufacturing
☐ Computer Components	☐ Retail
☐ Computer Entertainment	☐ Service
☐ Computer Education	☐ Wholesale
☐ Information Technologies	☐ SPECIFIC INDUSTRIES
☐ Computer Media	☐ Energy
☐ Software	☐ Environmental
☐ Internet	☐ Financial
☐ MEDICAL/HEALTHCARE	☐ Real Estate
☐ Biotechnology	☐ Transportation
☐ Healthcare Services	☐ Publishing
☐ Life Sciences	☐ Food
☐ Medical Products	☐ Franchises
☐ INDUSTRIAL	☒ DIVERSIFIED
☐ Advanced Materials	☐ MISCELLANEOUS
☐ Chemicals	
☐ Instruments & Controls	

STAGE PREFERENCE

☐ EARLY STAGE
☐ Seed
☐ Start-up
☐ 1st Stage
☒ LATER STAGE
☒ 2nd Stage
☒ Mature
☒ Mezzanine
☒ LBO/MBO
☐ Turnaround
☐ INT'L EXPANSION
☐ WILL CONSIDER ALL
☐ VENTURE LEASING

SBIC
Other Locations:

Affiliation:
Minimum Investment: $1 Million or more
Capital Under Management: Less than $100 Million

GEOGRAPHIC PREF

☐ East Coast
☐ West Coast
☒ Northeast
☐ Mid Atlantic
☐ Gulf States
☐ Northwest
☐ Southeast
☐ Southwest
☐ Midwest
☐ Central
☐ Local to Office
☐ Other Geo Pref

WASSERSTEIN ADELSON VENTURES

31 West 52nd Street
27th Floor
New York NY 10019

Phone (212) 969-2690   Fax (212) 702-5635

PROFESSIONALS	TITLE
W. Townsend Ziebold	Manager

INDUSTRY PREFERENCE

- ☒ INFORMATION INDUSTRY
- ☒ Communications
- ☒ Computer Equipment
- ☒ Computer Services
- ☒ Computer Components
- ☐ Computer Entertainment
- ☒ Computer Education
- ☒ Information Technologies
- ☒ Computer Media
- ☒ Software
- ☒ Internet
- ☒ MEDICAL/HEALTHCARE
- ☒ Biotechnology
- ☒ Healthcare Services
- ☒ Life Sciences
- ☒ Medical Products
- ☐ INDUSTRIAL
- ☐ Advanced Materials
- ☐ Chemicals
- ☐ Instruments & Controls

- ☐ BASIC INDUSTRIES
- ☐ Consumer
- ☐ Distribution
- ☐ Manufacturing
- ☐ Retail
- ☐ Service
- ☐ Wholesale
- ☐ SPECIFIC INDUSTRIES
- ☐ Energy
- ☐ Environmental
- ☐ Financial
- ☐ Real Estate
- ☐ Transportation
- ☐ Publishing
- ☐ Food
- ☐ Franchises
- ☒ DIVERSIFIED
- ☒ MISCELLANEOUS

STAGE PREFERENCE

- ☒ EARLY STAGE
- ☐ Seed
- ☒ Start-up
- ☒ 1st Stage
- ☒ LATER STAGE
- ☒ 2nd Stage
- ☐ Mature
- ☐ Mezzanine
- ☐ LBO/MBO
- ☐ Turnaround
- ☐ INT'L EXPANSION
- ☐ WILL CONSIDER ALL
- ☐ VENTURE LEASING

SBIC
Other Locations:

Affiliation:
Minimum Investment: $1 Million or more
Capital Under Management: $100 to $500 Million

GEOGRAPHIC PREF

- ☒ East Coast
- ☐ West Coast
- ☐ Northeast
- ☐ Mid Atlantic
- ☐ Gulf States
- ☐ Northwest
- ☐ Southeast
- ☐ Southwest
- ☐ Midwest
- ☐ Central
- ☐ Local to Office
- ☐ Other Geo Pref

WELSH, CARSON, ANDERSON & STOWE

320 Park Avenue
Suite 2500
New York NY 10022

Phone (212) 893-9500   Fax (212) 893-9575

PROFESSIONALS	TITLE
Patrick Welsh	General Partner
Anthony de Nicola	General Partner
Thomas McInerney	General Partner
Russell Carson	General Partner
Bruce Anderson	General Partner
Andrew Paul	General Partner
Paul Queally	General Partner
Lawrence Sorrel	General Partner
Richard Stone	General Partner

INDUSTRY PREFERENCE

- ☒ INFORMATION INDUSTRY
- ☐ Communications
- ☐ Computer Equipment
- ☒ Computer Services
- ☐ Computer Components
- ☐ Computer Entertainment
- ☐ Computer Education
- ☐ Information Technologies
- ☐ Computer Media
- ☐ Software
- ☐ Internet
- ☒ MEDICAL/HEALTHCARE
- ☐ Biotechnology
- ☒ Healthcare Services
- ☐ Life Sciences
- ☐ Medical Products
- ☐ INDUSTRIAL
- ☐ Advanced Materials
- ☐ Chemicals
- ☐ Instruments & Controls

- ☐ BASIC INDUSTRIES
- ☐ Consumer
- ☐ Distribution
- ☐ Manufacturing
- ☐ Retail
- ☐ Service
- ☐ Wholesale
- ☐ SPECIFIC INDUSTRIES
- ☐ Energy
- ☐ Environmental
- ☐ Financial
- ☐ Real Estate
- ☐ Transportation
- ☐ Publishing
- ☐ Food
- ☐ Franchises
- ☒ DIVERSIFIED
- ☒ MISCELLANEOUS

STAGE PREFERENCE

- ☐ EARLY STAGE
- ☐ Seed
- ☐ Start-up
- ☐ 1st Stage
- ☒ LATER STAGE
- ☐ 2nd Stage
- ☐ Mature
- ☐ Mezzanine
- ☒ LBO/MBO
- ☒ Turnaround
- ☐ INT'L EXPANSION
- ☐ WILL CONSIDER ALL
- ☒ VENTURE LEASING

Other Locations:

Affiliation:
Minimum Investment: $1 Million or more
Capital Under Management: Less than $100 Million

GEOGRAPHIC PREF

- ☐ East Coast
- ☐ West Coast
- ☐ Northeast
- ☐ Mid Atlantic
- ☐ Gulf States
- ☐ Northwest
- ☐ Southeast
- ☐ Southwest
- ☐ Midwest
- ☐ Central
- ☐ Local to Office
- ☐ Other Geo Pref

BANK OF AMERICA CAPITAL INVESTORS

100 N. Tryon Street
25th Floor
Charlotte NC 28255

Phone (704) 386-8063   Fax (704) 386-6432

PROFESSIONALS	TITLE
Walter W. Walker, Jr.	President

INDUSTRY PREFERENCE

- ☐ INFORMATION INDUSTRY
- ☐ Communications
- ☐ Computer Equipment
- ☐ Computer Services
- ☐ Computer Components
- ☐ Computer Entertainment
- ☐ Computer Education
- ☐ Information Technologies
- ☐ Computer Media
- ☐ Software
- ☐ Internet
- ☐ MEDICAL/HEALTHCARE
- ☐ Biotechnology
- ☐ Healthcare Services
- ☐ Life Sciences
- ☐ Medical Products
- ☐ INDUSTRIAL
- ☐ Advanced Materials
- ☐ Chemicals
- ☐ Instruments & Controls

- ☐ BASIC INDUSTRIES
- ☐ Consumer
- ☐ Distribution
- ☐ Manufacturing
- ☐ Retail
- ☐ Service
- ☐ Wholesale
- ☐ SPECIFIC INDUSTRIES
- ☐ Energy
- ☐ Environmental
- ☐ Financial
- ☐ Real Estate
- ☐ Transportation
- ☐ Publishing
- ☐ Food
- ☐ Franchises
- ☒ DIVERSIFIED
- ☐ MISCELLANEOUS

STAGE PREFERENCE

- ☐ EARLY STAGE
- ☐ Seed
- ☐ Start-up
- ☐ 1st Stage
- ☒ LATER STAGE
- ☒ 2nd Stage
- ☒ Mature
- ☒ Mezzanine
- ☒ LBO/MBO
- ☐ Turnaround
- ☐ INT'L EXPANSION
- ☐ WILL CONSIDER ALL
- ☐ VENTURE LEASING

SBIC
Other Locations:

Affiliation:
Minimum Investment: $1 Million or more
Capital Under Management: Less than $100 Million

GEOGRAPHIC PREF

- ☐ East Coast
- ☐ West Coast
- ☐ Northeast
- ☐ Mid Atlantic
- ☐ Gulf States
- ☐ Northwest
- ☐ Southeast
- ☐ Southwest
- ☐ Midwest
- ☐ Central
- ☐ Local to Office
- ☐ Other Geo Pref

BLUE RIDGE INVESTORS LTD. PARTNERSHIP

300 North Greene Street
Suite 2100
Greensboro NC 27401

Phone (336) 370-0576   Fax (336) 274-4984

PROFESSIONALS	TITLE
Edward C. McCarthy	Executive Vice President

INDUSTRY PREFERENCE

- ☒ INFORMATION INDUSTRY
- ☒ Communications
- ☒ Computer Equipment
- ☒ Computer Services
- ☒ Computer Components
- ☐ Computer Entertainment
- ☒ Computer Education
- ☒ Information Technologies
- ☐ Computer Media
- ☒ Software
- ☒ Internet
- ☐ MEDICAL/HEALTHCARE
- ☐ Biotechnology
- ☐ Healthcare Services
- ☐ Life Sciences
- ☐ Medical Products
- ☐ INDUSTRIAL
- ☐ Advanced Materials
- ☐ Chemicals
- ☐ Instruments & Controls

- ☒ BASIC INDUSTRIES
- ☐ Consumer
- ☒ Distribution
- ☒ Manufacturing
- ☐ Retail
- ☒ Service
- ☐ Wholesale
- ☒ SPECIFIC INDUSTRIES
- ☐ Energy
- ☐ Environmental
- ☐ Financial
- ☐ Real Estate
- ☐ Transportation
- ☐ Publishing
- ☐ Food
- ☐ Franchises
- ☒ DIVERSIFIED
- ☐ MISCELLANEOUS

STAGE PREFERENCE

- ☐ EARLY STAGE
- ☐ Seed
- ☐ Start-up
- ☐ 1st Stage
- ☒ LATER STAGE
- ☒ 2nd Stage
- ☒ Mature
- ☒ Mezzanine
- ☒ LBO/MBO
- ☐ Turnaround
- ☐ INT'L EXPANSION
- ☐ WILL CONSIDER ALL
- ☐ VENTURE LEASING

SBIC
Other Locations:

Affiliation:
Minimum Investment: $1 Million or more
Capital Under Management: Less than $100 Million

GEOGRAPHIC PREF

- ☐ East Coast
- ☐ West Coast
- ☒ Northeast
- ☒ Mid Atlantic
- ☐ Gulf States
- ☐ Northwest
- ☒ Southeast
- ☐ Southwest
- ☐ Midwest
- ☐ Central
- ☐ Local to Office
- ☒ Other Geo Pref
  Mid-Atlantic

CENTURA CAPITAL MARKETS

200 Providence Road - Suite 300
P.O. Box 6261
Charlotte NC 28207

Phone (704) 331-1451   Fax (704) 331-1761

PROFESSIONALS	TITLE
Robert R. Anders, Jr.	Managing Director
Robert H. Mitchell	Managing Director

INDUSTRY PREFERENCE

☐ INFORMATION INDUSTRY	☒ BASIC INDUSTRIES
☐ Communications	☐ Consumer
☐ Computer Equipment	☒ Distribution
☐ Computer Services	☒ Manufacturing
☐ Computer Components	☐ Retail
☐ Computer Entertainment	☒ Service
☐ Computer Education	☐ Wholesale
☐ Information Technologies	☐ SPECIFIC INDUSTRIES
☐ Computer Media	☐ Energy
☐ Software	☐ Environmental
☐ Internet	☐ Financial
☐ MEDICAL/HEALTHCARE	☐ Real Estate
☐ Biotechnology	☐ Transportation
☐ Healthcare Services	☐ Publishing
☐ Life Sciences	☐ Food
☐ Medical Products	☐ Franchises
☐ INDUSTRIAL	☒ DIVERSIFIED
☐ Advanced Materials	☐ MISCELLANEOUS
☐ Chemicals	
☐ Instruments & Controls	

STAGE PREFERENCE

☐ EARLY STAGE
☐ Seed
☐ Start-up
☐ 1st Stage
☒ LATER STAGE
☒ 2nd Stage
☒ Mature
☒ Mezzanine
☒ LBO/MBO
☐ Turnaround
☐ INT'L EXPANSION
☐ WILL CONSIDER ALL
☐ VENTURE LEASING

SBIC
Other Locations:

Affiliation:
Minimum Investment: Less than $1 Million
Capital Under Management: Less than $100 Million

GEOGRAPHIC PREF

☐ East Coast
☐ West Coast
☐ Northeast
☐ Mid Atlantic
☐ Gulf States
☐ Northwest
☒ Southeast
☐ Southwest
☐ Midwest
☐ Central
☐ Local to Office
☒ Other Geo Pref
NC, SC, VA

FIRST UNION CAPITAL PARTNERS, INC.

One First Union Center, 5th Floor
301 South College Street
Charlotte NC 28288-0732

Phone (704) 374-4791   Fax (704) 374-6711

PROFESSIONALS	TITLE
Tracy Chaffin	Chief Financial Officer

INDUSTRY PREFERENCE

☒ INFORMATION INDUSTRY	☒ BASIC INDUSTRIES
☒ Communications	☐ Consumer
☒ Computer Equipment	☐ Distribution
☒ Computer Services	☐ Manufacturing
☒ Computer Components	☒ Retail
☐ Computer Entertainment	☐ Service
☐ Computer Education	☐ Wholesale
☒ Information Technologies	☐ SPECIFIC INDUSTRIES
☒ Computer Media	☐ Energy
☒ Software	☐ Environmental
☒ Internet	☐ Financial
☐ MEDICAL/HEALTHCARE	☐ Real Estate
☐ Biotechnology	☐ Transportation
☐ Healthcare Services	☐ Publishing
☐ Life Sciences	☐ Food
☐ Medical Products	☐ Franchises
☐ INDUSTRIAL	☒ DIVERSIFIED
☐ Advanced Materials	☐ MISCELLANEOUS
☐ Chemicals	
☐ Instruments & Controls	

STAGE PREFERENCE

☒ EARLY STAGE
☐ Seed
☐ Start-up
☒ 1st Stage
☒ LATER STAGE
☒ 2nd Stage
☒ Mature
☒ Mezzanine
☒ LBO/MBO
☐ Turnaround
☐ INT'L EXPANSION
☐ WILL CONSIDER ALL
☐ VENTURE LEASING

SBIC
Other Locations:

Affiliation:
Minimum Investment: $1 Million or more
Capital Under Management: Less than $100 Million

GEOGRAPHIC PREF

☐ East Coast
☐ West Coast
☐ Northeast
☐ Mid Atlantic
☐ Gulf States
☐ Northwest
☐ Southeast
☐ Southwest
☐ Midwest
☐ Central
☐ Local to Office
☐ Other Geo Pref

INTERSOUTH PARTNERS

1000 Park Forty Plaza
Suite 290
Durham NC 27713

Phone (919) 544-6473   Fax (919) 481-0225

PROFESSIONALS	TITLE
Mitch Mumma	General Partner
Dennis J. Dougherty	General Partner

INDUSTRY PREFERENCE

- ☒ INFORMATION INDUSTRY
- ☒ Communications
- ☒ Computer Equipment
- ☒ Computer Services
- ☒ Computer Components
- ☒ Computer Entertainment
- ☐ Computer Education
- ☒ Information Technologies
- ☒ Computer Media
- ☒ Software
- ☒ Internet
- ☒ MEDICAL/HEALTHCARE
- ☒ Biotechnology
- ☒ Healthcare Services
- ☒ Life Sciences
- ☒ Medical Products
- ☒ INDUSTRIAL
- ☒ Advanced Materials
- ☒ Chemicals
- ☒ Instruments & Controls

- ☒ BASIC INDUSTRIES
- ☐ Consumer
- ☐ Distribution
- ☐ Manufacturing
- ☐ Retail
- ☒ Service
- ☐ Wholesale
- ☐ SPECIFIC INDUSTRIES
- ☐ Energy
- ☐ Environmental
- ☐ Financial
- ☐ Real Estate
- ☐ Transportation
- ☐ Publishing
- ☐ Food
- ☐ Franchises
- ☒ DIVERSIFIED
- ☐ MISCELLANEOUS

STAGE PREFERENCE

- ☒ EARLY STAGE
- ☒ Seed
- ☒ Start-up
- ☒ 1st Stage
- ☒ LATER STAGE
- ☒ 2nd Stage
- ☐ Mature
- ☐ Mezzanine
- ☐ LBO/MBO
- ☐ Turnaround
- ☐ INT'L EXPANSION
- ☐ WILL CONSIDER ALL
- ☐ VENTURE LEASING

Other Locations:

Affiliation:
Minimum Investment: Less than $1 Million
Capital Under Management: $100 to $500 Million

GEOGRAPHIC PREF

- ☐ East Coast
- ☐ West Coast
- ☐ Northeast
- ☐ Mid Atlantic
- ☐ Gulf States
- ☐ Northwest
- ☒ Southeast
- ☐ Southwest
- ☐ Midwest
- ☐ Central
- ☐ Local to Office
- ☐ Other Geo Pref

KITTY HAWK CAPITAL

2700 Coltsgate Road
Suite 202
Charlotte NC 28211

Phone (704) 362-3909   Fax (704) 362-2774

PROFESSIONALS	TITLE
W. Chris Hegele	Partner
Walker Wilkinson	Partner
Stephen W. Buchanan	Partner

INDUSTRY PREFERENCE

- ☒ INFORMATION INDUSTRY
- ☒ Communications
- ☒ Computer Equipment
- ☒ Computer Services
- ☒ Computer Components
- ☐ Computer Entertainment
- ☒ Computer Education
- ☒ Information Technologies
- ☒ Computer Media
- ☒ Software
- ☒ Internet
- ☐ MEDICAL/HEALTHCARE
- ☐ Biotechnology
- ☐ Healthcare Services
- ☐ Life Sciences
- ☐ Medical Products
- ☒ INDUSTRIAL
- ☒ Advanced Materials
- ☐ Chemicals
- ☒ Instruments & Controls

- ☒ BASIC INDUSTRIES
- ☒ Consumer
- ☒ Distribution
- ☒ Manufacturing
- ☒ Retail
- ☒ Service
- ☐ Wholesale
- ☒ SPECIFIC INDUSTRIES
- ☐ Energy
- ☐ Environmental
- ☒ Financial
- ☐ Real Estate
- ☐ Transportation
- ☐ Publishing
- ☐ Food
- ☐ Franchises
- ☒ DIVERSIFIED
- ☐ MISCELLANEOUS

STAGE PREFERENCE

- ☒ EARLY STAGE
- ☐ Seed
- ☒ Start-up
- ☒ 1st Stage
- ☒ LATER STAGE
- ☒ 2nd Stage
- ☒ Mature
- ☒ Mezzanine
- ☒ LBO/MBO
- ☐ Turnaround
- ☐ INT'L EXPANSION
- ☐ WILL CONSIDER ALL
- ☐ VENTURE LEASING

Other Locations:

Affiliation:
Minimum Investment: Less than $1 Million
Capital Under Management: $100 to $500 Million

GEOGRAPHIC PREF

- ☒ East Coast
- ☐ West Coast
- ☐ Northeast
- ☐ Mid Atlantic
- ☐ Gulf States
- ☐ Northwest
- ☒ Southeast
- ☐ Southwest
- ☐ Midwest
- ☐ Central
- ☐ Local to Office
- ☐ Other Geo Pref

NORTH DAKOTA SBIC, LP

51 Broadway
Suite 400
Fargo ND 58102

Phone (701) 298-0003   Fax (701) 293-7819

PROFESSIONALS	TITLE
John G. Cosgriff	Manager

INDUSTRY PREFERENCE

☐ INFORMATION INDUSTRY
☐ Communications
☐ Computer Equipment
☐ Computer Services
☐ Computer Components
☐ Computer Entertainment
☐ Computer Education
☐ Information Technologies
☐ Computer Media
☐ Software
☐ Internet
☐ MEDICAL/HEALTHCARE
☐ Biotechnology
☐ Healthcare Services
☐ Life Sciences
☐ Medical Products
☐ INDUSTRIAL
☐ Advanced Materials
☐ Chemicals
☐ Instruments & Controls

☐ BASIC INDUSTRIES
☐ Consumer
☐ Distribution
☐ Manufacturing
☐ Retail
☐ Service
☐ Wholesale
☐ SPECIFIC INDUSTRIES
☐ Energy
☐ Environmental
☐ Financial
☐ Real Estate
☐ Transportation
☐ Publishing
☐ Food
☐ Franchises
☒ DIVERSIFIED
☐ MISCELLANEOUS

STAGE PREFERENCE

☐ EARLY STAGE
☐ Seed
☐ Start-up
☐ 1st Stage
☒ LATER STAGE
☒ 2nd Stage
☒ Mature
☒ Mezzanine
☒ LBO/MBO
☐ Turnaround
☐ INT'L EXPANSION
☐ WILL CONSIDER ALL
☐ VENTURE LEASING
SBIC
Other Locations:

Affiliation:
Minimum Investment: Less than $1 Million
Capital Under Management: Less than $100 Million

GEOGRAPHIC PREF

☐ East Coast
☐ West Coast
☐ Northeast
☐ Mid Atlantic
☐ Gulf States
☐ Northwest
☐ Southeast
☐ Southwest
☐ Midwest
☐ Central
☐ Local to Office
☐ Other Geo Pref

ALPHA CAPITAL PARTNERS, INC.

310 West Monument
Suite 400
Dayton OH 45402

Phone (937) 222-2006   Fax (937) 228-0115

PROFESSIONALS	TITLE
Orval E. Cook	Sr. Vice President
Curtis D. Crocker	Vice President

INDUSTRY PREFERENCE

☒ INFORMATION INDUSTRY
☒ Communications
☒ Computer Equipment
☒ Computer Services
☒ Computer Components
☐ Computer Entertainment
☒ Computer Education
☒ Information Technologies
☐ Computer Media
☒ Software
☒ Internet
☒ MEDICAL/HEALTHCARE
☒ Biotechnology
☒ Healthcare Services
☒ Life Sciences
☒ Medical Products
☒ INDUSTRIAL
☒ Advanced Materials
☒ Chemicals
☒ Instruments & Controls

☒ BASIC INDUSTRIES
☒ Consumer
☒ Distribution
☒ Manufacturing
☒ Retail
☒ Service
☐ Wholesale
☐ SPECIFIC INDUSTRIES
☐ Energy
☐ Environmental
☐ Financial
☐ Real Estate
☐ Transportation
☐ Publishing
☐ Food
☐ Franchises
☒ DIVERSIFIED
☐ MISCELLANEOUS

STAGE PREFERENCE

☒ EARLY STAGE
☐ Seed
☐ Start-up
☒ 1st Stage
☒ LATER STAGE
☒ 2nd Stage
☒ Mature
☐ Mezzanine
☒ LBO/MBO
☐ Turnaround
☐ INT'L EXPANSION
☐ WILL CONSIDER ALL
☐ VENTURE LEASING

Other Locations: Chicago IL

Affiliation:
Minimum Investment: Less than $1 Million
Capital Under Management: Less than $100 Million

GEOGRAPHIC PREF

☐ East Coast
☐ West Coast
☐ Northeast
☐ Mid Atlantic
☐ Gulf States
☐ Northwest
☐ Southeast
☐ Southwest
☐ Midwest
☐ Central
☐ Local to Office
☐ Other Geo Pref

BLUE CHIP VENTURE COMPANY

**1100 Chiquita Center
250 East Fifth Street
Cincinatti OH 45202**

Phone (513) 723-2300   Fax (513) 723-2306

PROFESSIONALS

	TITLE
John C. McIlwraith	Manager
Z. David Patterson	Manager
John H. Wyant	Manager

INDUSTRY PREFERENCE

☐ INFORMATION INDUSTRY	☐ BASIC INDUSTRIES
☐ Communications	☐ Consumer
☐ Computer Equipment	☐ Distribution
☐ Computer Services	☐ Manufacturing
☐ Computer Components	☐ Retail
☐ Computer Entertainment	☐ Service
☐ Computer Education	☐ Wholesale
☐ Information Technologies	☐ SPECIFIC INDUSTRIES
☐ Computer Media	☐ Energy
☐ Software	☐ Environmental
☐ Internet	☐ Financial
☐ MEDICAL/HEALTHCARE	☐ Real Estate
☐ Biotechnology	☐ Transportation
☐ Healthcare Services	☐ Publishing
☐ Life Sciences	☐ Food
☐ Medical Products	☐ Franchises
☐ INDUSTRIAL	☒ DIVERSIFIED
☐ Advanced Materials	☒ MISCELLANEOUS
☐ Chemicals	
☐ Instruments & Controls	

STAGE PREFERENCE

☐ EARLY STAGE
☐ Seed
☐ Start-up
☐ 1st Stage
☒ LATER STAGE
☒ 2nd Stage
☐ Mature
☒ Mezzanine
☒ LBO/MBO
☐ Turnaround
☐ INT'L EXPANSION
☐ WILL CONSIDER ALL
☐ VENTURE LEASING

Other Locations:

Affiliation:
Minimum Investment: $1 Million or more
Capital Under Management: $100 to $500 Million

GEOGRAPHIC PREF

☐ East Coast
☐ West Coast
☐ Northeast
☐ Mid Atlantic
☐ Gulf States
☐ Northwest
☐ Southeast
☐ Southwest
☐ Midwest
☐ Central
☐ Local to Office
☒ Other Geo Pref
OH

BRANTLEY PARTNERS

**20600 Chagrin Boulevard
Suite 1150, Tower East
Shader Heights OH 44122**

Phone (216) 283-4800   Fax (216) 283-5324

PROFESSIONALS

	TITLE
Robert P. Pinkas	General Partner
Paul H. Cascio	General Partner
Michael J. Finn	General Partner
James R. Bergman	General Partner
Tab A. Keplinger	Chief Financial Officer

INDUSTRY PREFERENCE

☒ INFORMATION INDUSTRY	☒ BASIC INDUSTRIES
☒ Communications	☐ Consumer
☐ Computer Equipment	☒ Distribution
☒ Computer Services	☐ Manufacturing
☒ Computer Components	☐ Retail
☐ Computer Entertainment	☒ Service
☒ Computer Education	☐ Wholesale
☒ Information Technologies	☒ SPECIFIC INDUSTRIES
☐ Computer Media	☐ Energy
☒ Software	☒ Environmental
☐ Internet	☐ Financial
☒ MEDICAL/HEALTHCARE	☐ Real Estate
☐ Biotechnology	☐ Transportation
☒ Healthcare Services	☐ Publishing
☐ Life Sciences	☐ Food
☐ Medical Products	☐ Franchises
☒ INDUSTRIAL	☒ DIVERSIFIED
☒ Advanced Materials	☐ MISCELLANEOUS
☒ Chemicals	
☒ Instruments & Controls	

STAGE PREFERENCE

☐ EARLY STAGE
☐ Seed
☐ Start-up
☐ 1st Stage
☒ LATER STAGE
☒ 2nd Stage
☐ Mature
☒ Mezzanine
☒ LBO/MBO
☐ Turnaround
☐ INT'L EXPANSION
☐ WILL CONSIDER ALL
☐ VENTURE LEASING

Other Locations:

Affiliation:
Minimum Investment: $1 Million or more
Capital Under Management: $100 to $500 Million

GEOGRAPHIC PREF

☐ East Coast
☐ West Coast
☐ Northeast
☐ Mid Atlantic
☐ Gulf States
☐ Northwest
☐ Southeast
☐ Southwest
☐ Midwest
☐ Central
☐ Local to Office
☐ Other Geo Pref

CLARION CAPITAL CORP.

Ohio Savings Plaza
1801 East 9th Street, Suite 510
Cleveland OH 44114

Phone (216) 687-8941   Fax (216) 694-3545

PROFESSIONALS

Morton Cohen
Thomas Niehaus

TITLE

President

INDUSTRY PREFERENCE

- ☒ INFORMATION INDUSTRY
- ☒ Communications
- ☒ Computer Equipment
- ☒ Computer Services
- ☒ Computer Components
- ☐ Computer Entertainment
- ☒ Computer Education
- ☒ Information Technologies
- ☐ Computer Media
- ☒ Software
- ☒ Internet
- ☐ MEDICAL/HEALTHCARE
- ☐ Biotechnology
- ☐ Healthcare Services
- ☐ Life Sciences
- ☐ Medical Products
- ☐ INDUSTRIAL
- ☐ Advanced Materials
- ☐ Chemicals
- ☐ Instruments & Controls

- ☐ BASIC INDUSTRIES
- ☐ Consumer
- ☐ Distribution
- ☐ Manufacturing
- ☐ Retail
- ☐ Service
- ☐ Wholesale
- ☒ SPECIFIC INDUSTRIES
- ☐ Energy
- ☐ Environmental
- ☐ Financial
- ☐ Real Estate
- ☐ Transportation
- ☐ Publishing
- ☐ Food
- ☐ Franchises
- ☒ DIVERSIFIED
- ☐ MISCELLANEOUS

STAGE PREFERENCE

- ☐ EARLY STAGE
- ☐ Seed
- ☐ Start-up
- ☐ 1st Stage
- ☒ LATER STAGE
- ☒ 2nd Stage
- ☒ Mature
- ☒ Mezzanine
- ☒ LBO/MBO
- ☐ Turnaround
- ☐ INT'L EXPANSION
- ☐ WILL CONSIDER ALL
- ☐ VENTURE LEASING

SBIC
Other Locations:

Affiliation:
Minimum Investment: $1 Million or more
Capital Under Management: $100 to $500 Million

GEOGRAPHIC PREF

- ☐ East Coast
- ☐ West Coast
- ☐ Northeast
- ☐ Mid Atlantic
- ☐ Gulf States
- ☐ Northwest
- ☐ Southeast
- ☐ Southwest
- ☐ Midwest
- ☐ Central
- ☐ Local to Office
- ☐ Other Geo Pref

ENTERPRISE OHIO INVESTMENT COMPANY

8 North Main Street
Dayton OH 45402

Phone (937) 226-0457   Fax (937) 222-7035

PROFESSIONALS

Steven Budd

TITLE

President

INDUSTRY PREFERENCE

- ☐ INFORMATION INDUSTRY
- ☐ Communications
- ☐ Computer Equipment
- ☐ Computer Services
- ☐ Computer Components
- ☐ Computer Entertainment
- ☐ Computer Education
- ☐ Information Technologies
- ☐ Computer Media
- ☐ Software
- ☐ Internet
- ☐ MEDICAL/HEALTHCARE
- ☐ Biotechnology
- ☐ Healthcare Services
- ☐ Life Sciences
- ☐ Medical Products
- ☐ INDUSTRIAL
- ☐ Advanced Materials
- ☐ Chemicals
- ☐ Instruments & Controls

- ☒ BASIC INDUSTRIES
- ☐ Consumer
- ☐ Distribution
- ☐ Manufacturing
- ☒ Retail
- ☒ Service
- ☐ Wholesale
- ☒ SPECIFIC INDUSTRIES
- ☐ Energy
- ☐ Environmental
- ☐ Financial
- ☐ Real Estate
- ☐ Transportation
- ☐ Publishing
- ☐ Food
- ☒ Franchises
- ☒ DIVERSIFIED
- ☐ MISCELLANEOUS

STAGE PREFERENCE

- ☒ EARLY STAGE
- ☐ Seed
- ☐ Start-up
- ☒ 1st Stage
- ☒ LATER STAGE
- ☒ 2nd Stage
- ☒ Mature
- ☒ Mezzanine
- ☒ LBO/MBO
- ☐ Turnaround
- ☐ INT'L EXPANSION
- ☐ WILL CONSIDER ALL
- ☐ VENTURE LEASING

SSBIC
Other Locations:

Affiliation:
Minimum Investment: Less than $1 Million
Capital Under Management: Less than $100 Million

GEOGRAPHIC PREF

- ☐ East Coast
- ☐ West Coast
- ☐ Northeast
- ☐ Mid Atlantic
- ☐ Gulf States
- ☐ Northwest
- ☐ Southeast
- ☒ Southwest
- ☐ Midwest
- ☐ Central
- ☐ Local to Office
- ☒ Other Geo Pref
  OH

MORGENTHALER VENTURES

Terminal Tower
50 Public Square, Suite 2700
Cleveland OH 44113

Phone (216) 416-7500   Fax (216) 416-7501

PROFESSIONALS	TITLE
David Morgenthaler	Managing Partner
Paul S. Brentlinger	General Partner
John Lutsi	General Partner
Robert D. Pavey	General Partner
Keith M. Kerman	General Partner

INDUSTRY PREFERENCE

☒ INFORMATION INDUSTRY
☒ Communications
☒ Computer Equipment
☒ Computer Services
☒ Computer Components
☐ Computer Entertainment
☒ Computer Education
☒ Information Technologies
☐ Computer Media
☒ Software
☒ Internet
☒ MEDICAL/HEALTHCARE
☒ Biotechnology
☒ Healthcare Services
☒ Life Sciences
☒ Medical Products
☒ INDUSTRIAL
☐ Advanced Materials
☐ Chemicals
☒ Instruments & Controls

☒ BASIC INDUSTRIES
☐ Consumer
☐ Distribution
☒ Manufacturing
☐ Retail
☒ Service
☐ Wholesale
☐ SPECIFIC INDUSTRIES
☐ Energy
☐ Environmental
☐ Financial
☐ Real Estate
☐ Transportation
☐ Publishing
☐ Food
☐ Franchises
☒ DIVERSIFIED
☐ MISCELLANEOUS

STAGE PREFERENCE

☒ EARLY STAGE
☒ Seed
☒ Start-up
☒ 1st Stage
☒ LATER STAGE
☒ 2nd Stage
☒ Mature
☒ Mezzanine
☒ LBO/MBO
☐ Turnaround
☐ INT'L EXPANSION
☐ WILL CONSIDER ALL
☐ VENTURE LEASING

Other Locations: Menlo Park CA

Affiliation:
Minimum Investment: $1 Million or more
Capital Under Management: $100 to $500 Million

GEOGRAPHIC PREF

☐ East Coast
☐ West Coast
☐ Northeast
☐ Mid Atlantic
☐ Gulf States
☐ Northwest
☐ Southeast
☐ Southwest
☐ Midwest
☐ Central
☐ Local to Office
☐ Other Geo Pref

NATIONAL CITY CAPITAL CORPORATION

1965 East Sixth Street
Suite 1010
Cleveland OH 44114

Phone (216) 575-2491   Fax (216) 575-9965

PROFESSIONALS	TITLE
William H. Schecter	President
Jay A. Freund	Vice President
Christopher P. Dowd	Vice President
Carl E. Baldassarre	Managing Director
Richard Martinko	Managing Director

INDUSTRY PREFERENCE

☒ INFORMATION INDUSTRY
☐ Communications
☐ Computer Equipment
☐ Computer Services
☒ Computer Components
☐ Computer Entertainment
☐ Computer Education
☐ Information Technologies
☐ Computer Media
☐ Software
☐ Internet
☐ MEDICAL/HEALTHCARE
☐ Biotechnology
☐ Healthcare Services
☐ Life Sciences
☐ Medical Products
☐ INDUSTRIAL
☐ Advanced Materials
☐ Chemicals
☐ Instruments & Controls

☒ BASIC INDUSTRIES
☒ Consumer
☒ Distribution
☒ Manufacturing
☐ Retail
☒ Service
☒ Wholesale
☐ SPECIFIC INDUSTRIES
☐ Energy
☐ Environmental
☐ Financial
☐ Real Estate
☐ Transportation
☐ Publishing
☐ Food
☐ Franchises
☒ DIVERSIFIED
☐ MISCELLANEOUS

STAGE PREFERENCE

☐ EARLY STAGE
☐ Seed
☐ Start-up
☐ 1st Stage
☒ LATER STAGE
☒ 2nd Stage
☒ Mature
☒ Mezzanine
☒ LBO/MBO
☐ Turnaround
☐ INT'L EXPANSION
☐ WILL CONSIDER ALL
☐ VENTURE LEASING
SBIC
Other Locations:

Affiliation:
Minimum Investment: $1 Million or more
Capital Under Management: $100 to $500 Million

GEOGRAPHIC PREF

☐ East Coast
☐ West Coast
☐ Northeast
☐ Mid Atlantic
☐ Gulf States
☐ Northwest
☐ Southeast
☐ Southwest
☐ Midwest
☐ Central
☐ Local to Office
☐ Other Geo Pref

PRIMUS VENTURE PARTNERS

5900 Landerbrook Drive
Suite 200
Cleveland OH 44124-4020

Phone (440) 684-7300   Fax (440) 684-7342

PROFESSIONALS	TITLE
James T. Bartlett	Managing Director
Jonathan E. Dick	Managing Director
Loyal W. Wilson	Managing Director
William C. Mulligan	Managing Director
Kevin J. McGinty	Managing Director

INDUSTRY PREFERENCE

- ☒ INFORMATION INDUSTRY
- ☒ Communications
- ☐ Computer Equipment
- ☐ Computer Services
- ☐ Computer Components
- ☐ Computer Entertainment
- ☒ Computer Education
- ☐ Information Technologies
- ☐ Computer Media
- ☒ Software
- ☒ Internet
- ☒ MEDICAL/HEALTHCARE
- ☐ Biotechnology
- ☒ Healthcare Services
- ☐ Life Sciences
- ☒ Medical Products
- ☐ INDUSTRIAL
- ☐ Advanced Materials
- ☐ Chemicals
- ☐ Instruments & Controls

- ☒ BASIC INDUSTRIES
- ☒ Consumer
- ☐ Distribution
- ☐ Manufacturing
- ☒ Retail
- ☐ Service
- ☐ Wholesale
- ☒ SPECIFIC INDUSTRIES
- ☐ Energy
- ☐ Environmental
- ☒ Financial
- ☐ Real Estate
- ☐ Transportation
- ☐ Publishing
- ☐ Food
- ☐ Franchises
- ☒ DIVERSIFIED
- ☐ MISCELLANEOUS

STAGE PREFERENCE

- ☒ EARLY STAGE
- ☐ Seed
- ☐ Start-up
- ☒ 1st Stage
- ☒ LATER STAGE
- ☒ 2nd Stage
- ☒ Mature
- ☒ Mezzanine
- ☒ LBO/MBO
- ☐ Turnaround
- ☐ INT'L EXPANSION
- ☐ WILL CONSIDER ALL
- ☐ VENTURE LEASING

Other Locations:

Affiliation:
Minimum Investment: $1 Million or more
Capital Under Management: $100 to $500 Million

GEOGRAPHIC PREF

- ☐ East Coast
- ☐ West Coast
- ☐ Northeast
- ☐ Mid Atlantic
- ☐ Gulf States
- ☐ Northwest
- ☐ Southeast
- ☐ Southwest
- ☐ Midwest
- ☐ Central
- ☐ Local to Office
- ☐ Other Geo Pref

RIVER CITIES CAPITAL FUND

221 East Fourth Street
Suite 1900
Cincinnati OH 45202

Phone (513) 621-9700   Fax (513) 579-8939

PROFESSIONALS	TITLE
R. Glen Mayfield	Managing Partner
Edwin T. Robinson	Managing Partner
J. Eric Lanning	Principal
Murray R. Wilson	Principal
Frederick C. Keiser	Principal

INDUSTRY PREFERENCE

- ☐ INFORMATION INDUSTRY
- ☐ Communications
- ☐ Computer Equipment
- ☐ Computer Services
- ☐ Computer Components
- ☐ Computer Entertainment
- ☐ Computer Education
- ☐ Information Technologies
- ☐ Computer Media
- ☐ Software
- ☐ Internet
- ☐ MEDICAL/HEALTHCARE
- ☐ Biotechnology
- ☐ Healthcare Services
- ☐ Life Sciences
- ☐ Medical Products
- ☐ INDUSTRIAL
- ☐ Advanced Materials
- ☐ Chemicals
- ☐ Instruments & Controls

- ☐ BASIC INDUSTRIES
- ☐ Consumer
- ☐ Distribution
- ☐ Manufacturing
- ☐ Retail
- ☐ Service
- ☐ Wholesale
- ☐ SPECIFIC INDUSTRIES
- ☐ Energy
- ☐ Environmental
- ☐ Financial
- ☐ Real Estate
- ☐ Transportation
- ☐ Publishing
- ☐ Food
- ☐ Franchises
- ☒ DIVERSIFIED
- ☐ MISCELLANEOUS

STAGE PREFERENCE

- ☒ EARLY STAGE
- ☐ Seed
- ☐ Start-up
- ☒ 1st Stage
- ☒ LATER STAGE
- ☒ 2nd Stage
- ☒ Mature
- ☒ Mezzanine
- ☒ LBO/MBO
- ☐ Turnaround
- ☐ INT'L EXPANSION
- ☐ WILL CONSIDER ALL
- ☐ VENTURE LEASING

SBIC
Other Locations:

Affiliation:
Minimum Investment: Less than $1 Million
Capital Under Management: Less than $100 Million

GEOGRAPHIC PREF

- ☐ East Coast
- ☐ West Coast
- ☐ Northeast
- ☐ Mid Atlantic
- ☐ Gulf States
- ☐ Northwest
- ☐ Southeast
- ☐ Southwest
- ☐ Midwest
- ☐ Central
- ☐ Local to Office
- ☒ Other Geo Pref
- OH, KY, IN

BANCFIRST INVESTMENT CORPORATION

101 North Broadway
P.O. Box 26788
Oklahoma City OK 73126

Phone (405) 270-1044   Fax (405) 270-1089

PROFESSIONALS	TITLE
Randy Foraker	Manager

INDUSTRY PREFERENCE

- ☐ INFORMATION INDUSTRY
- ☐ Communications
- ☐ Computer Equipment
- ☐ Computer Services
- ☐ Computer Components
- ☐ Computer Entertainment
- ☐ Computer Education
- ☐ Information Technologies
- ☐ Computer Media
- ☐ Software
- ☐ Internet
- ☐ MEDICAL/HEALTHCARE
- ☐ Biotechnology
- ☐ Healthcare Services
- ☐ Life Sciences
- ☐ Medical Products
- ☐ INDUSTRIAL
- ☐ Advanced Materials
- ☐ Chemicals
- ☐ Instruments & Controls

- ☐ BASIC INDUSTRIES
- ☐ Consumer
- ☐ Distribution
- ☐ Manufacturing
- ☐ Retail
- ☐ Service
- ☐ Wholesale
- ☐ SPECIFIC INDUSTRIES
- ☐ Energy
- ☐ Environmental
- ☐ Financial
- ☐ Real Estate
- ☐ Transportation
- ☐ Publishing
- ☐ Food
- ☐ Franchises
- ☒ DIVERSIFIED
- ☐ MISCELLANEOUS

STAGE PREFERENCE

- ☒ EARLY STAGE
- ☐ Seed
- ☐ Start-up
- ☒ 1st Stage
- ☒ LATER STAGE
- ☒ 2nd Stage
- ☒ Mature
- ☐ Mezzanine
- ☒ LBO/MBO
- ☐ Turnaround
- ☐ INT'L EXPANSION
- ☐ WILL CONSIDER ALL
- ☐ VENTURE LEASING

SBIC
Other Locations:

Affiliation:
Minimum Investment: Less than $1 Million
Capital Under Management: Less than $100 Million

GEOGRAPHIC PREF

- ☐ East Coast
- ☐ West Coast
- ☐ Northeast
- ☐ Mid Atlantic
- ☐ Gulf States
- ☐ Northwest
- ☐ Southeast
- ☐ Southwest
- ☐ Midwest
- ☐ Central
- ☐ Local to Office
- ☒ Other Geo Pref
  OK

DAVIS, TUTTLE VENTURE PARTNERS LP

320 South Boston
Suite 1000
Tulsa OK 74103-3703

Phone (918) 584-7272   Fax (918) 582-2304

PROFESSIONALS	TITLE
Barry Davis	Managing General Partner
Elmer Wilening	General Partner

INDUSTRY PREFERENCE

- ☒ INFORMATION INDUSTRY
- ☒ Communications
- ☒ Computer Equipment
- ☒ Computer Services
- ☒ Computer Components
- ☐ Computer Entertainment
- ☒ Computer Education
- ☐ Information Technologies
- ☐ Computer Media
- ☐ Software
- ☐ Internet
- ☒ MEDICAL/HEALTHCARE
- ☒ Biotechnology
- ☒ Healthcare Services
- ☒ Life Sciences
- ☒ Medical Products
- ☒ INDUSTRIAL
- ☒ Advanced Materials
- ☒ Chemicals
- ☒ Instruments & Controls

- ☒ BASIC INDUSTRIES
- ☒ Consumer
- ☒ Distribution
- ☐ Manufacturing
- ☐ Retail
- ☐ Service
- ☐ Wholesale
- ☒ SPECIFIC INDUSTRIES
- ☒ Energy
- ☐ Environmental
- ☐ Financial
- ☐ Real Estate
- ☒ Transportation
- ☒ Publishing
- ☐ Food
- ☐ Franchises
- ☒ DIVERSIFIED
- ☒ MISCELLANEOUS

STAGE PREFERENCE

- ☐ EARLY STAGE
- ☐ Seed
- ☐ Start-up
- ☐ 1st Stage
- ☐ LATER STAGE
- ☐ 2nd Stage
- ☐ Mature
- ☐ Mezzanine
- ☐ LBO/MBO
- ☐ Turnaround
- ☐ INT'L EXPANSION
- ☐ WILL CONSIDER ALL
- ☐ VENTURE LEASING

Other Locations:

Affiliation:
Minimum Investment: $1 Million or more
Capital Under Management: $100 to $500 Million

GEOGRAPHIC PREF

- ☐ East Coast
- ☐ West Coast
- ☐ Northeast
- ☐ Mid Atlantic
- ☐ Gulf States
- ☐ Northwest
- ☐ Southeast
- ☒ Southwest
- ☐ Midwest
- ☐ Central
- ☐ Local to Office
- ☐ Other Geo Pref

NORTHERN PACIFIC CAPITAL CORPORATION

937 S.W. 14th Street, Suite 200
P.O. Box 1658
Portland OR 97207

Phone (503) 241-1255   Fax (503) 299-6653

PROFESSIONALS	TITLE
Joseph P. Tennant	President

INDUSTRY PREFERENCE

- ☐ INFORMATION INDUSTRY
- ☐ Communications
- ☐ Computer Equipment
- ☐ Computer Services
- ☐ Computer Components
- ☐ Computer Entertainment
- ☐ Computer Education
- ☐ Information Technologies
- ☐ Computer Media
- ☐ Software
- ☐ Internet
- ☐ MEDICAL/HEALTHCARE
- ☐ Biotechnology
- ☐ Healthcare Services
- ☐ Life Sciences
- ☐ Medical Products
- ☐ INDUSTRIAL
- ☐ Advanced Materials
- ☐ Chemicals
- ☐ Instruments & Controls

- ☐ BASIC INDUSTRIES
- ☐ Consumer
- ☐ Distribution
- ☐ Manufacturing
- ☐ Retail
- ☐ Service
- ☐ Wholesale
- ☐ SPECIFIC INDUSTRIES
- ☐ Energy
- ☐ Environmental
- ☐ Financial
- ☐ Real Estate
- ☐ Transportation
- ☐ Publishing
- ☐ Food
- ☐ Franchises
- ☒ DIVERSIFIED
- ☐ MISCELLANEOUS

STAGE PREFERENCE

- ☐ EARLY STAGE
- ☐ Seed
- ☐ Start-up
- ☐ 1st Stage
- ☒ LATER STAGE
- ☒ 2nd Stage
- ☒ Mature
- ☐ Mezzanine
- ☒ LBO/MBO
- ☐ Turnaround
- ☐ INT'L EXPANSION
- ☐ WILL CONSIDER ALL
- ☐ VENTURE LEASING

SBIC
Other Locations:

Affiliation:
Minimum Investment: Less than $1 Million
Capital Under Management: Less than $100 Million

GEOGRAPHIC PREF

- ☐ East Coast
- ☐ West Coast
- ☐ Northeast
- ☐ Mid Atlantic
- ☐ Gulf States
- ☒ Northwest
- ☐ Southeast
- ☐ Southwest
- ☐ Midwest
- ☐ Central
- ☐ Local to Office
- ☒ Other Geo Pref
    Pacific Northwest

OLYMPIC VENTURE PARTNERS

340 Oswego Pointe Drive
Suite 200
Lake Oswego OR 97034

Phone (503) 697-8766   Fax (503) 697-8863

PROFESSIONALS	TITLE
Gerry H. Langeler	General Partner

INDUSTRY PREFERENCE

- ☒ INFORMATION INDUSTRY
- ☒ Communications
- ☐ Computer Equipment
- ☐ Computer Services
- ☐ Computer Components
- ☐ Computer Entertainment
- ☐ Computer Education
- ☒ Information Technologies
- ☐ Computer Media
- ☒ Software
- ☒ Internet
- ☒ MEDICAL/HEALTHCARE
- ☒ Biotechnology
- ☐ Healthcare Services
- ☒ Life Sciences
- ☒ Medical Products
- ☐ INDUSTRIAL
- ☐ Advanced Materials
- ☐ Chemicals
- ☐ Instruments & Controls

- ☐ BASIC INDUSTRIES
- ☐ Consumer
- ☐ Distribution
- ☐ Manufacturing
- ☐ Retail
- ☐ Service
- ☐ Wholesale
- ☐ SPECIFIC INDUSTRIES
- ☐ Energy
- ☐ Environmental
- ☐ Financial
- ☐ Real Estate
- ☐ Transportation
- ☐ Publishing
- ☐ Food
- ☐ Franchises
- ☒ DIVERSIFIED
- ☐ MISCELLANEOUS

STAGE PREFERENCE

- ☒ EARLY STAGE
- ☒ Seed
- ☒ Start-up
- ☒ 1st Stage
- ☒ LATER STAGE
- ☒ 2nd Stage
- ☒ Mature
- ☐ Mezzanine
- ☒ LBO/MBO
- ☐ Turnaround
- ☐ INT'L EXPANSION
- ☐ WILL CONSIDER ALL
- ☐ VENTURE LEASING

Other Locations: Kirkland WA

Affiliation:
Minimum Investment: Less than $1 Million
Capital Under Management: $100 to $500 Million

GEOGRAPHIC PREF

- ☐ East Coast
- ☒ West Coast
- ☐ Northeast
- ☐ Mid Atlantic
- ☐ Gulf States
- ☒ Northwest
- ☐ Southeast
- ☒ Southwest
- ☐ Midwest
- ☐ Central
- ☐ Local to Office
- ☒ Other Geo Pref
    Pacific Northwest

SHAW VENTURE PARTNERS

400 Southwest Sixth Avenue
Suite 1100
Portland OR 97204

Phone (503) 228-4884   Fax (815) 352-1815

PROFESSIONALS	TITLE
Ralph R. Shaw	Managing General Partner
William Newman	General Partner
Judy Bannerman	Limited Partner

INDUSTRY PREFERENCE

- ☒ INFORMATION INDUSTRY
- ☒ Communications
- ☒ Computer Equipment
- ☒ Computer Services
- ☒ Computer Components
- ☐ Computer Entertainment
- ☒ Computer Education
- ☒ Information Technologies
- ☐ Computer Media
- ☒ Software
- ☒ Internet
- ☒ MEDICAL/HEALTHCARE
- ☒ Biotechnology
- ☒ Healthcare Services
- ☒ Life Sciences
- ☒ Medical Products
- ☒ INDUSTRIAL
- ☒ Advanced Materials
- ☐ Chemicals
- ☒ Instruments & Controls

- ☒ BASIC INDUSTRIES
- ☒ Consumer
- ☐ Distribution
- ☒ Manufacturing
- ☒ Retail
- ☒ Service
- ☐ Wholesale
- ☐ SPECIFIC INDUSTRIES
- ☐ Energy
- ☐ Environmental
- ☐ Financial
- ☐ Real Estate
- ☐ Transportation
- ☐ Publishing
- ☐ Food
- ☐ Franchises
- ☒ DIVERSIFIED
- ☐ MISCELLANEOUS

STAGE PREFERENCE

- ☒ EARLY STAGE
- ☒ Seed
- ☒ Start-up
- ☒ 1st Stage
- ☒ LATER STAGE
- ☒ 2nd Stage
- ☒ Mature
- ☒ Mezzanine
- ☒ LBO/MBO
- ☐ Turnaround
- ☐ INT'L EXPANSION
- ☐ WILL CONSIDER ALL
- ☐ VENTURE LEASING

SBIC
Other Locations:

Affiliation:
Minimum Investment: Less than $1 Million
Capital Under Management: Less than $100 Million

GEOGRAPHIC PREF

- ☐ East Coast
- ☐ West Coast
- ☐ Northeast
- ☐ Mid Atlantic
- ☐ Gulf States
- ☒ Northwest
- ☐ Southeast
- ☐ Southwest
- ☐ Midwest
- ☐ Central
- ☐ Local to Office
- ☐ Other Geo Pref

ADVANTA PARTNERS LP

Welsh & McKean Roads
P.O.   Box 844
Spring House PA 19477-0844

Phone (215) 444-6450   Fax (215) 444-6499

PROFESSIONALS	TITLE
Mitchell Hollin	Managing Director

INDUSTRY PREFERENCE

- ☒ INFORMATION INDUSTRY
- ☒ Communications
- ☒ Computer Equipment
- ☒ Computer Services
- ☒ Computer Components
- ☒ Computer Entertainment
- ☒ Computer Education
- ☒ Information Technologies
- ☒ Computer Media
- ☒ Software
- ☒ Internet
- ☐ MEDICAL/HEALTHCARE
- ☐ Biotechnology
- ☐ Healthcare Services
- ☐ Life Sciences
- ☐ Medical Products
- ☐ INDUSTRIAL
- ☐ Advanced Materials
- ☐ Chemicals
- ☐ Instruments & Controls

- ☐ BASIC INDUSTRIES
- ☐ Consumer
- ☐ Distribution
- ☐ Manufacturing
- ☐ Retail
- ☐ Service
- ☐ Wholesale
- ☐ SPECIFIC INDUSTRIES
- ☐ Energy
- ☐ Environmental
- ☐ Financial
- ☐ Real Estate
- ☐ Transportation
- ☐ Publishing
- ☐ Food
- ☐ Franchises
- ☐ DIVERSIFIED
- ☒ MISCELLANEOUS

STAGE PREFERENCE

- ☐ EARLY STAGE
- ☐ Seed
- ☐ Start-up
- ☐ 1st Stage
- ☒ LATER STAGE
- ☒ 2nd Stage
- ☐ Mature
- ☒ Mezzanine
- ☒ LBO/MBO
- ☐ Turnaround
- ☐ INT'L EXPANSION
- ☐ WILL CONSIDER ALL
- ☐ VENTURE LEASING

Other Locations: New York NY

Affiliation:
Minimum Investment: $1 Million or more
Capital Under Management: $100 to $500 Million

GEOGRAPHIC PREF

- ☐ East Coast
- ☐ West Coast
- ☐ Northeast
- ☐ Mid Atlantic
- ☐ Gulf States
- ☐ Northwest
- ☐ Southeast
- ☐ Southwest
- ☐ Midwest
- ☐ Central
- ☐ Local to Office
- ☐ Other Geo Pref

BACHOW & ASSOCIATES, INC.

Three Bala Plaza East
5th Floor
Bala Cynwyd PA 19004

Phone (610) 660-4900   Fax (610) 660-4930

PROFESSIONALS

Paul S. Bachow
Jay D. Seid
Frank H. Nowaczek
Salvatore Grasso

TITLE

Sr. Managing Director
Managing Director
Managing Director
Managing Director

INDUSTRY PREFERENCE

☒ INFORMATION INDUSTRY
☒ Communications
☒ Computer Equipment
☒ Computer Services
☒ Computer Components
☐ Computer Entertainment
☒ Computer Education
☒ Information Technologies
☐ Computer Media
☒ Software
☒ Internet
☒ MEDICAL/HEALTHCARE
☐ Biotechnology
☐ Healthcare Services
☐ Life Sciences
☐ Medical Products
☒ INDUSTRIAL
☐ Advanced Materials
☐ Chemicals
☒ Instruments & Controls

☒ BASIC INDUSTRIES
☐ Consumer
☐ Distribution
☒ Manufacturing
☐ Retail
☒ Service
☐ Wholesale
☐ SPECIFIC INDUSTRIES
☐ Energy
☐ Environmental
☐ Financial
☐ Real Estate
☐ Transportation
☐ Publishing
☐ Food
☐ Franchises
☒ DIVERSIFIED
☐ MISCELLANEOUS

STAGE PREFERENCE

☐ EARLY STAGE
☐ Seed
☐ Start-up
☐ 1st Stage
☒ LATER STAGE
☒ 2nd Stage
☒ Mature
☒ Mezzanine
☒ LBO/MBO
☒ Turnaround
☐ INT'L EXPANSION
☐ WILL CONSIDER ALL
☒ VENTURE LEASING

Other Locations:

Affiliation:
Minimum Investment: $1 Million or more
Capital Under Management: $100 to $500 Million

GEOGRAPHIC PREF

☒ East Coast
☐ West Coast
☐ Northeast
☐ Mid Atlantic
☐ Gulf States
☐ Northwest
☐ Southeast
☐ Southwest
☐ Midwest
☐ Central
☐ Local to Office
☐ Other Geo Pref

CEO VENTURE FUND

2000 Technology Center Drive
Suite 160
Pittsburgh PA 15219

Phone (412) 687-3451   Fax (412) 687-8139

PROFESSIONALS

William R. Newlin
James Colker
Glen F. Chatfield
Ned Renzi
Gene Yost
Gary Glausser

TITLE

Managing Partner
Managing Partner
General Partner
General Partner
General Partner
General Partner

ceofund@aol.com

INDUSTRY PREFERENCE

☒ INFORMATION INDUSTRY
☒ Communications
☐ Computer Equipment
☒ Computer Services
☒ Computer Components
☐ Computer Entertainment
☐ Computer Education
☒ Information Technologies
☒ Computer Media
☒ Software
☒ Internet
☒ MEDICAL/HEALTHCARE
☒ Biotechnology
☒ Healthcare Services
☒ Life Sciences
☒ Medical Products
☒ INDUSTRIAL
☒ Advanced Materials
☐ Chemicals
☒ Instruments & Controls

☒ BASIC INDUSTRIES
☐ Consumer
☐ Distribution
☐ Manufacturing
☐ Retail
☒ Service
☐ Wholesale
☐ SPECIFIC INDUSTRIES
☐ Energy
☐ Environmental
☐ Financial
☐ Real Estate
☐ Transportation
☐ Publishing
☐ Food
☐ Franchises
☒ DIVERSIFIED
☐ MISCELLANEOUS

STAGE PREFERENCE

☒ EARLY STAGE
☐ Seed
☒ Start-up
☒ 1st Stage
☒ LATER STAGE
☒ 2nd Stage
☐ Mature
☐ Mezzanine
☒ LBO/MBO
☐ Turnaround
☐ INT'L EXPANSION
☐ WILL CONSIDER ALL
☐ VENTURE LEASING

Other Locations:

Affiliation:
Minimum Investment: Less than $1 Million
Capital Under Management: Less than $100 Million

GEOGRAPHIC PREF

☒ East Coast
☐ West Coast
☐ Northeast
☐ Mid Atlantic
☐ Gulf States
☐ Northwest
☐ Southeast
☐ Southwest
☐ Midwest
☐ Central
☐ Local to Office
☐ Other Geo Pref

suite 410

ENERTECH

**700 The Safeguard Building
435 Devon Park Drive
Wayne PA 19087**

Phone (610) 254-4141   Fax (610) 254-4188

PROFESSIONALS	TITLE
David Lincoln	Managing Director
Scott Ungerer	Managing Director

INDUSTRY PREFERENCE

☒ INFORMATION INDUSTRY	☒ BASIC INDUSTRIES
☐ Communications	☐ Consumer
☐ Computer Equipment	☐ Distribution
☒ Computer Services	☐ Manufacturing
☐ Computer Components	☐ Retail
☐ Computer Entertainment	☒ Service
☐ Computer Education	☐ Wholesale
☒ Information Technologies	☒ SPECIFIC INDUSTRIES
☐ Computer Media	☒ Energy
☐ Software	☐ Environmental
☐ Internet	☐ Financial
☐ MEDICAL/HEALTHCARE	☐ Real Estate
☐ Biotechnology	☐ Transportation
☐ Healthcare Services	☐ Publishing
☐ Life Sciences	☐ Food
☐ Medical Products	☐ Franchises
☐ INDUSTRIAL	☒ DIVERSIFIED
☐ Advanced Materials	☒ MISCELLANEOUS
☐ Chemicals	Utilities
☐ Instruments & Controls	

STAGE PREFERENCE

☒ EARLY STAGE
☒ Seed
☒ Start-up
☒ 1st Stage
☒ LATER STAGE
☒ 2nd Stage
☒ Mature
☒ Mezzanine
☒ LBO/MBO
☒ Turnaround
☐ INT'L EXPANSION
☐ WILL CONSIDER ALL
☒ VENTURE LEASING

Other Locations:

Affiliation: Safeguard Scientifics, Inc.
Minimum Investment: Less than $1 Million
Capital Under Management: $100 to $500 Million

GEOGRAPHIC PREF

☐ East Coast
☐ West Coast
☐ Northeast
☐ Mid Atlantic
☐ Gulf States
☐ Northwest
☐ Southeast
☐ Southwest
☐ Midwest
☐ Central
☐ Local to Office
☐ Other Geo Pref

GREATER PHILADELPHIA VENTURE CAPITAL CORP.

**351 East Conestoga Road
Room 203
Wayne PA 19087**

Phone (610) 688-6829   Fax (610) 254-8958

PROFESSIONALS	TITLE
Fred S. Choate	Manager

INDUSTRY PREFERENCE

☐ INFORMATION INDUSTRY	☐ BASIC INDUSTRIES
☐ Communications	☐ Consumer
☐ Computer Equipment	☐ Distribution
☐ Computer Services	☐ Manufacturing
☐ Computer Components	☐ Retail
☐ Computer Entertainment	☐ Service
☐ Computer Education	☐ Wholesale
☐ Information Technologies	☐ SPECIFIC INDUSTRIES
☐ Computer Media	☐ Energy
☐ Software	☐ Environmental
☐ Internet	☐ Financial
☐ MEDICAL/HEALTHCARE	☐ Real Estate
☐ Biotechnology	☐ Transportation
☐ Healthcare Services	☐ Publishing
☐ Life Sciences	☐ Food
☐ Medical Products	☐ Franchises
☐ INDUSTRIAL	☒ DIVERSIFIED
☐ Advanced Materials	☐ MISCELLANEOUS
☐ Chemicals	
☐ Instruments & Controls	

STAGE PREFERENCE

☒ EARLY STAGE
☒ Seed
☒ Start-up
☒ 1st Stage
☒ LATER STAGE
☒ 2nd Stage
☐ Mature
☐ Mezzanine
☐ LBO/MBO
☐ Turnaround
☐ INT'L EXPANSION
☐ WILL CONSIDER ALL
☐ VENTURE LEASING
SSBIC
Other Locations:

Affiliation:
Minimum Investment: Less than $1 Million
Capital Under Management: Less than $100 Million

GEOGRAPHIC PREF

☐ East Coast
☐ West Coast
☐ Northeast
☐ Mid Atlantic
☐ Gulf States
☐ Northwest
☐ Southeast
☐ Southwest
☐ Midwest
☐ Central
☐ Local to Office
☒ Other Geo Pref
   Greater Philadelphia
   PA

GS CAPITAL LP

435 Devon Park Drive
Suite 612
Wayne Pa 19087

Phone (610) 293-9151   Fax (610) 293-1979

PROFESSIONALS	TITLE
Kenneth S. Sweet, Jr.	Principal
Reginald W. Wilkes	Principal
Richard J. Gessner, Jr.	Principal
Earl Layne	Principal

INDUSTRY PREFERENCE

☐ INFORMATION INDUSTRY	☐ BASIC INDUSTRIES
☐ Communications	☐ Consumer
☐ Computer Equipment	☐ Distribution
☐ Computer Services	☐ Manufacturing
☐ Computer Components	☐ Retail
☐ Computer Entertainment	☐ Service
☐ Computer Education	☐ Wholesale
☐ Information Technologies	☒ SPECIFIC INDUSTRIES
☐ Computer Media	☐ Energy
☐ Software	☐ Environmental
☐ Internet	☐ Financial
☐ MEDICAL/HEALTHCARE	☐ Real Estate
☐ Biotechnology	☐ Transportation
☐ Healthcare Services	☐ Publishing
☐ Life Sciences	☐ Food
☐ Medical Products	☒ Franchises
☐ INDUSTRIAL	☒ DIVERSIFIED
☐ Advanced Materials	☒ MISCELLANEOUS
☐ Chemicals	Franchises
☐ Instruments & Controls	

STAGE PREFERENCE

☒ EARLY STAGE
☒ Seed
☒ Start-up
☒ 1st Stage
☒ LATER STAGE
☒ 2nd Stage
☒ Mature
☒ Mezzanine
☒ LBO/MBO
☒ Turnaround
☐ INT'L EXPANSION
☐ WILL CONSIDER ALL
☒ VENTURE LEASING

SBIC SSBIC
Other Locations:

Affiliation:
Minimum Investment: Less than $1 Million
Capital Under Management: Less than $100 Million

GEOGRAPHIC PREF

☒ East Coast
☐ West Coast
☐ Northeast
☒ Mid Atlantic
☐ Gulf States
☐ Northwest
☐ Southeast
☐ Southwest
☐ Midwest
☐ Central
☐ Local to Office
☒ Other Geo Pref
   Mid-Atlantic

INTERNET CAPITAL GROUP

435 Devon Park Drive
Wayne PA 19087

Phone (610) 989-0111   Fax (610) 989-0112

PROFESSIONALS	TITLE
Walter W. Buckley III	President
Douglas A. Alexander	Managing Director
Richard Bunker	Managing Director

INDUSTRY PREFERENCE

☒ INFORMATION INDUSTRY	☐ BASIC INDUSTRIES
☐ Communications	☐ Consumer
☐ Computer Equipment	☐ Distribution
☐ Computer Services	☐ Manufacturing
☐ Computer Components	☐ Retail
☐ Computer Entertainment	☐ Service
☐ Computer Education	☐ Wholesale
☐ Information Technologies	☐ SPECIFIC INDUSTRIES
☐ Computer Media	☐ Energy
☐ Software	☐ Environmental
☒ Internet	☐ Financial
☐ MEDICAL/HEALTHCARE	☐ Real Estate
☐ Biotechnology	☐ Transportation
☐ Healthcare Services	☐ Publishing
☐ Life Sciences	☐ Food
☐ Medical Products	☐ Franchises
☐ INDUSTRIAL	☒ DIVERSIFIED
☐ Advanced Materials	☒ MISCELLANEOUS
☐ Chemicals	
☐ Instruments & Controls	

STAGE PREFERENCE

☒ EARLY STAGE
☐ Seed
☐ Start-up
☒ 1st Stage
☒ LATER STAGE
☒ 2nd Stage
☐ Mature
☐ Mezzanine
☐ LBO/MBO
☐ Turnaround
☐ INT'L EXPANSION
☐ WILL CONSIDER ALL
☐ VENTURE LEASING

Other Locations: Boston MA, San Francisco CA

Affiliation:
Minimum Investment: Less than $1 Million
Capital Under Management: $100 to $500 Million

GEOGRAPHIC PREF

☐ East Coast
☐ West Coast
☐ Northeast
☐ Mid Atlantic
☐ Gulf States
☐ Northwest
☐ Southeast
☐ Southwest
☐ Midwest
☐ Central
☐ Local to Office
☐ Other Geo Pref

KEYSTONE VENTURE CAPITAL

1601 Market Street
Suite 2500
Philadelphia PA 19103

Phone (215) 241-1200   Fax (215) 241-1211

PROFESSIONALS	TITLE
Kerry Dale	General Partner
Peter Ligeti	General Partner
John Regan	General Partner

INDUSTRY PREFERENCE

- ☒ INFORMATION INDUSTRY
- ☒ Communications
- ☒ Computer Equipment
- ☒ Computer Services
- ☐ Computer Components
- ☐ Computer Entertainment
- ☒ Computer Education
- ☒ Information Technologies
- ☒ Computer Media
- ☒ Software
- ☒ Internet
- ☒ MEDICAL/HEALTHCARE
- ☒ Biotechnology
- ☒ Healthcare Services
- ☒ Life Sciences
- ☒ Medical Products
- ☒ INDUSTRIAL
- ☒ Advanced Materials
- ☒ Chemicals
- ☒ Instruments & Controls

- ☒ BASIC INDUSTRIES
- ☐ Consumer
- ☐ Distribution
- ☐ Manufacturing
- ☐ Retail
- ☒ Service
- ☐ Wholesale
- ☒ SPECIFIC INDUSTRIES
- ☒ Energy
- ☐ Environmental
- ☐ Financial
- ☐ Real Estate
- ☐ Transportation
- ☒ Publishing
- ☐ Food
- ☐ Franchises
- ☒ DIVERSIFIED
- ☒ MISCELLANEOUS

STAGE PREFERENCE

- ☒ EARLY STAGE
- ☐ Seed
- ☐ Start-up
- ☒ 1st Stage
- ☒ LATER STAGE
- ☒ 2nd Stage
- ☐ Mature
- ☒ Mezzanine
- ☒ LBO/MBO
- ☐ Turnaround
- ☐ INT'L EXPANSION
- ☐ WILL CONSIDER ALL
- ☐ VENTURE LEASING

Other Locations:

Affiliation:
Minimum Investment: Less than $1 Million
Capital Under Management: $100 to $500 Million

GEOGRAPHIC PREF

- ☐ East Coast
- ☐ West Coast
- ☐ Northeast
- ☒ Mid Atlantic
- ☐ Gulf States
- ☐ Northwest
- ☐ Southeast
- ☐ Southwest
- ☐ Midwest
- ☐ Central
- ☐ Local to Office
- ☒ Other Geo Pref
  Mid-Atlantic

MELLON VENTURES, INC.

One Mellon Bank Center
Room 3200
Pittsburgh PA 15258-0001

Phone (412) 236-3594   Fax (412) 236-3593

PROFESSIONALS	TITLE
Larence Mock, Jr	President
Charles Billerbeck	Managing Director
Paul Cohn	Vice President

INDUSTRY PREFERENCE

- ☒ INFORMATION INDUSTRY
- ☒ Communications
- ☒ Computer Equipment
- ☒ Computer Services
- ☒ Computer Components
- ☒ Computer Entertainment
- ☒ Computer Education
- ☒ Information Technologies
- ☒ Computer Media
- ☒ Software
- ☒ Internet
- ☒ MEDICAL/HEALTHCARE
- ☐ Biotechnology
- ☒ Healthcare Services
- ☐ Life Sciences
- ☐ Medical Products
- ☒ INDUSTRIAL
- ☒ Advanced Materials
- ☒ Chemicals
- ☒ Instruments & Controls

- ☒ BASIC INDUSTRIES
- ☒ Consumer
- ☒ Distribution
- ☒ Manufacturing
- ☒ Retail
- ☒ Service
- ☒ Wholesale
- ☒ SPECIFIC INDUSTRIES
- ☐ Energy
- ☐ Environmental
- ☒ Financial
- ☐ Real Estate
- ☒ Transportation
- ☐ Publishing
- ☐ Food
- ☐ Franchises
- ☒ DIVERSIFIED
- ☒ MISCELLANEOUS

STAGE PREFERENCE

- ☐ EARLY STAGE
- ☐ Seed
- ☐ Start-up
- ☐ 1st Stage
- ☒ LATER STAGE
- ☐ 2nd Stage
- ☐ Mature
- ☒ Mezzanine
- ☒ LBO/MBO
- ☒ Turnaround
- ☐ INT'L EXPANSION
- ☐ WILL CONSIDER ALL
- ☒ VENTURE LEASING

SBIC
Other Locations: Radnor PA, Los Angeles CA, Atlanta GA

Affiliation: Mellon Bank , NA
Minimum Investment: $1 Million or more
Capital Under Management: Less than $100 Million

GEOGRAPHIC PREF

- ☐ East Coast
- ☐ West Coast
- ☐ Northeast
- ☐ Mid Atlantic
- ☐ Gulf States
- ☐ Northwest
- ☐ Southeast
- ☐ Southwest
- ☐ Midwest
- ☐ Central
- ☐ Local to Office
- ☐ Other Geo Pref

MELLON VENTURES, INC.

Five Radnor Corporate Center
100 Matsonford Road, Suite 170
Radnor PA 19087

Phone (610) 688-4600   Fax (610) 688-3930

PROFESSIONALS	TITLE
~~John Shoemaker~~	Managing Director
Robert W Driskell	

INDUSTRY PREFERENCE

☒ INFORMATION INDUSTRY
☒ Communications
☒ Computer Equipment
☒ Computer Services
☒ Computer Components
☒ Computer Entertainment
☒ Computer Education
☒ Information Technologies
☒ Computer Media
☒ Software
☒ Internet
☒ MEDICAL/HEALTHCARE
☐ Biotechnology
☒ Healthcare Services
☐ Life Sciences
☐ Medical Products
☒ INDUSTRIAL
☒ Advanced Materials
☒ Chemicals
☒ Instruments & Controls

☒ BASIC INDUSTRIES
☒ Consumer
☒ Distribution
☒ Manufacturing
☒ Retail
☒ Service
☒ Wholesale
☒ SPECIFIC INDUSTRIES
☐ Energy
☐ Environmental
☒ Financial
☐ Real Estate
☒ Transportation
☐ Publishing
☐ Food
☐ Franchises
☒ DIVERSIFIED
☒ MISCELLANEOUS

STAGE PREFERENCE

☐ EARLY STAGE
☐ Seed
☐ Start-up
☐ 1st Stage
☒ LATER STAGE
☐ 2nd Stage
☐ Mature
☒ Mezzanine
☒ LBO/MBO
☒ Turnaround
☐ INT'L EXPANSION
☐ WILL CONSIDER ALL
☒ VENTURE LEASING

SBIC
Other Locations: Pittsburgh PA, Los Angeles CA, Atlanta GA

Affiliation: Mellon Bank , NA
Minimum Investment: $1 Million or more
Capital Under Management: Less than $100 Million

GEOGRAPHIC PREF

☐ East Coast
☐ West Coast
☐ Northeast
☐ Mid Atlantic
☐ Gulf States
☐ Northwest
☐ Southeast
☐ Southwest
☐ Midwest
☐ Central
☐ Local to Office
☐ Other Geo Pref

MERIDIAN VENTURE PARTNERS

259 Radnor-Chester Road
Suite 140
Radnor PA 19087

Phone (610) 254-2999   Fax (610) 254-2996

PROFESSIONALS	TITLE
Robert E. Brown	General Partner
Elam M. Hitchner III	General Partner
Kenneth E. Jones	General Partner

INDUSTRY PREFERENCE

☒ INFORMATION INDUSTRY
☐ Communications
☐ Computer Equipment
☒ Computer Services
☐ Computer Components
☐ Computer Entertainment
☐ Computer Education
☒ Information Technologies
☒ Computer Media
☒ Software
☐ Internet
☒ MEDICAL/HEALTHCARE
☐ Biotechnology
☒ Healthcare Services
☐ Life Sciences
☐ Medical Products
☐ INDUSTRIAL
☐ Advanced Materials
☐ Chemicals
☐ Instruments & Controls

☒ BASIC INDUSTRIES
☒ Consumer
☒ Distribution
☒ Manufacturing
☒ Retail
☐ Service
☐ Wholesale
☐ SPECIFIC INDUSTRIES
☐ Energy
☐ Environmental
☐ Financial
☐ Real Estate
☐ Transportation
☐ Publishing
☐ Food
☐ Franchises
☒ DIVERSIFIED
☐ MISCELLANEOUS

STAGE PREFERENCE

☐ EARLY STAGE
☐ Seed
☐ Start-up
☐ 1st Stage
☒ LATER STAGE
☒ 2nd Stage
☒ Mature
☒ Mezzanine
☒ LBO/MBO
☐ Turnaround
☐ INT'L EXPANSION
☐ WILL CONSIDER ALL
☐ VENTURE LEASING

SBIC
Other Locations:

Affiliation:
Minimum Investment: $1 Million or more
Capital Under Management: Less than $100 Million

GEOGRAPHIC PREF

☒ East Coast
☐ West Coast
☐ Northeast
☐ Mid Atlantic
☐ Gulf States
☐ Northwest
☐ Southeast
☐ Southwest
☐ Midwest
☐ Central
☐ Local to Office
☐ Other Geo Pref

MID-ATLANTIC VENTURE FUNDS

125 Goodman Drive
Lehigh University
Bethlehem PA 18015

Phone (610) 865-6550   Fax (610) 865-6427

PROFESSIONALS	TITLE
Frederick J. Beste III	General Partner
Glen R. Bressner	General Partner

INDUSTRY PREFERENCE

- ☒ INFORMATION INDUSTRY
- ☒ Communications
- ☒ Computer Equipment
- ☒ Computer Services
- ☒ Computer Components
- ☐ Computer Entertainment
- ☒ Computer Education
- ☒ Information Technologies
- ☒ Computer Media
- ☒ Software
- ☒ Internet
- ☒ MEDICAL/HEALTHCARE
- ☐ Biotechnology
- ☒ Healthcare Services
- ☐ Life Sciences
- ☒ Medical Products
- ☒ INDUSTRIAL
- ☒ Advanced Materials
- ☒ Chemicals
- ☒ Instruments & Controls

- ☒ BASIC INDUSTRIES
- ☐ Consumer
- ☐ Distribution
- ☐ Manufacturing
- ☐ Retail
- ☒ Service
- ☐ Wholesale
- ☐ SPECIFIC INDUSTRIES
- ☐ Energy
- ☐ Environmental
- ☐ Financial
- ☐ Real Estate
- ☐ Transportation
- ☐ Publishing
- ☐ Food
- ☐ Franchises
- ☒ DIVERSIFIED
- ☐ MISCELLANEOUS

STAGE PREFERENCE

- ☒ EARLY STAGE
- ☒ Seed
- ☒ Start-up
- ☒ 1st Stage
- ☒ LATER STAGE
- ☒ 2nd Stage
- ☐ Mature
- ☐ Mezzanine
- ☒ LBO/MBO
- ☒ Turnaround
- ☐ INT'L EXPANSION
- ☐ WILL CONSIDER ALL
- ☒ VENTURE LEASING

Other Locations: Reston VA

Affiliation: formerly NEPA Venture Fund
Minimum Investment: Less than $1 Million
Capital Under Management: Less than $100 Million

GEOGRAPHIC PREF

- ☐ East Coast
- ☐ West Coast
- ☐ Northeast
- ☒ Mid Atlantic
- ☐ Gulf States
- ☐ Northwest
- ☐ Southeast
- ☐ Southwest
- ☐ Midwest
- ☐ Central
- ☐ Local to Office
- ☒ Other Geo Pref
  Mid-Atlantic

PATRICOF AND COMPANY

Executive Terrace Building
455 South Gulph Road, Suite 410
Radnor PA 19087

Phone (610) 265-0286   Fax (610) 265-4959

PROFESSIONALS	TITLE
George M. Jenkins	Managing Director

INDUSTRY PREFERENCE

- ☒ INFORMATION INDUSTRY
- ☒ Communications
- ☒ Computer Equipment
- ☒ Computer Services
- ☒ Computer Components
- ☐ Computer Entertainment
- ☒ Computer Education
- ☒ Information Technologies
- ☒ Computer Media
- ☒ Software
- ☒ Internet
- ☒ MEDICAL/HEALTHCARE
- ☒ Biotechnology
- ☒ Healthcare Services
- ☒ Life Sciences
- ☒ Medical Products
- ☒ INDUSTRIAL
- ☒ Advanced Materials
- ☒ Chemicals
- ☒ Instruments & Controls

- ☒ BASIC INDUSTRIES
- ☒ Consumer
- ☐ Distribution
- ☒ Manufacturing
- ☒ Retail
- ☒ Service
- ☐ Wholesale
- ☒ SPECIFIC INDUSTRIES
- ☒ Energy
- ☒ Environmental
- ☒ Financial
- ☐ Real Estate
- ☐ Transportation
- ☐ Publishing
- ☐ Food
- ☐ Franchises
- ☒ DIVERSIFIED
- ☐ MISCELLANEOUS

STAGE PREFERENCE

- ☒ EARLY STAGE
- ☒ Seed
- ☒ Start-up
- ☒ 1st Stage
- ☒ LATER STAGE
- ☒ 2nd Stage
- ☒ Mature
- ☒ Mezzanine
- ☒ LBO/MBO
- ☒ Turnaround
- ☐ INT'L EXPANSION
- ☐ WILL CONSIDER ALL
- ☒ VENTURE LEASING

Other Locations: New York NY, Palo Alto CA

Affiliation: MMG Patricof & Co., Inc.
Minimum Investment: Less than $1 Million
Capital Under Management: Over $500 Million

GEOGRAPHIC PREF

- ☐ East Coast
- ☐ West Coast
- ☐ Northeast
- ☐ Mid Atlantic
- ☐ Gulf States
- ☐ Northwest
- ☐ Southeast
- ☐ Southwest
- ☐ Midwest
- ☐ Central
- ☐ Local to Office
- ☐ Other Geo Pref

PENNSYLVANIA EARLY STAGE PARTNERS

~~800~~ The Safeguard Building
435 Devon Park Drive *Suite 510*
Wayne PA 19087

Phone (610) 293-4075   Fax (610) 254-4240

PROFESSIONALS
Michael Bolton

TITLE
Managing Director

INDUSTRY PREFERENCE

- ☒ INFORMATION INDUSTRY
- ☒ Communications
- ☒ Computer Equipment
- ☒ Computer Services
- ☒ Computer Components
- ☐ Computer Entertainment
- ☒ Computer Education
- ☒ Information Technologies
- ☒ Computer Media
- ☒ Software
- ☒ Internet
- ☒ MEDICAL/HEALTHCARE
- ☒ Biotechnology
- ☒ Healthcare Services
- ☒ Life Sciences
- ☒ Medical Products
- ☒ INDUSTRIAL
- ☒ Advanced Materials
- ☒ Chemicals
- ☒ Instruments & Controls

- ☒ BASIC INDUSTRIES
- ☐ Consumer
- ☐ Distribution
- ☐ Manufacturing
- ☐ Retail
- ☒ Service
- ☐ Wholesale
- ☐ SPECIFIC INDUSTRIES
- ☐ Energy
- ☐ Environmental
- ☐ Financial
- ☐ Real Estate
- ☐ Transportation
- ☐ Publishing
- ☐ Food
- ☐ Franchises
- ☒ DIVERSIFIED
- ☒ MISCELLANEOUS

STAGE PREFERENCE

- ☒ EARLY STAGE
- ☒ Seed
- ☒ Start-up
- ☒ 1st Stage
- ☐ LATER STAGE
- ☐ 2nd Stage
- ☐ Mature
- ☐ Mezzanine
- ☐ LBO/MBO
- ☐ Turnaround
- ☐ INT'L EXPANSION
- ☐ WILL CONSIDER ALL
- ☐ VENTURE LEASING

Other Locations:

Affiliation: Safeguard Scientifics, Inc.
Minimum Investment: Less than $1 Million
Capital Under Management: $100 to $500 Million

GEOGRAPHIC PREF

- ☐ East Coast
- ☐ West Coast
- ☐ Northeast
- ☐ Mid Atlantic
- ☐ Gulf States
- ☐ Northwest
- ☐ Southeast
- ☐ Southwest
- ☐ Midwest
- ☐ Central
- ☐ Local to Office
- ☒ Other Geo Pref
  PA

PHILADELPHIA VENTURES, INC.

The Bellevue - 8th Floor
200 South Broad Street
Philadelphia PA 19102

Phone (215) 732-4445   Fax (215) 732-4644

PROFESSIONALS
Walter Aikman
Thomas Morse
Charles Burton

TITLE
Managing Director
Managing Director
Managing Director

INDUSTRY PREFERENCE

- ☒ INFORMATION INDUSTRY
- ☒ Communications
- ☒ Computer Equipment
- ☒ Computer Services
- ☒ Computer Components
- ☒ Computer Entertainment
- ☒ Computer Education
- ☒ Information Technologies
- ☒ Computer Media
- ☒ Software
- ☒ Internet
- ☒ MEDICAL/HEALTHCARE
- ☒ Biotechnology
- ☒ Healthcare Services
- ☒ Life Sciences
- ☒ Medical Products
- ☒ INDUSTRIAL
- ☒ Advanced Materials
- ☒ Chemicals
- ☒ Instruments & Controls

- ☒ BASIC INDUSTRIES
- ☐ Consumer
- ☒ Distribution
- ☐ Manufacturing
- ☐ Retail
- ☐ Service
- ☐ Wholesale
- ☐ SPECIFIC INDUSTRIES
- ☐ Energy
- ☐ Environmental
- ☐ Financial
- ☐ Real Estate
- ☐ Transportation
- ☐ Publishing
- ☐ Food
- ☐ Franchises
- ☒ DIVERSIFIED
- ☒ MISCELLANEOUS

STAGE PREFERENCE

- ☒ EARLY STAGE
- ☐ Seed
- ☒ Start-up
- ☒ 1st Stage
- ☒ LATER STAGE
- ☒ 2nd Stage
- ☐ Mature
- ☒ Mezzanine
- ☒ LBO/MBO
- ☐ Turnaround
- ☐ INT'L EXPANSION
- ☐ WILL CONSIDER ALL
- ☐ VENTURE LEASING

Other Locations:

Affiliation:
Minimum Investment: Less than $1 Million
Capital Under Management: $100 to $500 Million

GEOGRAPHIC PREF

- ☐ East Coast
- ☐ West Coast
- ☐ Northeast
- ☐ Mid Atlantic
- ☐ Gulf States
- ☐ Northwest
- ☐ Southeast
- ☐ Southwest
- ☐ Midwest
- ☐ Central
- ☐ Local to Office
- ☐ Other Geo Pref

PNC EQUITY MANAGEMENT CORP.

3150 CNG Tower
625 Liberty Avenue
Pittsburgh PA 15222

Phone (412) 768-8661   Fax (412) 762-6233

PROFESSIONALS	TITLE
Gary J. Zentner	President
David McL. Hillman	Executive Vice President
David J. Blair	Vice President
Paul A. Giusti	Vice President
Peter V. Del Presto	Vice President

INDUSTRY PREFERENCE

☒ INFORMATION INDUSTRY	☒ BASIC INDUSTRIES
☐ Communications	☐ Consumer
☐ Computer Equipment	☒ Distribution
☐ Computer Services	☒ Manufacturing
☐ Computer Components	☒ Retail
☐ Computer Entertainment	☒ Service
☐ Computer Education	☐ Wholesale
☐ Information Technologies	☒ SPECIFIC INDUSTRIES
☒ Computer Media	☐ Energy
☐ Software	☐ Environmental
☐ Internet	☐ Financial
☒ MEDICAL/HEALTHCARE	☐ Real Estate
☐ Biotechnology	☐ Transportation
☒ Healthcare Services	☐ Publishing
☐ Life Sciences	☐ Food
☐ Medical Products	☐ Franchises
☐ INDUSTRIAL	☒ DIVERSIFIED
☐ Advanced Materials	☐ MISCELLANEOUS
☐ Chemicals	
☐ Instruments & Controls	

STAGE PREFERENCE

☒ EARLY STAGE
☐ Seed
☐ Start-up
☒ 1st Stage
☒ LATER STAGE
☒ 2nd Stage
☒ Mature
☒ Mezzanine
☒ LBO/MBO
☒ Turnaround
☐ INT'L EXPANSION
☐ WILL CONSIDER ALL
☒ VENTURE LEASING

SBIC
Other Locations:

GEOGRAPHIC PREF

☐ East Coast
☐ West Coast
☒ Northeast
☐ Mid Atlantic
☐ Gulf States
☐ Northwest
☐ Southeast
☐ Southwest
☐ Midwest
☐ Central
☐ Local to Office
☐ Other Geo Pref

Affiliation: PNC Financial Corp.
Minimum Investment: $1 Million or more
Capital Under Management: Over $500 Million

ROCK HILL VENTURES INC.

100 Front Street
Suite 1350
West Conshohocken PA 19428

Phone (610) 940-0300   Fax (610) 940-0301

PROFESSIONALS	TITLE
Hal Broderson	Partner
Charles Hadley	Partner

INDUSTRY PREFERENCE

☐ INFORMATION INDUSTRY	☐ BASIC INDUSTRIES
☐ Communications	☐ Consumer
☐ Computer Equipment	☐ Distribution
☐ Computer Services	☐ Manufacturing
☐ Computer Components	☐ Retail
☐ Computer Entertainment	☐ Service
☐ Computer Education	☐ Wholesale
☐ Information Technologies	☒ SPECIFIC INDUSTRIES
☐ Computer Media	☐ Energy
☐ Software	☐ Environmental
☐ Internet	☐ Financial
☒ MEDICAL/HEALTHCARE	☐ Real Estate
☒ Biotechnology	☐ Transportation
☒ Healthcare Services	☐ Publishing
☒ Life Sciences	☐ Food
☒ Medical Products	☐ Franchises
☐ INDUSTRIAL	☐ DIVERSIFIED
☐ Advanced Materials	☒ MISCELLANEOUS
☐ Chemicals	
☐ Instruments & Controls	

STAGE PREFERENCE

☒ EARLY STAGE
☒ Seed
☒ Start-up
☒ 1st Stage
☒ LATER STAGE
☒ 2nd Stage
☐ Mature
☒ Mezzanine
☒ LBO/MBO
☐ Turnaround
☐ INT'L EXPANSION
☐ WILL CONSIDER ALL
☐ VENTURE LEASING

Other Locations:

GEOGRAPHIC PREF

☒ East Coast
☐ West Coast
☐ Northeast
☐ Mid Atlantic
☐ Gulf States
☐ Northwest
☐ Southeast
☐ Southwest
☐ Midwest
☐ Central
☐ Local to Office
☐ Other Geo Pref

Affiliation:
Minimum Investment: $1 Million or more
Capital Under Management: $100 to $500 Million

SAFEGUARD INTERNATIONAL FUND

800 The Safeguard Building
435 Devon Park Drive
Wayne PA 19087

Phone (610) 293-0838   Fax (610) 293-0601

PROFESSIONALS	TITLE
Heinz C. Schimmelbusch	Managing Director
Michael R. Holly	Managing Director
Arthur Spector	Managing Director

INDUSTRY PREFERENCE

☐ INFORMATION INDUSTRY	☒ BASIC INDUSTRIES
☐ Communications	☐ Consumer
☐ Computer Equipment	☐ Distribution
☐ Computer Services	☒ Manufacturing
☐ Computer Components	☐ Retail
☐ Computer Entertainment	☐ Service
☐ Computer Education	☐ Wholesale
☐ Information Technologies	☒ SPECIFIC INDUSTRIES
☐ Computer Media	☒ Energy
☐ Software	☐ Environmental
☐ Internet	☐ Financial
☐ MEDICAL/HEALTHCARE	☐ Real Estate
☐ Biotechnology	☐ Transportation
☐ Healthcare Services	☐ Publishing
☐ Life Sciences	☐ Food
☐ Medical Products	☐ Franchises
☒ INDUSTRIAL	☒ DIVERSIFIED
☒ Advanced Materials	☒ MISCELLANEOUS
☒ Chemicals	Utilities
☒ Instruments & Controls	

STAGE PREFERENCE

☒ EARLY STAGE
☐ Seed
☒ Start-up
☒ 1st Stage
☒ LATER STAGE
☒ 2nd Stage
☒ Mature
☒ Mezzanine
☒ LBO/MBO
☒ Turnaround
☒ INT'L EXPANSION
☐ WILL CONSIDER ALL
☒ VENTURE LEASING

Other Locations:

Affiliation: Safeguard Scientifics, Inc.
Minimum Investment: Less than $1 Million
Capital Under Management: $100 to $500 Million

GEOGRAPHIC PREF

☐ East Coast
☐ West Coast
☐ Northeast
☐ Mid Atlantic
☐ Gulf States
☐ Northwest
☐ Southeast
☐ Southwest
☐ Midwest
☐ Central
☐ Local to Office
☐ Other Geo Pref

SANDHURST GROUP

351 E. Conestoga Road
Wayne PA 19087

Phone (610) 688-6829   Fax (610) 254-8958

PROFESSIONALS	TITLE
Fred G. Choate	General Manager

INDUSTRY PREFERENCE

☒ INFORMATION INDUSTRY	☒ BASIC INDUSTRIES
☐ Communications	☒ Consumer
☐ Computer Equipment	☐ Distribution
☐ Computer Services	☐ Manufacturing
☒ Computer Components	☐ Retail
☐ Computer Entertainment	☐ Service
☐ Computer Education	☐ Wholesale
☐ Information Technologies	☒ SPECIFIC INDUSTRIES
☐ Computer Media	☐ Energy
☐ Software	☐ Environmental
☐ Internet	☐ Financial
☐ MEDICAL/HEALTHCARE	☐ Real Estate
☐ Biotechnology	☐ Transportation
☐ Healthcare Services	☐ Publishing
☐ Life Sciences	☐ Food
☐ Medical Products	☐ Franchises
☒ INDUSTRIAL	☒ DIVERSIFIED
☐ Advanced Materials	☐ MISCELLANEOUS
☐ Chemicals	
☒ Instruments & Controls	

STAGE PREFERENCE

☐ EARLY STAGE
☐ Seed
☐ Start-up
☐ 1st Stage
☒ LATER STAGE
☒ 2nd Stage
☐ Mature
☐ Mezzanine
☒ LBO/MBO
☐ Turnaround
☐ INT'L EXPANSION
☐ WILL CONSIDER ALL
☐ VENTURE LEASING

Other Locations:

Affiliation:
Minimum Investment: Less than $1 Million
Capital Under Management: Less than $100 Million

GEOGRAPHIC PREF

☒ East Coast
☐ West Coast
☐ Northeast
☐ Mid Atlantic
☐ Gulf States
☐ Northwest
☐ Southeast
☐ Southwest
☐ Midwest
☐ Central
☐ Local to Office
☐ Other Geo Pref

SCP PRIVATE EQUITY PARTNERS, LP

300 The Safeguard Building
435 Devon Park Drive
Wayne PA 19087

Phone (610) 995-2900   Fax (610) 293-0601

PROFESSIONALS	TITLE
Winston J. Churchill	Managing General Partner
Samuel A. Plum	Managing General Partner

INDUSTRY PREFERENCE

☒ INFORMATION INDUSTRY	☒ BASIC INDUSTRIES
☒ Communications	☒ Consumer
☒ Computer Equipment	☐ Distribution
☒ Computer Services	☐ Manufacturing
☒ Computer Components	☐ Retail
☐ Computer Entertainment	☒ Service
☒ Computer Education	☐ Wholesale
☒ Information Technologies	☒ SPECIFIC INDUSTRIES
☒ Computer Media	☐ Energy
☒ Software	☐ Environmental
☒ Internet	☒ Financial
☒ MEDICAL/HEALTHCARE	☒ Real Estate
☒ Biotechnology	☐ Transportation
☒ Healthcare Services	☐ Publishing
☒ Life Sciences	☐ Food
☒ Medical Products	☐ Franchises
☐ INDUSTRIAL	☒ DIVERSIFIED
☐ Advanced Materials	☒ MISCELLANEOUS
☐ Chemicals	
☐ Instruments & Controls	

STAGE PREFERENCE

☒ EARLY STAGE
☐ Seed
☐ Start-up
☒ 1st Stage
☒ LATER STAGE
☒ 2nd Stage
☒ Mature
☒ Mezzanine
☒ LBO/MBO
☐ Turnaround
☐ INT'L EXPANSION
☐ WILL CONSIDER ALL
☐ VENTURE LEASING

Other Locations:

Affiliation: Safeguard Scientifics, Inc.
Minimum Investment: Less than $1 Million
Capital Under Management: $100 to $500 Million

GEOGRAPHIC PREF

☐ East Coast
☐ West Coast
☐ Northeast
☐ Mid Atlantic
☐ Gulf States
☐ Northwest
☐ Southeast
☐ Southwest
☐ Midwest
☐ Central
☐ Local to Office
☐ Other Geo Pref

SR ONE LTD.

Four Tower Bridge
200 Barr Harbor Drive, Suite 250
West Conshohocken PA 19428-2977

Phone (610) 567-1000   Fax (610) 567-1039

PROFESSIONALS	TITLE
Dr. Brenda D. ~~Gavta~~ Gavin	President
Dr. Barbara J. Dalton	Vice President
Dr. Raymond J. Whitaker	Vice President
Dr. Elaine V. Jones	Investment Manager
John N Braca	Chief Financial Officer

INDUSTRY PREFERENCE

☐ INFORMATION INDUSTRY	☐ BASIC INDUSTRIES
☐ Communications	☐ Consumer
☐ Computer Equipment	☐ Distribution
☐ Computer Services	☐ Manufacturing
☐ Computer Components	☐ Retail
☐ Computer Entertainment	☐ Service
☐ Computer Education	☐ Wholesale
☐ Information Technologies	☐ SPECIFIC INDUSTRIES
☐ Computer Media	☐ Energy
☐ Software	☐ Environmental
☐ Internet	☐ Financial
☒ MEDICAL/HEALTHCARE	☐ Real Estate
☒ Biotechnology	☐ Transportation
☒ Healthcare Services	☐ Publishing
☒ Life Sciences	☐ Food
☒ Medical Products	☐ Franchises
☐ INDUSTRIAL	☐ DIVERSIFIED
☐ Advanced Materials	☒ MISCELLANEOUS
☐ Chemicals	
☐ Instruments & Controls	

STAGE PREFERENCE

☒ EARLY STAGE
☒ Seed
☒ Start-up
☒ 1st Stage
☒ LATER STAGE
☒ 2nd Stage
☐ Mature
☒ Mezzanine
☒ LBO/MBO
☐ Turnaround
☐ INT'L EXPANSION
☐ WILL CONSIDER ALL
☐ VENTURE LEASING

Other Locations:

Affiliation: SmithKline Beecham
Minimum Investment: Less than $1 Million
Capital Under Management: $100 to $500 Million

GEOGRAPHIC PREF

☐ East Coast
☐ West Coast
☐ Northeast
☐ Mid Atlantic
☐ Gulf States
☐ Northwest
☐ Southeast
☐ Southwest
☐ Midwest
☐ Central
☐ Local to Office
☐ Other Geo Pref

TA ASSOCIATES, INC.

**One Oxford Center
Suite 4260
Pittsburgh PA 15219-1407**

Phone (412) 441-4949   Fax (412) 441-5784

PROFESSIONALS	TITLE
Jacqueline C. Morby	Managing Director

INDUSTRY PREFERENCE

- ☒ INFORMATION INDUSTRY
- ☒ Communications
- ☒ Computer Equipment
- ☒ Computer Services
- ☒ Computer Components
- ☐ Computer Entertainment
- ☒ Computer Education
- ☒ Information Technologies
- ☒ Computer Media
- ☒ Software
- ☒ Internet
- ☒ MEDICAL/HEALTHCARE
- ☐ Biotechnology
- ☒ Healthcare Services
- ☐ Life Sciences
- ☐ Medical Products
- ☒ INDUSTRIAL
- ☐ Advanced Materials
- ☐ Chemicals
- ☒ Instruments & Controls

- ☒ BASIC INDUSTRIES
- ☐ Consumer
- ☒ Distribution
- ☐ Manufacturing
- ☒ Retail
- ☒ Service
- ☐ Wholesale
- ☒ SPECIFIC INDUSTRIES
- ☒ Energy
- ☒ Environmental
- ☒ Financial
- ☐ Real Estate
- ☐ Transportation
- ☐ Publishing
- ☐ Food
- ☐ Franchises
- ☒ DIVERSIFIED
- ☐ MISCELLANEOUS

STAGE PREFERENCE

- ☐ EARLY STAGE
- ☐ Seed
- ☐ Start-up
- ☐ 1st Stage
- ☒ LATER STAGE
- ☒ 2nd Stage
- ☒ Mature
- ☒ Mezzanine
- ☒ LBO/MBO
- ☐ Turnaround
- ☐ INT'L EXPANSION
- ☐ WILL CONSIDER ALL
- ☐ VENTURE LEASING

Other Locations: Boston MA, Palo Alto CA

Affiliation:
Minimum Investment:$1 Million or more
Capital Under Management: Over $500 Million

GEOGRAPHIC PREF

- ☐ East Coast
- ☐ West Coast
- ☐ Northeast
- ☐ Mid Atlantic
- ☐ Gulf States
- ☐ Northwest
- ☐ Southeast
- ☐ Southwest
- ☐ Midwest
- ☐ Central
- ☐ Local to Office
- ☐ Other Geo Pref

TL VENTURES

**700 The Safeguard Building
435 Devon Park Drive
Wayne PA 19087**

Phone (610) 971-1515   Fax (610) 254-4188

PROFESSIONALS	TITLE
Robert E. Keith	Managing Director
Gary Anderson	Managing Director
Mark J. DeNino	Managing Director
Christopher Moller	Managing Director

INDUSTRY PREFERENCE

- ☒ INFORMATION INDUSTRY
- ☒ Communications
- ☒ Computer Equipment
- ☒ Computer Services
- ☒ Computer Components
- ☐ Computer Entertainment
- ☒ Computer Education
- ☒ Information Technologies
- ☒ Computer Media
- ☒ Software
- ☒ Internet
- ☒ MEDICAL/HEALTHCARE
- ☒ Biotechnology
- ☒ Healthcare Services
- ☒ Life Sciences
- ☒ Medical Products
- ☐ INDUSTRIAL
- ☐ Advanced Materials
- ☐ Chemicals
- ☐ Instruments & Controls

- ☐ BASIC INDUSTRIES
- ☐ Consumer
- ☐ Distribution
- ☐ Manufacturing
- ☐ Retail
- ☐ Service
- ☐ Wholesale
- ☒ SPECIFIC INDUSTRIES
- ☒ Energy
- ☐ Environmental
- ☐ Financial
- ☐ Real Estate
- ☐ Transportation
- ☐ Publishing
- ☐ Food
- ☐ Franchises
- ☒ DIVERSIFIED
- ☒ MISCELLANEOUS
  - Utilities

STAGE PREFERENCE

- ☒ EARLY STAGE
- ☒ Seed
- ☒ Start-up
- ☒ 1st Stage
- ☒ LATER STAGE
- ☒ 2nd Stage
- ☒ Mature
- ☒ Mezzanine
- ☒ LBO/MBO
- ☒ Turnaround
- ☐ INT'L EXPANSION
- ☐ WILL CONSIDER ALL
- ☒ VENTURE LEASING

Other Locations:

Affiliation: Safeguard Scientifics, Inc.
Minimum Investment: Less than $1 Million
Capital Under Management: $100 to $500 Million

GEOGRAPHIC PREF

- ☐ East Coast
- ☐ West Coast
- ☐ Northeast
- ☐ Mid Atlantic
- ☐ Gulf States
- ☐ Northwest
- ☐ Southeast
- ☐ Southwest
- ☐ Midwest
- ☐ Central
- ☐ Local to Office
- ☐ Other Geo Pref

FLEET EQUITY PARTNERS

50 Kennedy Plaza
12th Floor
Providence RI 02903

Phone (401) 278-6770   Fax (401) 278-6387

PROFESSIONALS	TITLE
Habib Gorgi	Partner
Robert M.VanDegna	Partner
Rory Smith	Partner
Greg Barr	Partner
Ted Mocarski	Partner

INDUSTRY PREFERENCE

- ☒ INFORMATION INDUSTRY
- ☒ Communications
- ☐ Computer Equipment
- ☐ Computer Services
- ☐ Computer Components
- ☐ Computer Entertainment
- ☐ Computer Education
- ☒ Information Technologies
- ☒ Computer Media
- ☐ Software
- ☐ Internet
- ☒ MEDICAL/HEALTHCARE
- ☐ Biotechnology
- ☒ Healthcare Services
- ☐ Life Sciences
- ☐ Medical Products
- ☐ INDUSTRIAL
- ☐ Advanced Materials
- ☐ Chemicals
- ☐ Instruments & Controls

- ☒ BASIC INDUSTRIES
- ☒ Consumer
- ☐ Distribution
- ☒ Manufacturing
- ☐ Retail
- ☒ Service
- ☐ Wholesale
- ☒ SPECIFIC INDUSTRIES
- ☐ Energy
- ☐ Environmental
- ☐ Financial
- ☐ Real Estate
- ☐ Transportation
- ☒ Publishing
- ☐ Food
- ☐ Franchises
- ☒ DIVERSIFIED
- ☐ MISCELLANEOUS

STAGE PREFERENCE

- ☐ EARLY STAGE
- ☐ Seed
- ☐ Start-up
- ☐ 1st Stage
- ☒ LATER STAGE
- ☒ 2nd Stage
- ☐ Mature
- ☐ Mezzanine
- ☒ LBO/MBO
- ☒ Turnaround
- ☐ INT'L EXPANSION
- ☐ WILL CONSIDER ALL
- ☒ VENTURE LEASING

SBIC
Other Locations:

Affiliation: Fleet Ventures Resources, Inc.
Minimum Investment: $1 Million or more
Capital Under Management: Over $500 Million

GEOGRAPHIC PREF

- ☐ East Coast
- ☐ West Coast
- ☐ Northeast
- ☐ Mid Atlantic
- ☐ Gulf States
- ☐ Northwest
- ☐ Southeast
- ☐ Southwest
- ☐ Midwest
- ☐ Central
- ☐ Local to Office
- ☐ Other Geo Pref

PROVIDENCE EQUITY PARTNERS

50 Kennedy Plaza
9th Floor
Providence RI 02903

Phone (401) 751-1700   Fax (401) 751-1790

PROFESSIONALS	TITLE
Johnathon Nelson	President
Glenn Creamer	Managing Director
Paul Salem	Managing Director

INDUSTRY PREFERENCE

- ☒ INFORMATION INDUSTRY
- ☒ Communications
- ☐ Computer Equipment
- ☐ Computer Services
- ☐ Computer Components
- ☐ Computer Entertainment
- ☐ Computer Education
- ☐ Information Technologies
- ☒ Computer Media
- ☐ Software
- ☒ Internet
- ☐ MEDICAL/HEALTHCARE
- ☐ Biotechnology
- ☐ Healthcare Services
- ☐ Life Sciences
- ☐ Medical Products
- ☐ INDUSTRIAL
- ☐ Advanced Materials
- ☐ Chemicals
- ☐ Instruments & Controls

- ☐ BASIC INDUSTRIES
- ☐ Consumer
- ☐ Distribution
- ☐ Manufacturing
- ☐ Retail
- ☐ Service
- ☐ Wholesale
- ☐ SPECIFIC INDUSTRIES
- ☐ Energy
- ☐ Environmental
- ☐ Financial
- ☐ Real Estate
- ☐ Transportation
- ☐ Publishing
- ☐ Food
- ☐ Franchises
- ☐ DIVERSIFIED
- ☒ MISCELLANEOUS

STAGE PREFERENCE

- ☐ EARLY STAGE
- ☐ Seed
- ☐ Start-up
- ☐ 1st Stage
- ☒ LATER STAGE
- ☒ 2nd Stage
- ☐ Mature
- ☒ Mezzanine
- ☒ LBO/MBO
- ☐ Turnaround
- ☐ INT'L EXPANSION
- ☐ WILL CONSIDER ALL
- ☐ VENTURE LEASING

Other Locations:

Affiliation:
Minimum Investment: $1 Million or more
Capital Under Management: Over $500 Million

GEOGRAPHIC PREF

- ☐ East Coast
- ☐ West Coast
- ☐ Northeast
- ☐ Mid Atlantic
- ☐ Gulf States
- ☐ Northwest
- ☐ Southeast
- ☐ Southwest
- ☐ Midwest
- ☐ Central
- ☐ Local to Office
- ☐ Other Geo Pref

TRANSAMERICA MEZZANINE FINANCING, INC.

7 North Laurens Street
Suite 603
Greenville SC 29601

Phone (864) 232-6198   Fax (864) 241-4444

PROFESSIONALS

Capers A. Easterby
William A. Litchfield
Roger G. Brook
Edward P. Stein

TITLE

President
Sr. Vice President
Vice President
Vice President

INDUSTRY PREFERENCE

☒ INFORMATION INDUSTRY
☒ Communications
☒ Computer Equipment
☒ Computer Services
☒ Computer Components
☐ Computer Entertainment
☒ Computer Education
☒ Information Technologies
☒ Computer Media
☒ Software
☒ Internet
☒ MEDICAL/HEALTHCARE
☐ Biotechnology
☒ Healthcare Services
☐ Life Sciences
☒ Medical Products
☐ INDUSTRIAL
☐ Advanced Materials
☐ Chemicals
☐ Instruments & Controls

☐ BASIC INDUSTRIES
☐ Consumer
☐ Distribution
☐ Manufacturing
☐ Retail
☐ Service
☐ Wholesale
☐ SPECIFIC INDUSTRIES
☐ Energy
☐ Environmental
☐ Financial
☐ Real Estate
☐ Transportation
☐ Publishing
☐ Food
☐ Franchises
☒ DIVERSIFIED
☒ MISCELLANEOUS

STAGE PREFERENCE

☐ EARLY STAGE
☐ Seed
☐ Start-up
☐ 1st Stage
☒ LATER STAGE
☐ 2nd Stage
☒ Mature
☒ Mezzanine
☒ LBO/MBO
☐ Turnaround
☐ INT'L EXPANSION
☐ WILL CONSIDER ALL
☐ VENTURE LEASING

SBIC
Other Locations:

Affiliation:
Minimum Investment: $1 Million or more
Capital Under Management: Less than $100 Million

GEOGRAPHIC PREF

☒ East Coast
☐ West Coast
☒ Northeast
☐ Mid Atlantic
☐ Gulf States
☐ Northwest
☒ Southeast
☒ Southwest
☐ Midwest
☐ Central
☐ Local to Office
☐ Other Geo Pref

COLEMAN SWENSON HOFFMAN BOOTH INC.

237 Second Avenue South
Franklin TN 37064

Phone (615) 791-9462   Fax (615) 791-9636

PROFESSIONALS

Larry Coleman
Dave Swenson
Jay Hoffman

TITLE

Managing General Partner
General Partner
General Partner

INDUSTRY PREFERENCE

☐ INFORMATION INDUSTRY
☐ Communications
☐ Computer Equipment
☐ Computer Services
☐ Computer Components
☐ Computer Entertainment
☐ Computer Education
☐ Information Technologies
☐ Computer Media
☐ Software
☐ Internet
☒ MEDICAL/HEALTHCARE
☐ Biotechnology
☒ Healthcare Services
☒ Life Sciences
☒ Medical Products
☐ INDUSTRIAL
☐ Advanced Materials
☐ Chemicals
☐ Instruments & Controls

☐ BASIC INDUSTRIES
☐ Consumer
☐ Distribution
☐ Manufacturing
☐ Retail
☐ Service
☐ Wholesale
☐ SPECIFIC INDUSTRIES
☐ Energy
☐ Environmental
☐ Financial
☐ Real Estate
☐ Transportation
☐ Publishing
☐ Food
☐ Franchises
☐ DIVERSIFIED
☒ MISCELLANEOUS

STAGE PREFERENCE

☒ EARLY STAGE
☒ Seed
☒ Start-up
☒ 1st Stage
☒ LATER STAGE
☒ 2nd Stage
☐ Mature
☐ Mezzanine
☐ LBO/MBO
☐ Turnaround
☐ INT'L EXPANSION
☐ WILL CONSIDER ALL
☐ VENTURE LEASING

Other Locations:

Affiliation:
Minimum Investment: $1 Million or more
Capital Under Management: $100 to $500 Million

GEOGRAPHIC PREF

☐ East Coast
☐ West Coast
☐ Northeast
☐ Mid Atlantic
☐ Gulf States
☐ Northwest
☐ Southeast
☐ Southwest
☐ Midwest
☐ Central
☐ Local to Office
☐ Other Geo Pref

FINOVA MEZZANINE CAPITAL

500 Church Street
Suite 200
Nashville TN 37219

Phone (615) 256-0701   Fax (615) 726-1208

PROFESSIONALS	TITLE
David Rosha	Sr. Vice President
Kathy Harris	National Manager
John Scott	Regional Manager

INDUSTRY PREFERENCE

☐ INFORMATION INDUSTRY
☐ Communications
☐ Computer Equipment
☐ Computer Services
☐ Computer Components
☐ Computer Entertainment
☐ Computer Education
☐ Information Technologies
☐ Computer Media
☐ Software
☐ Internet
☐ MEDICAL/HEALTHCARE
☐ Biotechnology
☐ Healthcare Services
☐ Life Sciences
☐ Medical Products
☐ INDUSTRIAL
☐ Advanced Materials
☐ Chemicals
☐ Instruments & Controls

☐ BASIC INDUSTRIES
☐ Consumer
☐ Distribution
☐ Manufacturing
☐ Retail
☐ Service
☐ Wholesale
☐ SPECIFIC INDUSTRIES
☐ Energy
☐ Environmental
☐ Financial
☐ Real Estate
☐ Transportation
☐ Publishing
☐ Food
☐ Franchises
☒ DIVERSIFIED
☐ MISCELLANEOUS

STAGE PREFERENCE

☒ EARLY STAGE
☐ Seed
☐ Start-up
☒ 1st Stage
☒ LATER STAGE
☒ 2nd Stage
☒ Mature
☒ Mezzanine
☒ LBO/MBO
☐ Turnaround
☐ INT'L EXPANSION
☐ WILL CONSIDER ALL
☐ VENTURE LEASING
SBIC
Other Locations:

Affiliation:
Minimum Investment: Less than $1 Million
Capital Under Management: $100 to $500 Million

GEOGRAPHIC PREF

☐ East Coast
☐ West Coast
☐ Northeast
☐ Mid Atlantic
☐ Gulf States
☐ Northwest
☐ Southeast
☐ Southwest
☐ Midwest
☐ Central
☐ Local to Office
☐ Other Geo Pref

INTERNATIONAL PAPER CAPITAL FORMATION, INC.

International Place II
6400 Poplar Avenue
Memphis TN 38197

Phone (901) 763-6282   Fax (901) 763-6076

PROFESSIONALS	TITLE
Bob J. Higgins	Vice President

INDUSTRY PREFERENCE

☐ INFORMATION INDUSTRY
☐ Communications
☐ Computer Equipment
☐ Computer Services
☐ Computer Components
☐ Computer Entertainment
☐ Computer Education
☐ Information Technologies
☐ Computer Media
☐ Software
☐ Internet
☐ MEDICAL/HEALTHCARE
☐ Biotechnology
☐ Healthcare Services
☐ Life Sciences
☐ Medical Products
☒ INDUSTRIAL
☒ Advanced Materials
☐ Chemicals
☐ Instruments & Controls

☐ BASIC INDUSTRIES
☐ Consumer
☐ Distribution
☐ Manufacturing
☐ Retail
☐ Service
☐ Wholesale
☒ SPECIFIC INDUSTRIES
☐ Energy
☒ Environmental
☐ Financial
☐ Real Estate
☐ Transportation
☐ Publishing
☐ Food
☐ Franchises
☒ DIVERSIFIED
☐ MISCELLANEOUS

STAGE PREFERENCE

☐ EARLY STAGE
☐ Seed
☐ Start-up
☐ 1st Stage
☒ LATER STAGE
☒ 2nd Stage
☒ Mature
☒ Mezzanine
☒ LBO/MBO
☐ Turnaround
☐ INT'L EXPANSION
☐ WILL CONSIDER ALL
☐ VENTURE LEASING
SSBIC
Other Locations: Purchase NY

Affiliation:
Minimum Investment: Less than $1 Million
Capital Under Management: Less than $100 Million

GEOGRAPHIC PREF

☐ East Coast
☐ West Coast
☐ Northeast
☐ Mid Atlantic
☐ Gulf States
☐ Northwest
☐ Southeast
☐ Southwest
☐ Midwest
☐ Central
☐ Local to Office
☐ Other Geo Pref

MASSEY BURCH CAPITAL CORP.

310 25th Avenue North
Suite 103
Nashville TN 37203

Phone (615) 329-9448   Fax (615) 329-9237

PROFESSIONALS	TITLE
Lucius E. Burch III	Chairman
Donald McLemore	Partner
William R. Earthman III	Partner
Donald M. Johnston	Partner

INDUSTRY PREFERENCE

- ☒ INFORMATION INDUSTRY
- ☒ Communications
- ☐ Computer Equipment
- ☐ Computer Services
- ☐ Computer Components
- ☐ Computer Entertainment
- ☐ Computer Education
- ☒ Information Technologies
- ☐ Computer Media
- ☐ Software
- ☐ Internet
- ☒ MEDICAL/HEALTHCARE
- ☐ Biotechnology
- ☒ Healthcare Services
- ☐ Life Sciences
- ☐ Medical Products
- ☐ INDUSTRIAL
- ☐ Advanced Materials
- ☐ Chemicals
- ☐ Instruments & Controls

- ☒ BASIC INDUSTRIES
- ☐ Consumer
- ☐ Distribution
- ☐ Manufacturing
- ☐ Retail
- ☒ Service
- ☐ Wholesale
- ☐ SPECIFIC INDUSTRIES
- ☐ Energy
- ☐ Environmental
- ☐ Financial
- ☐ Real Estate
- ☐ Transportation
- ☐ Publishing
- ☐ Food
- ☐ Franchises
- ☒ DIVERSIFIED
- ☐ MISCELLANEOUS

STAGE PREFERENCE

- ☒ EARLY STAGE
- ☒ Seed
- ☒ Start-up
- ☒ 1st Stage
- ☒ LATER STAGE
- ☒ 2nd Stage
- ☐ Mature
- ☐ Mezzanine
- ☒ LBO/MBO
- ☐ Turnaround
- ☐ INT'L EXPANSION
- ☐ WILL CONSIDER ALL
- ☐ VENTURE LEASING

Other Locations:

Affiliation: First Nashville Corp.
Minimum Investment: $1 Million or more
Capital Under Management: $100 to $500 Million

GEOGRAPHIC PREF

- ☐ East Coast
- ☐ West Coast
- ☐ Northeast
- ☐ Mid Atlantic
- ☐ Gulf States
- ☐ Northwest
- ☒ Southeast
- ☐ Southwest
- ☐ Midwest
- ☐ Central
- ☐ Local to Office
- ☐ Other Geo Pref

PETRA CAPITAL

172 Second Avenue North
Suite 112
Nashville TN 37201

Phone (615) 313-5999   Fax (615) 313-5990

PROFESSIONALS	TITLE
Michael Blackburn	Partner
Joseph O'Brien III	Partner
Robert Smith	Vice President

INDUSTRY PREFERENCE

- ☒ INFORMATION INDUSTRY
- ☒ Communications
- ☒ Computer Equipment
- ☒ Computer Services
- ☒ Computer Components
- ☐ Computer Entertainment
- ☒ Computer Education
- ☒ Information Technologies
- ☒ Computer Media
- ☒ Software
- ☒ Internet
- ☒ MEDICAL/HEALTHCARE
- ☐ Biotechnology
- ☒ Healthcare Services
- ☐ Life Sciences
- ☒ Medical Products
- ☒ INDUSTRIAL
- ☒ Advanced Materials
- ☐ Chemicals
- ☒ Instruments & Controls

- ☒ BASIC INDUSTRIES
- ☒ Consumer
- ☒ Distribution
- ☐ Manufacturing
- ☐ Retail
- ☐ Service
- ☐ Wholesale
- ☐ SPECIFIC INDUSTRIES
- ☐ Energy
- ☐ Environmental
- ☐ Financial
- ☐ Real Estate
- ☐ Transportation
- ☐ Publishing
- ☐ Food
- ☐ Franchises
- ☒ DIVERSIFIED
- ☒ MISCELLANEOUS

STAGE PREFERENCE

- ☐ EARLY STAGE
- ☐ Seed
- ☐ Start-up
- ☐ 1st Stage
- ☒ LATER STAGE
- ☐ 2nd Stage
- ☐ Mature
- ☒ Mezzanine
- ☐ LBO/MBO
- ☐ Turnaround
- ☐ INT'L EXPANSION
- ☐ WILL CONSIDER ALL
- ☐ VENTURE LEASING

Other Locations:

Affiliation:
Minimum Investment: $1 Million or more
Capital Under Management: $100 to $500 Million

GEOGRAPHIC PREF

- ☐ East Coast
- ☐ West Coast
- ☐ Northeast
- ☐ Mid Atlantic
- ☐ Gulf States
- ☐ Northwest
- ☐ Southeast
- ☐ Southwest
- ☐ Midwest
- ☐ Central
- ☐ Local to Office
- ☐ Other Geo Pref

RICHLAND VENTURES

200 31st Avenue North
Suite 200
Nashville TN 37203

Phone (615) 383-8030   Fax (615) 269-0463

PROFESSIONALS	TITLE
Jack Tyrrell	Partner
W. Patrick Ortale	Partner
John Chadwick	Partner
Mark Isaacs	Associate
Patrick Hale	Associate

INDUSTRY PREFERENCE

☒ INFORMATION INDUSTRY
☒ Communications
☒ Computer Equipment
☒ Computer Services
☐ Computer Components
☐ Computer Entertainment
☒ Computer Education
☒ Information Technologies
☒ Computer Media
☒ Software
☒ Internet
☒ MEDICAL/HEALTHCARE
☐ Biotechnology
☒ Healthcare Services
☐ Life Sciences
☐ Medical Products
☐ INDUSTRIAL
☐ Advanced Materials
☐ Chemicals
☐ Instruments & Controls

☒ BASIC INDUSTRIES
☒ Consumer
☐ Distribution
☐ Manufacturing
☐ Retail
☒ Service
☐ Wholesale
☐ SPECIFIC INDUSTRIES
☐ Energy
☐ Environmental
☐ Financial
☐ Real Estate
☐ Transportation
☐ Publishing
☐ Food
☐ Franchises
☒ DIVERSIFIED
☒ MISCELLANEOUS

STAGE PREFERENCE

☐ EARLY STAGE
☐ Seed
☐ Start-up
☐ 1st Stage
☒ LATER STAGE
☒ 2nd Stage
☒ Mature
☐ Mezzanine
☐ LBO/MBO
☐ Turnaround
☐ INT'L EXPANSION
☐ WILL CONSIDER ALL
☐ VENTURE LEASING

Other Locations:

Affiliation:
Minimum Investment: $1 Million or more
Capital Under Management: $100 to $500 Million

GEOGRAPHIC PREF

☐ East Coast
☐ West Coast
☐ Northeast
☐ Mid Atlantic
☐ Gulf States
☐ Northwest
☒ Southeast
☒ Southwest
☐ Midwest
☐ Central
☐ Local to Office
☒ Other Geo Pref
  TN

RIVER ASSOCIATES LLC

633 Chestnut Street
Suite 1640
Chattanooga TN 37450

Phone (423) 755-0888   Fax (423) 755-0870

PROFESSIONALS	TITLE
Mark Jones	Partner

INDUSTRY PREFERENCE

☐ INFORMATION INDUSTRY
☐ Communications
☐ Computer Equipment
☐ Computer Services
☐ Computer Components
☐ Computer Entertainment
☐ Computer Education
☐ Information Technologies
☐ Computer Media
☐ Software
☐ Internet
☐ MEDICAL/HEALTHCARE
☐ Biotechnology
☐ Healthcare Services
☐ Life Sciences
☐ Medical Products
☒ INDUSTRIAL
☒ Advanced Materials
☒ Chemicals
☒ Instruments & Controls

☒ BASIC INDUSTRIES
☐ Consumer
☒ Distribution
☐ Manufacturing
☐ Retail
☐ Service
☐ Wholesale
☐ SPECIFIC INDUSTRIES
☐ Energy
☐ Environmental
☐ Financial
☐ Real Estate
☐ Transportation
☐ Publishing
☐ Food
☐ Franchises
☒ DIVERSIFIED
☒ MISCELLANEOUS

STAGE PREFERENCE

☐ EARLY STAGE
☐ Seed
☐ Start-up
☐ 1st Stage
☒ LATER STAGE
☐ 2nd Stage
☐ Mature
☐ Mezzanine
☒ LBO/MBO
☒ Turnaround
☐ INT'L EXPANSION
☐ WILL CONSIDER ALL
☒ VENTURE LEASING

Other Locations:

Affiliation:
Minimum Investment: $1 Million or more
Capital Under Management: Less than $100 Million

GEOGRAPHIC PREF

☐ East Coast
☐ West Coast
☐ Northeast
☐ Mid Atlantic
☐ Gulf States
☐ Northwest
☐ Southeast
☐ Southwest
☐ Midwest
☐ Central
☐ Local to Office
☐ Other Geo Pref

SALIX VENTURES

30 Burton Hills Boulevard
Suite 370
Nashville TN 37215

Phone (615) 665-1409   Fax (615) 665-2912

PROFESSIONALS	TITLE
David Ward	Partner
Christopher Grant, Jr.	Partner

INDUSTRY PREFERENCE

- ☐ INFORMATION INDUSTRY
- ☐ Communications
- ☐ Computer Equipment
- ☐ Computer Services
- ☐ Computer Components
- ☐ Computer Entertainment
- ☐ Computer Education
- ☐ Information Technologies
- ☐ Computer Media
- ☐ Software
- ☐ Internet
- ☒ MEDICAL/HEALTHCARE
- ☐ Biotechnology
- ☒ Healthcare Services
- ☐ Life Sciences
- ☒ Medical Products
- ☐ INDUSTRIAL
- ☐ Advanced Materials
- ☐ Chemicals
- ☐ Instruments & Controls

- ☐ BASIC INDUSTRIES
- ☐ Consumer
- ☐ Distribution
- ☐ Manufacturing
- ☐ Retail
- ☐ Service
- ☐ Wholesale
- ☐ SPECIFIC INDUSTRIES
- ☐ Energy
- ☐ Environmental
- ☐ Financial
- ☐ Real Estate
- ☐ Transportation
- ☐ Publishing
- ☐ Food
- ☐ Franchises
- ☐ DIVERSIFIED
- ☒ MISCELLANEOUS

STAGE PREFERENCE

- ☒ EARLY STAGE
- ☐ Seed
- ☒ Start-up
- ☒ 1st Stage
- ☒ LATER STAGE
- ☒ 2nd Stage
- ☐ Mature
- ☐ Mezzanine
- ☐ LBO/MBO
- ☐ Turnaround
- ☐ INT'L EXPANSION
- ☐ WILL CONSIDER ALL
- ☐ VENTURE LEASING

Other Locations:

Affiliation:
Minimum Investment: $1 Million or more
Capital Under Management: Less than $100 Million

GEOGRAPHIC PREF

- ☐ East Coast
- ☐ West Coast
- ☐ Northeast
- ☐ Mid Atlantic
- ☐ Gulf States
- ☐ Northwest
- ☐ Southeast
- ☐ Southwest
- ☐ Midwest
- ☐ Central
- ☐ Local to Office
- ☐ Other Geo Pref

SSM VENTURE PARTNERS, LP

845 Crossover Lane
Suite 140
Memphis TN 38117

Phone (901) 767-1131   Fax (901) 767-1135

PROFESSIONALS	TITLE
C. Barham Ray	Partner
Ashley M. Mayfield	Partner
William Harrison	Partner
James D. Witherington, Jr	Partner
R. Wilson Orr III	Partner

INDUSTRY PREFERENCE

- ☒ INFORMATION INDUSTRY
- ☒ Communications
- ☐ Computer Equipment
- ☒ Computer Services
- ☐ Computer Components
- ☐ Computer Entertainment
- ☐ Computer Education
- ☒ Information Technologies
- ☐ Computer Media
- ☒ Software
- ☒ Internet
- ☒ MEDICAL/HEALTHCARE
- ☐ Biotechnology
- ☒ Healthcare Services
- ☐ Life Sciences
- ☐ Medical Products
- ☐ INDUSTRIAL
- ☐ Advanced Materials
- ☐ Chemicals
- ☐ Instruments & Controls

- ☒ BASIC INDUSTRIES
- ☒ Consumer
- ☐ Distribution
- ☐ Manufacturing
- ☐ Retail
- ☒ Service
- ☐ Wholesale
- ☐ SPECIFIC INDUSTRIES
- ☐ Energy
- ☐ Environmental
- ☐ Financial
- ☐ Real Estate
- ☐ Transportation
- ☐ Publishing
- ☐ Food
- ☐ Franchises
- ☒ DIVERSIFIED
- ☐ MISCELLANEOUS

STAGE PREFERENCE

- ☒ EARLY STAGE
- ☐ Seed
- ☒ Start-up
- ☒ 1st Stage
- ☒ LATER STAGE
- ☒ 2nd Stage
- ☒ Mature
- ☒ Mezzanine
- ☒ LBO/MBO
- ☐ Turnaround
- ☐ INT'L EXPANSION
- ☐ WILL CONSIDER ALL
- ☐ VENTURE LEASING

Other Locations:

Affiliation:
Minimum Investment: $1 Million or more
Capital Under Management: $100 to $500 Million

GEOGRAPHIC PREF

- ☐ East Coast
- ☐ West Coast
- ☐ Northeast
- ☐ Mid Atlantic
- ☐ Gulf States
- ☐ Northwest
- ☒ Southeast
- ☐ Southwest
- ☐ Midwest
- ☐ Central
- ☐ Local to Office
- ☒ Other Geo Pref
  TX

VALLEY CAPITAL CORP.

Suite 212, Krystal Building
100 W. Martin Luther King Boulevard
Chattanooga TN 37402

Phone (423) 265-1557   Fax (423) 265-1588

PROFESSIONALS	TITLE
Lamar J. Partridge	President

INDUSTRY PREFERENCE

☒ INFORMATION INDUSTRY	☐ BASIC INDUSTRIES	
☒ Communications	☐ Consumer	
☐ Computer Equipment	☐ Distribution	
☐ Computer Services	☐ Manufacturing	
☐ Computer Components	☐ Retail	
☐ Computer Entertainment	☐ Service	
☐ Computer Education	☐ Wholesale	
☐ Information Technologies	☐ SPECIFIC INDUSTRIES	
☐ Computer Media	☐ Energy	
☐ Software	☐ Environmental	
☐ Internet	☐ Financial	
☒ MEDICAL/HEALTHCARE	☐ Real Estate	
☐ Biotechnology	☐ Transportation	
☒ Healthcare Services	☐ Publishing	
☐ Life Sciences	☐ Food	
☐ Medical Products	☐ Franchises	
☐ INDUSTRIAL	☒ DIVERSIFIED	
☐ Advanced Materials	☐ MISCELLANEOUS	
☐ Chemicals		
☐ Instruments & Controls		

STAGE PREFERENCE

☒ EARLY STAGE
☐ Seed
☒ Start-up
☒ 1st Stage
☒ LATER STAGE
☒ 2nd Stage
☒ Mature
☒ Mezzanine
☒ LBO/MBO
☐ Turnaround
☐ INT'L EXPANSION
☐ WILL CONSIDER ALL
☐ VENTURE LEASING

SSBIC
Other Locations:

Affiliation:
Minimum Investment: Less than $1 Million
Capital Under Management: Less than $100 Million

GEOGRAPHIC PREF

☐ East Coast
☐ West Coast
☐ Northeast
☐ Mid Atlantic
☐ Gulf States
☐ Northwest
☒ Southeast
☐ Southwest
☐ Midwest
☐ Central
☐ Local to Office
☐ Other Geo Pref

ALLIANCE BUSINESS INVESTMENT COMPANY

1221 McKinney Street
Suite 3100
Houston TX 77010

Phone (713) 659-3131   Fax (713) 659-8070

PROFESSIONALS	TITLE
Leon Davis	Partner
Ross Davis	Partner
Lance Davis	Partner

INDUSTRY PREFERENCE

☒ INFORMATION INDUSTRY	☒ BASIC INDUSTRIES
☒ Communications	☐ Consumer
☐ Computer Equipment	☒ Distribution
☐ Computer Services	☒ Manufacturing
☐ Computer Components	☐ Retail
☐ Computer Entertainment	☐ Service
☐ Computer Education	☐ Wholesale
☐ Information Technologies	☒ SPECIFIC INDUSTRIES
☐ Computer Media	☒ Energy
☒ Software	☐ Environmental
☒ Internet	☐ Financial
☐ MEDICAL/HEALTHCARE	☒ Real Estate
☐ Biotechnology	☐ Transportation
☐ Healthcare Services	☐ Publishing
☐ Life Sciences	☐ Food
☐ Medical Products	☐ Franchises
☐ INDUSTRIAL	☒ DIVERSIFIED
☐ Advanced Materials	☐ MISCELLANEOUS
☐ Chemicals	
☐ Instruments & Controls	

STAGE PREFERENCE

☒ EARLY STAGE
☐ Seed
☒ Start-up
☒ 1st Stage
☒ LATER STAGE
☒ 2nd Stage
☒ Mature
☒ Mezzanine
☒ LBO/MBO
☐ Turnaround
☐ INT'L EXPANSION
☐ WILL CONSIDER ALL
☐ VENTURE LEASING

SBIC
Other Locations:

Affiliation:
Minimum Investment: Less than $1 Million
Capital Under Management: Less than $100 Million

GEOGRAPHIC PREF

☐ East Coast
☐ West Coast
☐ Northeast
☐ Mid Atlantic
☐ Gulf States
☐ Northwest
☐ Southeast
☒ Southwest
☐ Midwest
☒ Central
☐ Local to Office
☒ Other Geo Pref
South Central

ALLIANCE ENTERPRISE CORPORATION

North Central Plaza 1, Suite 710
12655 North Central Expressway
Dallas TX 75243

Phone (972) 991-1597   Fax (972) 991-1647

PROFESSIONALS	TITLE
Donald R. Lawhorne	President

INDUSTRY PREFERENCE

- ☒ INFORMATION INDUSTRY
- ☐ Communications
- ☐ Computer Equipment
- ☐ Computer Services
- ☒ Computer Components
- ☐ Computer Entertainment
- ☐ Computer Education
- ☐ Information Technologies
- ☐ Computer Media
- ☐ Software
- ☐ Internet
- ☐ MEDICAL/HEALTHCARE
- ☐ Biotechnology
- ☐ Healthcare Services
- ☐ Life Sciences
- ☐ Medical Products
- ☐ INDUSTRIAL
- ☐ Advanced Materials
- ☐ Chemicals
- ☐ Instruments & Controls

- ☒ BASIC INDUSTRIES
- ☐ Consumer
- ☐ Distribution
- ☒ Manufacturing
- ☐ Retail
- ☐ Service
- ☐ Wholesale
- ☒ SPECIFIC INDUSTRIES
- ☐ Energy
- ☐ Environmental
- ☐ Financial
- ☐ Real Estate
- ☐ Transportation
- ☐ Publishing
- ☒ Food
- ☐ Franchises
- ☒ DIVERSIFIED
- ☐ MISCELLANEOUS

STAGE PREFERENCE

- ☒ EARLY STAGE
- ☐ Seed
- ☐ Start-up
- ☒ 1st Stage
- ☒ LATER STAGE
- ☒ 2nd Stage
- ☒ Mature
- ☒ Mezzanine
- ☒ LBO/MBO
- ☐ Turnaround
- ☐ INT'L EXPANSION
- ☐ WILL CONSIDER ALL
- ☐ VENTURE LEASING
- **SSBIC**

Other Locations:

Affiliation:
Minimum Investment: Less than $1 Million
Capital Under Management: Less than $100 Million

GEOGRAPHIC PREF

- ☐ East Coast
- ☐ West Coast
- ☐ Northeast
- ☐ Mid Atlantic
- ☐ Gulf States
- ☐ Northwest
- ☐ Southeast
- ☒ Southwest
- ☐ Midwest
- ☐ Central
- ☐ Local to Office
- ☐ Other Geo Pref

AUSTIN VENTURES

1300 Norwood Tower
114 West 7th Street
Austin TX 78701

Phone (512) 485-1900   Fax (512) 476-3952

PROFESSIONALS	TITLE
Joseph C. Aragona	General Partner
Jeffery C. Garvey	General Partner
Ed Olkkola	General Partner
Kenneth P. Deangeus	General Partner
Blaine Wesner	General Partner

INDUSTRY PREFERENCE

- ☒ INFORMATION INDUSTRY
- ☒ Communications
- ☐ Computer Equipment
- ☐ Computer Services
- ☒ Computer Components
- ☐ Computer Entertainment
- ☐ Computer Education
- ☒ Information Technologies
- ☒ Computer Media
- ☒ Software
- ☒ Internet
- ☐ MEDICAL/HEALTHCARE
- ☐ Biotechnology
- ☐ Healthcare Services
- ☐ Life Sciences
- ☐ Medical Products
- ☐ INDUSTRIAL
- ☐ Advanced Materials
- ☐ Chemicals
- ☐ Instruments & Controls

- ☒ BASIC INDUSTRIES
- ☐ Consumer
- ☐ Distribution
- ☐ Manufacturing
- ☐ Retail
- ☒ Service
- ☐ Wholesale
- ☐ SPECIFIC INDUSTRIES
- ☐ Energy
- ☐ Environmental
- ☐ Financial
- ☐ Real Estate
- ☐ Transportation
- ☐ Publishing
- ☐ Food
- ☐ Franchises
- ☒ DIVERSIFIED
- ☐ MISCELLANEOUS

STAGE PREFERENCE

- ☒ EARLY STAGE
- ☒ Seed
- ☒ Start-up
- ☒ 1st Stage
- ☒ LATER STAGE
- ☒ 2nd Stage
- ☐ Mature
- ☐ Mezzanine
- ☐ LBO/MBO
- ☐ Turnaround
- ☐ INT'L EXPANSION
- ☐ WILL CONSIDER ALL
- ☐ VENTURE LEASING

Other Locations:

Affiliation:
Minimum Investment: Less than $1 Million
Capital Under Management: Over $500 Million

GEOGRAPHIC PREF

- ☐ East Coast
- ☐ West Coast
- ☐ Northeast
- ☐ Mid Atlantic
- ☐ Gulf States
- ☐ Northwest
- ☐ Southeast
- ☐ Southwest
- ☐ Midwest
- ☐ Central
- ☐ Local to Office
- ☒ Other Geo Pref
- TX

CAPITAL SOUTHWEST CORPORATION

12900 Preston Road
Suite 700
Dallas TX 75230

Phone (972) 233-8242 Fax (972) 233-7362

PROFESSIONALS	TITLE
William R. Thomas	President
Patrick F. Hamner	
Tim Smith	
Howard M. Thomas	
Susan K. Patterson	

INDUSTRY PREFERENCE

☒ INFORMATION INDUSTRY	☒ BASIC INDUSTRIES
☒ Communications	☐ Consumer
☒ Computer Equipment	☐ Distribution
☒ Computer Services	☒ Manufacturing
☒ Computer Components	☒ Retail
☐ Computer Entertainment	☒ Service
☐ Computer Education	☐ Wholesale
☒ Information Technologies	☐ SPECIFIC INDUSTRIES
☐ Computer Media	☐ Energy
☒ Software	☐ Environmental
☒ Internet	☐ Financial
☒ MEDICAL/HEALTHCARE	☐ Real Estate
☐ Biotechnology	☐ Transportation
☒ Healthcare Services	☐ Publishing
☐ Life Sciences	☐ Food
☐ Medical Products	☐ Franchises
☐ INDUSTRIAL	☒ DIVERSIFIED
☐ Advanced Materials	☐ MISCELLANEOUS
☐ Chemicals	
☐ Instruments & Controls	

STAGE PREFERENCE

☒ EARLY STAGE
☒ Seed
☒ Start-up
☒ 1st Stage
☒ LATER STAGE
☒ 2nd Stage
☒ Mature
☒ Mezzanine
☒ LBO/MBO
☐ Turnaround
☐ INT'L EXPANSION
☐ WILL CONSIDER ALL
☐ VENTURE LEASING
SBIC
Other Locations:

Affiliation:
Minimum Investment: $1 Million or more
Capital Under Management: $100 to $500 Million

GEOGRAPHIC PREF

☐ East Coast
☐ West Coast
☐ Northeast
☐ Mid Atlantic
☐ Gulf States
☐ Northwest
☐ Southeast
☒ Southwest
☐ Midwest
☐ Central
☐ Local to Office
☐ Other Geo Pref

CATALYST FUND, LTD. (THE)

Three Riverway
Suite 770
Houston TX 77056

Phone (713) 623-8133 Fax (713) 623-0473

PROFESSIONALS	TITLE
Richard L. Herrman	Manager
Ron Nixon	Manager

INDUSTRY PREFERENCE

☐ INFORMATION INDUSTRY	☐ BASIC INDUSTRIES
☐ Communications	☐ Consumer
☐ Computer Equipment	☐ Distribution
☐ Computer Services	☐ Manufacturing
☐ Computer Components	☐ Retail
☐ Computer Entertainment	☐ Service
☐ Computer Education	☐ Wholesale
☐ Information Technologies	☐ SPECIFIC INDUSTRIES
☐ Computer Media	☐ Energy
☐ Software	☐ Environmental
☐ Internet	☐ Financial
☐ MEDICAL/HEALTHCARE	☐ Real Estate
☐ Biotechnology	☐ Transportation
☐ Healthcare Services	☐ Publishing
☐ Life Sciences	☐ Food
☐ Medical Products	☐ Franchises
☐ INDUSTRIAL	☒ DIVERSIFIED
☐ Advanced Materials	☐ MISCELLANEOUS
☐ Chemicals	
☐ Instruments & Controls	

STAGE PREFERENCE

☐ EARLY STAGE
☐ Seed
☐ Start-up
☐ 1st Stage
☒ LATER STAGE
☒ 2nd Stage
☒ Mature
☒ Mezzanine
☒ LBO/MBO
☐ Turnaround
☐ INT'L EXPANSION
☐ WILL CONSIDER ALL
☐ VENTURE LEASING
SBIC
Other Locations:

Affiliation:
Minimum Investment: $1 Million or more
Capital Under Management: Less than $100 Million

GEOGRAPHIC PREF

☐ East Coast
☐ West Coast
☐ Northeast
☐ Mid Atlantic
☐ Gulf States
☐ Northwest
☐ Southeast
☐ Southwest
☐ Midwest
☐ Central
☐ Local to Office
☐ Other Geo Pref

CENTERPOINT VENTURES

**Two Galleria Tower
13455 Noel Road, Suite 1670
Dallas TX 75240**

Phone (972) 702-1101   Fax (972) 702-1103

PROFESSIONALS	TITLE
Bob Paluck	General Partner
Terry Rock	Partner

INDUSTRY PREFERENCE

☒ INFORMATION INDUSTRY	☐ BASIC INDUSTRIES
☒ Communications	☐ Consumer
☒ Computer Equipment	☐ Distribution
☒ Computer Services	☐ Manufacturing
☒ Computer Components	☐ Retail
☐ Computer Entertainment	☐ Service
☒ Computer Education	☐ Wholesale
☒ Information Technologies	☒ SPECIFIC INDUSTRIES
☒ Computer Media	☒ Energy
☒ Software	☐ Environmental
☒ Internet	☐ Financial
☒ MEDICAL/HEALTHCARE	☐ Real Estate
☒ Biotechnology	☐ Transportation
☐ Healthcare Services	☐ Publishing
☒ Life Sciences	☐ Food
☒ Medical Products	☐ Franchises
☐ INDUSTRIAL	☒ DIVERSIFIED
☐ Advanced Materials	☒ MISCELLANEOUS
☐ Chemicals	
☐ Instruments & Controls	

STAGE PREFERENCE

☒ EARLY STAGE	
☒ Seed	
☒ Start-up	
☒ 1st Stage	
☐ LATER STAGE	
☐ 2nd Stage	
☐ Mature	
☐ Mezzanine	
☐ LBO/MBO	
☐ Turnaround	
☐ INT'L EXPANSION	
☐ WILL CONSIDER ALL	
☐ VENTURE LEASING	

Other Locations: Austin, TX

Affiliation:
Minimum Investment: Less than $1 Million
Capital Under Management: $100 to $500 Million

GEOGRAPHIC PREF

☐ East Coast	
☐ West Coast	
☐ Northeast	
☐ Mid Atlantic	
☐ Gulf States	
☐ Northwest	
☐ Southeast	
☐ Southwest	
☐ Midwest	
☐ Central	
☐ Local to Office	
☒ Other Geo Pref	
TX	

CENTERPOINT VENTURES

**8920 Business Park Drive
Suite 100
Austin TX 78759-7405**

Phone (512) 231-1670   Fax (512) 651-6266

PROFESSIONALS	TITLE
Kent Fuka	Partner

INDUSTRY PREFERENCE

☒ INFORMATION INDUSTRY	☐ BASIC INDUSTRIES
☒ Communications	☐ Consumer
☒ Computer Equipment	☐ Distribution
☒ Computer Services	☐ Manufacturing
☒ Computer Components	☐ Retail
☐ Computer Entertainment	☐ Service
☒ Computer Education	☐ Wholesale
☒ Information Technologies	☒ SPECIFIC INDUSTRIES
☒ Computer Media	☒ Energy
☒ Software	☐ Environmental
☒ Internet	☐ Financial
☒ MEDICAL/HEALTHCARE	☐ Real Estate
☒ Biotechnology	☐ Transportation
☐ Healthcare Services	☐ Publishing
☒ Life Sciences	☐ Food
☒ Medical Products	☐ Franchises
☐ INDUSTRIAL	☒ DIVERSIFIED
☐ Advanced Materials	☒ MISCELLANEOUS
☐ Chemicals	
☐ Instruments & Controls	

STAGE PREFERENCE

☒ EARLY STAGE	
☒ Seed	
☒ Start-up	
☒ 1st Stage	
☐ LATER STAGE	
☐ 2nd Stage	
☐ Mature	
☐ Mezzanine	
☐ LBO/MBO	
☐ Turnaround	
☐ INT'L EXPANSION	
☐ WILL CONSIDER ALL	
☐ VENTURE LEASING	

Other Locations: Dallas, TX

Affiliation:
Minimum Investment: Less than $1 Million
Capital Under Management: $100 to $500 Million

GEOGRAPHIC PREF

☐ East Coast	
☐ West Coast	
☐ Northeast	
☐ Mid Atlantic	
☐ Gulf States	
☐ Northwest	
☐ Southeast	
☐ Southwest	
☐ Midwest	
☐ Central	
☐ Local to Office	
☒ Other Geo Pref	
TX	

HCT CAPITAL CORP.

4916 Camp Bowie Boulevard
Suite 200
Fort Worth TX 76107

Phone (817) 763-8706   Fax (817) 377-8049

PROFESSIONALS	TITLE
Vichy Woodward Young, Jr.	President

INDUSTRY PREFERENCE

- ☐ INFORMATION INDUSTRY
- ☐ Communications
- ☐ Computer Equipment
- ☐ Computer Services
- ☐ Computer Components
- ☐ Computer Entertainment
- ☐ Computer Education
- ☐ Information Technologies
- ☐ Computer Media
- ☐ Software
- ☐ Internet
- ☒ MEDICAL/HEALTHCARE
- ☐ Biotechnology
- ☒ Healthcare Services
- ☒ Life Sciences
- ☒ Medical Products
- ☐ INDUSTRIAL
- ☐ Advanced Materials
- ☐ Chemicals
- ☐ Instruments & Controls
- ☒ BASIC INDUSTRIES
- ☐ Consumer
- ☐ Distribution
- ☐ Manufacturing
- ☐ Retail
- ☒ Service
- ☐ Wholesale
- ☐ SPECIFIC INDUSTRIES
- ☐ Energy
- ☐ Environmental
- ☐ Financial
- ☐ Real Estate
- ☐ Transportation
- ☐ Publishing
- ☐ Food
- ☐ Franchises
- ☒ DIVERSIFIED
- ☐ MISCELLANEOUS

STAGE PREFERENCE

- ☒ EARLY STAGE
- ☒ Seed
- ☒ Start-up
- ☒ 1st Stage
- ☒ LATER STAGE
- ☒ 2nd Stage
- ☒ Mature
- ☒ Mezzanine
- ☒ LBO/MBO
- ☐ Turnaround
- ☐ INT'L EXPANSION
- ☐ WILL CONSIDER ALL
- ☐ VENTURE LEASING

SBIC
Other Locations:

Affiliation:
Minimum Investment: Less than $1 Million
Capital Under Management: Less than $100 Million

GEOGRAPHIC PREF

- ☐ East Coast
- ☐ West Coast
- ☐ Northeast
- ☐ Mid Atlantic
- ☐ Gulf States
- ☐ Northwest
- ☐ Southeast
- ☒ Southwest
- ☐ Midwest
- ☐ Central
- ☐ Local to Office
- ☐ Other Geo Pref

HOAK CAPITAL CORPORATION

13355 Noel Road
Suite 1050
Dallas TX 75240

Phone (972) 960-4848   Fax (972) 960-4899

PROFESSIONALS	TITLE
James Hoak, Jr.	Principal

INDUSTRY PREFERENCE

- ☒ INFORMATION INDUSTRY
- ☒ Communications
- ☒ Computer Equipment
- ☒ Computer Services
- ☒ Computer Components
- ☐ Computer Entertainment
- ☒ Computer Education
- ☒ Information Technologies
- ☒ Computer Media
- ☒ Software
- ☒ Internet
- ☐ MEDICAL/HEALTHCARE
- ☐ Biotechnology
- ☐ Healthcare Services
- ☐ Life Sciences
- ☐ Medical Products
- ☒ INDUSTRIAL
- ☐ Advanced Materials
- ☐ Chemicals
- ☒ Instruments & Controls
- ☐ BASIC INDUSTRIES
- ☐ Consumer
- ☐ Distribution
- ☐ Manufacturing
- ☐ Retail
- ☐ Service
- ☐ Wholesale
- ☐ SPECIFIC INDUSTRIES
- ☐ Energy
- ☐ Environmental
- ☐ Financial
- ☐ Real Estate
- ☐ Transportation
- ☐ Publishing
- ☐ Food
- ☐ Franchises
- ☒ DIVERSIFIED
- ☒ MISCELLANEOUS

STAGE PREFERENCE

- ☐ EARLY STAGE
- ☐ Seed
- ☐ Start-up
- ☐ 1st Stage
- ☒ LATER STAGE
- ☐ 2nd Stage
- ☐ Mature
- ☐ Mezzanine
- ☒ LBO/MBO
- ☒ Turnaround
- ☐ INT'L EXPANSION
- ☐ WILL CONSIDER ALL
- ☒ VENTURE LEASING

Other Locations:

Affiliation:
Minimum Investment: $1 Million or more
Capital Under Management: $100 to $500 Million

GEOGRAPHIC PREF

- ☐ East Coast
- ☐ West Coast
- ☐ Northeast
- ☐ Mid Atlantic
- ☐ Gulf States
- ☐ Northwest
- ☐ Southeast
- ☐ Southwest
- ☐ Midwest
- ☐ Central
- ☐ Local to Office
- ☐ Other Geo Pref

HOOK PARTNERS

13760 Noel Road
Suite 805
Dallas TX 75240

Phone (972) 991-5457   Fax (972) 991-5458

PROFESSIONALS	TITLE
David Hook	

INDUSTRY PREFERENCE

- ☒ INFORMATION INDUSTRY
- ☒ Communications
- ☒ Computer Equipment
- ☒ Computer Services
- ☒ Computer Components
- ☐ Computer Entertainment
- ☒ Computer Education
- ☒ Information Technologies
- ☒ Computer Media
- ☒ Software
- ☒ Internet
- ☒ MEDICAL/HEALTHCARE
- ☐ Biotechnology
- ☒ Healthcare Services
- ☒ Life Sciences
- ☒ Medical Products
- ☐ INDUSTRIAL
- ☐ Advanced Materials
- ☐ Chemicals
- ☐ Instruments & Controls

- ☐ BASIC INDUSTRIES
- ☐ Consumer
- ☐ Distribution
- ☐ Manufacturing
- ☐ Retail
- ☐ Service
- ☐ Wholesale
- ☐ SPECIFIC INDUSTRIES
- ☐ Energy
- ☐ Environmental
- ☐ Financial
- ☐ Real Estate
- ☐ Transportation
- ☐ Publishing
- ☐ Food
- ☐ Franchises
- ☒ DIVERSIFIED
- ☒ MISCELLANEOUS

STAGE PREFERENCE

- ☒ EARLY STAGE
- ☒ Seed
- ☒ Start-up
- ☒ 1st Stage
- ☐ LATER STAGE
- ☐ 2nd Stage
- ☐ Mature
- ☐ Mezzanine
- ☐ LBO/MBO
- ☐ Turnaround
- ☐ INT'L EXPANSION
- ☐ WILL CONSIDER ALL
- ☐ VENTURE LEASING

Other Locations:

Affiliation:
Minimum Investment: $1 Million or more
Capital Under Management: Less than $100 Million

GEOGRAPHIC PREF

- ☐ East Coast
- ☒ West Coast
- ☐ Northeast
- ☐ Mid Atlantic
- ☐ Gulf States
- ☐ Northwest
- ☐ Southeast
- ☒ Southwest
- ☐ Midwest
- ☐ Central
- ☐ Local to Office
- ☐ Other Geo Pref

HOUSTON PARTNERS

P.O. Box 2023
Houston TX 77752-2023

Phone (713) 222-8600   Fax (713) 222-8932

PROFESSIONALS	TITLE
Glenda Overbeck	General Partner
Harvard Hill, Jr.	General Partner

INDUSTRY PREFERENCE

- ☒ INFORMATION INDUSTRY
- ☐ Communications
- ☐ Computer Equipment
- ☐ Computer Services
- ☐ Computer Components
- ☐ Computer Entertainment
- ☐ Computer Education
- ☒ Information Technologies
- ☐ Computer Media
- ☐ Software
- ☐ Internet
- ☒ MEDICAL/HEALTHCARE
- ☐ Biotechnology
- ☒ Healthcare Services
- ☐ Life Sciences
- ☒ Medical Products
- ☐ INDUSTRIAL
- ☐ Advanced Materials
- ☐ Chemicals
- ☐ Instruments & Controls

- ☐ BASIC INDUSTRIES
- ☐ Consumer
- ☐ Distribution
- ☐ Manufacturing
- ☐ Retail
- ☐ Service
- ☐ Wholesale
- ☒ SPECIFIC INDUSTRIES
- ☐ Energy
- ☒ Environmental
- ☐ Financial
- ☐ Real Estate
- ☐ Transportation
- ☐ Publishing
- ☐ Food
- ☐ Franchises
- ☒ DIVERSIFIED
- ☐ MISCELLANEOUS

STAGE PREFERENCE

- ☐ EARLY STAGE
- ☐ Seed
- ☐ Start-up
- ☐ 1st Stage
- ☒ LATER STAGE
- ☒ 2nd Stage
- ☒ Mature
- ☒ Mezzanine
- ☒ LBO/MBO
- ☒ Turnaround
- ☐ INT'L EXPANSION
- ☐ WILL CONSIDER ALL
- ☒ VENTURE LEASING

SBIC
Other Locations:

Affiliation:
Minimum Investment: $1 Million or more
Capital Under Management: Less than $100 Million

GEOGRAPHIC PREF

- ☐ East Coast
- ☐ West Coast
- ☐ Northeast
- ☐ Mid Atlantic
- ☐ Gulf States
- ☐ Northwest
- ☒ Southeast
- ☒ Southwest
- ☐ Midwest
- ☒ Central
- ☐ Local to Office
- ☒ Other Geo Pref
   South Central

INTERWEST PARTNERS

**13355 Noel Road
Two Galleria Tower, Suite 1670
Dallas TX 75240**

Phone (972) 392-7279   Fax (972) 490-6348

PROFESSIONALS	TITLE
H. Berry Cash	General Partner
Alan W. Crites	General Partner

INDUSTRY PREFERENCE

☒ INFORMATION INDUSTRY	☒ BASIC INDUSTRIES
☒ Communications	☒ Consumer
☒ Computer Equipment	☐ Distribution
☒ Computer Services	☐ Manufacturing
☒ Computer Components	☐ Retail
☐ Computer Entertainment	☐ Service
☒ Computer Education	☐ Wholesale
☒ Information Technologies	☐ SPECIFIC INDUSTRIES
☒ Computer Media	☐ Energy
☒ Software	☐ Environmental
☒ Internet	☐ Financial
☒ MEDICAL/HEALTHCARE	☐ Real Estate
☒ Biotechnology	☐ Transportation
☒ Healthcare Services	☐ Publishing
☒ Life Sciences	☐ Food
☒ Medical Products	☐ Franchises
☒ INDUSTRIAL	☒ DIVERSIFIED
☒ Advanced Materials	☐ MISCELLANEOUS
☒ Chemicals	
☒ Instruments & Controls	

STAGE PREFERENCE

☒ EARLY STAGE
☒ Seed
☒ Start-up
☒ 1st Stage
☒ LATER STAGE
☒ 2nd Stage
☒ Mature
☒ Mezzanine
☒ LBO/MBO
☒ Turnaround
☒ INT'L EXPANSION
☐ WILL CONSIDER ALL
☒ VENTURE LEASING

Other Locations: Menlo Park CA

Affiliation: Berry Cash Southwest Partnership
Minimum Investment: Less than $1 Million
Capital Under Management: $100 to $500 Million

GEOGRAPHIC PREF

☐ East Coast
☐ West Coast
☐ Northeast
☐ Mid Atlantic
☐ Gulf States
☐ Northwest
☐ Southeast
☐ Southwest
☐ Midwest
☐ Central
☐ Local to Office
☐ Other Geo Pref

JARDINE CAPITAL CORP.

**7322 Southwest Freeway
Suite 787
Houston TX 77074**

Phone (713) 271-7077   Fax (713) 271-7577

PROFESSIONALS	TITLE
Lawrence Wong	President

INDUSTRY PREFERENCE

☐ INFORMATION INDUSTRY	☐ BASIC INDUSTRIES
☐ Communications	☐ Consumer
☐ Computer Equipment	☐ Distribution
☐ Computer Services	☐ Manufacturing
☐ Computer Components	☐ Retail
☐ Computer Entertainment	☐ Service
☐ Computer Education	☐ Wholesale
☐ Information Technologies	☐ SPECIFIC INDUSTRIES
☐ Computer Media	☐ Energy
☐ Software	☐ Environmental
☐ Internet	☐ Financial
☐ MEDICAL/HEALTHCARE	☐ Real Estate
☐ Biotechnology	☐ Transportation
☐ Healthcare Services	☐ Publishing
☐ Life Sciences	☐ Food
☐ Medical Products	☐ Franchises
☐ INDUSTRIAL	☒ DIVERSIFIED
☐ Advanced Materials	☐ MISCELLANEOUS
☐ Chemicals	
☐ Instruments & Controls	

STAGE PREFERENCE

☒ EARLY STAGE
☐ Seed
☐ Start-up
☒ 1st Stage
☒ LATER STAGE
☒ 2nd Stage
☒ Mature
☒ Mezzanine
☒ LBO/MBO
☐ Turnaround
☐ INT'L EXPANSION
☐ WILL CONSIDER ALL
☐ VENTURE LEASING
SSBIC
Other Locations:

Affiliation:
Minimum Investment: Less than $1 Million
Capital Under Management: Less than $100 Million

GEOGRAPHIC PREF

☐ East Coast
☐ West Coast
☐ Northeast
☐ Mid Atlantic
☐ Gulf States
☐ Northwest
☐ Southeast
☒ Southwest
☐ Midwest
☐ Central
☐ Local to Office
☐ Other Geo Pref

MESBIC VENTURES HOLDING CO.

**12655 N. Central Expressway
North Central Plaza I, Suite 710
Dallas TX 75243**

Phone (972) 991-1597   Fax (972) 991-1647

PROFESSIONALS

Donald R. Lawhorne
Linda Roack
Richard Vinegar
Divakar Kamath

TITLE

President
Sr. Vice President
Sr. Vice President
Executive Vice President

INDUSTRY PREFERENCE

- ☒ INFORMATION INDUSTRY
- ☐ Communications
- ☐ Computer Equipment
- ☐ Computer Services
- ☒ Computer Components
- ☐ Computer Entertainment
- ☐ Computer Education
- ☐ Information Technologies
- ☐ Computer Media
- ☐ Software
- ☐ Internet
- ☐ MEDICAL/HEALTHCARE
- ☐ Biotechnology
- ☐ Healthcare Services
- ☐ Life Sciences
- ☐ Medical Products
- ☐ INDUSTRIAL
- ☐ Advanced Materials
- ☐ Chemicals
- ☐ Instruments & Controls

- ☒ BASIC INDUSTRIES
- ☐ Consumer
- ☐ Distribution
- ☒ Manufacturing
- ☒ Retail
- ☐ Service
- ☐ Wholesale
- ☒ SPECIFIC INDUSTRIES
- ☐ Energy
- ☐ Environmental
- ☐ Financial
- ☐ Real Estate
- ☐ Transportation
- ☐ Publishing
- ☒ Food
- ☐ Franchises
- ☒ DIVERSIFIED
- ☒ MISCELLANEOUS
  Food Processing

STAGE PREFERENCE

- ☐ EARLY STAGE
- ☐ Seed
- ☐ Start-up
- ☐ 1st Stage
- ☒ LATER STAGE
- ☒ 2nd Stage
- ☒ Mature
- ☒ Mezzanine
- ☒ LBO/MBO
- ☒ Turnaround
- ☐ INT'L EXPANSION
- ☐ WILL CONSIDER ALL
- ☒ VENTURE LEASING
  SSBIC

Other Locations:

Affiliation: Alliance Enterprise Corp.
Minimum Investment: Less than $1 Million
Capital Under Management: Less than $100 Million

GEOGRAPHIC PREF

- ☐ East Coast
- ☐ West Coast
- ☐ Northeast
- ☐ Mid Atlantic
- ☐ Gulf States
- ☐ Northwest
- ☐ Southeast
- ☒ Southwest
- ☐ Midwest
- ☐ Central
- ☐ Local to Office
- ☐ Other Geo Pref

NATURAL GAS PARTNERS

**777 Main Street
Suite 2700
Fort Worth TX 76102**

Phone (817) 338-9235   Fax (817) 820-6650

PROFESSIONALS

Kenneth Hersch
Richard Couvington

TITLE

Managing Partner
Managing Partner

INDUSTRY PREFERENCE

- ☐ INFORMATION INDUSTRY
- ☐ Communications
- ☐ Computer Equipment
- ☐ Computer Services
- ☐ Computer Components
- ☐ Computer Entertainment
- ☐ Computer Education
- ☐ Information Technologies
- ☐ Computer Media
- ☐ Software
- ☐ Internet
- ☐ MEDICAL/HEALTHCARE
- ☐ Biotechnology
- ☐ Healthcare Services
- ☐ Life Sciences
- ☐ Medical Products
- ☐ INDUSTRIAL
- ☐ Advanced Materials
- ☐ Chemicals
- ☐ Instruments & Controls

- ☐ BASIC INDUSTRIES
- ☐ Consumer
- ☐ Distribution
- ☐ Manufacturing
- ☐ Retail
- ☐ Service
- ☐ Wholesale
- ☒ SPECIFIC INDUSTRIES
- ☒ Energy
- ☐ Environmental
- ☐ Financial
- ☐ Real Estate
- ☐ Transportation
- ☐ Publishing
- ☐ Food
- ☐ Franchises
- ☐ DIVERSIFIED
- ☒ MISCELLANEOUS

STAGE PREFERENCE

- ☒ EARLY STAGE
- ☐ Seed
- ☒ Start-up
- ☒ 1st Stage
- ☒ LATER STAGE
- ☒ 2nd Stage
- ☐ Mature
- ☐ Mezzanine
- ☒ LBO/MBO
- ☐ Turnaround
- ☐ INT'L EXPANSION
- ☐ WILL CONSIDER ALL
- ☐ VENTURE LEASING

Other Locations: Greenwich CT, Santa Fe NM

Affiliation:
Minimum Investment: $1 Million or more
Capital Under Management: Over $500 Million

GEOGRAPHIC PREF

- ☐ East Coast
- ☐ West Coast
- ☐ Northeast
- ☐ Mid Atlantic
- ☐ Gulf States
- ☐ Northwest
- ☐ Southeast
- ☐ Southwest
- ☐ Midwest
- ☐ Central
- ☐ Local to Office
- ☐ Other Geo Pref

PHILLIPS-SMITH SPECIALTY RETAIL GROUP

5080 Spectrum Drive
Suite 805 West
Addison TX 75001

Phone (972) 387-0725   Fax (972) 458-2560

PROFESSIONALS	TITLE
Cece Smith	Managing General Partner
Donald J. Phillips	Managing General Partner
G. Michael Machens	General Partner
Erik Anderson	Chief Financial Officer

INDUSTRY PREFERENCE

- ☒ INFORMATION INDUSTRY
- ☐ Communications
- ☐ Computer Equipment
- ☐ Computer Services
- ☐ Computer Components
- ☐ Computer Entertainment
- ☐ Computer Education
- ☐ Information Technologies
- ☐ Computer Media
- ☐ Software
- ☒ Internet
- ☐ MEDICAL/HEALTHCARE
- ☐ Biotechnology
- ☐ Healthcare Services
- ☐ Life Sciences
- ☐ Medical Products
- ☐ INDUSTRIAL
- ☐ Advanced Materials
- ☐ Chemicals
- ☐ Instruments & Controls

- ☒ BASIC INDUSTRIES
- ☐ Consumer
- ☐ Distribution
- ☐ Manufacturing
- ☒ Retail
- ☐ Service
- ☐ Wholesale
- ☒ SPECIFIC INDUSTRIES
- ☐ Energy
- ☐ Environmental
- ☐ Financial
- ☐ Real Estate
- ☐ Transportation
- ☐ Publishing
- ☐ Food
- ☐ Franchises
- ☒ DIVERSIFIED
- ☐ MISCELLANEOUS
- e-Commerce

STAGE PREFERENCE

- ☒ EARLY STAGE
- ☒ Seed
- ☒ Start-up
- ☒ 1st Stage
- ☒ LATER STAGE
- ☒ 2nd Stage
- ☒ Mature
- ☒ Mezzanine
- ☒ LBO/MBO
- ☐ Turnaround
- ☐ INT'L EXPANSION
- ☐ WILL CONSIDER ALL
- ☐ VENTURE LEASING

Other Locations: Bronxville NY, Colorado Springs CO

Affiliation:
Minimum Investment: $1 Million or more
Capital Under Management: $100 to $500 Million

GEOGRAPHIC PREF

- ☐ East Coast
- ☐ West Coast
- ☐ Northeast
- ☐ Mid Atlantic
- ☐ Gulf States
- ☐ Northwest
- ☐ Southeast
- ☐ Southwest
- ☐ Midwest
- ☐ Central
- ☐ Local to Office
- ☐ Other Geo Pref

PRIVATE EQUITY PARTNERS INC.

301 Commerce Street
Suite 1600
Fort Worth TX 76102

Phone (817) 332-1600   Fax (817) 336-7523

PROFESSIONALS	TITLE
Jeff Alexander	Principal
Scott Kleberg	Principal

INDUSTRY PREFERENCE

- ☐ INFORMATION INDUSTRY
- ☐ Communications
- ☐ Computer Equipment
- ☐ Computer Services
- ☐ Computer Components
- ☐ Computer Entertainment
- ☐ Computer Education
- ☐ Information Technologies
- ☐ Computer Media
- ☐ Software
- ☐ Internet
- ☐ MEDICAL/HEALTHCARE
- ☐ Biotechnology
- ☐ Healthcare Services
- ☐ Life Sciences
- ☐ Medical Products
- ☐ INDUSTRIAL
- ☐ Advanced Materials
- ☐ Chemicals
- ☐ Instruments & Controls

- ☐ BASIC INDUSTRIES
- ☐ Consumer
- ☐ Distribution
- ☐ Manufacturing
- ☐ Retail
- ☐ Service
- ☐ Wholesale
- ☐ SPECIFIC INDUSTRIES
- ☐ Energy
- ☐ Environmental
- ☐ Financial
- ☐ Real Estate
- ☐ Transportation
- ☐ Publishing
- ☐ Food
- ☐ Franchises
- ☒ DIVERSIFIED
- ☒ MISCELLANEOUS

STAGE PREFERENCE

- ☐ EARLY STAGE
- ☐ Seed
- ☐ Start-up
- ☐ 1st Stage
- ☒ LATER STAGE
- ☒ 2nd Stage
- ☐ Mature
- ☐ Mezzanine
- ☒ LBO/MBO
- ☒ Turnaround
- ☐ INT'L EXPANSION
- ☐ WILL CONSIDER ALL
- ☒ VENTURE LEASING

Other Locations:

Affiliation:
Minimum Investment: $1 Million or more
Capital Under Management: Less than $100 Million

GEOGRAPHIC PREF

- ☐ East Coast
- ☐ West Coast
- ☐ Northeast
- ☐ Mid Atlantic
- ☐ Gulf States
- ☐ Northwest
- ☒ Southeast
- ☒ Southwest
- ☐ Midwest
- ☐ Central
- ☐ Local to Office
- ☐ Other Geo Pref

R. CHANEY & CO.

909 Fannin Street
Suite 1800
Houston TX 77010

Phone (281) 356-7555   Fax (281) 750-0021

PROFESSIONALS	TITLE
Robert Chaney	Chairman

INDUSTRY PREFERENCE

☐ INFORMATION INDUSTRY
☐ Communications
☐ Computer Equipment
☐ Computer Services
☐ Computer Components
☐ Computer Entertainment
☐ Computer Education
☐ Information Technologies
☐ Computer Media
☐ Software
☐ Internet
☐ MEDICAL/HEALTHCARE
☐ Biotechnology
☐ Healthcare Services
☐ Life Sciences
☐ Medical Products
☐ INDUSTRIAL
☐ Advanced Materials
☐ Chemicals
☐ Instruments & Controls

☐ BASIC INDUSTRIES
☐ Consumer
☐ Distribution
☐ Manufacturing
☐ Retail
☐ Service
☐ Wholesale
☒ SPECIFIC INDUSTRIES
☒ Energy
☐ Environmental
☐ Financial
☐ Real Estate
☐ Transportation
☐ Publishing
☐ Food
☐ Franchises
☐ DIVERSIFIED
☒ MISCELLANEOUS

STAGE PREFERENCE

☐ EARLY STAGE
☐ Seed
☐ Start-up
☐ 1st Stage
☒ LATER STAGE
☒ 2nd Stage
☐ Mature
☒ Mezzanine
☐ LBO/MBO
☐ Turnaround
☐ INT'L EXPANSION
☐ WILL CONSIDER ALL
☐ VENTURE LEASING

Other Locations:

Affiliation:
Minimum Investment: Less than $1 Million
Capital Under Management: $100 to $500 Million

GEOGRAPHIC PREF

☐ East Coast
☐ West Coast
☐ Northeast
☐ Mid Atlantic
☐ Gulf States
☐ Northwest
☐ Southeast
☒ Southwest
☐ Midwest
☐ Central
☐ Local to Office
☐ Other Geo Pref

RICE SANGALIS TOOLE & WILSON

5847 San Felipe
Suite 4350
Houston TX 77057

Phone (713) 783-7770   Fax (713) 783-9750

PROFESSIONALS	TITLE
Don Rice	Managing Partner
Jeffrrey Sangalis	Managing Partner
Jeffrey Toole	Managing Partner
James Wilson	Managing Partner

INDUSTRY PREFERENCE

☐ INFORMATION INDUSTRY
☐ Communications
☐ Computer Equipment
☐ Computer Services
☐ Computer Components
☐ Computer Entertainment
☐ Computer Education
☐ Information Technologies
☐ Computer Media
☐ Software
☐ Internet
☐ MEDICAL/HEALTHCARE
☐ Biotechnology
☐ Healthcare Services
☐ Life Sciences
☐ Medical Products
☒ INDUSTRIAL
☒ Advanced Materials
☐ Chemicals
☒ Instruments & Controls

☒ BASIC INDUSTRIES
☒ Consumer
☒ Distribution
☐ Manufacturing
☐ Retail
☐ Service
☐ Wholesale
☐ SPECIFIC INDUSTRIES
☐ Energy
☐ Environmental
☐ Financial
☐ Real Estate
☐ Transportation
☐ Publishing
☐ Food
☐ Franchises
☒ DIVERSIFIED
☒ MISCELLANEOUS

STAGE PREFERENCE

☐ EARLY STAGE
☐ Seed
☐ Start-up
☐ 1st Stage
☒ LATER STAGE
☐ 2nd Stage
☐ Mature
☒ Mezzanine
☒ LBO/MBO
☒ Turnaround
☐ INT'L EXPANSION
☐ WILL CONSIDER ALL
☒ VENTURE LEASING

Other Locations:

Affiliation:
Minimum Investment: $1 Million or more
Capital Under Management: Over $500 Million

GEOGRAPHIC PREF

☐ East Coast
☐ West Coast
☐ Northeast
☐ Mid Atlantic
☐ Gulf States
☐ Northwest
☐ Southeast
☐ Southwest
☐ Midwest
☐ Central
☐ Local to Office
☐ Other Geo Pref

SBIC PARTNERS, LP

201 Main Street
Suite 2302
Fort Worth TX 76102

Phone (949) 729-3222   Fax (949) 729-3226

PROFESSIONALS	TITLE
Gregory Forrest	Manager
Jeffrey Brown	Manager

INDUSTRY PREFERENCE

☐ INFORMATION INDUSTRY
☐ Communications
☐ Computer Equipment
☐ Computer Services
☐ Computer Components
☐ Computer Entertainment
☐ Computer Education
☐ Information Technologies
☐ Computer Media
☐ Software
☐ Internet
☐ MEDICAL/HEALTHCARE
☐ Biotechnology
☐ Healthcare Services
☐ Life Sciences
☐ Medical Products
☐ INDUSTRIAL
☐ Advanced Materials
☐ Chemicals
☐ Instruments & Controls

☐ BASIC INDUSTRIES
☐ Consumer
☐ Distribution
☐ Manufacturing
☐ Retail
☐ Service
☐ Wholesale
☐ SPECIFIC INDUSTRIES
☐ Energy
☐ Environmental
☐ Financial
☐ Real Estate
☐ Transportation
☐ Publishing
☐ Food
☐ Franchises
☒ DIVERSIFIED
☐ MISCELLANEOUS

STAGE PREFERENCE

☒ EARLY STAGE
☐ Seed
☐ Start-up
☒ 1st Stage
☒ LATER STAGE
☒ 2nd Stage
☒ Mature
☒ Mezzanine
☒ LBO/MBO
☐ Turnaround
☐ INT'L EXPANSION
☐ WILL CONSIDER ALL
☐ VENTURE LEASING
SBIC
Other Locations:

Affiliation:
Minimum Investment: $1 Million or more
Capital Under Management: Less than $100 Million

GEOGRAPHIC PREF

☐ East Coast
☐ West Coast
☐ Northeast
☐ Mid Atlantic
☐ Gulf States
☐ Northwest
☐ Southeast
☐ Southwest
☐ Midwest
☐ Central
☐ Local to Office
☐ Other Geo Pref

SEVIN ROSEN MANAGEMENT CO.

13455 Noel Road
Suite 1670
Dallas TX 75240

Phone (972) 702-1100   Fax (972) 702-1103

PROFESSIONALS	TITLE
John V. Jaggers	General Partner
Jon W. Bayless	General Partner
Charles Phipps	General Partner

INDUSTRY PREFERENCE

☒ INFORMATION INDUSTRY
☒ Communications
☒ Computer Equipment
☒ Computer Services
☒ Computer Components
☐ Computer Entertainment
☒ Computer Education
☒ Information Technologies
☐ Computer Media
☒ Software
☒ Internet
☒ MEDICAL/HEALTHCARE
☒ Biotechnology
☒ Healthcare Services
☒ Life Sciences
☒ Medical Products
☒ INDUSTRIAL
☐ Advanced Materials
☒ Chemicals
☐ Instruments & Controls

☒ BASIC INDUSTRIES
☐ Consumer
☐ Distribution
☐ Manufacturing
☐ Retail
☒ Service
☐ Wholesale
☐ SPECIFIC INDUSTRIES
☐ Energy
☐ Environmental
☐ Financial
☐ Real Estate
☐ Transportation
☐ Publishing
☐ Food
☐ Franchises
☒ DIVERSIFIED
☐ MISCELLANEOUS

STAGE PREFERENCE

☒ EARLY STAGE
☒ Seed
☒ Start-up
☒ 1st Stage
☐ LATER STAGE
☐ 2nd Stage
☐ Mature
☐ Mezzanine
☐ LBO/MBO
☐ Turnaround
☐ INT'L EXPANSION
☐ WILL CONSIDER ALL
☐ VENTURE LEASING

Other Locations: Palo Alto CA

Affiliation: Sevin Rosen Funds
Minimum Investment: Less than $1 Million
Capital Under Management: $100 to $500 Million

GEOGRAPHIC PREF

☐ East Coast
☐ West Coast
☐ Northeast
☐ Mid Atlantic
☐ Gulf States
☐ Northwest
☐ Southeast
☐ Southwest
☐ Midwest
☐ Central
☐ Local to Office
☐ Other Geo Pref

STRATFORD CAPITAL PARTNERS, LP

200 Crescent Court
Suite 1600
Dallas TX 75201

Phone (214) 740-7377   Fax (214) 740-7393

PROFESSIONALS

Michael D. Brown
John Farmer

TITLE

Managing Partner
Managing Partner

INDUSTRY PREFERENCE

☐ INFORMATION INDUSTRY	☒ BASIC INDUSTRIES
☐ Communications	☐ Consumer
☐ Computer Equipment	☒ Distribution
☐ Computer Services	☒ Manufacturing
☐ Computer Components	☐ Retail
☐ Computer Entertainment	☐ Service
☐ Computer Education	☐ Wholesale
☐ Information Technologies	☐ SPECIFIC INDUSTRIES
☐ Computer Media	☐ Energy
☐ Software	☐ Environmental
☐ Internet	☐ Financial
☐ MEDICAL/HEALTHCARE	☐ Real Estate
☐ Biotechnology	☐ Transportation
☐ Healthcare Services	☐ Publishing
☐ Life Sciences	☐ Food
☐ Medical Products	☐ Franchises
☐ INDUSTRIAL	☒ DIVERSIFIED
☐ Advanced Materials	☐ MISCELLANEOUS
☐ Chemicals	
☐ Instruments & Controls	

STAGE PREFERENCE

☐ EARLY STAGE
☐ Seed
☐ Start-up
☐ 1st Stage
☒ LATER STAGE
☒ 2nd Stage
☒ Mature
☒ Mezzanine
☒ LBO/MBO
☐ Turnaround
☐ INT'L EXPANSION
☐ WILL CONSIDER ALL
☐ VENTURE LEASING
SBIC
Other Locations:

Affiliation:
Minimum Investment: $1 Million or more
Capital Under Management: $100 to $500 Million

GEOGRAPHIC PREF

☐ East Coast
☐ West Coast
☐ Northeast
☐ Mid Atlantic
☐ Gulf States
☐ Northwest
☐ Southeast
☐ Southwest
☐ Midwest
☐ Central
☐ Local to Office
☐ Other Geo Pref

SUNWESTERN INVESTMENT GROUP

12221 Merit Drive
Suite 935
Dallas TX 75251

Phone (972) 239-5650   Fax (972) 701-0024

PROFESSIONALS

Patrick Rivelli
James Silcock

TITLE

General Partner
General Partner

INDUSTRY PREFERENCE

☐ INFORMATION INDUSTRY	☐ BASIC INDUSTRIES
☐ Communications	☐ Consumer
☐ Computer Equipment	☐ Distribution
☐ Computer Services	☐ Manufacturing
☐ Computer Components	☐ Retail
☐ Computer Entertainment	☐ Service
☐ Computer Education	☐ Wholesale
☐ Information Technologies	☐ SPECIFIC INDUSTRIES
☐ Computer Media	☐ Energy
☐ Software	☐ Environmental
☐ Internet	☐ Financial
☐ MEDICAL/HEALTHCARE	☐ Real Estate
☐ Biotechnology	☐ Transportation
☐ Healthcare Services	☐ Publishing
☐ Life Sciences	☐ Food
☐ Medical Products	☐ Franchises
☐ INDUSTRIAL	☐ DIVERSIFIED
☐ Advanced Materials	☐ MISCELLANEOUS
☐ Chemicals	
☐ Instruments & Controls	

STAGE PREFERENCE

☐ EARLY STAGE
☐ Seed
☐ Start-up
☐ 1st Stage
☒ LATER STAGE
☒ 2nd Stage
☒ Mature
☐ Mezzanine
☒ LBO/MBO
☐ Turnaround
☐ INT'L EXPANSION
☐ WILL CONSIDER ALL
☐ VENTURE LEASING

Other Locations:

Affiliation:
Minimum Investment: Less than $1 Million
Capital Under Management: Less than $100 Million

GEOGRAPHIC PREF

☐ East Coast
☒ West Coast
☐ Northeast
☐ Mid Atlantic
☐ Gulf States
☐ Northwest
☐ Southeast
☒ Southwest
☐ Midwest
☐ Central
☐ Local to Office
☐ Other Geo Pref

TEXAS GROWTH FUND

111 Congress Avenue
Suite 2900
Austin TX 78701-4043

Phone (512) 322-3100   Fax (512) 322-3101

PROFESSIONALS	TITLE
Brent Humphries	Principal
Barry Twomey	Principal
Stephen Soileau	Principal
Jim Kozlowski	Principal

INDUSTRY PREFERENCE

☒ INFORMATION INDUSTRY	☒ BASIC INDUSTRIES
☒ Communications	☒ Consumer
☒ Computer Equipment	☒ Distribution
☐ Computer Services	☒ Manufacturing
☐ Computer Components	☐ Retail
☐ Computer Entertainment	☒ Service
☐ Computer Education	☐ Wholesale
☐ Information Technologies	☒ SPECIFIC INDUSTRIES
☐ Computer Media	☒ Energy
☐ Software	☐ Environmental
☐ Internet	☐ Financial
☒ MEDICAL/HEALTHCARE	☐ Real Estate
☒ Biotechnology	☐ Transportation
☒ Healthcare Services	☐ Publishing
☒ Life Sciences	☐ Food
☒ Medical Products	☐ Franchises
☐ INDUSTRIAL	☒ DIVERSIFIED
☐ Advanced Materials	☐ MISCELLANEOUS
☐ Chemicals	
☐ Instruments & Controls	

STAGE PREFERENCE

☐ EARLY STAGE
☐ Seed
☐ Start-up
☐ 1st Stage
☒ LATER STAGE
☒ 2nd Stage
☒ Mature
☒ Mezzanine
☒ LBO/MBO
☐ Turnaround
☐ INT'L EXPANSION
☐ WILL CONSIDER ALL
☐ VENTURE LEASING

Other Locations:

Affiliation:
Minimum Investment: $1 Million or more
Capital Under Management: Over $500 Million

GEOGRAPHIC PREF

☐ East Coast
☐ West Coast
☐ Northeast
☐ Mid Atlantic
☐ Gulf States
☐ Northwest
☐ Southeast
☒ Southwest
☐ Midwest
☐ Central
☐ Local to Office
☐ Other Geo Pref

UNITED ORIENTAL CAPITAL CORPORATION

908 Town & Country Boulevard
Suite 310
Houston TX 77024

Phone (713) 461-3909   Fax (713) 465-7559

PROFESSIONALS	TITLE
Jai Min Tai	President

INDUSTRY PREFERENCE

☐ INFORMATION INDUSTRY	☐ BASIC INDUSTRIES
☐ Communications	☐ Consumer
☐ Computer Equipment	☐ Distribution
☐ Computer Services	☐ Manufacturing
☐ Computer Components	☐ Retail
☐ Computer Entertainment	☐ Service
☐ Computer Education	☐ Wholesale
☐ Information Technologies	☐ SPECIFIC INDUSTRIES
☐ Computer Media	☐ Energy
☐ Software	☐ Environmental
☐ Internet	☐ Financial
☐ MEDICAL/HEALTHCARE	☐ Real Estate
☐ Biotechnology	☐ Transportation
☐ Healthcare Services	☐ Publishing
☐ Life Sciences	☐ Food
☐ Medical Products	☐ Franchises
☐ INDUSTRIAL	☒ DIVERSIFIED
☐ Advanced Materials	☐ MISCELLANEOUS
☐ Chemicals	
☐ Instruments & Controls	

STAGE PREFERENCE

☒ EARLY STAGE
☒ Seed
☒ Start-up
☒ 1st Stage
☐ LATER STAGE
☐ 2nd Stage
☐ Mature
☐ Mezzanine
☐ LBO/MBO
☐ Turnaround
☐ INT'L EXPANSION
☐ WILL CONSIDER ALL
☐ VENTURE LEASING
SSBIC
Other Locations:

Affiliation:
Minimum Investment: Less than $1 Million
Capital Under Management: Less than $100 Million

GEOGRAPHIC PREF

☐ East Coast
☐ West Coast
☐ Northeast
☐ Mid Atlantic
☐ Gulf States
☐ Northwest
☐ Southeast
☐ Southwest
☐ Midwest
☐ Central
☐ Local to Office
☒ Other Geo Pref
TX

VENTURES MEDICAL

16945 Northchase Drive
Suite 2150
Houston TX 77060

Phone (281) 873-5748   Fax (281) 873-5950

PROFESSIONALS	TITLE
William T. Mullaney	General Partner

INDUSTRY PREFERENCE

☐ INFORMATION INDUSTRY	☐ BASIC INDUSTRIES
☐ Communications	☐ Consumer
☐ Computer Equipment	☐ Distribution
☐ Computer Services	☐ Manufacturing
☐ Computer Components	☐ Retail
☐ Computer Entertainment	☐ Service
☐ Computer Education	☐ Wholesale
☐ Information Technologies	☐ SPECIFIC INDUSTRIES
☐ Computer Media	☐ Energy
☐ Software	☐ Environmental
☐ Internet	☐ Financial
☒ MEDICAL/HEALTHCARE	☐ Real Estate
☒ Biotechnology	☐ Transportation
☒ Healthcare Services	☐ Publishing
☒ Life Sciences	☐ Food
☒ Medical Products	☐ Franchises
☐ INDUSTRIAL	☐ DIVERSIFIED
☐ Advanced Materials	☐ MISCELLANEOUS
☐ Chemicals	
☐ Instruments & Controls	

STAGE PREFERENCE

☒ EARLY STAGE
☒ Seed
☒ Start-up
☒ 1st Stage
☐ LATER STAGE
☐ 2nd Stage
☐ Mature
☐ Mezzanine
☐ LBO/MBO
☐ Turnaround
☐ INT'L EXPANSION
☐ WILL CONSIDER ALL
☐ VENTURE LEASING

Other Locations:

Affiliation:
Minimum Investment: Less than $1 Million
Capital Under Management: Less than $100 Million

GEOGRAPHIC PREF

☐ East Coast
☐ West Coast
☐ Northeast
☐ Mid Atlantic
☐ Gulf States
☐ Northwest
☐ Southeast
☐ Southwest
☐ Midwest
☐ Central
☐ Local to Office
☐ Other Geo Pref

WINGATE PARTNERS

750 North Saint Paul
Suite 1200
Dallas TX 75201

Phone (214) 720-1313   Fax (214) 871-8799

PROFESSIONALS	TITLE
Jay (Bud) Applebaum	Principal

INDUSTRY PREFERENCE

☐ INFORMATION INDUSTRY	☒ BASIC INDUSTRIES
☐ Communications	☒ Consumer
☐ Computer Equipment	☒ Distribution
☐ Computer Services	☐ Manufacturing
☐ Computer Components	☒ Retail
☐ Computer Entertainment	☐ Service
☐ Computer Education	☐ Wholesale
☐ Information Technologies	☐ SPECIFIC INDUSTRIES
☐ Computer Media	☐ Energy
☐ Software	☐ Environmental
☐ Internet	☐ Financial
☒ MEDICAL/HEALTHCARE	☐ Real Estate
☐ Biotechnology	☐ Transportation
☒ Healthcare Services	☐ Publishing
☐ Life Sciences	☐ Food
☒ Medical Products	☐ Franchises
☒ INDUSTRIAL	☒ DIVERSIFIED
☒ Advanced Materials	☒ MISCELLANEOUS
☒ Chemicals	
☒ Instruments & Controls	

STAGE PREFERENCE

☐ EARLY STAGE
☐ Seed
☐ Start-up
☐ 1st Stage
☒ LATER STAGE
☐ 2nd Stage
☐ Mature
☐ Mezzanine
☒ LBO/MBO
☐ Turnaround
☐ INT'L EXPANSION
☐ WILL CONSIDER ALL
☐ VENTURE LEASING

Other Locations:

Affiliation:
Minimum Investment: $1 Million or more
Capital Under Management: $100 to $500 Million

GEOGRAPHIC PREF

☐ East Coast
☐ West Coast
☐ Northeast
☐ Mid Atlantic
☐ Gulf States
☐ Northwest
☐ Southeast
☐ Southwest
☐ Midwest
☐ Central
☐ Local to Office
☐ Other Geo Pref

FIRST SECURITY BUSINESS INVESTMENT CORP.

15 East 100 South
Suite 100
Salt Lake City UT 84111

Phone (801) 246-5737   Fax (801) 246-2670

PROFESSIONALS	TITLE
Butch Alder	Manager

INDUSTRY PREFERENCE

☐ INFORMATION INDUSTRY	☐ BASIC INDUSTRIES
☐ Communications	☐ Consumer
☐ Computer Equipment	☐ Distribution
☐ Computer Services	☐ Manufacturing
☐ Computer Components	☐ Retail
☐ Computer Entertainment	☐ Service
☐ Computer Education	☐ Wholesale
☐ Information Technologies	☐ SPECIFIC INDUSTRIES
☐ Computer Media	☐ Energy
☐ Software	☐ Environmental
☐ Internet	☐ Financial
☐ MEDICAL/HEALTHCARE	☐ Real Estate
☐ Biotechnology	☐ Transportation
☐ Healthcare Services	☐ Publishing
☐ Life Sciences	☐ Food
☐ Medical Products	☐ Franchises
☐ INDUSTRIAL	☒ DIVERSIFIED
☐ Advanced Materials	☐ MISCELLANEOUS
☐ Chemicals	
☐ Instruments & Controls	

STAGE PREFERENCE

☐ EARLY STAGE
☐ Seed
☐ Start-up
☐ 1st Stage
☒ LATER STAGE
☒ 2nd Stage
☒ Mature
☐ Mezzanine
☒ LBO/MBO
☐ Turnaround
☐ INT'L EXPANSION
☐ WILL CONSIDER ALL
☐ VENTURE LEASING

SBIC
Other Locations:

Affiliation:
Minimum Investment: Less than $1 Million
Capital Under Management: Less than $100 Million

GEOGRAPHIC PREF

☐ East Coast
☒ West Coast
☐ Northeast
☐ Mid Atlantic
☐ Gulf States
☐ Northwest
☐ Southeast
☐ Southwest
☐ Midwest
☐ Central
☐ Local to Office
☐ Other Geo Pref

UTAH VENTURES

423 Wakara Way
Suite 206
Salt Lake City UT 84108

Phone (801) 583-5922   Fax (801) 583-4105

PROFESSIONALS	TITLE
James Dreyfous	General Partner

INDUSTRY PREFERENCE

☒ INFORMATION INDUSTRY	☐ BASIC INDUSTRIES
☒ Communications	☐ Consumer
☒ Computer Equipment	☐ Distribution
☒ Computer Services	☐ Manufacturing
☒ Computer Components	☐ Retail
☐ Computer Entertainment	☐ Service
☒ Computer Education	☐ Wholesale
☒ Information Technologies	☒ SPECIFIC INDUSTRIES
☒ Computer Media	☐ Energy
☒ Software	☐ Environmental
☒ Internet	☐ Financial
☒ MEDICAL/HEALTHCARE	☐ Real Estate
☒ Biotechnology	☐ Transportation
☒ Healthcare Services	☐ Publishing
☒ Life Sciences	☐ Food
☒ Medical Products	☐ Franchises
☒ INDUSTRIAL	☒ DIVERSIFIED
☒ Advanced Materials	☒ MISCELLANEOUS
☒ Chemicals	
☒ Instruments & Controls	

STAGE PREFERENCE

☒ EARLY STAGE
☒ Seed
☒ Start-up
☒ 1st Stage
☒ LATER STAGE
☒ 2nd Stage
☐ Mature
☐ Mezzanine
☐ LBO/MBO
☐ Turnaround
☐ INT'L EXPANSION
☐ WILL CONSIDER ALL
☐ VENTURE LEASING

SBIC
Other Locations:

Affiliation:
Minimum Investment: Less than $1 Million
Capital Under Management: $100 to $500 Million

GEOGRAPHIC PREF

☐ East Coast
☒ West Coast
☐ Northeast
☐ Mid Atlantic
☐ Gulf States
☐ Northwest
☐ Southeast
☒ Southwest
☐ Midwest
☐ Central
☐ Local to Office
☐ Other Geo Pref

WASATCH VENTURE CORPORATION

1 South Main Street
Suite 1400
Salt Lake City UT 84133

Phone (801) 524-8939   Fax (801) 524-8941

PROFESSIONALS	TITLE
Todd J. Stevens	Managing Director
David Hemingway	President

INDUSTRY PREFERENCE

☒ INFORMATION INDUSTRY	☐ BASIC INDUSTRIES
☒ Communications	☐ Consumer
☒ Computer Equipment	☐ Distribution
☒ Computer Services	☐ Manufacturing
☒ Computer Components	☐ Retail
☐ Computer Entertainment	☐ Service
☒ Computer Education	☐ Wholesale
☒ Information Technologies	☐ SPECIFIC INDUSTRIES
☒ Computer Media	☐ Energy
☒ Software	☐ Environmental
☒ Internet	☐ Financial
☐ MEDICAL/HEALTHCARE	☐ Real Estate
☐ Biotechnology	☐ Transportation
☐ Healthcare Services	☐ Publishing
☐ Life Sciences	☐ Food
☐ Medical Products	☐ Franchises
☐ INDUSTRIAL	☐ DIVERSIFIED
☐ Advanced Materials	☐ MISCELLANEOUS
☐ Chemicals	
☐ Instruments & Controls	

STAGE PREFERENCE

☒ EARLY STAGE
☒ Seed
☒ Start-up
☒ 1st Stage
☐ LATER STAGE
☐ 2nd Stage
☐ Mature
☐ Mezzanine
☐ LBO/MBO
☐ Turnaround
☐ INT'L EXPANSION
☐ WILL CONSIDER ALL
☐ VENTURE LEASING

SBIC
Other Locations:

Affiliation:
Minimum Investment: Less than $1 Million
Capital Under Management: Less than $100 Million

GEOGRAPHIC PREF

☐ East Coast
☐ West Coast
☐ Northeast
☐ Mid Atlantic
☐ Gulf States
☐ Northwest
☐ Southeast
☐ Southwest
☐ Midwest
☐ Central
☐ Local to Office
☐ Other Geo Pref

GREEN MOUNTAIN CAPITAL, LP

RR 1, Box 1503
Waterbury VT 05676

Phone (802) 244-8981   Fax (802) 244-8990

PROFESSIONALS	TITLE
Michael Sweatman	General Manager

INDUSTRY PREFERENCE

☐ INFORMATION INDUSTRY	☐ BASIC INDUSTRIES
☐ Communications	☐ Consumer
☐ Computer Equipment	☐ Distribution
☐ Computer Services	☐ Manufacturing
☐ Computer Components	☐ Retail
☐ Computer Entertainment	☐ Service
☐ Computer Education	☐ Wholesale
☐ Information Technologies	☐ SPECIFIC INDUSTRIES
☐ Computer Media	☐ Energy
☐ Software	☐ Environmental
☐ Internet	☐ Financial
☐ MEDICAL/HEALTHCARE	☐ Real Estate
☐ Biotechnology	☐ Transportation
☐ Healthcare Services	☐ Publishing
☐ Life Sciences	☐ Food
☐ Medical Products	☐ Franchises
☐ INDUSTRIAL	☒ DIVERSIFIED
☐ Advanced Materials	☐ MISCELLANEOUS
☐ Chemicals	
☐ Instruments & Controls	

STAGE PREFERENCE

☐ EARLY STAGE
☐ Seed
☐ Start-up
☐ 1st Stage
☒ LATER STAGE
☒ 2nd Stage
☒ Mature
☐ Mezzanine
☒ LBO/MBO
☐ Turnaround
☐ INT'L EXPANSION
☐ WILL CONSIDER ALL
☐ VENTURE LEASING

SBIC
Other Locations:

Affiliation:
Minimum Investment: Less than $1 Million
Capital Under Management: Less than $100 Million

GEOGRAPHIC PREF

☐ East Coast
☐ West Coast
☒ Northeast
☐ Mid Atlantic
☐ Gulf States
☐ Northwest
☐ Southeast
☐ Southwest
☐ Midwest
☐ Central
☐ Local to Office
☐ Other Geo Pref

BLUE WATER CAPITAL LLC

8300 Greensboro Drive
Suite 440
McLean VA 22102

Phone (703) 790-8821   Fax (703) 448-1849

PROFESSIONALS	TITLE
Kim Cooke	Managing Director
Henry Barratt, Jr.	Managing Director
Reid Miles	Managing Director

INDUSTRY PREFERENCE

☒ INFORMATION INDUSTRY	☐ BASIC INDUSTRIES
☒ Communications	☐ Consumer
☒ Computer Equipment	☐ Distribution
☒ Computer Services	☐ Manufacturing
☒ Computer Components	☐ Retail
☐ Computer Entertainment	☐ Service
☒ Computer Education	☐ Wholesale
☒ Information Technologies	☐ SPECIFIC INDUSTRIES
☒ Computer Media	☐ Energy
☒ Software	☐ Environmental
☒ Internet	☐ Financial
☐ MEDICAL/HEALTHCARE	☐ Real Estate
☐ Biotechnology	☐ Transportation
☐ Healthcare Services	☐ Publishing
☐ Life Sciences	☐ Food
☐ Medical Products	☐ Franchises
☐ INDUSTRIAL	☐ DIVERSIFIED
☐ Advanced Materials	☒ MISCELLANEOUS
☐ Chemicals	
☐ Instruments & Controls	

STAGE PREFERENCE

☐ EARLY STAGE
☐ Seed
☐ Start-up
☐ 1st Stage
☒ LATER STAGE
☒ 2nd Stage
☒ Mature
☒ Mezzanine
☒ LBO/MBO
☐ Turnaround
☐ INT'L EXPANSION
☐ WILL CONSIDER ALL
☐ VENTURE LEASING

Other Locations: Birmingham MI

Affiliation:
Minimum Investment: $1 Million or more
Capital Under Management: Less than $100 Million

GEOGRAPHIC PREF

☐ East Coast
☐ West Coast
☐ Northeast
☐ Mid Atlantic
☐ Gulf States
☐ Northwest
☐ Southeast
☐ Southwest
☐ Midwest
☐ Central
☐ Local to Office
☐ Other Geo Pref

CALVERT SOCIAL VENTURE PARTNERS LP

402 Maple Avenue West
Suite C
Vienna VA 22180

Phone (301) 718-4272   Fax (301) 656-4421

PROFESSIONALS	TITLE
John May	General Partner

INDUSTRY PREFERENCE

☒ INFORMATION INDUSTRY	☐ BASIC INDUSTRIES
☐ Communications	☐ Consumer
☐ Computer Equipment	☐ Distribution
☐ Computer Services	☐ Manufacturing
☐ Computer Components	☐ Retail
☐ Computer Entertainment	☐ Service
☒ Computer Education	☐ Wholesale
☐ Information Technologies	☒ SPECIFIC INDUSTRIES
☐ Computer Media	☒ Energy
☐ Software	☒ Environmental
☐ Internet	☐ Financial
☒ MEDICAL/HEALTHCARE	☐ Real Estate
☐ Biotechnology	☐ Transportation
☒ Healthcare Services	☐ Publishing
☐ Life Sciences	☐ Food
☐ Medical Products	☐ Franchises
☐ INDUSTRIAL	☒ DIVERSIFIED
☐ Advanced Materials	☒ MISCELLANEOUS
☐ Chemicals	Offer positive social or
☐ Instruments & Controls	environmental impact

STAGE PREFERENCE

☒ EARLY STAGE
☒ Seed
☒ Start-up
☒ 1st Stage
☐ LATER STAGE
☐ 2nd Stage
☐ Mature
☐ Mezzanine
☐ LBO/MBO
☐ Turnaround
☐ INT'L EXPANSION
☐ WILL CONSIDER ALL
☐ VENTURE LEASING

Other Locations:

Affiliation:
Minimum Investment: Less than $1 Million
Capital Under Management: Less than $100 Million

GEOGRAPHIC PREF

☒ East Coast
☐ West Coast
☐ Northeast
☐ Mid Atlantic
☐ Gulf States
☐ Northwest
☐ Southeast
☐ Southwest
☐ Midwest
☐ Central
☐ Local to Office
☐ Other Geo Pref

COLUMBIA CAPITAL CORPORATION

201 North Union Street
Suite 300
Alexandria VA 22314-2642

Phone (703) 519-3581   Fax (703) 519-3904

PROFESSIONALS	TITLE
Robert Blow	Managing Director
James Fleming	Managing Director
R. Philip Herget	Managing Director
Harry F. Hopper	Managing Director
Mark Kington	Managing Director
David P. Mixer	Managing Director
James B. Murray, Jr.	Managing Director
Mark R. Warner	Managing Director

INDUSTRY PREFERENCE

☒ INFORMATION INDUSTRY	☐ BASIC INDUSTRIES
☒ Communications	☐ Consumer
☐ Computer Equipment	☐ Distribution
☐ Computer Services	☐ Manufacturing
☐ Computer Components	☐ Retail
☐ Computer Entertainment	☐ Service
☐ Computer Education	☐ Wholesale
☒ Information Technologies	☐ SPECIFIC INDUSTRIES
☐ Computer Media	☐ Energy
☐ Software	☐ Environmental
☒ Internet	☐ Financial
☐ MEDICAL/HEALTHCARE	☐ Real Estate
☐ Biotechnology	☐ Transportation
☐ Healthcare Services	☐ Publishing
☐ Life Sciences	☐ Food
☐ Medical Products	☐ Franchises
☐ INDUSTRIAL	☐ DIVERSIFIED
☐ Advanced Materials	☒ MISCELLANEOUS
☐ Chemicals	
☐ Instruments & Controls	

STAGE PREFERENCE

☒ EARLY STAGE
☒ Seed
☒ Start-up
☒ 1st Stage
☒ LATER STAGE
☒ 2nd Stage
☐ Mature
☐ Mezzanine
☐ LBO/MBO
☐ Turnaround
☐ INT'L EXPANSION
☐ WILL CONSIDER ALL
☐ VENTURE LEASING

Other Locations:

Affiliation:
Minimum Investment: Less than $1 Million
Capital Under Management: $100 to $500 Million

GEOGRAPHIC PREF

☐ East Coast
☐ West Coast
☐ Northeast
☐ Mid Atlantic
☐ Gulf States
☐ Northwest
☐ Southeast
☐ Southwest
☐ Midwest
☐ Central
☐ Local to Office
☐ Other Geo Pref

CONTINENTAL SBIC

4141 N. Henderson Road
Suite 8
Arlington VA 22203

Phone (703) 527-5200   Fax (703) 527-3700

PROFESSIONALS	TITLE
Arthur Walters	President

INDUSTRY PREFERENCE

☐ INFORMATION INDUSTRY	☐ BASIC INDUSTRIES
☐ Communications	☐ Consumer
☐ Computer Equipment	☐ Distribution
☐ Computer Services	☐ Manufacturing
☐ Computer Components	☐ Retail
☐ Computer Entertainment	☐ Service
☐ Computer Education	☐ Wholesale
☐ Information Technologies	☐ SPECIFIC INDUSTRIES
☐ Computer Media	☐ Energy
☐ Software	☐ Environmental
☐ Internet	☐ Financial
☐ MEDICAL/HEALTHCARE	☐ Real Estate
☐ Biotechnology	☐ Transportation
☐ Healthcare Services	☐ Publishing
☐ Life Sciences	☐ Food
☐ Medical Products	☐ Franchises
☐ INDUSTRIAL	☒ DIVERSIFIED
☐ Advanced Materials	☐ MISCELLANEOUS
☐ Chemicals	
☐ Instruments & Controls	

STAGE PREFERENCE

☒ EARLY STAGE
☒ Seed
☒ Start-up
☒ 1st Stage
☒ LATER STAGE
☒ 2nd Stage
☒ Mature
☒ Mezzanine
☒ LBO/MBO
☐ Turnaround
☐ INT'L EXPANSION
☐ WILL CONSIDER ALL
☐ VENTURE LEASING

SSBIC
Other Locations:

Affiliation:
Minimum Investment: Less than $1 Million
Capital Under Management: Less than $100 Million

GEOGRAPHIC PREF

☐ East Coast
☐ West Coast
☐ Northeast
☐ Mid Atlantic
☐ Gulf States
☐ Northwest
☐ Southeast
☐ Southwest
☒ Midwest
☐ Central
☐ Local to Office
☒ Other Geo Pref
    North, South, Midwest

EDISON VENTURE FUND

1420 Spring Hill Road
Suite 420
McClean VA 22102

Phone (703) 903-9546   Fax (703) 903-9528

PROFESSIONALS	TITLE
Gary Golding	General Partner
Tom Smith	General Partner

INDUSTRY PREFERENCE

☒ INFORMATION INDUSTRY	☒ BASIC INDUSTRIES
☒ Communications	☐ Consumer
☐ Computer Equipment	☐ Distribution
☒ Computer Services	☐ Manufacturing
☒ Computer Components	☐ Retail
☐ Computer Entertainment	☒ Service
☒ Computer Education	☐ Wholesale
☒ Information Technologies	☒ SPECIFIC INDUSTRIES
☒ Computer Media	☐ Energy
☒ Software	☐ Environmental
☒ Internet	☒ Financial
☐ MEDICAL/HEALTHCARE	☐ Real Estate
☐ Biotechnology	☐ Transportation
☐ Healthcare Services	☐ Publishing
☐ Life Sciences	☐ Food
☐ Medical Products	☐ Franchises
☒ INDUSTRIAL	☒ DIVERSIFIED
☒ Advanced Materials	☒ MISCELLANEOUS
☒ Chemicals	
☒ Instruments & Controls	

STAGE PREFERENCE

☒ EARLY STAGE	
☐ Seed	
☐ Start-up	
☒ 1st Stage	
☒ LATER STAGE	
☒ 2nd Stage	
☒ Mature	
☒ Mezzanine	
☒ LBO/MBO	
☐ Turnaround	
☐ INT'L EXPANSION	
☐ WILL CONSIDER ALL	
☐ VENTURE LEASING	

Other Locations: Lawrenceville NJ

Affiliation:
Minimum Investment: $1 Million or more
Capital Under Management: $100 to $500 Million

GEOGRAPHIC PREF

☒ East Coast	
☐ West Coast	
☐ Northeast	
☐ Mid Atlantic	
☐ Gulf States	
☐ Northwest	
☐ Southeast	
☐ Southwest	
☐ Midwest	
☐ Central	
☐ Local to Office	
☐ Other Geo Pref	

MID-ATLANTIC VENTURE FUNDS

1801 Reston Parkway
Suite 203
Reston VA 20190

Phone (703) 904-4120   Fax (703) 904-4124

PROFESSIONALS	TITLE
Marc F. Benson	Partner
Thomas A. Smith	Partner

INDUSTRY PREFERENCE

☒ INFORMATION INDUSTRY	☒ BASIC INDUSTRIES
☒ Communications	☐ Consumer
☒ Computer Equipment	☐ Distribution
☒ Computer Services	☐ Manufacturing
☒ Computer Components	☐ Retail
☐ Computer Entertainment	☒ Service
☒ Computer Education	☐ Wholesale
☒ Information Technologies	☐ SPECIFIC INDUSTRIES
☒ Computer Media	☐ Energy
☒ Software	☐ Environmental
☒ Internet	☐ Financial
☒ MEDICAL/HEALTHCARE	☐ Real Estate
☐ Biotechnology	☐ Transportation
☒ Healthcare Services	☐ Publishing
☐ Life Sciences	☐ Food
☒ Medical Products	☐ Franchises
☒ INDUSTRIAL	☒ DIVERSIFIED
☒ Advanced Materials	☒ MISCELLANEOUS
☒ Chemicals	
☒ Instruments & Controls	

STAGE PREFERENCE

☒ EARLY STAGE	
☒ Seed	
☒ Start-up	
☒ 1st Stage	
☒ LATER STAGE	
☒ 2nd Stage	
☐ Mature	
☐ Mezzanine	
☒ LBO/MBO	
☒ Turnaround	
☐ INT'L EXPANSION	
☐ WILL CONSIDER ALL	
☒ VENTURE LEASING	

Other Locations: Bethlehem PA

Affiliation: NEPA Management Corp.
Minimum Investment: Less than $1 Million
Capital Under Management: Less than $100 Million

GEOGRAPHIC PREF

☐ East Coast	
☐ West Coast	
☐ Northeast	
☒ Mid Atlantic	
☐ Gulf States	
☐ Northwest	
☐ Southeast	
☐ Southwest	
☐ Midwest	
☐ Central	
☐ Local to Office	
☒ Other Geo Pref	
Mid-Atlantic	

NEW ENTERPRISE ASSOCIATES

**One Fountain Square
Suite 580
Reston VA 20190**

Phone (703) 709-9499   Fax (703) 834-7579

PROFESSIONALS	TITLE
Peter Barris	Partner
Arthur Marks	

INDUSTRY PREFERENCE

☐ INFORMATION INDUSTRY
☐ Communications
☐ Computer Equipment
☐ Computer Services
☐ Computer Components
☐ Computer Entertainment
☐ Computer Education
☐ Information Technologies
☐ Computer Media
☐ Software
☐ Internet
☒ MEDICAL/HEALTHCARE
☒ Biotechnology
☒ Healthcare Services
☒ Life Sciences
☒ Medical Products
☐ INDUSTRIAL
☐ Advanced Materials
☐ Chemicals
☐ Instruments & Controls

☐ BASIC INDUSTRIES
☐ Consumer
☐ Distribution
☐ Manufacturing
☐ Retail
☐ Service
☐ Wholesale
☐ SPECIFIC INDUSTRIES
☐ Energy
☐ Environmental
☐ Financial
☐ Real Estate
☐ Transportation
☐ Publishing
☐ Food
☐ Franchises
☐ DIVERSIFIED
☒ MISCELLANEOUS

STAGE PREFERENCE

☒ EARLY STAGE
☒ Seed
☒ Start-up
☒ 1st Stage
☐ LATER STAGE
☐ 2nd Stage
☐ Mature
☐ Mezzanine
☐ LBO/MBO
☐ Turnaround
☐ INT'L EXPANSION
☐ WILL CONSIDER ALL
☐ VENTURE LEASING

Other Locations: Baltimore MD, Menlo Park CA

Affiliation:
Minimum Investment: Less than $1 Million
Capital Under Management: Over $500 Million

GEOGRAPHIC PREF

☐ East Coast
☐ West Coast
☐ Northeast
☐ Mid Atlantic
☐ Gulf States
☐ Northwest
☐ Southeast
☐ Southwest
☐ Midwest
☐ Central
☐ Local to Office
☐ Other Geo Pref

NOVAK BIDDLE VENTURE PARTNERS

**1897 Preston White Drive
Reston VA 20191**

Phone (703) 264-7904   Fax (703) 264-1438

PROFESSIONALS	TITLE
Roger Novak	Venture Partner
Jack Biddle	Venture Partner

INDUSTRY PREFERENCE

☒ INFORMATION INDUSTRY
☒ Communications
☒ Computer Equipment
☐ Computer Services
☒ Computer Components
☐ Computer Entertainment
☐ Computer Education
☒ Information Technologies
☒ Computer Media
☒ Software
☒ Internet
☐ MEDICAL/HEALTHCARE
☐ Biotechnology
☐ Healthcare Services
☐ Life Sciences
☐ Medical Products
☐ INDUSTRIAL
☐ Advanced Materials
☐ Chemicals
☐ Instruments & Controls

☐ BASIC INDUSTRIES
☐ Consumer
☐ Distribution
☐ Manufacturing
☐ Retail
☐ Service
☐ Wholesale
☐ SPECIFIC INDUSTRIES
☐ Energy
☐ Environmental
☐ Financial
☐ Real Estate
☐ Transportation
☐ Publishing
☐ Food
☐ Franchises
☐ DIVERSIFIED
☒ MISCELLANEOUS

STAGE PREFERENCE

☒ EARLY STAGE
☒ Seed
☒ Start-up
☒ 1st Stage
☒ LATER STAGE
☒ 2nd Stage
☐ Mature
☐ Mezzanine
☒ LBO/MBO
☐ Turnaround
☐ INT'L EXPANSION
☐ WILL CONSIDER ALL
☐ VENTURE LEASING

Other Locations:

Affiliation:
Minimum Investment: Less than $1 Million
Capital Under Management: Less than $100 Million

GEOGRAPHIC PREF

☐ East Coast
☐ West Coast
☐ Northeast
☐ Mid Atlantic
☐ Gulf States
☐ Northwest
☐ Southeast
☐ Southwest
☐ Midwest
☐ Central
☐ Local to Office
☐ Other Geo Pref

SPACEVEST

**11911 Freedom Drive
Suite 500
Reston VA 20190**

Phone (703) 904-9800   Fax (703) 904-0571

PROFESSIONALS	TITLE
John Higginbotham	Partner
Frank DiBello	Partner
Ransom Parker	Partner
Stephen Rochereau	Partner
Roger Widing	Partner

INDUSTRY PREFERENCE

☐ INFORMATION INDUSTRY
☐ Communications
☐ Computer Equipment
☐ Computer Services
☐ Computer Components
☐ Computer Entertainment
☐ Computer Education
☐ Information Technologies
☐ Computer Media
☐ Software
☐ Internet
☐ MEDICAL/HEALTHCARE
☐ Biotechnology
☐ Healthcare Services
☐ Life Sciences
☐ Medical Products
☐ INDUSTRIAL
☐ Advanced Materials
☐ Chemicals
☐ Instruments & Controls

☐ BASIC INDUSTRIES
☐ Consumer
☐ Distribution
☐ Manufacturing
☐ Retail
☐ Service
☐ Wholesale
☒ SPECIFIC INDUSTRIES
☐ Energy
☐ Environmental
☐ Financial
☐ Real Estate
☐ Transportation
☐ Publishing
☐ Food
☐ Franchises
☐ DIVERSIFIED
☒ MISCELLANEOUS
   Any Space Related
   Technologies

STAGE PREFERENCE

☒ EARLY STAGE
☐ Seed
☐ Start-up
☒ 1st Stage
☒ LATER STAGE
☒ 2nd Stage
☐ Mature
☐ Mezzanine
☐ LBO/MBO
☐ Turnaround
☐ INT'L EXPANSION
☐ WILL CONSIDER ALL
☐ VENTURE LEASING

Other Locations:

Affiliation:
Minimum Investment: Less than $1 Million
Capital Under Management: Less than $100 Million

GEOGRAPHIC PREF

☐ East Coast
☐ West Coast
☐ Northeast
☐ Mid Atlantic
☐ Gulf States
☐ Northwest
☐ Southeast
☐ Southwest
☐ Midwest
☐ Central
☐ Local to Office
☐ Other Geo Pref

VIRGINIA CAPITAL

**Nine South 12th Street
Suite 400
Richmond VA 23219**

Phone (804) 648-4802   Fax (804) 648-4809

PROFESSIONALS	TITLE
Frederick Russell	Managing Director
Thomas Deardorff	Vice President

INDUSTRY PREFERENCE

☒ INFORMATION INDUSTRY
☒ Communications
☐ Computer Equipment
☐ Computer Services
☐ Computer Components
☐ Computer Entertainment
☐ Computer Education
☐ Information Technologies
☐ Computer Media
☐ Software
☒ Internet
☒ MEDICAL/HEALTHCARE
☐ Biotechnology
☒ Healthcare Services
☐ Life Sciences
☒ Medical Products
☐ INDUSTRIAL
☐ Advanced Materials
☐ Chemicals
☐ Instruments & Controls

☒ BASIC INDUSTRIES
☐ Consumer
☐ Distribution
☐ Manufacturing
☐ Retail
☒ Service
☐ Wholesale
☒ SPECIFIC INDUSTRIES
☐ Energy
☒ Environmental
☐ Financial
☐ Real Estate
☐ Transportation
☐ Publishing
☐ Food
☐ Franchises
☒ DIVERSIFIED
☒ MISCELLANEOUS

STAGE PREFERENCE

☐ EARLY STAGE
☐ Seed
☐ Start-up
☐ 1st Stage
☒ LATER STAGE
☒ 2nd Stage
☒ Mature
☒ Mezzanine
☒ LBO/MBO
☐ Turnaround
☐ INT'L EXPANSION
☐ WILL CONSIDER ALL
☐ VENTURE LEASING
SBIC
Other Locations:

Affiliation:
Minimum Investment: $1 Million or more
Capital Under Management: Less than $100 Million

GEOGRAPHIC PREF

☐ East Coast
☐ West Coast
☐ Northeast
☐ Mid Atlantic
☐ Gulf States
☐ Northwest
☒ Southeast
☐ Southwest
☐ Midwest
☐ Central
☐ Local to Office
☐ Other Geo Pref

WALNUT CAPITAL CORP.

8000 Tower Crescent Drive
Suite 1070
Vienna VA 22182

Phone (703) 448-3771   Fax (703) 448-7751

PROFESSIONALS	TITLE
Joel Kanter	President

INDUSTRY PREFERENCE

☐ INFORMATION INDUSTRY	☐ BASIC INDUSTRIES
☐ Communications	☐ Consumer
☐ Computer Equipment	☐ Distribution
☐ Computer Services	☐ Manufacturing
☐ Computer Components	☐ Retail
☐ Computer Entertainment	☐ Service
☐ Computer Education	☐ Wholesale
☐ Information Technologies	☐ SPECIFIC INDUSTRIES
☐ Computer Media	☐ Energy
☐ Software	☐ Environmental
☐ Internet	☐ Financial
☐ MEDICAL/HEALTHCARE	☐ Real Estate
☐ Biotechnology	☐ Transportation
☐ Healthcare Services	☐ Publishing
☐ Life Sciences	☐ Food
☐ Medical Products	☐ Franchises
☐ INDUSTRIAL	☒ DIVERSIFIED
☐ Advanced Materials	☐ MISCELLANEOUS
☐ Chemicals	
☐ Instruments & Controls	

STAGE PREFERENCE

☒ EARLY STAGE
☐ Seed
☒ Start-up
☒ 1st Stage
☒ LATER STAGE
☒ 2nd Stage
☐ Mature
☒ Mezzanine
☒ LBO/MBO
☐ Turnaround
☐ INT'L EXPANSION
☐ WILL CONSIDER ALL
☐ VENTURE LEASING

SBIC
Other Locations:

Affiliation:
Minimum Investment: Less than $1 Million
Capital Under Management: Less than $100 Million

GEOGRAPHIC PREF

☐ East Coast
☐ West Coast
☐ Northeast
☐ Mid Atlantic
☐ Gulf States
☐ Northwest
☐ Southeast
☐ Southwest
☐ Midwest
☐ Central
☐ Local to Office
☐ Other Geo Pref

WATERSIDE CAPITAL CORPORATION

300 East Main Street
Suite 1380
Norfolk VA 23510

Phone (757) 626-1111   Fax (757) 626-0114

PROFESSIONALS	TITLE
Alan Lindauer	President
Martin Speroni	Director of Research

INDUSTRY PREFERENCE

☐ INFORMATION INDUSTRY	☐ BASIC INDUSTRIES
☐ Communications	☐ Consumer
☐ Computer Equipment	☐ Distribution
☐ Computer Services	☐ Manufacturing
☐ Computer Components	☐ Retail
☐ Computer Entertainment	☐ Service
☐ Computer Education	☐ Wholesale
☐ Information Technologies	☐ SPECIFIC INDUSTRIES
☐ Computer Media	☐ Energy
☐ Software	☐ Environmental
☐ Internet	☐ Financial
☐ MEDICAL/HEALTHCARE	☐ Real Estate
☐ Biotechnology	☐ Transportation
☐ Healthcare Services	☐ Publishing
☐ Life Sciences	☐ Food
☐ Medical Products	☐ Franchises
☐ INDUSTRIAL	☒ DIVERSIFIED
☐ Advanced Materials	☐ MISCELLANEOUS
☐ Chemicals	
☐ Instruments & Controls	

STAGE PREFERENCE

☒ EARLY STAGE
☐ Seed
☐ Start-up
☒ 1st Stage
☒ LATER STAGE
☒ 2nd Stage
☒ Mature
☒ Mezzanine
☒ LBO/MBO
☐ Turnaround
☐ INT'L EXPANSION
☐ WILL CONSIDER ALL
☐ VENTURE LEASING

SBIC
Other Locations:

Affiliation:
Minimum Investment: Less than $1 Million
Capital Under Management: Less than $100 Million

GEOGRAPHIC PREF

☐ East Coast
☐ West Coast
☐ Northeast
☐ Mid Atlantic
☐ Gulf States
☐ Northwest
☐ Southeast
☐ Southwest
☐ Midwest
☐ Central
☐ Local to Office
☐ Other Geo Pref

ARCH VENTURE PARTNERS

1000 Second Avenue
Suite 3700
Seattle WA 98104

Phone (206) 674-3028   Fax (206) 674-3026

PROFESSIONALS	TITLE
Steven Lazarus	Managing Director
Keith Crandell	Managing Director
Robert Nelsen	Managing Director
Alex Knight	Managing Director
Karen Kerr	Managing Director

INDUSTRY PREFERENCE

☒ INFORMATION INDUSTRY	☐ BASIC INDUSTRIES
☒ Communications	☐ Consumer
☒ Computer Equipment	☐ Distribution
☒ Computer Services	☐ Manufacturing
☐ Computer Components	☐ Retail
☐ Computer Entertainment	☐ Service
☐ Computer Education	☐ Wholesale
☐ Information Technologies	☒ SPECIFIC INDUSTRIES
☐ Computer Media	☒ Energy
☐ Software	☒ Environmental
☐ Internet	☐ Financial
☒ MEDICAL/HEALTHCARE	☐ Real Estate
☒ Biotechnology	☐ Transportation
☒ Healthcare Services	☒ Publishing
☒ Life Sciences	☐ Food
☒ Medical Products	☐ Franchises
☒ INDUSTRIAL	☒ DIVERSIFIED
☐ Advanced Materials	☒ MISCELLANEOUS
☐ Chemicals	Agriculture
☒ Instruments & Controls	

STAGE PREFERENCE

☒ EARLY STAGE
☒ Seed
☒ Start-up
☐ 1st Stage
☐ LATER STAGE
☐ 2nd Stage
☐ Mature
☐ Mezzanine
☐ LBO/MBO
☐ Turnaround
☐ INT'L EXPANSION
☐ WILL CONSIDER ALL
☐ VENTURE LEASING

Other Locations: Albuquerque NM, New York NY, Chicago IL

Affiliation:
Minimum Investment: $1 Million or more
Capital Under Management: $100 to $500 Million

GEOGRAPHIC PREF

☐ East Coast
☐ West Coast
☐ Northeast
☐ Mid Atlantic
☐ Gulf States
☐ Northwest
☐ Southeast
☐ Southwest
☐ Midwest
☐ Central
☐ Local to Office
☐ Other Geo Pref

FLUKE CAPITAL MANAGEMENT, LP

11400 Southeast 6th Street
Suite 230
Bellevue WA 98004

Phone (206) 453-4590   Fax (206) 453-4675

PROFESSIONALS	TITLE
Dennis P. Weston	Managing Partner

INDUSTRY PREFERENCE

☒ INFORMATION INDUSTRY	☒ BASIC INDUSTRIES
☒ Communications	☒ Consumer
☒ Computer Equipment	☐ Distribution
☒ Computer Services	☐ Manufacturing
☒ Computer Components	☒ Retail
☐ Computer Entertainment	☒ Service
☒ Computer Education	☐ Wholesale
☒ Information Technologies	☒ SPECIFIC INDUSTRIES
☒ Computer Media	☐ Energy
☒ Software	☒ Environmental
☒ Internet	☐ Financial
☒ MEDICAL/HEALTHCARE	☐ Real Estate
☒ Biotechnology	☐ Transportation
☒ Healthcare Services	☐ Publishing
☒ Life Sciences	☐ Food
☒ Medical Products	☐ Franchises
☐ INDUSTRIAL	☒ DIVERSIFIED
☐ Advanced Materials	☐ MISCELLANEOUS
☐ Chemicals	
☐ Instruments & Controls	

STAGE PREFERENCE

☒ EARLY STAGE
☐ Seed
☐ Start-up
☒ 1st Stage
☒ LATER STAGE
☒ 2nd Stage
☒ Mature
☒ Mezzanine
☒ LBO/MBO
☐ Turnaround
☐ INT'L EXPANSION
☐ WILL CONSIDER ALL
☐ VENTURE LEASING

Other Locations:

Affiliation:
Minimum Investment: Less than $1 Million
Capital Under Management: $100 to $500 Million

GEOGRAPHIC PREF

☐ East Coast
☐ West Coast
☐ Northeast
☐ Mid Atlantic
☐ Gulf States
☒ Northwest
☐ Southeast
☐ Southwest
☐ Midwest
☐ Central
☐ Local to Office
☐ Other Geo Pref

FRAZIER & CO.

601 Union Street
Suite 3300
Seattle WA 98101

Phone (206) 621-7200   Fax (206) 621-1848

PROFESSIONALS	TITLE
Alan Frazier	Managing General Partner
Jon Gilbert	General Partner
Nader Naini	General Partner
Fred Silverstein	General Partner

INDUSTRY PREFERENCE

☐ INFORMATION INDUSTRY
☐ Communications
☐ Computer Equipment
☐ Computer Services
☐ Computer Components
☐ Computer Entertainment
☐ Computer Education
☐ Information Technologies
☐ Computer Media
☐ Software
☐ Internet
☒ MEDICAL/HEALTHCARE
☒ Biotechnology
☒ Healthcare Services
☒ Life Sciences
☒ Medical Products
☐ INDUSTRIAL
☐ Advanced Materials
☐ Chemicals
☐ Instruments & Controls

☐ BASIC INDUSTRIES
☐ Consumer
☐ Distribution
☐ Manufacturing
☐ Retail
☐ Service
☐ Wholesale
☐ SPECIFIC INDUSTRIES
☐ Energy
☐ Environmental
☐ Financial
☐ Real Estate
☐ Transportation
☐ Publishing
☐ Food
☐ Franchises
☐ DIVERSIFIED
☒ MISCELLANEOUS

STAGE PREFERENCE

☐ EARLY STAGE
☐ Seed
☐ Start-up
☐ 1st Stage
☐ LATER STAGE
☐ 2nd Stage
☐ Mature
☐ Mezzanine
☐ LBO/MBO
☐ Turnaround
☐ INT'L EXPANSION
☐ WILL CONSIDER ALL
☐ VENTURE LEASING

Other Locations:

Affiliation:
Minimum Investment: Less than $1 Million
Capital Under Management: $100 to $500 Million

GEOGRAPHIC PREF

☐ East Coast
☐ West Coast
☐ Northeast
☐ Mid Atlantic
☐ Gulf States
☐ Northwest
☐ Southeast
☐ Southwest
☐ Midwest
☐ Central
☐ Local to Office
☐ Other Geo Pref

KIRLAN VENTURE CAPITAL

221 First Avenue West
Suite 108
Seattle WA 98119

Phone (206) 281-8610   Fax (206) 285-3451

PROFESSIONALS	TITLE
Bill Tenneson	President

INDUSTRY PREFERENCE

☒ INFORMATION INDUSTRY
☒ Communications
☒ Computer Equipment
☒ Computer Services
☐ Computer Components
☐ Computer Entertainment
☐ Computer Education
☒ Information Technologies
☐ Computer Media
☒ Software
☒ Internet
☒ MEDICAL/HEALTHCARE
☐ Biotechnology
☒ Healthcare Services
☒ Life Sciences
☒ Medical Products
☐ INDUSTRIAL
☐ Advanced Materials
☐ Chemicals
☐ Instruments & Controls

☐ BASIC INDUSTRIES
☐ Consumer
☐ Distribution
☐ Manufacturing
☐ Retail
☐ Service
☐ Wholesale
☐ SPECIFIC INDUSTRIES
☐ Energy
☐ Environmental
☐ Financial
☐ Real Estate
☐ Transportation
☐ Publishing
☐ Food
☐ Franchises
☒ DIVERSIFIED
☐ MISCELLANEOUS

STAGE PREFERENCE

☒ EARLY STAGE
☐ Seed
☐ Start-up
☒ 1st Stage
☒ LATER STAGE
☒ 2nd Stage
☐ Mature
☒ Mezzanine
☐ LBO/MBO
☐ Turnaround
☐ INT'L EXPANSION
☐ WILL CONSIDER ALL
☐ VENTURE LEASING

Other Locations:

Affiliation:
Minimum Investment: Less than $1 Million
Capital Under Management: Less than $100 Million

GEOGRAPHIC PREF

☐ East Coast
☒ West Coast
☐ Northeast
☐ Mid Atlantic
☐ Gulf States
☐ Northwest
☐ Southeast
☐ Southwest
☐ Midwest
☐ Central
☐ Local to Office
☐ Other Geo Pref

NORTHWEST VENTURE ASSOCIATES

221 N. Wall Street
Suite 628
Spokane WA 99201

Phone (509) 747-0728   Fax (509) 747-0758

PROFESSIONALS	TITLE
Tom Simpson	
Jean Balek-Miner	
Joe Herzog	
Mark Mecham	
Chris Brookfield	

INDUSTRY PREFERENCE

☒ INFORMATION INDUSTRY	☒ BASIC INDUSTRIES
☒ Communications	☒ Consumer
☒ Computer Equipment	☐ Distribution
☒ Computer Services	☐ Manufacturing
☒ Computer Components	☒ Retail
☐ Computer Entertainment	☐ Service
☒ Computer Education	☐ Wholesale
☒ Information Technologies	☒ SPECIFIC INDUSTRIES
☒ Computer Media	☐ Energy
☒ Software	☒ Environmental
☒ Internet	☐ Financial
☒ MEDICAL/HEALTHCARE	☐ Real Estate
☒ Biotechnology	☐ Transportation
☒ Healthcare Services	☐ Publishing
☒ Life Sciences	☐ Food
☒ Medical Products	☐ Franchises
☒ INDUSTRIAL	☒ DIVERSIFIED
☐ Advanced Materials	☒ MISCELLANEOUS
☐ Chemicals	
☐ Instruments & Controls	

STAGE PREFERENCE

☒ EARLY STAGE
☐ Seed
☐ Start-up
☒ 1st Stage
☒ LATER STAGE
☒ 2nd Stage
☐ Mature
☒ Mezzanine
☒ LBO/MBO
☐ Turnaround
☐ INT'L EXPANSION
☐ WILL CONSIDER ALL
☐ VENTURE LEASING

SBIC
Other Locations:

Affiliation:
Minimum Investment: Less than $1 Million
Capital Under Management: Less than $100 Million

GEOGRAPHIC PREF

☐ East Coast
☐ West Coast
☐ Northeast
☐ Mid Atlantic
☐ Gulf States
☒ Northwest
☐ Southeast
☐ Southwest
☐ Midwest
☐ Central
☐ Local to Office
☐ Other Geo Pref

OLYMPIC VENTURE PARTNERS

2420 Carillon Point
Kirkland WA 98033

Phone (425) 889-9192   Fax (425) 889-0152

PROFESSIONALS	TITLE
George H. Clute	General Partner
Charles P. Waite, Jr.	General Partner
William Miller	General Partner

INDUSTRY PREFERENCE

☒ INFORMATION INDUSTRY	☐ BASIC INDUSTRIES
☒ Communications	☐ Consumer
☐ Computer Equipment	☐ Distribution
☐ Computer Services	☐ Manufacturing
☐ Computer Components	☐ Retail
☐ Computer Entertainment	☐ Service
☐ Computer Education	☐ Wholesale
☒ Information Technologies	☐ SPECIFIC INDUSTRIES
☐ Computer Media	☐ Energy
☒ Software	☐ Environmental
☒ Internet	☐ Financial
☒ MEDICAL/HEALTHCARE	☐ Real Estate
☒ Biotechnology	☐ Transportation
☐ Healthcare Services	☐ Publishing
☒ Life Sciences	☐ Food
☒ Medical Products	☐ Franchises
☐ INDUSTRIAL	☒ DIVERSIFIED
☐ Advanced Materials	☐ MISCELLANEOUS
☐ Chemicals	
☐ Instruments & Controls	

STAGE PREFERENCE

☒ EARLY STAGE
☒ Seed
☒ Start-up
☒ 1st Stage
☒ LATER STAGE
☒ 2nd Stage
☐ Mature
☐ Mezzanine
☐ LBO/MBO
☐ Turnaround
☐ INT'L EXPANSION
☐ WILL CONSIDER ALL
☐ VENTURE LEASING

Other Locations: Lake Oswego OR

Affiliation:
Minimum Investment: Less than $1 Million
Capital Under Management: $100 to $500 Million

GEOGRAPHIC PREF

☐ East Coast
☒ West Coast
☐ Northeast
☐ Mid Atlantic
☐ Gulf States
☒ Northwest
☐ Southeast
☒ Southwest
☐ Midwest
☐ Central
☐ Local to Office
☒ Other Geo Pref
Pacific Northwest

PACIFIC HORIZON VENTURES

1001 Fourth Avenue Plaza
Suite 4105
Seattle WA 98154

Phone (206) 682-1181   Fax (206) 682-8077

PROFESSIONALS	TITLE
Donald Elmer	Managing General Partner
Doug Eplett, MD	General Partner
Burke Jackson	Special Partner

INDUSTRY PREFERENCE

☐ INFORMATION INDUSTRY
☐ Communications
☐ Computer Equipment
☐ Computer Services
☐ Computer Components
☐ Computer Entertainment
☐ Computer Education
☐ Information Technologies
☐ Computer Media
☐ Software
☐ Internet
☒ MEDICAL/HEALTHCARE
☒ Biotechnology
☒ Healthcare Services
☒ Life Sciences
☒ Medical Products
☐ INDUSTRIAL
☐ Advanced Materials
☐ Chemicals
☐ Instruments & Controls

☐ BASIC INDUSTRIES
☐ Consumer
☐ Distribution
☐ Manufacturing
☐ Retail
☐ Service
☐ Wholesale
☐ SPECIFIC INDUSTRIES
☐ Energy
☐ Environmental
☐ Financial
☐ Real Estate
☐ Transportation
☐ Publishing
☐ Food
☐ Franchises
☐ DIVERSIFIED
☒ MISCELLANEOUS

STAGE PREFERENCE

☒ EARLY STAGE
☐ Seed
☐ Start-up
☒ 1st Stage
☒ LATER STAGE
☒ 2nd Stage
☐ Mature
☐ Mezzanine
☐ LBO/MBO
☐ Turnaround
☐ INT'L EXPANSION
☐ WILL CONSIDER ALL
☐ VENTURE LEASING

Other Locations:

Affiliation:
Minimum Investment: Less than $1 Million
Capital Under Management: Less than $100 Million

GEOGRAPHIC PREF

☐ East Coast
☒ West Coast
☐ Northeast
☐ Mid Atlantic
☐ Gulf States
☐ Northwest
☐ Southeast
☐ Southwest
☐ Midwest
☐ Central
☐ Local to Office
☐ Other Geo Pref

PACIFIC NORTHWEST PARTNERS SBIC, LP

305 - 108th Avenue, NE
2nd Floor
Bellevue WA 98004

Phone (425) 455-9967   Fax (425) 455-9404

PROFESSIONALS	TITLE
Theodore M. Wight	General Partner

INDUSTRY PREFERENCE

☒ INFORMATION INDUSTRY
☐ Communications
☐ Computer Equipment
☐ Computer Services
☐ Computer Components
☐ Computer Entertainment
☐ Computer Education
☐ Information Technologies
☐ Computer Media
☒ Software
☐ Internet
☒ MEDICAL/HEALTHCARE
☐ Biotechnology
☒ Healthcare Services
☐ Life Sciences
☒ Medical Products
☐ INDUSTRIAL
☐ Advanced Materials
☐ Chemicals
☐ Instruments & Controls

☒ BASIC INDUSTRIES
☐ Consumer
☐ Distribution
☐ Manufacturing
☒ Retail
☒ Service
☐ Wholesale
☐ SPECIFIC INDUSTRIES
☐ Energy
☐ Environmental
☐ Financial
☐ Real Estate
☐ Transportation
☐ Publishing
☐ Food
☐ Franchises
☒ DIVERSIFIED
☐ MISCELLANEOUS

STAGE PREFERENCE

☒ EARLY STAGE
☒ Seed
☒ Start-up
☒ 1st Stage
☒ LATER STAGE
☒ 2nd Stage
☐ Mature
☐ Mezzanine
☐ LBO/MBO
☐ Turnaround
☐ INT'L EXPANSION
☐ WILL CONSIDER ALL
☐ VENTURE LEASING

SBIC
Other Locations:

Affiliation:
Minimum Investment: Less than $1 Million
Capital Under Management: Less than $100 Million

GEOGRAPHIC PREF

☐ East Coast
☐ West Coast
☐ Northeast
☐ Mid Atlantic
☐ Gulf States
☒ Northwest
☐ Southeast
☐ Southwest
☐ Midwest
☐ Central
☐ Local to Office
☐ Other Geo Pref

POLARIS VENTURE PARTNERS

701 Fifth Avenue
Suite 6850
Seattle WA 98104

Phone (206) 652-4555   Fax (206) 652-4666

PROFESSIONALS	TITLE
Stephen Arnold	General Partner
Brian Chee	Principal

INDUSTRY PREFERENCE

- ☒ INFORMATION INDUSTRY
- ☒ Communications
- ☒ Computer Equipment
- ☒ Computer Services
- ☒ Computer Components
- ☒ Computer Entertainment
- ☒ Computer Education
- ☐ Information Technologies
- ☒ Computer Media
- ☒ Software
- ☒ Internet
- ☒ MEDICAL/HEALTHCARE
- ☒ Biotechnology
- ☒ Healthcare Services
- ☒ Life Sciences
- ☒ Medical Products
- ☐ INDUSTRIAL
- ☐ Advanced Materials
- ☐ Chemicals
- ☐ Instruments & Controls

- ☐ BASIC INDUSTRIES
- ☐ Consumer
- ☐ Distribution
- ☐ Manufacturing
- ☐ Retail
- ☐ Service
- ☐ Wholesale
- ☐ SPECIFIC INDUSTRIES
- ☐ Energy
- ☐ Environmental
- ☐ Financial
- ☐ Real Estate
- ☐ Transportation
- ☐ Publishing
- ☐ Food
- ☐ Franchises
- ☒ DIVERSIFIED
- ☒ MISCELLANEOUS

STAGE PREFERENCE

- ☒ EARLY STAGE
- ☒ Seed
- ☒ Start-up
- ☒ 1st Stage
- ☒ LATER STAGE
- ☒ 2nd Stage
- ☐ Mature
- ☐ Mezzanine
- ☐ LBO/MBO
- ☐ Turnaround
- ☐ INT'L EXPANSION
- ☐ WILL CONSIDER ALL
- ☐ VENTURE LEASING

Other Locations: Waltham MA

Affiliation:
Minimum Investment: Less than $1 Million
Capital Under Management: $100 to $500 Million

GEOGRAPHIC PREF

- ☐ East Coast
- ☐ West Coast
- ☐ Northeast
- ☐ Mid Atlantic
- ☐ Gulf States
- ☐ Northwest
- ☐ Southeast
- ☐ Southwest
- ☐ Midwest
- ☐ Central
- ☐ Local to Office
- ☐ Other Geo Pref

CATTERTON-SIMON PARTNERS LP

10 Hale Street
Suite 205
Charleston WV 25301

Phone (203) 629-4901   Fax (203) 629-4903

PROFESSIONALS	TITLE
Frank Vest, Jr	Managing Partner

INDUSTRY PREFERENCE

- ☒ INFORMATION INDUSTRY
- ☐ Communications
- ☐ Computer Equipment
- ☐ Computer Services
- ☐ Computer Components
- ☐ Computer Entertainment
- ☒ Computer Education
- ☐ Information Technologies
- ☐ Computer Media
- ☐ Software
- ☒ Internet
- ☐ MEDICAL/HEALTHCARE
- ☐ Biotechnology
- ☐ Healthcare Services
- ☐ Life Sciences
- ☐ Medical Products
- ☐ INDUSTRIAL
- ☐ Advanced Materials
- ☐ Chemicals
- ☐ Instruments & Controls

- ☒ BASIC INDUSTRIES
- ☒ Consumer
- ☐ Distribution
- ☐ Manufacturing
- ☐ Retail
- ☐ Service
- ☐ Wholesale
- ☐ SPECIFIC INDUSTRIES
- ☐ Energy
- ☐ Environmental
- ☐ Financial
- ☐ Real Estate
- ☐ Transportation
- ☐ Publishing
- ☐ Food
- ☐ Franchises
- ☒ DIVERSIFIED
- ☒ MISCELLANEOUS

STAGE PREFERENCE

- ☐ EARLY STAGE
- ☐ Seed
- ☐ Start-up
- ☐ 1st Stage
- ☒ LATER STAGE
- ☒ 2nd Stage
- ☐ Mature
- ☐ Mezzanine
- ☒ LBO/MBO
- ☐ Turnaround
- ☐ INT'L EXPANSION
- ☐ WILL CONSIDER ALL
- ☐ VENTURE LEASING

Other Locations: Greenwich CT, Los Angeles CA

Affiliation:
Minimum Investment: $1 Million or more
Capital Under Management: $100 to $500 Million

GEOGRAPHIC PREF

- ☐ East Coast
- ☐ West Coast
- ☐ Northeast
- ☐ Mid Atlantic
- ☐ Gulf States
- ☐ Northwest
- ☐ Southeast
- ☐ Southwest
- ☐ Midwest
- ☐ Central
- ☐ Local to Office
- ☐ Other Geo Pref

WESTVEN LIMITED PARTNERSHIP

208 Capitol Street
Suite 300
Charleston WV 25301

Phone (304) 344-1794   Fax (304) 344-1798

PROFESSIONALS	TITLE
Thomas E. Loehr	President

INDUSTRY PREFERENCE

- ☒ INFORMATION INDUSTRY
- ☒ Communications
- ☒ Computer Equipment
- ☒ Computer Services
- ☒ Computer Components
- ☐ Computer Entertainment
- ☒ Computer Education
- ☒ Information Technologies
- ☐ Computer Media
- ☒ Software
- ☒ Internet
- ☐ MEDICAL/HEALTHCARE
- ☐ Biotechnology
- ☐ Healthcare Services
- ☐ Life Sciences
- ☐ Medical Products
- ☐ INDUSTRIAL
- ☐ Advanced Materials
- ☐ Chemicals
- ☐ Instruments & Controls

- ☒ BASIC INDUSTRIES
- ☐ Consumer
- ☐ Distribution
- ☒ Manufacturing
- ☐ Retail
- ☐ Service
- ☐ Wholesale
- ☒ SPECIFIC INDUSTRIES
- ☐ Energy
- ☐ Environmental
- ☐ Financial
- ☐ Real Estate
- ☐ Transportation
- ☐ Publishing
- ☐ Food
- ☐ Franchises
- ☒ DIVERSIFIED
- ☒ MISCELLANEOUS
- Wood Products

STAGE PREFERENCE

- ☒ EARLY STAGE
- ☐ Seed
- ☐ Start-up
- ☒ 1st Stage
- ☒ LATER STAGE
- ☒ 2nd Stage
- ☒ Mature
- ☐ Mezzanine
- ☒ LBO/MBO
- ☐ Turnaround
- ☐ INT'L EXPANSION
- ☐ WILL CONSIDER ALL
- ☐ VENTURE LEASING

SBIC
Other Locations:

Affiliation:
Minimum Investment: Less than $1 Million
Capital Under Management: Less than $100 Million

GEOGRAPHIC PREF

- ☒ East Coast
- ☐ West Coast
- ☐ Northeast
- ☐ Mid Atlantic
- ☐ Gulf States
- ☐ Northwest
- ☐ Southeast
- ☐ Southwest
- ☐ Midwest
- ☐ Central
- ☐ Local to Office
- ☐ Other Geo Pref

WHITNEY CAPITAL CORPORATION

707 Virginia Street East
Suite 1700
Charleston WV 25301

Phone (304) 345-2480   Fax (304) 345-7258

PROFESSIONALS	TITLE
Gale L. Gray	

INDUSTRY PREFERENCE

- ☐ INFORMATION INDUSTRY
- ☐ Communications
- ☐ Computer Equipment
- ☐ Computer Services
- ☐ Computer Components
- ☐ Computer Entertainment
- ☐ Computer Education
- ☐ Information Technologies
- ☐ Computer Media
- ☐ Software
- ☐ Internet
- ☐ MEDICAL/HEALTHCARE
- ☐ Biotechnology
- ☐ Healthcare Services
- ☐ Life Sciences
- ☐ Medical Products
- ☐ INDUSTRIAL
- ☐ Advanced Materials
- ☐ Chemicals
- ☐ Instruments & Controls

- ☐ BASIC INDUSTRIES
- ☐ Consumer
- ☐ Distribution
- ☐ Manufacturing
- ☐ Retail
- ☐ Service
- ☐ Wholesale
- ☐ SPECIFIC INDUSTRIES
- ☐ Energy
- ☐ Environmental
- ☐ Financial
- ☐ Real Estate
- ☐ Transportation
- ☐ Publishing
- ☐ Food
- ☐ Franchises
- ☒ DIVERSIFIED
- ☐ MISCELLANEOUS

STAGE PREFERENCE

- ☒ EARLY STAGE
- ☐ Seed
- ☐ Start-up
- ☒ 1st Stage
- ☒ LATER STAGE
- ☒ 2nd Stage
- ☒ Mature
- ☒ Mezzanine
- ☒ LBO/MBO
- ☐ Turnaround
- ☐ INT'L EXPANSION
- ☐ WILL CONSIDER ALL
- ☐ VENTURE LEASING

SBIC
Other Locations:

Affiliation:
Minimum Investment: Less than $1 Million
Capital Under Management: Less than $100 Million

GEOGRAPHIC PREF

- ☐ East Coast
- ☐ West Coast
- ☐ Northeast
- ☐ Mid Atlantic
- ☐ Gulf States
- ☐ Northwest
- ☐ Southeast
- ☐ Southwest
- ☐ Midwest
- ☐ Central
- ☐ Local to Office
- ☒ Other Geo Pref
- WV

BAIRD CAPITAL PARTNERS

227 East Wisconsin Avenue
Suite 2100
Milwaukee WI 53202

Phone (414) 765-3500   Fax (414) 298-7490

PROFESSIONALS	TITLE
Paul Carbone	Managing Director
Brian Anderson	Sr. Vice President
Dave Pelisek	Sr. Vice President
Andrew Brickman	Vice President

INDUSTRY PREFERENCE

- ☐ INFORMATION INDUSTRY
- ☐ Communications
- ☐ Computer Equipment
- ☐ Computer Services
- ☐ Computer Components
- ☐ Computer Entertainment
- ☐ Computer Education
- ☐ Information Technologies
- ☐ Computer Media
- ☐ Software
- ☐ Internet
- ☒ MEDICAL/HEALTHCARE
- ☐ Biotechnology
- ☒ Healthcare Services
- ☐ Life Sciences
- ☒ Medical Products
- ☒ INDUSTRIAL
- ☒ Advanced Materials
- ☒ Chemicals
- ☒ Instruments & Controls

- ☒ BASIC INDUSTRIES
- ☒ Consumer
- ☒ Distribution
- ☒ Manufacturing
- ☐ Retail
- ☒ Service
- ☐ Wholesale
- ☒ SPECIFIC INDUSTRIES
- ☐ Energy
- ☐ Environmental
- ☐ Financial
- ☐ Real Estate
- ☐ Transportation
- ☐ Publishing
- ☐ Food
- ☐ Franchises
- ☒ DIVERSIFIED
- ☒ MISCELLANEOUS
- Outsourcing

STAGE PREFERENCE

- ☐ EARLY STAGE
- ☐ Seed
- ☐ Start-up
- ☐ 1st Stage
- ☒ LATER STAGE
- ☐ 2nd Stage
- ☒ Mature
- ☐ Mezzanine
- ☒ LBO/MBO
- ☐ Turnaround
- ☐ INT'L EXPANSION
- ☐ WILL CONSIDER ALL
- ☐ VENTURE LEASING

Other Locations:

Affiliation:
Minimum Investment: $1 Million or more
Capital Under Management: Less than $100 Million

GEOGRAPHIC PREF

- ☐ East Coast
- ☐ West Coast
- ☒ Northeast
- ☐ Mid Atlantic
- ☐ Gulf States
- ☐ Northwest
- ☒ Southeast
- ☐ Southwest
- ☐ Midwest
- ☐ Central
- ☐ Local to Office
- ☐ Other Geo Pref

CAPITAL INVESTMENTS, INC.

1009 W. Glen Oaks Lane
Mequon WI 53092

Phone (262) 241-0303   Fax (262) 241-8451

PROFESSIONALS	TITLE
Steven Rippl	Executive Vice President

INDUSTRY PREFERENCE

- ☐ INFORMATION INDUSTRY
- ☐ Communications
- ☐ Computer Equipment
- ☐ Computer Services
- ☐ Computer Components
- ☐ Computer Entertainment
- ☐ Computer Education
- ☐ Information Technologies
- ☐ Computer Media
- ☐ Software
- ☐ Internet
- ☐ MEDICAL/HEALTHCARE
- ☐ Biotechnology
- ☐ Healthcare Services
- ☐ Life Sciences
- ☐ Medical Products
- ☐ INDUSTRIAL
- ☐ Advanced Materials
- ☐ Chemicals
- ☐ Instruments & Controls

- ☒ BASIC INDUSTRIES
- ☐ Consumer
- ☒ Distribution
- ☒ Manufacturing
- ☐ Retail
- ☐ Service
- ☐ Wholesale
- ☐ SPECIFIC INDUSTRIES
- ☐ Energy
- ☐ Environmental
- ☐ Financial
- ☐ Real Estate
- ☐ Transportation
- ☐ Publishing
- ☐ Food
- ☐ Franchises
- ☒ DIVERSIFIED
- ☐ MISCELLANEOUS

STAGE PREFERENCE

- ☐ EARLY STAGE
- ☐ Seed
- ☐ Start-up
- ☐ 1st Stage
- ☒ LATER STAGE
- ☒ 2nd Stage
- ☒ Mature
- ☒ Mezzanine
- ☒ LBO/MBO
- ☐ Turnaround
- ☐ INT'L EXPANSION
- ☐ WILL CONSIDER ALL
- ☐ VENTURE LEASING

SBIC
Other Locations:

Affiliation:
Minimum Investment: $1 Million or more
Capital Under Management: Less than $100 Million

GEOGRAPHIC PREF

- ☐ East Coast
- ☐ West Coast
- ☐ Northeast
- ☐ Mid Atlantic
- ☐ Gulf States
- ☐ Northwest
- ☐ Southeast
- ☐ Southwest
- ☐ Midwest
- ☐ Central
- ☐ Local to Office
- ☐ Other Geo Pref

HORIZON PARTNERS, LTD.

225 East Mason Street
Suite 600
Milwaukee WI 53202

Phone (414) 271-2200   Fax (414) 271-4016

PROFESSIONALS	TITLE
Paul W. Sweeney	Partner
Paul A. Stewart	Partner

INDUSTRY PREFERENCE

☒ INFORMATION INDUSTRY		☒ BASIC INDUSTRIES	
☐ Communications		☒ Consumer	
☐ Computer Equipment		☒ Distribution	
☐ Computer Services		☐ Manufacturing	
☐ Computer Components		☐ Retail	
☐ Computer Entertainment		☒ Service	
☐ Computer Education		☐ Wholesale	
☐ Information Technologies		☒ SPECIFIC INDUSTRIES	
☒ Computer Media		☐ Energy	
☐ Software		☐ Environmental	
☐ Internet		☒ Financial	
☐ MEDICAL/HEALTHCARE		☐ Real Estate	
☐ Biotechnology		☐ Transportation	
☐ Healthcare Services		☐ Publishing	
☐ Life Sciences		☐ Food	
☐ Medical Products		☐ Franchises	
☐ INDUSTRIAL		☒ DIVERSIFIED	
☐ Advanced Materials		☐ MISCELLANEOUS	
☐ Chemicals			
☐ Instruments & Controls			

STAGE PREFERENCE

☐ EARLY STAGE
☐ Seed
☐ Start-up
☐ 1st Stage
☒ LATER STAGE
☐ 2nd Stage
☐ Mature
☒ Mezzanine
☒ LBO/MBO
☐ Turnaround
☐ INT'L EXPANSION
☐ WILL CONSIDER ALL
☐ VENTURE LEASING

Other Locations:

Affiliation:
Minimum Investment: $1 Million or more
Capital Under Management: Less than $100 Million

GEOGRAPHIC PREF

☐ East Coast
☐ West Coast
☐ Northeast
☐ Mid Atlantic
☐ Gulf States
☐ Northwest
☐ Southeast
☐ Southwest
☐ Midwest
☐ Central
☐ Local to Office
☐ Other Geo Pref

LUBAR AND COMPANY

700 N. Water Street
Suite 1200
Milwaukee WI 53202

Phone (414) 291-9000   Fax (414) 291-9061

PROFESSIONALS	TITLE
Sheldon B. Lubar	Partner
William T. Donovan	Partner
David J. Lubar	Partner

INDUSTRY PREFERENCE

☒ INFORMATION INDUSTRY		☒ BASIC INDUSTRIES	
☒ Communications		☒ Consumer	
☒ Computer Equipment		☒ Distribution	
☒ Computer Services		☒ Manufacturing	
☒ Computer Components		☒ Retail	
☐ Computer Entertainment		☒ Service	
☒ Computer Education		☐ Wholesale	
☒ Information Technologies		☐ SPECIFIC INDUSTRIES	
☒ Computer Media		☐ Energy	
☒ Software		☐ Environmental	
☒ Internet		☐ Financial	
☒ MEDICAL/HEALTHCARE		☐ Real Estate	
☐ Biotechnology		☐ Transportation	
☐ Healthcare Services		☐ Publishing	
☐ Life Sciences		☐ Food	
☒ Medical Products		☐ Franchises	
☐ INDUSTRIAL		☒ DIVERSIFIED	
☐ Advanced Materials		☐ MISCELLANEOUS	
☐ Chemicals			
☐ Instruments & Controls			

STAGE PREFERENCE

☐ EARLY STAGE
☐ Seed
☐ Start-up
☐ 1st Stage
☒ LATER STAGE
☒ 2nd Stage
☐ Mature
☒ Mezzanine
☒ LBO/MBO
☐ Turnaround
☐ INT'L EXPANSION
☐ WILL CONSIDER ALL
☐ VENTURE LEASING

Other Locations:

Affiliation: Wisconsin Venture Capital Fund
Minimum Investment: Less than $1 Million
Capital Under Management: Less than $100 Million

GEOGRAPHIC PREF

☐ East Coast
☐ West Coast
☐ Northeast
☐ Mid Atlantic
☐ Gulf States
☐ Northwest
☐ Southeast
☐ Southwest
☐ Midwest
☐ Central
☐ Local to Office
☐ Other Geo Pref

VENTURE INVESTORS OF WISCONSIN INC.

505 South Rosa Road
University Research Park
Madison WI 53719

Phone (608) 441-2700   Fax (608) 441-2727

PROFESSIONALS

Roger H. Ganser
John Neis

TITLE

Managing Partner
Managing Partner

INDUSTRY PREFERENCE

⊠ INFORMATION INDUSTRY
⊠ Communications
⊠ Computer Equipment
⊠ Computer Services
⊠ Computer Components
☐ Computer Entertainment
⊠ Computer Education
⊠ Information Technologies
⊠ Computer Media
⊠ Software
⊠ Internet
⊠ MEDICAL/HEALTHCARE
⊠ Biotechnology
⊠ Healthcare Services
⊠ Life Sciences
⊠ Medical Products
⊠ INDUSTRIAL
☐ Advanced Materials
☐ Chemicals .
⊠ Instruments & Controls

⊠ BASIC INDUSTRIES
☐ Consumer
☐ Distribution
⊠ Manufacturing
☐ Retail
⊠ Service
☐ Wholesale
☐ SPECIFIC INDUSTRIES
☐ Energy
☐ Environmental
☐ Financial
☐ Real Estate
☐ Transportation
☐ Publishing
☐ Food
☐ Franchises
⊠ DIVERSIFIED
☐ MISCELLANEOUS

STAGE PREFERENCE

⊠ EARLY STAGE
⊠ Seed
⊠ Start-up
⊠ 1st Stage
☐ LATER STAGE
☐ 2nd Stage
☐ Mature
☐ Mezzanine
☐ LBO/MBO
☐ Turnaround
☐ INT'L EXPANSION
☐ WILL CONSIDER ALL
☐ VENTURE LEASING

Other Locations:

Affiliation:
Minimum Investment: Less than $1 Million
Capital Under Management: Less than $100 Million

GEOGRAPHIC PREF

☐ East Coast
☐ West Coast
☐ Northeast
☐ Mid Atlantic
☐ Gulf States
☐ Northwest
☐ Southeast
☐ Southwest
☐ Midwest
☐ Central
☐ Local to Office
☐ Other Geo Pref

INDEX

INDEX

BACCHARIS CAPITAL, INC. Menlo Park CA - 70

BACHOW & ASSOCIATES, INC. Bala Cynwyd PA - 323

BAIRD CAPITAL PARTNERS Chicago IL - 182

BAIRD CAPITAL PARTNERS Milwaukee WI - 368

BANCBOSTON VENTURES, INC Palo Alto CA - 71

BANCBOSTON VENTURES, INC Boston MA - 213

BANCFIRST INVESTMENT CORPORATION Oklahoma City OK - 320

BANK OF AMERICA CAPITAL INVESTORS Charlotte NC - 312

BANKAMERICA VENTURES Foster City CA - 71

BANKERS CAPITAL CORP. Kansas City MO - 251

BARCLAYS CAPITAL INVESTORS CORP. New York NY - 271

BASTION CAPITAL CORP. Los Angeles CA - 72

BATTERSON VENTURE PARTNERS, LLC Chicago IL - 183

BATTERY VENTURES San Mateo CA - 72

BATTERY VENTURES, L.P. Boston MA - 213

BAUSCH & LOMB INC Rochester NY - 271

BAY PARTNERS S B I C, L. P. Cupertino CA - 73

BCI ADVISORS INC. Teaneck NJ - 256

BEECKEN PETTY & CO. LLC Lisle IL - 183

BEHRMAN CAPITAL New York NY - 272

BENTLEY CAPITAL San Francisco CA - 73

BERKELEY INT'L CAPITAL CORPORATION San Francisco CA - 74

BERKSHIRE PARTNERS, LLC Boston MA - 214

BESSEMER VENTURE PARTNERS Menlo Park CA - 74

BESSEMER VENTURE PARTNERS Wellesley Hills MA - 214

BESSEMER VENTURE PARTNERS Westbury NY - 272

BEST FINANCE CORPORATION Los Angeles CA - 75

BIO-VENTURES WEST Tucson AZ - 62

BIO-VENTURES WEST Carlsbad CA - 75

BLUE CHIP VENTURE COMPANY Cincinatti OH - 316

BLUE RIDGE INVESTORS LTD. PARTNERSHIP Greensboro NC - 312

BLUE ROCK CAPITAL Wilmington DE - 167

BLUE WATER CAPITAL LLC Birmingham MI - 241

BLUE WATER CAPITAL LLC McLean VA - 356

BOSTON CAPITAL VENTURES Boston MA - 215

BOSTON MILLENNIA PARTNERS Boston MA - 215

BRAND EQUITY VENTURES Greenwich CT - 156

BRANTLEY PARTNERS Shader Heights OH - 316

BRENTWOOD ASSOCIATES Irvine CA - 76

BRENTWOOD ASSOCIATES Los Angeles CA - 76

BRENTWOOD ASSOCIATES Menlo Park CA - 77

BROADCAST CAPITAL, INC. Washington DC - 169

BT CAPITAL CORP. New York NY - 273

BURR, EGAN, DELEAGE & CO. San Francisco CA - 77

BURR, EGAN, DELEAGE & CO. INC ALTA COMM. Boston MA - 216

C

CALSAFE CAPITAL CORP. Alhambra CA - 78

CALVERT SOCIAL VENTURE PARTNERS LP Vienna VA - 356

CAMBRIDGE VENTURES, LP Indianapolis IN - 198

CANAAN PARTNERS Menlo Park CA - 78

CANAAN VENTURE PARTNERS Rowayton CT - 156

CANTERBURY MEZZANINE CAPITAL New York NY - 273

CAPITAL INVESTMENTS, INC. Mequon WI - 368

CAPITAL RESOURCE CO. OF CONNECTICUT Farmington CT - 157

CAPITAL RESOURCE PARTNERS Boston MA - 216

CAPITAL SOUTHWEST CORPORATION Dallas TX - 342

CAPSTONE VENTURES Menlo Park CA - 79

CAPSTONE VENTURES Minneapolis MN - 246

CARDINAL HEALTH PARTNERS Princeton NJ - 256

CATALYST FUND, LTD. (THE) Houston TX - 342

CATTERTON-SIMON PARTNERS LP Los Angeles CA - 79

CATTERTON-SIMON PARTNERS LP Greenwich CT - 157

CATTERTON-SIMON PARTNERS LP Charleston WV - 366

D

E

F

J-K-L

M

N

O

OLYMPIC VENTURE PARTNERS Lake Oswego OR - 321

OLYMPIC VENTURE PARTNERS Kirkland WA - 364

ONELIBERTY VENTURES Boston MA - 230

ONSET VENTURES Menlo Park CA - 117

OPEN PRAIRIE VENTURES Champaign IL - 191

OPPORTUNITY CAPITAL CORPORATION Fremont CA - 117

ORION PARTNERS Wellesley MA - 230

OXFORD BIOSCIENCE PARTNERS Costa Mesa CA - 118

OXFORD BIOSCIENCE PARTNERS Westport CT - 163

P

PACIFIC CAPITAL LP Ann Arbor MI - 243

PACIFIC HORIZON VENTURES Seattle WA - 365

PACIFIC MEZZANINE FUND, L.P. Emeryville CA - 118

PACIFIC NORTHWEST PARTNERS S B I C, L P Bellevue WA - 365

PACIFIC VENTURE CAPITAL LTD. Honolulu HI - 179

PACIFIC VENTURE GROUP Encino CA - 119

PACIFIC VENTURE GROUP Redwood Shores CA - 119

PACIFIC VENTURE GROUP Irvine CA - 120

PAPPAJOHN CAPITAL RESOURCES Des Moines IA - 201

PARAGON VENTURE PARTNERS Menlo Park CA - 120

PARIBAS PRINCIPAL INCORPORATED New York NY - 299

PARTECH INTERNATIONAL San Francisco CA - 121

PATRICOF AND COMPANY Palo Alto CA - 121

PATRICOF AND COMPANY New York NY - 300

PATRICOF AND COMPANY Radnor PA - 328

PAUL CAPITAL PARTNERS San Francisco CA - 122

PENINSULA CAPITAL PARTNERS Detroit MI - 244

PENMAN PARTNERS Chicago IL - 192

PENNSYLVANIA EARLY STAGE PARTNERS Wayne PA - 329

PENNY LANE PARTNERS LP Princeton NJ - 264

PETRA CAPITAL Nashville TN - 337

PFINGSTEN PARTNERS, LP Deerfield IL - 192

PHILADELPHIA VENTURES, INC Philadelphia PA - 329

PHILLIPS-SMITH SPECIALTY RETAIL GROUP Colorado Springs CO - 152

PHILLIPS-SMITH SPECIALTY RETAIL GROUP Bronxville NY - 300

PHILLIPS-SMITH SPECIALTY RETAIL GROUP Addison TX - 348

PHOENIX GROWTH CAPITAL CORP. San Rafael CA - 122

PINECREEK CAPITAL PARTNERS LP Newport Beach CA - 123

PIPER JAFFRAY VENTURES, INC. Minneapolis MN - 249

PLATINUM VENTURE PARTNERS Oakbrook Terrace IL - 193

PNC EQUITY MANAGEMENT CORP. Pittsburgh PA - 330

POLARIS VENTURE PARTNERS Waltham MA - 231

POLARIS VENTURE PARTNERS Seattle WA - 366

PORTAGE VENTURE PARTNERS, LLC Northfield IL - 193

POSITIVE ENTERPRISES, INC. San Francisco CA - 123

PREMIER MEDICAL PARTNER FUND San Diego CA - 124

PRIMUS VENTURE PARTNERS Cleveland OH - 319

PRINCE VENTURES Westport CT - 164

PRISM VENTURE PARTNERS Westwood MA - 231

PRIVATE EQUITY PARTNERS INC Fort Worth TX - 348

PROSPECT STREET VENTURES New York NY - 301

PROVIDENCE EQUITY PARTNERS Providence RI - 334

Q-R

QUEST VENTURES San Francisco CA - 124

R CHANEY & CO Houston TX - 349

RADIUS VENTURES, LLC New York NY - 301

RAND CAPITAL CORP. Buffalo NY - 302

RECOVERY EQUITY INVESTORS, L.P. San Mateo CA - 125

REGENT CAPITAL PARTNERS New York NY - 302

REPRISE CAPITAL CORP Westbury NY - 303

ORDERING AN ELECTRONIC VERSION OF THIS DIRECTORY

An electronic text file, containing the data in this directory, is available via e-mail for $149 or on diskette for $199 including USPS Priority mail. This offer expires May 31, 2001. Visit http://www.findingmoney.com/order1 for current pricing and new products.

Both e-mail and diskette versions contain the following information:

Name	Website URL
Title	Telephone number
Company	Fax number
Address	Minimum investment
Suite/Floor	Fund size
City	Industry preferences
State	Life stage preferences
Zip	Geographic preferences

To Order:

1. E-mail Venture Capital Directory Orders
To order via the Internet, complete the order form at http://www.findingmoney.com/order1.

2. Diskette Venture Capital Directory Orders
To order a copy of the data in this directory on a diskette complete the following form and mail to: INVESTECH, 6743 Montia Court, Suite 100, Carlsbad CA 92009
or fax to: (fax) 760-931-2664. After August 2000 use 442-931-2664.

Sorry, no CODs or checks. Credit card or money orders only, please.

Name: _____

Company: _____

Address: _____

Suite: _____

City: _____ State: _____ Zip: _____

Phone: _____ Fax: _____

Credit Card # _____ Expiration Date _____

Signature _____ Today's Date _____

Where did you purchase your copy of this book? _____